Privatization in Latin America

MYTHS AND REALITY

Edited by

Alberto Chong
Florencio López-de-Silanes

A COPUBLICATION OF STANFORD ECONOMICS AND FINANCE,
AN IMPRINT OF STANFORD UNIVERSITY PRESS, AND THE WORLD BANK

A copublication of Stanford Economics and Finance, an imprint of Stanford University Press, and the World Bank.

Stanford University Press	The World Bank
1450 Page Mill Road	1818 H Street, NW
Palo Alto, CA 94304	Washington, DC 20433

The findings, interpretations, and conclusions expressed herein are those of the author(s) and do not necessarily reflect the views of the Board of Executive Directors of the World Bank or the governments they represent.

The World Bank does not guarantee the accuracy of the data included in this work. The boundaries, colors, denominations, and other information shown on any map in this work do not imply any judgment on the part of the World Bank concerning the legal status of any territory or the endorsement or acceptance of such boundaries.

ISBN 0-8213-5882-0	(World Rights except North America)
ISBN (soft cover) 0-8047-5242-7	(North America)
ISBN (hard cover) 0-8047-5241-9	(North America)

Library of Congress Cataloging-in-Publication Data

Privatization in Latin America : myths and reality / Alberto Chong, Florencio López-de-Silanes [editors].
    p. cm.—(Latin American development forum)
Includes bibliographical references and index.
ISBN 0-8213-5882-0
    1. Privatization—Latin America. I. Chong, Alberto. II. López-de-Silanes, Florencio.   III. Latin American development forum.

HD4010.5.P754 2005
338.98'05—dc22

2004062831

Latin American Development Forum Series

This series was created in 2003 to promote debate, disseminate information and analysis, and convey the excitement and complexity of the most topical issues in economic and social development in Latin America and the Caribbean. It is sponsored by the Inter-American Development Bank, the United Nations Economic Commission for Latin America and the Caribbean, and the World Bank. The manuscripts chosen for publication represent the highest quality in each institution's research and activity output and have been selected for their relevance to the academic community, policymakers, researchers, and interested readers.

Advisory Committee Members

About the Contributors

Francisco Anuatti-Neto is a professor in the Department of Economics at the Universidade de São Paulo and FIPE (Fundação Instituto de Pesquisas Econômicas), Brazil.

Milton Barossi-Filho is a professor in the Department of Economics at the Universidade de São Paulo and FIPE (Fundação Instituto de Pesquisas Econômicas), Brazil.

Katherina Capra is a researcher at the Unidad de Análisis de Políticas Sociales y Económicas (UDAPE), La Paz, Bolivia.

Alberto Chong is a senior research economist in the Research Department at the Inter-American Development Bank, Washington, D.C.

Ronald Fischer is a professor in the Department of Economics at the Universidad de Chile, Santiago.

Sebastián Galiani is a professor in the Department of Economics at the Universidad de San Andrés, Buenos Aires, Argentina.

Mauricio Garrón is a coordinator at the Organización Latinoamericana de Energía, Quito, Ecuador.

Paul Gertler is a professor at the Haas School of Management, University of California at Berkeley.

Antonio Gledson de Carvalho is a professor in the Department of Economics at the Universidade de São Paulo and FIPE (Fundação Instituto de Pesquisas Econômicas), Brazil.

Rodrigo Gutiérrez is a professor in the Department of Economics at the Universidad de Chile, Santiago.

Florencio López-de-Silanes is a professor in the School of Management at Yale University and an associate with the National Bureau of Economic Research, Cambridge, Mass.

Roberto Macedo is a professor in the Department of Economics at the Universidade de São Paulo and FIPE (Fundação Instituto de Pesquisas Econômicas), Brazil.

Carlos Machicado is a researcher and PhD student in the Latin American Program of the Universidad de Chile (Santiago)/Instituto Tecnológico Autónomo de México (Distrito Federal)/Universidad Torcuato di Tella (Buenos Aires, Argentina).

Carlos Pombo is a professor in the Department of Economics, Universidad del Rosario, Bogotá, Colombia.

Manuel Ramírez is a professor in the Department of Economics at the Universidad del Rosario, Bogotá, Colombia.

Ernesto Schargrodsky is a professor in the Business School at the Universidad Torcuato Di Tella, Buenos Aires, Argentina.

Pablo Serra is a professor in the Department of Economics at the Universidad de Chile, Santiago.

Federico Sturzenegger is dean of the Business School at the Universidad Torcuato Di Tella, Buenos Aires, Argentina.

Máximo Torero is a senior researcher at Grupo de Análisis para el Desarrollo (GRADE), Lima, Peru, and International Food Policy Research Institute, Washington, D.C.

Contents

FIGURES

Foreword

In the 1980s, a number of Latin American countries launched significant privatization programs. Following decades of statist economic policies, trade protection, heavy-handed regulation, and even nationalization, privatizations were introduced as the linchpin of Washington consensus policies. Indeed, not only countries in Latin America, but many transition economies and other developing economies expected privatization to ignite economic growth.

A decade later, many privatizations in Latin America were completed, but the process reached a standstill. The initial hope and optimism gave way to doubt, disappointment, and a widely shared belief that privatization had failed. Indeed, the alleged failures of privatization became central to the denunciations of Washington consensus policies. So what happened? Has privatization delivered benefits or not? Were the critics scholars or demagogues?

This volume discusses a number of criticisms of privatization and then painstakingly assembles empirical data designed to evaluate them. A broad range of evidence, collected from a variety of countries, points to increased productivity and profitability, accelerating restructuring and output growth, mounting tax revenues, and improving product quality following privatization. In the cases where privatizations failed, the problems appear to be linked to continued state involvement and regulation, as well as a weak corporate governance framework. Indeed, the volume provides substantial evidence that improved corporate governance and regulatory environment are complementary to privatization. In general, private ownership delivers the same significant benefits in Latin America as it does in other parts of the world.

But do the increased shareholder profits of privatized firms come at the expense of other stakeholders? The evidence provides no support for the view that increased profitability comes from monopoly pricing, exploitation of workers, or reductions in tax payments. To the contrary, increased profitability comes from productivity growth rather than redistribution.

The studies in this volume also show that the manner in which privatization is carried out matters. Transparency and homogeneity of procedures, speed, and moderation in preprivatization restructuring lead to better outcomes and allow less room for corruption.

The evidence presented in this volume amounts to a compelling case that privatization in Latin America has been a success. To the extent that they pay attention to the evidence, critics of privatization in Latin America must recognize the basic fact that benefits have been substantial. It is hoped that these studies advance the course of privatization and capitalism in other parts of the world as well.

Andrei Shleifer
Whipple V.N. Jones Professor of Economics, Harvard University
January 2005

Acknowledgments

THIS BOOK WAS WRITTEN WITH THE SUPPORT of the Latin American Research Network at the Inter-American Development Bank (IDB). Created in 1991, this network aims to leverage the IDB's research department's capabilities, improve the quality of research performed in the region, and contribute to the development policy agenda in Latin America and the Caribbean. Through a competitive bidding process, it provides grant funding to leading Latin American research centers to conduct studies on the economic and social issues of greatest concern to the region today. The network currently comprises nearly 300 research institutes all over the region and has proven to be an effective vehicle for financing quality research to enrich the public policy debate in Latin America and the Caribbean.

Many individuals provided comments and suggestions: César Calderón, Guillermo Calvo, Virgilio Galdo, Arturo Galindo, Magdalena López-Morton, Eduardo Lora, William Megginson, Alejandro Micco, Ugo Panizza, Andrei Shleifer, and Luisa Zanforlin. The authors also thank Bank and Yale University colleagues who participated in formal and informal discussions and workshops on background papers, and who provided comments during revisions. Valuable input was also provided in the production of this book by Norelis Betancourt, Madison Boeker, Adriana Cabrera, Rita Funaro, Raquel Gómez, Martha Grotton, Maria Helena Melasecca, Mariela Semidey, and John Dunn Smith. Book design, editing, and print production were coordinated by Santiago Pombo, Janet Sasser, and Monika Lynde in the World Bank's Office of the Publisher.

The views and opinions expressed in this book are those of the authors and do not necessarily reflect the official position of the IDB, its Board of Directors, or the Advisory Committee.

1

The Truth about Privatization in Latin America

Alberto Chong and Florencio López-de-Silanes

AFTER DECADES OF POOR PERFORMANCE and inefficient operations by state-owned enterprises, governments all over the world have earnestly embraced privatization. Beginning in the 1980s, thousands of state-owned enterprises have been turned over to the private sector in Africa, Asia, Latin America, and eastern and western Europe. This trend was spurred by the well-documented poor performance and failures of state-owned enterprises and the efficiency improvements after privatization around the world.[1] Privatization efforts have greatly stalled in recent years, however, despite worldwide evidence that points to improved performance, firm restructuring, fiscal benefits, increased output, and quality improvements following privatization.

Academia, politicians, and the media have recently attacked privatization, voicing concerns about its record, the sources of the gains, and its impact on social welfare and the poor.[2] The negative reaction to privatization is reflected in opinion polls and some governments' reluctance to further their privatization programs.[3] Popular support for privatization, as for other structural policies, generally follows a J curve, declining at first and recovering when the policy matures (Przeworski 1991). If politicians retreat from the now-unpopular effort to restructure the role of the state in the economy, the window of opportunity for deepening privatization efforts may close.[4] Many countries have implemented large privatization programs, but in many others the state retains a large presence, often across many sectors of the economy (La Porta, López-de-Silanes, and Shleifer 2002). In these circumstances, it is imperative to analyze the real record of privatization and draw lessons from it.

This chapter evaluates the privatization experience and assesses the empirical validity of the main concerns voiced against it. We focus on Latin America because after the transition economies of eastern Europe, Latin

America is the region with the largest decline in the state's share of production in the past 20 years. The extent of privatization in Latin America and the quality of the data allow researchers to produce comprehensive analyses that provide appropriate academic responses to some of the main criticisms raised.

Overall, the empirical record shows that privatization leads not only to higher profitability but also to large output and productivity growth, fiscal benefits, and even quality improvements and better access for the poor. Instances of failure exist, but in light of the overwhelming evidence, these failures should not be turned into an argument to stop privatization. The analysis in this chapter suggests that privatization failures can be understood in a political economy framework. Their roots can be traced to substantial state participation in opaque processes, poor contract design, inadequate reregulation, and insufficient deregulation and corporate governance reform that increase the cost of capital and limit firm restructuring in a competitive environment.

The chapter is organized as follows. The next section gives a brief overview of the rationale and extent of privatization around the world. The rest of the sections are structured around what we consider the four main areas of concern about privatization. The first hurdle is to confirm that the profitability increases recorded by the literature are robust, unbiased, and not solely explained by sample selection of the best firms. The first generation of privatization papers suffered from this problem. A recent series of Latin American studies analyzed here, however, uses comprehensive firm-level data that provide robust evidence on performance changes after privatization. The second hurdle is to address criticisms of privatization concerning the welfare of workers, consumers, and the state, which we do by exploring who pays for the profitability gains. The evidence suggests that although labor cost reductions and price increases account for part of the gains, the bulk of the profitability improvement lies in deep firm restructuring and productivity growth. The third hurdle is to examine concerns about the proper role of the state in firm restructuring before privatization and about the opacity of procedures, which may lead to collusion and corruption. Our final hurdle is to assess the role of complementary policies such as deregulation, reregulation, and corporate governance reform. We place particular attention on sectors with market power and inefficient regulation following privatization. The final section concludes, providing some policy implications from the privatization record thus far.

A Brief Look at the Privatization Experience around the World

In the mid-1900s many famous economists and politicians favored state ownership of firms in several industries, where monopoly power and externalities often produced market failures. In the 1990s, however, the evidence on the failures of state-owned enterprises around the world and developments in contract and ownership theory led to a reassessment of the benefits of state ownership in production (Shleifer 1998). The literature emphasizes two reasons for the poor record of state ownership. One strand of the literature focuses on managerial shortcomings; it reflects the idea that imperfect monitoring and poor incentives for managers of state-owned enterprises translate into inferior performance. There are many reasons to believe this would be so. The average state-owned firm is not traded on the stock market; the threat of a takeover does not exist since control rests in the hands of the state. Discipline from creditors does not play much of a role either, because most loans to state-owned enterprises are public debt, and losses are typically covered by subsidies from the treasury. Additionally, the boards of directors rarely implement good corporate governance practices, and management turnover obeys political rather than market forces (Vickers and Yarrow 1988).

The other strand of the literature emphasizes the political economy aspects of state production. The political view highlights the inherent conflict of interest in running state-owned enterprises, as managers seek to maximize their political capital and thus pursue inefficient decisions. Political interference in the firm's production results in excessive employment, poor choices of products and location, and inefficient investment (Shleifer and Vishny 1996; La Porta and López-de-Silanes 1999). State-owned enterprises face soft budget constraints that allow them to implement such practices, since governments may not want to risk the political cost of firms going bust (Sheshinski and López-Calva 2003). The basic claims of the two strands of the literature have been validated by empirical research on state-owned enterprises and firm performance after privatization around the world (see Boardman and Vining 1989; Megginson, Nash, and van Randenborgh 1994; Ehrlich and others 1994; La Porta and López-de-Silanes 1999; Frydman and others 1999; Dewenter and Malatesta 2001; and Chong and López-de-Silanes 2004, among others).

Motivated by the evidence on the failures of state-owned enterprises, governments in more than 100 countries have undertaken privatization programs since the mid-1980s (Megginson and Netter 2001). Throughout the world annual revenues from privatization soared during the late 1990s, peaking in 1998 at over $100 billion (OECD 2001).[5] Industrial countries have pursued privatization less vigorously than have developing nations. Between 1984 and 1996 the participation of state-owned enterprises in industrial countries declined from a peak of 8.5 percent to about 5.0 percent of gross domestic product (GDP), while production from state-owned companies declined more steeply in developing countries (figure 1.1). According to Sheshinski and López-Calva (2003), the activities of state-owned enterprises as a percentage of GDP decreased from about 11 percent in 1980 to 5 percent in 1997 in middle-income countries and from 15 to 3 percent in low-income economies. Developing

Figure 1.1 Economic Activity of State-Owned Enterprises, 1978–97

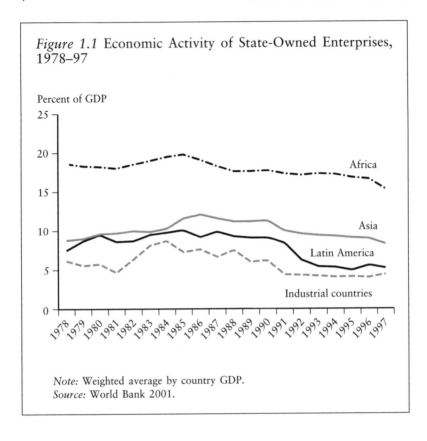

Percent of GDP

Note: Weighted average by country GDP.
Source: World Bank 2001.

countries also saw large reductions in employment among state-owned enterprises during the same period. In middle-income countries such employment fell from a peak of 13 percent of total employment to about 2 percent, and in low-income countries it dropped from more than 20 percent to about 9 percent.

These averages mask great regional variation in the size and economic importance of the remaining state-owned production. In Sub-Saharan Africa only a few governments have openly adopted an explicit divestment strategy for state-owned enterprises. The African privatization effort has been significant in only a handful of countries, and state production still accounts for more than 15 percent of GDP in the region.[6] Asia also features large variation, in that several Asian countries have not consistently pursued a privatization strategy. China, for example, only recently committed to privatizing all but the largest state enterprises. In India, where privatization has thus far not figured prominently in the agenda, the state still owns 43 percent of the country's capital stock. Many governments in

Table 1.1 Proceeds from Privatization in Developing Countries, 1990–99
(US$ billions)

Year	East Asia and Pacific	Latin America	Eastern Europe and Central Asia	Middle East and North Africa	South Asia	Sub-Saharan Africa
1990	376	10,915	1,262	2	29	74
1991	834	18,723	2,551	17	996	1,121
1992	5,161	15,560	3,626	69	1,557	207
1993	7,155	10,488	3,988	417	974	641
1994	5,508	8,199	3,957	782	2,666	605
1995	5,410	4,616	9,742	746	916	473
1996	2,680	14,142	5,466	1,478	889	745
1997	10,385	33,897	16,537	1,612	1,794	2,348
1998	1,091	37,685	8,002	1,000	174	1,356
1999	5,500	23,614	10,335	2,074	1,859	694
1990–1999	44,100	177,839	65,466	8,197	11,854	8,264

Source: World Bank 2001.

the region continue to hang on to their assets in sectors such as energy, telecommunications, transportation, and banking, although private equity funds and multinationals were expecting large state-owned fire sales after the Asian crisis of 1997.[7]

In contrast, transition economies and Latin American countries have been very active in privatization. Transition economies in eastern Europe and central Asia accounted for 21 percent of total privatization revenues in developing countries during the 1990s, second only to Latin America (table 1.1). To facilitate their shift to a market economy, most transition countries launched mass privatization programs that resulted in dramatic reductions of state ownership. These programs, however, have sometimes been unpopular, accused of corruption and foot-dragging on implementing corporate governance reforms, and thus affording poor protection for new minority investors.

Even against the backdrop of massive economic transformations in transition economies, the privatization record of Latin America seems remarkable. Latin America accounted for 55 percent of total privatization revenues in the developing world in the 1990s. The decline in the economic activity of state-owned enterprises has been more substantial in Latin America than in Asia and Africa, bringing levels close to those of industrialized countries. In recent years, however, Latin America has virtually halted its privatization process.

The privatization impetus has also faded in other regions, leaving the bureaucrats very much in business. State-owned enterprises still account for more than 20 percent of investment worldwide and about 5 percent of formal employment (Kikeri 1999). Governments may own or control much more than is apparent at first sight. A clear example is the case of government ownership of banks. Data for the late 1990s indicate that after bank privatization programs had been completed in many countries, the world mean of government ownership of the top 10 banks was still 42 percent, 39 percent if former or current socialist countries were excluded (La Porta, López-de-Silanes, and Shleifer 2002). Thus, while government ownership has decreased with privatization, it has not fallen to negligible levels.

Dramatic differences in the extent of privatization are also evident within regions. In Latin America, for example, countries with large state-owned sectors, such as Ecuador, Nicaragua, and Uruguay, barely privatized at all in the 1990s, while others, such as Argentina, Bolivia, Guyana, Panama, and Peru, raised revenues from comprehensive privatization programs that exceeded 10 percent of GDP (figure 1.2). The difference in the extent of privatization across countries and the large amount of assets in the hands of the state heighten the importance of understanding the privatization record so far and of developing lessons for future privatization programs.[8]

Which Firms Are Up for Sale?
Concerns about What Is Privatized

Privatization studies typically analyze the impact on firm performance by comparing firm-level data before and after privatization. This literature has established worldwide evidence on the benefits of privatization from increased firm profitability driven primarily by increased efficiency (Megginson, Nash, and van Randenborgh 1994; Boubakri and Cosset 1998, 1999; Dewenter and Malatesta 2001). Critics suggest, however, that these results may reflect sample selection bias or result from the use of noncomparable data.

Sample Selection Bias

Sample selection bias can arise from five basic sources. First, politicians who conduct privatization have the incentive to sell only the healthiest firms—what critics refer to as the crown jewels. According to this hypothesis, politicians sell only viable assets and keep poor performers, allowing investors to engage in cherry-picking (Bayliss 2002). Second, several studies are based on information about firms privatized through public offerings on the stock exchange. Such samples are thus biased

Figure 1.2 Revenues from Privatization in Latin America, 1990–2000

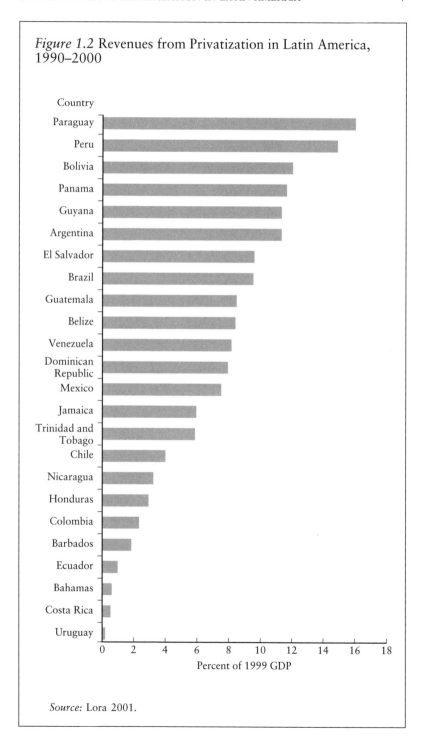

Source: Lora 2001.

toward the largest, and probably the best-performing, firms. A third source of sample selection comes from the greater availability of data from industrialized countries, which may have relatively better-performing firms. Cross-country firm-level analyses are therefore biased because their samples include a disproportionate share of well-performing firms.[9] The fourth source emerges from the intense focus of the studies on oligopolistic or heavily regulated industries, where the gains from privatization may come from market power. Finally, survivorship bias is introduced when firms that went bankrupt after privatization are excluded from the sample that compares performance before and after privatization.

Several early studies on firm performance after privatizations in Latin America suffer from these biases (table 1.2). Some of these papers are specific case studies of a limited number of large firms (see, for example, Galal and others 1994 and Chong and Sánchez 2003). Others do not include econometric or statistical analysis (Sánchez and Corona 1993; Hachette and Lüders 1994; Birch and Haar 2000). Still others are econometric studies of one or two heavily regulated sectors (Ramamurti and Vernon 1991; López-de-Silanes and Zamarripa 1995; Pinheiro 1996; Ramamurti 1996, 1997). Finally, some provide evidence from cross-country analysis of oligopolistic sectors such as telecommunications (Petrazzini and Clark 1996; Ramamurti 1996; Ros 1999; Wallsten 2000).

Overcoming sample selection bias is empirically difficult and requires large amounts of pre- and postprivatization information for nearly complete cross-industry samples of privatized firms of all sizes. La Porta and López-de-Silanes (1999) deal with these issues by collecting information from 95 percent of nonfinancial firms privatized in Mexico in the period 1983–92.[10] Mexico undertook a comprehensive privatization program in which the goal was to eliminate state ownership across the board, with the exceptions of electricity and oil. As a result, the sample contains large, medium-size, and small firms that span more than 40 sectors covering mining, manufacturing, agricultural products, and services as varied as night clubs and soccer teams. These characteristics make it a good sample for testing the validity of the concerns raised above. The study concludes that sample selection bias does not explain the positive results reached by privatization, as profitability of privatized firms increases across sectors and firm sizes, even considering bankrupt firms. The median firm experienced an increase in operating profitability of 24 percentage points. Moreover, the Mexican government did not sell the crown jewels, given that this oil-rich nation retained petroleum and some petrochemicals as state assets.[11]

A recent research effort across Latin America expands the detailed privatization analysis for the region, using comprehensive data and a methodology similar to that described above for Mexico to examine the programs of Argentina, Bolivia, Brazil, Chile, Colombia, and Peru and to update the data and findings for Mexico These studies, gathered together

Table 1.2 Recent Studies on Firm Performance after Privatization in Latin America

Study	Sample, period, and methodology	Summary of findings and conclusions
Birch and Haar 2000	Uses a descriptive study of the privatization experience in the last two decades in Argentina, Brazil, Chile, Colombia, Mexico, Peru, Venezuela, and some Caribbean countries.	Finds sizable effects of privatization on short- and long-run macroeconomic conditions; shows a positive effect of privatization on productivity and a negative effect on employment.
Chisari, Estache, and Romero 1999	Assesses macroeconomic and distributional effects of privatization in Argentina's gas, electricity, telecommunications, and water sectors using a computable general equilibrium model.	Concludes that privatization of utilities accounts for total gains of about $3.3 billion (at 1993 prices) or the equivalent of 1.25 percent of GDP. Privatization cannot be blamed for increased unemployment, which may be caused by ineffective regulation.
Chong and Sánchez 2003	Uses a detailed analysis of the contractual arrangements of privatizations and concessions in infrastructure in Brazil, Chile, Colombia, and Peru.	Concludes that clear, homogeneous, transparent, and credible institutional processes during privatization yield positive outcomes.
Clarke and Cull 1999	Tests econometrically how political constraints affect transactions during bank privatization, based on evidence from the privatization program of provincial banks in Argentina during the 1990s.	Finds that provinces with high fiscal deficits were willing to accept layoffs and guarantee a larger part of the privatized bank's portfolio in return for a higher sale price.
Galal and others 1994	Compares postprivatization performance of 12 large firms (mostly airlines and regulated utilities) from Chile and Mexico.	Finds net welfare gains in 11 of 12 cases covered, with average gains equal to 26 percent of the firms' predivestiture sales; uncovers no case in which workers were made worse off and three cases in which workers' conditions improved.

(Table continues on the following page.)

Table 1.2 (continued)

Study	Sample, period, and methodology	Summary of findings and conclusions
Hachette and Lüders 1994	Analyzes the difference in 10 performance indicators of 144 private, public, and privatized firms in Chile in 1974–87.	Finds no significant differences in behavior among public, private, and privatized firms that operate under similar sets of rules and regulations.
Petrazzini and Clark 1996	Uses International Telecommunications Union data through 1994 to test whether deregulation and privatization affect the level and growth of telephone density, prices, service quality, and employment; sample covers 26 developing countries, including some Latin American nations.	Deregulation and privatization are both associated with significant improvements in the level and growth of telephone density but have no consistent impact on the quality of service. Deregulation is associated with lower prices and increased employment; privatization has the opposite effect.
Pinheiro 1996	Analyzes the performance of 50 Brazilian firms before and after privatization, using data through 1994; variables used are net sales, net profits, net assets, investment, employment, and indebtedness.	Concludes that privatization has improved the performance of the firms; shows that the null hypothesis of no change in behavior is rejected for the production, efficiency, profitability, and investment variables; and finds a significant negative impact on employment.
Ramamurti 1996	Surveys four telecommunications, two airlines, and one toll-road privatization program in 1987–91; discusses political and economic issues and methods used to overcome bureaucratic and ideological opposition to divestiture.	Concludes that privatization had positive results for telecommunications, partly owing to the scope for improvement of technology, capital investment, and attractiveness of offer terms; observes little improvement in airlines and toll road, which had less room for productivity enhancement.
Ramamurti 1997	Examines the restructuring and privatization of Ferrocarriles Argentinos in 1990, testing whether	Documents a 370 percent improvement in labor productivity and a 78.7 percent decline in

Study	Description	Findings
	productivity, employment, and the need for operating subsidies changed after divestiture.	employment; an improvement and expansion in services, combined with a reduction in the cost to consumers; and the elimination of the need for operating subsidies.
Ros 1999	Uses International Telecommunications Union data and panel data regressions to examine the effects of privatization and competition on network expansion and efficiency in 110 countries in 1986–95.	Countries with at least 50 percent private ownership in the main telecommunications firm have significantly higher telephone density levels and growth rates. Both privatization and competition increase efficiency, but only privatization is positively associated with network expansion.
Sánchez and Corona 1993	Uses a descriptive case-study approach to analyze the privatization experiences of Argentina, Chile, Colombia, and Mexico, focusing on the preparatory measures taken prior to privatization; valuation, sale mechanisms, regulation, and supervision; and the fiscal and macroeconomic impact of privatization.	Finds great differences in the effects of privatization in the countries covered; concludes that firms, institutions, and regulations need sufficient time to prepare for the privatization process to be successful.
Trujillo and others 2002	Uses pooled and panel data with fixed and random effects to examine the macroeconomic effects of private sector participation in infrastructure, based on a sample of 21 Latin American countries in 1985–98.	Finds that private sector involvement in utilities and transport has minimal positive effects on GDP. Private investment is crowded out, and private participation reduces recurrent expenditures—except in transport, where it has the opposite effect. The net effect on the public sector account is uncertain.

(Table continues on the following page.)

Table 1.2 (continued)

Study	Sample, period, and methodology	Summary of findings and conclusions
Wallsten 2001	Explores the impact of privatization, competition, and regulation on telecommunications firms' performance in 30 African and Latin American countries in 1984–97.	Indicates that competition is significantly associated with increases in per capita access to telecommunications services and with decreases in its costs, while privatization is helpful only if coupled with effective, independent regulation. Concludes that competition combined with privatization is best and that privatizing a monopoly without regulatory reforms should be avoided.

Comprehensive sample country studies in Latin America

Study	Country sample, period, and methodology	Summary of findings and conclusions
Galiani and others 2005	Argentina. Covers 21 federal nonfinancial state-owned firms plus all privatized banks in Argentina, which account for 74 percent of total privatization revenues; tests whether performance indicators of state-owned firms improved after privatization. Period: 1991–2000.	Profitability of nonfinancial firms increased 188 percent after privatization. Investment increased at least 350 percent while employment decreased approximately 40 percent; there was no impact on prices.
Capra and others 2005	Bolivia. Covers 32 firms, which account for 60 percent of total transactions in Bolivia; tests whether performance indicators of state-owned firms improved after privatization. Period: 1992–99.	Privatization had a significant impact in operating efficiency as profitability increased by over 100 percent and costs per unit dropped by a third. Employment fell by 15 percent, but wages for remaining blue- and white-collar workers doubled.

Study	Description	Findings
Anuatti-Neto and others 2005	Brazil. Includes 102 publicly traded firms (equivalent to 94 percent of total value of transactions in the country); tests whether performance indicators improved after privatization. Period: 1987–2000.	Privatization improved the firms' profitability (14 percent) and reduced their unit costs (33 percent) and investment-to-sales ratio (41 percent).
Fischer, Gutiérrez and Serra, 2005	Chile. Covers only 37 nonfinancial firms, owing to political and economic turbulence in the 1970s and changes in accounting standards; tests whether performance indicators improved after privatization. Period: 1979–2001.	Profitability did not increase significantly after privatization, and productivity did not vary among regulated and unregulated sectors. Study finds no evidence that firms fired workers after privatization, although layoffs occurred prior to privatization.
Pombo and Ramírez 2005	Colombia. Analyzes 30 former firms in the Institute for Industrial Promotion program, which account for 95 percent of the total accumulated privatization sales; tests whether performance indicators improved after privatization. Period: 1974–98.	Firms were profitable before privatization. Labor productivity grew 13 percent and investment fell from 5.9 to 2.5 percent per year owing to previous overinvestment; employment was reduced by 23 percent.
La Porta and López-de-Silanes 1999; Chong and López-de-Silanes 2005	Mexico. Assesses whether the performance of 218 privatized firms improved after divestment; compares performance with industry-matched firms; splits improvements documented between industry- and firm-specific results. Period: 1983–1991.	The output of privatized firms increased 54.3 percent, while employment declined by half (though wages for remaining workers increased). Firms achieved a 24 percentage point increase in operating profitability, eliminating the need for subsidies that amounted to 12.7 percent of GDP. Higher product prices explain 5 percent of improvements; transfers from laid-off workers, 31 percent; and incentive-related productivity gains, 64 percent.

(Table continues on the following page.)

Table 1.2 (continued)

Study	Country sample, period, and methodology	Summary of findings and conclusions
Torero 2005	Peru. This study covers 36 nonfinancial firms, which account for 90 percent of privatization cases and 86 percent of total transactions. In addition, it includes a separate analysis for the financial sector. It tests whether performance indicators improved after privatization. Period: 1986–2000.	Profitability, operational efficiency, and output increased after privatization. The ratio of sales to employees increased by 50 percent in telecommunications, 69 percent in electricity, and 25 percent in the financial sector. After privatization, 36 percent of employees retained their jobs.

Source: Megginson and Netter 2001; Chong and López-de-Silanes 2004.

in this volume, compare firm performance before and after privatization, and they adjust for macroeconomic and industry effects with matching firms. Figure 1.3 summarizes the data collection efforts of this series of papers. With the exception of Brazil, where access to preprivatization data for firms that are not publicly traded was denied, the coverage across firm sizes for all countries is enough to put to rest the main concerns regarding sample selection. The samples used for Bolivia and Chile are the smallest, around 66 percent in terms of value, while the samples for the rest of the countries cover 80, 90, and even 95 percent of transaction values and number of privatization contracts.

Extensive groundwork and creative ways of accessing nonpublic information allowed researchers to collect comprehensive pre- and postprivatization data. In Peru, for example, Torero obtained preprivatization information from so-called White Books, or original privatization documents that were available to prospective bidders when state-owned enterprises were being privatized. He was able to collect comprehensive postprivatization data from privatization dossiers, as well as from the National Supervisory Commission of Firms and Securities and other regulatory agencies. All in all, Torero collected information for nearly 90 percent of privatized firms in Peru. For Argentina, Galiani, Gertler, Schargrodsky, and Sturzenegger drew a comprehensive sample based on information from individual companies, the Ministry of Economic Affairs, and regulatory agencies. In Colombia, which has smaller privatization programs than those of Argentina and Peru, Pombo and Ramírez collected comprehensive information on the privatization from the Institute for Industrial Promotion.[12] They constructed an unbalanced panel data set with records from the Annual Manufacturing Survey starting in 1974 and ending in 1998. Their panel features over 140 variables covering 94 specific groups based on the International Standard Industrial Classification, together with survey information on about 6,000 establishments. For Mexico, Chong and López-de-Silanes use the same database as did La Porta and López-de-Silanes (1999), which combines information from the original privatization White Books with information collected from surveys sent to privatized firms and data from the various census bureaus. The information for Mexico basically covers the whole program, with 218 nonfinancial, state-owned enterprises privatized between 1983 and 1992.

In Bolivia, information on privatized state-owned enterprises is particularly difficult to gather owing to the relatively small size of firms and the lackadaisical record-keeping efforts in the country.[13] Capra, Chong, Garrón, López-de-Silanes, and Machicado complement original information from government institutions with information collected through a survey sent to privatized firms. For Chile, Fischer, Serra, and Gutiérrez faced significant complications in collecting data owing to the long privatization period (1979–2001) and the change in accounting standards in 1982. Despite these problems, their data provide systematic

Figure 1.3 Availability of Privatization Data on Latin America

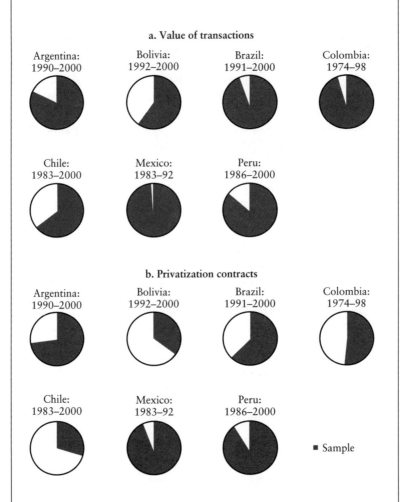

a. Value of transactions

Argentina:
1990–2000

Bolivia:
1992–2000

Brazil:
1991–2000

Colombia:
1974–98

Chile:
1983–2000

Mexico:
1983–92

Peru:
1986–2000

b. Privatization contracts

Argentina:
1990–2000

Bolivia:
1992–2000

Brazil:
1991–2000

Colombia:
1974–98

Chile:
1983–2000

Mexico:
1983–92

Peru:
1986–2000

■ Sample

Note: On the pie charts, the gray area indicates sample coverage; the value of transactions is given as a percentage of the total value of privatization transactions in each country; the number of privatization contracts is given as a percentage of the total number of privatization contracts in the country.
Source: Chapters 2–8.

evidence that complements more descriptive work by others such as Lüders (1991) and Sáez (1992). Finally, Brazil proved to be the most difficult case, since Anuatti-Neto, Barossi-Filho, Gledson de Carvalho, and Macedo were denied access to all preprivatization information for firms that are not publicly traded and were thus restricted to using information on firms traded on the stock exchange. Although their results may suffer from some sample selection bias, their study represents one of the most comprehensive data sets in Brazil, covering close to 95 percent of the total value of privatization transactions (chapter 4).

Overall, the coverage and industry-matching techniques of this recent series of privatization studies in Latin America demonstrate that the increased profitability of privatized firms is not the result of sample selection bias.

Noncomparable Data

There are two additional problems with data collection procedures relating to the comparability of firms before and after the sale. In several countries governments either split existing state-owned enterprises to sell them as independent units or grouped separate firms together to form packages to be sold as a unit. In both cases large amounts of data are needed to conduct a firm-by-firm analysis of the pre- and postprivatization period. Having information disaggregated at the plant level and gaining access to financial statements prepared before the sale are essential for keeping units comparable across time. A second set of problems with the data emerges from changes in the sample after privatization, since the state-owned firm may be merged with the acquiring firm or with one of its subsidiaries. Such a merger creates a new entity and thus makes it difficult, if not impossible, to make meaningful comparisons.

Table 1.3 summarizes the different problems faced by the researchers who recently undertook the comprehensive privatization analyses in seven Latin American countries. All countries presented the issues raised above to different degrees. In most cases, the problem was solved using detailed firm- or plant-level accounting information provided by auditing companies before privatization. That was the case for Argentina, Colombia, Mexico, and Peru. In Peru, the author also took advantage of privatization agreements that required firms to keep separate books for different units, thereby allowing data aggregation. Other methods included estimating proxy financial information or disassembling firms into their original constituents.[14]

When none of these efforts could be undertaken, firms were discarded from the sample to ensure clean estimates. The resulting samples typically excluded the following:

• Cases of state-owned enterprises for which data from the preprivatization period were missing, often as a result of mergers or spinoffs

Table 1.3 Reasons for Firm Exclusion from the Privatization Sample

Country	Merger with private firm	Sale of small minority partici- pation	Firm was liqui- dated	Missing informa- tion	Recent sale	Change in accounting standards
Argentina	Yes	Yes	Yes	Yes	—	—
Bolivia	Yes	—	—	Yes	Yes	Yes
Brazil	Yes	Yes	—	Yes	Yes	—
Chile	Yes	—	Yes	Yes	—	Yes
Colombia	Yes	—	—	Yes	—	—
Mexico	Yes	—	Yes	Yes	—	—
Peru	Yes	—	Yes	Yes	—	—

Note: This table shows the main reasons for excluding some firms from the final sample in each country. "Yes" means some firms were excluded for that particular reason. — means that the study does not suffer from the potential loss.
Source: Chapters 2–8 of this volume.

• A few instances of very small state ownership shares being sold (Argentina and Chile), firms that underwent changes in accounting (Bolivia and Chile), and some very recent privatization cases (Bolivia and Brazil)
• Firms that were liquidated after privatization, although robustness checks were applied to ensure results would not be significantly changed with their inclusion.

To summarize, several early privatization studies suffered from biases introduced by incomplete samples and the use of poor data when the nature of the firm changed with privatization. Today these concerns have largely been put to rest thanks to the recent Latin American studies outlined in this chapter and other efforts, mainly for eastern European countries, that use comprehensive firm-level data across sectors and company sizes.[15]

Evidence from Comprehensive Data Samples on Privatization in Latin America

This section outlines the evidence on performance changes after privatization emerging from the Latin American countries included in our compilation. As previously explained, the data are some of the most comprehensive and up-to-date for the region, allowing us to address many of the concerns raised about privatization. We analyze profitability, operating efficiency, the behavior of inputs, output, and taxes. Latin American studies find improvements in firms' profitability, which is in line with earlier worldwide evidence (Megginson, Nash, and van Randenborgh 1994; Boubakri and Cosset 1998, 1999; D'Souza and Megginson 1999). These increases are typically accompanied by reductions in unit costs, boosts in output, and reduced or constant levels of employment and investment. The evidence suggests that higher efficiency, achieved through firm restructuring and productivity improvements, underpins profitability gains. The raw results on firm performance are followed by industry-adjusted information to verify their robustness. Whenever possible, we show the data for median firms, as they are less affected by outliers.

Raw Data

The evidence from Latin America shows substantial gains in profitability after privatization, measured by ratios of net income to sales and operating income to sales (figure 1.4). For the countries in the sample, the median net-income-to-sales ratio increased 14 percentage points, while the operating-income-to-sales ratio increased 12 percentage points. The largest gains are in Argentina and Peru, where median changes in the ratio of net income to sales reached about 20 percentage points, and in Bolivia, where the ratio of operating income to sales increased more than 15 percentage points. Brazil shows the second smallest gains, between 2 and 3 percentage points depending on the ratio. Colombian state-owned enterprises, unlike their counterparts in other countries, were highly profitable before privatization, which is largely explained by the protective industrial policy implemented by the Colombian government during the 1980s. There is some evidence that profitability in Colombia dropped because firms were already efficient, and privatization was coupled with market liberalization, which brought increased competition.

   The data for Latin America suggest that the main reason behind the profitability gains is the improved operating efficiency brought about by privatization. In figure 1.5 we explore this issue using costs per unit, the ratio of sales to assets, and the ratio of sales to employment. Costs per unit plummet, with the median decline equivalent to about 16 percent for the countries with available data. The results are statistically significant at 1 percent for all countries except Chile. State-owned enterprises were highly unprofitable before privatization in five of the seven countries, with losses above 10 percent of sales in terms of net income over sales. The exceptions are Chile, whose state-owned enterprises exhibited slightly positive profitability ratios, and Colombia, where the state-owned sector was very profitable compared with private competitors.

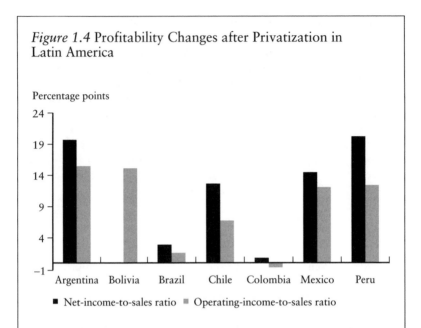

Figure 1.4 Profitability Changes after Privatization in Latin America

Note: The components of the variables are defined as follows: net income is equal to operating income minus interest expenses and net taxes paid, as well as the cost of any extraordinary items; operating income is equal to sales minus operating expenses, minus cost of sales, and minus depreciation; and sales are equal to the total value of products and services sold, nationally and internationally, minus sales returns and discounts. For Bolivia, the net-income-to-sales ratio is not available.
    Source: Chapters 2–8.

The sales-to-asset ratios similarly show a rising trend in four out of five countries. The median country increase in this ratio is 16 percent. Colombia and Peru are the only countries with a fall in sales to assets (about 30 and 20 percent, respectively); in both countries privatized enterprises engaged in large investments that overtook output increases. Finally, the impact on the sales-to-employment ratio is dramatic, with a median gain of 65 percent. Chile and Mexico show the most impressive results, in that sales per employee doubled. Information for Colombia suggests that state-owned enterprises also underwent restructuring with significant efficiency gains. The mean (median) manufacturing firm in Colombia experienced a 48 (65) percent gain in its sales-to-employment ratio and a 2.4 percent per year increase in its total factor productivity index.

Figure 1.5 Operating Efficiency Changes after Privatization in Latin America

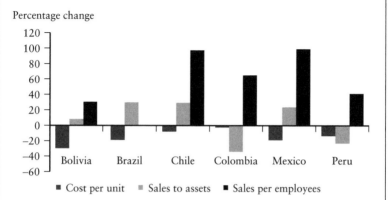

Note: Cost per unit is defined as the ratio of cost of sales to sales. The components of the variables are defined as follows: cost of sales is equal to the direct expense involved in the production of a good (or provision of a service), including raw material expenditure plus total compensation paid to blue-collar workers; sales are equal to the total value of products and services sold nationally and internationally minus sales returns and discounts; employees corresponds to the total number of workers (paid and unpaid) who depend directly on the company; and assets are defined as property, plant, and equipment (PPE), which is equal to the value of a company's fixed assets adjusted for inflation. For Brazil, the sales-per-employees ratio is not available.
Source: Chapters 3–8.

As figure 1.6 shows, labor retrenchment is a significant component of the privatization experience in Latin America. Privatized firms reduced a substantial percentage of their work force in almost all countries. The exception to this trend is Chile, where the mean number of workers in privatized firms increased by 15 percent and the median fell by 5 percent. In general, the median country reduced 24 percent of its work force. Privatized state-owned enterprises in Bolivia, Colombia, Mexico, and Peru show significant reductions: the median firm fired 13 percent, 24 percent, 57 percent, and 56 percent of the work force, respectively. The magnitude of employment reductions in these countries speaks of state-owned firms with bloated work forces, providing evidence in line with the political economy view of the benefits of privatization. The evidence on labor cuts suggests

Figure 1.6 Percentage Changes in Employment after Privatization in Latin America

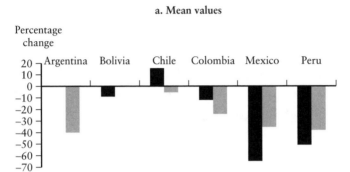

a. Mean values

Percentage change

■ Number of employees ■ Industry-adjusted number of employees

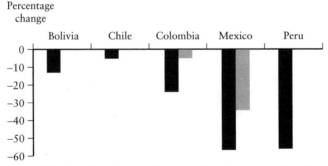

b. Median values

Percentage change

■ Number of employees ■ Industry-adjusted number of employees

Note: The number of employees corresponds to the total number of workers (paid and unpaid) who depend directly on the company. The industry-adjusted number of employees is computed by augmenting the preprivatization number by the difference between the cumulative growth rate of the number of employees of the firm and the cumulative growth rate of the number of employees of the control group in the postprivatization period relative to the average number of employees before privatization. For Argentina, the mean number of employees is not available; for Chile and Peru, the median industry-adjusted information is not available; for Bolivia, the industry-adjusted information is not available.

Source: Chapters 2, 3, 5, 6, 7, and 8.

that transfers from workers to shareholders may be a significant component of the success of privatization. We explore this issue later in the chapter.

A priori, the impact of privatization on investment is not clear. One could expect privatized firms to avoid new investments since state-owned enterprises usually had ample idle capacity. At the same time, if the production process used by the state-owned firm is outdated, one could expect a large increase in investment. The data for Latin America confirm the initial hypothesis, since investment exhibits modest gains or statistically insignificant changes. The exception is Argentina, where investment increased by more than 350 percent.

Our analysis so far suggests that the profitability gains of privatized firms stem mostly from efficiency gains. Most countries show drastic cuts in employment and fairly consistent capital stocks. Perhaps the most striking finding is that the output of privatized state-owned enterprises increased dramatically, despite dwindling employment and modest investment (figure 1.7). The median firm in our sample increased output by over 40 percent, with the largest gains achieved by Mexico and Colombia, where median output increased 68 percent and 59 percent, respectively. The country with the lowest, albeit significant, increase in output is Brazil, where real sales went up 17 percent.

Adjusted Ratios

Latin America underwent major economic transformations in the 1990s as countries embraced liberal policies and opened up their borders. Most of these countries expanded and contracted at various points, leading to concerns about the interpretation of the evidence just discussed. In particular, one might argue that the large profitability and output increases and the rapid growth in productivity can only be the result of macroeconomic and industry changes in the region. To isolate the role of privatization, the series of studies in our compilation present industry-adjusted measures, which support the patterns discussed so far.

The data displayed in figure 1.7, for example, allow us to rule out macroeconomic factors as the driving force behind postprivatization output growth: median industry-adjusted sales grew 27.5 percent in the region. In Brazil and Peru, matching private firms basically stagnated, while the median industry-adjusted output of privatized firms in those countries increased at about the same rate as the raw numbers. Meanwhile, the improved economic conditions and industry factors in Mexico and Colombia accounted for about one-fifth and three-fifths of output growth, respectively.

Relative to industry benchmarks, the median (mean) employment of privatized firms fell roughly 20 (35) percent in the region (see figure 1.6). In contrast, relative investment behavior differs across countries. Ratios of median industry-adjusted investment to sales and investment to assets fell

Figure 1.7 Median Changes in Output after Privatization in Latin America

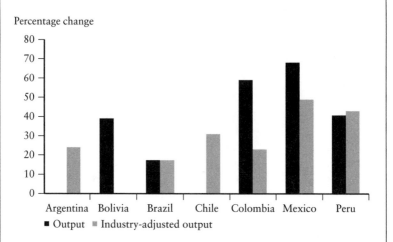

Note: Output is defined as the monetary value of sales. The industry-adjusted output is computed by augmenting the preprivatization value by the difference between the cumulative growth rate of output of the firm and the cumulative growth rate of output of the control group in the postprivatization period relative to the average level of output before privatization. For Colombia, the information corresponds to mean values; for Peru, industry-adjusted output information is expressed in mean values; for Argentina and Chile, output information is not available; for Bolivia, industry-adjusted output information is not available.

Source: Chapters 2–8.

considerably in Brazil and Mexico but showed a marked increase in Argentina, Chile, and Colombia.

The second most important finding of this section involves the closing performance gap between privatized and comparable private firms after privatization (figure 1.8). Mexico offers the most dramatic example of convergence: the net-income-to-sales gap between state-owned and private firms disappeared with privatization and even turned slightly in favor of the privatized enterprises. The Argentine data, although not in a comparable format, also show a similar pattern of catching up. The industry-adjusted net-income-to-sales ratio increased 188 percent after privatization, while the operating-income-to-sales ratio rose 129 percent. The profitability gap

Figure 1.8 Net-Income-to-Sales Gap between Privatized and Private Firms before and after Privatization

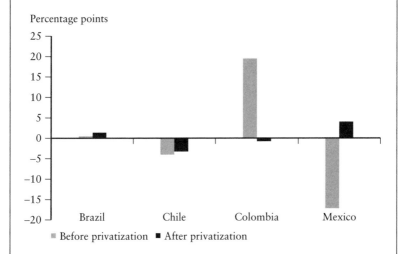

Percentage points

Note: Net income is equal to operating income minus interest expenses and net taxes paid, as well as the cost of any extraordinary items; sales are equal to the total value of products and services sold nationally and internationally, minus sales returns and discounts. For Colombia, information is from the energy sector.
Source: Chapters 4, 5, 6, and 7.

between Colombian privatized and private firms also closed, albeit from a different starting point.[16] Before privatization, the median firm in manufacturing was almost 4 percent more profitable than its private counterparts, while in the state-owned energy sector, this difference was about 20 percent. Substantially lower levels of protection of these firms explain the narrowing gap with the private sector after privatization. Finally, the Brazilian and Chilean privatized samples also improved their relative profitability with respect to their industry competitors. In the case of Brazil, privatized state-owned enterprises became slightly more profitable than their private competitors, while the gap between Chilean privatized and private firms narrowed by about 20 percent.

The gap between privatized and private firms also closed in terms of unit costs (figure 1.9). Brazilian privatized firms quickly reduced a gap of

Figure 1.9 Cost-per-Unit Gap between Privatized and Private Firms before and after Privatization

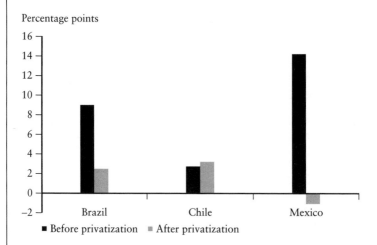

Percentage points

■ Before privatization   ■ After privatization

Note: Cost per unit is defined as the ratio of costs of sales to net sales. Cost of sales is equal to the direct expense involved in the production of a good (or provision of a service), including raw material expenditure plus total compensation paid to blue-collar workers. Sales are equal to the total value of products and services sold, nationally and internationally, minus sales returns and discounts.
Source: Chapters 4, 5, and 7.

9 percentage points to about 2 percentage points. In Chile, this gap was 2–3 percentage points both before and after privatization. In Argentina, industry-adjusted unit costs for privatized firms declined 10 percent. Meanwhile, Mexico's privatized state-owned enterprises substantially cut costs to eliminate a large 14 percentage point gap with private competitors. The catching-up effect of privatization is explained by the large gains in operating efficiency that more than survive industry adjustments. Relative to industry benchmarks, median sales per employee went up 9 percent in Argentina, 30 percent in Bolivia, and a massive 88 percent in Mexico. Similarly, median industry-adjusted sales-to-asset ratios increased 20 percent in Mexico, 34 percent in Brazil, and 49 percent in Chile. All of these numbers suggest that a large component of the higher profitability comes from improved efficiency, lining up with the rest of the evidence presented in the following section.

Who Wins and Loses from Privatization? Concerns about Exploitation of Market Power, Workers, and the Government

Some of the main criticisms of privatization are based on the belief that the gains in firm profitability are achieved at the expense of society. These gains are claimed to be extracted from consumers through the use of market power, from workers by means of lower salaries, and from the government (Campbell-White and Bhatia 1998; Bayliss 2002). In this section we use the recent empirical evidence from Latin America and elsewhere to assess the sources of profitability gains of privatized state-owned enterprises.

Government Revenues

Critics of privatization often argue that the government, and thus society at large, loses from privatization because it gives up a positive stream of cash flows and puts it in the hands of private buyers. The argument is extended to claim that the sale of state-owned enterprises is equivalent to a privatization of gains and a socialization of losses. In other words, well-connected groups are able to reap the profits of privatized firms and receive government-sponsored bailouts when things go wrong. The evidence used to support these claims comes mostly from case studies of profitable state-owned enterprises that were privatized, unprofitable state-owned enterprises that turned out to be great moneymakers after privatization, and state-owned enterprises that became money losers and went into financial distress. This perception has swayed public opinion because of the excessive costs levied on society in some cases of botched privatizations. In Mexico, for example, the bailouts granted to keep banks and highways from going bankrupt increased public debt from less than 25 percent of GDP to over 50 percent (López-Calva 2004).

The underlying logic of these arguments is similar to that undergirding the arguments for the economic benefits of state production, which in the 1950s and 1960s justified the existence of state-owned enterprises on the grounds that they help solve market failures by taking into account the social costs of their actions. Today, academic evidence of the opposite abounds in at least three areas. First, systematic evidence shows that state-owned enterprises are less efficient than private firms in industrial and developing countries (Shleifer and Vishny 1994; Shleifer 1998). Second, the inefficiency of state-owned enterprises may be the natural result of political meddling when governments use them to achieve political objectives. This political use of state production leads to excessive employment, inefficient investments, and inadequate location of production sites, among other things (López-de-Silanes, Shleifer, and Vishny 1997). Finally, the large body of empirical work generated since the mid-1990s (reviewed in previous sections) shows that by and large privatization leads to substantial increases in the profitability of firms.

Criticisms of privatization that center on what the government gives up disregard the fact that state-owned enterprises are typically money-losing entities before privatization. Moreover, the visible losses may underestimate the real bottom line, because their precise magnitude is obscured by large cross-subsidies from other state-owned enterprises and soft loans from the government. In fact, tax collection from state-owned enterprises improved after privatization in most Latin American countries analyzed here. Brazil, the country with the smallest gains in profitability, experienced a 1 percentage point decrease in its net-taxes-to-sales ratio, although that ratio was still positive after privatization (the difference is not statistically significant). In Mexico, the same ratio increased 7.6 percentage points. We do not have direct information for Argentina, Chile, and Peru, but given that net income over sales increased between 12 and 20 percentage points, it is safe to assume that net taxes over sales also increased by a few percentage points. Increased fiscal revenues mean more resources that can be channeled to address pressing social needs, thereby benefiting society at large.

Higher tax revenues, if managed appropriately, should allow governments an increased capability for welfare-improving activities to benefit the poorest segments of society. Argentina, Mexico, and Peru are examples of countries where privatization revenues and the increased tax receipts from firms that formerly did not make profits were probably large enough to offset the costs of job losses (Rama 1999; Chong and López-de-Silanes 2003). Privatization revenues need not be a blessing, however, if they are misused. Anuatti-Neto and his coauthors point out that in Brazil privatization brought about high macroeconomic costs because the revenues it produced may have delayed fiscal adjustment and helped prop up an overvalued currency. This is obviously not an argument against privatization but rather an argument against the political misuse of the resources it generates.

Overall, the empirical literature on privatization shows that it affects the government's budget by reducing previous subsidies to state-owned enterprises, raising substantial revenue from the sale, and generating taxes on the increased profits. The benefits of a well-managed privatization program could be substantial not only for the privatized firm but also for society.

Worker Exploitation

The second potential source of gains after privatization is transfers from workers to shareholders, because cuts in labor costs may account for a large fraction of reduced total costs. Labor cost reductions can come from two sources: fewer workers, or lower wages and benefits. As explained above, the set of papers presented here finds that direct employment by the median state-owned firm falls between 5 and 57 percent after privatization depending on the country (see figure 1.6). Layoffs explain part of the cost reduction and thus higher profits after privatization. The other potential component is cuts in wages and benefits. The hypothesis that privatization leads to redistribution of income from workers to the new owners predicts a reduction in real wages and benefits for those workers who remain in the firm. Data on wages at the firm level are scarce, but for those countries with available information (Argentina, Bolivia, Colombia, Mexico, and Peru), the evidence shows the exact opposite: an increase in the real and industry-adjusted wages of workers in privatized firms (figure 1.10). Both real and industry-adjusted wages for the median firm increased by about 100 percent in Mexico and Peru. Bolivia enjoyed real wage increases of almost 110 percent, while in Argentina the industry-adjusted increase was about 70 percent. Colombia shows the smallest increase, but even here workers in privatized firms increased their wages more than others in the private sector.

The two components of the transfers from workers to profits move in opposite directions. The fraction of profitability changes that may be attributed to labor cost savings thus encompasses the lower costs stemming from layoffs and the higher costs from wage increases for the remaining workers. Following the methodology in La Porta and López-de-Silanes (1999), the studies on Argentina, Bolivia, Mexico, and Peru compute the impact on profits from lower labor costs after privatization. The evidence from these four countries shows that even with the extreme assumption that laid-off workers had zero productivity, the median savings from labor costs is equivalent to 16 percent of the gains in net income to sales after privatization or 20 percent of the gains in operating income to sales. The range of calculations extends from close to 5 percent in Peru to 45 percent in Mexico (figure 1.11). If we assume that these workers are half as productive as those retained by the firm, the median savings from reduced labor costs for the countries with data falls to 8 percent of the gains in net income to sales and 10 percent of the gains in operating income to sales. Overall, the evidence indicates that labor cost reductions are a source of the gains after privatization, but these savings do not explain the bulk of the higher observed profitability.

The welfare of displaced workers after privatization is another issue for consideration. The calculations above overstate the losses to workers to the extent that some of those laid off found alternative employment or attach some value to leisure. There is evidence that this is in fact the case; Galiani and his coauthors, for example, carried out a survey among displaced workers in Argentina. They found that the labor force

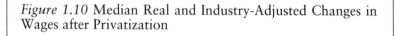

Figure 1.10 Median Real and Industry-Adjusted Changes in Wages after Privatization

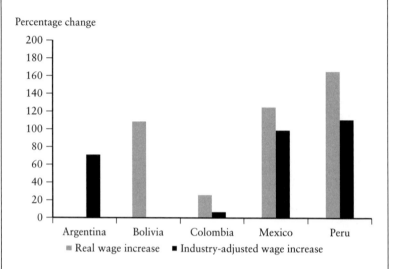

Note: Real average wages are defined as the inflation-adjusted total compensation paid to the average worker. The Consumer Price Index was used as a deflator to calculate real wages. Industry-adjusted wages are computed by augmenting the preprivatization value by the difference between the cumulative growth rate of real wages per worker of the firm and the cumulative growth rate of real wages per worker of the control group in the postprivatization period relative to the average real wage per worker before privatization. For Bolivia, Mexico, and Peru, information is for a subsample of firms that have available wage evidence.
Source: Chapters 2, 3, 6, 7, and 8.

participation rate was high among such workers and that although unemployment rates were above those of the rest of the population, many displaced workers found alternative jobs in which they felt their situation was stable. Taking all factors into account, these authors estimate the welfare loss to displaced workers was equivalent to 39–51 percent of their earnings before privatization and that 40 percent thought they were not worse off after privatization. This is surprising, since most theories and evidence suggest that workers in state-owned enterprises are overpaid and have very low productivity. Further work is needed in this area to provide clearer

Figure 1.11 Transfers from Workers as a Percentage of Increased Profitability after Privatization

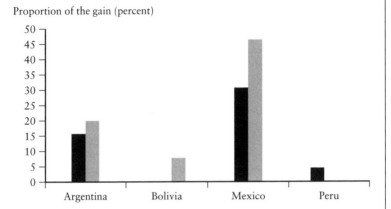

Proportion of the gain (percent)

■ Net-income-to-sales ratio   ■ Operating-income-to-sales ratio

Note: The figure shows the median gain in net income to sales and operating income to sales explained by savings in labor costs stemming from layoffs after privatization. Savings from layoffs are calculated as follows:

$$\frac{\text{WAGE}_{bp}(L_{bp} - L_{ap})}{\text{SALES}_{ap}}$$

where WAGE_{bp} is the average wage of employees in state-owned enterprises before privatization; L_{bp} is the number of workers employed before privatization; L_{ap} is the number of workers employed after privatization; and $SALES_{ap}$ is the monetary value of sales after privatization. The resulting number is thus expressed as a fraction of sales. We then divide by the percentage point increase in the operating-income-to-sales ratio to determine the percentage of the increase that results from transfers from workers. For Bolivia, Mexico, and Peru, information is for a subsample of firms that have available wage evidence. For Bolivia, net-income-to-sales data are not available. For Peru, data on savings in labor costs as a percentage of operating income to sales are not available.

Source: Chapters 2, 3, 7, and 8.

evidence on the extent of welfare losses to workers, but the available evidence thus far suggests that while laid-off workers do lose in this process, the losses may not be as large as previously thought.

Finally, privatization could also have compositional effects on the labor force and hurt unskilled workers disproportionately. The empirical evidence on this issue is inconclusive for the two Latin American countries with disaggregated wage and employment data, but it suggests that blue-collar workers actually fare better than their white-collar counterparts. In Bolivia, only 5 percent of blue-collar workers were laid off, while over 27 percent of white-collar workers were fired by the median firm. Moreover, unskilled workers who remained saw their real wages increase 103 percent, compared with a 99 percent rise for skilled workers. In Mexico, blue-collar workers suffered higher layoffs than white-collar ones in the median firm: 61 percent (32 percent industry-adjusted) for blue-collar workers versus 46 percent (31 percent industry-adjusted) for white-collar workers. Wages again exhibited the same trend as in Bolivia, with sharp rises in blue-collar real and industry-adjusted wages (148 percent and 122 percent, respectively) and smaller, though still substantial, wage increases for white-collar workers (100 percent real and 48 percent industry-adjusted). Therefore, for neither of these countries can we conclude that unskilled workers fared worse than skilled labor as a result of privatization.

Abuse of Market Power and Consumer Exploitation

The last concern about the sources of postprivatization gains is that the increase in firm profitability may come at the expense of consumers through weak regulation and abuse of market power. The papers presented here provide useful data for assessing these claims. If market power is a significant determinant of the gains, we should expect firms in noncompetitive sectors to experience large gains in operating income owing to higher product prices. Since profits are likely to be higher in noncompetitive sectors than in competitive sectors both before and after privatization, the relevant comparison for establishing the facts for this section is relative changes among privatized firms in competitive and noncompetitive sectors.

For the Latin American countries with data disaggregated by competitive and noncompetitive sectors, we find that changes in profitability are generally larger in the competitive sector than among noncompetitive industries. This evidence goes against the hypothesis that market power explains most of the gains. As figure 1.12 shows, the median ratio of operating income to sales in Mexico increased 14.5 percentage points for privatized firms in the competitive sector and only 7.5 points for firms in noncompetitive industries. Competitive firms in Colombia performed relatively better than their noncompetitive counterparts: their median

Figure 1.12 Median Changes in Profitability of Privatized Firms in Competitive and Noncompetitive Industries in Latin America

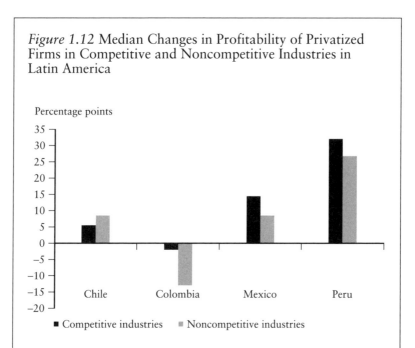

Note: Profitability is defined as the median ratio of operating income to sales, except for Peru where it is the mean net-income-to-sales ratio. For Chile, firms are classified as noncompetitive if they are in telecommunications, electricity, or social services sectors; and as competitive if they are not. For Colombia, noncompetitive firms are those in the energy sector; all other sectors are considered competitive. For Mexico, firms are classified into competitive and noncompetitive based on the description of the industry provided by the privatization prospectus of the firm. For Peru, the noncompetitive sectors are electricity, financial, and telecommunications, and the data for the competitive industries show aggregate information for the whole sample. For Peru, the information is expressed in mean values.
Source: Chapters 5–8.

profitability decreased by only 2 percentage points, compared with the 13 point drop for noncompetitive sectors, which underwent severe deregulation. Data for Peru reinforce this trend. Firms in noncompetitive sectors increased their profitability by an average of 27 percentage points, while the mean increase in the whole sample was 32 percentage points. In Chile, although the noncompetitive sectors' profitability increased more (8.5 percentage points), the increase is not statistically different from the 5.5 percentage point increase in competitive sectors.

Regression analysis for Peru using concentration proxies also contributes to assessing the role of market power. Confirming the trend
above, market concentration in Peru was found not to be a significant determinant of profits. Finally, information on firms' product prices before
and after privatization in Mexico also suggests that market power is not a
large source of gains. Cumulative price increases in the noncompetitive
sector in Mexico were only 6 percent higher than the growth of the industry-matched producer price index over the postprivatization period. La
Porta and López-de-Silanes (1999) use these product price data to draw a
quick calculation of the contribution of changes in prices to the observed
change in profitability of the whole sample of privatized firms. Their data
show that price increases accounted for only 5 (7) percent of the change in
mean (median) operating income to sales after privatization.[17]

If market power were an important source of profits for privatized
firms, those in noncompetitive sectors would show lower growth in employment, investment, and output than firms in competitive sectors (La
Porta and López-de-Silanes 1999). Available evidence for Latin America
does not support these claims (figure 1.13). In Mexico and Colombia, employment dropped 46 percent and 24 percent, respectively, for firms in the
competitive sector, and it decreased only 19 percent and 10 percent for
noncompetitive firms. In Chile, the pattern is even more striking: employment increased in both sectors, rising 16 percent in competitive industries
and 32 percent in noncompetitive sectors. For Peru, employment data
show no divergence in results between competitive and noncompetitive
sectors, as employment fell 50 percent in noncompetitive sectors and 51
percent for the whole sample. Output growth data for Mexico and Peru
reinforce this trend. In Peru, output growth for both sectors was very similar, with noncompetitive firms increasing sales 47 percent and the sales of
the whole sample going up 50 percent. Similarly, in Mexico, output of
competitive firms increased 56 percent, while sales in the noncompetitive
sector went up 78 percent.

Additional evidence comes from investment patterns. Investment per
employee grew 49 percent and 154 percent in the noncompetitive sectors
of Mexico and Colombia, respectively. Meanwhile, the same ratio grew
only 29 percent in competitive sectors of Mexico and stagnated in Colombia's competitive industries. The evidence for Chile here runs in the opposite direction, but it is hardly conclusive of market power abuse. Although
investment per employee grew 74 percent in Chile's competitive sectors, it
also grew almost 50 percent in noncompetitive industries.

Overall, the Latin American evidence presented in this section does not
support the claim that consumer exploitation is a significant source of privatization gains. These studies suggest that a large source of the gains may
lie in deep firm restructuring that leads to lower costs and higher efficiency. Evidence from Chile and Mexico is suggestive of this pattern. Unit
costs in the competitive sector fell 3 percent in Chile and 13 percent in

Figure 1.13 Changes in Employment and Output of Privatized Firms in Competitive and Noncompetitive Industries in Latin America

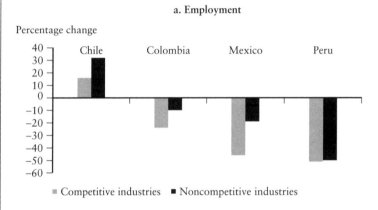

a. Employment

Percentage change

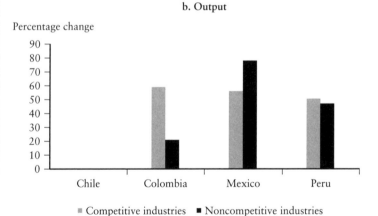

b. Output

Percentage change

Note: Employment corresponds to the total number of workers (paid and unpaid) who depend directly on the company; output is the monetary value of sales. For definitions of competitive and noncompetitive firms, see figure 1.12. For Chile, output information is not available. For Peru, the information is expressed in mean values.

Source: Chapters 5–8.

Mexico, while those of noncompetitive industries decreased 8 percent and 24 percent, respectively. Abuse of market power may be an issue for some firms, but the bulk of the evidence suggests it is not the main explanation of privatization gains across the board.

Dimensions of Consumer Welfare beyond the Effect on Prices

Beyond its effect on prices, privatization may affect consumer welfare through decreased access, worsened distribution, and reduced quality of goods and services (Akram 2000; Bayliss and Hall 2000; Bayliss 2001; Birdsall and Nellis 2002; Freije and Rivas 2002). These concerns are significant because the poorest segments of society are generally the main consumers of goods and services previously produced by state-owned enterprises. The evidence presented earlier on increased output, firm restructuring, and prices should alleviate some of these concerns, particularly for the case of standardized goods and products. Output and price are suitable proxies for measuring the availability of most of these goods. In the area of public utilities and services, however, access and distribution may still be a concern, since some segments of the population may lack access to the network and may thus be unable to purchase these services regardless of their price. Similarly, the quality of services such as water, electricity, telecommunications, or transportation may be reduced to try to meet price regulations. In all of these circumstances, consumer welfare may suffer as a result of privatization.

Some reviews of privatization cases are pessimistic about its success in the utilities sector. Bayliss (2002) points to examples of botched privatizations in Puerto Rico and Trinidad and Tobago, where water privatization led to price hikes and no apparent improvement in provision. Similarly, the privatization of the electricity sector in the Dominican Republic is claimed to have led to frequent blackouts and increases in utility prices, culminating in civil unrest and the deaths of several demonstrators (Bayliss 2002). One can always find cases of failure and cases of success. Therefore, the only way to address this question fully is to gather data that allow a systematic and economically robust analysis.

A first generation of privatization studies sheds light on this subject by analyzing case studies in several countries. Galal and others (1994), for example, analyze 12 privatization cases in Chile, Malaysia, Mexico, and the United Kingdom, including firms in sectors such as airlines and telecommunications. Their results indicate that privatization led to welfare gains of about 25 percent of preprivatization sales in 11 of the 12 cases. Early work on the privatization experience in Argentina also shows significant gains in access to services such as water, power, and port infrastructure (Carbajo and Estache 1996; Crampes and Estache 1996; Estache and Rodríguez 1996). Ramamurti (1996, 1997) concludes that privatization had a positive effect on Latin American telecommunications and railroad infrastructure because it led to a technological overhaul of the sectors and increased both access and the quality of service. Similarly, Ros (1999) examines the effect of privatization on the telecommunications sector in 110 countries and finds that the transfer of control from the public to the private sector led to significantly higher telephone density levels. Although the level of competition had a positive effect on industry efficiency, only privatization was related to network expansions.

A new generation of studies based on more detailed data and new econometric approaches corroborates the early results in terms of access and quality. For instance, Torero and Pasco-Font (2001) show that the number of telephone lines in Peru increased from 2.9 to 7.8 per 100 inhabitants and that the electrification coefficient jumped from 48 to 70 percent between 1993 and 1998. A study by Torero, Schroth, and Pasco-Font (2003) tests the impact of the privatization of telecommunications on the welfare of urban consumers in Peru; the authors find significant welfare gains and dramatic improvements in terms of efficiency, access, and quality of service. Similarly, Fischer, Gutiérrez, and Serra, in chapter 5, find improvements in access and service quality in the telecommunications sector in Chile, where the number of phone lines in operation increased sixfold, bringing density levels from 4.7 lines per 100 inhabitants in 1987 to 23.1 lines in 2001. The average length of the waiting period for a new phone line dropped from 416 days in 1993 to only 6 days in 2001, while the waiting list for a phone dropped from a peak of 314,000 households in 1992 to only 32,000 by 2001.[18]

The region offers a number of similar examples of improvements in access to water, electricity, telecommunications, and other services that have created benefits beyond lower prices. Nonetheless, one may still be concerned about the distributional impacts of the increased coverage, as it may not be reaching the poorest sectors of society. Bayliss (2002) recognizes that privatization has the potential for welfare-enhancing outcomes if it allows low-income households to gain access to the service network. However, her review of cases suggests that the drive to seek higher profits in the private provision of services will almost invariably lead to a loss for the poor. Birdsall and Nellis (2002) also argue that privatization may lead to improvements in efficiency and profitability while worsening income distribution and wealth.[19] They conclude that the gains in profitability are probably not worth the distributive effects they create.

Recent detailed econometric analyses with better samples provide some answers to these concerns. In chapter 2 Galiani and his coauthors offer some of the best data available for the municipal level in Argentina, where about 30 percent of localities privatized water delivery services. Their results show a significant increase in the proportion of households connected to water services in municipalities that privatized compared with those that did not. Their regression estimates suggest that the number of households connected to the water network increased by 11.6 percent as a result of privatization (with the exception of Buenos Aires, where 98 percent of households were already connected). Using less comprehensive data from Bolivia, Barja, McKenzie, and Urquiola (2002) find that privatization increased access to water relative to both the existing trend and nonprivatized areas. They further report that the relative benefits of water privatization are greatest for the poorest segments of the population, who gained from the largest increases in access.

For Argentina, Galiani and his coauthors cleverly design tests that map water delivery to infant mortality in an effort to directly address the concerns about quality after privatization. Their regressions show that, controlling for other factors, child mortality fell by 5 to 7 percent more in areas of Argentina that privatized water services than in those that did not. The effect was largest in the poorest municipalities that privatized, where child mortality fell 24 percent. Privatization translated into 375 child deaths prevented per year. McKenzie and Mookherjee (2003) provide an overview of four studies from Argentina, Bolivia, Mexico, and Nicaragua that use household surveys to measure the impact of privatization on welfare. They conclude that the sale of state-owned enterprises brought positive welfare effects and that the poorest segments of the population appear to be relatively better off. In Argentina, for example, they report falling electricity prices that improved the welfare of all income deciles. For Bolivia, they report welfare gains from increased electricity access for all but the top income deciles; the gains exceeded 100 percent for the lowest deciles despite real price increases. The price of electricity increased in Nicaragua, but the welfare loss to households that already had access was less than 1 percent of their per capita expenditure, because the budget share allocated to electricity is typically low. At the same time, the value of gaining access to electricity was positive and of a larger magnitude for lower-income deciles that had relatively less access before privatization. The net positive impact of electricity privatization for these low-income groups reached nearly 16 percent of per capita expenditure.

So far, we have provided evidence that counters most of the criticisms of privatization. What remains unaddressed, however, is how to make sense of the cases of privatization failures pointed out by several authors (see Bayliss 2002 and Birdsall and Nellis 2002 for reviews). It will always be possible to find instances of failed privatizations, but analysts should not distort this information and turn it into an argument against privatization itself. The overwhelming evidence showing that it can be done right suggests that we should look for the reasons why it failed in certain instances. In the next two sections, we argue that many of these failures have two roots: the role of politicians in the privatization process, which may lead to corruption, renegotiation, and opportunistic behavior; and the lack of an appropriate postprivatization regulatory and corporate governance framework that sets the boundaries for nonabusive corporate behavior and facilitates investment.

What Is the Best Approach for Selling? Concerns about the Privatization Process

Privatization requires heavy government involvement because the politicians involved are frequently setting up the method and running the sale process. This may lead to favoritism and nepotism (Perotti 1995; Bortolotti, Fantini, and Scarpa 2001; Biais and Perotti 2002; Earle and Gehlbach 2003). Looking at the privatization process in this light shows the relevance of understanding the impact of the process's characteristics and the opportunities for corruption they may provide. Privatization may be the last chance for politicians to appropriate cash flows or deliver favors that further their political objectives. The role of politicians in privatization is central in three areas: the method of privatization chosen, the restructuring of firms before they are sold off, and the types of contracts written.

The Method of Privatization

The way the privatization process is carried out is of utmost importance. A successful program can increase social welfare and bring about efficiency gains across the board, while a botched process may create opportunities for inefficiency and corruption. In Argentina, as in other countries, an obscure bidding process raised suspicions of corruption and political favoritism. When governments fail to ensure a crystal clear process, the perception of corruption can breed unease among the public and may lead to a backlash against privatization. In principle, a clear and homogeneous privatization process should be established from the start, and special emphasis should be placed on making the auction results as transparent as possible. In reality, however, only a handful of countries have followed this path. Many fail to establish clear guidelines because their privatization programs were originally planned as small affairs or because they lack the necessary skills to do so. Alternatively, politicians may have strong incentives to create obscure and arbitrary privatization mechanisms that allow them to extract high rents for themselves or their constituencies. To analyze the validity of such claims empirically, one could use systematic evidence of the impact of the privatization process on sale prices and on subsequent firm performance. This is difficult although not impossible.

The existing empirical literature has taken two approaches to address these issues. The first approach uses cross-country comparisons. Chong and Riaño (2003), for example, analyze 285 privatizations in industrial and developing countries and find that bureaucratic quality, lack of corruption, and privatization prices are positively related. Their results show that when they control for macroeconomic conditions and firm characteristics, a 1 point increase in their 10 point index of bureaucratic quality is associated with a 10.2 percent increase in the price paid per dollar of assets in privatizations, while a similar increase in the 10 point lack-of-corruption index results in a 9.6 percent rise in the price paid per dollar of assets. Bortolotti, Fantini, and Scarpa (2001), who analyze data for 49 countries, conclude that strong legal institutions and adequately developed capital markets substantially contribute to successful privatizations. Finally, Chong and Sánchez (2003) provide data for infrastructure privatization contracts in Brazil, Chile, Colombia, and Peru to show that establishing a clear and transparent contractual arrangement helped achieve the privatization objectives set out by these governments. These results together suggest that the success or failure of privatization programs is influenced by the honesty and efficiency of the government and by the simplicity and transparency of contractual agreements.

The second approach to analyzing the impact of the method of privatization is to use within-country data. López-de-Silanes (1997) for Mexico and Arin and Okten (2002) for Turkey are able to control for potentially omitted variables and therefore provide a full analysis of the impact of several restructuring measures and privatization mechanisms on the net price of state-owned enterprises.[20] The case of Mexico is a good illustration of the impact of specific differences in the privatization process, since the program lasted for more than a decade and was executed by different administrations. An additional benefit of this sample is that although the general method of a first-price sealed-bid auction was the rule throughout the period, certain firms were privatized with specific requirements that provide useful variations to analyze. Between 1982 and 1988 privatization was not conducted as a centralized program, but rather each ministry was allowed to sell enterprises in its realm of operations. This resulted in a plethora of requirements for bidders and methods of payment. The administration that took power in 1988 established a centralized privatization office and developed a homogeneous process, which improved transparency by mandating public disclosure of the bidding stages through the press. Econometric estimations show that once the analyst controls for macroeconomic and firm-level characteristics, firms privatized during the second period sold at a premium of about 15 percent (López-de-Silanes 1997). The gains in efficiency owing to improved coordination and the presumably reduced room for corruption and political meddling have a clear mapping in the price received for enterprises sold.

Econometric work with firm-level data from Mexico also shows that different auction requirements make a substantial difference in the net price received by the government for state-owned enterprises. Firms sold under restrictions banning foreign bidders, requiring a prequalification stage, or asking for cash-only payments brought significantly lower prices per dollar of assets sold. Such requirements thus have an effect that is independent of the fact that they reduce competition in the auction; this evidence suggests that idiosyncratic and arbitrary privatization processes come at a direct cost to the government in terms of the price paid for state-owned enterprises.

The speed at which each privatization takes place may also have an impact on net prices raised. The theoretical literature is split between the benefits and costs of a short process. While rushing a sale carries potential costs such as not attracting enough bidders or not having enough time to set up an appropriate regulatory framework, the advocates of a speedy process point to the benefits of quickly disposing of money-losing firms and avoiding costly restructuring (Coes 1998). The recent literature addresses this issue by measuring the impact of the length of the privatization process on the price paid for the specific state-owned enterprise. Some believe that a lengthy privatization process should come at no cost, either because managers' concern for their reputation will lead them to run the firm efficiently or because the announcement of privatization may improve stakeholders' incentives and thus boost company performance (Caves 1990; Bolton and Roland 1992). Conversely, to the extent that the privatization process is similar to the situation of a firm in financial distress, the privatization announcement may be followed by a deterioration of incentives and performance (Altman 1984; Wruck 1990).

Within-country firm-level panel data are ideally set up for resolving this dispute. Evidence from Mexico and Turkey shows that after one controls for firm and industry characteristics, lengthy privatization processes come at a substantial cost to the government. The announcement of privatization in these countries brought a considerable deterioration in performance, which is probably attributable to the collapse of managers' incentives and to the performance of disgruntled workers who see their futures as highly uncertain.[21]

Restructuring Firms before Privatization

Government restructuring of state-owned enterprises before their sale is an issue likely to be fraught with political difficulties given that this is probably the last chance for government officials to extract benefits. As with other policies, restructuring programs can be defended rationally on grounds that they may increase revenues from the sale or ensure that firms are sent out to the market in the best condition to minimize layoffs and secure their survival (Nellis and Kikeri 1989; Kikeri, Nellis, and Shirley 1992; Kikeri 1999). As a result, there is great ambivalence about the optimal policy approach toward restructuring before privatization.

López-de-Silanes (1997) summarizes the theoretical arguments for and against various measures of prior restructuring and suggests that the issue should be resolved empirically. This is not a straightforward proposition, however, even with firm-level data. Restructuring measures are not undertaken randomly but are selectively targeted to firms that need them most. We would expect the government to absorb the debt of highly indebted state-owned enterprises, to fire workers when firms face serious overemployment, and to invest in new machinery when production processes are outdated. If the endogenous nature of these measures is not considered, we run the risk of reaching the wrong conclusions because regression coefficients would capture not only the effect of the restructuring measure, but also the negative effects of being in distress or having a bloated work force.

Available empirical evidence strongly suggests that restructuring policies do not lead to better net prices per dollar of assets sold. For the case of Mexico, López-de-Silanes (1997) shows that, after he controls for endogeneity, the optimal policy seems to be to refrain as much as possible from engaging in the restructuring of state-owned enterprises. Some of the most popular measures, such as debt absorption, do not increase net prices, while measures such as the establishment of investment and efficiency programs actually reduce net prices. These facts may be the result of politicians themselves carrying out the restructuring programs and emphasizing their political preferences when deciding what to invest in and what to do with existing infrastructure. It is disingenuous to think that the government can satisfy the desires of the new owners better than they could themselves. In Mexico's case, a few changes to the privatization mechanism could have yielded large benefits: emphasizing speed, firing the chief executive officer before privatization, and refraining from costly restructuring measures would have increased net prices by 135 percent. A similar study by Chong and Galdo (2004) analyzes a cross-country sample of telecommunications firms that were privatized between 1985 and 2000; the authors' ordinary least squares (OLS) and instrumental variables (IV) regressions yield no evidence that streamlining before privatization is linked to higher net prices. Finally, evidence from Turkey also supports the conclusion that restructuring measures are either useless or counterproductive in raising net prices (Arin and Okten 2002).

One of the most sensitive topics in the area of firm restructuring before privatization is that of labor force retrenchment. To analyze the impact of such retrenchment policies beyond their effects on privatization prices, we construct (in an earlier paper, Chong and López-de-Silanes 2003) a worldwide privatization database containing detailed preprivatization firm and labor force characteristics, labor restructuring measures undertaken by the government, and information on postprivatization labor rehiring policies, among other things. Table 1.4 shows that despite heavy unionization rates, most governments around the world downsize the labor force of state-owned enterprises before privatization. Labor retrenchment occurred in 78 percent of the sample, while only 33 percent of all firms experienced voluntary downsizing programs. Employment guarantees were established as part of privatization in 28 percent of the cases, while pay cuts before privatization were infrequent (7.5 percent). Asia is the only region of the world with a significantly lower frequency of labor downsizing before privatization. Governments in Latin America deviated little from the general pattern; the only notable exception is the low frequency of employment guarantees, which was used in only 8 percent of all firms privatized in the region. Table 1.4 also shows that state-owned enterprises in Latin America were heavily unionized and active: two-thirds of state-owned enterprises privatized in the region experienced labor strikes in the three years before privatization.

Following our earlier methodology, we ran OLS and instrumental variables regressions for the 94 state-owned enterprises privatized in Latin America to test whether labor restructuring policies in this region translated into higher net prices per dollar of firm sales. The first column of table 1.5 shows the OLS results, which suggest that labor downsizing before privatization has a significant negative impact, equivalent to 28 percent of the average net price per dollar of sales. The instrumental variables results in column 2 show that once we control for endogeneity, the coefficient drops essentially to zero and loses all significance.[22] The results for Latin America reflect those for other regions: labor downsizing before privatization is not priced by the buyers. From the point of view of increased government revenues, if a state-owned enterprise is overstaffed, it is probably best for governments to wait and let the new owners make the decisions after they buy the firm.

The other two regressions in table 1.5 focus on the effect of labor retrenchment in the form of voluntary downsizing programs in which governments offer monetary incentives for workers to quit. Even after controlling for endogeneity, voluntary downsizing leads to a marginally significant discount in the net price paid by private buyers. This negative effect might be explained by adverse selection, in that workers with the highest productivity or the best chances of finding alternative work are more likely to leave. Voluntary downsizing may therefore hurt firms, since it tends to result in the termination of valuable workers and the retention of less productive ones (Fallick 1996; Rama 1999). Despite the fact that voluntary separation programs are politically palatable, the findings here show that these programs may weaken firms and distort the composition of the work force, as predicted by theoretical models (Kahn 1985; Diwan 1994; Jeon and Laffont 1999).

To shed further light on the "quality of firing" carried out by governments before privatization, we collected data on the hiring policies of state-owned enterprises after privatization (Chong and López-de-Silanes 2003). While hiring new workers probably responds to the legitimate business needs of privatized firms, rehiring previously fired workers

Table 1.4 Labor Restructuring before Privatization, by Region

Indicator	Latin America	Asia	Africa and Middle East	Developed countries	Transition economies	All
Sample size, unionization, and strikes before privatization						
Number of firms	101	24	64	77	42	308
Firms with unions before privatization	92.1	58.3	81.2	83.1	88.1	84.4
Firms with strikes before privatization	66.3	29.2	45.3	29.8	47.6	47.4
Type of restructuring measure before privatization						
Downsizing	82.2	58.3	79.7	79.2	76.2	78.2
Voluntary downsizing	32.5	12.5	45.3	28.6	14.3	32.5
Employment guarantee	8.4	20.1	51.6	13	52.4	28.2
Pay cut	8.9	0	1.6	13	7.1	7.5

Note: The table shows the number of firms included for each region, the regularity of unions and strikes, and the frequency of restructuring measures undertaken before privatization. The variables are defined as follows: (1) firms with unions before privatization is the percentage of privatized state-owned enterprises that had a union up to three years before privatization; (2) firms with strikes before privatization is of state-owned enterprises that suffered any kind of protest such as picketing or strikes during the three years before privatization; (3) downsizing is a dummy variable equal to 1 if the firm undertook any downsizing of the labor force up to three years before privatization, and 0 otherwise; downsizing may be classified as voluntary or compulsory, and may be neutral (no particular group targeted) or targeted according to age (age-biased downsizing), skills (skill-biased downsizing), or gender (female-biased downsizing); (4) voluntary downsizing is a dummy variable equal to 1 if the state-owned enterprise reduced its labor force in an exclusively noncoercive manner during the three years before privatization, and 0 otherwise; the most common methods of voluntary downsizing are incentive-based measures such as severance packages and pension enhancements; (5) employment guarantee is a dummy variable equal to 1 if the state-owned enterprise made any promise regarding the employment status of workers during the three years before privatization, and 0 otherwise; (6) pay cut is a dummy variable equal to 1 if there were any reductions in the salary or wage of workers during the three years before privatization, and 0 otherwise.

Source: Chong and López-de-Silanes (2003).

Table 1.5 Labor Restructuring and Privatization Prices in Latin America

| | Dependent variable: net price | | | |
Variable	OLS (1)	IV (2)	OLS (3)	IV (4)
Firm and privatization characteristics				
Net total liabilities	0.0176	0.0168	0.0216	0.0153
	(0.041)	(0.043)	(0.040)	(0.042)
Mining	0.3265***	0.3406***	0.293***	0.3466***
	(0.071)	(0.067)	(0.074)	(0.061)
Industry	0.2580***	0.2711***	0.2104***	0.277***
	(0.076)	(0.074)	(0.075)	(0.065)
Services	0.4106***	0.4232***	0.3565***	0.4177***
	(0.069)	(0.066)	(0.072)	(0.057)
Foreign	0.0561*	0.0737**	0.0666**	0.0856**
	(0.033)	(0.036)	(0.033)	(0.038)
Labor characteristics				
Unions	-0.1592	-0.1821	-0.1878	-0.1814
	(0.131)	(0.149)	(0.122)	(0.143)
Labor policies				
Downsizing	-0.1683***	-0.0201		
	(0.044)	(0.027)		
Voluntary downsizing			-0.1213***	-0.0558*
			(0.038)	(0.032)

(Table continues on the following page.)

Table 1.5 (continued)

Variable	Dependent variable: net price			
	OLS	IV	OLS	IV
	(1)	(2)	(3)	(4)
Macroeconomic variable				
Gross domestic product	0.0673***	0.0681*	0.0687***	0.0713***
	(0.010)	(0.010)	(0.010)	(0.011)
Constant	−1.2120***	−1.3512*	−1.2715***	−1.4746***
	0.334	0.341	0.311	0.350***
Observations	94	94	94	94
R^2	0.47	0.38	0.53	0.41
F	11.36	10.32	11.59	12.35
Prob > F	0.000	0.000	0.000	0.000

* Significant at the 10 percent level.
** Significant at the 5 percent level.
*** Significant at the 1 percent level.

Note: IV = instrumental variables and OLS = ordinary least square. The dependent variable is the net privatization price/sales, which is defined as the amount that accrues to the government from the sale of the state-owned enterprise after all privatization and restructuring costs are taken into account, adjusted by the percentage of company shares sold and divided by the average net sales of the state-owned enterprise during the three years before its privatization. The present value of the resulting number as of 2000 is used. The independent variables are defined as follows: (1) net total liabilities is a dummy variable equal to 1 if net total liabilities of the firm were greater than 0 up to three years before privatization, and 0 otherwise; (2) dummy variables for sectors (mining, industry, and services) are equal to 1 if the state-owned enterprise is part of that sector, and 0 otherwise; (3) foreign is a dummy variable equal to 1 if foreign firms were allowed to bid on the sale of the state-owned enterprise, and 0 otherwise; (4) unions is a dummy variable equal to 1 if the state-owned enterprise had a union up to three years before privatization, and 0 otherwise; (5) downsizing is a dummy variable equal to 1 if the firm undertook any downsizing of the labor force up to three years before privatization, and 0 otherwise; downsizing may be classified as voluntary or compulsory, and may be targeted according to age (age-biased downsizing), skills (skill-biased downsizing), or gender (female-biased downsizing) or may be neutral (no particular group targeted); (6) voluntary downsizing is a dummy variable equal to 1 if the state-owned enterprise reduced its labor force in an exclusively noncoercive manner during the three years before privatization, and 0 otherwise; the most common methods of voluntary downsizing are incentive-based measures such as severance packages and pension enhancements; (7) gross domestic product is the log of the average GDP in the country (in U.S. dollars at purchasing power parity) during the three years before privatization. All regressions include firm size controls. Columns 1 and 3 provide estimates from OLS regressions, while columns 2 and 4 show the second stage of the two-step instrumental variables procedure used in order to account for the endogenous nature of the labor downsizing variables. The instrumental variables approach is carried out according to the procedure outlined in Chong and López-de-Silanes (2004). Robust standard errors are given in parentheses.

Source: Chong and López-de-Silanes 2003.

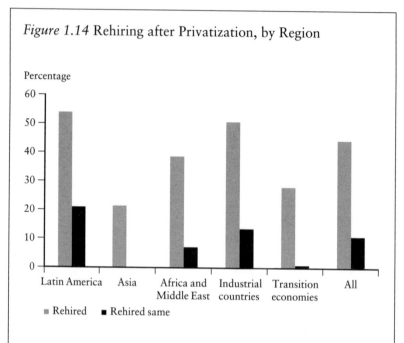

Figure 1.14 Rehiring after Privatization, by Region

Note: Variables are defined as follows: rehired is a dummy variable
equal to 1 if the privatized firm rehired previously fired workers up to
18 months after privatization, and 0 otherwise; rehired same is a dummy
variable equal to 1 if the privatized firm rehired previously fired workers
and placed them in the same department from which they were fired up
to 18 months after privatization, and 0 otherwise. Previously fired
workers are those who were terminated during the three years before
privatization.
Source: Chong and López-de-Silanes 2003.

could mean that the downsizing programs before privatization went too
far. After all, why else would a firm rehire a worker who was deemed
expendable a relatively short time before? Figure 1.14 shows that close
to 45 percent of all firms that underwent labor retrenchment programs
in the three years before privatization hired back some of the fired workers after privatization. Across countries, only 10 percent of firms with
government-run retrenchment programs ended up hiring back some of
those workers to their previous positions within 18 months after privatization. Latin America is the region with the highest percentage of firms
rehiring workers (53 percent) and rehiring to the same jobs that they had
previously held (20 percent).

Table 1.6 analyzes the determinants of the probability that the privatized state-owned firm with labor retrenchment programs before privatization would hire new workers (new hires) or former workers previously fired by the government (rehires). Results show that the existence of a voluntary downsizing program before privatization does not predict a higher probability of firms hiring new workers after privatization (column 1), but it increases by 34 percentage points the probability that the private buyer will rehire some of the workers who were previously fired by the government (column 2).[23]

The hiring behavior of firms in the postprivatization period says a great deal about the quality of the firing process and provides further evidence against the wisdom of government restructuring before privatization. Based on the evidence in this section, governments should think hard before restructuring the work force of state-owned enterprises intended for privatization. The political costs are high, the impact on net prices is low, and the firm could end up losing some of its most valuable employees.

Type of Privatization Contract

The type of privatization contract written is another potential area that may leave room for opportunistic behavior from politicians and private buyers. The simplest contracts are straightforward, outright sales of assets in which the government disconnects itself completely from the operational future of the privatized firm. Other types of contracts may actually lead to a perverse relationship between the privatized firm and the state as managers and bureaucrats collude to serve their own interests at the expense of consumers and taxpayers. These contracts could take the form of the provision of services, the construction of infrastructure projects, or the establishment of joint ventures between private companies and the government. The common element in all of these cases is that the umbilical cord between the government and the firm has not been severed, leaving ample room for a complex set of problems. Shleifer and Vishny (1994) develop a theoretical model to help understand the incentives faced by firms in instances of partial privatization. When privatized firms depend significantly on the state, they may not restructure as expected because it is easier for them to extract rents from the government than to undergo painful reforms. At the same time, politicians have incentives to keep them afloat by subsidizing them and shielding them from competition. These arrangements persist because they are beneficial for both parties, although they reduce social welfare. As Bayliss (2002) points out, water privatization programs in Guinea and Côte d'Ivoire are examples of poor deals in which the private sector was able to make substantial profits controlling the distribution and fee collection of the service, while the government spent resources maintaining the infrastructure.

Table 1.6 New Hires and Rehires in Privatized Firms in
Latin America

Indicator	Dependent variable: new hires		Dependent variable: rehires	
	Probit (1)	dF/dX	Probit (2)	dF/dX
Voluntary	0.6035	[0.1600]	0.9004**	[0.3370]
downsizing	(0.3835)		(0.3826)	
Strikes	0.6026	[0.1408]	1.0382**	[0.3961]
	(0.431)		(0.423)	
Foreign	−0.3092	[−0.0852]	−0.2469	[−0.0943]
participation	(0.4074)		(0.3879)	
Collective	−0.2898	[−0.0767]	−0.8634*	[−0.3340]
relations	(0.4835)		(0.5221)	
laws				
Constant	0.1453		−10.1961**	
	(4.2973)		(4.3490)	
Observations	76	76		
Log likelihood	−29.49	−33.99		
Wald chi^2	6.58	13.60		

* Significant at the 10 percent level.
** Significant at the 5 percent level.
*** Significant at the 1 percent level.
Note: The dependent variable in the first regression is new hires, which is a
dummy variable equal to 1 if the privatized firm hired new workers up to 18
months after privatization, and 0 otherwise; in the second regression, it is rehires,
which is a dummy variable equal to 1 if the privatized firm rehired previously fired
workers up to 18 months after privatization, and 0 otherwise. The independent
variables are defined as follows: (1) voluntary downsizing is a dummy variable
equal to 1 if the state-owned enterprise cut its labor force in an exclusively
noncoercive manner during the three years before privatization, and 0 otherwise;
the most common methods of voluntary downsizing are incentive-based measures
such as severance packages and pension enhancements; (2) strikes is a dummy
variable equal to 1 if there were any protests, picketing, or strikes up to three years
before privatization, and 0 otherwise; (3) foreign participation is a dummy variable
equal to 1 if foreign firms were allowed to bid for the state-owned enterprise, and
0 otherwise; (4) the collective relations laws index ranges from 0 to 3 and measures
the level of protection granted to workers by labor and employment laws (higher
values of the index represent more stringent laws regarding worker protection); it
measures the areas of collective bargaining, worker participation in management,
and collective disputes. All regressions include a partial privatization dummy,
sectoral dummies, and country macroeconomic controls. Standard errors and
marginal effects are given in parentheses and brackets, respectively.
Source: Data collected by the authors; Chong and López-de-Silanes 2003; Botero and
others 2005.

To find a solution to the complications that these relationships generate, Engel, Fischer, and Galetovic (1999, 2001) analyze the Chilean infrastructure concessions of the 1990s and note that franchising programs can
provide a better alternative to the traditional approach of full state financing for infrastructure projects, particularly for governments that are
financially and politically constrained. The regulatory framework, however, must be effective if governments are to reap the potential benefits of
franchising and avoid falling into hold-up problems in which firms under-
bid to get the contracts but then threaten bankruptcy if a renegotiation is
not granted.

Guasch (2001) provides empirical evidence that renegotiations in concessions are fairly common. He analyzes more than 1,000 concessions
granted in Latin American countries during the 1990s and finds that more
than 60 percent of them were substantially renegotiated within three
years. Infrastructure projects are usually very risky because of the difficulty inherent in forecasting demand. Firms therefore press for income
guarantees and other explicit or implicit insurance mechanisms that end
up costing the government too much. It may occasionally be in a country's
best interest to give out these guarantees, but they should be explicit and
transparent, and they should ideally be made in exchange for a fee (Engel,
Fischer, and Galetovic 2003).

In all of these situations, the solution should also include very clear disclosure and monitoring mechanisms to avoid related-party transactions at
unfair terms. Such transactions may end up bankrupting the joint venture
or the asset that the government has an interest in keeping afloat to the
benefit of the private corporation, as happened in the case of highways
and commercial banks in Chile and Mexico (Ramírez 1998; Johnson and
others 2000; La Porta, López-de-Silanes, and Zamarripa 2003). These are
not easy issues to solve, and many of the failures of privatization can be
linked to perverse incentives provided by misguided privatization concession contracts.

The evidence in this section can be understood from a political economy perspective. Privatization involves politicians with incentives and
objectives. Therefore, the design of the privatization process, the contracts
ultimately written, the restrictions attached to the sale of state-owned enterprises, and the restructuring measures adopted before privatization
should be understood as opportunities for politicians to extract rents and
hand out favors. This perspective helps rationalize instances in which corruption in privatization leads to disastrous results. The policy lesson is
clear: a transparent and expeditious privatization process leaves less room
for corruption and collusion among politicians and businessmen who may
try to benefit from opaqueness. One must also consider the time needed to
set up an effective privatizing agency and build the regulatory framework
that should be in place before state-owned enterprises with market power
are sold. We turn to this topic in the next section.

Complementary Policies: Reregulation and Corporate Governance

The previous section analyzed some of the main privatization failures emerging from policies or decisions taken before or at the time of privatization. In this section, we turn to the impact of the regulatory and institutional framework after privatization. Privatization should not be looked at in isolation. Its success is likely to depend on at least two sets of complementary policies. The first is deregulation and reregulation of sectors with market power or in which government ownership represented a substantial percentage of total assets before privatization. The second is the establishment of a set of institutions that promote good corporate governance, which facilitates access to capital and allows recently privatized firms to finance their growth without dependence on the state. Many privatization failures can be explained by a lack of careful consideration of these two complementary sets of policies.

Privatization, Reregulation, and Deregulation

An appropriate regulatory framework after privatization is a key component of the success or failure of the program, particularly in utilities and services. A common element across many failed examples of privatization is inadequate regulation leading to suboptimal levels of competition or situations in which producers are allowed to keep the gains from privatization without sharing them with consumers (Boubakri and Cosset 1999; Megginson and Netter 2001). The classic position of critics is to turn this into an argument against further privatization. However, the ample empirical evidence surveyed here shows that privatization can be done correctly and can lead to social gains. This evidence should be enough to discard a simplistic interpretation of cases of failures.

Regulation should be carefully revised in conjunction with privatization in two prominent situations: industries characterized as natural monopolies or by the presence of oligopolistic markets, and industries in which the government owns most of the assets in the industry even if no individual firm has substantial market power. Sectors with heavy state presence tend to be protected by a web of regulations originally instituted to cut the losses of state-owned firms and reduce fiscal deficits. In some of these cases, the necessary regulatory effort can be best understood as deregulation to eliminate protective structures that shield companies from competition and allow privatized firms to make extraordinary gains at the cost of consumers. As explained in both the early and more recent literature, competition and deregulation should be carefully considered in privatization (Yarrow 1986; Allen and Gale 2000). Winston (1993) argues that deregulation has the power to produce efficiency improvements, which can benefit consumers and producers. There is no reason to believe that deregulation should lead to different outcomes in the case of privatization of overprotected industries.[24] In sectors with oligopolistic power, the deregulation effort needs to be complemented by a reregulation that clearly establishes a new package of rules and disclosures that will enhance supervision and reduce abuse of market power.

Reregulation of oligopolistic sectors is complicated because of weaknesses in regulatory governance. As Fischer and Serra (2002) explain, regulators are often subject to pressures from populist politicians and industry lobbyists, and their low salaries make them susceptible to capture. Moreover, regulatory systems often operate within the context of an inefficient and perhaps even corrupt judicial system.

Deregulation complements privatization in two ways (La Porta and López-de-Silanes 1999). First, product market competition provides a tool for weeding out the least efficient firms. This process may take too long—or not work at all—if regulation inhibits new entry or makes exit costly. Wallsten (2001) undertakes an econometric analysis of the effects of telecommunications privatization and regulation in a panel of 30 countries in Latin America and Africa. His results show that competition from mobile operators and privatization combined with the existence of a separate regulator are significantly associated with increases in labor efficiency, mainlines per capita, and connection capacity. A casual interpretation of his results suggests that privatization of oligopolistic industries without concurrent reforms may not necessarily improve welfare.

Second, deregulation may also complement privatization by raising the cost of political intervention. Whereas an inefficient monopoly can squander its rents without endangering its existence, an inefficient firm in a competitive industry would have to receive a subsidy to stay afloat. The introduction of competition forces politicians to pay firms directly to engage in politically motivated actions, whereas previously the costs of these measures were absorbed by a state-owned firm that did not have to worry about market performance. In fact, competition is often restricted precisely because it raises the costs of political influence. Colombia and Mexico provide good examples of deregulatory policy actions that, when coupled with privatization, can be used as a lever to transform the economic landscape and reduce political interference in the economy. In the early 1990s Colombia began an economic openness program through the promotion of market competition and deregulation. As Pombo and Ramírez describe in chapter 6, privatization was perceived as an instrument for economic deregulation and the promotion of market competition. A decade earlier Mexico started to transform its previously closed economy characterized by capital controls, price regulation, restrictions on foreign direct investment, high tariffs, import quotas, and a large state-owned public sector. As in the case of Colombia, privatization coupled with deregulation played a key role in the drive to restructure the economy and help privatized state-owned enterprises catch up to their private peers (La Porta and López-de-Silanes 1999).

Generally speaking, reregulation or deregulation can take place at three different moments: before privatization, at the time of privatization, or after the state-owned enterprise has been sold. The literature emphasizes the importance of having efficient regulation at an early stage. Reregulation or deregulation before privatization of the industry may increase the pace of divestiture and help sell companies at a higher price if it reduces regulatory risk.[25] Wallsten (2002) finds that countries that established a separate regulatory authority in telecommunications before privatization not only benefited from increased telecommunications investment and telephone penetration but also gained from investors' willingness to pay more for the telecommunications firms.[26] Establishing effective preprivatization regulation is not easy, however, for at least three reasons. First, changes to the regulatory regime before privatization are likely to lower the profits of state-owned enterprises, which translates into higher financial needs for the government at a very difficult time. Second, the political will for a true regulatory reform might not materialize without the pressure of imminent privatization. Finally, governments with little experience in privatization often find it difficult to carry out an effective preprivatization regulatory reform.

Deregulation and reregulation at the time of privatization solve the first two problems and reduce regulatory risk discounts. As long as a suitable regulatory framework is in place at or before the time of privatization, consumers and the government should benefit from the process. Chisari, Estache, and Romero (1999) use a computable general equilibrium model for Argentina to show that the gains from efficient regulation are nontrivial. Their model estimates the gains from the private operation of utilities at about 0.9 percent of GDP and those of effective regulation at an additional 0.35 percent of GDP. Moreover, the distribution of the gains across income classes is driven by the effectiveness of the regulators. In short, they claim that clear reregulation is good for the poor.

Lack of regulatory capabilities at the time of privatization, coupled with a desire to maximize price at the time of the sale, has led several governments to postpone full and clear reregulation. Establishing an adequate regulatory scheme after privatization, however, may be problematic from a political economy perspective. Since the agency in charge of enforcing and regulating the contracts is often the same as or subordinated to the agency that carried out the privatization, the people involved have an incentive to implement lax enforcement to avoid exposing past mistakes. Chong and Sánchez (2003) document that for a broad number of concessions in infrastructure projects, the private sector was able to bargain and keep protective regulation after privatization because of the threat of bankruptcy, withdrawal, or desertion of future investment commitments. All of these affect the reputation and credibility of privatizing politicians. According to Guasch (2001), concession contracts in developing countries often led to renegotiations over the last 15 years. In Latin America and the Caribbean, 40 percent of all concession contracts were renegotiated just over 2.2 years after they were signed. Engel, Fischer, and Galetovic (2003) argue that opportunistic renegotiations of concessions are common because of a "privatize now, regulate later" approach. Cost overruns in concessions and unclear rules governing contingencies provide private owners with the opportunity to extract economic rents from the government. Finally, attempting to substantially alter the regulatory framework after the sale is further complicated by the fact that new constituencies against reregulation are created at the time of privatization. Shareholders and managers of privatized state-owned enterprises are joined by workers and even consumers who could benefit from the protective regulatory status of firms.

The political economy approach explains why it is hard to bring about changes in regulation after privatization and why privatized firms are frequently able to renegotiate their contracts on more favorable terms. It is therefore advisable to push for changes in the regulatory framework at the time of privatization or earlier, if possible. Perfecting the new regulatory framework may take a lot of time, however, and this should not be used as an excuse for postponing the privatization of money-losing entities.

Privatization and Corporate Governance

The last issue we address in this paper is the connection between the success of privatization and the establishment of an institutional framework that promotes good corporate governance. The absence of this framework increases the cost of capital and thus prevents privatized firms from undertaking the investments needed to operate in a more competitive environment. Access to alternative sources of finance at a low cost allows firms to survive and grow without state help.

The development and appropriate functioning of stock and credit markets need a solid regulatory framework that promotes investor protection and disclosure. Recent research shows a strong link between a firm's access to capital and efficiently enforced laws (La Porta and others 1997, 1998, 2000b, 2002; La Porta, López-de-Silanes, and Shleifer 2003). In countries where large numbers of firms have been sent out to the private market and deregulation has increased competition and lowered trade barriers, there is an urgent need for institutions that can efficiently channel resources to the new private sector. The old laws and institutions might have been efficient in covering the needs of state-owned enterprises, but private enterprises and privatized firms require different services and stand to benefit from the development of deep stock and credit markets. Ariyo and Jerome (1999) argue that the absence of developed capital markets and the lack of appropriate legal and judicial structures have hindered the success of privatization in Africa.

Before privatization, government banks are typically used as a source of financing. Yet in most privatization programs, the banking sector is one of those turned over to private hands. If financing for privatized state-owned enterprises is expected to come from privatized banks—or from any other private credit institution—then creditor rights, embedded in bankruptcy laws, and the efficiency of courts must be strengthened and streamlined. Without proper bankruptcy procedures that allow for the expedient recovery of assets, financial institutions will be reluctant to lend for fear of potential losses, and they may end up failing to satisfy the financial needs of the private sector. The banking system itself is rendered more vulnerable to crises without effective creditor rights, since it loses its ability to repossess collateral expediently (La Porta, López-de-Silanes, and Zamarripa 2003).

The development of large stock markets where firms can access long-term funds is also an important complementary measure to privatization. In some cases governments have provided a boost to stock markets by privatizing state-owned enterprises through initial public offerings. This is not enough, however, to ensure the development of the market and its usefulness as a source of future financing for these firms. Privatization without a commitment to improve shareholder rights in corporate and securities laws will probably lead to widespread abuse and appropriation of benefits by managers or those in control, with only small gains for minority investors in the form of dividends, for example (La Porta and others 2000a; López-de-Silanes 2002; La Porta, López-de-Silanes, and Shleifer 2003). The failure to institute appropriate securities laws and effective enforcement may be responsible for many of the scandals that are now blamed on privatization in countries such as the Czech Republic (Dyck 2001; Glaeser, Johnson, and Shleifer 2001). An additional benefit of corporate governance reform is that the improvement in disclosures and accounting standards facilitates the work of regulators. As Carey and others (1994) and Campos-Méndez, Trujillo, and Estache (2001) argue, postprivatization regulators end up relying on standard accounting data instead of imposing specific regulatory accounting needs. If this is the case, enhanced accounting standards should be of great benefit to regulators of privatized firms, particularly in the area of disclosure of related-party transactions and conflicts of interest.

The reform of corporate governance institutions through the establishment and enforcement of effective securities, corporate, and bankruptcy laws should become an essential complementary policy to prevent expropriation by controlling investors and to promote the development of stable sources of funds to which privatized firms can turn to finance their growth. Bear in mind that many financially troubled private firms became state owned in the last 50 years when limited access to capital pushed them to seek government financing (López-de-Silanes 1994).

Conclusions

The push for privatization and the drive to restructure the role of the state in production have lost their appeal. A large political backlash to privatization has been brewing for some time, and public opinion and policymakers in Latin America and other regions of the world have now turned against privatization. The goal of this chapter is to help set the privatization record straight by analyzing systematic evidence emerging from comprehensive studies around the world. In this quest, we benefit from a recent series of academic papers focusing on the Latin American experience. Given their extensive coverage and systematic econometric approach, these papers are able to address the series of concerns voiced against privatization.

The evidence lines up: countries that privatize benefit, and the gains not only are kept by firm owners—they are also distributed to society. These findings do not mean that failures do not occur, but rather that they are not the norm. Most instances of failure can be explained by three factors. First, opaque processes with heavy state involvement open the door to corruption and opportunistic behavior. Second, poor contract design and regulatory capture are linked to a lack of deregulation and inadequate reregulation. Third, deficient corporate governance institutions raise the cost of capital, hamper restructuring efforts, and may throw firms back into the hands of the state. The understanding of the political economy mechanisms behind the causes of failure should be used to improve privatization, not to stop it.

Notes

The authors gratefully acknowledge comments from Eduardo Bitrán, Eduardo Engel, Luis Felipe López-Calva, John Nellis, Máximo Torero, and Andrés Velasco. They would also like to thank Patricio Amador, José Caballero, Cecilia Calderón, Virgilio Galdo, Magdalena S. López-Morton, Alejandro Ponce, and Alejandro Riaño for outstanding research assistance.

1. On the poor performance of state-owned enterprises, see Boardman and Vining (1989) and Mueller (1989); on improvements after privatization, see Megginson, Nash, and van Randenborgh (1994); Ehrlich and others (1994); Frydman and others (1999); La Porta and López-de-Silanes (1999); Dewenter and Malatesta (2001); Megginson and Netter (2001); Sheshinski and López-Calva (2003); and Chong and López-de-Silanes (2004).

2. See Bayliss (2002) and Birdsall and Nellis (2002) for recent cross-country reviews of privatization failures. Criticism about specific countries or industries includes Coes (1998), Nellis (1999), Harper (2000), Wallsten (2001), and Stiglitz (2002).

3. Polls show that privatization is becoming less popular even in the United Kingdom, which led the privatization effort in the 1980s. In 1983 around 43 percent of people wanted more privatization, but that number was down to 24

percent by 1992, and it barely reached 19 percent in 2002 ("The End of Privatization," *The Economist*, June 13, 1998, 53–54).

4. Earle and Gehlbach (2003) provide a framework that rationalizes why policymakers may pay too much attention to public sentiment and thus refrain from potentially welfare-improving actions.

5. All dollar amounts are in U.S. dollars unless otherwise specified.

6. Recent research shows that the privatization effort in Africa may have been highly underestimated. Bennell (1997) argues that most papers studying privatization in Africa are based on low-quality or outdated samples. Based on a comprehensive survey of privatization transactions that spans 16 years (1980–95) and includes over 2,000 privatizations, he concludes that African privatization programs are larger than previously thought and that they increased substantially in the 1990s.

7. "State-Owned Stockpiles," *The Economist*, March 31, 2001, 58–59.

8. The analysis in this paper covers only the privatization experience at the country or federal level—that is, assets sold by the central or federal government—which accounts for the majority of assets sold around the world so far. A different sample and experience is that of the privatization of services at the local, municipal, or county level, where local governments "privatize" the public provision of services. These programs have taken place in only a few nations, such as the United States (López-de-Silanes, Shleifer, and Vishny 1997) and England, where public service provision by the private sector has become a central issue.

9. Differences in accounting procedures may also be problematic in determining adequate measures of operating performance (Megginson and Netter 2001).

10. Financial firms privatized in Mexico are analyzed in a separate paper (López-de-Silanes and Zamarripa 1995).

11. Sheshinski and López-Calva (2003) make similar claims after they analyze privatization programs and remaining state-owned assets around the world.

12. The role of the Institute for Industrial Promotion in creating new manufacturing enterprises was central during the 1950s and 1960s. The largest private capital enterprises in the steel, chemical, paper, fertilizer, metalworking, and automobile sectors today were companies formerly associated with the institute.

13. Not surprisingly, chapter 3 represents the first formal empirical study of the impact of privatization on firm performance in Bolivia.

14. For example, Pombo and Ramírez used the first method in Colombia, whereas Anuatti-Neto and and his coauthors (Brazil) and Fischer, Serra, and Gutiérrez (Chile) employed both methods.

15. Comprehensive privatization studies for eastern European countries also find higher profitability results, although the accounting data for such countries are more problematic. Some examples are Claessens, Djankov, and Pohl (1997) for the Czech Republic; Dyck (1997) for East Germany; and Frydman and others (1999) for the Czech Republic, Hungary, and Poland. For most of these cases, accounting differences before and after privatization are of greater concern than in Latin America, where the state-owned enterprises filed and collected information similar to that of private firms.

16. Data for Colombia are from the energy sector.

17. To isolate the contribution of changes in relative prices as a factor behind the observed profitability gains, the calculation compares the observed percentage point increase in operating income to sales with what would have taken place if privatized firms had increased output but left real prices unchanged at preprivatization levels. Specifically, the formula used for the price contribution is

$$\text{PRICECONTRIB} = \frac{\text{SALES}_{ap} - \text{COST}_{ap}}{\text{SALES}_{ap}} - \frac{\left[\text{SALES}_{ap} \Big/ \left(1 + \pi\right)\right] - \text{COST}_{ap}}{\text{SALES}_{ap} \Big/ (1 + \pi)},$$

where $SALES_{ap}$ represents sales in the postprivatization period, $COST_{ap}$ represents operating costs in the postprivatization period, and π is the increase in real prices.

18. Trujillo and others (2002) provide evidence for 21 Latin American countries between 1985 and 1998 and find that private sector involvement in utilities and transportation yielded marginally positive results on per capita GDP.

19. Birdsall and Nellis (2002) indicate that these results are less valid for Latin America than for transition economies and less relevant for utilities than for banks or oil.

20. The net price in these studies is defined as the net privatization price (after the costs of privatization and restructuring are deducted) divided by the dollar value of the firms' assets. The benefit of focusing on this measure is that it provides a useful framework for comparing across firms and gives a benchmark against which to think about the relative price of other privatization goals pursued by the government. Privatization programs are typically designed with the aim of pursuing revenue generation, to get out of a fiscal crisis, or to serve redistributive purposes. For Brazil, Colombia, Mexico, and Peru, the price paid was a crucial motivation in selecting winners for almost all privatized state-owned enterprises (see López-de-Silanes 1997, Torero 2002, and the chapters in this volume on Brazil and Colombia). Furthermore, economists generally endorse the goal of maximizing revenues. Bolton and Roland (1992) show that a policy of maximizing net sales revenue is likely to be consistent with a policy of maximizing social welfare since the proceeds from the sale can be used to subsidize employment, investment, a social safety net, and other public goods.

21. López-de-Silanes 1997; Arin and Okten 2002. The evidence for the case of Turkey should be regarded as tentative since the lack of data has thus far prevented a robust instrumental variables analysis for this country.

22. We apply a two-step instrumental variables approach by estimating a nonlinear reduced-form equation that describes the probability that a particular labor restructuring policy will be implemented. The instruments used are classified in two groups: firm-level and macroeconomic-level determinants. The firm-level variables included the presence of a leading agent bank, involvement of a ministry before privatization, the political affiliation of unions, and sectoral dummies. The macroeconomic variables include the average GDP growth rate and the degree of openness in the three years before privatization, as well as the legal origin of the country. None of these variables are statistically significant when included in the price equation. The F statistic for the excluded instruments is statistically significant at 1 percent in all cases.

23. Regressions control for labor rigidities coming from the collective relations laws from each country, as the incidence of rehires after privatization could also reflect the firing costs and rigidities of the labor market.

24. For the case of Mexico, La Porta and López-de-Silanes (1999) find that deregulation—particularly the removal of price or quantity controls and trade barriers—is linked to faster convergence of privatized firms to industry benchmarks.

25. See Bortolotti, Fantini, and Siniscalco (2001) for the case of the electricity sector.

26. Chong and Galdo (2004) find similar results.

References

Akram, Tanweer. 2000. "Publicly Subsidized Privatization: A Simple Model of Dysfunctional Privatization." *Applied Economics* 32 (13): 1689–99.

Allen, Franklin, and Douglas Gale. 2000. "Corporate Governance and Competition." In Xavier Vives, ed., *Corporate Governance: Theoretical and Empirical Perspectives*. Cambridge, U.K.: Cambridge University Press.

Altman, Edward. 1984. "A Further Empirical Investigation of the Bankruptcy Cost Question." *Journal of Finance* 39 (4): 1067–89.

Arin, Kermin, and Cagla Okten. 2002 "The Determinants of Privatization Prices: Evidence from Turkey." Working Paper. Louisiana State University, Baton Rouge, La.

Ariyo, Ademola, and Afeikhena Jerome. 1999. "Privatization in Africa: An Appraisal." *World Development* 27 (1): 201–13.

Barja, Gover, David McKenzie, and Miguel Urquiola. 2002. "Capitalization and Privatization in Bolivia." Cornell University, Ithaca, N.Y.

Bayliss, Kate. 2001. "Privatization of Electricity Distribution: Some Economic, Social and Political Perspectives." Report 2001-04-E-Distrib. University of Greenwich, Public Services International Research Unit, Greenwich, U.K.

———. 2002. "Privatization and Poverty: The Distributional Impact of Utility Privatization." *Annals of Public and Cooperative Economics* 73 (4): 603–25.

Bayliss, Kate, and David Hall. 2000. "Privatization of Water and Energy in Africa." Report 2000-09-U-Afr. University of Greenwich, Public Services International Research Unit, Greenwich, U.K.

Bennell, Paul. 1997. "Privatization in Sub-Saharan Africa: Progress and Prospects during the 1990s." *World Development* 25 (11): 1785–803.

Biais, Bruno, and Enrico Perotti. 2002. "Machiavellian Privatization." *American Economic Review* 92 (1): 240–58.

Birch, Melissa, and Jerry Haar, eds. 2000. *The Impact of Privatization in the Americas*. Boulder, Colo.: North-South Center Press.

Birdsall, Nancy, and John Nellis. 2002. "Winners and Losers: Assessing the Distributional Impact of Privatization." Working Paper 6. Center for Global Development, Washington, D.C.

Boardman, Anthony, and Aidan R. Vining. 1989. "Ownership and Performance in Competitive Environments: A Comparison of the Performance of Private, Mixed, and State-Owned Enterprises." *Journal of Law and Economics* 32 (1): 1–33.

Bolton, Patrick, and Gerald Roland. 1992. "Privatization Policies in Central and Eastern Europe." *Economic Policy* 6 (15): 275–303.

Bortolotti, Bernardo, Marcella Fantini, and Carlo Scarpa. 2001. "Privatization: Politics, Institutions and Financial Markets." *Emerging Markets Review* 2 (2): 109–36.

Bortolotti, Bernardo, Marcella Fantini, and Domenico Siniscalco. 2001. "Regulation and Privatization: The Case of Electricity." In Giuliano Amato and Laraine L. Laudati, eds., *The Anti-Competitive Impact of Regulation*. Northampton, U.K.: Elgar Press.

Botero, Juan, and others. 2005. "The Regulation of Labor." *Quarterly Journal of Economics,* forthcoming.

Boubakri, Narjess, and Jean Claude Cosset. 1998. "The Financial and Operating Performance of Newly Privatized Firms: Evidence from Developing Countries." *Journal of Finance* 53 (3): 1081–110.

———. 1999. "Does Privatization Meet the Expectations? Evidence from African Countries." Working Paper. École des Hautes Etudes Commerciales, Montreal.

Campbell-White, Oliver, and Anita Bhatia. 1998. "Privatization in Africa." Directions in Development Report 17972. World Bank, Washington, D.C.

Campos-Méndez, Javier, Lourdes Trujillo, and Antonio Estache. 2001. "Processes, Information and Accounting Gaps in the Regulation of Argentina's Private Railways." Working Paper 2636. World Bank, Washington, D.C.

Carbajo, José, and Antonio Estache. 1996. "Competing Private Ports: Lessons from Argentina." Viewpoint Note 100. World Bank, Washington, D.C.

Carey, Alan, and others. 1994. "Accounting for Regulation in U.K. Utilities." London: Institute of Chartered Accountants of England and Wales.

Caves, Richard. 1990. "The Concentration-Margins Relationship Reconsidered: Comments." *Brookings Papers on Economic Activity: Microeconomics* 322–24.

Chisari, Omar, Antonio Estache, and Carlos Romero. 1999. "Winners and Losers from the Privatization and Regulation of Utilities: Lessons from a General Equilibrium Model of Argentina." *World Bank Economic Review* 13 (2): 357–78.

Chong, Alberto, and Virgilio Galdo. 2004. "Streamlining and Privatization Prices in the Telecommunications Industry." *Economica.*

Chong, Alberto, and Florencio López-de-Silanes. 2003. "Privatization and Labor Restructuring around the World." Yale University, School of Management, New Haven, Conn.

————. 2004. "Privatization in Latin America: What Does the Evidence Say?" *Economía* 4(2): 37–94.

Chong, Alberto, and Alejandro Riaño. 2003. "Institutions and Privatization Prices." Inter-American Development Bank, Washington, D.C.

Chong, Alberto, and Jose Miguel Sánchez, eds. 2003. *Medios privados para fines publicos: arreglos contractuales y participacion privada en infraestructura en America Latina.* Washington, D.C.: Inter-American Development Bank.

Claessens, Stjin, Simeon Djankov, and Gerhard Pohl. 1997. "Ownership and Corporate Governance: Evidence from the Czech Republic." Policy Research Paper 1737. World Bank, Washington, D.C.

Clarke, George, and Robert Cull. 1999. "Bank Privatization in Argentina: A Model of Political Constraints and Differential Outcomes." Working Paper 2636. World Bank, Washington, D.C.

Coes, Donald. 1998. "Beyond Privatization: Getting the Rules Right in Latin America's Regulatory Environment." *Quarterly Review of Economics and Finance* 38 (3): 525–32.

Crampes, Claude, and Antonio Estache. 1996. "Regulating Water Concessions: Lessons from the Buenos Aires Concession." Viewpoint Note 91. World Bank, Washington, D.C.

D'Souza, Juliet, and William L. Megginson. 1999. "The Financial and Operating Performance of Newly Privatized Firms in the 1990s." *Journal of Finance* 54 (4): 1397–438.

Dewenter, Kathryn L., and Paul H. Malatesta. 2001. "State-Owned and Privately-Owned Firms: An Empirical Analysis of Profitability, Leverage and Labor Intensity." *American Economic Review* 91 (1): 320–34.

Diwan, Ishac. 1994. "Public Sector Retrenchment and Severance Pay: Nine Propositions." In Shahid Chaudhry, Gary Reid, and Waleed Malik, eds., *Civil Service*

Reform in Latin America and the Caribbean: Proceedings of a Conference. Technical Paper 259. Washington, D.C.: World Bank.

Dyck, Alexander. 1997. "Privatization in Eastern Germany: Management Selection and Economic Transition." *American Economic Review* 87 (4): 565–97.

————. 2001. "Privatization and Corporate Governance: Principles, Evidence and Future Challenges." *World Bank Research Observer* 16 (1): 59–84.

Earle, John, and Scott Gehlbach. 2003. "A Spoonful of Sugar: Privatization and Popular Support for Reform in the Czech Republic." *Economics and Politics* 15 (1): 1–32.

Ehrlich, Isaac, and others. 1994. "Productivity Growth and Firm Ownership: An Empirical Investigation." *Journal of Political Economy* 102 (5): 1006–38.

Engel, Eduardo, Ronald Fischer, and Alexander Galetovic. 1999. "The Chilean Infrastructure Concessions Program: Evaluation, Lessons, and Prospects for the Future." Working Paper 60. Centro de Economía Aplicada, Santiago, Chile.

————. 2001. "Least-Present-Value-of-Revenue Auctions and Highway Franchising." *Journal of Political Economy* 109 (5): 993–1020.

————. 2003. "Privatizing Highways in Latin America: Fixing What Went Wrong." *Economía* 4 (1): 129–64.

Estache, Antonio, and Martín Rodríguez. 1996. "Regulatory Lessons from Argentina's Power Concessions." Viewpoint Note 99. World Bank, Washington, D.C.

Fallick, Bruce. 1996. "A Review of the Recent Empirical Literature on Displaced Workers," *Industrial and Labor Relations Review* 50 (1): 5–16.

Fischer, Ronald, and Pablo Serra. 2002. "Regulating the Electricity Sector in Latin America." *Economía* 1 (1): 155–98.

Freije, Samuel, and Luis Rivas. 2002. "Privatization, Inequality and Welfare: Evidence from Nicaragua." Instituto de Estudios Superiores de Administración, Centro de Desarrollo Humano y Organizaciones, Caracas, Venezuela.

Frydman, Roman, and others. 1999. "When Does Privatization Work? The Impact of Private Ownership on Corporate Performance in Transition Economies." *Quarterly Journal of Economics* 114 (4): 1153–91.

Galal, Ahmed, Leroy Jones, Pankay Tandon, and Ongo Vogelsang. 1994. *Welfare Consequences of Selling Public Enterprises.* Oxford, U.K.: Oxford University Press.

Glaeser, Edward, Simon Johnson, and Andrei Shleifer. 2001. "Coase versus the Coasians." *Quarterly Journal of Economics* 116 (3): 853–99.

Guasch, José Luis. 2001. "Concessions and Regulatory Design: Determinants of Performance—Fifteen Years of Evidence." Policy Research Paper. World Bank, Washington, D.C.

Hachette, Dominique, and Rolf J. Lüders. 1994. *Privatization in Chile: An Economic Appraisal.* San Francisco, Calif.: ICS (International Center for Economic Growth) Press.

Harper, Joel T. 2000. "The Performance of Privatized Firms in the Czech Republic." Working Paper. Florida Atlantic University, Boca Raton, Fla.

Jeon, Doh-Shin, and Jean-Jacques Laffont. 1999. "The Efficient Mechanism for Downsizing the Public Sector." *World Bank Economic Review* 13 (1): 67–88.

Johnson, Simon, and others. 2000. "Tunneling." *American Economic Review* 90 (May, *Papers and Proceedings, 1999)*: 22–27. Reprinted in Klaus J. Hopt, ed., *Capital Markets and Company Law*. Oxford, U.K.: Oxford University Press, 2002.

Kahn, Charles. 1985. "Optimal Severance Pay with Incomplete Information." *Journal of Political Economy* 93 (3): 435–51.

Kikeri, Sunita. 1999. "Privatization and Labor: What Happens to Workers When Governments Divest?" Technical Paper 396. World Bank, Washington, D.C.

Kikeri, Sunita, John Nellis, and Mary Shirley. 1992. "Privatization: The Lessons of Experience." Policy Views. World Bank, Country Economics Department, Washington, D.C.

La Porta, Rafael, and Florencio López-de-Silanes. 1999. "The Benefits of Privatization: Evidence from Mexico." *Quarterly Journal of Economics* 114 (4): 1193–242.

La Porta, Rafael, Florencio López-de-Silanes, and Andrei Shleifer. 2002. "Government Ownership of Banks." *Journal of Finance* 57 (1): 265–302.

———. 2003. "What Works in Securities Laws?" Working Paper 9882. National Bureau of Economic Research, Cambridge, Mass.

La Porta, Rafael, Florencio López-de-Silanes, and Guillermo Zamarripa. 2003. "Related Lending." *Quarterly Journal of Economics* 118 (1): 231–68.

La Porta, Rafael, Florencio López-de-Silanes, Andrei Shleifer, and Robert Vishny. 1997. "Legal Determinants of External Finance." *Journal of Finance* 52 (3): 1131–50.

———. 1998. "Law and Finance." *Journal of Political Economy* 106 (6): 1113–55.

———. 2000a. "Agency Problems and Dividend Policies around the World." *Journal of Finance* 55 (1): 1–33.

———. 2000b. "Investor Protection and Corporate Governance." *Journal of Financial Economics* 58 (1): 3–27.

———. 2002. "Investor Protection and Corporate Valuation." *Journal of Finance* 57 (3): 1147–70.

López-Calva, Luis F. 2004 "Comments to Privatization in Latin America: What Does the Evidence Say?" *Economía* 4(2): 95–111.

López-de-Silanes, Florencio. 1994. "A Macro Perspective on Privatization: The Mexican Program." In Santiago Levy and Lars E. O. Svensson, eds., *Macroeconomic Aspects of Privatization*. Washington, D.C.: World Bank.

———. 1997. "Determinants of Privatization Prices." *Quarterly Journal of Economics* 107 (4): 965–1025.

———. 2002. "The Politics of Legal Reform." *Economía* 2 (2): 91–152.

López-de-Silanes, Florencio, and Guillermo Zamarripa. 1995. "Deregulation and Privatization of Commercial Banking." *Revista de Análisis Económico* 10 (2): 113–64.

López-de-Silanes, Florencio, Andrei Shleifer, and Robert W. Vishny. 1997. "Privatization in the United States." *Rand Journal of Economics* 28 (3): 447–71.

Lora, Eduardo. 2001. "Structural Reforms in Latin America: What Has Been Reformed and How to Measure It." Working Paper W-466, Inter-American Development Bank, Research Department, Washington, D.C.

Lüders, Rolf J. 1991. "Chile's Massive SOE Divestiture Program, 1975–1990: Failures and Successes." *Contemporary Policy Issues* 9 (4): 1–19.

64 CHONG AND LÓPEZ-DE-SILANES

McKenzie, David, and Dilip Mookherjee. 2003. "The Distributive Impact of Privatization in Latin America: Evidence from Four Countries." *Economía* 3 (2): 161–218.

Megginson, William, and Jeffry Netter. 2001. "From State to Market: A Survey of Empirical Studies on Privatization." *Journal of Economic Literature* 39 (2): 321–89.

Megginson, William, Robert Nash, and Matthias van Randenborgh. 1994. "The Financial and Operating Performance of Newly Privatized Firms: An International Empirical Analysis." *Journal of Finance* 49 (2): 403–52.

Mueller, Denis G. 1989. *Public Choice.* Cambridge, U.K.: Cambridge University Press.

Nellis, John. 1999. "Time to Rethink Privatization in Transition Economies?" Discussion Paper 38 International Finance Corporation, Washington, D.C.

Nellis, John, and Sunita Kikeri. 1989. "Public Enterprise Reform: Privatization and the World Bank." *World Development* 17 (5): 659–72.

OECD (Organisation for Economic Cooperation and Development). 2001. "Recent Privatization Trends in OECD Countries." Paris.

Perotti, Enrico. 1995. "Credible Privatization." *American Economic Review* 85 (4): 847–59.

Petrazzini, Ben, and Theodore H. Clark. 1996. "Costs and Benefits of Telecommunications Liberalization in Developing Countries." Working Paper. Hong Kong University of Science and Technology, Hong Kong, China.

Pinheiro, Armando C. 1996. "Impactos microeconômicos da privatização no Brasil." *Pesquisa e Planejamento Econômico* 26 (3): 357–97.

Przeworski, Adam. 1991. *Democracy and the Market: Political and Economic Reforms in Eastern Europe and Latin America.* Cambridge, U.K.: Cambridge University Press.

Rama, Martin. 1999. "Efficient Public Sector Downsizing." *World Bank Economic Review* 13 (1): 1–22.

Ramamurti, Ravi. 1996. *Privatizing Monopolies: Lessons from the Telecommunications and Transport Sectors in Latin America.* Baltimore: Johns Hopkins University Press.

———. 1997. "Testing the Limits of Privatization: Argentine Railroads." *World Development* 25 (12): 1973–93.

Ramamurti, Ravi, and Raymond Vernon. 1991. "Privatization and Control of State-Owned Enterprises." EDI (Economic Development Institute) Development Studies. World Bank, Washington, D.C.

Ramírez, Miguel D. 1998. "Privatization and Regulatory Reform in Mexico and Chile: A Critical Overview." *Quarterly Review of Economics and Finance* 38 (3): 421–39.

Ros, Agustin. 1999. "Does Ownership or Competition Matter? The Effects of Telecommunications Reform on Network Expansion and Efficiency." *Journal of Regulatory Economics* 15 (1): 65–92.

Sáez, Raul. 1992. "An Overview of Privatization in Chile: The Episodes, the Results, and the Lessons." Consultancy report, CIEPLAN (Corporación de Investigaciones Económicas para América Latina), Santiago, Chile.

Sánchez, Manuel, and Rossana Corona. 1993. "Privatization in Latin America." Inter-American Development Bank, Centers for Research in Applied Economics, Washington, D.C.

Sheshinski, Eytan, and Luis F. López-Calva. 2003. "Privatization and Its Benefits: Theory and Evidence." In K. Basu, P. Nayak, and R. Ray, eds., *Markets and Governments*. Oxford, U.K.: Oxford University Press.

Shleifer, Andrei. 1998. "State versus Private Ownership." *Journal of Economic Perspectives* 12 (4): 133–50.

Shleifer, Andrei, and Robert W. Vishny. 1994. "Politicians and Firms." *Quarterly Journal of Economics* 109 (4): 995–1025.

———. 1996. "A Survey of Corporate Governance." Working Paper 5554. Cambridge, Mass.: National Bureau of Economic Research.

Stiglitz, Joseph. 2002. *Globalization and Its Discontents*. New York: Norton.

Torero, Máximo. 2002. "Impacto de la privatización sobre el desempeño de las empresas en el perú." Documento de Trabajo 41. Grupo de Analisis para el Desarrollo, Lima, Perú.

Torero, Máximo, and Alberto Pasco-Font. 2001. "El impacto social de la privatización y de la regulación de los servicios públicos en el Perú." Working Paper 35. Grupo de Análisis para el Desarrollo, Lima, Perú.

Torero, Máximo, Enrique Schroth, and Alberto Pasco-Font. 2003. "The Impact of Telecommunications Privatization in Peru on the Welfare of Urban Consumers." *Economía* 4 (1): 99–128.

Trujillo, Lourdes, Noelia Martin, Antonio Estache, and Javier Campos. 2002. "Macroeconomic Effects of Private Sector Participation in Latin America's Infrastructure." Policy Research Working Paper 2906. World Bank, Washington, D.C.

Vickers, John, and George Yarrow. 1988. *Privatization: An Economic Analysis*. Cambridge, Mass.: MIT Press.

Wallsten, Scott. 2000. "Telecommunications Privatization in Developing Countries: The Real Effect of Exclusivity Periods." SIEPR Policy Paper 99-21, Stanford, Calif.

———. 2001. "An Empirical Analysis of Competition, Privatization, and Regulation in Africa and Latin America." *Journal of Industrial Economics* 49 (1): 1–19.

———. 2002. "Does Sequencing Matter? Regulation and Privatization in Telecommunications Reforms." Policy Research Working Paper 2817. World Bank, Washington, D.C.

Winston, Clifford. 1993. "Deregulation: Days of Reckoning for Microeconomists." *Journal of Economic Literature* 31 (3): 1263–89.

World Bank. 2001. *World Bank Privatization Database*. Washington, D.C.

Wruck, Karen. 1990. "Financial Distress, Reorganization, and Organizational Efficiency." *Journal of Financial Economics* 27 (2): 419–44.

Yarrow, George. 1986. "Privatization in Theory and Practice." *Economic Policy* 2 (4): 324–64.

2

The Benefits and Costs of Privatization in Argentina: A Microeconomic Analysis

Sebastián Galiani, Paul Gertler, Ernesto Schargrodsky, and Federico Sturzenegger

SINCE THE BEGINNING OF THE 1980S, THE world has undergone a major shift in thinking about the appropriate economic role of the state. Privatization of state-owned enterprises (SOEs) has been at the core of this change ever since Britain and France initiated privatization planning. In the last two decades, several countries have launched ambitious privatization programs. Although the extent, form, and pace of change have varied from country to country, the general trend has been similar: the state has gradually withdrawn from directly producing goods and services. Despite the importance of this experience, we still have little empirical knowledge about how well privatization works in practice.

Few studies have analyzed the impact of privatizations. Early empirical research found mixed results about the relative performance of private versus public firms (Caves 1990; Vining and Boardman 1992). More recent research finds private ownership to be generally more efficient than public ownership (see, for example, Megginson, Nash, and van Randenborgh 1994). These studies focus only on the question of productive efficiency. Recently, however, La Porta and López-de-Silanes (1999) studied Mexico's experience with privatization in the 1980s and early 1990s. They analyzed how privatization changed the performance of SOEs over a broad set of outcomes. Additionally, these authors considered the possibility that the increased profitability of privatized companies came at the expense of society through higher prices or layoffs.

In this chapter, we follow La Porta and López-de-Silanes (1999) to evaluate the Argentine privatization program. Thus, we study the effects of privatization on profitability, operating efficiency, productivity, output, investment, employment, wages, and prices. The structure of the Argentine public firms, however, was very different from the privatized Mexican public sector. In Argentina the state primarily owned a few large natural monopolies. In Mexico the state ran a large number of firms across several productive sectors. Thus, although both privatization programs were massive, the Mexican experience was richer in the number of cases compared with the Argentine experience, while the Argentine privatization program was enormous relative to the size of the economy. Mexico privatized around 1,000 firms of various sizes in sectors throughout the economy, but some of the largest public companies such as PEMEX, the oil monopoly, or the electricity companies were not privatized. In contrast, Argentina privatized a smaller number of firms of much larger average size (Lustig 1992; Galiani and Petrecolla 1996, 2000).

The particular features of the Argentine privatization process allow us to study the direct impact of privatization in sectors in which, because the state was a monopolist, the whole industry was transferred to the private sector. In such cases, laid-off workers may not be able to use their sector-specific human capital in other sectors of the economy, or consumers may have no choice in their suppliers. We go beyond the impact of privatization on firms to measure the direct impact of privatization on consumers' and workers' welfare.

We propose two direct measures of the welfare impact of privatizations. First, the Argentine program involved the privatization of local water and sewerage firms. Changes in the health of the population associated with these privatizations would provide a measure of the impact of privatization that goes beyond transfers of consumer surplus. We evaluate how the privatization of local water and sewerage firms affected both access to these services and child mortality. Second, the Argentine program involved massive layoffs. Profitability gains in privatized firms may have been obtained at the expense of workers (Shleifer and Summers 1988). We measure the effect of privatizations on workers' wages by comparing the wages of a random sample of workers before and after they were laid off from the former state oil company (Yacimientos Petrolíferos Fiscales, or YPF) with a matched counterfactual group built up using data gathered from an ongoing household survey.

In short, in this chapter we address three questions:

• How did privatization affect the performance of firms and through which channels—market power or productivity gains?

• Are there direct welfare impacts of privatization that can be rigorously identified in an econometric sense? In particular, has the privatization of water and sewerage services improved or worsened the health of the population?

• Part of the efficiency gains of privatized firms may have come from the breach of explicit and implicit contracts between workers and firms. What is the evidence of this for Argentina? What has been the effect of the privatization of YPF on the earnings of laid-off workers?

This chapter assesses both the efficiency and some significant distributional impacts of the Argentine privatization program. This is done by considering privatization as a policy instrument and by exploiting the fact that the group of economic units (that is, SOEs, public banks, households, and workers) exposed to privatization varied both by unit and by year. That enables us to use a similar statistical identification strategy to document some of the benefits and costs of privatization. Although we are not able to identify all the efficiency and distributional impacts of privatization by applying this treatment-and-control-group approach, our main contribution to the literature is to document causal effects of privatization on measures of efficiency and distribution.[1]

Our results show that the profitability of the nonfinancial firms increased after their privatization. Both the ratio of operating income to sales and the ratio of net income to sales increased significantly as a result of privatization. Large increases in operating efficiency underpin these gains in profitability. Thus, we find a huge overall increase in the operating efficiency of the privatized firms in Argentina. Employment cuts are a big part of the story, however. Employment decreased approximately 40 percent as a result of privatization. Labor productivity increased not only because employment decreased, but also because privatized firms increased production. Privatization also had a big impact on investment; all the measures of investment analyzed were positively and significantly affected by privatization. Investment itself increased at least 350 percent as a result of privatization. Finally, we do not find any statistically significant effect of privatization on prices. Nevertheless, after the privatization, prices did not decrease. The efficiency gains we documented imply that prices should have fallen if the quality improvements were not large enough.

Contrary to the case of nonfinancial firms, we do not find large overall increases in operating efficiency after the privatization of public banks. However, some indicators of efficiency performed well because of privatization. Output per employee increased 20 percent, while the average number of employees per branch decreased 37 percent as a result of privatization. As in the case of nonfinancial firms, employment cuts are a big part of the story. Employment decreased approximately 36 percent because of privatization. Thus, on several indicators, the privatized banks seem to be more efficient after the privatization than they were before. Finally, the average capitalization ratio (the ratio of net worth to assets) increased 5 percent because of privatization. The higher capitalization rate of the privatized banks means a more solvent system, which is quite important in countries as vulnerable to external shocks as Argentina.

On the direct measures of welfare analyzed, we find a negative and statistically significant effect of the privatization of water services on child
mortality. The estimated coefficient implies a decrease of approximately
5 percent in child mortality rates induced by the privatization of water
provision. Our estimates of earnings losses of displaced workers indicate
that a huge redistribution cost is associated with the privatizations of
SOEs: displaced workers incur substantial earnings losses. We estimate
that after taking unemployment into account, the earnings losses because
of privatization were approximately 50 percent of the real earnings of the
workers before privatization.

In this chapter, we limit ourselves to analyzing the effects of privatization on several measures of firm performance, and on consumers' and employees' welfare in a partial equilibrium analysis. An important caveat is
that we do not evaluate general equilibrium effects of the massive privatization program implemented in Argentina.[2] Indeed, it would be possible to
argue that the deep macroeconomic crisis that the country is suffering is to
some extent related to the previous privatization policies. For example, if
the privatization package distorted the equilibrium path of the exchange
rate, it could have induced a severe and unsustainable misallocation of resources in the economy. Moreover, the debt financing associated with acquisition of the privatized firms contributed to the large increase in the
country indebtedness. In addition, the massive layoffs that accompanied
privatization may have contributed to the severe increase in unemployment. Rather than a macroeconomic study, however, we conduct an exclusively microeconomic analysis in the industries and markets in which
privatization took place.

The chapter is organized as follows. In the next section, we document
the Argentine privatization program, followed by a sample of privatized
firms. The next two sections present the results of the effect of privatization on the performance of both financial and nonfinancial firms. We then
study the impact of the privatization of water and sewerage companies on
both access to these services and child mortality, followed by an analysis
of the impact of privatization on the earnings of long-term displaced
workers. The last section presents our conclusions.

The Argentine Privatization Program

In 1989 Argentina was in the midst of an acute hyperinflation driven by
the monetization of large fiscal deficits. The administration of recently
elected president Carlos Menem launched an ambitious privatization
program. A remarkable characteristic of the Argentine privatization
program was its extent and speed. The program included most SOEs as
well as other state assets that had not previously been operated as independent firms (Galiani and Petrecolla 1996, 2000; Heymann and

Kosacoff 2000). The privatization program was launched together with other structural reforms, such as financial and trade liberalization, the implementation of a monetary currency board in 1991 (Plan de Convertibilidad), the independence of the central bank (Banco Central de la Republica Argentina, or BCRA), the decentralization of health and education services, and other pro-market actions such as a general deregulation of economic activities.

The fiscal revenues from the privatization of the SOEs constituted a crucial instrument of the stabilization programs launched by the Menem government. According to Gerchunoff (1992), the main objective of the privatization program, at least at the beginning, was to solve Argentina's (intertemporal) fiscal problems. Company-specific reasons also drove the privatization process. After a long period of negative net investments, the SOEs needed high levels of capital investment to improve both the quality of and access to their services. The public sector had no means to fund those investments. In addition to its direct effects, the privatization program signaled a clear change in the direction of the economic development of the country.

For the most part, SOEs in Argentina were large, vertically integrated, natural monopolies. These characteristics implied that Argentina privatized a small number of very large firms and that the Argentine privatization program was huge relative to the size of the economy. Under the priority of raising privatization revenues, in many sectors the authorities decided to maintain a monopolistic structure in order to make the new private companies more attractive to the new buyers. With the same objective, prices for the services or products were raised in the immediate preprivatization period. The tax structure to which the new companies were going to be exposed was simplified. Moreover, the state absorbed the companies' liabilities before transferring the companies to private hands. Finally, the new companies enjoyed considerable regulatory freedom at the beginning of the program. The creation of regulatory agencies was delayed or neglected during the early years of the privatization program.

The transfer of companies and assets to private control took several forms, such as total sale through open international auctions, concessions, public offer of shares, licensing, leases with or without purchase options, management contracts, and the issue of exploration permits. The government obtained revenues in the form of cash and external debt bonds. A positive fiscal impact also resulted from a reduction in current losses, which were previously financed by the public budget, and a positive flow of taxes from the privatized companies. Table 2.1 presents the revenues from privatizations by sector in federal and provincial transfers according to the Ministerio de Economía (2000). The table shows the income for every sale (annual fees paid for concessions are not included).

Table 2.1 Privatization Revenues in Argentina, by Sector
(US$ millions, unless otherwise indicated)

Sector	Total income	Percent of . total	Cash	Bonds, market value	Bonds, nominal value	Other revenues
Federal privatizations						
Petroleum and gas	7,594	39.1	6,716	878	1,271	n.a.
Electricity	3,908	20.1	1,989	1,451	2,586	468
Communications	2,982	15.4	2,279	703	5,150	n.a.
Gas	2,950	15.2	1,553	1,397	3,116	n.a.
Transportation	756	3.9	284	183	1,314	290
Petrochemical	438	2.3	418	20	132	n.a.
Banks and financial services	394	2.0	394	n.a.	n.a.	n.a.
Steel	158	0.8	143	14	30	n.a.
Derivatives from petroleum and gas	116	0.6	116	n.a.	n.a.	n.a.
Pipelines	77	0.4	77	n.a.	n.a.	n.a.
Construction	20	0.1	20	n.a.	n.a.	n.a.
Other manufacturing industries	11	0.1	11	n.a.	n.a.	n.a.
Hotels and restaurants	8	0.0	3	5	13	n.a.
Chemical	5	0.0	3	2	3	n.a.
Electronics	2	0.0	1	n.a.	1	1
Agriculture	2	0.0	2	n.a.	n.a.	n.a.
Total federal	19,422	100.0	14,009	4,653	13,615	759
Provincial privatizations						
Electricity	2,085	47.1	2,068	n.a.	n.a.	18
Petroleum and gas	1,703	38.5	1,703	n.a.	n.a.	n.a.
Water and sewerage	589	13.3	589	n.a.	n.a.	n.a.
Paper	50	1.1	50	n.a.	n.a.	n.a.
Total provincial	4,427	100.0	4,410	n.a.	n.a.	18

n.a. Not applicable.

Note: Income from every privatization sale is included, but annual concession fees are not. *Other revenues* includes the use of trusts and liabilities assumed by the companies.

Source: Ministerio de Economía 2000.

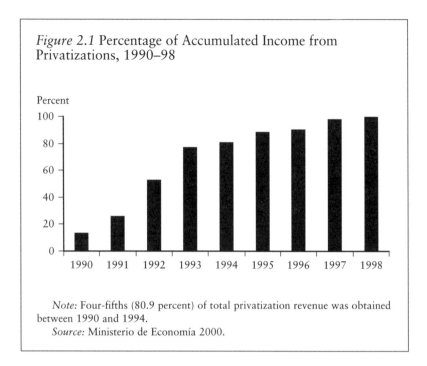

Figure 2.1 Percentage of Accumulated Income from Privatizations, 1990–98

Note: Four-fifths (80.9 percent) of total privatization revenue was obtained between 1990 and 1994.
Source: Ministerio de Economía 2000.

Figure 2.1 shows the accumulation of privatization revenues during the 1990s. Nearly 81 percent of total revenues from privatizations was obtained between 1990 and 1994. Mostly small companies and some residual shares of large companies were sold in the second half of the decade.

The Sample

According to official statistics (CEP 1998 and the Central Bank), 154 privatization contracts were signed during the 1990s. However, the sample of privatized SOEs analyzed in our study is smaller than the number of signed contracts for several reasons:

• Several SOEs were split vertically and horizontally into smaller units or assets and privatized separately. In the majority of these cases, it is not possible to obtain preprivatization financial statements and performance indicators reported separately according to the criteria used to break up the SOEs.[3] This reduces the number of observations, since our unit of analysis has to be the SOE and not the private companies that emerged out of the process.

• Concessions of roads, freeways, and docks cannot be analyzed because no financial statements are available for the preprivatization period. Roads, freeways, and docks were not organized as companies under public ownership.

• The sale of state minority participation in private companies is not considered in our study since the privatization itself did not imply a change in the management objectives of those firms.

• Within the oil sector, some contracts involved exploration permits of areas where the state oil company had not previously operated (*áreas petroleras marginales*).

• Several SOEs were liquidated or ceased operation.

• In a few cases, data for the SOEs are not available.

Given these constraints, we have been able to collect data for 21 federal nonfinancial SOEs and for all the privatized banks. Our database for nonfinancial SOEs accounts for 81.7 percent of the revenues from the sale of companies that continued operating as separate companies after being privatized and for 72.4 percent of the total privatization revenues.[4] Appendix 2A describes the industrial structure and data sources for the sectors included in our study.

As stated above, our units of analysis are the SOEs. Therefore, we aggregate the information from all the companies that resulted from the privatization of each SOE, with the exception of Ferrocarriles Argentinos, the one company where it was possible to find data by business unit for the preprivatization period. Table 2.2 presents the set of nonfinancial companies included in our study. The smaller nonfinancial privatized firms not considered in our study are listed in table 2.3, along with the reason they were excluded.

Finally, we construct a separate database for the banking sector, where for regulatory reasons we have monthly data for an extended number of variables, and for which we have a control group comprised of nonprivatized public banks and private banks. The privatized provincial banks are listed in table 2.4

Results for Nonfinancial Firms

With the objective of analyzing the benefits and costs of privatization, in this section we report the effects of privatization of nonfinancial firms on profitability, operating efficiency, productivity, output, investment, employment, wages, and prices. In doing so, we document the effects of privatization on several measures of firm performance.

Suppose one is interested in estimating the influence of a policy instrument on an outcome for a group—in our case, for example, the effect of privatization on productivity. Thus, the group consists of state-owned

Table 2.2 Nonfinancial Companies Included in the Database

State-owned company name	Private company name	Years with data	
		Public	Private
Obras Sanitarias	Aguas Argentinas	1988–92	1993–97
ENTEL	Telefónica	1985–90	1991–99
	Telecom		
Ferrocarriles Argentinos	Trenes de Buenos Aires		
	Metrovías		
	Ferrovías		
	Transp. Metropolitanos Gral. Roca	Cargo:	Cargo:
	Transp. Metropolitanos Gral. San Martín	1989–92	1993–99
	Transp. Metropolitanos Belgrano Sur		
	Ferroexpreso Pampeano	Urban passenger:	Urban passenger:
	Ferrosur Roca	1991–92	1993–99
	Ferrocarril Mesopotámico		
	Nuevo Central Argentino		
	Buenos Aires al Pacífico		
Aerolíneas Argentinas	Aerolíneas Argentinas	1986–89	1992–94
Gas del Estado	TGS		
	TGN		
	Dist. de gas Metropolitana	1987–92	1993–99
	Dist. de gas Buenos Aires Norte		
	Dist. de gas Noroeste		
	Dist. de gas del Centro		

(Table continues on the following page.)

Table 2.2 (continued)

State-owned company name	Private company name	Years with data	
		Public	Private
Gas del Estado	Dist. de gas del Litoral Dist. de gas Cuyana Dist. de gas Pampeana Dist. de gas del Sur	1987–92	1993–99
YPF	YPF	1987–90	1991–99
Hidronor	Transener Hidroeléctrica Piedra del Aguila Hidroeléctrica Cerros Colorados Hidroeléctrica Alicura Hidroeléctrica El Chocón	1986–91	1993–99
SEGBA	Edenor Edesur Edelap Central Costanera Central Puerto	1986–91	1992–95
SOMISA	SIDERAR	1987–91	1995–98
Encotel	Correo Argentino	1989–96	1997–2000
Tandanor	Tandanor	1988–91	1994–99

Note: For full names of companies and other information about the database, see appendix 2A.
Source: Authors' data.

Table 2.3 Nonfinancial Privatizations in Argentina Not Included in the Database

Divested assets from YPF	Ceased to operate or liquidated	Not operating as companies in public period	Information not found
86 oil marginal areas	Astillero Domecq Garcia	Administración General de Puertos (AGP) – 6 Docks	Altos Hornos Zapla
Area Petrolera Aguaragüe	Carboquímica Argentina	Elevador Terminal del Puerto de Quequen	Canal 11
Area Petrolera El Huemul–Koluel Kaike	Fabricaciones Militares (Acido Sulfúrico, de armas Matheu, Pilar, Río Tercero Cargas, San Francisco)	Elevadores Puerto de Buenos Aires	Canal 13
Area Petrolera Palmar Largo		Elevadores Puerto Diamante	Fabricaciones Militares (San Martin, ECA, Tolueno Sintético, Área Militar Córdoba)
Area Petrolera Puesto Hernández	ELMA	Elevadores Terminales de Rosario	
Area Petrolera Santa Cruz I	Empresa de Desarrollos Especiales	Highways	Hipódromo Argentino
Area Petrolera Santa Cruz II	Entesa	Hotel Llao Llao	Interbáires
Area Petrolera Tierra del Fuego	Forja Argentina	Navigation waterways	Petroquímica Bahía Blanca
Area Petrolera Tordillo	Hipasam	Unidad Portuaria San Pedro	Radio Belgrano
Area Petrolera Vizcacheras	Induclor		
Buques Tanque (YPF)	Intesa		
Destilería Dock Sud (YPF)	Radio Excelsior		
Destilería San Lorenzo (YPF)	Sateena		
Oleoductos del Valle (YPF— 70 percent)	Sidinox		

(Table continues on the following page.)

Table 2.3 (continued)

Divested assets from YPF	Ceased to operate or liquidated	Not operating as companies in public period	Information not found
Planta de Aerosoles Dock Sud (YPF)	Sisteval		
Puerto Rosales (YPF—70 percent)	Sitea		
Refinería Campo Durán	Tanque Argentino Mediano		
	Tecnología Aeroespacial		

Note: Divested assets from YPF are assets that were part of YPF (Yacimientos Petrolíferos Fiscales) before the privatization but not afterward. Includes areas that were not operated before their concession. No data were available for companies that ceased to operate or were liquidated after the privatization process or for privatized companies that were not operated as independent organizations before privatization. Records for the companies in the last column could not be found.

Source: Authors' data.

Table 2.4 Privatized Banks in Argentina Included in the Database

| Bank | Privatization date | Number of available monthly observations | |
		Before privatization	After privatization
Caja de Ahorro	March 1994	8	62
Chaco	November 1994	14	58
Entre Ríos	January 1995	17	57
Formosa	December 1995	29	45
Misiones	January 1996	23	23
Río Negro	March 1996	30	41
Salta	March 1996	31	43
Tucumán	July 1996	35	39
San Luis	August 1996	37	25
Santiago del Estero	September 1996	38	36
San Juan	November 1996	34	34
Previsión Social de Mendoza	November 1996	41	18
Mendoza	November 1996	41	27
Jujuy	February 1998	47	20
Municipal de Tucumán	August 1998	60	14
Santa Cruz	December 1998	53	10
Santa Fe	January 1999	50	9

Note: Privatized provincial banks are included in the sample. In May 1998 the Bank of Mendoza acquired the privatized Banco de Previsión Social de Mendoza.
Source: Authors' data.

enterprises $i = 1 \ldots N$ observed over a sample horizon $t = 1 \ldots T$. Suppose further that the policy instrument (that is, the privatization of a firm) changes in a particular period t for a segment of the group (or, as in our case, that it changes for all the SOEs but at different points in time). Let dP_{it} be a 0–1 indicator that equals unity if the privatization was operative for firm i in period t. Firms of the group that experience privatization react according to a parameter α. The standard statistical model to estimate α is the following two-way fixed effect error component model:[5]

$$y_{it} = \alpha \, dP_{it} + \lambda_t + \mu_i + \varepsilon_{it} \qquad (2.1)$$

where μ_i is a time-invariant effect unique to firm i that also captures industry differences, λ_t is a time effect common to all firms in period t, and ε_{it} is an individual time-varying error distributed independently across individuals and time and independently of all μ_i and λ_t (Chamberlain 1984; Heckman and Robb 1985).

The difference-in-difference estimator of α answers the question we are interested in: how the expected value of a specific variable y (that is, the dependent variable in equation 2.1) changes in any period if the SOE is privatized. Thus, $\alpha = E(y_{it} \mid dP_{it} = 1) - E(y_{it} \mid dP_{it} = 0)$ for all i and t. This estimator assumes that, in the absence of privatization, the mean change in the privatized and nonprivatized firms would have been the same. Thus, the change in the outcome measured in the comparison group serves to benchmark common period effects among SOEs.[6]

As explained in the previous section, the privatizations in our data set occurred at different points in time.[7] The Argentine privatization program induced some exogenous variation in the transfer of enterprises across SOEs and time. Thus, our identification strategy exploits the fact that exposure to privatization varied both by firm and by year.[8]

As we do not have information for the whole period for every company, our 21 nonfinancial firms compose an unbalanced panel:

Year	1985	1986	1987	1988	1989	1990	1991	1992
Public	1	4	7	10	15	14	18	14
Private	0	0	0	0	0	0	2	4

Year	1993	1994	1995	1996	1997	1998	1999	2000
Public	1	1	1	1	0	0	0	0
Private	18	19	19	18	19	18	16	1

We are interested in analyzing the change in performance of our sample of firms following privatization. We rely on six broad indicators of performance: profitability, operating efficiency, employment and wages, capital investment, total output, and prices. Appendix tables 2B.1 and 2B.2 describe our variables. We express nominal variables in 1999 pesos, deflating them by the aggregate consumer price index (CPI).[9]

Following La Porta and López-de-Silanes (1999), we calculate two profitability ratios: operating income to sales and net income to sales. Evaluating changes in operating income offers a superior measure of efficiency gains, whereas evaluating changes in net income provides a useful summary statistic of the full impact of privatization on the performance of the SOEs. We could also have evaluated the impact of privatization on the ratio of operating (net) income to fixed assets, but our measure of fixed assets (property, plant, and equipment, or PPE) is not reliable because of the difficulties in consistently measuring PPE in periods of extreme price instability. We observed that PPE adjusts dramatically downward after privatizations. Moreover, it is likely that PPE could have been overstated in the SOEs' balance sheets because the cost of public investment projects used to be extremely high.

We also examine three indicators of operating efficiency to capture changes in the ability of firms to produce output from any given level of inputs (compare La Porta and López-de-Silanes 1999). We compute the logarithm of unit costs (defined as the ratio of the cost of labor and intermediate inputs to sales), the logarithm of sales per employee, and the logarithm of output per employee.

We also analyze the impact of privatization on labor variables: the logarithm of total employment and the logarithm of real average wages. To assess the impact of privatization on capital formation, we examine the level of investment.[10] Here, we consider the logarithm of investment, the logarithm of investment to sales, the logarithm of investment to total employment, and the logarithm of investment to fixed assets (PPE). Finally, we examine the behavior of output and prices.

Before analyzing the impact of privatization on these indicators, we need to discuss some econometric issues. Although it is customary to study the influence of a policy instrument on a (conditional) mean outcome, it is advisable in our case to also study the influence of privatization on the (conditional) median of the distribution of the firm performance indicators studied. Let:

$$y_{it} = \alpha_\theta \, dP_{it} + \lambda_{\theta t} + \mu_{\theta i} + \varepsilon_{\theta it} \qquad (2.2)$$

with $Q_\theta(y_{it} \,|\, dP_{it}, \lambda_t) = \alpha_\theta \, dP_{it} + \lambda_{\theta t} + \mu_{\theta i}$, where $Q_\theta(y_{it} \,|\, dP_{it}, \lambda_t)$ denotes the θth conditional quantile of y given dP for a given unit i and period t. This is the quantile regression model of Koenker and Basset (1978). The quantile regression model is concerned with the distribution of a scalar random variable y conditional on a vector of covariates $\mathbf{x}$ when the θ-quantile of y conditional on $\mathbf{x}$ is a linear function in $\mathbf{x}$. For example, consider the case where θ equals 0.5. This is the median regression. This estimator is obtained by minimizing the sum of absolute errors and is referred to as the least absolute deviation (LAD) estimator.

The LAD estimator is a robust alternative to the ordinary least squares (OLS) estimator for estimating the parameters of a linear regression function.[11] A potentially serious problem in our data set is the presence of severe outliers in many of the measures of firm performance that we analyze. The LAD estimator protects us against outliers in the dependent random variable y and is preferable over the OLS estimator in this respect.

Moreover, the impact of privatizations on any outcome considered in our study is likely to be heterogeneous across SOEs, and this heterogeneity is unlikely to be successfully parameterized. Thus, the OLS estimate of α in equation 2.1 is likely to estimate a mixture of different population parameters (different privatization impacts across industries) with a severely skewed distribution. The median impact of privatization on any outcome will be less influenced by extreme observations (impacts) than the mean impact of privatization on any outcome. Thus, the impacts of privatization on any performance indicator are likely to be better represented by its median than by its mean. In that case, equation 2.2 could instead be estimated with θ equal to 0.5 and the consequent redefinition of the parameter of interest.

The heterogeneity of impacts of privatization across SOEs also leads us to study the percentage change of any variable y with respect to privatization instead of the level impact of privatization on these variables whenever that is practical.[12] It is reasonable to assume that the former parameter is much less heterogeneous across industries than the latter one.

Turning now to the results, note first that the profitability of privatized firms increased dramatically after the privatization period. The SOEs in our sample were highly unprofitable during the preprivatization period. La Porta and López-de-Silanes (1999) find similar results for Mexico. Table 2.5 shows simple comparisons before and after privatization for the mean and median operating-income-to-sales and net-income-to-sales ratios. Both profitability performances show statistically significant increases after privatization. The huge differences that exist between the mean and median statistics, especially in the preprivatization period, suggest that the parameter of interest in equation 2.2 is more appealing than the one in equation 2.1.

In table 2.6 we report the estimate of the impacts of privatization on both the conditional mean and the conditional median of the set of indicators we propose to analyze. Thus, we report the difference-in-difference estimates of the impact of privatization on the set of indicators proposed.

Table 2.5 Changes in Profitability for the Sample of Nonfinancial Privatized Firms

Variable	Mean before privatization	Mean after privatization	t-statistic for change in mean	Median before privatization	Median after privatization	Z-statistic for change in median
Operating income to sales	−0.579	−0.158	2.59***	−0.100	0.055	4.32***
Net income to sales	−0.479	0.030	3.49***	−0.157	0.040	15.90***

*** Significant at the 1 percent level.

Note: See appendix table 2B.1 for definitions of variable. The number of (firm-year) observations is 170.

Source: Authors' calculations.

Table 2.6 Changes in Performance for the Sample of Nonfinancial Privatized Firms

Variable	Number of observations	Mean regressions	Median regressions
Profitability			
Operating income/sales	168	0.75*	0.83***
		(0.41)	(0.01)
Net income/sales	168	1.03**	1.06***
		(0.45)	(0.01)
Operating efficiency			
Log(unit cost)	126	−5.63***	−0.1***
		(1.46)	(0.06)
Log(sales/employment)	145	1.02	0.09***
		(0.69)	(0.02)
Log(production/employment)	111	4.53***	0.38***
		(1.33)	(0.07)
Labor			
Log(employment)	148	−0.65**	−0.50***
		(0.31)	(0.04)
Log(average real wage per employee)	72	0.096	−0.34***
		(0.35)	(0.07)
Investment			
Log(investment)	88	1.7*	1.51***
		(1.03)	(0.22)
Log(investment/sales)	88	1.3	0.29***
		(0.87)	(0.09)
Log(investment/employment)	71	4.25***	2.21***
		(1.5)	(0.07)
Log(investment/noncurrent assets)	86	2.07***	1.8***
		(0.79)	(0.06)
Output			
Log(production)	150	6.4***	0.22***
		(0.96)	(0.03)
Prices			
Log(prices)	155	−0.11	−0.02
		(0.19)	(0.03)

* Significant at the 10 percent level.
** Significant at the 5 percent level.
*** Significant at the 1 percent level.

Note: See appendix table 2B.1 for definitions of variables. All regressions include year and firm fixed effects. Standard errors are in parentheses. Obviously, the observations for 1985 and 2000 are excluded from the estimated regression functions since the models include year effects. The number of observations varies across regressions because information is not available for all variables for every firm during the sample period. For each firm, we exclude from the sample the observation for the year in which the company was privatized due to the lack of reliable data during the transition period. Results are similar if we also exclude the two years before privatization. None of the results changes qualitatively if we exclude the data for 1989 from the analysis. In that case the estimates become more precise.

Source: Authors' calculations.

The distinction between these estimates and the before-and-after estimates reported in table 2.5 is that the difference-in-difference estimates also control for the common aggregate effects (year effects) on the dependent variables. We confirm the significant increase in profitability after privatization. Both operating income to sales and net income to sales increased significantly as a result of privatization. This result and, indeed, all the results reported in table 2.6 are qualitatively robust to the parameter analyzed (mean or median).

Large increases in operating efficiency underpin these gains in profitability. The impact of privatization on the (conditional) median unit costs shows a reduction in the latter of 10 percent. This effect is close to the effect found by La Porta and López-de-Silanes (1999) for Mexico. The impact of privatization on (conditional) mean unit costs, however, is implausibly large. Most likely, it shows the pervasive upshot of extreme effects in some SOEs. Because this occurs with other variables as well, we emphasize the report of the impacts of privatization on the conditional median of the performance measures studied, although none of the reported results changes qualitatively if we concentrate on the impact of privatization on the conditional mean of the performance measures. The ratio of median sales to employment also increases 10 percent because of the privatization of the SOEs. Finally, the impact of privatization on labor productivity, measured by the ratio of production to total employment, is dramatic. The impact of privatization on the median level of productivity shows an increase of 46 percent. Thus, we find a huge overall increase in the operating efficiency of the privatized firms in Argentina.

As in the Mexican case, employment cuts explain a large part of the increase in profitability. Employment decreased approximately 40 percent as a result of privatization. It is likely that this figure underestimates the layoffs experienced by privatized firms because in some SOEs, employment was already falling during the immediate preprivatization period. For example, a significant proportion of the layoffs at YPF occurred two years before the privatization of the big oil company. Nevertheless, our results show that a substantial proportion of the layoffs occurred after the firms were privatized.

Labor productivity increased not only because employment decreased but also because privatized firms increased production. The median level of production increased 25 percent because of privatization.

The impact of privatization on the real average wage for a pool of workers is unlikely to be identified because the composition of workers' human capital probably changed with the layoffs accompanying the privatizations. On the one hand, many workers were laid off in early retirement plans and hence, on average, SOE workers had more tenure than the average remaining worker in the privatized firms.[13] Additionally, positions created through nepotism and cronyism disappeared because of privatization, and these positions had likely been rewarded above the average wage. On the other hand, casual evidence shows that managers' real wages increased substantially because the privatized firms had to pay competitive wages to attract skilled executives to replace the previous, politically appointed SOE directors. Thus, when we consider the impact of privatization on average wages at the firm level, the fixed effect assumption of the difference-in-difference estimator breaks down because the composition of the workers' human capital likely changed with the privatization of the SOEs. Nevertheless, the estimated impact of privatization on average real wages seems to be negative or null.[14] This impact appears to vary greatly across firms, reaffirming our suspicion that the identified effect of privatization on wages is mainly driven by composition effects instead of productivity effects (see also La Porta and López-de-Silanes 1999).

Following La Porta and López-de-Silanes (1999), we evaluate the contribution of layoffs to the changes in profitability. We compute operating income for the postprivatization period for each SOE maintaining the employment at the preprivatization level. Then, we estimate equation 2.2 for the operating-income-to-sales ratio. The coefficient of the privatization dummy variable drops to 0.67.[15] Only 20 percent of the estimated increase in the ratio of median operating income to sales seems to be attributable to workers' layoffs, a figure considerably lower than the one estimated by La Porta and López-de-Silanes (1999) for Mexico.[16]

Regarding the impact of privatization on investment, all the measures analyzed are positively and significantly affected by privatization. Investment itself increased at least 350 percent as a result of privatization. This effect is enormous and well above the one found in Mexico by La Porta and López-de-Silanes. This result is consistent with the view that one of the main motives for privatizing the SOEs in Argentina was to reestablish investment.

Finally, we consider the behavior of prices. The main difficulty in identifying the impact of privatization on prices is that prices were usually increased before the firms were privatized, substantially so in some cases, to make the companies attractive to private investors. Moreover, prices were not increased immediately before every privatization but rather when the privatization package was launched at the beginning of the 1990s. Thus, there is not enough variability across both firms and time in the changes in prices as a result of privatization to identify the effect of the latter on the former. Furthermore, we lack enough data in the immediate preprivatization period to document this effect. Additionally, the quality of several products supplied by the privatized firms increased significantly after privatization. These changes in quality are difficult to measure but well known in several sectors such as telecommunications and electricity.[17]

Under these restrictions, we do not find any statistically significant effect of privatization on prices. Nevertheless, prices did not decrease in the postprivatization period, when the efficiency gains we documented imply that prices should have fallen if the improvements in quality were not large enough. These results thus suggest that there is an important pending regulatory mission to accomplish in Argentina.[18]

Results for Banks

The Argentine banking sector went through an important transformation after the Tequila financial crisis of 1995 following the devaluation of the Mexican peso in December of 1994. Under the currency board, the central bank, BCRA, faced severe limits on its ability to act as a lender of last resort. Thus, it could not bail out banks that were having solvency problems. Instead, BCRA helped these banks to be acquired, merged, or, in the case of public banks, privatized. This process led to a significant reduction in the total number of banks operating in the country, from 168 in December 1994 to 122 two years later (Burdisso, D'Amato, and Molinari 1998).

The data set used in this study was compiled by BCRA and contains monthly financial information for all the entities that participated in the Argentine Financial System from June 1993 to September 1999. It includes the basic balance sheet accounts, the net income structure, and some physical data such as the number of employees and branches for each bank. Although the data set covers the period during which almost all privatizations took place, not all the information is available for every bank variable at every moment. In particular, more disaggregated data are available for the more recent periods.

These data have the advantage of being perfectly comparable across institutions, as well as before and after the privatizations, as BCRA, acting as regulator of the financial system, requires the entities to present their balance sheets with the same accounts and criteria.

In 1991 there were 35 public banks in Argentina, 27 owned by the provinces and 8 owned by national and municipal governments. Between 1992 and 1999, 19 of these public banks were privatized and 2 others were merged with privatized banks, leaving only 14 banks under public ownership by September 1999. We include 17 of the 19 privatized banks in our study, since no preprivatization information was available for two banks in the data set. These were the Banco de La Rioja (privatized in July 1994) and Banco de Corrientes (May 1993). The privatization of the Banco Hipotecario Nacional is also not covered here because it was done after September 1999. The variables used in our study are detailed in appendix table 2B.2.

When an SOE is privatized, the government usually tries to make the firm more attractive to buyers and ends up selling it—after a restructuring process—without the "undesired" assets and liabilities. In the case of the Argentine public banks, most of the provincial governments formed a residual entity with the low-quality assets and liabilities. To be able to cope with the short-term liabilities, the Argentine government, the Inter-American Development Bank, and the World Bank created the Fondo Fiduciario para el Desarrollo Provincial (FFDP) to lend money and give technical assistance to the provinces for privatizing their banks. In short, the privatization of provincial banks involved the creation of residual entities with the purpose of keeping the low-quality assets and liabilities that would not be attractive to potential buyers. Because of these ownership changes, stock variables such as total assets and deposits are worthless for detecting changes in performance. Instead, we consider performance ratios.

We rely on five broad indicators of performance: profitability, operating efficiency, employment, capitalization, and loan growth. We express nominal variables in 1999 pesos, deflating them by the aggregate CPI index.

The results show, first, that most profitability indicators of privatized banks increased dramatically in the postprivatization period. Table 2.7 shows simple before-and-after comparisons for the mean and median profitability indicators. Looking at the profitability ratios, almost every indicator is negative before the privatization period and turns positive after it. The median increase in the profit margin, operating margin, interest margin, return on equity (ROE), and return on assets (ROA) are all statistically significant.[19] However, the median operating income per branch decreased after privatization.

We now analyze the influence of the privatization of banks on the set of selected performance indicators estimating the model described in equation 2.1. In contrast with the case of nonfinancial firms, not all the public banks were privatized during the 1990s. Following our definition of the parameter α in the previous section, we include only public banks in the control group. In table 2.8, we present two different estimates of the impact of the privatization of banks on their performance. The data one year before and one year after the privatizations are not included in the analysis shown in the first column, whereas they are in the second column. The data just before privatization could be misleading since the government could be trying to restructure the banks before privatization to increase their attractiveness or, in case of corruption, could have modified the financial records to favor its friends in the auctions (the "cooked-books" hypothesis). The year after privatization could be considered as one dedicated to the restructuring process (see La Porta and López-de-Silanes 1999).

We report the difference-in-difference estimates of the impact of privatization on the set of indicators proposed. Most results are similar across samples. Thus, we find no evidence to support the claim that results are attributable to misleading accounting conducted before privatization.

The overall positive impact of privatization on profitability is not confirmed. Even though we find a statistically significant increase on ROA

Table 2.7 Changes in Profitability for the Sample of Privatized Banks

Variable	Mean before privatization	Mean after privatization	t-statistic for change in mean	Median before privatization	Median after privatization	Z-statistic for change in median
Profit margin (percent)	−27.07	22.32	1.09	−15.51	7.53	100.62***
Operating margin (percent)	−37.56	−15.52	0.56	−22.67	5.96	109.99***
Interest margin (percent)	−0.83	0.79	3.41***	0.20	0.55	101.71***
Operating income per branch	142	123	−0.61	145	107	11.47***
ROA (percent)	−0.007	0.002	4.93***	−0.002	0.001	167.20***
ROE (percent)	−2.305	1.224	0.66	−1.141	1.149	98.91***

*** Significant at the 1 percent level.

Note: ROA = return on assets and ROE = return on equity. See appendix table 2B.2 for definitions of variables. Number of (firm-month) observations: profit margin = 987; operating margin = 955; interest margin = 985; operating income per branch = 723; ROA = 1,148; ROE = 1,148.

Source: Authors' calculations.

Table 2.8 Changes in Performance for Privatized Public Banks

| | Column 1 | | Column 2 | |
| | Number of observa- | | Number of observa- | |
Variable	tions	Coefficient	tions	Coefficient
Profitability				
ROA	2,007	0.01***	2,246	0.01***
		(0.002)		(0.001)
ROE	2,007	0.031	2,246	0.04
		(0.03)		(0.05)
Profit margin	1,724	1.22	1,923	1.24*
		(0.94)		(0.77)
Operating margin	1,666	0.30	1,864	−0.06
		(1.08)		(0.84)
Interest margin	1,675	0.02***	1,874	0.03***
		(0.004)		(0.01)
Operating income/ branch	1,311	−227.67*** (73.73)	1,462	−199.45*** (59.90)
Operating efficiency				
Log(average cost)	1,859	0.01	2,089	−0.02
		(0.03)		(0.03)
Log(administrative expenses)	1,996	0.31*** (0.02)	2,226	0.44*** (0.02)
Log(output/ employee)	1,392	0.19*** (0.03)	1,581	0.14*** (0.03)
Log(employees/ branch)	1,507	−0.46*** (0.02)	1,694	−0.55*** (0.02)
Employment				
Log(employees)	1,513	−0.45***	1,702	−0.59***
		(0.02)		(0.02)
Other				
Capitalization	2,010	0.07***	2,249	0.08***
		(0.01)		(0.01)
Loan growth (percent)	1,922	0.03*** (0.01)	1,462	0.07*** (0.01)

* Significant at the 10 percent level.
*** Significant at the 1 percent level.
Note: ROA = return on assets and ROE = return on equity. See appendix table 2B.2 for definitions of variables. Column 1 does not include data for one year before and one year after privatization. Column 2 includes all observations.
Source: Authors' calculations.

upon privatization, we do not find any statistically significant impact on ROE, and the impact on operating income per branch is negative and statistically significant. The interest margin has also increased in association with the privatization of banks. The evidence suggests, however, that the privatization impact on both the profit and operating margins is not statistically significant.

Contrary to the case of nonfinancial firms, we do not find large increases in operating efficiency after the privatization of public banks. The impact of privatization on the (conditional) mean average costs is null. In addition, the impact of privatization on the mean administrative expenses is positive and statistically significant. They have increased 36 percent as a result of privatization. However, other indicators of efficiency performed better because of privatization. Output per employee increased 20 percent, while the average number of employees per branch decreased 37 percent. As in the case of the nonfinancial firms, employment cuts are a big part of the story. Thus, on several indicators, the privatized banks seem to be more efficient after the privatization than before. This result is in line with the results found in Burdisso, D'Amato, and Molinari (1998).

The privatization process also implied a supply increase in the credit market. Finally, solvency improved in privatized banks. The average capitalization ratio (net worth to assets) increased 5 percent because of privatization. This increase in capitalization is statistically significant. The average capitalization of the banks in the year before privatization was −10 percent, a fact that helps explain the reasons for undertaking privatization. The higher capitalization rate of the privatized banks means a more solvent system, which is quite important in countries as vulnerable to external shocks as Argentina. This is in line with the consensus that the reforms taken by the BCRA after the Tequila crisis regarding the approval of mergers, liquidation of bankruptcy banks, and privatizations helped to strengthen the financial system.

Privatization of Water and Sewerage Companies: Access to Services and Welfare

In this section, we study the impact of the privatization of water and sewerage companies on both access to service and child mortality. There are three reasons to focus our analysis on the privatization of water and sanitation services.

First, access to water supply and sanitation is a fundamental need. The significance of water, as distinct from other infrastructure industries, derives from the fact that human survival depends on access to water that is free of pollutants. The health and economic benefits of water and sanitation supply to households and individuals (and especially to children) are well documented. The lack of improved domestic water supply leads to disease through two principal transmission routes: waterborne disease that occurs from drinking contaminated water, and water-washed disease that occurs from a lack of water. Diarrhea, which can be both waterborne and water-washed, is the most important public health problem affected by the quality of and access to water and sanitation. Approximately 4 billion cases of diarrhea each year cause 2.2 million deaths throughout the world, mostly among children under the age of five. These deaths represent approximately 15 percent of all deaths of children under the age of five in developing countries (WHO 2000). Water, sanitation, and hygiene interventions can reduce diarrheal disease, on average, by between one-fourth and one-third (Esrey and others 1991). Thus, of all privatizations, the transfers of the provision of water and sanitation services are the ones that potentially could have the highest impact on a direct measure of welfare like health.

Second, the proportion of people in the world with access to water and sanitation facilities remained constant during the 1990s despite all the efforts and programs to increase the access of the poor to these services (WHO 2000). Thus, it is of special interest to test whether the privatization of water and sanitation services increased access to those services.

Third, water and sanitation services are a natural monopoly, where declining long-run average costs mean that it is most efficient for only a single firm to serve the market. Moreover, water differs from other natural monopolies in the importance of the externalities present. Both the natural monopoly feature and the health effects of water and sanitation force high public interest in the sector (Shirley 2000).

Between 1991 and 2000, several provincial privatizations in the water sector occurred, in addition to the privatization of the federal Obras Sanitarias de la Nación (OSN), which transferred the responsibility for water and sanitation service in the Buenos Aires metropolitan area to a private company, Aguas Argentinas, in May 1993.[20] The provision of water has been privatized in localities covering approximately 60 percent of the population of the country (as of the 1991 census). Water and sanitation privatizations were dispersed throughout the decade. Thus, there are localities in Argentina where privatization has not taken place. In those localities where privatization occurred, there is variability across both localities and time. This exogenous variation in the provision of water and sanitation services across time and space can be exploited to identify the causal effect of water and sanitation privatization on both access to water and child mortality.

Table 2.9 shows the access to connection to both water and sanitation services in urban areas in 1991. Connection to the water network is high (approximately 70 percent of the population) but certainly far from full coverage like the one achieved in the Argentine capital, Capital Federal (Ciudad de Buenos Aires). Connection to the sewerage network is much lower (approximately 37 percent of the population). Localities do not

Table 2.9 Access to Water and Sewerage Services, 1991
(percent)

	Water service		Sewerage service	
Sample	Urban population with connection	Urban households with connection	Urban population with connection	Urban households with connection
Total	70	73	37	41
Localities privatized between 1990 and 1999	71	74	40	45
Localities not privatized between 1990 and 1999	69	70	29	32
Capital Federal (privatized in 1993)	98	98	94	94

Note: The data are obtained from the 1991 Census of Households and Population. Urban population is the population living in all localities with more than 5,000
inhabitants in 1991. A locality is in the privatized group if the privatization of water
services occurred between 1990 and 1999.
Source: 1991 Census of Households and Population.

show substantial differences in the proportion of the population (households) with access to connection to the water network, whether it is public or private.

Artana, Navajas, and Urbiztondo (1999) analyze the first two privatizations of water and sewerage services in Argentina: Aguas Argentinas
and Aguas de Corrientes. Using official data for the period 1991 to 1995,
they report that the number of water connections in the area covered by
Aguas de Corrientes rose by 22 percent and the number of sewerage connections by 50 percent. That translates into an additional 7 percentage
points of the population covered with water services and 12 percentage
points of the population covered with sewerage services. These increases
in coverage are outstanding by any standard. For Aguas Argentinas, we
obtained similar data from the regulator for the period 1980 to 1999, and
we estimated the following regression function (where the notation is self-
explanatory, and t equals 1, 2, 3, . . . , 20):

$$\text{Log (Population served)} = \text{const.} + 0.0064\ t + 0.042\ (t - 14)\ I_{(t>14)}$$
$$(0.001)^a \qquad\qquad (0.006)^a$$
$$R^2 = 0.94$$

The results of the estimation are shown in figure 2.2.

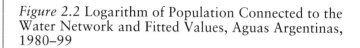

Figure 2.2 Logarithm of Population Connected to the Water Network and Fitted Values, Aguas Argentinas, 1980–99

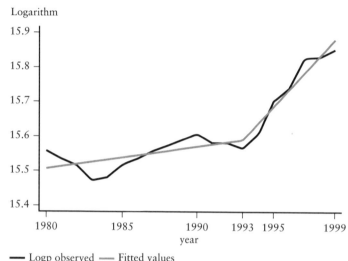

Note: The fitted values come from a simple regression including a constant, a linear time trend, and an indicator variable for the postprivatization period, beginning in 1993, as explained in the text. Fitted values closely follow the actual data.
Source: Authors' calculations.

The increase in the access to water services in the area covered by Aguas Argentinas after privatization also seems to be exceptional. After 1993 the population with access to water services increased by approximately 3 percent annually.[21]

These figures are not estimates of the causal effect of privatization of water on access to service, however. First, there is a measurement error problem since the firms know exactly where connections were expanded, but this knowledge translates noisily into population served. We have only household data on access to service from the 1991 census and from a random survey conducted in 1996–97 (by Encuesta de Desarrollo Social, or EDS) that covered all urban localities with more than 5,000 habitants and that asked the same questions about access to water connections as the

1991 census did. Second, and more important, connections could have also expanded without privatization. Thus, to identify the causal effect of privatization on access to water, we exploit the fact that between 1991 and 1997, the two dates for which we possess household access information, some privatizations affecting several localities had already occurred. Thus, for the localities that were randomly chosen in the EDS survey, we perform a test of the difference in difference of the proportion of households with access to the water network in 1991 and 1997 between urban localities where water provision had been privatized and those where it had not. The results are reported in table 2.10.

Thus, we find a statistically significant increase in the access to water services caused by the privatization of firms. Similar results are found in

Table 2.10 Difference in Difference of the Proportion of Households with Access to Water Connection, 1991–97
(percent)

	Water	
Localities	*All localities with access*	*Excluding Capital Federal*
Localities not privatized: 1991 census data	86.6	86.6
Localities not privatized: 1997 EDS, survey data	89.8	89.8
Localities not privatized: Difference 1997 − 1991	3.2	3.2
Localities privatized: 1991 census data	73.0	64.0
Localities privatized: 1997 EDS, survey data	78.0	71.4
Localities privatized: Difference 1997 − 1991	5.0	7.4
Difference-in-difference estimate	1.8	4.2
Z-test for difference in the changes in proportions	2.83***	5.78***

*** Significant at the 1 percent level.
Note: Difference in difference of the proportion of households with access to water between 1991 and 1997, between the localities where water services were privatized and those where it was not. Only the localities randomly chosen in the EDS (Encuesta de Desarrollo Social) survey are included in the 1991 estimates. Sampling weights are used to estimate the proportions reported in the table. A locality is in the privatized group if the privatization of water services occurred between 1990 and 1996.
Source: Authors' calculations.

terms of population. Note that the increase is higher when we exclude Capital Federal where access was already full before the privatization. Also, note that the increase in the access to water services in the privatized regions is approximately 11 percent (from 64.0 percent to 71.4 percent, excluding Capital Federal). This increase is consistent with the increase in access to water services that we estimated for OSN for 1993–97. Because the network expansion induced by privatization is phased over a longer period (1991–97) than the one covered by the test we conduct, it is reasonable to conclude that the causal impact of privatizations on access to water services is greater than our estimate.

Finally, we evaluate the impact of the privatization of water services on child mortality. Mortality data, compiled in Argentina by the Ministerio de Salud, are constructed at the local level disaggregated by age. Although the data are not publicly available, we have been able to access the data for the 66 localities in the country with 100,000 or more inhabitants. These localities account for 58.6 percent of the total population and for 64.4 percent of the urban population. We focus on child mortality (mortality of children below five years of age) because children are more vulnerable to water-related diseases such as diarrhea (WHO 2000). We divide the number of deaths by the number of children of that age to obtain mortality rates, the dependent variable of the following analysis.

Consider the evaluation of the impact of the privatization of water provision on child mortality.[22] The difference-in-difference estimator of the impact of privatization on mortality, α, is obtained by estimating the following regression function:

$$\text{Mortality Rates}_{it} = \alpha \, dPriv_{it} + \beta x_{it} + \lambda_t + \mu_i + \varepsilon_{it} \qquad (2.3)$$

where Mortality Rates$_{it}$ are the mortality rates of children below five years of age in locality i and year t, x_{it} is a set of control variables—income and inequality[23]—that vary across both localities and time, and $dPriv_{it}$ is a 0–1 indicator that equals unity if in locality i and period t the main provider of water services is a private firm. When $dPriv_{it}$ is 0, the main provider of water services in locality i and period t may be a public firm or a cooperative. Finally, μ_i is a time-invariant effect unique to locality i, λ_t is a time effect common to all localities in period t, and ε_{it} is a locality time-varying error distributed independently across locality and time, and independently of all μ_i and λ_t.

We report the results of this exercise in table 2.11. We find that privatization of water services has a negative and statistically significant effect on child mortality. The estimated coefficient implies that privatization induces a decrease of approximately 5 percent in child mortality rates. Thus, we find that the privatization of water services both increased access to water services and reduced child mortality.

Table 2.11 The Effect of Privatization on Child Mortality Rates, 1990–99

Impact	Dependent variable: mortality rates
$dPriv_{it}$	−0.21*
	(0.12)
Number of observations	658
Number of localities	66

* Significant at the 10 percent level.

Note: Standard errors are in parentheses. $dPriv_{it}$ is a 0–1 indicator that equals unity if in locality *i* and period *t* the main provider of water services is a private firm. When $dPriv_{it}$ is 0, the main provider of water services in locality *i* and period *t* may be a public firm or a cooperative. The regression includes year and province fixed effects. It also includes local income and inequality as control variables.

Source: Authors' calculations.

Privatization and Worker Displacement: Wages and the Distribution of Welfare

A great deal of attention in recent years has been devoted to the consequences of worker displacement for individual labor market performance (see, among others, Hamermesh 1989 and Hall 1995). Displaced workers are generally defined as those workers who were permanently laid off without cause. This type of involuntary rupture in employment relationships is usually associated with structural change, sectoral reallocation, or technological innovation. Displacement is usually followed by a period of slow rebuilding of employment relationships, as workers displaced from long-term jobs require time to find new acceptable jobs (Hall 1995). Therefore, the emphasis of our study is on long-term welfare losses after displacement. The workers displaced by the privatization of SOEs constitute a valuable alternative source for studying the consequences of worker displacement for individual labor market performance.

One good reason to study worker displacement is that its consequences can yield insights into the wage determination process. Human capital theory predicts that to the extent that experience and skills acquired on the job are general, displaced workers should not suffer large wage losses upon reemployment. In contrast, workers with accumulated industry or firm-specific capital or workers extracting industry or firm-specific rents are likely to sustain large pay cuts when changing firms or sectors.[24] Thus, even if the privatization of SOEs results in a socially efficient reduction in the level of employment in the privatized firms, the laid-off workers may still be badly harmed. If that is the case, then part of the efficiency gains of privatized firms may have come from the breach of implicit and explicit contracts between workers and firms. In this section, we explore to what extent workers displaced by privatization suffered long-term earnings losses. We rely on a survey of a random sample of displaced workers from the former state oil company YPF.

Privatization and Worker Displacement

One of the salient characteristics of the Argentine privatization program is the huge reduction in employment associated with it. Employment fell approximately 40 percent as a result of privatization. A very important question in itself but also as part of a broader study of the microeconomic benefits and costs of privatization, is the following: What has been the effect of the privatizations on the earnings of laid-off workers? To assess this question, we use a survey of a random sample of workers displaced from YPF in 1991 as part of the restructuring process of the firm before its privatization. The frame of the survey was a list of all displaced workers from YPF during 1991. The survey was conducted during the first week of August of 2001. The sample size is 504 observations.

It is likely that workers in state-owned enterprises were extracting rents and that their wages therefore did not reflect their productivity. In such a case, a long-term earnings loss because of privatization estimates a dimension of the distributive cost of privatization and is not necessarily a destruction of workers' specific human capital. Thus, our concern is with the distribution of the costs of what otherwise appears to be an efficient reform. Nonetheless, the impact of privatization on long-term earnings is not a minor point in society's perceptions of the benefits and costs of privatization.

Certainly, the welfare of workers depends not only on their earnings but also, among other things, on their fringe benefits, health insurance, and the stability of their jobs. Thus, we think it is informative to consider the overall subjective impact of privatization on the displaced workers' welfare. We find that approximately 60 percent of the displaced workers in our sample consider that they were adversely affected by displacement.[25] Nevertheless, even if revealing, this is only a subjective appraisal of the overall costs of displacement.

In addition to the earnings losses, the jobless rate for laid-off workers in the United States is higher than it is for unemployed workers who were not laid off (Ruhm 1991). In our sample, even in the long term, we also find that this is the case.

The primary factor to consider is the age distribution of the displaced workers in our sample. Displacement because of privatization was concentrated among workers older than 40 years; 30 percent of the surveyed individuals were older than 59 years at the time of the survey. Indeed, 60 percent of the sampled individuals were between 39 and 59 years, and none of the displaced workers was younger than 28 years at the time of the survey.

To draw inferences about this sample of displaced workers, we construct comparison groups from the ongoing household survey. The household survey is conducted twice a year, in May and October, in the main 28 urban agglomerates of the country.

The male labor force participation rate among the individuals displaced from YPF younger than 60 years is 90 percent.[26] Preferably, we shall compare the statistics obtained from the survey of YPF displaced workers with the same statistics estimated from the May 2001 wave of the household survey in all urban agglomerates.[27] Unfortunately, at the time of writing, only the data tapes of Greater Buenos Aires were available for May 2001. It is preferable to contrast estimates of 2001 with statistics obtained using data from the same year since the recession deepened during 2001. Thus, we compare the statistics obtained from the sample of displaced workers with the same statistics estimated using the data of Greater Buenos Aires for May 2001.[28] The labor force participation rate among males between 28 and 59 years in Greater Buenos is 96.3 percent. The participation rate in this control group and in the displaced workers' sample differs at the 1 percent level of significance. Similarly, we find that the unemployment rate among males displaced from YPF is 26.4 percent, while unemployment in the control group is 13.9 percent. Thus, we find that even though the labor force participation rate of the displaced workers, 10 years after displacement, is slightly below the labor force participation rate of a comparable group in the population, their unemployment rate is twice as high as the population unemployment rate.[29]

The Long-Term Impact of Job Displacement on Earnings

The bulk of the evidence on worker displacement comes from the United States; there is no evidence at all from Latin America. Even using different methods and data sets, the evidence from the United States is unambiguous: in addition to the direct income loss associated with unemployment, workers face large and persistent earnings losses after displacement (see, for example, Jacobson, LaLonde, and Sullivan 1993).

Most of the U.S. research on the impact of job displacement on earnings assumes that workers' earnings at a given date depend on the time since displacement through a set of dummy variables for the number of quarters after (and possible before) displacement (see, for example, Jacobson, LaLonde, and Sullivan 1993).

Consider the simplest case where we observe earnings at time t_0 before displacement and at time t_h. At time t_j, where $h > j > 0$, a group of workers was displaced from their jobs. If a longitudinal data set were available, we would estimate the displaced workers' earning losses as the difference between their actual and expected earnings had the events that led to their job losses not occurred. Thus, we would estimate a two-way fixed-effect error component model like the following:

$$y_{it} = \alpha \, dDP_{it} + \beta_t \, x_{it} + \lambda_t + \mu_i + \varepsilon_{it} \qquad (2.4)$$

where $t = 0$ or h; y_{it} is the logarithm of earnings of worker i in period t, x_{it} is a set of control variables—the standard human capital variables included in a earnings equation—that vary across both individuals and time, and dDP_{it} is a 0–1 indicator that equals unity in period h if individual i in period j was displaced from his or her job. Finally, μ_i is a time-invariant effect unique to individual i, λ_t is a time effect common to all individuals in period t, and ε_{it} is an individual time-varying error distributed independently across individuals and time, and independently of all μ_i and λ_t. Note that, in general, β is not allowed to be a time-varying parameter. Indeed, by default, the regression equation 2.4 models the "returns to education" as time-invariant. This assumption is not free of problems since it assumes that the growth rate of earnings is not affected by the change in relative prices.

The control group would be the workers not displaced. Thus, it is critical that displacement represents an event exogenous to the wage profile of the displaced individuals and hence, the expected wages of the control group are the same as the expected wages of the displaced workers had they instead stayed in their jobs. Although, in principle, displacement caused by privatization seems to be an event exogenous to workers' decisions, in practice, it is not. Displaced workers are older than workers who are not displaced, and displacement is dominated by selection based on individual characteristics. The main problem with the counterfactual group, however, is that their wages are not the same as the expected wages of the displaced workers if privatization had not taken place; that is because privatization affects the functioning of the entire firm including productivity and real wages. Furthermore, since our parameter of interest measures long-term earnings losses because of displacement from privatization, the control group would be made up of individuals who have remained in their jobs since privatization occurred; the control group would thus comprise an unusual group of workers that is not likely to be comparable to the group of workers displaced by privatization.

In this study, therefore, we focus on a family of alternative parameters—namely, the parameters of interest in a study of the benefits and costs of privatization. First, we define displaced workers' earnings losses (DWEL) to be the difference between the actual and expected earnings of a displaced worker where the expected earnings are assumed to be those taken from the population of similar individuals in terms of observable socioeconomic variables (DWEL I) instead of from the workers not displaced from a privatized firm. We argue that, in general, this parameter is the appropriate evaluation of the earnings costs of displacement caused by privatization. Argentina, however, has a relatively generous system of severance pay (Galiani and Nickell 1999). Thus, when displaced, workers received a nontrivial severance payment that they could invest and from which they could obtain a flow of income. Naturally, workers may invest their severance differently and have different returns as a result. Nonetheless, they could invest the severance in secure coupon bonds with a fixed interest rate and constant, regular repayment of interest (U.S. Treasury bonds, for example). Thus, an alternative estimate of the displaced workers' earnings losses is the difference between their actual and expected earnings where their actual earnings also incorporate the potential flow of interest on a coupon bond over the severance payment received at the time of displacement and where the expected earnings are defined in the same way as before (DWEL II).

To estimate our parameters of interest, consider the data-generating process of the earnings of a typical displaced worker. In period 0, they are given by:

$$y_{i0} = c_0 + \beta_0 x_{i0} + \mu_i + \varepsilon_{i0} \tag{2.5}$$

while in period h they are given by:

$$y_{ih} = c_h + \beta_h x_{ih} + \alpha + \mu_i + \varepsilon_{ih} \tag{2.6}$$

Thus, if we knew the parameter vector $\{c_t, \beta_t\}_{t=0,h}$, a consistent estimate of α would be given by the following before-and-after estimator: $\hat{\alpha} = \Delta\omega_{it}$, where $\omega_{it} = y_{it} - c_t - \beta_t x_{it}$. Thus, $\hat{\alpha} = \Delta\omega_{it} = \alpha + \Delta\varepsilon_{it}$. However, we do not know $\{c_t, \beta_t\}_{t=0,h}$. To circumvent this lack of knowledge, we estimate an earning equation in a sample representative of the population in periods 0 and h. Thus, we estimate the parameter vector $\{c_t, \beta_t\}_{t=0,h}$ using a control group. Note that our estimator of α is the simplest version of the conditional difference-in-difference matching estimator (see Heckman, Ichimura, and Todd 1997).

In our sample, $t = 1991$ and 2001. We estimate the parameter vector $\{c_t, \beta_t\}_{t=1991,2001}$ by estimating earnings equations using household survey data from the Greater Buenos Aires agglomerate for the waves of October 1991 and May 2001. We sample males between 18 and 59 years old who have a job at the time these household surveys were conducted. The dependent variable is the logarithm of the monthly earnings of the workers in their main occupations. We exclude unpaid workers from the sample. The conditioning variables are a set of schooling dummies and the age and the age squared of the sampled individuals. The schooling dummy variables measure the maximum level of the educational system attended by an individual and whether or not it was completed. The base category in the regression function is the complete primary school.

Table 2.12 The Effect of Privatization on Displaced Workers'
Earnings Flows

DWEL I (α)	DWEL II (α)
−0.73***	−0.54***
(0.055)	(0.052)
Number of displaced workers' observations: 150	Number of displaced workers' observations: 139

*** Significant at 1 percent level.
Note: DWEL refers to the change in the excess workers earn over their estimated market wages. Market wages are estimated from an earnings regression on the household survey. Only displaced workers currently working in 2001 are considered. DWEL I considers only current earnings. DWEL II adds the potential interest income on the severance payment (estimated at a monthly rate of 0.5 percent). The logarithm of earnings is used for the estimation. The estimate of DWEL II does not change at all if we do not impute the potential monthly flow of interests because of investing the severance payment in a secure coupon bond to a few observations that report they actually obtain monetary profits from the investment they did with the severance payment they received after displacement. Standard errors, in parentheses, are computed by assuming that our estimate of $\{c_t, \beta_t\}_{t=1991,2001}$ coincides with the true parameter values.
Source: Authors' calculations.

Since the household survey obtains data only on earnings in the month previous to the survey, we consider only the earnings of the displaced workers that were occupied at the time they were surveyed in 2001. To estimate DWEL II, we assume a monthly interest rate of 0.5 percent on the severance payment. In table 2.12 we present our best estimates of DWEL I and DWEL II.

The results are unambiguous: displaced workers face long-term substantial earnings losses. Our estimate of our statistic DWEL I is 51.8 percent of the earnings before privatization.[30] This estimate is substantially higher than the one obtained by applying the before-and-after estimator to the displaced workers' data set, which is 39.4 percent. However, there are two reasons why this latter measure does not capture the full effect of displacement on workers' earnings. First, it does not control for macroeconomic factors that cause changes in workers' earnings regardless of whether they are displaced. Second, this measure does not account for the earnings growth that would have occurred in the absence of job loss; in the long term, workers' earnings may return to their levels before displacement, but not to the levels expected before their job losses (see Jacobson, LaLonde, and Sullivan 1993).

As expected, our statistic DWEL II is somewhat lower than DWEL I. It is 41.7 percent; still, we estimate quite a substantial earnings loss after displacement, well above the earnings losses because of displacement estimated in the United States. Thus, it appears that there is a huge re-distribution cost associated with the privatizations of SOEs: displaced workers incur substantial earnings losses. What is more, since unemployment is higher among displaced workers than among a comparison group in the population, the earnings losses because of displacement are higher than the ones estimated by our statistic DWEL II. Indeed, we estimate that after taking into account unemployment, the earnings losses because of privatization are approximately 50 percent of the real earnings of the workers before privatization.

Finally, it is worth considering where the earnings losses of the displaced workers come from. Figure 2.3 shows the correlation of our estimates of

---

Figure 2.3 Displaced Workers' Earnings Rents: 1991 and 2001

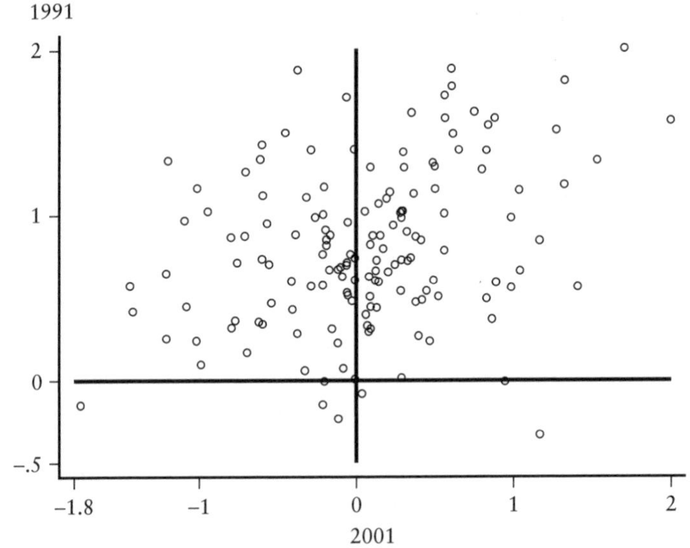

Note: Figure shows a correlation between displaced workers' rents in 1991 and 2001 (before and after their displacement). Rents are measured as the difference between their earnings and the expected earnings from an earnings regression for all workers in the household survey. Most workers enjoyed positive rents before their displacement, but roughly half of them did in 2001. (Earnings of 2001 do not include interest flow.)

Source: Authors' calculations.

ω_{1991} and ω_{2001}. Notice that ω_t measures the rent of a worker (that is, the difference between what an employed worker gets from his/her employment relationship and his/her *outside option*). As can be observed, almost all workers extracted (positive) rents in 1991, while only half of them were still obtaining (positive) rents in 2001.

Conclusions

In this chapter, we evaluated both the efficiency and some significant distributional impacts of the Argentine privatization program. This was done by considering privatization as a policy instrument and by exploiting the fact that exposure to privatization of a group of economic units (SOEs, public banks, households, and workers) varied both by unit and by year. We then used a similar statistical identification strategy to document some of the benefits and costs of privatization. Although we were not able to identify all the efficiency and distributional impacts of privatization by applying this treatment and control group approach, we contributed to the literature by documenting a wide set of causal effects of privatization on measures of efficiency and distribution.

Following La Porta and López-de-Silanes (1999), we studied the effects of privatization on profitability, operating efficiency, productivity, output, investment, employment, wages, and prices for both financial and nonfinancial privatized firms in Argentina during the 1990s. We also studied two direct measures of the welfare impact of privatizations. First, the Argentine program involved the privatization of local water and sewerage firms. Changes in the health of the population associated with these privatizations would provide a measure of the impact of privatization that goes beyond transfers of consumer surplus. We evaluated how the privatization of local water and sewerage firms affected both access to service and child mortality. Second, the Argentine program involved massive layoffs. Profitability gains in privatized firms may have been obtained at the expense of workers. We measured the effect of privatizations on workers' earnings by comparing the before-and-after wages of a random sample of laid-off workers from YPF with a matched counterfactual group build up using data gathered from the ongoing household survey.

Before discussing our results, a caveat is in order. We perform here a partial equilibrium analysis. This chapter analyzes the effects of privatization on several measures of firm performance and on the welfare of consumers and employees in the markets affected by the privatizations. We do not evaluate the potential macroeconomic effects of a privatization program as massive as the one implemented in Argentina.

We found that profitability of nonfinancial firms increased after privatization. Both operating income to sales and net income to sales increased significantly as a result of privatization. Large increases in operating efficiency underpin these gains in profitability. The impact of privatization on (conditional) median unit costs shows a reduction in median costs of 10 percent. The median sales-to-employment ratio also increased 10 percent because of the privatization of the SOEs. Finally, the impact of privatization on the median level of productivity shows an increase of 46 percent. Thus, we find a huge overall increase in the operating efficiency of privatized firms in Argentina. However, employment cuts are a big part of the story. Employment decreased approximately 40 percent as a result of privatization. Labor productivity increased not only because employment decreased but also because privatized firms increased production. The median level of production increased 25 percent because of privatization. Regarding the impact of privatization on investment, all the measures analyzed are positively and significantly affected by privatization. Investment itself increased at least 350 percent as a result of privatization. Finally, we do not find any statistically significant effect of privatization on prices. Nevertheless, after the privatization period, prices did not decrease, when the efficiency gains we documented indicate that they should have fallen if quality improvements were not large enough. This suggests that there is a pending important regulatory mission to accomplish in Argentina.

Contrary to the case of nonfinancial firms, we do not find large increases in operating efficiency after the privatization of public banks. The impact of privatization on (conditional) mean average costs is null. In addition, the impact of privatization on mean administrative expenses is positive and statistically significant. They have increased 36 percent as a result of privatization. However, other indicators of efficiency performed better because of privatization. Output per employee increased 20 percent, while the average number of employees per branch decreased 37 percent as a result of privatization. As in the case of the nonfinancial firms, employment cuts are a big part of the story. Thus, on several indicators, privatized banks seem to be more efficient after the privatization than before. The privatization of public banks has also implied an increase in credit supply. Finally, the average capitalization ratio (net worth to assets) increased 5 percent because of privatization. The higher capitalization rate of the privatized banks means a more solvent system, which is quite important in countries as vulnerable to external shocks as Argentina.

On the direct measures of welfare analyzed, we find that the privatization of water services had a negative and statistically significant effect on child mortality. The estimated coefficient implies a decrease of approximately 5 percent in child mortality rates induced by the privatization of water provision. Turning to our estimate of displaced workers' earnings losses, it appears that there is a huge redistributive cost associated with the privatization of SOEs: displaced workers incur substantial earnings losses. The earnings losses due to displacement, after taking into account unemployment, are approximately 50 percent of the real earnings of workers before privatization.

We have identified extraordinary increases in the efficiency of the privatized firms. We have also found that privatization has succeeded in satisfying other important objectives such as restoring investment and enhancing the solvency of the financial system. Finally, we considered some direct impacts of privatization on welfare and found mixed results. Thus, although we found important benefits of privatization, we also found direct costs associated with them. Overall, however, our results are much in favor of privatization.

Appendix 2A: Sector Structure and Data Sources

Gas

Gas del Estado, a vertically integrated monopoly, was privatized in December 1992 and vertically divided into several production companies, two transport companies, and eight distribution companies. The transport and distribution companies operate as local monopolies. ENARGAS (Ente Nacional Regulador del Gas) is the national regulatory authority. Competition is allowed only in the market for large users, who can buy gas directly from producers.

Financial statements of Gas del Estado were obtained from ENARGAS; financial statements for the private companies were obtained from the Buenos Aires Stock Exchange (if the firms were publicly traded) and from Inspección General de Justicia.

Telecommunications

ENTEL (Empresa Nacional de Telecomunicaciones), which was transferred to private hands in November 1990, was divided into two new companies, Telecom and Telefónica de Argentina, to provide telecommunications services in the northern and southern parts of the country, respectively. The companies operated as regional monopolies until 1999, when entry into the long-distance market was deregulated. Entry in local markets was deregulated in 2000. The regulatory authority is the Comisión Nacional de Comunicaciones (CNC).

The sources of information were the financial statements of ENTEL obtained from SIGEN (Sindicatura General de la Nacion), the financial statements of Telecom and Telefónica de Argentina, Heymann and Kosacoff (2000), and statistical information from the International Telecommunications Union for 1991 and 2001. No official financial statements were produced for ENTEL for the years 1989 and 1990. The price structure changed several times during the 1990s, making price comparisons difficult. We use the telecommunications index of the CPI as our price variable.

Electricity

In the electricity sector, the largest SOEs were SEGBA (Servicios Eléctricos del Gran Buenos Aires), Agua y Energía Eléctrica, and Hidronor (Hidroeléctrica Norpatagónica). SEGBA was the distributor in the Buenos Aires metropolitan area, but it also generated part of the energy it distributed. Agua y Energía Eléctrica and Hidronor were basically generators of electricity. With the privatization, the electrical sector was vertically divided into generation, transport, and distribution. SEGBA was divided into three distributors (Edenor, Edesur, and Edelap) and five generators (Central Puerto, Central Costanera, Central Dock Sud, Central Dique, and Central Pedro de Mendoza). Hidronor and Agua y Energía Eléctrica were divided into 6 transport companies and 22 generators. Competition occurs, mainly, in the generation activities. The sector is now subject to regulation by the secretary of energy, ENRE (Ente Nacional Regulador de la Electricidad), and CAMMESA (Compañía Administradora del Mercado Mayorista Eléctrico SA). The secretary of energy is responsible for the norms in the sector, ENRE is responsible for the application of these norms, and CAMMESA is responsible for the coordination among the different participants in the market (generators, transporters, and distributors).

We obtained SEGBA financial statements for the period 1986–91 from SIGEN and Ministerio de Economía, and the financial statements of Edenor, Edesur, Edelap, Central Puerto and Central Costanera (the firms that resulted from SEGBA divestiture) for the period 1992–94 from ENRE. For Hidronor, we obtained two audit statements for 1987 and 1988 and the final financial statement for 1991. We also obtained data for 99.92 percent (in terms of privatization revenues) of the generator companies that emerged from the privatization of Hidronor. We were able to find information for three of the six transportation companies; the three account for 91.7 percent of the privatization revenues of the electricity transportation companies. Our sources of information were Ministerio de Economía, SIGEN, ENRE, Buenos Aires Stock Exchange, and the companies that were willing to collaborate.

Water and Sewerage

Obras Sanitarias de la Nación was the provider of water and sewerage services in the Buenos Aires metropolitan area and was transferred to private hands in 1992. Aguas Argentinas is the private company that provides these services under a 35-year concession. The regulatory authority for the Buenos Aires metropolitan area is Ente Tripartito de

Obras y Servicios Sanitarios. In other parts of the country water and sewerage services are provided by a large and heterogeneous group of companies (cooperatives, and municipal and provincial companies), several of which were also privatized.

We focus on Obras Sanitarias de la Nación and Aguas Argentinas. The data for these companies were obtained from official financial statements from Ministerio de Economía and SIGEN. Most of the local providers that are or were (before privatization) cooperatives or local companies do not have financial statements.

Airlines

Aerolíneas Argentinas was privatized in 1990. It operates as an unregulated oligopoly in the domestic market and competes in the international market. Information on Aerolíneas Argentinas was obtained from Ministerio de Economía (before privatization) and the official financial statements of the company (after privatization).

Railroads

Ferrocarriles Argentinos was the SOE that managed the railroad system for the entire country. In a first stage toward privatization, the company was divided into three segments: cargo, urban passengers, and long-distance passengers. The cargo segment was finally divided into five private companies, which obtained 30-year concessions for the payment of an annual canon and a preset investment schedule. These companies are Buenos Aires al Pacífico San Martín SA, Nuevo Central Argentino SA, Ferrocarril Mesopotámico, Ferrosur Roca, and Ferroexpreso Pampeano.

In the urban passenger sector, a new company, Ferrocarriles Metropolitanos SA, was created in April 1991 and then divided into seven lines according to the old Ferrocarriles Argentinos lines. One company, Trenes de Buenos Aires SA, operates two lines (Mitre and Sarmiento). Thus, in this segment six companies operate seven railway lines. The private companies have an investment schedule, and they receive an annual subsidy, because it was thought that they would not be able to make profits.

The long-distance passenger segment was unprofitable and deemed unlikely to be attractive to the private sector. The federal government instead offered the operation to the provinces interested in maintaining the service. Only seven provinces accepted this offer, and the rest of the services were discontinued. The regulatory authority is the Comisión Nacional Reguladora del Transporte.

The data for the railways companies were obtained from SIGEN (before privatization) and from the official financial statements of the companies and Ministerio de Economía (after privatization).

Postal Services

The SOE was Empresa Nacional de Correos y Telégrafos, which was transformed into Empresa Nacional de Correos y Telégrafos SA in December 1992 and privatized in September 1997. Since December 1997 it has been controlled and operated privately as Correo Argentino SA. This private group has a 30-year concession in return for an annual fee. The regulatory authority is the CNC.

The data for postal services were obtained from SIGEN (before privatization) and from the official financial statements of the company (after privatization).

Oil

YPF (Yacimientos Petrolíferos Fiscales) was the SOE sold to the private sector in 1992. Many of YPF's assets, such as tankers, fleet, two refineries, and most of the primary and secondary drilling areas, were sold separately. The company has operated in an unregulated market since 1991. Repsol of Spain acquired it in 1999.

Because so many of YPF's assets were sold separately, any comprehensive comparison between the performance of YPF as a public entity and YPF as a private entity is impossible. Bearing this in mind, we were able to provide some comparisons of the public YPF to what remained of YPF in private hands. The data for both the public and private YPF were obtained from official financial statements from Ministerio de Economía and the firm's Web site.

Other

Two SOEs that were privatized were under the control of Ministerio de Defensa. SOMISA (Sociedad Mixta Siderurgica Argentina) was the main steel manufacturer in Argentina. Between 1991 and 1995, a "transition company," Aceros Paraná, was formed, which was privatized as SIDERAR in 1995. Tandanor (Talleres Navales Dársena Norte), a shipyard, was transferred to private ownership in December 1991. Both SOMISA and Tandanor operate in unregulated markets.

The data found for SOMISA are incomplete, since the only source of information is an audit report. No data were available for the transition company Aceros Paraná. The data for Tandanor were obtained from SIGEN (before privatization) and from Inspección General de Justicia (after privatization).

Banks

Even though the major economic reforms in Argentina took place during the first half of the 1990s, the banking sector went through an important

Appendix Table 2B.1 Description of the Variables Used to Evaluate the Impact of Privatization on the Performance of Nonfinancial Firms

Variable	Description
Fixed assets (property, plant, and equipment, or PPE)	Value of the company's fixed assets adjusted for inflation. PPE is measured by noncurrent assets.
Sales	Total value of products and services sold, minus sales returns and discounts.
Operating income	Sales minus operating expenses, cost of sales, and depreciation.
Operating income/sales	Ratio of operating income to sales. Operating income is equal to sales minus operating expenses, cost of sales, and depreciation. Sales equal the total value of products and services sold, minus sales returns and discounts.
Net income	Operating income plus other normal income minus other normal expenses. Note that extraordinary results and income taxes are excluded.
Net income/sales	Ratio of net income to sales. Net income equals operating income plus other normal income minus other normal expenses. (Note that extraordinary results and income taxes are excluded.) Sales equal the total value of products and services sold, minus sales returns and discounts.
Unit costs	Ratio of total cost of sales to sales. Cost of sales equals the direct expense involved in the production of a good (or provision of a service). Sales equal the total value of products and services sold, minus sales returns and discounts.
Employment	Total number of employees. Employees are taken to be all workers who depend directly on the company.
Wages per worker	Ratio of the total wage schedule paid by the firm to the total number of workers who depend directly on the company.
Sales/employment	Ratio of sales to total employment. Sales equal the total value of products and services sold, minus sales returns and discounts. Employment takes into account all workers who depend directly on the company.
Operating income/ employment	Ratio of operating income to total employment. Operating income is equal to sales minus

(Table continues on the following page.)

Appendix Table 2B.1 (continued)

Variable	Description
	operating expenses, minus cost of sales, and minus depreciation. Employment takes into account all workers who depend directly on the company.
Prices	In most cases, ratio of sales to physical output. For multiproduct firms or firms where prices are two- or three-part tariffs, the variable equals the price index of the product constructed by INDEC (Instituto Nacional de Estadísticas y Censos). This latter definition applies only to Obras Sanitarias de la Nación, Entel, Encotel, SOMISA, and YPF.
Production	Total output of the firm. For some multiproduct firms, this variable is the ratio of total sales to prices, where prices are constructed by INDEC (Instituto Nacional de Estadísticas y Censos). This latter definition applies only to Obras Sanitarias de la Nación, Entel, Encotel, SOMISA, and YPF.
Production/ employment	Ratio of production to total employment. Production equals total output of the firm. For some multiproduct firms, this variable is the ratio of total sales to prices, where prices are constructed by INDEC (Instituto Nacional de Estadísticas y Censos). This latter definition applies only to Obras Sanitarias de la Nación, Entel, Encotel, SOMISA, and YPF. Employment takes into account all workers who depend directly on the company.
Investment	Value of expenditure to acquire property, equipment, and other capital assets that produce revenue (gross investment).
Investment/sales	Ratio of investment to sales. Investment equals the value of expenditure to acquire property, equipment, and other capital assets that produce revenue. Sales equal the total value of products and services sold, minus sales returns and discounts.
Investment/ employment	Ratio of investment to total employment. Investment equals the value of expenditure to acquire property, equipment, and other capital assets that produce revenue. Employment takes into account all workers who depend directly on the company.

Appendix Table 2B.2 Description of the Variables Used to
Evaluate the Impact of Privatization on the Performance of
Financial Firms

Variable	Description
ROA	Return on assets. Ratio of net income to assets. Net income equals operating income plus other normal income minus other normal expenses. (Note that extraordinary results and income taxes are excluded.) Assets equal the sum of cash holdings ($ + US$), public titles, loans, participation in other societies, fixed assets, other assets, intangible assets, and foreign subsidiaries.
ROE	Return on equity. Ratio of net income to net worth. Net income equals operating income plus other normal income minus other normal expenses. (Note that extraordinary results and income taxes are excluded.) Net worth equals total assets minus total liabilities.
Profit margin	Ratio of net income to total revenue. Net income equals operating income plus other normal income minus other normal expenses. (Note that extraordinary results and income taxes are excluded.) Total revenue is equal to financial income plus service income plus irrecoverable charges.
Operating margin	Ratio of financial income plus irrecoverable charges plus services income plus financial expenditures plus services expenditures plus administrative expenses to financial income plus irrecoverable charges plus other income.
Interest margin	Ratio of financial incomes plus financial expenditures plus irrecoverable charges to loans plus public titles.
Branches	Number of branches per institution.
Employees	Number of employees per institution.
Output	Cash holdings ($ + US$) plus public titles plus loans plus deposits.
Average cost	Ratio of administrative expenses to output. Administrative expenses include wages, tax payments, and asset depreciation. Output equals the sum of cash holdings ($ + US$), public titles, loans, and deposits.
Capitalization	Ratio of capital to assets. Assets equal the sum of cash holdings ($ + US$), public titles, loans, participation in other societies, fixed assets, other assets, intangible assets, and foreign subsidiaries.
Operating income	Operating income equals the sum of financial incomes, irrecoverable charges, and service income.
Loan growth	Growth in total loans, calculated as the logarithm of loans in year t minus the logarithm of loans in year $t - 1$.

transformation after the Tequila crisis of December 1994. From the 35 public banks that started the decade, 19 were privatized between 1992 and 1999, 2 were merged with privatized banks, and 14 banks continued to be owned by the public sector. We analyze the privatization of 17 banks. The data set we used was provided by BCRA (the central bank) and contains monthly financial information of all the entities that operated in the Argentine Financial System for the period June 1993 through September 1999. It includes the basic balance sheet accounts, income structure, and some physical data such as the number of employees and branches. Although the data set covers the period in which almost all the bank privatizations took place, not all the information is available for every moment. Particularly, more disaggregated and better quality data are available only for more recent periods.

Notes

The authors are grateful for the comments of Alberto Chong, Florencio López-de-Silanes, and Máximo Torero. Matias Cattaneo, María Eugenia Garibotti, Hernán Moscosco, Mariano Tappata, and German Sturzenegger provided excellent research assistance.

1. Although several studies describe the privatization process in Argentina, none of them attempts to identify the causal effects of privatization on broad measures of performance (see, for example, Gerchunoff 1992; FIEL 1999; and Galiani and Petrecolla 2000).

2. The effects of the numerous accusations of corruption associated with the privatization of the Argentine public firms are also excluded from our analysis.

3. The only exception was Ferrocarriles Argentinos, the railway public enterprise. The company was divided into 11 units (operating lines or corridors) given in concession, and it was possible to find data by business unit for the preprivatization period.

4. Income from concessions is not considered in these calculations. Aguas Argentinas and the railway companies were privatized under this legal form. Information on total revenues from concessions is not available.

5. Possibly including a set of control regressors that vary across both units and time.

6. La Porta and López-de-Silanes (1999) use a difference-in-difference estimator to isolate the contribution of privatization to firm performance. As a control group, they form industry control groups (three-digit Standard Industrial Classification, or SIC, code level) using all private firms trading in the Mexican Stock Market (they used economywide aggregates where no matching firms were found). In our case, since most of the privatizations are the only firm in the sector, we have to rely on the nonprivatized firms to assess the counterfactual scenario of the privatized ones. Thus, our estimates of equations 2.1 and 2.2 are the closest we can get to their mean and median sector-adjusted estimates.

7. As explained before, some small privatized firms are not included in our data set. However, even if we had information on those small privatizations, the appropriateness of pooling small and large firms in our econometric analysis would be arguable.

8. Naturally, the number of observations included in the control group each year decreases every time a firm is privatized. Nevertheless, it is worth noting that

if the statistical model specified to identify the impact of privatization on the random variable *y* is correct, this is not a nuisance.

9. For several variables, however, the data are not that reliable because of the severe difficulties of producing consistent balance sheet accounts in periods of extreme price instability. We have detected some outliers in 1989. In addition, other outliers are dispersed across the data set. We do not exclude them from the regressions. Instead, as we explain later in the chapter, we present the results from a median regression, which are robust to outliers in the dependent variable.

10. We do not attempt to measure directly the impact of privatization on the stock of fixed assets because of the severe measurement errors in this variable already discussed.

11. In this context, robust connotes a certain flexibility of the statistical procedures to deviations from the distributional assumptions of the hypothesized models (see Koenker and Bassett 1978).

12. The percentage change of any variable *y* with respect to privatization is given by 100 [Exp(α) − 1], where α is the estimated coefficient in the regression equation 2.1 or 2.2 when the dependent variable is the natural logarithm of *y*.

13. For example, in the case of YPF, a random sample of laid-off workers shows that in 1991, just before the privatization of the firm in 1993, the mean (median) age of these workers was 43 (43) years while the mean (median) age of the employees in the manufacturing sector was 34 (33) years (household survey, all urban agglomerates). Only 10 percent of the laid-off workers from YPF were younger than 30 years, while 43 percent of the employees in the manufacturing sector were younger than 30 years in 1991.

14. At least 60 percent of the estimated (conditional) median impact of the privatizations on real wages may be explained by the change in the average age of the workers if the data from YPF are representative of all privatizations. We estimated an earnings function using wage data from the random sample of displaced workers from YPF for the year 1991 and computed the implied decrease in average real wages as the result of the estimated change in the average age of the workers of YPF after privatization.

15. It is still statistically different from 0 at the 1 percent level of significance.

16. This statistic may overestimate the contribution of layoffs to profits because it assumes that the laid-off workers were completely unproductive.

17. For example, our results on the effect of privatization on child mortality, discussed later in the chapter, may come from a mix of better access and improved water quality.

18. FIEL (1999) also finds that most of the real prices of the goods and services provided by the former SOEs did not increase during the 1990s even though most of them were increased at the beginning of the 1990s. Nevertheless, the prices of the goods and services of most privatized firms are indexed by the U.S. consumer price index. This implies that the prices of the privatized firms could have increased 18.5 percent since 1995 with respect to the domestic CPI. However, these changes in prices are not identified as a result of the privatization even though they are caused by the regulatory framework. Clearly, this regulatory pricing policy is inconsistent with a fixed exchange rate policy like the one adopted by Argentina during the 1990s.

19. The changes in the interest margins are mainly caused by the reduction in the share of nonperforming loans after the privatization. When we perform a test of mean differences on the interest margin without netting the nonperforming loans, we reject the hypothesis of equal means only at the 10 percent significance level. This improvement in the loan performance after privatization could result because the private banks managed credit decisions better or because the "bad loans" were placed in the residual entity. In the latter case, again, the bank fixed-effect assumption in the before-and-after estimator breaks down.

20. The first potable water service of Argentina was provided by Obras Sanitarias de la Nación in 1870. It initially served 30,000 people, and coverage continued to expand until 1960. In the 1980s coverage as a share of population actually contracted. OSN's jurisdiction was nationwide until 1980. At that point, it was restricted to Capital Federal and 13 localities of Greater Buenos Aires. Responsibility for service in the rest of the country was transferred to provincial governments (Artana, Navajas, and Urbiztondo 1999).

21. According to our estimates, the served population increased 4.8 percent a year, while population itself increased approximately 1.7 percent a year.

22. Most privatizations also included the provision of sanitation services.

23. Data on household income and inequality (the ratio of the top 10 percent to the bottom 10 percent of the distribution of per capita family income) are obtained from the Permanent Household Survey.

24. By rent, we mean the difference between what an employed worker can get from his/her employment relationship and his/her *outside option.*

25. Individuals were asked to consider the overall impact of displacement from YPF on their welfare, taking into account that they received a severance payment at the time of displacement. Approximately 80 percent of the sample reported that the major benefit lost was the health insurance package. Of the displaced workers who were employed at the time of the survey, half considered that they were in a permanent (stable) job, while 37 percent thought their job was transitory. The remaining 13 percent were unsure how to characterize the stability of their current employment.

26. The female labor force participation rate is 70 percent, although the sample included only 33 females younger than 60 years.

27. Alternatively, we could compare the statistics obtained from the survey conducted to the displaced workers from YPF with the same statistics estimated from the May 2001 wave of the household survey using data from the urban agglomerates of Chubut, Greater Buenos Aires, La Plata, Mendoza, Neuquen, and Salta. These regions match geographically the places where our sample of displaced workers resides.

28. The data gathered at the beginning of May 2001 and at the beginning of August 2001 are perfectly comparable. It was only after October 2001 that the level of economic activity in Argentina imploded.

29. These differences are even greater for skilled workers (those with at least some college or a tertiary degree). The unemployment rate among male unskilled (at most high school) workers displaced from YPF is 28 percent, while the male skilled unemployment rate in the same sample is 20 percent. The same statistics in the control group are, respectively, 15.8 and 6.4 percent.

30. Remember that the percentage change of y with respect to privatization is given by $100 [\text{Exp}(\alpha) - 1]$.

References

Artana, D., F. Navajas, and S. Urbiztondo. 1999. "Governance and Regulation in Argentina." In W. Savedoff and P. Spiller, eds., *Spilled Water.* Washington, D.C.: Inter-American Development Bank.

Burdisso, T., L. D'Amato, and A. Molinari. 1998. "Privatización de Bancos en la Argentina: ¿Un Camino hacia una Banca más Eficiente?" Documento de Trabajo 4. Banco Central de la República Argentina, Buenos Aires.

Caves, Richard. 1990. "Lessons from Privatization in Britain: State Enterprise Behavior, Public Choice, and Corporate Governance." *Journal of Economic Behavior and Organization* 13: 145–69.

CEP (Centro de Estudios Públicos). 1998. "Privatizaciones: Un Balance Cuantitativo." Ministerio de Economía, Buenos Aires (www.minproduccion.gov.ar).

Chamberlain, G. 1984. "Panel Data." In Zvi Griliches and M. Intriligator, eds., *Handbook of Econometrics.* Amsterdam: North-Holland.

Esrey, S. A., J. B. Potash, L. Roberts, and C. Shiff. 1991. "Effects of Improved Water Supply and Sanitation on Ascariasis, Diarrhoea, Dracunculiasis, Hookworm Infection, Schistosomiasis and Trachoma." *Bulletin of the World Health Organization* 69: 609–21.

FIEL (Fundación de Investigaciones Económicas Latinoamericanas). 1999. *La Regulación de la Competencia y de los Servicios Públicos.* Buenos Aires.

Galiani, Sebastián, and S. Nickell. 1999. "Unemployment in Argentina in the 1990s." Working Paper DTE 219. Instituto Torcuato Di Tella, Buenos Aires.

Galiani, Sebastián, and D. Petrecolla. 1996. "The Changing Role of the Public Sector: An Ex-post View of the Privatization Process in Argentina." *Quarterly Review of Economics and Finance* 36: 131–52.

———. 2000. "The Argentine Privatization Process and Its Aftermath: Some Preliminary Conclusions." In Melissa Birch and Jerry Haar, eds., *The Impact of Privatization in the Americas.* Boulder, Colo.: North-South Center Press.

Gerchunoff P., ed. 1992. *Las Privatizaciones en Argentina—Primera etapa.* Buenos Aires: Instituto Torcuato Di Tella.

Hall, B. 1995. "Lost Jobs." *Brookings Papers on Economic Activity*, pp. 221–73. Washington, D.C.: Brookings Institution.

Hamermesh, D. 1989. "What Do We Know about Worker Displacement in the United States." *Industrial Relations* 28: 51–59.

Heckman, J., and R. Robb. 1985. "Alternative Methods for Evaluating the Impact of Interventions: An Overview." *Journal of Econometrics* 30: 239–67.

Heckman, J., H. Ichimura, and P. Todd. 1997. "Matching as an Econometric Evaluation Estimator: Evidence from Evaluating a Job Training Programme." *Review of Economic Studies* 64: 605–54.

Heymann D., and B. Kosacoff. 2000. *La Argentina de los Noventa–Tomo II–Desempeño Económico en un Entorno de Reformas.* Buenos Aires: Editorial Universitaria de Buenos Aires.

Jacobson, L., R. LaLonde, and D. Sullivan. 1993. "Earnings Losses of Displaced Workers." *American Economic Review* 83: 685–709.

Koenker, R., and G. Basset. 1978. "Regression Quantiles." *Econometrica* 46: 33–50.

La Porta, Rafael, and Florencio López-de-Silanes. 1999. "The Benefits of Privatization: Evidence from Mexico." *Quarterly Journal of Economics* 114: 1193–242.

Lustig, Nora. 1992. *Mexico: The Remaking of an Economy.* Washington, D.C.: Brookings Institution.

Megginson, William, Robert Nash, and Matthias van Randenborgh. 1994. "The Financial and Operating Performance of Newly Privatized Firms: An International Empirical Analysis." *Journal of Finance* 49: 403–52.

Ministerio de Economía, Government of Argentina. 2000. "El Proceso de Privatizaciones en la Argentina desde una Perspectiva del Balance de Pagos." Buenos Aires.

Ruhm, C. 1991. "Are Workers Permanently Scared by Job Displacement?" *American Economic Review* 81: 319–24.

Shirley, M. 2000. "Reforming Urban Water Systems: A Tale of Four Cities." In L. Manzetti, ed., *Regulatory Policy in Latin America: Post-Privatization Realities.* Miami: North-South Center Press.

Shleifer, Andrei, and Lawrence Summers. 1988. "Breach of Trust in Hostile Takeovers." In Alan Auerbach, ed., *Corporate Takeovers: Causes and Consequences*. Chicago: University of Chicago Press.

Vining, Aidan R., and Anthony Boardman. 1992. "Ownership vs. Competition: Efficiency in Public Enterprises." *Public Choice* 73: 205–39.

WHO (World Health Organization). 2000. *Global Water Supply and Sanitation Assessment 2000 Report*. Geneva.

3

Privatization and Firm Performance in Bolivia

Katherina Capra, Alberto Chong,
Mauricio Garrón, Florencio López-de-Silanes,
and Carlos Machicado

FOLLOWING THE EXAMPLE SET BY THE Thatcher government in Britain in the early 1980s, the transfer of state-owned enterprises (SOEs) to the private sector has become widespread. By the end of the 1990s, more than 100 countries had adopted some kind of privatization program (Megginson and Netter 2001). The wide acceptance of this policy in Latin America resulted from a recognition that the state failed to deliver on its promises more often than not and that more efficient alternatives were available. In particular, the acceptance of market mechanisms meant the abandonment of the import substitution paradigm that had been the region's defining policy during the previous decades.

In recent years, however, privatization has come under severe criticism, as the benefits of the program have often gone unnoticed, while its failures have been prominently publicized. Critics argue that the benefits of privatization are exaggerated; that when they do arise, they result from exploitation of workers and consumers by the private sector; and that it is always the poor or the government that foots the bill for misconceived privatization schemes. Given the rising backlash against privatization in Bolivia, as well as most of the rest of Latin America, a systematic analysis of the evidence is in order to ensure that the right conclusions are reached and that appropriate decisions are made regarding whether privatization should be rolled back, as the critics propose, or instead be expanded and deepened.

Bolivia, like many other Latin American countries, undertook privatization with enthusiasm. Measured by both the number of firms sold and their average size, Bolivia's privatization program is small by international standards but important relative to its economy. During the 1990s Bolivia received privatization revenues equivalent to approximately 12 percent of its 1999 gross domestic product (GDP)—a greater share than Argentina, Brazil, or Mexico (see chapter 1).

Our sample of Bolivian firms reflects the mostly small and medium state-owned enterprises that were sold to the private sector and that may be thought to react differently to privatization than the typically large firms privatized in other countries. In addition to shedding light on the Bolivian privatization program, our study may serve as a guide for other countries seeking to privatize small- or medium-size firms.

The remainder of this chapter is structured as follows. The next section presents a review of the privatization conceptual framework, as well as the different arguments for and against privatization. We also review some of the recent literature and survey the existing studies for privatization in Bolivia. We then describe the Bolivian privatization program and classify it into three waves, which coincide with three different administrations under which the programs were undertaken. Next, we describe our data sample and the efforts conducted to collect information. We discuss the firms considered in the study, as well as the reasons for the exclusion of the remaining observations. We then present our main results regarding the raw and industry-adjusted performance effects of privatization. Finally, we conclude with the policy implications that arise from our main findings.

Privatization: Conceptual Framework

This section provides a brief overview of the most common goals pursued through privatization, a description of the theoretical framework that underpins most of the recent research, and an overview of the existing studies analyzing the effects of privatization with a special emphasis on Bolivia.

The Objectives Pursued with Privatization

Privatization can be undertaken for many reasons. As shown in table 3.1, it can result from economic considerations (with a micro- or macroeconomic emphasis), political reasons, firm-related considerations, or a desire to improve consumer welfare.[1] Although many of the goals listed in table 3.1 are interrelated, in some cases tradeoffs have to be made.

In a first attempt to evaluate the Bolivian privatization program, we chose to follow the footsteps of other recent studies and assume that the main objective behind the program was to improve the efficient use of resources by privatized firms (see, among many others, Wiltshire 1987, Moore 1990, and Nellis 1991).

Table 3.1 Common Objectives for Privatizations

Economic Goals
Achieve higher productivity and efficiency
Strengthen the role of the private sector in the economy
Improve the public sector's financial health
Provide autonomy to satisfy financing requirements
Political Goals
Release the enterprise from political interference
Free resources for allocation in other priority areas
Make it possible for employees to participate as shareholders
Firm-Oriented Goals
Improve performance of specific firms
Consumer-Oriented Goals
Improve services and goods
Lower prices and improve quality

Source: Authors.

The Arguments for and against Privatization

In recent years developments in the field of contract property theory have brought researchers' attention to the debate regarding public versus private provision of goods and services (Shleifer and Vishny 1996; Shleifer 1998). According to contract theory, the government could draw up an agreement, which includes all possible contingencies, so that the contractor would always deliver the expected results. Under these assumptions, it is completely irrelevant whether a good or service is provided by a public or a private entity. However, once we consider the costs in both time and money involved in drawing up a contract that tries to foresee all possible contingencies and once we acknowledge that enforcement of contracts is costly, the applicability of the predictions of this model seems unlikely.

In response to the incompleteness of contracts, property theory argues that asset ownership is the foundation for control and thus determines the incentive structure that can explain the performance of firms and managers.[2] Within this framework, two lines of argument, the social view and the agency view, emerge to explain why a change in ownership can lead to shifts in the performance of privatized firms. The social view argues that SOEs play an important role in counteracting market failures by implementing pricing policies that take social marginal costs into account. Thus, the increased profitability of privatized firms may reflect not only efficiency gains but also consumer exploitation through the use of market power (Shapiro and Willig 1990).

The agency view, in contrast, argues that the benefits of privatization stem from an ownership structure that provides adequate incentives. It begins by acknowledging that firms under state control pursue political, social, and economic objectives simultaneously and are thus almost guaranteed to perform at a lower level than firms in the private sector (Sheshinski and López-Calva 1999).

Within this second view, there are two complementary explanations about the inadequate incentive structure for SOEs, depending on who the critical agency conflict lies with—the manager or the politician. The managerial view argues that managers of SOEs may lack high-powered incentives or the necessary monitoring authority to ensure that the firm is run effectively (Vickers and Yarrow 1988). The political perspective stresses that when politicians have control over a firm, they are likely to pursue a multitude of objectives and relegate efficiency considerations to a secondary role (Shleifer and Vishny 1994; López-de-Silanes, Shleifer, and Vishny 1997). The inclusion of political and social goals is likely to diminish the pursuit of economic ones. Also, the frequent changing of the relative importance of these priorities is likely to affect negatively the long-term performance of SOEs. In this sense, privatization can promote efficiency by allowing the objectives of the enterprise to be more focused and thus reducing the ambiguity attached to these objectives, and by facilitating long-term planning (Commander and Killick 1988).

Empirical Studies on Privatization

Most empirical studies can be classified into three broad groups: case studies, intercountry studies, and cross-section studies. The first group includes studies such as Ramamurti (1997) and D`Souza (1998), who find that privatization increased productivity and reduced the work force in specific sectors (railroads and telecommunications, respectively); Eckel, Eckel, and Singal (1997), who document significant price decreases in the airline sector following the privatization of British Airways; and Newberry and Pollitt (1997), who find that the producers and shareholders benefit the most from privatization, while consumers and the government benefit only marginally.

Among the most prominent cross-section studies are those by Galal and others (1994), Megginson, Nash, and van Randenborgh (1994), Frydman and others (1998), and Boubakri and Cosset (1998). All these studies find that the performance of privatized companies significantly improved. However, another study by Pohl, Claessens, and Djankov (1997), using a sample of 6,300 firms, shows that privatization's positive effects on corporate performance are not uniform among different types of firms and performance measures.

Finally, among the most prominent examples of intercountry studies are Martín and Parker (1995); Barberis and others (1996); Claessens and Djankov (1998); and La Porta and López-de-Silanes (1999). The major findings of these studies are that privatized firms improved their performance, that the change in management contributed to an increase in the value of the firms, and that the greater business profitability was largely explained by improvements in productivity and not by higher sale prices or reductions in labor costs.

Relatively little has been written on Bolivia's privatization program, especially regarding the first privatization phase from 1992 to 1994. Some recent studies provide valuable information for understanding the privatization program in Bolivia; among these are Montero (1994), Reordenamiento de las Empresas Públicas (1994), and Requena (1996). Their contributions, however, are limited to a descriptive analysis of the privatization process or a useful, albeit partial, analysis of the financial performance of former SOEs. Another important study is that of Barja and Urquiola (2001), who analyze the impact of capitalizations and the regulatory reforms implemented in conjunction with privatization in order to assess their impact on access and availability of services to low-income households.

Deeper studies of Bolivia's privatization usually stall because of the scarcity of information, mainly financial data, regarding firms' situation before and after the process. This is precisely the gap this chapter tries to fill by collecting comparable information from a wide sample of privatized firms during the period 1992–2000.

The Bolivian Privatization Program

The privatization program was very successful in attracting foreign investment, which reached levels heretofore unseen in Bolivia. The increase in foreign investment came primarily from capital investments in gas, electricity, and telecommunications. These increases, together with reforms in the financial sector, caused second-round increases in private domestic investment and consumption. This boom in investment drove economic growth throughout the mid-1990s to the late 1990s.

The increased social investment can be understood only in the context of the state reform in which it was implemented. The method of investment delivery changed from an overwhelmingly centralized provision of services to a provision based on municipalities. This reform was implemented by a wide-ranging decentralization reform, enacted as part of the Ley de Participación Popular and the Ley de Decentralizacion. The motivation behind this reform was to make expenditures in social investment more efficient by better matching expenditures to local needs. The underlying hypothesis was that communities are better able than the central government to assess their needs and select how best to make investments that address those needs. From its inception the decentralization was supported by the Inter-American Development Bank and the

World Bank, both through credit and lending activities and, more generally, in the context of the Heavily Indebted Poor Countries Initiative and the corresponding Bolivian Poverty Reduction Strategy Paper. The Inter-American Development Bank in particular focused on loans to strengthen municipalities and their ability to plan and execute investment projects.

Before 1992 the government sought, through the use of shared risk contracts, an increased private involvement in certain sectors (such as mining and hydrocarbons) that had traditionally been reserved for the public sector. These contracts typically transferred assets of SOEs to private administrators, who would then have to undertake the necessary investments to modernize the business or complete the project. Within this framework, the state received a flat fee for the leased assets, and the private firm could claim any residual profits. The first contracts of this nature were signed during the 1980s and are still used today. Although the size of many of these agreements makes them an important object of study, they reflect a qualitatively different phenomenon than the privatizations that would later take place.

In 1994 the Bolivian government decided to privatize its state-owned enterprises, which controlled seven industries: oil and gas, petroleum refining, tin mines, railways, electrical power, telephones, and airlines. In some instances, the government used traditional privatization; under this method, the government transfers majority ownership of an SOE to the private sector and has freedom over how to spend the proceeds. More often, however, the Bolivian government relied on capitalization. Under capitalization, the state transfers 50 percent of a company's shares to the investor with the winning bid. It transfers an additional 45 percent of the shares to a private pension fund for the accrued benefit of the public in general, with the remaining 5 percent going to the company employees. The investor takes over the management of the firm and commits to *invest* the amount it offered to acquire its 50 percent share, in the development of the firm. It must carry out this investment within a specific time period (typically 6–8 years). In addition, the investor agrees to fulfill obligations that encompass expansion and quality goals, to operate under tariff regulation, and to fulfill other clauses specified in a long-term contract (typically 40 years).

This method of privatization was selected by the center-right political faction led by Gonzalo Sanchez de Lozada because previous privatizations had been strongly criticized. This plan attempted to elicit popular support by distributing shares to the electorate; however, not everyone was happy with the plan. Some said it was unfair to those younger than 21 years of age, who were left out of the distribution. Others objected that their shares went into a pension fund that they would benefit from only in the future or maybe not at all if they died before retirement. Others objected to the sale of strategic industries to foreigners.

The period analyzed here starts in 1992 and ends in the early 2000s. It can be broken into three privatization waves, which are associated with different governments and reflect the major pushes given to privatization in Bolivia.[3] The first wave started in 1992 with the enactment of the Privatization Law.[4] The second wave began in 1994 and introduced the capitalization schemes. And the third wave started in 1998 and constituted a return to the straight sales seen during the first wave.

First Wave

With the enactment of the Privatization Law in April 1992, Bolivia began its privatization process. The process was characterized by the complete transfer of companies, which operated in competitive markets and were considered "small" businesses. Under this wave, 34 SOEs were privatized. All were considered to be nonperforming before their sale, they had ample excess capacity and bloated work forces, and most received subsidies from the government (Ministerio de Capitalización 1994). A list of these 34 SOEs can be found in appendix table 3A.1 and includes, for the most part, hotels, bus terminals, milk-processing plants, flour-collection businesses, and similar enterprises.

Enterprises transferred to the private sector in this first wave were sold through public auctions and public bidding processes. In a few cases workers were offered the option of purchasing shares in the business, but this was the exception rather than the rule. Outside consultants were used to help assess the value of the largest enterprises; however, several firms were so small that no proper valuation was carried out. The objectives were to reduce the public deficit by cutting subsidies; increase the efficient use of assets by transferring them to the private sector; and increase social investment in health, education, and basic infrastructure by directing the proceeds of the privatization to these ends. Most firms were sold without any prior restructuring and with the government paying, in advance, for any social benefits owed to existing workers.[5]

Second Wave

The second privatization wave began in 1994, when capitalization was adopted as the method of privatization.[6] Capitalization contracts differed from the way in which SOEs had been privatized previously in two important ways. First, the private investor acquired complete managerial control but only 50 percent of the equity. Second, in contrast to a traditional privatization, which involves the sale of the enterprise, no sale was involved and, hence, the national treasury did not receive any proceeds from the transfer. What capitalization called for was an injection of capital to the enterprises under consideration. Thus, through this process, the equity of the enterprise doubled, the private investor held 50 percent of the equity in the capitalized enterprise, and the state transferred the other 50 percent to company employees and as nontransferable shares to two newly established private pension funds.

Capitalizations were used for the largest SOEs, which had traditionally been considered strategic, and often resulted in the breakdown of state monopolies. For example, the state hydrocarbon enterprise, Yacimientos Petrolíferos Fiscales Bolivianos (YPFB), was capitalized as several different units. Similarly, the generating units of the national power company Empresa Nacional de Electricidad (ENDE) and two units (Andina and Oriental) of the railroad enterprise Empresa Nacional de Ferrocarriles (ENFE), were capitalized independently. At the same time, other state monopolies were capitalized as a single entity, such as the telecommunications enterprise, Empresa Nacional de Telecomunicaciones (ENTEL), and the national airline, Lloyd Aéreo Boliviano (LAB). Appendix table 3A.1 lists the 10 capitalizations carried out during the second wave, as well as 35 traditional privatizations.

The idea behind the capitalizations was to encourage private firms to invest in and run what had been key SOEs. The government's main objectives were to attract private investment on a large scale; accelerate job creation; improve managerial and technological efficiency by transferring control to the private sector; and create a long-term saving mechanism to directly redistribute the gains from the privatization into pensions instead of using the gains for public spending. To make the enterprises more attractive for bidders, the commercial debts of capitalized firms were often transferred to the national treasury.

As evident from the list above, capitalizations were used mainly for firms in noncompetitive markets and especially for those involved in the provision of public services. These firms also employed the largest number of workers and consequently were home to the most active labor unions. According to a study undertaken by the Ministerio de Capitalización (1994), before the capitalization of SOEs, all of these enterprises had productivity and efficiency indicators below international benchmarks.

Third Wave

The third wave saw an end to the capitalization program and a return to the classical approach to privatization. From 1998 to 2003, the third wave included the sale of 14 SOEs including a petroleum refinery, several mining firms, a cement factory, and other assorted enterprises (see appendix table 3A.1). Because of the nature of the firms sold, the third wave also included significant regulation and deregulation of relevant sectors to ensure that consumers would not be exploited by firms with market power.

Reforms in Specific Sectors

Capitalization was introduced relatively late in Bolivia's road to liberalization and was seen not as a means to cover deficits but rather as an option for attracting foreign investment and improving management in key areas of the economy. Indeed, this process raised significant amounts of capital. Total commitments were about $2 billion, roughly equivalent to 30 percent of GDP, thus contributing to a significant increase in investment.[7] This process was complemented with changes to some sectors' industrial organization and with the implementation of a regulatory framework seeking to promote competition and efficiency. The main tool in this regard was the Sistema de Regulación Sectorial (SIRESE) Law in 1994, which created a regulatory system for the entire infrastructure sector. In essence, this legislation defined the regulatory institutional structure, including the role of five regulatory agencies (*superintendencias*) for the electricity, telecommunications, hydrocarbons, potable water, and transportation sectors. It also established an oversight agency responsible for systemwide coordination and evaluation, and introduced market competition as one of the foundations of the infrastructure sector. Last, the law formulated the procedures for appeals, hearings, and conflict resolution.

This framework is supplemented by four specific laws—covering electricity (1994), telecommunications (1995), hydrocarbons (1996), and potable water (2000)—that introduced changes in the organization of each sector. These laws govern issues related to tariff regulation, entry, service quality, and sanctions and are administered by the sectoral regulatory agencies of SIRESE.

Electricity. The reform of Bolivia's electricity sector is considered one of the most successful to date. Bolivia opted for both vertical and horizontal separations. ENDE, the largest power company, was divided into three generation units and a transmission grid. The generation units were capitalized, and the transmission grid was privatized as a common carrier. In distribution, the Empresa de Luz y Fuerza Electrica de Cochabamba (ELFEC, the Cochabamba electricity distribution company) was also privatized, while the Compania Boliviana de Energia Electrica (COBEE, the second largest generator and distribution company in La Paz) was already private. Among the other major cities, the Cooperativa Rural de Electrificacion (CRE, the Santa Cruz distribution company) remains a cooperative and is considered to be well run along commercial lines. Many of the smaller electric systems, which are cooperatively owned, have yet to be corporatized (that is, to become *sociedades anonimas*).

In reforming its electricity industry, Bolivia broke away from some of the accepted models for reform prevailing at that time and became the first country to restructure and privatize the power sector using the capitalization method. This decision was prompted not by a desire to flout current fashionable practice, but rather because it suited the country that way and because the resulting reform program constituted an appropriate and timely response to the situation in Bolivia at that time. Instead of copying other countries' models, Bolivia wisely adopted some of the principles underlying current reform trends all over the world and applied them in the degree and form that best suited its own position.

By adopting the capitalization approach, Bolivia not only privatized electricity supply but also transferred one-half of the industry's ownership to Bolivian citizens. The shares allocated to Bolivians were entrusted to special pension funds, which were responsible for managing the shares within certain trading parameters. This process developed both the pension funds and the local capital markets. It also ensured that capitalization took place through timely investments that were equal in size to the contributions made by private investors. This approach differs from the previous attempts at privatization in the United Kingdom (England and Wales) and Chile. In fact, the Bolivian case might be labeled as a "reverse Chilean" process because the pension funds were used to *manage* the shares rather than to buy them.

Hydrocarbons. Before the reforms, the hydrocarbons industry (oil and natural gas) was dominated by Yacimientos Petrolíferos Fiscales Bolivianos, a vertically integrated monopoly involved in all activities of the industry. Limited private participation was possible through joint ventures with YPFB. Since the reform, the governmental priority has been to remove YPFB from production activities and to promote foreign investment to foster a natural gas export industry directed mainly to southern Brazil. The state intends this industry to become the engine of development for other sectors of the national economy. With this goal in mind, reforms and foreign investment were targeted to exploration and the creation of new infrastructure. The opening of a pipeline to Brazil in 1999 made this vision a reality. A general policy promoting private control of all phases of hydrocarbons, including retail commercialization, was adopted for the domestic market.

To implement these objectives, the Hydrocarbons Law places few restrictions on the export and import of petroleum products and stipulates that exploration, production, and commercialization be executed through joint ventures with YPFB. The administration of gas and oil pipelines was transferred, without exclusive rights, to the capitalized Transredes. The administration of other pipelines was entrusted to the private Oil Tanking. Most of YPFB's refining units were transferred to the private Empresa Boliviana de Refinación, while YPFB continues to run the wholesale operations for petroleum products.

Telecommunications. In the preprivatization era, the telecommunications industry was divided among the state monopoly, Empresa Nacional de Telecomunicaciones, which provided national and international long-distance communication services, 15 cooperatives with monopolies in fixed local telephone services, and Telecel, a private monopoly in the cellular market. The Telecommunications Law maintained this division until the end of 2001, when entry was liberalized. Until then, ENTEL and the cooperatives had exclusive rights, but the cellular market was opened to competition with the entry of ENTELMovil (a division of capitalized ENTEL). The Telecommunications Law also encompassed incentives for the exploitation of economies of scope by the most efficient firms. This objective is pursued through two mechanisms: cooperatives failing to achieve improvement goals lose a percentage of their market to ENTEL; and authorization for mergers, acquisitions, and stock swaps.

The entry of Nuevatel, a joint venture between COMTECO (the Cochabamba cooperative) and Western Wireless International, has been the only modification to this industrial structure. Nuevatel was created for the purpose of acquiring a PCS (personal communications services) license and began operations in December 2000, intensifying competition in the mobile phone market.

Water. While other sectors underwent capitalization and the introduction of regulation, the water industry experienced limited changes and encountered several difficulties. The intention of the reform in this sector was the creation of several concessions (as opposed to actual privatization) for the administration of state assets. In practice, however, only one municipal firm, SAMAPA (La Paz-El Alto), was transferred to the private sector in 1997 for administration by Aguas del Illimani, a private firm. It was expected that within a prudent period of time, the necessary legislation would be in place to conform the remaining public water firms to a similar model. However, the long delay in formulating the Potable Water and Sewerage Law (finally approved in 2000), together with a significant failure to create a second concession through the transfer of a municipal firm to a consortium, Aguas del Tunari, in Cochabamba, has deferred reforms and somewhat redirected change in this sector. Nevertheless, during 1998 and 1999, the water regulatory agency was able to incorporate the new regulatory regime and sign concessions with the existing municipal water firms in Santa Cruz, Oruro, Sucre, and other smaller cities.

Under the new model, the concession approach seeks to improve internal efficiency and achieve expansion and quality goals. The new Potable Water and Sewerage Law has four important elements:

• Responsibility for the provision of these services is assigned to the municipal governments but can be transferred to water and sewerage providers (WSPs) that are private, municipal, or mixed firms, cooperatives, or other civil associations recognized by law.

• The territory is divided into concession and nonconcession areas: the concession areas are financially sustainable, and services are provided only by WSPs, while nonconcession areas are not financially sustainable, and the service can be provided by a local government.

• Regulation of WSPs includes tariff regulation using the rate-of-return criteria, investment and efficiency targets, and a five-year regulatory lag.

• Universal access in nonconcession areas is to be supported by public investment.

The contract signed with Aguas del Illimani reflects these aims. Objectives for the 1997–2001 period include 100 percent access to potable water or sewerage (public fountains excluded) in the areas of Achachicala and Pampahasi, which cover the city of La Paz; 82 percent access to potable water in the city of El Alto by 2001, of which 50 percent was to consist of expansion connections, and 41 percent access to sewerage; and compliance with the goal of expanding, over time, the percentage of households with potable water coverage and sanitation services.

Quality control includes norms related to the source of water; its quality, abundance, and pressure; continuity of service; infrastructure efficiency; consumer service; and emergencies. Regulated prices are calculated to assist the company to meet its contractual obligations and expansion goals. Although the five-year lag promotes internal efficiency, no productivity factors were incorporated. Furthermore, tariffs were set in dollar terms, payable in bolivianos.

Data Sample

The task of collecting information for this chapter required the collaboration of various public and private institutions. Several sources of information were used. From the National Statistical Institute and the National Tax Service, we obtained financial information for the period in which the companies were part of the public sector. The statistical agency provided information on approximately 30 percent of the companies in the study. The National Service of Commerce Registry and the General Superintendency helped with postprivatization information. The former provided information on owners of the businesses, while the latter provided annual reports of the capitalized companies. We also carried out a survey to complete the financial information needed for this study. Other information came from the Reorganization Unit, the Vice Ministry of Budget and Accounting, and the National Chamber of Hotels.

Data were not always strictly compatible across sources, and an extra effort to confirm sources had to be made. When differences were encountered, data and sources were selected based on the series that matched existing trends most closely.[8] The sample's small size also implies that few results are statistically significant. Nonetheless, the data set we constructed constitutes, to our knowledge, the most serious and comprehensive data on the transfer of SOEs to the private sector in Bolivia.

Because of the small size of many privatized firms (more than 90 percent were small or medium-size enterprises), financial and performance information was not always collected or kept up-to-date either before or after privatization. Unlike other countries, very few privatized firms were listed on the stock exchange either before or after their transfer to private hands. This explains the lack of a single source of comprehensive data and the multiplicity of sources needed to construct our database.

According to the Reorganization Unit, 94 public enterprises were transferred to the private sector between 1992 and 2003.[9] Of these, 83 were privatized under the traditional method, 10 through capitalizations, and 1 as a concession.[10] While the number of privatized firms seems large, only 31 firms had sufficient information to include in the final sample. Table 3.2 summarizes the number of firms in the sample and the reason for excluding those that were not analyzed in the study.

Four firms were excluded because they were too small and did not have proper accounting records. We were unable to confirm if these firms had effectively been privatized, much less to capture their financial and employment information. Another 9 firms, all from the first wave, were sold as stripped assets, making a comparison impossible. Twenty-nine firms had no financial statements from the period in which they were in public hands, and we were unable to obtain the information from our surveys. Eleven firms were created from disintegrated monopolies from which we were unable to construct separate financial books to measure performance of the relevant units before privatization. We were therefore forced to exclude them from the sample. Finally, 10 firms from the third wave were left out of the sample because the sale was too recent for any meaningful postprivatization comparison to be made.

Table 3.2 Reasons for Excluding Firms from the Sample

Reason	Number of firms
Firms too small	4
Firms sold as stripped assets	9
No financial statements from the period when firms were public	29
Firms created from disintegrated monopolies	11
Sale too recent	10
Enterprises not included in the study	63
Enterprises included in the study	31
Total	94

Source: Authors' data.

Results

Following the methodology of La Porta and López-de-Silanes (1999), this section seeks to measure the change in performance of the privatized firms by comparing performance indicators before and after privatization. We divide our indicators into the following five groups: profitability, operating efficiency, labor, assets and investment, and output.

To calculate estimates that take into account the sometimes large differences among industries, a difference-in-difference analysis was carried out using information from firms that had been private all along. As a control group, we used data from the Manufacturing Industry Survey (CIIU), using the corresponding industrial classification for each firm; for firms that could not be classified within a corresponding CIIU code, we used an aggregate measure of the whole manufacturing industry as an economy-wide control. *Before privatization* refers to the average for the four years before privatization, or for the years with available data, while the term *after privatization* corresponds to the average value for 1999 and 2000, or for the last two years for which information is available.[11]

Raw Data

Table 3.3 presents the results from our unadjusted ratios. Several interesting results can be appreciated. The first is that both mean and median profitability increased by 15 percentage points. Privatized firms' ratio of operating income to sales increased from a mean (median) of slightly over 20.1 (12.8) percentage points before privatization to 35.1 (27.9) percentage points after privatization. Moreover, this increase is statistically significant at the 10 percent level.

The next set of indicators suggests that the increase in profitability was primarily driven by improvements in efficiency. Our cost-per-unit indicator suggests that privatized firms underwent significant restructuring and streamlining following privatization. The mean (median) firm reduced its costs by 18.3 (20.8) percentage points, with the difference being significant at the 5 percent level. Moreover, the magnitude of this increase in efficiency suggests that efficiency gains by themselves can account for the increased profitability of privatized firms. Other indicators of operating efficiency provide additional circumstantial evidence to suggest that transfers from workers and market power are not a source of improved profitability of privatized firms. The mean (median) firm increased its ratio of sales to property, plant, and equipment (PPE) by 36.5 (8.1) percent and its ratio of sales to employees by 48.2 (30.4) percent. The most remarkable results, however, are those for the subsample of firms for which we can calculate the ratio of operating income to employees. In this case, the interaction of greater labor efficiency and reduced costs allowed

Table 3.3 Changes in Performance of the Sample of Privatized Firms on Bolivia

Variable	N	Before privatization Mean Median	After privatization Mean Median	t-statistic	Z-statistic
Profitability					
Operating income/sales	28	0.2010	0.3511	1.71*	1.64
		0.1281	0.2793		
Operating income/PPE	20	0.2063	0.2858	0.42	−0.37
		0.1048	0.1074		
Operating efficiency					
Cost per unit	28	0.8217	0.6386	−2.40**	−2.26**
		0.9110	0.7032		
Log(sales/PPE)	23	−0.4628	−0.0981	1.26	1.09
		−0.4735	−0.3925		
Log(sales/employees)	23	11.6759	12.1581	1.59	1.52
		11.8141	12.1181		
Operating income/employees (thousands)	19	12.6049	73.6712	1.89*	1.76*
		10.1750	39.7259		
Labor					
Log(employees)	24	4.6709	4.5811	−0.19	−0.46
		4.7405	4.6094		
Log(blue-collar workers)	20	4.1466	4.0935	−0.12	−0.28
		4.2853	4.2377		
Log(white-collar workers)	20	1.4807	1.3572	−0.25	−0.61
		1.1705	0.8959		
Average wage per worker (thousands)	16	10.8515	19.9102	2.49**	2.26**
		9.0361	18.8589		

(Table continues on the following page.)

Table 3.3 (continued)

Variable	N	Before privatization Mean Median	After privatization Mean Median	t-statistic	Z-statistic
Average wage per blue-collar worker (thousands)	16	9.5054 7.7061	16.0569 15.6106	2.24**	2.04**
Average wage per white-collar worker (thousands)	16	26.1511 22.4439	59.9427 44.5518	2.38**	2.33**
Assets and investment					
Log(PPE)	23	17.1634 16.6764	16.8574 16.9574	−0.43	−0.25
Investment/sales	18	0.0499 0.0177	0.0560 0.0110	0.18	−1.27
Investment/employees (thousands)	15	10.8727 2.5556	10.1345 1.0845	−0.09	−1.763*
Investment/PPE	17	0.0288 0.0137	0.0232 0.0073	−0.34	−0.95
Log(PPE/employees)	18	12.4286 12.1583	12.2558 12.1274	−0.47	−0.35
Output					
Log(sales)	31	15.9962 15.5094	16.1039 15.8996	0.16	0.12

* Significant at the 1 percent level.
** Significant at the 5 percent level.
*** Significant at the 10 percent level.

Note: N = number and PPE = property, plant, and equipment. This table presents raw results for the sample of 31 privatized firms. For each empirical proxy, the table presents the number of usable observations and the mean and the median values before and *after privatization. Before privatization* refers to the average value for the four years before privatization; after privatization refers to the average value for 1999 and 2000, or for the last two years for which information is available. We report *t*-statistics and Z-statistics (Wilcoxon rank sum) as the test for significance for the change in mean and median values, respectively. Definitions for each variable can be found in appendix 3A.2.

Source: Authors' calculations.

the median firm to increase its operating income per worker by a staggering 290 percent.

Privatization usually leads to employment cuts across the board, which encourages critics to argue that the gains in profitability are merely transfers from workers to the new owners. In the case of Bolivia, the mean (median) firm reduced its work force by 9.0 (13.1) percent, significantly less than the labor reduction experienced in other countries. For example, La Porta and López-de-Silanes (1999) found that the mean (median) firm in Mexico fired 64.9 (56.8) percent of its work force, while Torero (chapter 8) documents employment cuts of 51.0 (56.1) percent for Peru. Moreover, once we consider that the average wage per worker increased by a mean (median) of 83.5 (108.7) percent, it is clear that firms did not increase profits by exploiting workers. Even though the fall in employment is not statistically significant, the increase in wages is significant at the 5 percent level.

An additional criticism of privatization is that even if firms do restructure and become more efficient, it is the poorest workers who bear the brunt of the restructuring burden. Privatization is thus opposed not because of concerns regarding its aggregate effect but because it is thought to have a negative redistributive effect. By breaking up employment cuts and wage increases into white-collar and blue-collar workers, we can shed some light on this issue. Regarding employment, the evidence conclusively shows that blue-collar workers fare better than their white-collar colleagues. While the mean (median) firm fired 12.3 (27.5) percent of its white-collar workers, it fired only 5.3 (4.8) percent of its blue-collar ones. This evidence suggests that it is false to assume, at least in the case of Bolivia, that privatization hurt unskilled workers disproportionately. Regarding wages, the evidence is mixed but still does not support the view that unskilled workers were exploited. Average wages of white-collar workers increased 129.2 percent, significantly more than the 68.9 percent increase observed for blue-collar workers. However, the median change in wages, arguably a better gauge as it is less susceptible to outlier observations, shows virtually identical increases of about 100 percent for both types of workers. Moreover, even if wages for white-collar workers increased more than those of blue-collar ones, an average real increase of 70 to 100 percent in wages and greater job stability can hardly be considered a disproportionate burden for unskilled workers.

Regarding investment, there seems to be no clear-cut trend—the mean and median values of our investment ratios move in opposite directions. It is difficult to know a priori what to expect from investment following privatization. On the one hand, firms usually have ample spare capacity and thus room to increase production by using assets more efficiently. On the other hand, production processes may be outdated and require significant investments to bring them up-to-date. Bolivia presents a good example of this ambivalence, as many of its privatized firms clearly suffered from overcapacity.

However, some of the larger firms were privatized under capitalization schemes, the precise purpose of which was to increase investment. In any case, the only statistically significant result is the median for the ratio of investment to employees, which shows a decrease of almost 60 percent.

Finally, our results corroborate other studies of privatization showing that notwithstanding a reduced work force and no general increases in investment, the mean (median) firm was able to increase output—in the case of Bolivia, by 10.8 (39.0) percent.[12] This growth in real sales is the final piece in the puzzle, demonstrating that the main effect of privatization is a substantial improvement in efficiency, which permeates through as higher profits for firms, higher wages for workers, and increased output for consumers.

Industry-Adjusted Data

Toward the end of the 1990s, the Bolivian economy experienced important fluctuations in its growth rate and underwent great sectoral transformations. For example, its average growth rate ranged from a high of 4.8 percent in 1995–98 to just 0.44 percent in 1999.[13] One may, therefore, wonder whether the strong increases in output, profitability, and wages observed in our sample can be explained by general macroeconomic trends or sector-specific events. To isolate the role of privatization, we present industry-adjusted ratios in table 3.4. In short, we find that the performance improvements observed in the previous section are not explained by industrywide or macroeconomic changes and that in fact some of our industry-adjusted indicators show a more favorable picture of performance by privatized firms than that suggested by the raw indicators described in the previous section.

The first result is that industry-adjusted indicators show that output at the median privatized firm increased by 26.7 percent. This would imply that about 70 percent of the raw increase in output results from privatization, while only 30 percent can be explained by industry or macroeconomic changes. Focusing on the mean firm yields an even more favorable interpretation, with industry-adjusted output in privatized firms increasing 32.4 percent.

Regarding profitability, the results show that privatized firms first converged to the levels of their industry peers and then surpassed them. The mean (median) ratio of operating income to sales shows that SOEs underperformed their industry groups by 14.4 (18.3) percentage points and that after privatization they overperformed the same control group by 13.7 (5.9) percentage points. As expected, these gains in profitability stem from larger cost savings and efficiency gains than those experienced by other firms. Industry-adjusted costs per unit dropped by a mean (median) of 6.4 (5.0) percentage points, while the ratio of sales to employees increased 51 (9.6) percent.

Table 3.4 Industry-Adjusted Changes in Performance for the Sample of Privatized Firms

Variable	N	Before privatization Mean Median	After privatization Mean Median	t-statistic	Z-statistic
Profitability					
Operating income/sales	28	−0.1442 −0.1830	0.1373 0.0594	3.52***	3.15***
Operating efficiency					
Cost per unit	28	0.2216 0.2399	0.1573 0.1905	−0.72	−0.23
Log(sales/employees)	22	7.8357 8.5944	8.3456 8.6909	0.74	0.96
Labor					
Index of total employees	24	100.00 100.00	70.33 58.98	−3.01***	−5.29***
Index of industry-adjusted real wages per worker	16	100.00 100.00	238.02 131.86	1.76*	−0.65
Output					
Log(sales)	31	−5.6182 −6.3877	−5.2942 −6.1206	0.53	0.67

* Significant at the 10 percent level.
** Significant at the 5 percent level.
*** Significant at the 1 percent level.

Note: N = number. This table presents industry-adjusted results for the sample of 31 privatized firms. See text for an explanation of the way these results were computed. For each empirical proxy, the table presents the number of usable observations and the mean and median values before and after privatization. *Before privatization* refers to the average value for the four years before privatization; *after privatization* refers to the average value for 1999 and 2000, or for the last two years for which information is available. We report t-statistics and Z-statistics (Wilcoxon rank sum) as the test for significance for the change in mean and median values, respectively. Definitions for each variable can be found in appendix table 3A.2.

Source: Authors' calculations.

Finally, our industry-adjusted indicators show that employment cuts after privatization are more significant than the raw data suggested, but the wage increases observed are robust. The mean (median) index of total employees dropped 29.7 (41.0) percent following privatization, significantly above the 9.0 (13.1) percent decrease observed in the raw data. This implies that firms in the control group hired a substantial number of workers over the period analyzed. Meanwhile, the industry-adjusted real wages per worker show a robust increase for the mean (median) firm of 138.0 (31.9) percent following privatization.

All in all, our industry-adjusted indicators show that macroeconomic conditions and industry-specific changes cannot explain the large performance gains documented for privatized firms. Although in some cases a part of the gains can be explained by industry changes, the bulk of the improvement in firm performance is due to restructuring and efficiency gains. In fact, the raw indicators may be underestimating the true impact of privatization as industry-adjusted improvements are larger than the ones shown by the raw indicators.

Conclusions

This study assembled a comprehensive database for firm characteristics before and after privatization. Despite severe information limitations, we were able to collect sufficient data for one-third of the firms privatized between 1992 and 2003. Our sample contains firms of all sizes, with an emphasis on medium and small ones; this sample reflects the structure of privatization in Bolivia.

Our results broadly mirror those found for other countries: privatization leads to a significant increase in efficiency and a corresponding rise in firm profitability. Although privatization results in a decrease in employment, the Bolivian experience shows only mild changes relative to those found for other countries. Notably, real wages increase by almost 100 percent, suggesting that SOEs employed too many workers and used them ineffectually but did not overpay them. In this sense it is likely that these jobs were sought after not because they paid well but because they did not require much effort. Investment shows no clear trend; the mean and median values move in opposite directions. This is probably a reflection of Bolivia's esoteric two-tiered structure of privatization in which most firms sold were suffering from overcapacity, but a few of the largest were sold under capitalization schemes, which by definition were aimed at increasing investment. Finally, we also find that despite a reduced work force and the ambivalent behavior of investment, firms were able to increase output substantially. These results carry through when we look at industry-adjusted indicators, and in fact, in some cases, shed a more favorable light on the performance of privatized firms.

This study provides a valuable contribution for two reasons. First, it represents the first systematic study of the change in performance of Bolivian SOEs following privatization. Although previous authors have analyzed specific privatizations and others have written descriptive analyses of the program, this chapter represents, to our knowledge, the most comprehensive effort to collect employment and financial information for privatized firms in Bolivia. Second, the sample of firms privatized in Bolivia, unlike most other countries, is composed mostly of medium and small firms. In this sense, the results obtained from this analysis shed some light as to what other countries with similar characteristics may expect from privatization. Our results imply that there seem to be no significant differences in the benefits of privatization to small and medium-size firms than those observed for larger SOEs in other countries.

Appendix Table 3A.1 List of Privatized Firms, 1992–2001

First wave

1 Fondo Ganadero del Beni y Pando	18 Fábrica de Cerámica Roja de Cobija
2 Fábrica de Objetos de Peltre	19 Hotel Prefectural Liriuni
3 Empresa Forestal Pecuaria Tariquia	20 Centro de Acopio Yamparaez
4 Planta Industrializadora de Quinua	21 Centro de Acopio Redención Pampa
5 Planta de Alimentos Balanceados Portachuelo	22 Centro de Acopio Tomina
6 Empresa Nacional de La Castaña	23 Hacienda Ganadera Santa Martha
7 Industrias Metálicas (Inmetal)	24 Hotel Prefectural de Caranavi
8 Línea Aérea Imperial	25 Cabaña Lechera Todos Santos Paz
9 Pait - Pl Procesadora de Caranavi	26 Hotel Prefectural de Pando
10 Cadenas Andinas sam	27 Centro de Acopio Totora
11 Criadero de Truchas Piuisilla	28 Centro de Acopio Lourdes
12 Pollos Bb	29 Centro de Acopio Betanzos
13 Taller de Cerámica Artesanal Chuquisaca	30 Fabrica de Aceites Comestibles Villamontes
14 Fábrica Nal. de Fósforos	31 Fábrica Boliviana de Cerámica
15 Hotel La Paz (Ex-Sheraton)	32 Fábrica de Cerámica Roja de Oruro
16 Hotel Crillon	33 Hotel Prefectural de Tarija
17 Fábrica de Cerámica Roja de Trinidad	34 Ingenio Azucarero Guabira

(Table continues on the following page.)

Appendix Table 3A.1 (continued)

Second wave (sale)

35 Empresa Transportadora de Electricidad (TDE)	55 Planta de Alimentos Balanceados Tarija
36 Empresa de generación eléctrica Luz y Fuerza de Cochabamba (ELFEC)	56 Planta Industrializadora de Leche – Scz
	57 Planta Industrializadora de Leche Pil – La Paz
37 Hilandería Santa Cruz Sam	
38 Planta Laminadora de Goma Sam	58 Planta Industrializadora de Leche Pil – Cbba
39 Bien Inmueble	59 Planta Industrializadora de Leche Pil – Tarija
40 Planta de Hilandería Viacha (Phv)	60 Planta Industrializadora de Leche Pil – Sucre
41 Hotel Balneario Asahi	
42 Hotel Prefectural Caranavi	61 Ingenio Azucarero Guabira
43 Hotel Prefectural de Copacabana	62 Fabrica de Aceites Comestibles Villamontes
44 Hotel Prefectural de Coroico	63 Planta Elaboradora de Quesos San Javier
45 Hotel Prefectural de Sorata	
46 Hotel Prefectural Viscachani	64 Planta de Alimentos Balanceados Tarija
47 Hotel Prefectural de Urmiri	
48 Hotel Prefectural de Chulumani	65 Producción de Harinas Compuestas – Tarhui
49 Hotel Terminal de Oruro	
50 Terminal de Buses Oruro	66 Cabaña de Porcinos "El Zapallar"
51 Terminal de Buses Sucre	
52 Terminal de Buses Cochabamba	67 Hilandería Pulacayo
53 Producción de Alimentos de Maiz Mairana	68 Multipropósito Gran Chaco
	69 Fábrica Boliviana de Cerámica
54 Planta de Alimentos Balanceados de Chuquisaca	70 Fábrica de Cerámica Roja de Oruro

Second wave (capitalization)

71 Empresa Generadora de Electricidad (CORANI)	76 Lloyd Aéreo Boliviano
	77 Empresa Petrolera Andina
72 Empresa Nacional de Telecomunicaciones (ENTEL)	78 Empresa Petrolera Chaco
	79 Transportadora de hidrocarburos (TRANSREDES)
73 Empresa Ferroviaria Andina	
74 Empresa Ferroviaria Oriental	80 Empresa Generadora de Electricidad (Valle Hermoso)
75 Empresa Generadora de Electricidad (GUARACACHI)	

Third wave

81 Refinería de Petróleo (EBR)	83 Estaciones de servicio de aeropuertos
82 Planta de almacenaje de carburantes y Poliductos	84 Gasolineras

Appendix Table 3A.1 (continued)

Third wave	
85 Empresa Minera Vinto – Antimonio	90 Empresa Metalúrgica Vinto – Estaño
86 Financiera de Desarrollo S.A.	91 Empresa Minera Huanuni
87 Campo Geotérmico Laguna Colorada	92 Planta Industrial Oruro
	93 Empresa Minera Colquiri
88 Fábrica Nacional de Explosivos Sam	94 Planta de Productos Lácteos Milka
89 Fábrica Nacional de Cemento	

Source: Authors.

Appendix Table 3A.2 Description of the Variables Used in Tables 3.3 and 3.4

Variable	Description
Operating income/sales	The ratio of operating income to sales. Operating income is equal to sales minus operating costs and minus depreciation. Sales are equal to the total value of products and services sold, nationally and internationally. Operating costs is equal to the direct expense involved in the production of a good (or provision of a service). This includes the day-to-day expenses incurred in running a business, such as sales and administration. It is also called operating expenses.
Operating income/PPE	The ratio of operating income to property, plant, and equipment. Operating income is equal to sales minus operating costs and minus depreciation. Operating costs is equal to the direct expense involved in the production of a good (or provision of a service). Property, plant, and equipment is equal to the value of a company's fixed assets adjusted for inflation.
Cost per unit	The ratio of operating costs to sales. Operating costs is equal to the direct expense involved in the production of a good (or provision of a service). This includes the day-to-day expenses incurred in running a business, such as sales and administration. Sales are equal to the total value of products and services sold, nationally and internationally.
Log(sales/PPE)	Natural logarithm of the ratio of sales to property, plant, and equipment. Sales are equal to the total value of products and services sold, nationally and

(Table continues on the following page.)

Appendix Table 3A.2 (continued)

Variable	Description
	internationally. Property, plant, and equipment is equal to the value of a company's fixed assets adjusted for inflation.
Log(sales/ employees)	Natural logarithm of the ratio of sales to total number of employees. Sales are equal to the total value of products and services sold, nationally and internationally. Employees corresponds to the total number of workers who depend directly on the company.
Operating income/ employees	The ratio of operating income to total number of employees. Operating income is equal to sales minus operating costs and minus depreciation. Employees corresponds to the total number of workers who depend directly on the company.
Log(employees)	Natural logarithm of the total number of employees. Employees corresponds to the total number of full time workers who depend directly on the company. It does not include individuals who are retired or working on commission.
Log(blue-collar workers)	Natural logarithm of the total number of blue-collar workers. Blue-collar workers perform un- or semi-skilled labor for modest to low wages. They perform tasks directly related to the (mass) production process or menial services. Typically, they are factory-line or maintenance workers.
Log(white-collar workers)	Natural logarithm of the total number of white-collar workers. White-collar workers perform skilled labor and administrative tasks for modest to high salaries. They are individuals involved in sales, administration, and management.
Average wage per worker	The average wage paid per worker in each firm. The consumer price index was used as a deflator to calculate real wages. A similar procedure is used for the calculation of real wages per blue-collar and white-collar workers.
Log(PPE)	Natural logarithm of property, plant, and equipment. Property, plant, and equipment is equal to the value of a company's fixed assets adjusted for inflation.
Investment/sales	The ratio of investment to sales. Investment is equal to the value of expenditure to acquire property, equipment, and other capital assets that produce revenue. Sales are equal to the total value of products and services sold, nationally and internationally.

Appendix Table 3A.2 (continued)

Variable	Description
Investment/ employees	The ratio of investment to employees. Investment is equal to the value of expenditure to acquire property, equipment, and other capital assets that produce revenue. Employees corresponds to the total number of workers (paid) who depend directly on the company.
Investment/PPE	The ratio of investment to property, plant, and equipment. Investment is equal to the value of expenditure to acquire property, equipment, and other capital assets that produce revenue. Property, plant, and equipment is equal to the value of a company's fixed assets adjusted for inflation.
Log(PPE/ employees)	Natural logarithm of the ratio of property, plant, and equipment to total number of employees. Property, plant, and equipment is equal to the value of a company's fixed assets adjusted for inflation. Employees corresponds to the total number of workers who depend directly on the company.
Log(sales)	Natural logarithm of sales. Sales are equal to the total value of products and services sold, nationally and internationally.
Index of total employees	For each firm, the index takes value of 100 for the preprivatization period. The average of the last two years after privatization value is computed by augmenting the preprivatization value by the difference between the cumulative growth rate of employment of the firm and the cumulative growth rate of employment of the control group in the postprivatization period relative to the average employment in the four years that preceded privatization. Industry control groups are given by an index of economywide total employment.
Index of industry-adjusted real wages per worker	For each firm, the index takes value of 100 for the preprivatization period. The average of the last two years after privatization value is computed by augmenting the preprivatization value by the difference between the cumulative growth rate of real wages per worker of the firm and the cumulative growth rate of real wages per worker of the control group in the postprivatization period relative to the average real wage per worker in the four years that preceded privatization. Industry control groups are given by an index of economywide real wages per worker.

Source: Authors.

Notes

The authors are indebted to Patricio Amador, Jose Caballero, Cecilia Calderon, Gabriela Enrique, Paola Espinoza, Jesús Mogrovejo, and Monica Yanez for providing skillful research assistance.

1. For a detailed discussion of privatization effects on these objectives as well as their interrelation, see Sheshinski and López-Calva (1999).

2. Some extensions to these two initial arguments analyze more deeply the relationship between property, efficiency, and contracts. These include agency theory, public choice theory, property rights theory, and transactions costs analysis; see Commander and Killick (1988) and Hodge (1999), among others.

3. From 1989 to 1993, the government of Jaime Paz Zamora; from 1993 to 1997, the government of Gonzalo Sanchez de Lozada; and from 1997 to 2001, the government of Hugo Banzer Suarez.

4. Privatization Law 1330, April 24, 1992.

5. See López-de-Silanes (1997) for a discussion of prior restructuring measures and their effect on the price paid for privatized SOEs.

6. The Capitalization Law that made this type of privatization possible was enacted on March 21, 1994.

7. All dollar values are U.S. dollars unless otherwise indicated.

8. Many of the differences resulted from the application of distinct accounting systems, as many of the balance sheets and income statements were not audited.

9. This number includes one concession. The Reorganization Unit is a unit within the Ministry of Investment and Privatization and serves as the government's agency responsible for privatization. As such, it maintains records of the privatizations undertaken in Bolivia.

10. The number of capitalized enterprises can be counted in two different ways: as the number of enterprises before capitalization (5), or as the number of enterprises resulting from the capitalization process (10). For this chapter we have adopted the second measure.

11. For the purpose of calculating the average of the last two years, we consider the year of privatization as a postprivatization year.

12. For example, the median increase in output of privatized firms was 17.4 percent in Brazil, 69.0 percent increase in Colombia, 68.2 percent in Mexico, and 40.8 percent in Peru; see chapters 4, 6, and 8, and La Porta and López-de-Silanes 1999.

13. During the 1990s increased openness brought a greater influx of foreign capital. This, in turn, favored the growth of the economy, raised employment levels, and increased mean labor productivity (Jiménez, Pereira, and Hernany 2002).

References

Barberis, Nicholas, Maxim Boycko, Andrei Shleifer, and Natalia Tsukanova. 1996. "How Does Privatization Work? Evidence from the Russian Shops." *Journal of Political Economy* 104: 764–90.

Barja, Gover, and Miguel Urquiola. 2001. "Capitalization, Regulation, and the Poor: Access to Basic Services in Bolivia." Working Paper, funded by the United Nations University/World Institute for Development Economics Research. Helsinki.

Boubakri, Narjess, and Jean-Claude Cosset. 1998. "The Financial and Operating Performance of Newly Privatized Firms: Evidence from Developing Countries." *Journal of Finance* 53: 1081–110.

Claessens, Stijn, and Simeon Djankov. 1998. "Politicians and Firms in Seven Central and Eastern European Countries." Policy Research Working Paper 1954. World Bank, Washington, D.C.

Claessens, Stijn, Simeon Djankov, and Gerhard Pohl. 1997. "Ownership and Corporate Governance: Evidence from the Czech Republic." Policy Research Paper 1737. World Bank, Washington, D.C.

Commander, Simon, and Tony Killick. 1988. "Privatisation in Developing Coutries: a Survey of the Issues." In Paul Cook and Colin Kirkpatrick, eds., *Privatisation in Less Developed Countries*. New York: St. Martin's Press.

D'Souza, Juliet. 1998. "Privatization of Telecommunication Companies: An Empirical Analysis." Working Paper, Mercer University, Macon, Ga.

Eckel, Catherine, Doug Eckel, and Vijay Singal. 1997. "Privatization and Efficiency: Industry Effects of the Sale of British Airways." *Journal of Financial Economics* 43: 275–98.

Frydman, Roman, Cherryl W. Gray, Marek Hessel, and Andrzej Rapaczynski. 1998. "Private Ownership and Corporate Performance: Some Lessons from Transition Economies." Working Paper. New York University, C.V. Starr Center for Applied Economics, New York.

Galal, Ahmed, Leroy Jones, Pankay Tandon, and Ongo Vogelsang. 1994. *Welfare Consequences of Selling Public Enterprises*. Oxford, U.K.: Oxford University Press.

Hodge, Graeme A. 1999. *Privatization: An International Review of Performance*. Boulder, Colo.: Westview Press.

Jiménez Wilson, Rodney Pereira, and Werner Hernany. 2002. "Bolivia: Efecto de la Liberalización Sobre el Crecimiento, Empleo, Distribución y Pobreza." In *Liberalizacion, Desigualdad y Pobreza: America Latina y el Caribe en los 90*, Capitulo 5. Programa de las Naciones Unidas para el Desarrollo (PNUD), Comision Economica para America Latina y el Caribe (CEPAL).

La Porta, Rafael, and Florencio López-de-Silanes. 1999. "The Benefits of Privatization: Evidence from Mexico." *Quarterly Journal of Economics* 114 (4): 1193–242.

López-de-Silanes, Florencio. 1997. "Determinants of Privatization Prices." *Quarterly Journal of Economics* 107 (4): 965–1025.

López-de-Silanes, Florencio, Andrei Shleifer, and Robert Vishny. 1997. "Privatization in the United States." *Rand Journal of Economics* 28 (3): 447–71.

Martín, Stephen, and David Parker. 1995. "Privatization and Economic Performance Throughout the UK Business Cycle." *Managerial and Decision Economics* 16: 225–37.

Megginson, William L., and Jeffry M. Netter. 2001. "From State to Market: A Survey of Empirical Studies on Privatization." *Journal of Economic Literature* 39: 321–89.

Megginson, William L., Robert C. Nash, and Matthias van Randenborgh. 1994. "The Financial and Operating Performance of Newly Privatized Firms: An International Empirical Analysis." *Journal of Finance* 49 (2): 403–52.

Ministerio de Capitalización. 1994. "Monitor de la Capitalización, números especiales." La Paz, Bolivia.

Montero, Marcelo. 1994. "Análisis Financiero Nacional, Regional e Individual de las Empresas Privatizadas." Ley N° 1178 SAFCO (Sistema de Administración Financiera y Control Gubernamental). La Paz.

Moore, Jacqueline. 1990. "Privatization: The Liberals View to Improving Efficiency and Performance of Industry." I. I. Pty, Ltd., Sydney.

Nellis, John. 1991. "Privatization in Reforming Socialist Economies." In J. Bohn and V. Kreacic, eds., *Privatization in Eastern Europe: Current Implementation Issues*. Yugoslavia: International Centre for Public Enterprises in Developing Countries.

Newberry, David, and Michael G. Pollitt. 1997. "The Restructuring and Privatization of Britain's CEGN – Was It Worth It?" *Journal of Industrial Economics* 45: 269–303.

Pohl, Gerhard, Stijn Claessens, and Simeon Djankov. 1997. "Privatization and Restructuring in Central and Eastern Europe: Evidence and Policy Options." Technical Paper 368. World Bank, Washington, D.C.

Ramamurti, Ravi. 1997. "Testing the Limits of Privatization: Argentine Railroads." *World Development* 25: 1973–93.

Reordenamiento de las empresas públicas. 1994. Government of Bolivia, La Paz.

Requena, Mario. 1996. "La Experiencia de Privatización y Capitalización en Bolivia." Serie de Reformas de Política Pública 38, Comisión Económica para América Latina y El Caribe, Santiago, Chile.

Shapiro, Carl, and Robert Willig. 1990. "Economic Rationales for the Scope of Privatization." In B. N. Suleiman and J. Waterbury, eds., *The Political Economy of Public Sector Reform and Privatization*, 55–87. London: Westview Press.

Sheshinski, Eytan, and Luis F. Lopez-Calva. 1999. "Privatization and Its Benefits: Theory and Evidence." HDII Discussion Paper 698. Harvard University, Cambridge, Mass.

Shleifer, Andrei. 1998. "State Versus Private Ownership." *Journal of Economic Perspectives* 12(4): 133–50.

Shleifer, Andrei, and Robert Vishny. 1994. "Politicians and Firms." *Quarterly Journal of Economics* 109 (4): 995–1025.

———. 1996. "A Theory of Privatization." *Economic Journal* 106: 309–19.

SIRESE (Sistema de Regulación Sectorial). 2000. "La Regulación Sectorial en Bolivia." Annual Report, Superintendencia General, La Paz.

Vickers, John, and George Yarrow. 1988. "Privatization: An Economic Analysis." Cambridge, Mass.: MIT Press.

Wiltshire, Kenneth. 1987. "Privatization: The British Experience: An Australian Perspective." Committee for Economic Development of Australia and Longman Cheshire, Melbourne.

4

Costs and Benefits of Privatization: Evidence from Brazil

Francisco Anuatti-Neto, Milton Barossi-Filho, Antonio Gledson de Carvalho, and Roberto Macedo

THE BRAZILIAN PRIVATIZATION PROGRAM has been a major undertaking by international standards. Between 1991 and July 2001, the state transferred its control of 119 firms and minority stakes in a number of companies to the private sector. The auctions produced $67.9 billion in revenues, plus the transfer of $18.1 billion in debt. The government also sold $6 billion in shares of firms that remained under state control, obtained $10 billion from new concessions of public services to the private sector, and sold $1.1 billion in scattered, noncontrolling stakes in various private companies owned by BNDES, the National Social and Economic Development Bank. The magnitude of the Brazilian privatization program is among the largest in the world, making it worthy of closer analysis.

The Brazilian program has also been large in relative terms. Lora and Panizza (2002) compared the cumulative value of the privatization efforts between 1988 and 1999 as a proportion of gross domestic product (GDP) in 10 South and Central American countries (Argentina, Bolivia, Brazil, Costa Rica, Ecuador, El Salvador, Honduras, Paraguay, Peru, and Uruguay). Brazil came in third with a rate of 5 percent of GDP, above the average of 2.7 percent, and was surpassed only by Peru (6 percent) and Bolivia (9 percent).[1] The value of privatizations in 5 of the other countries did not exceed 1 percent of GDP.

Despite its magnitude, the Brazilian program has been largely ignored in the international literature. For instance, a survey by Megginson and Netter (2001, p. 326) recognized the Brazilian program as "likely to remain very influential," because of its scale and the size of the country. Their survey did not include any specific analysis of the Brazilian program, however, largely because of the paucity of studies and because most of the literature that does exist has been published only in Brazil and in Portuguese. Furthermore, the existing studies have their shortcomings, as their review in this chapter makes clear. Therefore, there is room for adding to both the Brazilian and the international literature.

It is also important to disseminate findings among the Brazilian public at large. The economy's performance was very disappointing in the 1990s. Some groups, among them politicians and journalists, have often expressed their frustration with privatization and other reform and adjustment policies, blaming them for the sluggish growth of the economy. In part because of this, the program all but stalled after 1998. Thus, it is crucial to show the results of the privatization program to shed light on a discussion largely based on unwarranted conclusions.

With regard to theoretical aspects, privatization is the subject of a wider and continuing debate on the role of the government in the economy. The analysis in this chapter is primarily focused on the relative effectiveness of private versus public ownership of companies that underwent privatization in Brazil. As a working hypothesis, the chapter tests the proposition that private ownership is more effective, but it also looks at the ways in which privatization results in increased profits, such as higher prices and reduced employment. Moreover, it discusses the management of the privatization process in terms of its macroeconomic implications and its objective of democratizing capital ownership, among other issues. In this fashion, the chapter provides empirical evidence important to understanding the role of public ownership in the country, as well as the process by which the state has been stepping back from an entrepreneurial role.

The next section describes the Brazilian privatization program and surveys the literature on it. The chapter then presents the variables and the data set used in the empirical analysis. The methodology and the empirical results are summarized and other benefits and costs are discussed. The chapter then examines public opinion on the privatization program in Brazil and compares these views with those in other countries in the same region. It also evaluates the perspectives for new privatization efforts in the country, before summarizing the major conclusions.

The Brazilian Privatization Program and the Literature

The Brazilian privatization program has three components: the federal National Program of "Destatization" (NPD), which started in 1991; similar programs at the state level, which began in 1996; and the privatization program of the telecommunications industry.[2] This last component was launched in 1997 as a program at the federal level, separate from the NPD but running parallel to it. We refer to it here as the telecom program. Its auctions, mostly taking place in 1997 and 1998, produced a total of

$28.8 billion in revenues plus $2.1 billion in debt transfers. The NPD yielded a total of $28.2 billion in revenues plus $9.2 billion in debt transfers, while the state-level program produced a total of $27.9 billion in revenues plus $6.8 billion in debt transfers.[3]

Altogether, electricity accounted for 31 percent of the total value of the auctions; telecommunications, 31 percent; steel, 8 percent; mining, 8 percent; oil and gas, 7 percent; petrochemicals, 7 percent; financial, 6 percent; and others, 2 percent. Largely because of the telecom program, the value of privatizations reached a peak in 1997–98, a period that accounted for 69 percent of the total value as of July 2001. This statistic has important implications for our later analysis of the effect the privatization program had on Brazil's fiscal crises and external imbalances.[4]

In any discussion of privatization, it is important to know what enterprises the government owned before the privatization, which enterprises were privatized, and which remained under government control. We have little information on the initial situation in the various Brazilian state governments and on what remains to be privatized there. We therefore focus on the federal level only, the most important part of the program, where our information covers the whole program, except for the concession of public services.

An Overview of Privatization at the Federal Level

In 1980 the federal government undertook a survey of all its "entities," including companies, foundations, port authorities, research institutes, and councils in charge of professional registration. There were 560 such institutions, of which 250 were organized as firms (mainly in the form of corporations). In the 1980s some minor privatizations occurred, and a few firms were also closed. At the start of the program in 1991, other entities had also ceased to exist. As a result, the program was launched with 186 firms still under government control. At the end of 2000, mainly because of the privatization program, this number was reduced to 102.

Appendix table 4A.1 lists the companies privatized by the federal government since 1990. Appendix table 4A.2 lists the firms privatized on behalf of some states by BNDES, some minority controlling stakes formerly held by the federal government, and firms privatized by the state of São Paulo. In both tables, we list the firms included in our sample and the revenue obtained from their privatization. Note is also made of the companies that were listed on the São Paulo stock exchange before privatization.

Appendix table 4A.3 lists the enterprises owned by the federal government that were not privatized. The group includes, among others, hospitals, port authorities, the postal service, an agricultural research firm, and BNDES. Among the industries where companies remain to be privatized are the electricity industry, where privatization of several major companies has been postponed; the oil industry; and the financial sector, in which a few federal banks and most state banks have already been privatized (the latter group having been federalized for this purpose). The table also lists a group of entities organized as corporations over which the government exercises 100 percent control. Some of these entities are government agencies disguised as corporations. These firms are directly linked to the federal budget, from which they receive practically all the resources they use.

The privatization program has made little progress since 1998. Among other reasons, privatization and other liberalization measures coincided with sluggish growth, which weakened support for the program. Moreover, some accusations that the government had used excessive methods to bring interested groups to the telecom auctions caused a furor in the press and led the minister of telecommunications to resign in 1998. Furthermore, if continued, the program would extend into politically sensitive areas such as electricity, where the states are very strong; oil, where the gigantic Petrobrás still arouses strong nationalistic feelings; and the almost 200-year-old Banco do Brasil, which plays an important role in financing farmers and therefore enjoys strong political support.

The Brazilian Literature on Privatization

In reviewing this literature, we concentrate on the studies that have addressed the status of the state-owned enterprises (SOEs) before and after privatization, as that is the major focus of this chapter. At a later point we refer to the literature on other issues as well.

Three studies are worth reviewing. Pinheiro and Giambiagi (1997) of BNDES presented an overall evaluation of the preprivatization performance of federal SOEs in the 1981–94 period. They showed disappointing figures for the SOEs, in terms of both profitability and dividends received by the national treasury. Over that entire period, the ratio of profits to net assets was −2.5 percent, on average. Moreover, from 1988 to 1994, years for which data on dividends were available, the ratio of profits to assets accounted for only 0.4 percent of the equity capital owned by the federal government in the SOEs.

One of the causes of this disappointing performance was the SOEs' wage policies. Macedo (1985) undertook a comprehensive analysis of wage differentials between private firms and SOEs. His data consisted of wages and other characteristics of individual workers, obtained from forms filled out by firms every year, as required by the Ministry of Labor.[5] He compared the wages of the workers in private firms and SOEs of approximately the same size in 10 industries. After controlling for differences in education, age, gender, and experience, he found sizable wage differentials in favor of the workers at the SOEs.[6]

The third study is Pinheiro (1996). He analyzed the performance of 50 former SOEs before and after privatization, using data up to 1994. His data covered one to four years before and after privatization for each company and came from data sets similar to those used in this study but that were complemented by questionnaires filled out by the firms and delivered to BNDES for that purpose. Unfortunately, the bank's policy prevents the use of the data by outsiders. The study covered eight variables: net sales, net profit, net assets, investment, fixed investment, number of employees, debt, and an index of liquidity. From these variables, another six were derived to measure efficiency: sales and profit by employee, the rate of return measured by the ratios of profit to sales and profit to net assets, and the propensity to invest, with respect to both sales and assets. No comparison was made with the performance of the private sector as a control group, nor was a distinction made between companies listed on the stock exchange and those that were unlisted.

Pinheiro (1996) concluded that "in general, the obtained results confirm that privatization brings a significant improvement . . . [in] the performance of the firms. Thus, for most of the variables, the null hypothesis of no change in behavior is rejected in favor of the alternative hypotheses that privatization increases the production, the efficiency, the profitability and the propensity to invest, reduces employment and improves the financial indicators of the firms."[7]

In the current study, we add to this literature in various respects. The study was carried out by an independent team, whereas most of the previous major studies were produced by staff members of BNDES. The study covers a larger number of firms, looks at privatization up to the year 2000, and uses data that can be disclosed. We took explicit care to avoid a selection bias by including both large and small privatized firms, SOEs, and firms in which the state held minority control, as well as firms listed on the stock exchange and firms that were unlisted. In addition to tests of means, the empirical work also employs panel data analysis. Moreover, the analysis of performance before and after privatization is also compared with the indicators observed in the private sector during the same periods.

The importance of this last feature must be underscored, as the Brazilian economy underwent various cycles in the pre- and postprivatization periods. In summary, after strong growth in 1994 and 1995, when a modest number of companies were privatized, the economy's performance was sluggish until a strong recovery took hold in 2000, after the privatization program had passed its peak. Thus, economic cycles might have affected the performance of former SOEs. The absence of control for this effect could have blurred the results of the impact of privatization.

The Data Set and the Variables

Our data set is based on the annual financial statements (balance sheets, income statements, and cash flows) of the former SOEs and of a number of private companies used as a control group. Brazilian accounting standards and procedures, as established by law and regulatory agencies, have remained the same for the whole period, thus facilitating our analysis.[8] The data range from 1987 to 2000. The financial statements were obtained from two consulting firms (Economática and Austin Assis) and a nongovernmental organization (the Getúlio Vargas Foundation). All three collect financial statements from several sources, including newspapers. We excluded from our analysis the privatizations in the financial sector, as that sector has a unique structure, involves specific issues, and would have required specialized analysis. We also excluded the cases in which BNDES sold minor, noncontrolling participations in scattered companies as part of its portfolio as a development bank. Thus, we focused only on sales of control packages, both of a majority and of a minority nature. Table 4.1 explains the coverage of the sample.

To proceed, it is necessary to distinguish privatization contracts (or auctions) from privatized enterprises. A number of former SOEs were sold as a block, and the successful bidder for an operational holding company was also given access to the control of its subsidiaries. In the case of the telecommunications sector, for instance, five amalgamated blocks of privatization auctions covered the entire local, cellular, long-distance, and international restructured segments.

As a result, the data set of the sampled companies covers 66 privatization contracts, corresponding to 102 firms. From the figures given in table 4.1,

Table 4.1 Description of the Privatization Program and Coverage of the Sample, 1991–2000

Type of privatization	Number of contracts	Number of companies	Auction results (US$ millions)[a]
Privatization program			
Financial sector	9	9	5,112.30
Minority sales in SOEs	6	6	6,164.10
BNDES participations	—	—	1,146.00
Control package sales	103	147	76,878.20
Total	118	162	89,439.20
Companies included in sample			
State minority control	16	16	1,299.20
State majority control	50	86	70,709.80
Total	66	102	72,009.00

Note: SOEs = state-owned companies and BNDES = National Social and Economic Development Bank.

a. These values include transferred debt ($17.8 billion) and offers to employees in the telecommunications industry ($0.3 billion) but exclude concessions of new services ($7.7 billion).

Source: Authors' calculations.

it can be inferred that the sample covers 64 percent of the control packages, 69 percent of the firms they include, and 94 percent of the total value of the auctions. The smaller number of companies in the mean and median tests is explained by the methodology adopted and described in the next section.

No information was available from the sources listed above for the 37 contracts not included, which correspond to 45 companies and yielded proceeds of $4.9 billion, as listed in appendix table 4A.1. Attempts to gather information from BNDES White Books were frustrated by nondisclosure and confidentiality rules governing data held by the bank.[9] Table 4.2 summarizes the number of Brazilian companies privatized according to industry classification, along with their value at the auctions and the percentage they represented of the total value of each industry.

All but three of the electricity companies were included in the sample. The sample includes one of the three gas distribution companies that were privatized at the state level. More petrochemical, fertilizer, and chemical plants are included in the sample than are excluded. The excluded group includes various limited liability companies, which are not required to make their balance sheets and income statements public.

Although they are not important in economic size, the release of information on the privatized railways and ports could yield interesting case studies, as privatization accompanied the restructuring of these industries even as the government retained an active role in them. The railways were operated under regional branches of the federal railway network and were split into regional companies for privatization purposes only. The regional port facilities had been separate companies, operating under a federal holding company. In this case, privatization led to the creation of specialized terminals to be leased to private operators, with part of the infrastructure facilities remaining in the hands of SOEs. Thus, if data were available, one could compare the performance of both private firms and SOEs working side by side.

The companies under the heading "others" include miscellaneous activities such as bus terminals, data processing, and ferryboats or small firms that are not organized as corporations and are also not required to make their balance sheets and income statements public.

Thus, what was left outside of our sample represents only a minor part of the program, but not an uninteresting group for industry- and firm-specific studies. Their absence, due to insurmountable difficulties, does not jeopardize the relevance of our sample as representative of the companies that underwent privatization in Brazil. When the information was available, as it was for most of the companies and the most important ones, it was included in the sample.

Our data set involves essentially the same variables used by La Porta and López-de-Silanes (1999) in their study of the Mexican case. Fifteen financial indicators, according to seven criteria, make up this set of variables, as described in table 4.3.

Table 4.2 Privatized Brazilian Companies by Industry Classification

Industry classification	Companies included in sample	Auction value (US$ millions)	Percent included	Companies excluded from sample	Auction value (US$ millions)	Percent excluded
Aviation	1	455.0	100.0	0	0.0	0.0
Bank and financial industry[a]	0	0.0	0.0	8	5,107.0	100.0
Electricity and power plants	23	29,959.1	96.35	3	1,134.0	3.65
Fertilizers	2	452.0	91.50	3	42.0	8.50
Mining	2	6,864.0	100.0	0	0.0	0.0
Oil and gas	3	5,538.0	97.44	1	146.0	2.56
Others	0	0.0	0.0	7	809.0	100.0
Petrochemicals	17	2,156.0	75.86	7	686.0	24.14
Ports and container terminals	0	0.0	0.0	9	461.0	100.0
Railways	2	1,076.0	62.50	6	646.0	37.50
Steel	6	8,187.0	100.0	0	0.0	0.0
Telecommunications	44	23,858.0	100.0	0	0.0	0.0
Water and sewage	2	592.0	100.0	0	0.0	0.0
Total	102	79,137.1	89.75	44	9,031.0	10.25

a. All information about this industry is excluded from the sample as in La Porta and López-de-Silanes (1999).
Source: Authors' calculations.

Table 4.3 Summary of Results

	Appendix tables			
Indicator	4C.1	4C.2	4C.3	4C.4
Profitability				
Operating income/sales	+	−	+	+
Operating income/PPE	+	+	+	+
Net income/sales	−	−	+	+
Return on assets	+	+	+	+
Return on equity	+	+	+	+
Operating efficiency				
Log(sales/PPE)	+	+	+	+
Operating cost/sales	−	−	−	−
Assets				
Log(PPE)	−	−	−	−
Investment/sales	−	−	−	−
Investment/PPE	−	−	+	+
Output				
Log(sales)	+	+	+	+
Shareholders				
Payout	−	−	−	−
Finance				
Current	+	+	+	+
Long-term debt/equity	+	−	+	−
Net taxes				
Net taxes/sales	−	−	−	−

Note: PPE = property, plant, and equipment. See appendix 4B for definitions of the variables. See appendix 4C for full results of the mean tests. Appendix tables 4C.1 and 4C.2 refer to the results obtained upon the calculation of mean and median values for two years before and two years after privatization (Method 1). The adjustments on these calculated values are made for comparisons with the private sector and produce the results in appendix table 4C.2. The results in appendix tables 4C.3 and 4C.4 are based on the same procedure, but the mean and median values are calculated for all years before and after privatization (Method 2). The shading means the indicator mean difference is significant at least at the 10 percent level. The sample size of companies taken for the mean and median tests is 73. Auction results amount to $68.1 billion.

Empirical Analysis

Two different approaches were adopted to examine changes in performance after privatization: mean and median tests, and panel data analysis.

Mean and Median Tests

For the mean and median tests, two different methods were used. Under the first method, for each indicator a comparison is made between the mean and median values of the two years following privatization and their values in the two years before privatization.[10] The second method fully utilizes the information in the data set by comparing the mean and medians of all years after privatization with their values in the years before.

The Brazilian economy experienced cycles over the course of the period during which privatization took place. Thus, changes in performance could reflect cyclical movements of the economy, rather than the impact of privatization. To circumvent this problem, in each method we also used, as an alternative procedure, a control group of private companies. The performance of the privatized companies was adjusted by taking the difference between the indicator for the privatized enterprise and the average of the indicator for the control group. Thus, we followed a procedure close to the one used by La Porta and López-de-Silanes (1999, p. 1211), who adopted, in their words, "industry-adjusted changes in performance for the sample of privatized firms."[11]

Table 4.3 summarizes the results in terms of their signs and statistical significance. The complete results are presented in appendix 4C.

Profitability. In general, the results indicate an improvement in the profitability of the privatized companies. Considering the ratio of operating income to property, plant, and equipment (PPE), return on assets (ROA), and return on equity (ROE), performance after privatization improves regardless of the comparison method we used. The increase of operating income to PPE is evident once the change in the mean or median is always positive and significant, at least at the 10 percent level. The statistics for ROE and ROA are also always positive. In the case of ROE, three of the four statistics are significant, while for ROA only two reveal significance.

A slightly different picture appears when we consider the ratio of operating income to sales. Looking at the sign of the change, this indicator improves after privatization under the second method but not under the first and not in comparison with the private sector, when the change becomes negative and significant at the 10 percent level (appendix table 4C.2). Little can be said about the ratio of net income to sales. The sign of the coefficients varies across methods and fails to present statistical significance.

At the firm level, various reasons could account for results of this kind. At this point, the method's weakness in investigating in detail the sources of variance becomes apparent, underscoring the importance of using a different approach to test explanatory variables other than privatization, as is done shortly by using panel data analysis.

Operating Efficiency. The results strongly suggest an improvement in efficiency. In all tables we observe an increase in the ratio of sales to PPE and a reduction in the ratio of operating costs to sales. In the case of sales to PPE, all the statistics are positive and significant, strongly suggesting that privatized firms became more efficient in the use of their assets. Regarding operating costs to sales, all the statistics present a negative sign, while only one of them lacks significance at the 10 percent level. As illustrated in appendix table 4C.1, operating costs dropped by one-third in the two years after privatization, compared with the two years before privatization, thus providing evidence of improved efficiency at the operational level.

Assets and Output. Apparently, privatization had a negative impact on investment. In all the tables, the Log (PPE) and investment-to-sales statistics present a negative sign. These results seem consistent with the increase in efficiency we found. When considering the ratio of investment to PPE, which reflects the rate of investment, there is no clear picture: the sign changes across the two methods and the private sector adjustment, but none of the statistics is significant.

The effect of privatization on sales is a small but significant increase, observed in all tables. The statistics that test for difference in average are significant at the 1 percent level (appendix tables 4C.1 and 4C.3). There is a small increase in sales even after the adjustment to the performance of the private sector is made (appendix tables 4C.2 and 4C.4).

Finance and Shareholders. With respect to the payout ratio—that is, the ratio of total dividends paid to net operating income—no conclusive evidence was obtained. The sign of the coefficient is consistently negative although never significant. A lack of information could be responsible for this finding, since this variable could be calculated only for a reduced number of firms (45).[12]

A clearer picture emerges with the financial management indicators. We observe an increase in the ratio of current assets to current liabilities, both in absolute terms and in comparison with the private firms in our control group. The statistics for the difference in average are consistently positive and significant. Moreover, the adjusted mean and median are negative (appendix tables 4C.2 and 4C.4), meaning that former SOEs, when compared with the control group, continued to present lower short-term solvency. The overall improvement indicates that SOEs, having government backing, are less concerned with achieving sound financial performance.

With respect to the ratio of long-term debt to equity, we observe that when privatized firms are seen in isolation, privatization has a positive impact, as the coefficients are significant and show an increase (appendix tables 4C.1 and 4C.3). When compared with the performance of the private firms, however, the change in coefficients becomes negative, and a different picture emerges (appendix tables 4C.2 and 4C.4). In any case, in the same tables the mean values after privatization (0.108 and −0.002, respectively) indicate that the leverage of former SOEs converged to values observed in the private sector.

The results regarding financial structure are similar to those reported by La Porta and López-de-Silanes (1999) and can be explained by the almost null probability of insolvency of state-owned enterprises, since their credit status is guaranteed by the government. Having lost government backing, these firms were forced to adjust by decreasing their long-term-debt-to-equity ratio and increasing their current-assets-to current-liabilities ratios.

Net Taxes. Our results indicate a clear decrease in the ratio of net taxes to sales. All the coefficients are negative and significant at the 1 percent level. There are two reasons for finding a clear and significant decrease in net taxes after privatization in Brazil. This variable is defined as the difference between calculated taxes and allowed deductions. Because the allowed deductions do not come in the form of explicit subsidies, it is worthwhile to describe them in detail to interpret the results more accurately.

Three general categories of deductions apply: fiscal incentives, compensation for previous losses, and tax credits. Losses incurred in one particular year may be deducted from income tax over several years. This, in particular, affected companies that were highly dollar-indebted when the devaluation of the Brazilian real occurred in early 1999. In fact, losses of this sort were also responsible for a decrease in net taxes even for the control group in 2000.

With respect to tax credits, an important dimension is the legal treatment of the premium paid on asset value in mergers and acquisitions. Brazilian corporate law recognizes the premium, and it was regulated in the mid-1990s. The acquiring company is allowed to set up a reserve account for the premium and amortize it over a period of 5 to 10 years. When the reason for the premium paid over assets is based on expected future profits, the rebate is allowed for a period of up to 5 years. This benefit applies to mergers and acquisitions in general. Thus, both the overall private sector under restructuring and the privatized companies have been beneficiaries of these rebates. The existence of an explicit provision setting out the premium paid for concessions as expected future profits facilitates the use of this sort of tax credit in privatization. Therefore, reasonable explanations exist for our finding that net tax payments have decreased after privatization.

In particular, evidence provided by individual data in the iron and steel industry supports this argument. On average, most of the firms in that industry were subjected to Brazilian government rules concerning income tax before the privatization, which established the amount of tax that was due. After privatization, the pattern of this indicator changes a great deal. This result is readily observable since the individual data for this industry stretch over more years than any other in our sample, which allows us to state that Companhia Siderúrgica de Tubarão (CST) and Usiminas started paying more income tax after their privatization in 1993 and 1992, respectively. Clearly, four out of six firms in this industry did the same as CST and Usiminas: Acesita, Aço Minas Gerais, COSIPA, and CSN, suggesting that the tax credit for premiums paid on assets would explain this unexpected decrease in taxes.

Taken as a whole, these results support the view that privatization brought improvements in the performance of the firms. However, as pointed out, the mean and median tests leave room for a more comprehensive analysis that fully utilizes the variance of the data set and allows for examining other aspects of the privatization process. This is the focus of the next section.

Panel Data Analysis

We start with a brief description of the technique used in this subsection. It is a dynamic version of panel data analysis and focuses on individual heterogeneities over time, in particular the discontinuous effect of privatization. This approach is an alternative to generalizations of constant-intercept-and-slope models for panel data, which introduce dummy variables to account for effects of variables that are specific to individual cross-sectional units, but stay constant over time, together with the effects that are specific to each time period, but the same for all cross-sectional units. The analysis is dynamic because the lagged value of the independent variable is included in the model, and the panel is unbalanced as the data set is missing some observations for some firms.

Many economic relationships are dynamic in nature, and another advantage of the panel data approach is that it allows for a better understanding of the dynamics of adjustment of a particular variable. However, the inclusion of a lagged dependent variable in the model causes problems, which are well known in the literature.[13] Following it, we opted to apply the Arellano and Bond (1991) GMM-IV (generalized method of moments instrumental variables) method to estimate the parameters of the panel data model used in the empirical analysis.[14]

The Model and Variables. To assess the effect of privatization on each performance indicator listed in appendix table 4B.1, we relied on the following econometric model:

$$I_{it} = \alpha_i + \phi\, I_{it-1} + \lambda\, P_{it} + \beta\, X_{it} + \delta\, M_{pt} + e_{it},$$

where:

I_{it} represents the performance indicator for firm i in year t;

I_{it-1} represents the performance indicator for firm i in year $t-1$;

P_{it}, referred to as PRIVATIZATION, is a dummy variable that assumes a value of 1 if company i had already been privatized in year t, and 0 otherwise;

X_{it} is a set of control variables that are also firm specific (see appendix 4D for definitions of control variables); and

M_{pt}, referred to as PRIVATE MEAN, is the mean value of the performance indicator for the group of privatized firms listed in appendix 4A, defined only over time, that is, assuming for every year the same value across the cross-sections of privatized firms.

Empirical Results. The panel results are shown in table 4.4. Before discussing them, it should be noted that it is possible to decompose the X_{it} vector of the model into two groups. The first group comprises the dummy variables that are associated with the environment confronted by the firms and that are effective for all companies in the sample (TRADABLE, REGULATED, and LISTED). The other contains firm-specific variables that affect only the companies that are the focus of the study (PRIVATIZATION, SPLIT/MERGER, and MINORITY CONTROL).

In the case of firms operating in TRADABLE industries, one observes the predominance of an inferior performance compared with those in nontradable industries. This is found in the indicators of profitability, operational efficiency, output, sales, and indebtedness. Firms also seem to pay higher net taxes to sales. The reason for an underperforming tradable sector is that, for most of that period, the country was promoting trade liberalization, a process aggravated from 1995 to 1998 by an exchange rate overvaluation.

Because the effects of REGULATION are likely to be different in the various industries, a more detailed analysis would be required to investigate them. In any case, the comparative analysis of regulated industries versus unregulated ones shows a slightly better performance among regulated industries in terms of profitability, investment, sales, and indebtedness. A possible explanation for this is that regulation encouraged companies to improve their performance, in particular, by setting more realistic prices for the regulated activities.

For the privatized companies that underwent restructuring in the form of SPLIT/MERGERS, no discernible effect was found on profitability indicators. Moreover, the same companies present evidence of inferior results in terms of operational efficiency, assets and outputs, indebtedness, and net taxes. Notice that this dummy variable is in effect only for the period in which the intervention occurred and it is associated with the privatization intervention. So the inferior results would have to be interpreted with respect to the performance of firms that were privatized without restructuring. There is an open debate on the virtue of government-led adjustments in debt, labor force, and firm activities before privatization (Megginson and Netter 2001).

The MINORITY CONTROL dummy shows two significant coefficients for profitability performance indicators, but it also shows mixed results for operational efficiency, with a relatively large ratio of sales to PPE and a somewhat high ratio of operational costs to sales. Firms privatized

Table 4.4 Changes in Performance: GMM-IV Panel Data Analysis

							Performance indicators							
Variable	OI/S	OI/PPE	NI/S	ROA	ROE	Log (S/PPE)	OC/S	Log (PPE)	I/S	I/PPE	Log (S)	Current	LTD/E	NT/S
Privatization	0.056***	0.033	0.003	0.016***	0.062***	0.070***	−0.015***	−0.012***	−0.032***	0.057***	0.008	0.140***	−0.029*	−0.006***
	0.008	0.055	0.005	0.003	0.005	0.009	0.003	0.004	0.009	0.010	0.004	0.015	0.020	0.001
Tradable	−0.001	0.030***	−0.006***	−0.007***	−0.030***	−0.026***	−0.005***	−0.005**	0.003	−0.034***	−0.010***	0.019	0.028***	0.006***
	0.003	0.007	0.002	0.002	0.004	0.005	0.002	0.002	0.005	0.007	0.003	0.017	0.010	0.0005
Regulation	0.032***	0.013	0.003	−0.0006	0.011**	−0.030***	−0.035***	0.027***	0.003	0.015	0.024***	−0.056	0.130***	−0.004***
	0.005	0.016	0.003	0.003	0.005	0.007	0.002	0.003	0.007	0.009	0.003	0.019	0.017	0.001
Split/mergers	0.028	−0.070	0.010	0.0007	0.005	−0.041***	0.032***	0.018***	0.055***	−0.066***	0.004	−0.102***	−0.235***	−0.004**
	0.039	0.105	0.010	0.004	0.004	0.010	0.006	0.005	0.020	0.012	0.004	0.022	0.022	0.001
Minority control	0.016	−0.066	0.040***	0.007	0.026***	0.065***	0.008*	−0.011	−0.021	0.065***	−0.016***	0.348***	−0.137***	0.023***
	0.018	0.097	0.011	0.007	0.011	0.012	0.005	0.009	0.022	0.022	0.005	0.062	0.041	0.005
Listed	0.057*	−0.063	0.067***	0.018***	0.029***	0.035***	−0.016***	0.008*	0.122***	0.115***	0.007**	0.016	0.085***	−0.004***
	0.034	0.065	0.014	0.003	0.005	0.013	0.006	0.004	0.020	0.011	0.003	0.016	0.024	0.001
Private mean	1.287***	1.070***	0.425***	0.751***	0.710***	0.520***	0.770***	0.101***	0.954***	0.970***	0.115***	0.635***	0.887***	1.070***
	0.053	0.041	0.040	0.040	0.037	0.037	0.061	0.008	0.032	0.024	0.008	0.055	0.030	0.067
Lagged variable	0.195***	0.080***	0.556***	0.035***	0.172***	0.831***	0.555***	0.912***	0.304***	0.075***	0.926***	0.458***	0.186***	0.040***
	0.019	0.020	0.015	0.005	0.016	0.007	0.017	0.004	0.012	0.013	0.006	0.013	0.041	0.011
Exchange rate[a]								−0.020***			−0.012***			
								0.003			0.004			
Constant	−0.137***	−0.015	−0.062***	−0.022***	−0.070***	−0.210***	−0.022***	0.029	−0.120***	−0.164***	−0.220***	−0.299***	−0.122	0.004
	0.034	0.052	0.015	0.004	0.008	0.019	0.014	0.043	0.024	0.0187	0.050	0.080	0.032	0.003
N	1798	2158	1960	2257	1903	2044	1580	2561	1702	2185	2073	2120	2256	1598
Pseudo R^2	0.332	0.352	0.441	0.397	0.468	0.554	0.561	0.373	0.491	0.538	0.725	0.584	0.610	0.447

(Table continues on the following page.)

Table 4.4 (continued)

	Performance indicators													
Variable	OI/S	OI/PPE	NI/S	ROA	ROE	Log (S/PPE)	OC/S	Log (PPE)	I/S	I/PPE	Log (S)	Current	LTD/ E	NT/S
Sargan Test[b] (Prob > χ^2)	0.000	0.000	0.001	0.002	0.000	0.000	0.005	0.000	0.010	0.004	0.000	0.000	0.000	0.012

* Significant at the 10 percent level.
** Significant at the 5 percent level.
*** Significant at the 1 percent level.

Note: GMM-IV = generalized method of moments instrumental variables. For definitions of the performance indicators, see appendix 4B. The table shows the estimated coefficients for unbalanced panel data regressions, corresponding to each performance indicator. See text for explanation. Error terms are shown in parentheses.

a. Dummy variable introduced in order to overcome a devaluation bias in those variables that are defined in absolute terms after 1999. Though this effect has caused impacts in all of the performance indicators, they can be overcome for those which are defined as a ratio of two variables.

b. Sargan Test for Over-Identifying Restrictions. All the null hypotheses were rejected, validating the use of the instruments chosen.

with these characteristics pay the highest net taxes relative to sales of all privatized firms and have lower indebtedness, indicating that they did not benefit as much from the corporate tax credits that came with privatization and that they had inferior access to credit compared with other privatized companies.

The dummy LISTED reveals a clearer positive effect for all criteria of performance. In particular, coefficients for four of the five profitability indicators presented positive and significant signs. Listed companies also showed better indicators for operational efficiency, output, and assets, as well as the largest indicator for long-term debt to equity. The net-tax-to-sales indicator has a negative sign again, indicating corporate tax benefits for listed companies. Thus, the results presented by this dummy caution against the bias in selecting only firms listed on the stock exchange for privatization studies.

It is possible now to assess the net effects of PRIVATIZATION as a change in the intercept of each indicator. In general, its impact comes as hypothesized and stronger than the one revealed by the mean and median tests. As it is the key variable under investigation, the results for the various indicators of performance are discussed in more detail.

Profitability. Three out of the five indicators of profitability presented in table 4.4 clearly reveal the improvement that comes with privatization, as its estimated parameters are positive and significant at the 1 percent level. Privatization coefficients for the ratio of operating income to sales (OI/S), return on assets (ROA), and return on equity (ROE) show an increase of 5.6 percent, 1.6 percent, and 6.2 percent, respectively.

Operational Efficiency. Significant at the 1 percent level, the coefficients of the privatization dummy show the expected sign, that is, an increase of 7 percent in the ratio of sales to PPE, or Log(S/PPE), and a reduction of 1.5 percent in the ratio of operating costs to sales (OC/S).

Assets and Output. Significant PPE and sales are the only indicators measured by their absolute values, which are measured in dollars. The Brazilian currency suffered a major devaluation early in 1999 that was not reversed in 2000. To capture the negative effect on these indicators, we introduced a dummy variable taking the value of 1 in those years, and 0 otherwise. For both Log(PPE) and Log(S) the estimated coefficients were negative and significant at 1 percent. In the Log(S) equation adjusted in this fashion, the impact of privatization on sales is smaller (0.8 percent) than in the Log(PPE) equation.

Even after taking devaluation into account, the privatization coefficient for the property, plant, and equipment indicator, or Log(PPE), is negative, indicating a reduction of 1.2 percent in the productive assets of the firms. This result is consistent with the coefficients for privatization with respect to other asset indicators. An increase in the ratio of sales to

PPE, or Log(S/PPE), intensifies the use of productive assets, so a reduction of 3.2 percent in the investment-to-sales (I/S) ratio is likely. As the ratio of investment to PPE (I/PPE) shows a positive coefficient of 5.7 percent for privatization, the indication is that investments after privatization are moving into working capital.

The indication of an increase in investments in the form of working capital is confirmed by a strong impact of privatization on the ratio of current assets to current liability: a 14 percent increase, significant at the 1 percent level. With respect to the ratio of long-term debt to equity (LTD/E), a likely outcome is that the privatized companies will seek to reduce the cost of capital, combining equity and debt in an efficient way. Conversely, state-owned enterprises are likely to increase debt, saving the national treasury from investing in their equity as their credit status, guaranteed by the government, has a small probability of default. This situation may lead to large LTD/E ratios. After privatization and the loss of government backing, privatized firms are forced to adjust by decreasing this ratio and increasing the ratio of current assets to current liabilities. Accordingly, the privatization coefficient for LTD/E shows a reduction in indebtedness of 2.9 percent, significant at the 10 percent level. It is interesting to observe the LTD/E coefficients estimated for SPLIT/MERGERS (−23.5 percent) and MINORITY CONTROL (−13.7 percent), which magnify the impact of losing government backing.

With respect to net taxes, the coefficient of privatization is negative and significant at the 1 percent level. The reasons are those presented in the mean and median tests, now confirmed by a panel data analysis.

Other Variables in the Model. The coefficient of the private mean is positive and significant for all indicators, reflecting the impact of overall business and macroeconomic conditions. It also cautions against another distortion of some studies on privatization in which the impact of privatization from the changes in these conditions over time is not isolated.

The coefficients of the lagged variable, instrumented by its two-period version, are all positive and significant, revealing that the past behavior of firms' indicators has a strong influence on their current performance. On top of this effect, other variables exert influence, such as those encountered above.

Finally, we emphasize once more that the obtained evidence on decreasing tax revenue, mainly after privatization, is a special phenomenon due to tax credits. It therefore does not reflect a permanent reduction in income for the Brazilian government.

Other Benefits and Costs of the Program

The improvement in the performance of privatized firms shown in the previous section can be viewed as a benefit, as it contributes to the efficiency of the economy as a whole. This section addresses other benefits, as well as some costs, of the privatization program. It also seeks to identify some sources of the gains made by privatized firms in the form of reductions in employment and increases in prices.

Employment

One of the weaknesses of the Brazilian data is that no comprehensive, reliable, and unified record of the number of employees exists for the privatized companies either before or after their sale. Financial statements and annual reports, including those of listed firms, are not required to include information on employment, and companies provide it at their own discretion. There are also no uniform requirements for including payroll information in these reports and statements, which bundle wage and salary costs together with other operational costs.

Even when employment and payroll data are available, their analysis is handicapped for other reasons. In Brazil, there are strong incentives for the adoption of outsourced services, such as security, cleaning, maintenance, and accounting. Outsourcing has become a widespread means of reducing labor costs, as service providers are usually smaller firms and pay lower wages. In addition, one often finds workers disguised as business owners to avoid heavy taxation of wages and salaries.[15] Most workers prefer formal contracts with employers; firms and unions also press for this and are more successful with SOEs. It is therefore very likely that privatization has led to an extension of outsourcing. Thus, a reduction of employment in a company would not necessarily mean a reduction in the jobs generated by its activities along its chain of suppliers.[16]

Given this picture, we first examine the employment effects at the industry level, where there are aggregate data. Then, for a limited number of former SOEs, we focus on employment data from the files of *Exame,* a business magazine that collects financial statements and reports of Brazilian firms, as well as scattered employment data from the magazine and other sources.

In Brazil the most important source of data on formal employment is the Annual Survey of Social Data (RAIS) from the Ministry of Labor and Employment. All firms and the government are required annually to list workers and their characteristics such as year of entrance, white-collar versus blue-collar, unionized, level of education, and so forth. Individual firms cannot be identified in the samples. This source has consistent data for the period 1995 to 1999.

Table 4.5 shows data on employment for the industries in which the most important privatizations have occurred. One can see that until 1997 the private sector was responsible for less than one-twentieth of employment in electricity, about one-third in water and sewage, a quarter in telecommunications, and a fifth in piped gas distribution. By 1999, in both the telecommunications and the gas distribution sectors, the larger part of

Table 4.5 Employment in Selected Industries, by Public or Private Ownership, 1995–99

Industry	1995			1996			1997			1998			1999		
	Public (%)	Private (%)	Total	Public (%)	Private (%)	Total	Public (%)	Private (%)	Total	Public (%)	Private (%)	Total	Public (%)	Private (%)	Total
Mining	18	82	39,131	18	82	38,060	1	99	31,447	1	99	39,955	1	99	35,763
Petroleum	76	24	14,442	82	18	21,546	72	28	16,963	62	38	13,923	39	61	10,590
Fertilizers	18	82	6,460	9	91	7,145	11	89	8,395	1	99	12,563	1	99	11,907
Petro-chemicals	5	95	15,739	2	98	14,947	0	100	19,018	1	99	26,263	1	99	28,935
Iron and steel	5	95	376,220	5	95	369,234	2	98	385,064	2	98	429,965	2	98	446,949
Electricity	97	3	149,100	97	3	128,545	95	5	99,871	64	36	111,225	55	45	95,870
Gas distribution	92	8	3,257	89	11	2,640	83	17	1,551	60	40	1,763	31	69	1,437
Water and sewage	68	32	135,313	72	28	146,791	66	34	159,588	66	34	145,375	62	38	149,822
Telecommunications	80	20	107,689	77	23	113,126	75	25	117,740	19	81	105,284	26	74	109,478

Note: Number of employees as of December 31.
Source: Ministry of Labor and Employment, 1995 Survey of Social Data.

employment moved to private companies. In the electricity and water and sewage sectors, employment is still largely in SOEs and public enterprises but now with a significant mix of private firms. The table shows a clear reduction in employment following privatization in the electricity and piped gas distribution industries. In telecommunications, the effect of privatization on reducing employment is less clear, in part because the provision of services expanded very rapidly after privatization. Worth mentioning is the case of the water and sewage industry: still largely in the hands of the government and not expanding as quickly as telecommunications, its employment ranks high in stability among the industries shown in the table. Note also the recovery of employment in petrochemicals and in iron and steel, showing that after employment adjusts following privatization, the growth of investment and production leads to new jobs.

The employment data from *Exame*'s files cover companies privatized in the period 1995–2000; some data are missing, but enough are available to allow a comparison between the pre- and postprivatization years. Figure 4.1 shows data for 49 companies in the form of a box-plot diagram. The impact of privatization on employment emerges clearly from the plotted data, with 43 companies showing a reduction in employment after privatization and only 6 revealing an increase. Tests were performed by taking the average number of employees in at least two years before and after privatization. The Wilcoxon signed rank test, calculated for the difference in means, is equal to –5.217 and significant at the 1 percent level. A parametric *t*-test is also calculated and equals 3.906, which is significant at the 5 percent level.

Our conclusion is that a share of the costs of privatization has been borne by some of the workers directly employed by the former SOEs who lost their jobs either in the process of adjustment for the sale or thereafter. This is an inevitable outcome of privatization as new owners seek higher efficiency. Thus, this reduction in employment was one of the sources of gains from privatization. However, as privatized firms invest and expand their activities, at some point employment begins to increase, although the same workers are not necessarily rehired, and some of them might continue to suffer the costs of displacement and reallocation. In the Brazilian case, the widespread use of outsourced services often blurs the picture, as positive impacts are not necessarily captured by the direct employment data of privatized firms, particularly in the telecommunications industry.

Prices

Following privatization, newly established regulatory agencies moved to encourage more realistic prices, particularly in the areas of electricity and telecommunications. The government had to announce this policy during the privatization process to guarantee the success of the auctions. Moreover,

Figure 4.1 Formal Employment before and after Privatization, 1995–99

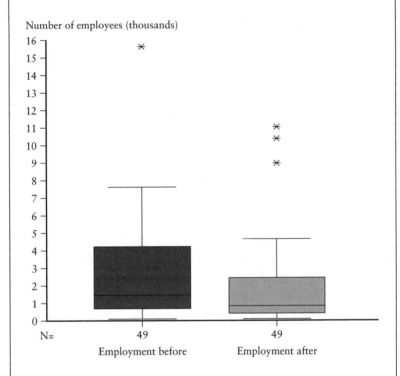

Note: The figure shows a box plot for the lower and upper bounds of the number of employees in our sample before and after privatization. The shaded region represents the percentile while the black line inside represents the median. The two lines at the extremes are the percentiles, and the stars stand for outlier observations beyond two standard deviations. See the text and table 4.5 for a more detailed explanation.
Source: Authors' calculations.

the overvaluation of the Brazilian real and the trade liberalization reforms undertaken since the early 1990s meant that the tradable industries were exposed to increased competition.

To show some of the relevant changes in relative prices, we made a comparison of various price indexes at the industry level with an overall price index, the CPI-A calculated by the Brazilian census bureau. We took

August 1994 prices as a reference for the other indexes. In the tradable industries, such as iron and steel, nonferrous metals, nonmetallic minerals, fertilizers, and plastics, which are greatly affected by the overvaluation of the real, domestic prices lagged behind CPI-A variations for the years 1994 to 1998. After devaluation, prices in these industries clearly caught up to the CPI-A. This sheds light on one of the results of the previous section, where it was found that firms in these industries had shown a shakier performance than firms in other industries, in part because of the restraint imposed by the overvalued real.

For telephone rates, the price effects started when the telecommunications industry was being prepared for privatization, as early as 1996. In particular, the minimum monthly fee for access to a line increased sharply. This has been a source of gains to the telephone companies, but no one in Brazil would dispute that it was followed by a massive expansion of services to the point of destroying the market that previously existed for trading telephone lines, at prices sometimes reaching $2,000–$3,000, or even more when the dollar was overvalued.

In electricity, the rate restructuring began in 1995. Privatization itself started in 1997, and the concessionaries signed an incentive contract with a clause allowing a pass-through of noncontrollable costs. Thus, with the devaluation in 1999, they were allowed to adjust prices for the dollar-denominated contracts they had, for instance, with suppliers from Paraguay.

Our conclusion is that prices have been a source of gains to privatized firms in the telecommunications and electricity industries. Regulation combined with privatization made prices follow contracts and other rules, thus reducing the scope for political manipulation that existed when the government played a larger entrepreneurial role in these industries. In the telecommunications industry, this government role practically ceased to exist, but it is still strong in electricity, particularly in power generation.

A Social Cost: No Democratization of Capital Ownership

Macedo (2000) points out that some groups in Brazilian society were excluded from the privatization auctions and therefore from the opportunities to gain from them. As a rule, the privatization program did not resort to public offers to any significant degree. Moreover, some public sector liabilities could have been exchanged for shares of the SOEs being privatized. Among these liabilities are the unfunded ones of the present and future pensioners of the social security system and the deposits that formal workers hold in their accounts of the Workers' Tenure Guarantee Fund. This fund, known as FGTS (Fundo de Garantia de Tempo de Serviço), accumulates on a monthly basis a percentage of wages and salaries, to be used in case of termination or dismissal of the workers. Macedo's conclusion was that because of this discrimination, the privatization process failed in one of its stated objectives: democratizing capital ownership in Brazil. Only recently were workers allowed to use their FGTS deposits in successful public offers for a block of Petrobrás shares and another block of remaining state-owned shares of the Vale do Rio Doce mining company.

Effects on the Development of Capital Markets

A goal of the program was to maximize the revenue from sales. Many of the former SOEs were structured as public companies and therefore subject to laws governing the stock market. Before 1996 minority investors in Brazil were protected with features such as "tag-along" (giving minority investors the right to sell their shares at the same price as the managing block in case of change in control) and oppressed minority rights (having their shares bought back at book value in cases of restructuring, such as mergers or divestitures). Because some companies had to be restructured for privatization (for instance, Telebrás, the state holding company for telecommunications, was split into 12 different firms), there was a fear that lawsuits from minority shareholders might hamper the privatization process or reduce the revenues from auctions, or both. This concern led the government to reform the legislation in such a way that the amendments to the corporate law revoked the tag-along and the oppressed minority rights clauses. To mitigate the impact, the legislation entitled nonvoting shares to an additional 10 percent in dividends over those paid to voting shares. In any case, as the postprivatization experience has shown, without the protective clauses, minority shareholders have in several cases been victims of controlling groups' opportunistic behavior.

At the end of the 1990s, influential works such as those of La Porta and others (1997), Levine (1997), and Levine and Zervos (1998) helped to confirm the view that the development of capital markets is important to promote economic growth, and that protecting minority investors' rights is the best way to promote capital markets. In 2000 and 2001 the Brazilian Congress discussed a bill to increase minority shareholders' rights, including restoring the tag-along and oppressed minority rights. Unfortunately, the new law that emerged establishes tag-along for only 80 percent of the minority shares, and the new oppressed minority rights have been extensively criticized as inadequate. Thus, the adverse effect of privatization on stock markets is likely to last.

A Macroeconomic Cost: No Effective Debt Reduction and Delayed Devaluation

Macedo (2000) also claims that privatization had a macroeconomic cost because the generated revenues to the government budget, and to the external accounts through foreign direct investment, delayed a genuine fiscal adjustment and the necessary devaluation of the real. It is important to understand the details of this argument because it warns of the risks of misusing privatization resources in conditions of fiscal and external imbalances and in the presence of soft budget constraints.

Privatization was intended to help the fiscal crisis and the external imbalance, but this intended benefit was lost because in its first term (1995–98), the administration of Fernando Henrique Cardoso increased the fiscal deficit. Moreover, the new currency, the real, had clearly become overvalued immediately after its release in 1994. With its political capital linked to price stabilization, the government opted for defending the real, afraid of the impact of devaluation on prices. Very high interest rates were the main policy instrument. These developments had the effect of seriously aggravating the budget deficit and debt, the payment of debt interest, and the external imbalance. Thus, public debt increased from 29.2 percent of gross domestic product (GDP) in 1994 to 52.5 percent in 2001; debt interest grew from 5.8 percent of GDP in 1996 to 11.8 percent in 2001; and the current account deficit went from less than 0.5 percent of GDP in 1994 to around 4 percent in 1997 and has remained at that level.[17]

Thus, the privatization program did not accomplish the objective of reducing public debt. On the contrary, public expenses increased, more than offsetting the inflow of resources from the privatization auctions.[18] Macedo (2000) also argues that privatization allowed the financing of higher current account deficits, particularly in 1997 and 1998 when the privatization program peaked and attracted substantial foreign investment. Although this inflow is usually considered a positive consequence of the process, it also contributed to the postponement of a badly needed devaluation of the Brazilian currency.[19]

Privatization as a Tool for Imposing Fiscal Discipline: The Case of the States

The fiscal policies of Brazilian states also contributed to the ballooning fiscal deficits and debt from 1994 to 1997. Tight public-sector budgets as a whole came only after 1998, when the size of the debt started to cause discomfort in the financial markets, and the external imbalance continued to deteriorate. The federal government then started to generate huge primary surpluses and was also increasingly able to impose fiscal discipline on the states. Privatization of the states' assets played an important role in this process. The states had their debt transferred to the federal government, to which they became indebted themselves, but at more favorable interest rates. To obtain this benefit, the states had to make commitments to restrain further indebtedness on their part and also to privatize. Thus, the federal government was able to impose a tight fiscal constraint on the states that it had not adopted itself.

Public Opinion

Privatization has not been popular in Brazil. A 2001 Latinbarómetero public opinion survey conducted in 16 Latin American countries reported that 53 percent of the respondents in Brazil believed that privatization had not been beneficial to the country (Lora and Panizza 2002). Nonetheless, Brazilian public opinion about privatization was found to be more favorable than that of its neighbors: on average 63 percent of the respondents in all the surveyed countries believed that privatization had not been beneficial to their nations. The countries in which the public appeared to be less discontented with privatization were Chile (47 percent expressed dissatisfaction) and Venezuela (46 percent). For all the other countries, approval ratings were lower than in Brazil.[20] Several factors contributed to the unpopularity. In most cases the average citizen is not able to identify fully the benefits of privatization such as those analyzed in this chapter. The creation of nonbanking SOEs in Brazil, such as steel and mining, followed the Second World War, when the main motivation was the belief that the state had to play a major role in "strategic" industries, the products of which tend to be remote from the pressing concerns of the population. Thus, one cannot expect the public to be concerned with the outcome of privatization in these industries or to be inclined to evaluate its technicalities.

The total privatization of the telecommunications industry and the partial privatization of the electricity SOEs produced mixed outcomes for consumers. Both were followed by higher rates, which have blurred the favorable impact of a major expansion of telecommunications services. In electricity, a further negative impact emerged in 2001, when the country had to face rationing due to the low levels of the reservoirs of the hydroelectric plants, which constitute the basis of power generation in the country. Opponents of privatization were eager to blame it for the crisis.

It is also important to highlight that privatization coincided with sluggish growth, particularly after the program peaked in 1997–98. Therefore, dissatisfaction with lower economic gains or even losses, such as those emerging from the higher rates of unemployment, are likely to have developed into criticisms of government policies in general and privatization in particular.

Moreover, as already pointed out, the government failed in its objective of using the program to democratize capital ownership. Only recently has it resorted to successful public offerings in which workers were entitled to participate by using their FGTS deposits. Thus, as a rule the common citizen was left out of the process and its benefits in the form of rewards to the controllers and shareholders.

Opposition to the program also resulted from its unfavorable treatment in the media, court battles to impede the auctions, attempts to disrupt the auctions themselves, sometimes followed by police intervention, and so forth. The news coverage of the privatization of the telecommunications industry was particularly negative, as there were accusations that some government authorities had been involved in arm-twisting to attract and assemble groups to participate in the auctions. Recorded tapes of conversations held by government authorities among themselves and with interested parties reached the press. Even though the legal battles were decided in favor of privatization, the uproar was serious enough to cause the minister of communications to resign in November 1998.

News of this sort has inevitably aroused suspicions that the process has been tainted by wrongdoings. Lora and Panizza (2002) found that opposition to privatization, again measured by the percentage of those who do not consider it beneficial, was lower in Brazil than in its neighbors. Generally approval ratings are higher in those countries with extensive privatization and limited corruption. In this respect, Brazil ranks second only to Chile in an evaluation involving the above-mentioned group of 16 countries. In any case, although privatization is faring better in relative terms, clearly it is not popular in the country, a finding that is not surprising given the reasons discussed here.

Although the privatization program has not been popular in general, a different picture emerges from a study by Lamounier and De Souza (2002), which focused only on the opinion of a group called the "Brazilian elites," composed of 500 businessmen (including leaders of associations of small and medium firms), union leaders, congressmen, high-ranking members of the executive and judiciary branches of government, journalists, religious leaders, directors of nongovernmental organizations, and intellectuals. On average, 62 percent responded that they approved or tended to approve of privatization. The rates ranged between 87 percent for members of the executive branch of government to 13 percent for union leaders, whose rate was the only one below 45 percent. Another question was directed at the performance of the companies after privatization. In this case, the approval rate (percentage of good or above) showed large variations by industries.[21]

Perspectives

The overall unpopularity and its causes are among the reasons for the privatization program's having come to a virtual standstill since 1998. According to BNDES, the proceeds from the auctions, including new concessions of public services, fell from $26.3 billion in 1997 and $35.7 billion in 1998 to $4.2 billion in 1999, $10.2 billion in 2000 (this figure includes the privatization of a state bank, Banespa, which totaled $3.6 billion and had been in the pipeline for a long time), $2.8 billion in 2001, and $2.2 billion in 2002.[22]

Other factors also explain the current status of the program. First, moving ahead would mean including those SOEs that have stronger political patronage than those privatized thus far. For example, on the list of remaining SOEs is the almost two-century-old Banco do Brasil, a commercial bank of which the federal government is the controlling shareholder. It holds the government's accounts and is the key player in providing agricultural credit, which is subsidized by the federal budget. As a result, it has built a major constituency, as private banks have refrained from being more active in agricultural credit. Its staff, traditionally selected by public examinations, is a breeding ground for government officers. Some of them have reached the ministerial level or have become members of Congress and are very influential. Moreover, the bank is not wholly state-owned but also has private shareholders who act as a group to maintain its current status.

Another example is the giant oil company Petrobrás. The company was established in 1954, following a strong nationalist stance against foreign oil companies. Petrobrás proved effective in finding oil in Brazil. It moved into offshore drilling in the 1980s and has set worldwide records in deep-water exploitation. Domestic production that currently accounts for 90 percent of the country's needs is seen as a sign of success. It had a monopoly in prospecting, production, and importing in the upstream market until 1995. Since then, it continues to have a virtual monopoly in these activities, as well as in refining. Because oil is associated with national security issues, the military sees continuing government control of Petrobrás as crucial. Moreover, the company also has private shareholders who support its current and very profitable status.

In the electricity industry, the privatization process occurred mainly in the distribution sector. A few important companies in this sector were kept by state governments unwilling to move in the direction of privatization. With respect to the generation segment, the state of São Paulo privatized a large part of its assets. At the federal level, only one subsidiary of a federal holding company, Eletrobrás, was privatized. The three remaining subsidiaries control around 60 percent of the country's generation. After the 2001 drought, which led to rationing, the process of sector restructuring stalled. The rationing stimulated industry and households to adopt energy-saving measures, and in the aftermath demand has not recovered its previous levels. Both rationing and demand reduction brought losses to the industry, exacerbating the dollar indebtedness of some privatized companies since 1999. With distribution and generation companies currently suffering huge losses, the federal government, which regulates the entire industry, is preparing a new sector arrangement. At the same time, BNDES has to find a way to manage huge debts by companies on the verge of default. Thus, it is an industry in disarray, not attractive to private investors, and in need of reorganization before any discussion of a new round of privatizations.

Despite these shortcomings, there are no plans to reverse the privatization that has occurred in Brazil, either at the moment or in the foreseeable future. The new federal government, inaugurated in 2003, is for the first time led by the Worker's Party, which won the presidential election as an opposition party. It fought privatization in Congress and in the courts in the 1990s, but since taking power it has adopted conservative fiscal and monetary policies and avoided condemning privatization. In this context, there is no room for privatization reversal, nor has the government even been suggesting it in discourse. Apparently, the government is likely to keep the program stalled, that is, no privatization reversal but no further advances.

Even in light of these new political developments, the possibility of resuming the privatization effort should not be ignored: a serious fiscal problem remains in the form of large and difficult-to-manage public deficits and debt. They have been kept under control at the cost of huge increases in the tax burden, which moved from 25.7 percent of GDP in 1993 to a record level of 35.9 percent in 2002, an exceptionally high rate for a developing country.[23] Under such conditions, a new start of the privatization program could help to alleviate the fiscal accounts. Moreover, since the new government has been willing to reconsider many of the cherished dogmas it subscribed to when in opposition, there is a chance that even its current stance against new privatization efforts might be reconsidered as well. Thus, to give new life to privatization, it is important to continue monitoring the process and publicizing the results of the program and the inefficiencies of the remaining SOEs. In addition, the objective of democratizing capital ownership by means of public offers should be brought to the front line, both for its own merits and to attract wider political support, in particular by making privatization more appealing to President Lula da Silva's government.

Summary and Conclusions

This chapter has focused mainly on the changes in the performance of companies that have been privatized in Brazil since 1991. It confirmed previous findings that the firms became more efficient after privatization. It has contributed to the literature, first by bringing to a wider audience studies available only in Brazil and in Portuguese. It is also more up-to-date than previous studies, since it covers data up until 2000. In terms of the companies covered, it is the most comprehensive study thus far. In the sample, a selection bias was avoided by including both large and small firms, as well as those listed and unlisted on the stock exchange. All companies for which information was available have been included in the analysis. In addition to tests of means and medians, the research also resorted to panel data analysis in an attempt to utilize fully the information provided by the data. Moreover, the analysis of performance before and after privatization was also compared with that of the private sector, taken as a control group over time. Finally, this study was undertaken by an independent team, whereas most of the previous ones were done by staff members of BNDES.

In addition to the findings of improved efficiency, the chapter has identified some sources of gains made by privatized firms in the form of reduced direct employment and increased prices. The chapter has also shown costs in the sense that the benefits of privatization could have been higher had the government not used the revenues to sustain its misguided policy of enlarging fiscal deficits and adopting high interest rates to defend the real. Moreover, foreign investment attracted by privatization and the high interest rates also contributed to the postponement of devaluation. In any case, what is to blame are the fiscal, interest rate, and exchange rate policies, not privatization itself.

The benefits could also have been greater had the government not neglected the opportunity privatization offered for democratizing capital ownership. In the capital markets, privatization also brought costs in the form of reducing the rights of minority shareholders, thereby hampering the development of these markets.

The study has also shown that although there is evidence that a majority of the Brazilian elite approve of privatization, the majority of the general population does not view privatization as beneficial, as revealed by public opinion surveys. After pointing out some of the reasons behind this unpopularity and looking at the current status of the program, the chapter concludes that the door to new privatization efforts remains open. One suggestion is to give the program popular appeal in the form of public offers in which workers would be entitled to participate with their own financial assets, including the deposits they hold in the FGTS.

With respect to future research, it is particularly necessary to further clarify costs, to look at the impact of privatization at the industry level, and to examine the role of the regulatory agencies that have emerged in the wake of the state's backing away from its role as an entrepreneur.

To conclude, we return to Megginson and Netter (2001), quoted at the start of this chapter. The Brazilian privatization program is indeed likely to remain influential because of its scale and the size of the country. We hope that privatization will continue to have an impact because of the successes and benefits of the program, not for the mistakes that have been made.

Appendix 4A

Table 4A.1 Federal State Enterprises Privatized, 1991–2000

Auction	Company name	Date of auction	Auction result (US$ million)[a]	Included in sample[b]	Listed before privatization[b]
USIMINAS	Usinas Siderúrgicas de Minas Gerais (Usiminas)	10/24/91	2,310	1	1
	Usiminas Mecânica (Usimec)[c]				
CELMA	Cia. Eletromecânica	11/01/91	96	0	0
MAFERSA	Mafersa S.A.	11/11/91	50	0	0
COSINOR	Cia. Siderúrgica do Nordeste (Cosinor)	11/14/91	15	0	0
	Cosinor Distribuidora (Cosinor Dist.)[c]				
SNBP	Serviço de Navegação da Bacia do Prata	1/14/92	12	0	0
INDAG	Indag Fertilizantes	1/23/92	7	0	0
AFP	Aços Finos Piratini	2/14/92	109	1	0
PETROFLEX	Petroflex Indústria e Comércio S.A.	4/10/92	255	1	1
COPESUL	Cia. Petroquímica do Sul	5/15/92	871	1	1
CAN	Cia. Nacional de Álcalis	7/15/92	87	0	0
	Álcalis Rio Grande do Norte (Alcanorte)[c]			0	0
CST	Cia. Siderúrgica de Tubarão	7/16/92 to 7/23/92	837	1	1
NITRIFLEX	Nitriflex	8/6/92	35	1	0
FOSFÉRTIL	Fertilizantes Fosfatados S.A.	8/12/92	226	1	1

(Table continues on the following page.)

Table 4A.1 (continued)

Auction	Company name	Date of auction	Auction result (US$ million)[a]	Included in sample[b]	Listed before privatization[b]
POLISUL	Polisul	9/11/92	188	0	0
PPH	PPH	9/29/92	94	0	0
GOIASFÉRTIL	Goiás Fertilizantes S.A.	10/8/92	22	0	0
ACESITA	Cia. Aços Especiais Itabira	10/23/92	697	1	1
	Acesita Energética (Energética)[c]			0	0
	Forjas Acesita (Fasa)[c]			0	0
CBE	Cia Brasileira de Estireno	12/3/92	11	1	0
	Poliolefinas[c]	3/19/93	87	0	0
CSN	Cia. Siderúrgica Nacional	4/2/93	2,028	1	1
	Fábrica de Estruturas Metálicas S.A.[c]			0	0
ULTRAFÉRTIL	Ultrafértil S.A. Indústria e Comércio de Fertilizantes	6/24/93	226	1	0
COSIPA	Cia. Siderúrgica Paulista	8/20/93	1,470	1	1
AÇOMINAS	Aço Minas Gerais S.A.	9/10/93	721	1	0
OXITENO	Oxiteno	9/15/93	56	1	1
PQU	Petroquímica União S.A.	1/25/94	328	1	1
ARAFÉRTIL	Arafértil Fertilizantes – ARAFÉRTIL	4/15/94	13	0	0
CARAÍBA	Mineração Caraíba LTDA	7/28/94	6	1	0
ACRINOR	Acrinor	8/12/94	13	0	0
COPERBO	Coperbo	8/16/94	32	0	0
CIQUINE	Ciquine	8/17/94	30	1	1
POLIALDEN	Polialden	8/17/94	19	1	1

POLITERO	Politeno	8/18/94	73	1	1
EMBRAER	Empresa Brasileira de Aeronáutica (Embraer)	12/7/94	455	1	1
	Embraer Aircraft Corporation (EAC)^c			0	0
	Embraer Aviation International (EAI)^c			0	0
	Indústria Aeronáutica Neiva (Neiva)^c			0	0
ESCELSA	Espírito Santo Centrais Elétricas S.A.	7/11/95	522	1	1
COPENE	Cia. Petroquímica do Nordeste	8/15/95	745	1	1
CPC	CPC	9/29/95	161	0	0
CQR	CQR	10/5/95	2	1	0
SALGEMA	SALGEMA	10/5/95	183	0	0
NITROCARBONO	Nitrocarbono	12/5/95	37	1	1
PRONOR	Pronor	12/5/95	99	1	1
POLIPROPILENO	Polipropileno	2/1/96	86	1	1
KOPPOL	Koppol	2/1/96	70	0	0
LIGHT	Light Serviços de Eletricidade S.A.	5/21/96	3,094	1	1
DETEN	Deten	5/22/96	12	1	0
POLIBRASIL	Polibrasil^c	8/27/96	111	0	0
EDN	Estireno do Nordeste- EDN	9/26/96	16	1	1
CVRD	Cia. Vale do Rio Doce	5/6/97	6,858	1	1
CODESP	Terminal de Contêiners Tecon 1 (Codesp)	9/17/97	251	0	0
CDRJ	CDRJ – Porto de Angra do Reis	11/5/98	8	0	0
CDRJ	CDRJ-Terminal de Contêineres 1 – Porto de Sepetiba	9/3/98	79	0	0
CDRJ	CDRJ-Terminal Roll-on Roll-off do Porto do Rio	11/3/98	26	0	0

(Table continues on the following page.)

Table 4A.1 (continued)

Auction	Company name	Date of auction	Auction result (US$ million)[a]	Included in sample[b]	Listed before privatization[b]
CDES	Cia. Docas do Espírito Santo- Casi de Capuaba	5/6/98	26	0	0
CDES	Cia. Docas do Espírito Santo –Casi de Paul	5/13/98	9	0	0
CODEBA	Cia. Docas da Bahia	12/21/99	21	0	0
RFF	Rede Ferroviária Federal S.A. (Nordeste)	7/18/97	15	0	0
RFF	Rede Ferroviária Federal S.A. (Oeste)	3/5/96	63	0	0
RFF	Rede Ferroviária Federal S.A. (SP)	11/10/98	206	1	0
RFF	Rede Ferroviária Federal S.A. (Sudeste)	9/20/96	870	1	0
RFF	Rede Ferroviária Federal S.A. (Sul)	12/13/96	209	0	0
RFF	Rede Ferroviária Federal S.A. (Tereza Crisitina)	11/22/96	18	0	0
RFF	Rede Ferroviária Federal S.A. (Centro-Leste)	6/14/96	316	0	0
MERIDIONAL	Banco Meridional do Brasil S.A.	12/4/97	240	0	0
EMBRATEL	Embratel	7/29/98	2,276	1	1
TELESP	Telesp Operacional, Borda do Campo	7/29/98	4,967	2	1
CENTRO SUL	Telepar, Telebrasília, Telegoiás, and other four closed companies: CTMR, Telemat, Teleron, Teleacre	7/29/98	1,778	3	3

NORTE LESTE	Telerj, Telebahia, Telemig, Telpe, Telma, Telest, Teleceará, Teleamazon, and other nine closed companies	7/29/98	2,949	16	8
	Aggregate transferred debt of these companies		2,125		
	Telecom offers to employees		293		
TELESP CEL.	Telesp Celular	7/29/98	3,082	1	0
SUDESTE CEL.		7/29/98	1,168	1	0
TELEMIG CEL.		7/29/98	649	1	0
CELULAR SUL		7/29/98	601	4	0
NORDESTE CEL.		7/29/98	567	7	0
LESTE CEL.		7/29/98	368	2	0
CENT. OESTE CEL.	Telegoiás Celular and other five closed companies	7/29/98	378	3	1
TELE NORTE C		7/29/98	161	2	0
GERASUL	Centrais Geradoras do Sul do Brasil S.A.	9/15/98	1,962	1	0
GUARARAPES	GUARARAPES	12/7/98	0.1	1	1
DATAMEC	Datamec S.A.	6/23/99	49	0	0
BANESPA	Banco do Estado de São Paulo	11/20/00	3,604	0	0
Petrobrás	Petrobrás[d]	8/9/00	4,032	1	1
Total			56,841.20	75	38

a. Includes transferred debt; values are current U.S. dollars.
b. These two columns show the number of companies included in the sample and the number of representative companies with shares traded at BOVESPA, respectively.
c. Sold with mother company.
d. Minority shares privatization in remaining state-owned enterprise.
Source: BNDES.

Table 4A.2 Companies Privatized by BNDES on Behalf of Brazilian States, Minority Shares Privatized by Federal Government, and São Paulo State Privatization Program

Company name	Date of auction	Auction result (US$ million)[a]	Included in sample	Listed before privatization
Banco Banerj S.A. – BANERJ	6/26/97	289	0	0
Banco de Crédito de Minas Gerais S.A – Credireal	8/7/97	112	0	0
Banco do Estado da Bahia – BANEB	7/22/99	147	0	0
Banco do Estado de Minas Gerais – BEMGE	9/14/98	494	0	0
Banco do Estado de Pernambuco S.A.	11/17/98	153	0	0
Banco do Estado de Santa Catarina – BESC	9/30/97	28	0	0
Centrais Elétricas Cachoeira Dourada	9/5/97	854	1	1
Centrais Elétricas do Pará S.A. – CELPA	7/9/98	504	0	0
CELPE	2000	1,135	1	1
Centrais Elétricas Matogrossenses S.A. – CEMAT	11/27/97	814	1	1
CESP Paranapanema	7/28/99	1,164	1	1
CESP TIETÊ	11/1/99	1,140	1	1
Cia de Gás de São Paulo – COMGÁS	4/14/99	1,076	1	1
Cia União de Seguros Gerais	11/20/97	45	0	0
Cia. Centro Oeste de Dist. de Energia Elétrica – (AES-SUL)	10/21/97	1,436	1	1
Cia. De Eletricidade de Minas Gerais – CEMIG[b]	5/28/97	1,053	1	1
Cia. De Eletricidade do Estado da Bahia – COELBA	7/31/97	1,965	1	1
Cia. De Eletricidade do Rio de Janeiro – CERJ	11/20/96	951	1	1
Cia. De Navegação do Rio de Janeiro – CONERJ	2/5/98	29	0	0
Cia. De Saneamento Básico de São Paulo – SABESP[b]	7/31/97	375	1	1
Cia. De Saneamento Básico do Paraná – SANEPAR[b]	6/8/98	217	1	1
Cia. Energética de Brasília – CEB[b]	4/30/97	74	1	1

Cia. Energética do Ceará – COELCE	4/2/98	1,338	1	1
Cia. Estadual de Gás do Rio de Janeiro – CEG	7/14/97	430	1	0
Cia. Fluminense de Trens Urbanos	7/15/98	240	0	0
Cia. Metropolitano do Rio de Janeiro[b]	12/19/97	262	0	0
Cia. N. NE de Dist. de Energia Elétrica – CEEE – (RGE)	10/21/97	1,635	1	1
Cia. Paranaense de Energia – COPEL[b]	9/20/96	413	1	1
Cia. Paulista de Força e Luz – CPFL	11/5/97	2,833	1	1
Cia. Riograndense de Telecomunicações – CRT	6/19/98	2,496	1	1
COSERN	12/12/97	718	1	0
EBE – BANDEIRANTE DE ENERGIA	9/17/98	1,235	1	0
Elektro Eletricidade e Serviços S.A. – ELEKTRO	7/16/98	1,917	1	0
Eletricidade de São Paulo S.A. – Metropolitana	4/15/98	3,445	1	0
Empresa Energética de Mato Grosso do Sul – ENERSUL	11/19/97	783.0	1	0
Empresa Energética de Sergipe – ENERGIPE	12/3/97	560	0	0
Estrada de Ferro Paraná Oeste S.A. – Ferroeste	12/10/96	25	0	0
Riogás S.A.	7/14/97	146	0	0
Terminal Garagem Menezes Côrtes	10/28/98	67	0	0
Total		32,598	24	18

Note: BNDES = National Social and Economic Development Bank.
a. Includes transferred debt; values are current U.S. dollars.
b. Minority shares in remaining state-owned enterprises.
Source: BNDES.

Table 4A.3 Remaining State-Owned Enterprises

Productive sectors
Eletrobrás group (Electricity)
• Centrais Elétricas Brasileiras S.A. – ELETROBRÁS
  Boa Vista Energia S.A. – BOVESA
  Centrais Elétricas de Rondônia S.A. – CERON
  Centrais Elétricas do Norte do Brasil S.A. – ELETRONORTE
  Centro de Pesquisas de Energia Elétrica – CEPEL
  Companhia de Eletricidade do Acre – ELETROACRE
  Companhia de Geração Térmica de Energia Elétrica – CGTEE
  Companhia Energética de Alagoas – CEAL
  Companhia Energética do Amazonas – CEAM
  Companhia Energética do Piauí – CEPISA
  Companhia Hidro Elétrica do São Francisco – CHESF
  Eletrobrás Termonuclear S.A. – ELETRONUCLEAR
  Empresa Transmissora de Energia Elétrica do Sul do Brasil S.A. –
    ELETROSUL
  FURNAS Centrais Elétricas S.A.
  LIGHTPAR – Light Participações S.A.
  Manaus Energia S.A. – MANAUS ENERGIA

Petrobrás group (Oil)
• Petróleo Brasileiro S.A. – PETROBRÁS
  Braspetro Oil Services Company – BRASOIL
  Petrobrás Distribuidora S.A. – BR
  Petrobrás Gás S.A. – GASPETRO
  Petrobrás Internacional S.A. – BRASPETRO
  Petrobras International Finance Company – PIFCO
  Petrobrás Química S.A. – PETROQUISA
  Transportadora Brasileira Gasoduto Bolívia-Brasil S.A. – TBG
  Indústria Carboquímica Catarinense S.A. – ICC (Em Liquidação)
  Petrobrás Transporte S.A. – TRANSPETRO
  Fronape International Company – FIC

Ports
Companhia Docas do Ceará – CDC
Companhia Docas do Espírito Santo – CODESA
Companhia das Docas do Estado da Bahia – CODEBA
Companhia Docas do Estado de São Paulo – CODESP
Companhia Docas do Maranhão – CODOMAR
Companhia Docas do Pará – CDP
Companhia Docas do Rio de Janeiro – CDRJ
Companhia Docas do Rio Grande do Norte – CODERN
Transportation
Rede Ferroviária Federal S.A. – RFFSA (In process of liquidation)
Rede Federal de Armazéns Gerais Ferroviários S.A. – AGEF (In process of
  liquidation)

Table 4A.3 (continued)

Other
BB-Administradora de Cartões de Crédito S.A. – BB-CAR
BB-Corretora de Seguros e Administradora de Bens S.A. – BB-COR
BB-TUR Viagens e Turismo Ltda.
BEM Serviços Gerais Ltda. – BEM SG

BEM Vigilância e Transporte de Valores S.A. – BEM VTV
Casa da Moeda do Brasil – CMB
Centrais de Abastecimento de Minas Gerais S.A. – CEASA/MG
Companhia de Armazéns e Silos do Estado de Minas Gerais – CASEMG
Companhia de Entrepostos e Armazéns Gerais de São Paulo – CEAGESP
COBRA – Computadores e Sistemas Brasileiros S.A.
Empresa Brasileira de Correios e Telégrafos – ECT
Empresa Brasileira de Infra-Estrutura Aeroportuária – INFRAERO
Empresa de Processamento de Dados da Prev. Social – DATAPREV
Empresa Gerencial de Projetos Navais – EMGEPRON
Hospital Cristo Redentor S.A. – REDENTOR
Hospital Fêmina S.A. – FÊMINA
Hospital Nossa Senhora da Conceição S.A. – CONCEIÇÃO
Indústria de Material Bélico do Brasil – IMBEL
Sistema de Processamento de Dados, Planej. e Adm. de Cartões de Crédito
   Ltda. – SISPLAN
Telecomunicações Brasileiras S.A. – TELEBRÁS

Financial sector
• Banco do Brasil S.A. – BB
   BB-Banco de Investimento S.A. – BB-BI
   BB-Distribuidora de Títulos e Valores Mobiliários S.A. – BB-DTVM
   BB-Financeira S.A., Crédito, Financ. e Investimento – BB-FIN
   BB-Leasing Company Ltd. – BB-LEASING
   BB-Leasing S.A. Arrendamento Mercantil – BB-LAM
   Brasilian American Merchant Bank – BAMB
• Banco Nacional de Desenvolvimento Econômico e Social – BNDES
   Agência Especial de Financiamento Industrial – FINAME
   BNDES Participações S.A. – BNDESPAR
• Banco do Estado de Goiás S.A. – BEG
   BEG Distribuidora de Títulos e Valores Mobiliários S.A. – BEG DTVM
• Banco do Estado de Santa Catarina S.A. – BESC
   BESC Distribuidora de Títulos e Valores Mobiliários S.A. – BESCVAL
   BESC Financeira S.A. Crédito, Financiamento e Investimento –
      BESCREDI
   BESC S.A. Arrendamento Mercantil – BESC LEASING
• Banco do Estado do Ceará S.A. – BEC
   BEC Distribuidora de Títulos e Valores Mobiliários S.A. – BEC DTVM

(Table continues on the following page.)

Table 4A.3 (continued)

- Banco do Estado do Maranhão S.A. – BEM
  BEM Distribuidora de Títulos e Valores Mobiliários Ltda. – BEM DTVM
  Banco da Amazônia S.A. – BASA
  Banco do Estado do Amazonas S.A. – BEA
  Banco do Estado do Piauí S.A. – BEP
  Banco do Nordeste do Brasil S.A. – BNB
  Caixa Econômica Federal – CEF
  IRB-Brasil Resseguros S.A. – IRB-BRASIL RE
  Financiadora de Estudos e Projetos – FINEP

Enterprises included in the fiscal budget
Companhia Brasileira de Trens Urbanos – CBTU
Companhia de Desenvolvimento de Barcarena – CODEBAR
Companhia de Desenvolvimento dos Vales do São Francisco e do Parnaíba –
  CODEVASF
Companhia de Navegação do São Francisco – FRANAVE
Companhia de Pesquisa de Recursos Minerais – CPRM
Companhia Nacional de Abastecimento – CONAB
Empresa Brasileira de Comunicação S.A. – RADIOBRÁS
Empresa Brasileira de Pesquisa Agropecuária – EMBRAPA
Empresa Brasileira de Planejamento de Transportes – GEIPOT
Empresa de Trens Urbanos de Porto Alegre S.A. – TRENSURB
Hospital de Clínicas de Porto Alegre – HCPA
Indústrias Nucleares do Brasil S.A. – INB
Nuclebrás Equipamentos Pesados S.A. – NUCLEP
Serviço Federal de Processamento de Dados – SERPRO
VALEC - Engenharia, Construções e Ferrovias S.A.

Other
Centrais de Abastecimento do Amazonas S.A. – CEASA/AM
Petrobrás America Inc. – AMERICA
Petrobrás U.K. Limited – BUK

Source: Ministry of Planning, Budget and Administration, Department of Coordination and Control of State Enterprises, Executive Secretary.

Appendix 4B

Table 4B.1 Description of the Variables

Variable	Definition
Profitability	
Operating income/sales (OI/S)	Ratio of operating income to sales. Operating income is equal to sales minus operating expenses, cost of sales, and depreciation. Sales are equal to total value of products and services sold minus sales returns and discounts.

Table 4B.1 (continued)

Variable	Definition
Operating income/ property, plant and equipment (OI/PPE)	Ratio of operating income to property, plant, and equipment, which is the value of a company's fixed assets adjusted for inflation. Operating income is equal to sales minus operating expenses, cost of sales, and depreciation.
Net income/sales (NI/S)	Ratio of net income to sales. Net income is equal to operating income minus interest expenses and net taxes paid. Sales are equal to total value of products and services sold minus sales returns and discounts.
Return on assets (ROA)	Ratio of operating income, which is equal to sales operating expenses, cost of sales, and depreciation minus interest expenses and net taxes paid, to total assets.
Return on equity (ROE)	Ratio of operating income, which is equal to sales minus operating expenses, cost of sales, and depreciation minus interest expenses and net taxes paid, to equity.
Operating efficiency Log(sales/PPE)	Log of the ratio of total value of products and services sold minus sales returns and discounts to property, plant, and equipment, which is the value of a company's fixed assets adjusted for inflation.
Operating costs/sales (OC/S)	Ratio of operating expenses to sales, defined as the total value of products and services sold minus sales returns and discounts.
Assets Log(PPE)	Log of property, plant, and equipment, which is the value of a company's fixed assets adjusted for inflation.
Investment/sales (I/S)	Ratio of investment to sales, defined as the total value of products and services sold minus sales returns and discounts. Investment is calculated as the difference of property, plant, and equipment along time.
Investment/PPE (I/PPE)	Ratio of investment to property, plant, and equipment, which is the value of a company's fixed assets adjusted for inflation.
Output Log(sales)	Log of sales, the total value of products and services sold minus sales returns and discounts.

(Table continues on the following page.)

Table 4B.1 (continued)

Variable	Definition
Shareholders	
Payout ratio	Ratio of total dividends to operating income minus interest expenses and net taxes paid.
Finance	
Current	Ratio of current assets to current liabilities.
Long-term debt/equity (LTD/E)	Ratio of long-term debt to equity
Net taxes	
Net taxes/sales (NT/S)	Ratio of net taxes to sales. Net taxes are equal to corporate income taxes paid net of direct subsidies or tax credits received during the fiscal year.

Source: Authors' calculations.

Appendix 4C

Table 4C.1 Change in Performance: Tests of Means and Medians (Two Years before Privatization versus Two Years after, without Adjustment)

Variable	N	Mean and median before	Mean and median after	Z-test
Profitability				
Operating income/sales	66	0.037	0.042	0.536
		0.072	0.108	0.523
Operating income/PPE	67	0.092	0.141	3.556***
		0.035	0.107	3.566***
Net income/sales	66	0.000	−0.008	−0.595
		0.034	0.039	0.677
Return on assets	70	−0.860	0.008	0.291
		0.014	0.011	−1.287
Return on equity	70	−1.152	0.046	0.662
		0.019	0.039	0.862

Table 4C.1 (continued)

Variable	N	Mean and median before	Mean and median after	Z-test
Operating efficiency				
Log(sales/PPE)	63	−0.273	−0.006	5.520***
		−0.201	0.009	5.492***
Operating costs/sales	58	0.375	0.251	−2.631***
		0.200	0.196	−2.917***
Assets				
Log(PPE)	67	6.001	5.946	−1.981*
		5.891	5.813	−1.983*
Investment/sales	57	0.295	−0.032	−2.550**
		0.158	0.093	−2.476**
Investment/PPE	57	0.115	0.094	−1.202
		0.101	0.104	0.202
Output				
Log(sales)	66	5.644	5.876	4.335**
		5.403	5.643	4.301**
Shareholders				
Payout ratio	45	71.40	55.99	−0.089
		30.78	48.66	0.166
Finance				
Current	70	0.847	1.009	2.755***
		0.745	0.866	3.089***
Long-term debt/equity	63	0.636	0.701	2.506**
		0.181	0.269	2.506**
Net taxes				
Net taxes/sales	65	0.024	−0.010	−3.834***
		0.017	0.007	−3.343***

* Significant at the 10 percent level.
** Significant at the 5 percent level.
*** Significant at the 1 percent level.

Note: N = number; PPE = property, plant, and equipment. The table presents, for each empirical proxy, the number of usable observations and the mean and median values before and after privatization. The full sample contains 102 privatized companies. Before privatization refers to the average of the two years before the sale; after privatization refers to the average of the two years following privatization. We report Z-statistics for signed rank tests and Wilcoxon rank sum tests for change in mean and median values, respectively. Definitions for each variable can be found in appendix table 4B.1.

Source: Authors' calculations.

Table 4C.2 Change in Performance: Tests of Means and Medians
(Two Years before Privatization versus Two Years after, with
Adjustment)

Variable	N	Mean and median before	Mean and median after	Z-test (1)
Profitability				
Operating income/sales	66	0.097	−0.430	−2.944***
		0.084	0.019	−2.944***
Operating income/PPE	67	−0.092	0.141	3.556***
		0.005	0.222	5.713***
Net income/sales	66	−0.004	−0.105	−1.476
		0.020	0.012	−1.534
ROA	70	−0.870	−0.014	0.824
		0.003	−0.012	−1.369
ROE	70	−1.194	0.025	1.768*
		−0.030	0.021	1.698*
Operating efficiency				
Log(sales/PPE)	63	−0.548	−0.298	3.980**
		−0.522	−0.218	3.876**
Operating costs/sales	58	0.174	0.065	−1.837
		0.014	0.021	−0.809
Assets				
Log(PPE)	67	1.445	1.002	−1.286
		0.955	0.871	−1.370
Investment/sales	57	0.223	−0.058	−1.887**
		0.117	0.066	−1.795*
Investment/PPE	57	0.038	0.024	−0.774
		0.026	0.039	0.264
Output				
Log(sales)	66	0.774	0.901	3.306***
		0.274	0.457	3.598***
Shareholders				
Payout ratio	45	0.309	−0.263	−0.229
		−28.62	−5.805	0.299
Finance				
Current	70	−0.510	−0.250	3.238***
		−0.605	−0.250	3.768**
LTD/equity	63	0.254	0.108	−0.210
		−0.142	−0.325	−0.021

(Table continues on the following page.)

Table 4C.2 (continued)

Variable	N	Mean and median before	Mean and median after	Z-test (1)
Net taxes				
Net taxes/sales	65	0.018	−0.014	−3.578***
		0.005	0.003	−3.575***

* Significant at the 10 percent level.
** Significant at the 5 percent level.
*** Significant at the 1 percent level.

Note: N = number; PPE = property, plant, and equipment; ROA = return on assets; ROE = return on equity; and LTD = long-term debt. The table presents, for each empirical proxy, the number of usable observations and the mean and median values before and after privatization, adjusted to take into account unstable macroeconomic policies. See text for full explanation. The full sample contains 102 privatized companies. *Before privatization* refers to the average of the two years before the sale; *after privatization* refers to the average of the two years following privatization. We report Z-statistics for signed rank tests and Wilcoxon rank sum tests for change in mean and median values, respectively. Definitions for each variable can be found in appendix table 4B.1.

Source: Authors' calculations.

Table 4C.3 Change in Performance: Tests of Means and Medians (All Years before and after Privatization, without Adjustment)

Variable	N	Mean and median before	Mean and median after	Z-test (1)
Profitability				
Operating income/sales	71	−0.052	0.050	1.511
		0.080	0.096	1.037
Operating income/PPE	70	0.057	0.291	3.042***
		0.045	0.097	3.408***
Net income/sales	71	−0.067	−0.042	0.815
		0.010	0.039	0.889
ROA	73	−0.812	0.017	2.967***
		0.003	0.026	2.311**
ROE	73	−1.109	0.021	2.258**
		0.008	0.038	2.150**
Operating efficiency				
Log(sales/PPE)	64	−0.247	−0.076	5.600***
		−0.285	0.012	5.244***

(Table continues on the following page.)

Table 4C.3 (continued)

Variable	N	Mean and median before	Mean and median after	Z-test (1)
Operating costs/sales	64	0.428	0.245	−3.138***
		0.255	0.207	−2.756***
Assets				
Log(PPE)	70	6.889	5.994	−1.141
		5.911	5.809	−0.952
Investment/sales	62	0.191	0.038	−1.406
		0.202	0.113	−1.157
Investment/PPE	62	−0.017	0.118	−1.288
		0.085	0.098	0.168
Output				
Log(sales)	71	5.823	6.004	2.032*
		5.800	5.974	1.956*
Shareholders				
Payout ratio	59	34.406	30.860	−0.138
		38.848	42.268	1.232
Finance				
Current	73	0.849	1.106	2.662***
		0.843	0.905	2.642***
LTD/equity	66	0.529	0.576	3.192***
		0.167	0.298	3.302***
Net taxes				
Net taxes/sales	68	0.015	0.009	−3.821***
		0.018	0.006	−4.296***

* Significant at the 10 percent level.
** Significant at the 5 percent level.
*** Significant at the 1 percent level.
Note: N = number; PPE = property, plant, and equipment; ROA = return on assets; ROE = return on equity; and LTD = long-term debt. The table presents, for each empirical proxy, the number of usable observations and the mean and median values before and after privatization. The full sample contains 102 privatized companies. *Before privatization* refers to the average of all the years before the sale; *after privatization* refers to the average of all the years following privatization. We report Z-statistics for signed rank tests and Wilcoxon rank sum tests for change in mean and median values, respectively. Definitions for each variable can be found in appendix table 4B.1.
Source: Authors' calculations.

Table 4C.4 Change in Performance: Tests of Means and Medians
(All Years before and after Privatization, with Adjustment)

Variable	N	Mean and median before	Mean and median after	Z-test (1)
Profitability				
Operating income/sales	71	−0.050	−0.005	0.107
		0.072	0.036	−0.241
Operating income/PPE	70	−0.003	0.385	6.112***
		−0.010	0.207	6.387***
Net income/sales	71	−0.084	−0.064	0.693
		0.005	0.014	0.262
ROA	73	−0.831	−0.003	3.130***
		−0.017	0.003	2.736***
ROE	73	−1.159	−0.012	3.236***
		−0.440	0.014	3.223***
Operating efficiency				
Log(sales/PPE)	63	−0.677	−0.255	5.226***
		−0.600	−0.264	4.914***
Operating costs/sales	64	0.236	0.066	−3.199***
		0.090	0.025	−2.819***
Assets				
Log(PPE)	69	1.380	1.017	−2.001*
		1.111	0.993	−1.885*
Investment/sales	62	0.098	0.011	−0.394
		0.123	0.086	−0.730
Investment/PPE	62	−0.018	0.055	−1.385
		0.022	0.029	1.072
Output				
Log(sales)	71	0.906	1.178	2.333***
		0.855	1.029	2.599***
Shareholders				
Payout ratio	59	0.082	−5.963	−0.731
		−29.35	−9.292	1.169
Finance				
Current	73	−0.526	−0.232	3.653***
		−0.503	−0.313	3.937***
LTD/equity	66	0.233	−0.002	−2.086**
		−0.107	−0.238	−2.286**

(Table continues on the following page.)

Table 4C.4 (continued)

Variable	N	Mean and median before	Mean and median after	Z-test (1)
Net taxes				
Net taxes/sales	68	0.007	0.005	3.173***
		0.007	0.002	−3.534***

* Significant at the 10 percent level.
** Significant at the 5 percent level.
*** Significant at the 1 percent level.

Note: N = number; PPE = property, plant, and equipment; ROA = return on assets; ROE = return on equity; and LTD = long-term debt. The table presents, for each empirical proxy, the number of usable observations and the mean and median values before and after privatization, adjusted to take into account unstable macroeconomic policies. See text for full explanation. The full sample contains 102 privatized companies. *Before privatization* refers to the average of all the years before the sale; *after privatization* refers to the average of all the years following privatization. We report Z-statistics for signed rank tests and Wilcoxon rank sum tests for change in mean and median values, respectively. Definitions for each variable can be found in appendix table 4B.1.

Source: Authors' calculations.

Appendix 4D

Table 4D.1 Definition of the Control Variables Included in the Vector of the Econometric Model

Variable	Definition	Expected impact on i_{it}
Split/merger	A dummy variable that takes the value 1 if the company had been split or merged as a result of its privatization, and 0 otherwise.	(+) or (−)
Minority control	A dummy variable that takes the value 1 if the government, owned only a minority participation before privatization, and 0 otherwise.	(+)
Listed	A dummy variable that takes the value 1 if the privatized enterprise was listed on the São Paulo stock exchange before privatization, and 0 otherwise.	(+)

(Table continues on the following page.)

Table 4D.1 (continued)

Variable	Definition	Expected impact on i_{it}
Tradable	A dummy variable that assumes the value 1 if the privatized firm is in a tradable goods industry, following three criteria: its typical product is included in the international classification of tradable goods; it is free from nontariff restrictions; and its effective protection tariff is not redundant, and 0 otherwise.	$(-)$
Regulated[a]	A dummy variable that assumes a value of 1 if the privatized firm is in a regulated industry, and 0 otherwise.	$(+)$ or $(-)$
Private mean	The yearly average of each performance indicator based on private companies only.	$(+)$ or $(-)$

a. *Regulated* refers to privatized firms that belong to an industry whose prices have been controlled by the government before and after privatization.
Source: Authors' calculations.

Notes

The authors acknowledge financial support from Fundação Instituto de Pesquisas Econômicas (FIPE) and the Latin American and Caribbean Research Network Program (LACRNP) of the Inter-American Development Bank; the assistance of Economática; Austin Assis, and the Getúlio Vargas Foundation for providing the data sets; and the research assistance of Renata Domingos and Alan de Genaro Dario.

1. These numbers, as well as others quoted from the same study, have been rounded.
2. This section draws from Macedo (2000) and updates and extends his analysis.
3. These values exclude concessions of public services. All dollar amounts are U.S. dollars.
4. The major source of data on the Brazilian privatization program is BNDES, which was given the task of managing it, including a part developed at the state level. The reports and other documents used as sources are BNDES 1999a, 1999b, and 2001.
5. The same kind of data is used later in the analysis of employment effects. This data base is known as RAIS (Relação Anual das Informações Sociais, or Annual Survey of Social Data).

6. The differential, net of the workers' characteristics, reached a peak of 80 percent when the workers' characteristics were valued according to the private sector criteria, as measured by the regression coefficients of the workers' characteristics in the wage equation of that sector.

7. More recently, in a seminar sponsored by BNDES to celebrate the 10th anniversary of the privatization program, Pinheiro (2000) presented some additional and updated results, again based on data that cannot be disclosed, this time covering 55 firms. The analysis simply compared the performance of the firms before and after privatization, thus not relating their performance to that of the private firms. Pinheiro found sizable increases in net operational revenues, investment, net profit, productivity, and tax collections as well as a reduction in employment, in some cases compensated by an expansion in contracted-out services.

8. High rates of inflation plagued the economy from 1986 to 1994, a period in which indexation following legal rules was widespread. Because the analysis is developed in terms of ratios based on flow variables, such as operating income to sales, the problems of inflation and indexation are circumvented. For a few cases in which the absolute value of the indicator is used, the original values in Brazilian currency were converted into U.S. dollars.

9. In the process of privatization, BNDES franchised to interested bidders the existing information on the firms. The files are kept by BNDES, but they are considered a proprietary right of the winning bidder. BNDES has also occasionally used questionnaires to gather information from firms after privatization. BNDES responded to our request for both types of data saying that it could not make them available to third parties.

10. This procedure differs from that of La Porta and López-de-Silanes (1999) in that they used one fixed year for the period after privatization. In the Mexican case, privatization was heavily concentrated in a few years. In Brazil it has extended over a decade and more. Therefore, a fixed year for comparison would be inadequate.

11. Our adjustment, however, could not be done by industry, as some privatized enterprises do not have a corresponding match in the private sector. This is the case, for instance, with the major mining company (Companhia Vale do Rio Doce), the telecommunications companies, and many companies in the energy sector.

12. This information was available only for listed companies.

13. According to Baltagi (1995), inclusion of a lagged dependent variable renders the OLS (ordinary least squares) estimator biased and inconsistent even if the error terms are not serially correlated. Baltagi (1995) and Hsiao (1986) also demonstrate that the same problem affects GLS (generalized least squares) and FGLS (feasible generalized least squares) estimators. Finally, the instrumental variable (IV) estimation method alone leads to consistent, but not necessarily efficient, estimates of the parameters in the model, because it does not make use of all the available moment conditions (Ahn and Schmidt 1995).

14. For the lagged dependent variables, this method resorts to instrumental variables that are obtained in a dynamic panel data model once existing orthogonality conditions between these lagged values and the disturbances are taken into account. A set of valid instruments is represented by all the dependent variables lagged more than one period. In this chapter, the parameter estimates were obtained by using as an instrument the independent variable lagged two years.

15. The incentives gained strength after new "social rights" were established by the constitution of 1988, as detailed by Fernandes (1998).

16. Pinheiro (2000) tackled both the direct impact and the effect of contracting out on employment, on the basis of questionnaires sent to the privatized firms by BNDES. He found a 33 percent reduction in the total number of formal workers.

For production workers, the reduction was 29.5 percent, evidence that overstaffing was concentrated in white-collar workers. In absolute numbers, he found that, excluding telecommunications, the total reduction was 10,000 workers in the year of privatization and 35,000 in the year before, thus showing adjustment by SOEs before privatization. In the telecommunications sector, he found that 145,000 new jobs were contracted out to expand services. This number might sound high, but notice that in this country of 170 million inhabitants, the number of fixed telephone lines increased from 9.6 per 100 people in 1996 to 21.4 in 2000, while the number of cellular phones rose from 1.6 per 100 people to 12.9, an expansion that has required a lot of labor, particularly in the case of fixed lines.

17. Data obtained from the Brazilian Central Bank and Department of Treasury.

18. Macedo (2000) compares the fiscal picture at that time to what Kornai (1979) calls a soft budget constraint, typical of centralized governments whose budgets are only vaguely monitored or controlled by Congress and society, if at all. Under such conditions, the only effective constraint emerges when markets react to the piling up of debt and the interest rate becomes a problem in itself.

19. Interestingly enough, the devaluation in early 1999 came after the telecommunications privatization auction in 1998, in which the presence of foreign direct investment was stronger. These investments were seen by the market as a sign that the government could hold on to the overvalued real. As the program came to a halt, devaluation came sooner than expected.

20. The other countries are Argentina, Bolivia, Colombia, Costa Rica, Ecuador, El Salvador, Guatemala, Honduras, Mexico, Nicaragua, Paraguay, Peru, and Uruguay.

21. The highest ratings were given to the aviation industry (80 percent), in which Embraer, the only former SOE, has been very successful; steel (65 percent); and telecommunications (58 percent). The lowest ratings were received by railroads (9 percent), electricity (13 percent), and one airline (11 percent)—a small company that belonged to the state of São Paulo and was individually privatized in the mid-1980s.

22. In 2000, for the first time since the program started, the federal government resorted to a public offer of minority shares in Petrobrás, totaling $4 billion, in which workers were also allowed to participate with their FGTS deposits. The operation was very successful, as was another public offer of a remaining state-owned block of minority shares of Companhia Vale do Rio Doce, sold in 2002 for $1.9 billion.

23. The source of the tax burden data is the Secretary of Federal Revenue, Ministry of Finance, as published by Folha de São Paulo (May 10, 2003).

References

Ahn, S. C., and P. Schmidt. 1995. "Efficient Estimation of Models for Dynamic Panel Data." *Journal of Econometrics* 68: 5–27.

Arellano, M., and S. Bond. 1991. "Some Tests of Specification for Panel Data: Monte Carlo Evidence and an Application to Employment Equations." *Review of Economic Studies* 58: 277–97.

Baltagi, B. H. 1995. *Econometric Analysis of Panel Data*. New York: John Wiley & Sons.

BNDES (Banco Nacional de Desenvolvimento Econômico e Social). 1999a. *Privatizações no Brasil – 1991/99*. Rio de Janeiro.

————. 1999b. *Sistema de Informações*. Rio de Janeiro.

————. 2001. "Privatização, www.gov.br.

Fernandes, R. 1998. "Encargos Sociais e Demanda por Trabalho no Setor Formal da Economia." *Economia Aplicada* 2(3): 553–78.

Hsiao, C. 1986. *Analysis of Panel Data*. Cambridge, U.K.: Cambridge University Press.

Kornai, J. 1979. "Resource vs. Demand-Oriented Systems." *Econometrica* 47 (4): 801–19.

La Porta, Rafael, and Florencio López-de-Silanes. 1999. "The Benefits of Privatization: Evidence from Mexico." *The Quarterly Journal of Economics* (November): 1193–242.

La Porta, Rafael, Florencio López-de-Silanes, Andrei Shleifer, and Robert Vishny. 1997. "Legal Determinants of External Finance." *Journal of Finance* 52 (3): 1131–50.

Lamounier, B., and A. De Souza. 2002. "As Elitres Brasileiras e o Desenvolvimento Nacional: Fatores de Consenso e Dissenso." *Relatório de Pesquisa*. São Paulo: IDESP (Instituto de Estudos Econômicos, Sociais e Políticos).

Levine, Ross. 1997. "Financial Development and Economic Growth: Views and Agenda." *Journal of Economic Literature* (35): 688–726.

Levine, Ross, and S. Zervos. 1998. "Stock Markets, Banks, and Economic Growth." *American Economic Review* (88): 537–58.

Lora, Eduardo, and U. Panizza. 2002. "Structural Reforms in Latin America under Scrutiny." Paper prepared for the seminar "Reforming Reforms," held at the annual meeting of the Board of Governors, Inter-American Development Bank, Fortaleza, Brazil. Available at www.iadb.org/res.

Macedo, R. 1985. *Os Salários nas Empresas Estatais*. São Paulo: Nobel.

————. 2000. "Privatization and the Distribution of Assets and Income in Brazil." Working Paper 14. Carnegie Endowment for International Peace, Washington, D.C.

Megginson, William L., and Jeffry M. Netter. 2001. "From State to Market: A Survey of Empirical Studies of Privatization." *Journal of Economic Literature* 39 (June): 321–89.

Megginson, William L., Robert C. Nash, and Matthais van Randenborgh. 1994. "The Financial and Operating Performance of Newly Privatized Firms: An International Empirical Analysis." *Journal of Finance* 49 (2): 403–52.

Pinheiro, Armando C. 1996. "Impactos Microeconômicos da Privatização no Brasil." *Pesquisa e Planejamento Econômico* 26 (3): 357–98.

————. 2000. "Após a Privatização." Rio de Janeiro: BNDES. Presentation in Powerpoint format available at www.bndes.gov.br.

Pinheiro, Armando C., and F. Giambiagi. 1997. "Lucratividade, Dividendos e Investimentos das Empresas Estatais: Uma Contribuição para o Debate sobre Privatização no Brasil." *Revista Brasileira de Economia* 51 (January–March): 93–131.

5

The Effects of Privatization on Firms: The Chilean Case

*Ronald Fischer, Rodrigo Gutiérrez,
and Pablo Serra*

THIS CHAPTER EVALUATES THE EFFECTS OF privatization on the efficiency of firms and institutions in Chile. One of the chief characteristics of the Chilean privatization process is that it has been all-encompassing. In the three decades that followed the fall of the government of the socialist president Salvador Allende (December 1970–December 1973), all the banks and firms that had been acquired or expropriated by the Allende administration were either privatized or liquidated. Farms that had been expropriated after the agrarian reform of 1965 were privatized, as well as a majority of the firms that were state-owned before December 1970.

The military government of Augusto Pinochet also privatized the pension system and a part of the health insurance system. It promoted vouchers for subsidized private schools and allowed free entry of new institutions into university and other tertiary education. Finally, the private sector improved or built and undertook the operation of most large infrastructure projects such as highways, seaports, airports, water reservoirs, and even jails. In addition, in a bid to decentralize government, local governments (municipalities) became responsible for the lowest level of the public health care system as well as for public schooling.

The privatization effort has been part of a much wider process of economic liberalization that Chile initiated in 1974. The process represents a major reversal of the policies the country had followed since the 1940s, when the state played a role not only through the public firms, but also through regulations and other mechanisms (Galetovic 1998). The government set interest rates and exchange rates, as well as regulating almost 3,000 prices for goods and services. As part of its import substitution strategy, the state protected those sectors deemed essential. All of these mechanisms started to disappear in 1974 with the country's shift toward a market economy in which the price system was the main determinant of resource allocation and the private sector was the centerpiece of the economy. Moreover, many traditional supervisory activities were surrendered to the private sector.

It is possible to distinguish three main phases of the privatization process, even though any chronological division is arbitrary. In the first phase, which covers the period 1974–83, 259 firms that were expropriated or illegally taken during the Allende administration were restored to their original owners. The government also sold or liquidated an additional 112 nonfinancial firms acquired in the same period (retaining 1 in that category). In addition, 33 of the 65 firms owned by the government before 1970 were also privatized or liquidated. Nevertheless, in 1983 the government still owned 45 firms, some of them because they were considered of strategic importance and some because there were no takers. These included all of the major telecommunications and electric power firms, as well as copper mining companies.

In the second phase, from 1984 to 1989, the state privatized the telecommunications and electric power firms as well as most of the firms previously considered strategic: the CAP steel works, the national airline LAN Chile, and other major firms. It also finished selling the last few firms that had been acquired by the socialist government. By 1989 only 19 of the 65 firms dating from the pre-Allende period were still state-owned.

The privatization of state-owned enterprises (SOEs) slowed down in the 1990–2001 period. However, the government sold the three main water and sewage companies and completed the privatization of the electricity sector. The distinguishing feature of this period, however, is the privatization—through concession contracts—of infrastructure management. Since 1993, the main highways and airports have been built, maintained, and operated by private investors. The main state-owned ports have also been franchised to private firms.

Most analysts ascribe the strong growth of the Chilean economy that began in 1985 (after a severe crisis in the first half of the decade) to economic liberalization. If we accept this premise, we may still question the specific contribution of privatization. So many systemic changes occurred at the same time that it is difficult to evaluate the individual contribution of a particular policy. Nevertheless, Larraín and Vergara (1995) suggest that the rest of the program would not have been credible in the absence of a privatization process. Moreover, privatization was important in helping balance the budget and in developing capital markets.[1] In this chapter, however, we focus on the direct effect of privatization on the efficiency of privatized sectors and therefore do not look at the global effects on the rest of the economy.

Privatization of SOEs

The Chilean privatization of SOEs has been a long-lasting and yet unfinished process. There are still 38 firms—most of them of economic importance—that remain in public hands. They include ENAP, the monopoly oil refinery; Codelco, a copper mining concern that is the largest company in Chile; ENAMI, a copper refinery; Banco del Estado, the fourth largest commercial bank; the post office; the subway; the Chilean mint; the rail lines; 10 ports; Zofri, a free trade zone; and other minor companies, representing, in all, around 9 percent of total gross domestic product (GDP) in 1998 (Hachette 2000). The perception that Chile has advanced further along the privatization route than most other countries is probably due to the fact that the bulk of traditional infrastructure and social services has been privatized rather than to the extent to which the state has retired from the productive sector.

As can be seen from table 5.1, 125 firms were privatized between 1974 and 2001. Most of these firms, however, were owned by the state for only a short time, and only 65 of these stayed in public hands long enough to count as true SOEs. Most of the firms acquired during the socialist administration (1970–73) were privatized by 1978, and by 1983 only 1 of those firms was still state-owned. At least 55 other firms controlled by the government have been liquidated. Several of these were viable only while protected by large tariffs and other nontariff barriers, and thus became nonviable after the opening of the economy (Hachette and Lüders 1994). Note also that in the 1979–89 period many state-owned firms were created by the breaking up of larger firms and were later sold.

Table 5.1 Nationalization and Privatization of Firms in Chile, 1970–2001

Number of firms	1970–73	1974–78	1979–83	1984–89	1990–2001
Beginning of period	65	179	82	45	44
Acquired	113	1	0	0	0
Created	1	0	10	29	12
Privatized	0	70	14	27	14
Liquidated	0	28	20	3	4
No information	0	0	13	0	0
End of period	179	82	45	44	38

Note: The table does not include Pehuenche, which was privatized as a project. It does include Corporación del Cobre (Codelco) and 10 seaports originating in the breakup of Emporchi.
Source: Authors.

Compared with later processes (in Mexico, for instance, see La Porta and López-de-Silanes 1999), privatization in Chile was not transparent in its early stages. This can be explained partially by the violent social convulsions that affected Chile from 1970 through 1982. This era saw a coup overthrowing the socialist government and bringing in a dictatorship, three large economic crises (1973, 1975, and 1982), and major structural changes in the economy. Furthermore, policymakers explored untried policies in the absence of a free press—there is almost no record of privatizations that took place in the 1970s. Moreover, accounting books convey little about the value of a firm as inflation rates reached levels of more than 500 percent in some years, and bookkeeping regulations were loose and not upgraded until the 1982 crisis. Therefore, most of the usable data on privatization for Chile correspond to the firms privatized since the early 1980s that remained public corporations (that is, that trade shares on the stock market), because they were required to publish financial information. More than half of these firms provide public services, and their data are contaminated by the effects of regulation, while the remaining firms are usually dominant in their markets or have sizable market shares.

The most important conclusion we draw in this section is that contrary to other documented cases (see La Porta and López-de-Silanes 1999), most SOEs in Chile were fairly efficient before being sold, except perhaps in the sense of overinvestment in the electric power sector. As a matter of fact, employment increased after privatization in most firms. As a result, privatization did not substantially improve the behavior of privatized firms, and by many measures, investment was lower than average for their sectors after privatization.[2] A second conclusion is that in the case of several variables of interest, the main divide is that between firms operating in a regulated market and those acting in a competitive market. In particular, privatized firms that face competition have had lower profit rates, with profitabilities that are similar to those of their respective industries, while firms in the regulated sector have had significantly higher profit rates than the average for their industries at the 2-digit SIC (Standard Industrial Classification) level. In the case of the regulated sectors, the effects of privatization may result from differences in management efficiency or from the introduction of new regulations on the sector, or from the interplay of those two factors. Thus, it is necessary to evaluate the regulations in order to understand the impact of privatization.

Privatization of Regulated Sectors

This section focuses on the privatization of utilities that occurred in the 1980s and on the private infrastructure franchises of the 1990s. In these sectors the government switched from the role of provider to the role of regulator. The government was aware that in some cases adequate incentives were required in order for privatization to increase welfare. For that reason the regulations that were introduced before privatization tended to promote competition whenever it was feasible and to stimulate efficient behavior when competition was impossible.

Privatization of Utilities

In this section we analyze the postprivatization performance of regulated utilities and relate it to regulatory legislation. We focus on the electricity and telecommunications companies that were privatized in the 1980s.[3] The gains in efficiency from privatization derive both from the differential efficiency between the public and private management and from the effect of the rules and regulations that were imposed on the sector.

During the 1980s Chile reformed and liberalized its electricity and telecommunications sectors. The process started in the late 1970s, with the establishment of new regulatory bodies and the introduction of new legislation in 1982, and culminated in the privatization of the major firms between 1985 and 1989. One trait that infrastructure-based sectors share is that competitive segments coexist with other segments that constitute a natural monopoly. Chile's policy has been to introduce competition wherever possible and to regulate noncompetitive segments of industry. The government believed that market discipline played an essential role in economic policy, so much so that one of the first economic laws it introduced (in October 1973) was a thorough revamping of antitrust legislation.

With respect to the Chilean electricity sector, the cornerstone of the reform process was the introduction of competition in the wholesale contract market for energy. The unbundling of transmission services was a prerequisite for wholesale competition to survive. Thus, it was necessary to introduce the principle of open access to the transmission network. The second major change was that investment in power generation was left to market forces. It was assumed that existing firms or potential entrants would invest in generation capacity whenever a project had a return on capital that was commensurate with the sector's risk. The third major regulatory innovation was the introduction of incentive regulation to calculate the distribution rates. This implies that prices are set so that an efficient distribution company attains a predetermined rate of return (Fischer and Serra, 2000). The legislation regulating the telecommunications sector follows a similar pattern. These laws allow for free market prices in all sectors deemed competitive but regulate rates of basic phone services considered to be local monopolies. As the local network is considered an essential facility for competitors, the 1982 law requires local telephone service operators to provide access to their network to any other operator that requests the service.

On average, SOEs increased their profitability and efficiency after privatization, following the trend of the national economy, but the behavior

of firms providing regulated services stood out. Their labor productivity—
and consequently their profitability—increased more than that of the unregulated firms. Hence, there is some evidence that the incentive mechanisms worked and provided incentives for efficiency. At the same time, the
high profit rates of these firms are also evidence of regulatory failure. In
fact, the available evidence shows that a large fraction of the efficiency
gains was not transferred to consumers as prescribed by the regulatory
model. Nonetheless, this situation has changed since the turn of the century as regulators have become more forceful and competition has made
its mark even on sectors previously considered to be natural monopolies.

The Privatization of Infrastructure

Despite the existence of some early plans to franchise infrastructure during the Pinochet government, it was the democratically elected Aylwin
administration (1990–94) that managed to pass a law allowing private
franchises of highways and other infrastructure projects. Because of initial delays and practical hurdles, it was not until the Frei administration
(1994–2000) that the groundwork was completed and the franchising of
infrastructure went into full swing. For the next six years, during and after the Frei administration, most profitable private projects were franchised to national and international firms. Projects worth more than $4
billion are operational or are close to being operational. An additional
$2.5 billion in projects was auctioned or was scheduled for auction dur-
ing 2002, but construction had not yet started; another $650 million was
under consideration at the time of this writing but had not been evaluated
in detail.

By the mid-1990s, the government discovered that it faced bottlenecks
in seaports—a serious problem since most Chilean international cargo is
transported by sea. Each port had multiple private cargo transfer and storage operators, but there was little investment in equipment, and activities
were not well coordinated. The government decided to franchise port terminals (frentes de atraque) to private operators.[4] Given the scarcity of
ports in Chile because of geographical reasons, terminals can be considered essential facilities. To increase efficiency and investment in the ports,
the main terminals were auctioned under restrictions on horizontal and
vertical integration designed to prevent monopolization of the ports.

Overall, the program of infrastructure franchising has been successful.
The highway program has encountered few problems, especially compared with the experience of Mexico, which eventually cost taxpayers an
estimated $8 billion. By now Chile can boast of a substantially upgraded
road infrastructure and lower transportation costs. Moreover, since franchise auctions were open and competitive, tolls (user prices) should be
close to average cost, which is the second-best outcome in the presence
of economies of scale. There are, however, potential problems with the

traffic guarantees the government has included in contracts to facilitate access to loans, since they represent unaccounted contingent liabilities of the government that are pro-cyclical. Finally, there have been noticeable improvements in the efficiency of the privatized ports. The loading and unloading process has become twice as fast in just one year, having a multiplier effect on transportation costs since shorter stays in port mean that more efficient and more capital-intensive ships can afford to operate from Chile.

In this chapter we report the effects of privatization on 37 nonfinancial firms that were privatized between 1979 and 1999. During this period 13 additional nonfinancial firms were privatized, but the available data for those entities were insufficient. This is symptomatic of one of the negative features of the Chilean privatization process: the lack of transparency (Hachette and Lüders 1994). There are no public records for privatizations that occurred during the 1970s. Some of these firms subsequently went bankrupt or became private corporations (that is, with no publicly traded shares) and did not publish accounting information. Therefore, most of the usable data on privatization for Chile correspond to the now publicly traded firms that were privatized starting in the early 1980s, which are required to publish financial information. Nineteen of the 37 firms in the sample belong to regulated sectors, so their data are contaminated by the effects of regulation, while the remainder are usually dominant firms in their markets or have sizable market shares.[5] In this chapter we report both absolute and normalized (adjusted) changes in various performance ratios before and after privatization. The normalization allows us to compare the behavior of privatized firms to the performance of the sector to which they belong.

The rest of the chapter is organized as follows. The next three sections analyze the privatization of state-owned firms and its effect on their performance, efficiency, and other parameters. That is followed by a section devoted to a qualitative assessment of privatization of regulated sectors. First, we analyze the privatized utilities and their sectors in more detail. Then we look at the private provision of infrastructure through franchises. The last section concludes.

A Brief History of the Privatization of Public Enterprises

The Era of State Intervention

State participation in the economy has had a long history in Chile, although it has only been truly significant since 1940. After the crisis of the 1930s—according to Mamalakis (1976), Chile was one of the countries that suffered most heavily in the crisis—the country chose an import substitution strategy and more state intervention. Thirty years later, the government

Table 5.2 State-Owned and State-Seized Firms, 1970–2001

Type of firm	1970	1973	1983	1989	2001
Enterprises	65	179	45	44	38
Banks	1	19	2	1	1
Seized	0	259	0	0	0

Note: Between 1970 and 1973, the government increased from 2 to 68 the number of firms in which it had minority stakes.
Source: Corporación de Fomento de la Producción; Hachette and Lüders (1994). Data for 2000 compiled by the authors.

owned or had a controlling interest in 65 firms (and 1 bank), 21 of which were created by law and 44 that were controlled by the Corporación de Fomento (CORFO), a government organization created to promote industrial production (table 5.2). These firms either operated only in sectors that the state deemed too important to be left to the market or were originally private firms that had gone bankrupt until government intervention saved them.[6]

CORFO was set up in 1939 to spur economic development through the promotion of investment. It operated through loans and loan guarantees to the private sector, through research and development of projects, and eventually, through their implementation. CORFO established firms that were deemed essential for Chile's development,[7] among them Empresa Nacional de Electricidad (ENDESA, 1944), Compañía de Acero del Pacífico (CAP, 1946), Industria Azucarera Nacional (IANSA, 1953), Empresa Nacional de Telecomunicaciones (ENTEL, 1964), Petroquímica Chilena (Petrox, 1967), Sociedad Química y Minera de Chile (Soquimich, 1968), Celulosa Constitución (Celco, 1969), Celulosa Arauco (1967), and Industrias Forestales SA (Inforsa, 1970). There were minority private shareholders in these firms (43 percent in the case of CAP). CORFO was also a minority shareholder in two other firms.

Among the firms created by law are Correo y Telégrafos, which has been public since before independence; Ferrocarriles del Estado, founded in 1851; Línea Aérea Nacional (LAN), created in 1931; Empresa Nacional del Petróleo (ENAP), established in 1950; the Empresa Marítima del Estado, spun off from Ferrocarriles in 1953; the Banco del Estado, established in 1953 by the merger of state-owned financial institutions established in the previous century; Empresa Nacional de Minería, created in 1960; and the Empresa Portuaria de Chile, split off from the customs office in 1960.

A change of policy occurred in the late 1960s when the government began a modest process of acquiring private firms. Previously, all SOEs had been created by the state itself, except for those troubled firms unable to repay the CORFO loans. Codelco was established in 1968 to acquire 50

Table 5.3 Number of State-Owned Firms, by Year, 1973–2001

Date	1973	1978	1983	1989	2001
State-owned pre-1970	65	46	32	19	15
Acquired 1970–73	113	34	1	0	0
Created 1970–73	1	1	1	1	0
Acquired 1974–78		1	1	0	0
Created 1979–83			10	2	1
Created 1984–89				22	13
Created 1990–2001					10
Total	179	82	45	44	38

Note: The table does not include Pehuenche, which was privatized as a project. It does includes Corporación del Cobre (Codelco) and 10 seaports originating in the breakup of Emporchi.
Source: Authors' computations based on Hachette and Lüders (1994) and Corporación de Fomento de la Producción.

percent of the shares of the four largest copper mines (copper represented more than 80 percent of all exports). In 1970 Chilectra was acquired by CORFO, which meant that the state owned almost the entire electric power sector. Moreover, in the 1965–70 period, 22 percent of the arable land (4.1 million hectares) was expropriated in a land reform process. Most of the land was not transferred by deed to the peasants (except for 2,600 hectares), but was kept in public hands (Rosende and Reinstein 1986).

The pace of state intervention in the economy accelerated in December 1970 when the socialist Allende administration took office with the professed aim of creating a vast state-owned sector. The target was to acquire all firms whose equity exceeded $500,000 in current dollars, as well as all of the banking sector, the import-export sector, and all utilities. A majority in the Chilean congress opposed this plan, so the executive branch resorted to administrative measures and legal loopholes. First, CORFO offered to buy shares in any bank or publicly traded firm. Given the uncertainty of the times, many investors decided to sell out (table 5.3).

In the 1971–73 period CORFO managed to buy a majority share in 113 industrial firms and 14 banks, as well as a minority shareholding in 68 other firms and 5 banks, while creating only 1 new firm (Transmarchilay). Therefore, in September 1973 the state was a majority controller in 179 firms and 15 banks and was a minority shareholder in 70 firms and 4 banks. Another 259 firms were intervened in or nationalized. In this case the administration used preexisting legislation that allowed intervention or expropriation of firms when there was a threat of shortages. In the case of strikes, firms stopped operating, so a risk of shortage existed, allowing the intervention of the government.

To recapitulate, by September 1973 the government controlled 441 firms and 15 banks, and there were few important companies in private hands (the firms under control of the state represented almost 40 percent of GDP). In addition, 66 agro-industrial plants were built or operated, or both, by Socoagro, a subsidiary of CORFO. The state owned 8,979,000 hectares, of which 5,873,000 had been expropriated in 1971–73 (Larroulet 1984), and the share of the economy in the hands of the state was growing apace.

The First Round of Privatization

After the coup of September 1973, the military government in power began to develop a strategy of economic liberalization. One of its aspects was the return to the original owners of the firms in which the government had intervened. During 1974, 202 firms were returned to their owners; 39 were given back the next year, leaving only 18 firms to be normalized in the next few years. Most of these firms that were returned to their original owners by 1975 had been in the hands of the government for only a few years and are therefore not representative of SOEs (Meller 1996; Sáez 1996). At the same time, the land that had been expropriated was privatized: 28 percent of the land that had been expropriated illegally was returned to its original owners, another 52 percent was divided into small landholdings and sold to the peasants at subsidized prices (many of the peasants later resold the land), while the remainder was privatized through public auction or was transferred to the Corporación Nacional Forestal (Hachette and Lüders 1994).

Between 1975 and 1977 the government privatized most of the firms that had been acquired in 1971–73. Most of the shareholdings in banks were sold in 1976, leaving a few to be sold the next year. In the 1975–77 period, 70 state-controlled firms were privatized, while 28 other firms were closed and their assets auctioned off (table 5.4). By 1980 the state had control over only 10 of the firms acquired by the socialist government. At the same time, the military dictatorship decided to keep the largest electricity and telecommunications companies. The same strategic reasons made the military government buy a controlling interest in the main telephone company in 1974 (thus obtaining control of 100 percent of the telecommunications sector).

Of those SOEs that dated to the period before 1970, only 46 were still owned by the state by the end of the 1970s, with the government having either sold or liquidated 30 of them. The state retained the 22 companies that had been created by a special law, but the number of CORFO companies shrank from 44 to 11. CORFO sold all of the firms it had acquired through debt capitalization and kept only a portion of the companies it had created. Thus, by the end of the 1970s the state owned the major electric utilities, telecommunications companies, the big mining companies, and a large fraction of the transportation industry (railways, two shipping

Table 5.4 Privatized State-Owned Enterprises, 1972–2001

Privatized SOEs	1974–78	1979–83	1984–89	1990–2001
Pre-1970 SOEs	10	7	10	3
Acquired 1970–73	60	7	1	0
Created 1970–73	0	0	0	1
Acquired 1974–78	0	0	1	0
Created 1979–83		0	8	1
Created 1984–89			7	7
Created 1990–2001				2
Total	70	14	27	14

Source: Authors' computations based on Hachette and Lüders (1994) and Corporación de Fomento de la Producción.

companies, and the national airline) as well as the steel mill. The status of 13 firms is unclear, since they either were liquidated or went bankrupt shortly after privatization.

The larger firms were sold at public auctions, although there were postauction negotiations with the auction winners (Hachette and Lüders 1994). The smaller firms were sold directly. Overall, the objective seems to have been to maximize state revenue, which explains why the government usually offered a controlling interest (generally all of the shares owned by CORFO), rather than selling small lots of shares in the open market. In the case of the banks, the government tried to diversify ownership by setting a limit of 1.5 percent on holdings, but this limit was raised after being easily evaded by buyers using shell companies. No serious attempts were made to attract foreign investors.

The objective of maximizing revenue from sales led to a policy of lending money to the buyers. Thus, only 10–20 percent of the bid was required immediately, and there was a one-year grace period, plus seven years for full repayment, with a low (for those times) real interest rate of 8–12 percent per year. The government asked for a loan guarantee of 150 percent of the loan value, but the guarantee could be in the form of shares in the company. In the case of the banks, the minimum payment was 20 percent (on average 23 percent was paid up front), and the loan had to be paid in full within two years at a real interest rate of 8 percent. The government offered such easy conditions because the private sector was still undercapitalized due to the effects of the policies of the early 1970s.

The Crisis of the Early 1980s

Most financial firms, as well as several banks that had been privatized from 1975 to 1979, were taken over by the state during the economic crisis of 1981–83. Beginning in 1981 several banks became effectively insolvent because they could not recover loans from troubled companies, many of them related firms, which were either bankrupt or had suffered severe losses.[8] The government took over four banks in November 1981 and two more the following year, all of which were later closed. In January 1983 the government had to take over eight additional banks that had failed to repay international loans (three of these banks were later closed down). Ironically, most of the financial institutions that had been privatized during 1975 and 1976—representing 55 percent of all financial assets—were again being run by the state in the early 1980s (Rosende and Reinstein 1986).

By December 1984 the accumulated losses of the financial sector represented more than 200 percent of the sector's equity and reserves and 18 percent of GDP (Valenzuela 1989). To continue to have access to international credit markets, the government had to guarantee all foreign loans of the banks that it had taken over while rescuing local depositors. The government also took over many nonfinancial companies, as well as the private pension funds (Administradoras de Fondos de Pensiones [AFPs]) that were linked to the troubled banks, either because they had unpaid loans from the banks or because they were owned by the same economic conglomerates (Rosende and Reinstein 1986). Between 40 and 90 firms were taken over by the state, giving rise to the so-called *área rara* ("gray sector"). Hence in the 1982 crisis, the state once more became the controller of many previously privatized firms. This new period of state control was fairly short-lived, and firms were not considered to be truly state-owned.

The trigger of the crisis may have been international in origin (a large rise in the prime lending rate in 1981 plus a moderate fall in the terms of trade), but the impact was amplified by mistakes in economic policy, some of which were related to the privatization process. The Chilean financial system was sufficiently fragile that the rise in interest rates, coupled with the stoppage in capital inflows, weakened the new conglomerates, most of which had high debt-to-asset ratios. The mechanisms used for privatization in the 1970s led to concentrated property holdings and gave rise to conglomerates that were highly leveraged (Sanfuentes 1984). In many cases, the buyers of banks used bank deposits to pay the loans incurred in acquiring the banks. When nonfinancial firms were privatized in 1976–77, the new owners of banks also used their clients' deposits or loans from other financial institutions to buy the firms. As mentioned, the buyers were required to put up collateral for 150 percent of the loan used to buy state-owned firms, but shares in the firm could be used as collateral. In this way, large and highly indebted conglomerates were formed.

The lack of regulation in the banking system made it easy for the banks to lend money to related firms, and even when restrictions were imposed on related lending, they were easily eluded. In the case of the two main banks, 21 percent and 50 percent of all loans went to conglomerate members.

Bank regulators did not keep track of the quality of the loan portfolios. Ideology played its part in the lack of regulation, since government economists argued that if the banks were receiving deposits, private investors must have decided that the projects to which the banks were loaning money were profitable, and regulation was unnecessary. However, the regulators failed to realize the effect of implicit deposit insurance on their assumptions. In 1976 depositors in a failing newly privatized bank had been protected from losses, which created the perception among depositors of the existence of implicit state insurance. Moreover, investors in the conglomerates believed that they were too large to fail (Vergara 1996). Regulatory changes to monitor the quality and supervise the concentration of bank loans were put in place only in 1982; a stringent new banking law was not introduced until 1986.

In addition to the financial resources from their affiliated banks, the two largest conglomerates managed mutual funds (82 percent), insurance companies (53 percent), and pension funds (68 percent) that granted them even more control over the economy (Sanfuentes 1984). These institutions bought shares of firms in the conglomerate, thus raising share prices. The indebtedness of the conglomerates resulted in part from the level of real interest rates in the 1975–81 period, which was high because of the excessive demands for credit from the conglomerates to buy even more privatized firms. The high real rates were compensated by capital gains in the stock market. In 1981 the government allowed banks to contract loans abroad, which led to a rapid increase in indebtedness. Firms that had access to international loans obtained credit at much lower rates than could smaller firms with no access. In less than two years foreign debt doubled, with the two largest groups holding 52 percent of the debt.

Starting in 1985 the banks that had been taken over began to be privatized once again. Preferred shares representing 70 percent of equity were sold to new buyers. The banks sold their bad loans to the central bank and were recapitalized. In return, the central bank became a claimant on future profits of the banks.[9] When selling the two major banks, the government strove to create a broad-based class of shareholders for two reasons: to provide stability and to make it more difficult to reverse the privatization process. The mechanism was so-called "popular capitalism": buyers were required to put only 5 percent down, while CORFO gave them a 15-year loan for the remainder. There was a 1-year grace period at a zero real interest rate, a 30 percent discount for timely repayment of the loan, and generous tax benefits. The number of shares per buyer was limited (and limits were enforced). Three additional banks were sold to groups of investors.

The two main conglomerates had been the owners of the larger AFPs (Provida, Santa María, San Cristóbal, and Alameda), which held 68 percent of workers' pension funds. The two largest (Provida and Santa María) were sold under the popular capitalism scheme (without the tax benefits).

Aetna, which owned 49 percent of AFP Santa María, bought enough shares to get control, while the rest went to small buyers. Banker's Trust bought 40 percent of the shares in Provida, with the remaining shares going to small buyers. The other two Afps were merged and auctioned under the name of AFP Unión.

After their recapitalization, the government also auctioned the other firms it had taken over. In most cases, a controlling package was auctioned, but in contrast to the procedures of the 1970s, the government required that payment be up-front. Local conglomerates in association with foreign investors bought the major companies. To make the auctions more attractive to foreigners, they were allowed to pay with Chilean bonds that were selling in the market at 60 percent of par value. Unfortunately, little information is available about the details of the transactions of that period, as there seem to be no clear records.

The Privatization of the Historic SOEs (1985–89)

In the period 1985–89, the government privatized 27 firms and closed down 3 other companies, while creating 29 companies by splitting up larger SOEs. Only 3 of the SOEs created were entirely new (Zofri, Metro, and Cotrisa). In particular, 11 water and sewage companies were created from the national water works. The firms that were sold in this period

Table 5.5 Revenues from Privatization of Chilean Public Enterprises, 1985–89
(US$ million)

Firm	1985	1986	1987	1988	1989	Total
Electricity firms (13)	16.4	124.3	393.0	632.5	77.9	1,244.1
Telecommunications firms (3)	0.9	55.6	35.5	344.0	192.1	628.1
Soquimich	4.7	85.4	71.5	60.9	0.0	222.5
CAP	12.1	139.5	53.2	0.0	0.0	204.8
ECOM	3.2	0.2	0.0	0.0	2.8	6.2
IANSA	0.0	8.8	1.0	50.8	8.0	68.6
Lab. Chile	0.0	2.8	3.8	18.1	3.1	27.8
Schwager	0.0	0.0	6.1	2.2	7.0	15.3
ENAEX	0.0	13.4	0.0	0.0	0.0	13.4
Isegen	0.0	0.0	0.0	0.0	5.6	5.6
LAN Chile	0.0	0.0	0.0	7.0	75.9	82.9
Chilefilms	0.0	0.0	0.0	4.5	0.0	4.5
Isevida	0.0	0.0	0.0	0.0	8.8	8.8
Total	37.3	430.0	564.1	1,120.0	381.2	2,532.6

Source: Corporación de Fomento (CORFO) annual reports.

were pre-1970 SOEs or firms that were spin-offs of pre-1970s SOEs that were created in order to be privatized. The state sold 12 pre-1970s SOEs and 14 firms that were spin-offs of SOEs, as well as two other firms that were acquired in the 1970s and had been kept for strategic reasons. Most of the firms sold in this period were utilities and included 13 electric and 3 telecommunications companies (table 5.5).

Four different privatization mechanisms were used in this period. The first was through best price offers for the firm or for controlling packages in open international auctions. The second mechanism was the auction of noncontrolling packages of shares on the stock market. A third mechanism was the direct sale of shares to the workers of privatized companies, public employees, and small investors—the so-called labor and popular capitalism. Workers and public employees financed the purchases of shares by using their severance benefits and loans from public institutions at subsidized interest rates. Private pension funds participated in the privatization process through the acquisition of packages of shares in the stock market. Finally, public utility users that needed to connect to the system or increase the capacity of their connection were required to pay for the infrastructure in return for shares in the company (Bitrán and Sáez 1994).

Privatization during the 1990s

The first elected government after the military regime (1990–94) stopped the privatization process almost completely, in contrast to the second elected government (1994–2000), which gave new life to the privatization process. From 1994 to 2001, 14 companies were privatized while 4 others were closed down. During the same period 12 new firms were created, 10 of them being subdivisions of Emporchi, the port authority. By late 2001, 38 firms remained in public hands; 14 of these were pre-1970 SOEs, and 24 had been created after 1980, mainly by splitting up traditional SOEs. The current SOEs include the largest copper mining company, the oil refinery, 9 regional water and sewage companies, the post office, the subway, a copper refinery, 10 ports, the post office, and a commercial bank.

Between 1994 and 2000 the government used public auctions to sell the state-owned transportation companies: two shipping companies (Empremar and Transmarchilay), a cargo railway company in the northern part of the country (Ferronor), and the cargo railway company in the central zone (Fepasa). It also sold the remaining 27 percent of the national airline on the stock exchange. Ferronor bought the northern rail system, which consists of several lines that run from mines in the Andes to ports and carry minerals. It has been a successful company. Fepasa got the cargo concession in the rail system south of Santiago, but the lines were kept by the state (which also kept the money-losing passenger rail system). Unfortunately for this second company, the rail lines were in worse shape than expected, as was the case with the rolling equipment. Moreover, its hold-ing company had financial problems, and initially Fepasa made some busi-ness mistakes. Hence, it is only after several years in private hands that it has been able to achieve positive operational flows.

During this period, the state also completed the privatization of the electric power sector. Edelnor was privatized in the 1991–94 period. In 1995 Codelco, the state-owned copper mining company, hived off and then sold its thermal power plant (Tocopilla). A 37.5 percent stake in Col-bún was sold in 1996. Before the sale just over 15 percent of Colbún was traded on the stock market. In December 1997 the government auctioned 4.65 percent of Colbún in the stock market, selling its remaining shares in 2001.[10]

The two most important privatizations of the 1990s were those of the three largest water and sewage companies. Unlike other public services, the military regime did not privatize sanitation services. The need to raise rates significantly before it became feasible to privatize these services was a hindrance to the sale of the water companies. The military government felt that privatization followed by a substantial price hike would have been politically unpopular. In fact, in the late 1980s, water rates were on aver-age less than half of what was needed to finance provision of the service, with prices covering less than 20 percent of outlays in the desertic north-ern regions. Before privatization, however, rates had to be raised so that the water companies could cover their costs.

Modernization of the water and sewer sector began in 1977 with the creation of the Servicio Nacional de Obras Sanitarias (Sendos). This en-tity absorbed several agencies belonging to different ministries and made it possible to reduce the work force from 10,000 to 3,000. Apart from regulatory responsibilities for the whole sector, Sendos was charged with providing water services to the regions. In the same year, state-owned wa-ter companies were set up based on preexisting companies both in the Santiago metropolitan region (Emos) and in the central zone, or Region V (Esval). In 1989, 11 regional joint-stock companies affiliated with CORFO were created out of Sendos.

In 1988 a new regulatory framework was set up for the sector, closely matching its electricity sector counterpart. The new rate system allowed for the self-financing of efficient firms. Pricing zones with relatively homoge-neous costs were also established. The new pricing system was introduced gradually in 1990, and charges rose by an average of 90 percent in real terms between 1990 and 1994, although the rate adjustment process was still not complete in all regions. The rise in prices was steeper in areas with higher costs, exceeding 500 percent in some cases, and by 1998 average re-gional water rates ranged from $0.43 to $1.21 per cubic meter. Arrears were cut from 7.9 percent in 1990 to 2.9 percent in 1994, as a result of a business-oriented approach and by the possibility of cutting off service to customers in arrears. In 1994 the average rate of return on equity among public water companies was 6.3 percent.

The Frei administration decided to privatize water companies. However, it wanted to strengthen the regulatory framework before selling the firms, since it was not totally satisfied with the way the regulation of privatized public utilities was working. In 1995 the administration sent a bill to Congress improving the rate settlement process. Congress approved the bill in December 1997 after a prolonged and heated debate, since it was assumed that the bill was in preparation for privatization.

The privatization of the water sector began in 1998. Since then the three major water and sewerage companies have been sold. A scheduled rate revision took place in the two major sanitation companies after privatization. The revision resulted in a 20 percent increase in the rates of both firms. The increase is more or less in line with the 10 percent cost of capital estimated for the sector (the public firms had a 7 percent rate of return on equity), and the sale prices reflect these numbers. The privatized firms are investing in sewage treatment plants and this will lead to further rate hikes. In 2002 the government was in the process of franchising its remaining water and sewerage companies.

Data on Privatized Chilean Firms

Given the history of the privatization process described above, the data are difficult to obtain in usable form. We excluded from our analysis privatizations that took place between 1975 and 1979, first, because most firms that were privatized during that period were managed by the government for only a few years. Second, the political and economic turbulence of the 1970s renders available information highly idiosyncratic. In fact, economic data from 1971 to 1973 show significant distortions, and the economic recovery did not start until 1976. Moreover, accounting standards were lax and were changed in 1982. Hence, in this chapter we focus on the 54 firms privatized from 1979 to 2001. Two of these are insurance companies and are thus excluded from the sample, which includes only nonfinancial firms. Two water companies that were privatized in 1999 have also been excluded, since there is only one year of postprivatization data. Of the remaining 50 firms, only 34 are publicly traded on the stock exchange and thus are required to provide financial information to the public, while the other 16 have no public disclosure requirements.[11] However, we were able to access the information of 3 of the firms in the latter group (Empremar, Fepasa, and Ferronor) and they have been included in the sample.[12] This leaves 37 firms for which we have usable data.

Data Problems

The basic source of information is the so-called FECUs (Ficha Estadística Codificada Uniforme), the standardized quarterly reports that companies with publicly traded shares (plus some other firms designated by law) must provide the Chilean Securities and Exchange Commission. The December FECU typically includes the annual financial report and other information, including the number of workers in the firm.[13] FECUs have been required since 1982 and are available in digital form.[14] Before the important changes in the accounting standards introduced in 1982,[15] the accounting information of firms was not standardized; it is thus less descriptive of the true financial status of firms. An additional source of information is the annual company reports. However, the data in the annual reports are not standardized and are therefore less useful.

No source exists for the following data at the firm level: number of white- and blue-collar workers, average wages, salary differentials, and output price indexes. Another important data limitation is the lack of readily available physical data, since the output of some products is described only in the annual reports; the products themselves change between annual reports; and, finally, we have no price index of these products. As an example, a steel company might produce steel in ingots and as sheets and bars, iron ore, and other products. Should we assume that physical productivity has gone down because steel ingots per worker have fallen, or does that decline result from a change in the demand for ingots as compared to steel bars and iron ore, for instance?

In principle, one might look at sales per worker as an index of productivity, and we do this. However, most of the firms we analyze either are regulated or face very few competitors, so that prices are not determined in a free market environment. More sales per employee after privatization could therefore be attributable to either higher prices or higher productivity, or to a combination of both factors. In our analysis, in addition to working with the whole sample of firms, we analyze the performance of the group of regulated and unregulated firms. Our definition of a regulated firm is slightly ad hoc: a firm is regulated if the government, through interventions in the market or through rate regulation, has the ability to change its profitability.[16] This implies that all electric distribution companies are regulated for our purposes, as are local and long-distance telephone companies.[17] IANSA, the sugar refining monopoly, is a doubtful case, since high trade barriers protect it. IANSA was assumed to be unregulated, but results do not change if we group it among the regulated firms.

We have defined investment as the difference between net physical assets (that is, accumulated depreciation is subtracted from accumulated investment) at time t minus the same variable at $t - 1$.

To measure the impact of privatization on firms, we exclude the two years immediately before and after privatization. As described in La Porta and López-de-Silanes (1999), there is a potential cleansing effect in the accounts before the sale of the company, while the two years following privatization might not be representative of the postprivatization performance if the firm is still undergoing a reorganization process. Hence, we compare years three to five before privatization with years three to five after privatization. Nevertheless, we have examined the data in the three years before privatization to get a feeling for the cleansing effect.

Treatment of Mergers and Divestitures

Using data three to five years before and after privatization creates its own set of problems. Some firms were spun off just a short period before being privatized. For instance, Chilectra was divided into three firms before privatization. Six regional distribution companies, Colbún, and smaller generating companies were spun off from ENDESA. The problem is that preprivatization FECUs for the newly independent firms do not exist, and determining the change in performance caused by privatization is therefore not straightforward. Similarly, in the case of mergers, we do not have postprivatization independent FECUs. In these cases we have to rework the data in order to assign the assets of the original firms to each daughter firm. Conversely, when the firms are merged, we have to "disassemble" the merged firm into its original constituents.

The procedure we follow is to assign the different variables in proportion to their fraction of the merged firm at the time of privatization. For example, suppose that firm A splits off from firm Z and both are privatized. To obtain data on a variable prior to privatization, we take the data at privatization and consider the proportions of that variable for the combined firm. We then assign the data in the combined FECU or variables not in the FECU (before privatization) in those proportions. A similar procedure is used to analyze data for merged firms.

Data Adjustments

To eliminate the effect of economic conditions on the performance of firms, we also present normalized comparisons. Subtracting the average values of the performance ratios for the two-digit SIC group to which they belong normalizes firm performance ratios. Although the two-digit decomposition encompasses widely differing industries, going to more digits in the decomposition would not have been useful, since the firms in question represent most if not all of the industry at more detailed SIC levels. We have subtracted the two-digit averages rather than using ratios because of the extreme variations in these ratios, which would have given excessive weight to some observations. Moreover, the interpretation is simple: if an adjusted ratio for a privatized firm is negative, the ratio for that firm is worse than the average of that variable in its (two-digit) sector. Some two-digit average ratios have been treated differently because of the extreme variation in the data. For example, consider the ratio of net income to sales (or to property, plant, and equipment) for a small timber company in the control group that sells a forest. This is nonoperational income, there are very few sales, and the ratio of net income to sales is astronomical. In these cases we have taken the sum of net income for firms in the control group and divided it by total sales of the firms in the control group to obtain a more reasonable result.

Effects of Privatization on Chilean Firms

We analyze the firms before and after privatization both in terms of absolute performance and by comparing them to a benchmark given by the average behavior of their sector at the two-digit level, as mentioned previously. The first part of the analysis in each subsection is devoted to unadjusted data. Perhaps the most interesting result we obtain is the difference between the performance of regulated and unregulated firms. Detailed tables and figures showing the pre- and postprivatization performance appear in the appendix.

Profitability

Before privatization, in contrast to Mexico (see La Porta and López-de-Silanes 1999), Chilean SOEs were fairly profitable. That was the case for most of the large SOEs that were privatized, as shown in table 5.6, so the firms did not have to go through the large changes that were required in other countries. Even though, on average, privatized firms were profitable, several smaller firms (and a few large ones such as ENDESA in 1985) did have losses before privatization. If anything, at the time there were complaints that the government was selling the crown jewels. Hence, the scope for efficiency benefits from privatization was relatively small.

Table 5.6 Net Income to Equity for Privatized Firms before Privatization, 1970–86

Firm	1970	1974	1979	1983	1986	Year privatized
CAP	10.9	0.5	0.2	0.7	2.3	1986
Chilectra	0.5	−3.2	2.6	4.6	—	1986
CTC	0.7	−4.1	1.7	11.9	10.9	1987
ENDESA	0.3	−4.3	2.4	6.4	4.9	1988
ENTEL	−0.7	−3.4	12.3	13	35.4	1988
IANSA	−9.3	12.1	−9.8	−24	5.5	1988
Lab. Chile	4.1	7.9	0.5	−196.4	12.8	1989
Soquimich	−65.3	11.9	−7.9	10.1	30.8	1986

— Not available.
Source: Sáez 1996.

Using table 5A.1 of the appendix, which is analogous to the first part of table IV in La Porta and López-de-Silanes (1999), we can analyze profitability before and after privatization. If we consider the profitability variables—operating income to sales (OI/S), operating income to physical assets (OI/PPE, or property, plant, and equipment), net income to sales (NI/S), and net income to physical assets (NI/PPE)—we observe that there seems to be a significant change in the profitability ratios before and after privatization. In particular, we observe that NI/S rose from less than 2 percent to 13 percent, on average, and that NI/PPE rose from less than 4 percent to more than 16 percent. Moreover, the profitability measures are strongly positive.

This change in profitability, however, comes mainly from the change in the results of regulated firms. While the profitability ratios improve for the group of unregulated firms, there is enough variation in the results that we cannot show that the change is significant. The important ratio NI/PPE increases from a low of 4 percent to a fairly reasonable rate slightly above 12 percent. By contrast, in the case of regulated firms the change in profitability ratios is far more important. The ratio NI/PPE rises from 3.5 percent to 20.5 percent, and the same pattern of large increases in profitability of regulated firms occurs for the other profitability ratios.

When we consider adjusted variables (appendix table 5A.4), obtained by normalizing the profitability ratios by subtracting the average ratio of their sector, we find that the improvement is less significant. This implies that part of the improvement observed in the unadjusted data can be explained largely by a simultaneous improvement in the average profitability of the sector. Nevertheless, the ratio NI/PPE for the sample of firms rises from 1.5 percent above the average in the sector to almost 10 percent. What is interesting is that the profitability ratios with respect to sales are not significantly different from those of the industry as a whole, which seems to indicate that the increased profitability is related to better use of physical assets or, alternatively, to overinvestment before privatization.

As in the case of unadjusted variables, most of the change in profitability results from the increase in the profitability ratios of the regulated firms. While adjusted profitability of unregulated firms increases after privatization, the increase is insignificant. Moreover, the profitability of these firms is not significantly different from that of the other firms in their sector. By contrast, all adjusted profitability ratios except for NI/S increase significantly after privatization in the group of regulated firms. Moreover, these firms, which had average profitability similar to that of their sectors, became much more profitable afterward, seeming to indicate that the regulators were unable to pass the gains in efficiency on to consumers.

Efficiency

Efficiency is described by the ratios of cost per unit (cost/sales) and sales to physical assets (S/PPE), shown in appendix table 5A.2. The cost-per-unit ratio falls by a small but significant amount at the 10 percent level for the sample of privatized firms. The S/PPE ratio falls slightly but insignificantly. Once again, there is a large difference in the behavior of regulated and unregulated firms. Cost per unit falls significantly for regulated firms, while it barely changes for unregulated firms. Similarly, the S/PPE ratio increases significantly (at 10 percent) for the regulated firms, whereas it falls for unregulated firms.

When we examine adjusted efficiency ratios (appendix table 5A.5), we observe that there is no difference between the privatized firms and the cost per unit in their sectors, and there is no change postprivatization. Moreover, for this ratio there is no difference between regulated and unregulated firms. Things are different for the S/PPE ratio, since the privatized firms seem to have much higher ratios than the average for their sector.

Assets and Investment

Appendix table 5A.3 shows variables related to assets and investment. We use net investment, defined as the year-to-year difference in the depreciated stock of fixed assets. The average value of the logarithm of physical assets (the log of the geometric mean of PPE) shows a slight increase, which is not significant, after privatization.[18] The change is concentrated in the regulated firms, where the effect is statistically significant. The investment to sales ratio (I/S) fell after privatization but not significantly. This would seem to indicate that firms invested more productively. An alternative explanation is that SOEs that operated in a competitive setting were investing efficiently before privatization so there was not that much scope for improvement.

The ratio of investment to physical assets (I/PPE) for the whole set of firms fell, but again, the effect is not statistically significant. There was a fall in this ratio for the unregulated firms and an increase for regulated firms (again, insignificant). The ratios of investment per employee (I/employee) increased, but not significantly. Physical assets per employee (PPE/employee) increased significantly after privatization. This seems to imply that workers had access to better equipment, but what is interesting here is that it is in the unregulated firms that the increase is more significant (at 10 percent).

When we consider adjusted ratios (appendix table 5A.6), no significant changes appear in the behavior before and after privatization, except for the investment-to-sales (I/S) ratio, which is lower than average in the sector before privatization and approaches the average—but is still lower—

after privatization. This effect is significant both for the whole sample of firms and for the regulated firms.

Productivity

In appendix table 5A.2 we show the labor productivity ratios of sales to employees and operating income to employees. Both of these ratios show that productivity increased significantly as firms became private, as expected. Once again, however, most of the change was attributable to the behavior of regulated firms, for which sales-to-employment ratios increased by 88 percent and operating-income-to-employment ratios rose by 325 percent. We were unable to obtain employment data for all the firms in a sector at the two-digit level, so we have not been able to compare the growth in productivity of privatized firms with the other firms in their sectors.

We have also examined physical productivity for firms for which we could obtain measures of physical product (tons, passengers per kilometer, gigawatt hours [GWh], and so forth) as shown in appendix table 5A.8. We have used these variables to construct productivity ratios, and then we have taken the percentage difference before and after privatization. The results show that firms increased their productivity by about 25 percent on average after privatization, but there is enough variation in the data that this is not significant for the whole sample nor for regulated or unregulated firms separately. Some caution is required in the use of these data, however: most firms have more than one line of production, and therefore a fall in physical productivity on the basis of one product may mean nothing. As an example, the airline LAN Chile seems to have decreased its productivity in terms of passengers per kilometer after privatization. However, after privatization, the firm launched a successful cargo branch, the revenues of which are generally on par with those of the passenger segment of the company. Therefore, the data in this section may show that productivity has increased in physical terms, but without the prices of these different products and their production, this comparison is not very informative.

Employment

As can be seen from table 5.7, there is no evidence that firms fired workers during the 1983–92 period, which includes the years in which the firms were privatized. In fact, it appears that firms took on more workers on aggregate. Moreover, it is clear that SOEs reduced their employment levels several years before they were privatized (more than three years in most cases). However, different firms were privatized at different times, and therefore it is interesting to see if this continues to hold for the complete sample of privatized firms, considering the time at which they were privatized. To examine this issue, we use appendix table 5A.7. Again, there is

Table 5.7 Employment Changes in Privatized Firms, 1970–92

Firm	1970	1973	1979	1983	1986	1992	Year privatized
CAP	7,025	11,637	9,321	6,519	6,667	9,643	1986
Chilectra	NA	4,250	4,196	3,846	4,133	4,712	1986
CTC	5,887	7,252	7,206	6,338	6,938	8,504	1987
ECOM	188	341	333	165	149	—	1986
ENAEX	344	340	394	388	470	—	1987
ENDESA	6,512	8,504	4,270	2,705	2,905	2,980	1988
ENTEL	1,161	1,458	1,236	1,338	1,402	1,748	1988
IANSA	2,827	2,881	1,597	1,079	2,027	1,561	1988
Lab. Chile	3,608	4,546	2,059	1,372	883	797	1989
Soquimich	10,814	10,684	7,109	4,096	4,704	3,242	1986

— Not available.

Note: ECOM went bankrupt before 1992.

Source: Sáez (1996), except data for 1992, which is from the FECUs (Ficha Estadística Codificada Uniforme). Data for ENDESA (apart from 1970) from Hachette and Lüders (1994). Data for Chilectra from Sáez (1996), except for 1986 and 1992. Those years obtained by aggregation of all the firms that were originally part of the firms in 1980 using data in Hachette and Lüders (1994) for 1986.

no evidence that firms fired workers after privatization. Employment increased slightly but not significantly after privatization: the average firm grew from 1,193 to 1,381 employees. Both regulated and unregulated firms grew in size. Note that on average, unregulated firms are larger.

Privatization of Regulated Sectors: The Efficiency of Privatized Utilities

In this section we provide an assessment of the privatization-cum-regulation process of electricity and telecommunications companies carried out between 1985 and 1989. The evaluation considers the aims of the privatization efforts, namely, to provide capital for expansion of utilities that the state was not able to fund at the necessary level, to enhance the efficiency of enterprises, and to transfer those efficiency gains to consumers. In the previous section we showed that SOEs increased their profitability and efficiency after privatization. These changes, however, are in line with those of their corresponding industries in the case of unregulated firms. But firms that provide regulated services stand apart. Their profitability increased more than did that of their unregulated counterparts. This difference must be attributed to the interplay between privatization and regulation.

The Privatization Process

The government privatized most of the telecommunications and electricity industries between 1985 and 1989. Some of the smallest companies were sold through public auctions. Larger firms were privatized through a variety of mechanisms: sale of shares on the stock market; the periodic auction of packages of shares on the stock market; and the direct sale of shares to employees of privatized firms (labor capitalism), public employees, and small investors (popular capitalism).

In the late 1970s the telecommunications industry was dominated by two public enterprises: CTC, which provided basic telephone service throughout almost the entire country, and ENTEL, the only international long-distance provider. These two companies shared the domestic long-distance market. The state also owned two regional local telephone companies (CNT and Telcoy) and Correos y Telégrafos, which provided telegraph service. In 1982 the government sold CNT and Telcoy through public bidding. However, the privatization of the large telecommunications firms started only in 1985. By the end of 1987, 25 percent of the equity of CTC was in private hands. In 1988 the government sold 45 percent of the ownership of the company to a foreign investor. In the case of ENTEL, in 1985 and 1986 the government sold 30 percent and 3 percent, respectively, of its shares, most of which were acquired by pension funds. In 1988 the state further reduced its stake in ENTEL to 37.7 percent. This time, company workers were the main purchasers (12.5 percent). The revenues from the privatization process of the main telecommunications firms appear in table 5.8.

The privatization of the two largest electric power companies (ENDESA and Chilectra) started in 1986. To create competition in the wholesale electricity market, they were restructured before privatization. The restructuring involved separating distribution from generation. ENDESA, the largest company, was divided into six generating companies, six distribution companies, and two small, isolated companies combining generation and distribution in the southern part of the country.

Table 5.8 Privatization of Chilean Telecommunications Firms, 1984–89
(US$ million)

Firm	1985	1986	1987	1988	1989	Total
ENTEL	0.2	36.7	8.4	81.8	105.0	232.2
CTC	0.7	4.7	27.1	262.2	87.1	381.7
Telex	0	14.2	0	0	0	14.2
Total	0.9	55.6	35.5	344.0	192.1	628.1

Source: Corporación de Fomento (CORFO) annual reports.

Table 5.9 Privatization of Electric Power Firms, 1984–89
(US$ million)

Firm	1985	1986	1987	1988	1989	Total
Distribution						
Chilmetro	10.0	36.0	83.3	0	0	129.3
Chilquinta	2.4	11.1	18.7	0	0	32.2
Emec	0	6.0	7.5	0	0	13.5
Emel	0	7.9	0	0	0	7.9
Emelat	0	0	9.7	0.9	0	10.6
Emelari	0	0	0	0	3.1	3.1
Eliqsa	0	0	0	0	4.8	4.8
Elecda	0	0	0	0	6.1	6.1
Generation[a]						
Endesa	0	0	180.0	585.4	63.8	829.2
Pullinque	0	0	62.0	0	0	62.0
Chilgener	4.0	22.2	31.8	33.8	0	91.8
Pilmaiquen	0	41.1	0	0	0	41.1
Integrated						
Edelmag	0	0	0	4.8	0.1	4.9
Total	16.4	124.3	393.0	624.9	77.9	1,236.5

a. Excludes Pehuenche, which was sold as a project for $7.6 million.
Source: Corporación de Fomento (CORFO) annual reports.

Chilectra was divided into three firms: a generating company and two distribution companies. Most of the firms were under private control by 1989. The revenues from the privatization process of the main electricity firms appear in table 5.9.

The Regulatory Framework

Some services provided by utilities were considered to be natural monopolies, and therefore the development of regulatory institutions preceded their privatization. Regulatory bodies were created in the late 1970s for each sector: the National Energy Commission (CNE) and the Undersecretariat of Telecommunications, respectively. They are responsible for granting operating licenses, monitoring technical standards, and setting rates for services where competition is insufficient. Regulation, operation, and, to some extent, policymaking had previously been in the hands of the SOEs themselves. Moreover, new regulatory legislation was introduced in 1982. The aims of these laws were to create the conditions for competition to arise whenever possible and to guarantee, in cases where there was insufficient competition, that the efficiency gains expected from privatization would be transferred to consumers.

Under these rules, concessions to operate utility services are not exclusive, and objective, nondiscriminatory criteria govern the granting of licenses. Only technical reasons, as in the case of mobile telephony, may limit the number of operators. At the same time, legislation mandates that service be provided within the area of the concession, defines continuity and quality standards, and requires interconnection with other firms when regulators deem this to be necessary. Rates of regulated services are based on the long-term marginal cost of a hypothetical efficient firm. Prices are set every four (electricity distribution) or five (basic telephony) years, and within the price-setting periods they are indexed to the prices of the main inputs used to provide the service. The separation of rates from current costs is intended to create an incentive for firms to be efficient.

Chile's regulations did provide for open access to essential facilities but did not initially regulate access charges. Moreover, Chilean legislation does not preclude vertical integration. Thus, in 1992 Enersis, a holding company that owned distribution companies supplying 44.4 percent of the market in the Central Interconnected System, took control of ENDESA, the largest power generation company, which in turn owned the main transmission system. It is fairly well known that regulated monopolies that are vertically integrated into unregulated segments may have an incentive to sabotage their downstream competitors (Beard, Kaserman, and Mayo 2001). Accusations by their competitors that integrated monopolies were discriminatory led to regulatory changes. In 1994 the telecommunications law was amended to mandate the regulation of access charges to the local telephone network. In 1997 the Antitrust Commission instructed ENDESA to recharter its transmission subsidiary as a public corporation and open its ownership to the participation of other shareholders. ENDESA sold the transmission subsidiary in 1999.

The Electricity Sector. Legislation regulating the electric power sector distinguishes among three distinct activities: generation, transmission, and distribution. Only distribution firms need concessions. Distribution licenses are granted for indefinite periods but may be canceled if the quality of service falls below the legal standard. Power-generating firms and transmission companies within the same area must interconnect, and they must coordinate their operations through an economic load dispatch center (CDEC). This center's aims are to guarantee the most economical operation of all generating facilities, to guarantee the right of power-generation companies to sell energy at any point in the system, and to safeguard the security of the system. All plants must be available for dispatch (refusal to provide energy when requested can lead to severe penalties), unless maintenance has been scheduled. The optimal operation of the various facilities, independently of existing supply contracts, calls for transfers of energy to be made between power generators at the so-called *spot price*, which is the operational (or marginal) cost of the most expensive plant in operation at a given time.

The Chilean regulatory system distinguishes between large and small customers. Large customers, with maximum power demands above 2 megawatts (MW), are free to negotiate the terms of their supply with the various generating firms. Small customers, in contrast, purchase energy from distribution companies at regulated prices, which are made up of two components: the node price, at which the distribution firms buy energy from power-generation firms, and the value added of distribution, which pays for distribution services. Distribution charges are computed for the various urban or rural areas in such a way that an efficient firm operating in an area with those characteristics would make a 10 percent return on the net replacement value of its assets. This charge is calculated as a weighted average of the findings of outside studies contracted by the industry and the national energy commission, respectively, with the commission study accounting for two-thirds. This figure is applied to the real firms to calculate average profit levels for the industry over the net replacement value of assets. If these average profit ratios are more than 14 percent or less than 6 percent, distribution costs are adjusted to the nearest of the two ranges.

The node price, in turn, has two components: the price of energy and the price of peak power. To guarantee stable rates for small consumers, the price of energy is computed every 6 months as an average of the marginal costs expected over the next 48 months, using projections of demand, fuel prices, water reserve levels, generating plants under construction, and the indicative investment plan drawn up by the national energy commission. The price of peak power is defined as the annual cost of increasing power during peak hours with the least expensive type of plant. This cost is increased to take into account the reserve margin (or security level) of the system.

Large customers (including distribution companies) are required to have contracts with generating companies. In turn, every power-generation company must have the capacity to meet the yearly energy contracts, bearing in mind potential dry spells that would affect the hydroelectric plants and the average capacity of thermal-generation units. Power-generation firms must also be able to satisfy peak demand, measured as the average gross hourly demand they have undertaken to supply their customers at the system's peak times. A yearly determination is made of power and energy deficits or surpluses incurred by the generation companies with respect to their supply contracts that would give rise to transfers between producers. The terms of energy transfer arrangements are negotiated between the firms, while transfers of peak power are made at the price set by the regulatory commission.

Finally, power-generating firms pay the marginal cost plus a fee (the "basic" fee) for the use of the transmission lines. Given that there are significant economies of scale in building lines, marginal-cost pricing does not allow for recovery of all transmission costs. The difference between the total cost of a line and the revenue collected through marginal costs is designated as the basic fee. Then, for each line, the basic fee has to be distributed among the various power-generating firms. The basic fee is negotiated between the transmission company and the generating company, and disagreements must be settled by arbitration. The assignment of the basic fee cost of a line among the various generating firms is based on the firm's demand at the moment of maximum total demand. The foregoing criteria have no solid conceptual basis, particularly with respect to the assignment of the entire transmission cost to the generating firms.

Telecommunications. The legislation governing telecommunications generally provides for free market pricing of telecommunications services. However, rates are regulated for those services that the Antitrust Commission considers to be provided under conditions of inadequate competition.[19] The telephone companies themselves, on the basis of guidelines set by Subtel (Subsecretaría de Telcomunicaciones, a department under the Ministry of Transportation and Telecommunications), carry out the studies that are used to set rates. The companies hand in these studies to Subtel, which has 120 days to present its objections and counterproposals. A committee of three experts arbitrates disagreements between the companies and Subtel, with respect to both guidelines and objections. The company appoints one member of the committee, the regulator appoints the second one, and the two parties agree on the third. Although the regulators make the final decision, they tend to follow the recommendations of the experts, since the companies are otherwise likely to go to court.

The ambiguities of the 1982 law had created a legal monopoly in the long-distance service market. In 1989 a number of companies applied to Subtel for licenses to operate this service. The final decision was not handed down for several years because of the indecisiveness of the courts as to whether or not vertical integration of local and long-distance service should be allowed. Finally, in 1993 the Antitrust Commission authorized the participation of local telephone companies in the long-distance market. In 1994 the law was modified to introduce competition to long-distance service through a multicarrier system, and following the ruling of the commission, it imposed restrictions on local telephone companies that wished to operate in the long-distance market. In the first place, they had to do so through subsidiaries organized as independent joint-stock companies, subject to supervision by the Superintendent of Securities and Insurance (the Chilean Securities and Exchange Commission). The law also required that local telephone firms not discriminate among long-distance carriers with respect to quality of service and information on long-distance traffic demand. Moreover, the charges to access the local network were regulated.

In 1988 the government set standards for mobile telephone service, although an early entrant had had a concession since 1981. The new regulations created two concession areas for mobile service, with two licenses in each area, to be granted on a first-come, first-served basis. In November 1996 Subtel granted three nationwide personal communications system (PCS) licenses, using a "beauty contest" in which geographic coverage was the key bidding variable. Until 1999 subscribers had to pay the same fee for both the calls they made and the calls they received, which was a disincentive to the use of mobile phones. In February 1999 the regulator introduced a "calling party pays" principle, under which callers pay for all charges (including the regulated access charges) when using mobile phones.

Evaluation of Privatization in the Regulated Sectors

An assessment of the privatization efforts carried out at electricity and telecommunications companies between 1985 and 1989 should consider the objectives of the process. As we mentioned earlier, the goals were to increase the efficiency of these firms and to invest in new capacity. Therefore, a complete evaluation of the privatization-cum-regulation process would require, as a counterfactual, a prediction on how the privatized firms would have developed had they remained in the public sector. Here we take a more modest approach. We analyze, for each sector, the post-privatization evolution of a set of variables and relate their behavior to the regulatory changes. In particular, the comparison between regulated utilities and those that operate in competitive markets makes it possible to draw inferences regarding the effectiveness of the regulatory system. In some cases, the differences are so significant that inferences can be drawn despite the obvious limitations of this approach.

The Electricity Sector. Between 1988 and 2000 electricity generation grew from 16,914 GWh to 39,142 GWh, and installed capacity rose from 4,016 MW to 10,045 MW. In the Central Interconnected System, capacity grew less than electric generation, as peak demand grew at a lower rate during those years because of the use of peak-demand pricing.[20] Moreover, power-generating firms have generally invested earlier than required under the government's indicative investment plan. Despite the installation of new capacity ahead of the plan, there have been periods of energy shortages in the system because of its heavy dependence on hydroelectric power (in rainy years, such as 1992, 97 percent of generation is provided by hydroelectric power). These outages, however, seem to have been caused by regulatory failures.

Small customers face regulated (forward-looking) energy prices. This price inflexibility, however, should not be an obstacle to market clearing even in very dry years. If generating companies were to compensate users by an amount equal to the outage cost per unit of undelivered energy during a severe drought, this would make users indifferent to a reduction in their energy consumption, so that in theory, the supply deficit should be eliminated.[21] Unfortunately, this compensation mechanism has never been used. Changes to the law (introduced at the suggestion of the largest hydroelectric operator) eliminated these compensations when the drought is more severe than in the driest year that is used in computing the node price, leaving an incomplete price system. Moreover, no procedures were introduced to deal with that case. After the 1998 blackouts the law was modified and now imposes compensations under all circumstances. In response, generators have not renewed their contracts with distributors to supply energy at the node price, leading to an impasse.

Labor productivity in the privatized companies has improved considerably. In ENDESA power generated per worker rose from 2.2 GWh in 1989 to 18.1 GWh in 2001 (table 5.10). If we consider only employees working in the holding company and in the generation subsidiaries, the power generated per worker rose from 6.3 GWh in 1991 to 28.7 GWh in 2000. Labor productivity in electricity distribution also grew substantially after privatization. For example, Chilectra, the largest distributor, has more than doubled its annual sales of electricity since privatization, from 3,612 GWh in 1987 to 9,253 GWh in 2001, and its customer base has grown from 973,000 to 1,289,000. The number of workers, meanwhile, fell from 2,587 to 722, and the number of clients per worker grew from 376 in 1987 to 1,785 in 2001. In addition, energy losses fell from 19 percent to 5.4 percent in the same period (table 5.11).

Table 5.12 shows the node prices in the two main interconnected systems (Sistema Interconectado Central and Sistema Interconectado del Norte Grande) in current dollars and pesos. There has been a clear downward trend in energy prices since generating firms were privatized. In constant pesos, the drop is approximately 33 percent for the central system and 73 percent for the northern system. This drop is explained primarily by the decline in the prices of fuels used at the thermoelectric plants (partly due to the appreciation of the peso), which play a part in determining marginal prices. In the central system, the fall was particularly sharp from 1997 onward, owing to the anticipation of the arrival of natural gas supplies from Argentina (recall that the regulated price of energy is forward-looking). A greater load factor as a fraction of installed capacity (that is, the system operates closer to capacity) and the transfer to consumers of these gains in productivity also help explain the lower prices. The profits of the main power-generating company have increased moderately since privatization, reaching a peak of 15.7 percent return on equity in 1995 and declining in the following years. This decline is a result of unfavorable hydrological

Table 5.10 ENDESA: Investment, Power Generation, and Labor Productivity

Year	Investment, domestic (US$ million)	Investment, foreign (US$ million)	Domestic generation (GWh)	Local workers		Labor productivity[a]	
				All	Generation[b]	All	Generation
1988	—	—	7,420	—	—	—	—
1989	110	—	6,649	2,980	—	2.2	—
1990	—	—	6,608	2,883	—	2.3	—
1991	131	—	8,521	2,445	1,357	3.5	6.3
1995	180	119	11,783	2,255	1,038	5.2	11.4
1999	301	362.4	13,672	1,383	711	9.9	19.2
2000	145	78	15,346	888[c]	574	17.3	26.7
2001	—	—	15,741	—	—	—	—

— Not available.

Note: GWh = gigawatt hours.

a. In GWh per worker.

b. Assumes that 30.5 percent of employees work in transmission in 1991 and 1992 (the 1993 figure).

c. The reduction in the labor force is partially explained by the sale of the transmission subsidiary.

Source: ENDESA (Empresa Nacional de Electricidad) annual reports.

Table 5.11 Chilectra: Sales, Employees, Labor Productivity, and Energy Loss

Item	1987	1988	1989	1990	1995	2000	2001
Sales (GWh)	3,612	3,844	4,070	4,230	6,676	8,854	9,523
Customers	973	1,008	938	935	1,100	1,262	1,289
Employees	2,587	2,565	2,144	2,159	1,801	867	722
Labor productivity[a]	376	393	437	433	610	1,455	1,785
Sales per worker[b]	1.4	1.5	2	2	3.7	10.2	12.8
Energy losses (percent)	19.8	18.8	16	14	9	5.2	5.4

Note: GWh = gigawatt hour.
a. Customers per worker.
b. GWh per worker.
Source: Chilectra annual reports.

Table 5.12 Change in Node Prices and Residential Rates

	Node price			Residential	
Year	Central[a]	North[a]	Central[b]	North[b]	Central[b]
1987	22.2	53.4	2.4	5.9	14.73
1988	26.1	49.7	2.9	5.6	15.87
1989	26.8	51.7	3.3	6.4	16.97
1990	22.6	59.5	3.0	7.9	18.15
1991	19.3	47.8	2.6	6.5	15.83
1992	18.9	36.9	2.9	5.6	15.72
1993	20.4	37.8	3.1	5.7	15.08
1994	21.1	34.7	3.7	6.1	15.31
1995	18.4	23.1	3.7	4.6	15.44
1996	15.4	23.5	3.1	4.8	14.65
1997	12.7	18.8	2.7	4.0	13.77
1998	10.7	14.0	2.1	2.8	12.16
1999	11.4	11.4	2.1	2.1	12.16
2000	14.9	13.7	2.6	2.4	—

— Not available.
a. October 2,000 pesos per kilowatt hour.
b. Current US cents per kilowatt hour.
Source: National Energy Commission (CNE).

conditions and the fact that the installation of more efficient combined-cycle gas turbines and the arrival of natural gas from Argentina have reduced the economic value of existing plants.[22] Note that the fall in profitability in generation led to further labor productivity gains in the late 1990s.

Regulation of distribution firms has been less successful. According to data from the Ministry of Economics, the value added (that is, the charge to consumers) of distribution for Chilectra fell by 18 percent in the rate-setting process of 1992 and by an additional 5 percent in the rate-setting process of 1996. However, this price reduction does not match the efficiency gains achieved after privatization. This situation led to increases in the profits of distribution companies. The return on equity obtained by Chilectra increased from 8 percent in 1988 to 32 percent in 1996–98. In the 2000 rate-setting process, rates were reduced by a further 18 percent, which led to lower profit margins at first. In response, Chilectra increased labor productivity substantially. The rest of the industry has gone through a similar process.

The profit levels in distribution are much higher than those of the generating companies, which in any event are subject to greater risks, both for lack of a secure market (they operate under competition) and because of the potential for droughts (table 5.13). Some of the distribution industry profits come from unregulated services that are unlikely to become competitive, because they are closely related to regulated services, as in the case of the renting of meters. Distribution companies also obtain significant returns by allowing phone and cable TV companies to hang cables on their poles. However, these returns are not considered when estimating the income of the efficient firm, so, in effect, consumers can pay more than twice for the same infrastructure.

Telecommunications. Since privatization, the telecommunications sector has experienced rapid growth, as shown by all indicators. Between 1987 and 2001, the number of lines in service rose by a factor of almost six, so the line density rose from 4.7 to 23.1 lines per 100 inhabitants (table 5.14). In the main local phone company (Telefónica), which accounts for 76 percent of all subscribers, average installation time was reduced from 416 days in 1993 to 6 days in 2001, and the waiting list, which in 1987 included 236,000 people, had been reduced to 32,000 by 2001, having reached a peak of 314,000 in 1992. Digital conversion rose from 36 percent in 1987 to 100 percent in 1993. Long-distance traffic also grew significantly. Outgoing international traffic rose by a factor of 10, from 21.2 million minutes in 1987 to 241.0 million minutes in 2001. Growth was especially rapid after the introduction of competition in long-distance services (table 5.14). The number of lines per worker in the largest telecommunications firm grew from 74 in 1987 to 845 in 2001 (table 5.15).

This period also saw the emergence of new services, such as beepers, data transmission, private networks, and the Internet. However, the new

Table 5.13 Profits of the Main Electric Sector Companies: 1987–2000
(percent)

	Distribution				Generation			
Year	Chilectra	CGE	Chilquinta	Saesa	ENDESA	Gener	ElectroAndina	Edelnor
1987	—	18.5	8.8	17.6	5.2	3.1	—	−7.7
1988	7.4	19.7	12.4	19.9	13.7	7.8	—	−2.8
1989	21.3	17.8	19.5	25.9	7.7	8.4	—	−0.7
1990	22.9	17.5	19.5	25.2	6.4	9.4	—	3.3
1991	19.4	16.5	21.7	26.6	10.4	7.4	—	3.0
1992	17.3	16.7	42.3	24.9	13.5	7.3	—	3.4
1993	14.5	18.3	15.7	27.1	11.0	8.6	—	3.4
1994	17.9	17.1	7.9	22.5	15.7	8.4	—	7.2
1995	27.6	21.1	9.5	24.8	14.5	11.6	—	2.3
1996	32.1	22.0	19.8	26.3	12.7	9.5	—	0.1
1997	31.8	20.0	11.8	22.2	9.9	10.3	5.6	2.5
1998	31.6	20.2	9.3	18.6	3.6	5.9	8.2	2.6
1999	20.6	16.9	111.3ᵃ	16.4	−13.5	0.8	6.2	−0.9
2000	16.0	15.3	8.9	29.2	9.1	0.3	8.8	−3.9

— Not available.
a. Profits of Chilquinta in 1999 include nonrecurring profits from sales of shares.
Source: Authors' computations from FECUs (Ficha Estadística Codificada Uniforme).

Table 5.14 Telecommunications Statistics, 1987–2000

Year	Lines in service (thousands)	Density (lines/100 inhabitants)	Mobile phones (thousands)	International traffic (millions of minutes)
1980	363	—	—	8.0
1985	537	—	—	13.4
1988	631	4.9	—	27.5
1989	689	5.4	4.9	29.9
1990	864	6.5	13.9	38.8
1991	957	7.8	36.1	47.0
1992	1,283	9.6	64.4	53.1
1993	1,521	10.9	85.2	59.5
1994	1,634	11.6	115.7	63.5
1995	1,891	13.2	197.3	113.6
1996	2,264	15.6	319.5	144.2
1997	2,693	18.3	409.7	198.8
1998	2,947	20.4	964.2	215.0
1999	3,109	20.6	2,260.7	210.2
2000	3,365	22.0	3,401.5	222.5
2001[a]	3,581	23.1	5,271.5	241.0

— Not available.
a. December 2001 (estimated).
Source: Subtel.

service that has had the greatest impact is mobile services. At the end of 1997, 16 years after the entry of the first operator, there were only 410,000 subscribers. This number rose sharply with the fall in prices brought about by the entry of new PCS concessionaires. By mid-1998, the number of subscribers had risen to 650,000. With the introduction of the "calling party pays" system in February 1999, the number of subscribers jumped again. By the end of 2001 the number of subscribers had reached 5.3 million.[23] This explosion in the number of mobile phones is partially explained by the high level of the access charge to mobile companies set by the regulator. This charge was set too high, so mobile phone companies have been willing to give away the phones in order to benefit from the access charge paid on incoming calls.

Real residential local telephone charges have increased by about 5 percent since privatization (table 5.16). However, there was a simultaneous rebalancing of rates, which makes it difficult to reach definite conclusions about the evolution of charges. Before 1993 phones rates were much higher for business subscribers than for residential clients. Moreover, clients have benefited from the extension of basic phone

Table 5.15 Telefónica-CTC: Basic Fixed Phone Statistics

Year	Lines (thousands)	Share	Workers[a]	Lines per worker[a]	Installation time (days)	Waiting list (thousands)
1980	360	99.3	6,911	52	—	150
1985	505	94.1	6,894	73	—	181
1988	592	93.7	7,518	79	—	236
1989	646	93.8	7,366	88	—	284
1990	812	94.0	7,530	108	—	308
1991	997	94.3	7,994	125	—	241
1992	1,213	94.5	7,991	152	—	314
1993	1,437	94.5	8,133	177	416.0	198
1994	1,545	94.6	7,424	208	208.9	117
1995	1,754	92.8	7,449	235	169.8	52
1996	2,056	90.8	7,073	291	55.4	72
1997	2,394	88.9	6,898	347	38.6	97
1998	2,650	89.9	6,917	383	35.4	58
1999	2,592	83.4	5,649	459	15.4	27
2000	2,701	80.3	4,639	582	4.3	10
2001	2,723	76.1	3,223	845	5.7	32

— Not available.
a. Excludes employees working in subsidiaries.
Source: Subtel and CTC annual reports.

zones. In fact, many calls that were previously considered long-distance calls are now considered local calls. In 1993 rates were 8.6 percent higher than they were in 1987 as a result of the 1988 rate-setting process. In the 1993 rate-setting process residential rates were further increased by 9.8 percent. This rate hike was explained by the need to compensate for the partial elimination of subsidies from long-distance service to local service and the unification of residential and commercial rates. Starting in 1994 access charges for long-distance calls were substantially reduced.

The 1999 rate-setting process can be considered a turning point. Basic phone rates were reduced by 11 percent, at the same time that access charges to the local network were reduced by an average of 72 percent. As a result, in 2001 basic phone rates for an average family were still 5 percent higher than in 1987, but access charges for long-distance calls were much lower. The deregulation of long-distance service in 1994 eliminated the need for rate-setting in that market. Deregulation coupled with the reduction in access charges to the local network led to a dramatic fall in long-distance rates. This is illustrated by the value of a one-minute call to the United States, a route that represents 42 percent of international traffic. In 1987 the average per minute cost of a call to the United States was

Table 5.16 Cost of Local Monthly Telephone Service for the Average Family

Year (May)	US$	May 1987 pesos
1987	11.62	9,853
1988	11.00	9,151
1989	11.24	8,347
1990	13.44	9,475
1991	15.69	10,213
1992	17.75	10,156
1993	18.91	10,817
1994	19.96	11,742
1995	24.36	11,584
1999	23.57	11,432
2000	19.43	10,137
2001	17.11	10,340

Note: Fixed charge plus variable consumption, including value added tax.
Source: National Institute of Statistics (1987–98), authors' estimations for 1999–2001.

$1.51. If the regulated rate-setting process had remained in place, the price today during normal hours would have been $2.40, instead of the current price of about $0.10.[24]

Since long-distance companies, as well as other telecommunications operators, require access to local networks in order to provide service, it became crucial to regulate fees for access to the public network. In the 1994 rate-setting process, the regulator established the rule that the access charge for incoming and outgoing domestic long-distance calls and outgoing international calls would be 0.63 times the charge for a local call, which is higher than the real cost of providing the service. Even worse, the per minute access charge for incoming international calls was set at a rate that was 14 times the local rate during normal hours and 84 times the local rate during reduced-rate hours. High access charges to local networks, coupled with strong competition in the industry on the part of the market leader, Telefónica-CTC, meant that many long-distance operators had serious financial difficulties during the 1994–99 period. The local telephony companies, which were allowed to operate in the long-distance market through subsidiaries, had incentives to charge below cost on long-distance calls, since by lowering rates long-distance traffic would increase and the companies would benefit from the higher revenue arising from access charges to the local network, a reward that the other long-distance companies did not have. In response, the 1999 rate-setting process reduced access rates by an additional 62.7 percent on national and international outgoing calls. In the case of incoming international traffic, the charge was reduced by 97.5 percent in normal hours and by 99.6 percent in off-peak periods (from the previous high levels). The average reduction in regulated access charges was about 72 percent.

Prices of mobile telephony have also declined sharply with increased competition. At the end of 1997 subscribers paid a fixed charge of 15,000 pesos plus 130 pesos per minute for calls made as well as calls received. The entry of ENTEL PCS in March 1998 led to a marketing war among operators that entailed heavy spending on advertising and brought about a significant decline in prices. In early 1998 Telefónica-CTC offered 60 free calling minutes for a fixed monthly charge of 7,080 pesos and billed additional outgoing minutes at 124 pesos during normal hours and 80 pesos during reduced-rate hours. In addition, customers who signed a two-year contract received the mobile phone for free. Other plans offered 200 free calling minutes for 16,000 pesos. Clearly, increased competition significantly reduced rates.

The profitability of Telefónica-CTC increased after privatization and remained high until 1997, as shown in table 5.17. Regulators were unsuccessful in passing Telefónica-CTC's efficiency gains on to customers. This state of affairs changed in 1998, as Telefónica-CTC began to shift investment toward competitive sectors such as mobile telephony and long-distance. The rate-setting process of 1999 that lowered local rates and access charges to the local network also had a large impact on

Table 5.17 Profits of Telecommunications Enterprises, 1987–2000
(percent return on equity)

Year	CTC	CNT	Telcoy	ENTEL	Telex	BellSouth
1987	11.5	20.1	20.5	56.4	n.a.	n.a.
1988	12.7	26.7	23.9	73.6	n.a.	n.a.
1989	17.8	18.7	26.2	73.8	57.4	n.a.
1990	12.9	20.2	15.6	52.7	21.9	n.a.
1991	16.2	22.7	16.7	50.5	14.5	n.a.
1992	19.4	29.2	22.8	49.7	28.3	n.a.
1993	23.0	30.2	30.4	37.4	58.9	n.a.
1994	18.7	24.9	32.2	17.2	16.5	0.0
1995	17.3	13.7	29.2	8.4	10.2	−70.4
1996	20.9	21.0	37.3	2.4	5.6	−250.3
1997	18.7	18.6	39.0	5.1	−29.9	−1.0
1998	10.8	24.1	47.8	−3.8	−41.5	62.6
1999	−3.8	24.6	36.3	7.0	−30.1	−3.0
2000	−8.5	15.7	20.0	6.3	−45.1	1.1

n.a. Not applicable.
Source: Authors' figures, based on companies' annual reports.

Telefónica-CTC. Moreover, Telefónica-CTC suffered from the devalu-ation of the peso (20–30 percent) that began in 1998, since it had not hedged its dollar-denominated debt. Another negative effect was the decline in demand growth and the increase in nonpaying clients attribut-able to the economic slowdown that began in late 1998. Finally, Telefónica-CTC is responsible for the access charges to mobile phone companies of its nonpaying clients, and these access charges are 20 times higher than those that Telefónica-CTC can charge.

Telefónica-CTC has implemented a strict cost reduction plan, which in-cludes a drastic reduction in the number of workers. This cutback results from the elimination of inefficiencies in the firm as well as the reduction in planned investment made necessary by the decline in profitability brought on by the new rates and slower economic growth. This increase in effi-ciency allowed the company to achieve modest profits in 2001 after two years of large losses. Since severance payments are large, part of the ex-planation for the losses is the cost of scaling back the level of employment in the company.

The two basic regional telephone companies that are dominant in their respective areas (Telcoy and CNT) were less affected by the rate-setting process and have maintained their profit levels. ENTEL is in the opposite situation. While it was a regulated monopoly provider of long-distance services, its rates were much higher than the cost of providing service, which allowed it to have profit levels of above 50 percent for several years. Deregulation led to dramatic falls in long-distance rates and profits (see table 5.17). In 1998 the company reported losses result-ing from the strong competition in long distance, its restructuring costs, and the cost of entry into the mobile telephony market, where it has be-come one of the key players. In 1999 and 2000 the firm showed profits once again, in part because of the asymmetric access rates between the fixed and mobile networks and its successful marketing approach in mobile telephony.

In short, the telecommunications sector has been one of the most active in the last few years, and only since 2001 has a slowdown become noticeable. The increased competition in the sector has had a favorable effect on consumers, who are spoiled for choice. Even in local calls, a market that is monopolized in most countries, the market share of Tele-fónica-CTC has declined from 94 percent in 1987 to 76 percent in the year 2001. There are substantial unresolved regulatory problems, how-ever. The most important revolve around the principles that should guide the regulation of access charges. The central issue is that, apart from the direct effect on the profitability of the company, high access rates present a cost on competitors. One dilemma is whether access charges should be based on costs adjusted for the demand facing a company—a principle that Telefónica-CTC claims represents a subsidy to the competition and that the competition deems essential for survival—or if rates should be symmetric for identical services. The inclusion of fixed costs is also an issue in this regard: should they be included in the cost calculations? Finally, a further issue is whether time-metering of calls or access is appropriate when capacity is not a constraint (at least for standard telephone calls) due to technological change.

The underlying problem is that in the case of access charges, price competition can break down. Consider a situation in which users value outgoing calls more than incoming calls and Telefónica-CTC's access rates are set low, while its smaller rivals have high regulated rates due to their higher costs. A Telefónica-CTC client would pay the regulated rate for calls within the Telefónica-CTC network, but a higher rate for calls to Telefónica-CTC's rivals. Conversely, a rival's client faces a cheaper rate to call a Telefónica-CTC phone. Since Telefónica-CTC is by far the largest company, with 76 percent of all telephone lines, most of the other providers' calls end up on Telefónica-CTC's network in any case. Since the competitors pay a low access rate for these calls, they might be able to charge a low rate for phone service even though their own networks are more expensive. Thus, the rivals can gain market share at the expense of Telefónica-CTC by having high access charges. Of course, if users also value incoming calls, this incentive to raise access charges is smaller since clients will not appreciate the fact that people are reluctant to call them because it is expensive. Nevertheless, on balance, heavy users of outgoing calls are more attractive to firms than clients who put more weight on incoming calls.

At the same time, the last mile is an essential facility in telecommunications. Last-mile technology is any telecommunications technology, such as wireless radio, that carries signals from the telecommunications facility along the relatively short distance (hence, the "last mile") to and from the home or business. Cable companies usually have access to the last mile, but other operators (long-distance, mobile telephony, Internet access providers) require access to the local telephone network (or to the cable network) to reach consumers. A wireless fixed system, WLL, has not been as successful as expected. Since Telefónica-CTC faces regulated rates, it has incentives to become a monopoly in the competitive sectors (Beard, Kaserman, and Mayo 2001). It can achieve a monopoly by nonprice discrimination against the other operators. To reduce this risk and preserve competition in the other markets, the regulator may prefer to incur the social cost of having more than one last-mile service provider. Which option is better depends on the extent of economies of phone-line density.

Infrastructure Franchises

By the early 1990s continuous high growth rates for the preceding years had led to congestion and severe quality problems in highways, seaports, and airports. Even though the government had increased the expenditure in infrastructure several times over the minuscule amounts spent during the 1980s, they were insufficient. Therefore, franchising became the hope for rehabilitating and expanding public infrastructure. In 1992 a franchise law was passed allowing the private sector to finance and operate highways, airports, and other infrastructure.

Franchises have other advantages in addition to solving the problems of governments that do not have the resources (financial, managerial, and supervisory) to provide for infrastructure needs.[25] First, when the same firm is in charge of construction and maintenance, it has better incentives to invest in nonverifiable quality; second, justifying cost-based tolls is politically easier when the project is a private concession; third, the cost of the project is imposed on users and not on the rest of society; and fourth, there is a built-in screening mechanism against socially wasteful projects, since a project with a negative private return will most likely also have a negative social return. Moreover, when franchise auctions are open and competitive, tolls or user prices should be close to average cost, which is second-best optimal in the presence of economies of scale.

From 1994 and 2004, 32 projects were auctioned for a total of about $5 billion; about 18 are already operational. In addition, in 1997 a law was passed allowing franchises of the infrastructure of public ports. Currently, more than 2,000 kilometers of interurban highways together with the main airports and seaports are privately managed. Even though the system has been remarkably successful, several challenges remain. One of these is how to incorporate flexibility in order to react to changed conditions (for instance, unexpected permanent increases in traffic that require widening a road or raising the toll) while at the same time keeping a reputation for not renegotiating contracts when the franchise is losing money or for not expropriating money-making franchises. Another problem is that most of the profitable private projects have been franchised, and the projects that remain require government subsidies to attract interested bidders. The existence of government subsidies, however, negates many of the advantages of infrastructure franchises, and the optimal approach to franchising in this case is equivalent to the traditional approach of franchising the building of the road out to the lowest bidder and financing it up-front with public funds (Engel, Fischer, and Galetovic 2002).

Highways and Airports

The private sector has financed the construction of new highways and airports through build-operate-transfer concessions (table 5.18). More recently the government has extended the range of concession contracts to the building of water reservoirs for irrigation and to penal complexes

Table 5.18 Concessions in Operation

Project name	Project origin	Investment (US$ million)	Franchise length (years)
Northern access to Concepción	Public	214	28
Access to Santiago's Airport	Public	9	12
La Serena Airport	Public	4	10
Route 78, Santiago— San Antonio	Public	172	23.7
Road of La Madera	Public	31	25
Road Nogales— Puchuncaví	Public	12	22
Road Santiago— Los Andes	Private	131	28
Route 5, Chillán— Collipulli	Public	192	21
Route 5, Los Vilos— La Serena	Public	244	25
Route 5, Santiago— Los Vilos	Public	251	23
Route 5, Talca— Chillán	Public	171	12.5
Route 5, Temuco— Río Bueno	Public	211	25
Carriel Sur Airport, Concepción	Private	25	16.5
El Loa Airport, Calama	Private	4	12
El Tepual Airport, Puerto Montt	Public	6	12
Iquique Airport	Public	6	12
El Melón tunnel	Public	50	23

Source: Ministerio de Obras Publicas.

(appendix tables 5A.9 and 5A.10).[26] In general the auction process for concessions has operated as follows. The government sets the minimum technical specifications of the project and grants a concession for 20 or 30 years to the bidder offering to charge the lowest user price for building, operating, and maintaining the project. Bidders must first go through a technical vetting process that qualifies them to make an economic bid. A ceiling and a floor price are imposed. If the ceiling is reached, the bidders compete on the minimum subsidy requested. If the floor price is reached, the firm that offers the largest payment to the state wins the concession.

The first project, a $42 million tunnel, was put out to tender at the end of 1992, was completed on time at very close to the budgeted cost, and was inaugurated in 1995. The most important franchised highway project has been the improvement of the Pan-American Highway, with a total investment estimated at $2.4 billion and total length of 1,511 kilometers. The project was divided into eight segments and put out to tender, with concessions awarded over a two-year period. The final stretch, adjudicated in May 1998, runs from Santiago to Talca, with an estimated cost of $750 million. The concession will last 25 years. Starting in 1995 contracts for building and operating the cargo and passenger terminals of the eight main airports were awarded in a public bidding process. Airport concession-holders have invested about $271 million, of which $200 million were spent in Santiago.

Concessions raise important regulatory issues. There are end-point problems, especially regarding maintenance close to the end of the concession period. The length of infrastructure concessions and the rigidity of the contract rules pose a major dilemma. For instance, in cases of congestion, welfare maximization may require increases in the user fee set in the original contract. The question is how to share the increased income, since the firm bid on a lower price and unless it gets a fraction of the increased revenue, prefers to keep the lower price. However, when bidders expect contracts to be renegotiated, the benefits of competitive bidding are largely lost, since the firm's ability to negotiate, or its lobbying capacity, counts as much as or more than its efficiency (Williamson 1976). Shortening the concession period is not a solution, since concessionaires would not have enough time to recoup their investments, necessitating government subsidies.

The Melón Tunnel illustrates these problems. Although it had no cost overruns and was built on time, it has not been successful and is unlikely to recoup the original investment (the firm has been incurring annual losses of about $1.5 million). The successful bidder fell victim to the winner's curse (fairly common in a newly developed system such as infrastructure concessions), having offered to pay substantially more than the runner-up. The concessionaire overestimated the demand for the road at the toll ceiling, since a significant percentage of drivers choose the old alternative road.[27] The winner claims that the lower-than-estimated demand results from the construction of new alternative roads and offers to reduce the toll if the government lowers the annual payment. Such an agreement would almost certainly be socially beneficial in the short run, but the government has refused to renegotiate on the grounds that it would set a dangerous precedent.

Franchise-holders have discovered that willingness to pay is less than anticipated when an alternative free route is available, even if an economic computation shows that the savings in time and wear and tear on the vehicle compensate for the toll. Even in cases in which alternatives are not competitive at all, demand can be highly variable and depend on macroeconomic and regional effects. Moreover, the traffic on a specific road depends on the other links in the highway network. Thus, government may affect the demand on a particular route when it alters the rest of the network, and government flexibility in this respect is obviously required.[28] The government dealt with this problem by introducing minimum traffic guarantees, which promise that if traffic flows fall below predetermined levels (usually equivalent to the toll revenues that would pay 70 percent of estimated construction costs), the government will make up the shortfall.

Giving guarantees to concession-holders makes it easier for bidders to obtain loans in the financial system, which translates into a larger number of bidders and therefore greater competition. At the same time, state guarantees have some disadvantages. First, they increase the chances that projects that are neither privately nor socially profitable will be undertaken. Private investors might push for higher estimated construction costs so that the guarantee covers all of their actual construction costs, even though they know that actual traffic would probably be much lower (given that the guarantee covers 70 percent of estimated construction costs). Second, it is inconvenient to eliminate all risks from the concession-holder during the highway operation period, because it would mean losing the benefits of private management. Third, guarantees create contingent liabilities for the government, but they are seldom valued and are excluded in the year-to-year budget or counted as government debt. However, guarantees carry a seldom-observed political economy advantage: if traffic falls far below expectations, the government can always point to the guarantees as a way of reducing the pressure to renegotiate the franchise contract.

To avoid some of the problems associated with standard auctions, the government has been experimenting with a new mechanism advocated by Engel, Fischer, and Galetovic (forthcoming) for auctioning infrastructure concessions.[29] In their proposal, the regulator sets the maximum toll that the concession-holder can charge and then awards the concession to the firm demanding the least present value of revenue (PVR) for building and then operating the highway until the required revenue is collected through toll payments. Hence, the duration of the concession is endogenous. This auction mechanism reduces the risk faced by the franchise-holder, because the present value of the total income the concession-holder will receive is known in advance.

An additional advantage of PVR auctions is that they are inherently flexible. Early termination of a concession is not a problem, if required, for instance, to widen the highway. If the government compensates the operator with the amount remaining to be collected minus estimated savings on maintenance and operation costs, this is a fair compensation to the franchise-holder. Hence, PVR greatly reduces the scope for disagreement. The authority could also adjust the toll charged by the franchise-holder to more closely approximate the optimal toll given the level of congestion.[30]

The highway linking Santiago and Valparaíso was auctioned using the PVR method. In February 1998, a Spanish consortium won the concession. It sought a present value revenue of UF (Unidades de Fomento) 11,938,207, or approximately $400 million, an amount it expects to collect in 15 years. The price-cap for the toll is 1,800 Chilean pesos (about $3). In this instance, the rules required that bidders seeking a minimum guaranteed income would have had to pay the government for this guarantee. Remarkably, two out of four bidders, including the winner, did not seek the guarantee. Thus, in principle, the state did not assume any risk.

Starting in 1999 the government has awarded four urban highway concessions in Santiago that represent a total investment of about $1.4 billion (two franchises for the improvement of a road that rings Santiago and two that cross Santiago in the north-south and east-west directions). Auctioning urban highways has proven more difficult than expected. First, in urban highways the range of government decisions influencing traffic is much broader than in interurban highways. The construction of access roads, the use of complementary or substitute routes, the expansion of the subway system, or the introduction of tolls on congested streets can affect traffic patterns. Moreover, the construction of highways generates urban problems. The construction of large-capacity urban expressways can cause the deterioration of the surrounding area. In Santiago people living in a well-to-do residential area adjacent to a proposed highway mounted a strong campaign against its construction. Although they could not prevent its construction, they forced major changes that increased the cost substantially. Ecologists have opposed urban highways because they believe highways will encourage car use and thereby increase pollution; instead they favor investing in public transport. While the argument is correct when the highways are free, it no longer holds when these highways have tolls that depend on the level of congestion.

Concessions for Port Management and Operation

There are 10 state-owned ports and 22 private ports in Chile. The state-owned seaports have natural advantages because of their better geographical locations. In general the private ports are used for bulk cargo, so they need less infrastructure than the state-owned ports, which tend to specialize in general cargo (normally in containers). This type of cargo requires calm waters for loading and unloading, so extensive works usually protect the state-owned ports.

Private participation in state-owned ports started in 1981 when private firms were allowed to perform the duties of loading and unloading ships at the docks, as well as on-port storage services. This change greatly increased efficiency in cargo handling, making it unnecessary to invest in expanding these ports, even though previously, under public operation, the ports were always congested. The port authority (Empresa Portuaria de Chile, or Emporchi), however, retained the management of all state-owned port infrastructure, that is to say, docking sites and storage facilities (Foxley and Mardones 2000).

In the mid-1990s, it became evident that rapid growth in foreign trade would, in the short term, render inadequate the cargo transfer capacity of state-owned ports. This was particularly true of ports located in the central zone of the country where, for geographic reasons, there is little potential for development of new ports. Chile has only a few well-protected bays and inlets, and most of these lie in the middle of urban centers. Expanding the number of docking sites at existing ports is possible, at least in the case of the port of San Antonio, but costly. In addition to these stumbling blocks, a dearth of stacking and storage space at the ports further compounds problems, since urban growth and sprawl have severely limited the ability of these port service areas to expand.[31] Finally, having multiple private operators conspired against the coordination of activities and investment in specialized gantry cranes for containers.

The government feared that inefficient port operations would have a multiplier effect on the costs of the transportation chain. Ships range from large, fast, and expensive types to slower, more sea-worn vessels. Since an efficient ship costs tens of millions of dollars, from the point of view of a shipping company the main cost of an inefficient port is not the fees for docking, loading, and unloading but rather the capital cost of the ship. Inefficient ports tend to be able to receive only slower, older, and smaller ships with higher operational costs. Hence, even in addition to having high docking and loading costs, inefficient ports raise the total transport cost of traded goods by much more and render a country uncompetitive in the international market for its goods. This was one of the fears of the Chilean government, since Chile is an open economy that depends on remaining competitive for its future growth.

The government believed that it was possible to expand the transfer capacity of the state-owned ports by increasing private participation in port administration and operation. Moreover, the government began to think of ports as consisting of terminals, known as *frentes de atraque*, which combine groups of docking sites and storage space that could function as independent units. By coordinating activities and internalizing all the benefits of investment in new equipment, a single operator would be the best way of operating a terminal. Based on this assessment, a bill was introduced in Congress for modernization of the state-owned port sector, which was enacted in December 1997. The law split Emporchi into 10 different SOEs or port authorities, one for each state-owned port, which were granted the power to award concessions to multiple or single private companies for the administration and operation of port infrastructure.

Granting concessions for state-owned port administration and operations posed certain risks to the sector's competitiveness. There are only three ports in the central zone of Chile (Region V), which is where most of the general cargo enters and leaves the country. Two of these ports are state-owned (Valparaíso and San Antonio), while one (Ventanas) is privately owned. Altogether, these three ports are endowed with seven *frentes de atraque*, but not all of these are able to berth large vessels. Additionally, it is necessary to consider that some terminals are especially built for transfer of containers, others for bulk cargo (where there is no lack of competition), and still others, for standard cargo.

In other countries, large-scale port users, mainly shipping companies, own their own cargo terminals, because such an arrangement provides operational advantages. In Chile, however, so few *frentes de atraque* are available that only a small number of users of significant size would be able to own their terminal. This would, of course, place other users at a great disadvantage. Even though regulations make it mandatory for prices to be made public and set on a nondiscriminatory basis, concessionaires can use subtle ways of discriminating against nonintegrated shippers that are difficult to prove and therefore to penalize. These methods include assigning the choice spaces in the holding areas to one company over another, providing one company with better service than others, using insider information, and manipulating docking reservations.

In drafting the port modernization law (Law 19.542), legislators took these problems into account and included several clauses designed to safeguard competition in the sector. First, the law requires that concessions be awarded through public auctions and for no more than 30 years. Second, concessionaires must be incorporated as publicly owned companies that are engaged in a single line of business. Third, the rates set by concessionaires must be made public and established on a nondiscriminatory basis. Fourth, proposed by-laws and internal regulations for concessions are required as an integral part of the rules of bidding. These rules must conform to objective technical and nondiscriminatory standards, especially with regard to assignment of spaces and reserve capacity.

The two port authorities in Region V put up for simultaneous public bidding three out of the six docking areas they owned. Two of these were the *frentes de atraque* capable of berthing the largest vessels at each port, while the third was the bulk terminal of San Antonio. The port authorities, in consultation with the Antitrust Prevention Commission, imposed additional conditions on concession-holders to prevent risks of abuse of a dominant position, as provided for by the law. Their conditions included ceilings on horizontal integration, restrictions on vertical integration, additional rules of transparency, reserving the right to set maximum prices to prevent low bidder turnout, and quality standards.

The rules specified, for instance, that significant users (defined as those that shipped more than 15 percent of the cargo in the region) should not own more than 40 percent of the stock or voting shares in the firms that operated the port franchises. According to the port authorities, it was necessary to limit significant users to a minority position in the company in order to reduce the possibility of discrimination. Concessionaires are required to grant any interested party expeditious access to information such as cargo contracts, service priorities, and types of cargo and consignees, so that all of the interested parties would have the same information. Finally, the port authorities can impose penalties for low quality of service. Minimum transfer speeds and maximum waiting times for ships are specified in the concession contracts.

The concessions were awarded in July 1999. In principle, each one was to be awarded to the bidder that offered the lowest maximum port transfer rate index, which was an average of four transfer charges. Nonetheless, in fairness to private port competitors, the rules of bidding for each docking front specified a minimum rate floor index. Moreover, the minimum rate floor has the beneficial effect of creating ex-post rents for the nonintegrated port, which implies that the incentives for underhand integration with a shipper and then discriminating against its competition are reduced. In the event that more than one bidder offered the minimum rate index established in the rules, a tie-breaking payment was to be offered in addition.[32] This payment was over and above the leasing payment that was established in the rules of bidding for the port infrastructure and was calculated on the basis of the economic value of the property.

The bidding attracted a great deal of interest, and a total of 21 bids were tendered by consortia made up of leading domestic and foreign companies, of which 19 included the minimum rate index, plus the additional tie-breaking payment. All terminals were awarded in the end on the basis of the tie-breaking payment amount. Consequently, the average rates for port services were reduced by more than 10 percent in the *frentes de atraque* that were awarded in concession, and the government was also able to take in revenues of $267 million, tripling its expectations (Foxley and Mardones 2000).

The results of the first years of operation have also satisfied the government's expectations, as can be seen with data for the Port of

Table 5.19 Valparaíso: Time Spent Loading and Unloading and Transfer Speed

Productivity measure	1999	2001	2002 (est.)
Loading, unloading (hours)	45.0	26.3	21.0
Transfer speed (containers per hour)	25.5	43.7	54.8

Note: Loading and unloading time is for a Eurosal vessel with 1,150 cargo movements.
Source: Empresa Puerto Valparaíso.

Valparaíso (table 5.19). The efficiency in port services increased substantially. Similarly, the transfer speed at the port of Iquique increased by 41 percent in just half a year.[33] Finally, at the franchised terminal at San Antonio, the main port, the transfer speed rose from 475 tons an hour to 635 tons an hour, an increase of 34 percent.[34] At the Valparaíso concession, investment in new cranes, computer software, and other equipment during 2001 topped $8 million, with another $27.5 million expected by 2006.

Conclusions

This section collects our results and presents some hypotheses that offer consistent explanations for these results. Unfortunately, the lack of information limits the verifiability of these hypotheses. First, we find that privatized firms experienced significant improvements in efficiency, but this improvement is no different from the change experienced by other private firms in their respective economic sectors. This allows us to conclude that Chilean SOEs were efficient before privatization, at least if we compare them with private firms in their respective sectors. Hachette and Lüders (1994) have noted this previously. This conclusion is consistent with the fact that employment levels in privatized firms were stable for several years before privatization and rose afterward. This is not surprising given that many years before privatization, state-owned enterprises had undergone reorganizations that were especially geared toward reducing the number of workers (see table 5.7).

Second, we find that there are significant differences in the postprivatization performance of regulated and unregulated firms. Hence, we report separate results for each group. We give an account of adjusted results, that is, where we have normalized the performance of firms with respect to the performance of their economic sectors at the 2-digit SIC levels. We focus first on the behavior of firms that were not regulated. Results for this group show no major changes in efficiency measured as unit costs and sales over physical assets after privatization. Since these firms operated in competitive sectors and their efficiency did not grow compared with other firms in their sectors, adjusted profitability should not show major changes after privatization, as is the case.

The postprivatization performance of regulated firms is quite different. The profitability of regulated firms grew after privatization. In fact, the ratio of net income over PPE rose substantially, while the ratio of income to sales also increased, though at a more modest rate. These firms enjoyed efficiency gains after privatization, but those gains are not statistically significant. Similarly, the cost per unit indicator shows a slight decrease, while the ratio of sales to PPE shows a modest increase. These results are consistent with efficiency gains resulting primarily from a more efficient use of capital (and probably a minor increase in regulated prices). There is some evidence that before privatization, regulated SOEs had overinvested in physical assets. This implies that privatization should result in higher profits rates, as observed.

The implication is that Chile's approach to incentive regulation has paid off, promoting efficiency in regulated firms. As shown, the efficiency gains in the regulated sectors that were privatized do not lag behind those of the unregulated privatized sectors. However, regulators have been unable to transfer all these efficiency gains to consumers. This should not come as a complete surprise. It is well known that regulation is an imperfect substitute for competition, and Chile is no exception. Moreover, the ability of regulators to transfer gains to consumers has recently improved substantially.

Certain aspects of the Chilean regulatory legislation and practice should be improved. In particular, the transparency of the rate-setting process should increase. Currently, regulators in the electricity and telecommunications sectors can exchange the information used to set rates only with the regulated companies; this prevents consumer organizations from countering the lobbying pressures of the regulated enterprises. The recent law regarding the water and waste treatment sector takes the opposite approach: all the information used in setting rates must be made public. However, it is not clear that this new law has been effective in restraining lobbying while at the same time limiting the possibility of regulatory takings.

The regulatory process requires improvement in access to information on the regulated firm. It also necessitates modeling an efficient firm, but this in turn requires information that is uniquely available to the real firm, since costs depend, among other factors, on topography, geographic density of customers, and demand. Regulators have encountered major problems in gaining access to company data, because legislation does not provide specific penalties for failure to deliver information or for submitting false information. Currently, when a company refuses to hand over information, the regulator must go to the courts, where the process is lengthy and penalties are low.

Another lesson that may be learned from the Chilean experience is the importance of properly regulating essential facilities. A 1982 law, for example, required the dominant local telephone operators to provide interconnection access for other operators requesting it, with the cost of access to be negotiated by the parties. However, the negotiation of these charges led to prolonged lawsuits that made it difficult for new companies to enter the market. A 1994 law solved the problem by regulating all interconnection charges. Similarly, Chilean legislation guarantees power-generating firms access to the transmission system, but the fact that the largest power-generating company owned the transmission system, combined with the fact that transmission tolls are negotiated, created some problems. In June 1997 the Antitrust Commission ruled that the power-generating company should divest its transmission assets to an independent company.

Other types of natural monopolies were also privatized: those related to infrastructure. In those cases, the rate-setting problem was solved by competition for the field (Demsetz 1968), auctioning franchises to the firms that asked for the lowest user fee. It has been a successful system. The main highways have been completely overhauled and their capacity has increased substantially, reducing internal transportation costs and making the country as a whole more efficient. Only a few potential problems remain. First, the traffic guarantees offered by the government to successful bidders created unaccounted liabilities; and, second, franchise-holders might be successful in lobbying the government for changes in the terms of their contracts. In fact, many contracts have already been renegotiated because the highway projects were awarded through agreements that omitted important details and thus had to be revised. This has meant a substantial (but not overwhelming) increase in the cost of the projects. At the same time, the government was able to remain firm when Tribasa (a company that had received three important highway concessions) failed to complete one of its projects on time, and this is an encouraging sign.

Seaport franchises have also been successful so far: investment has increased, port efficiency is higher, and ships require much shorter periods for loading and unloading. There have been no complaints from shipping companies that they are discriminated against in the franchised ports, so it appears that the horizontal and vertical integration restrictions on the port operators have served their purpose. Despite these favorable results, however, it is too soon to have a fair evaluation of the port franchises.

To summarize, privatization has benefited the country, even in the case of the regulated sectors. Market imperfections mean that it is not always easy to align the interests of private providers in regulated sectors and those of society as a whole. However, regulation has partially succeeded in this goal, in part because of ongoing fine-tuning.

Appendix 5A

Table 5A.1 Changes in Profitability of Privatized Firms

Variable	N	Mean before Median before	Mean after Median after	t-statistic for change in mean	Z-statistic for change in median	Test for mean before = 0 median before = 0	Test for mean after = 0 median after = 0
All firms							
Operating income/sales	37	0.1182 0.0835	0.2051 0.1512	3.6298*	−2.5459*	3.6213* 0.0000*	7.6211* 5,12E−09*
Operating income/PPE	37	0.0969 0.0624	0.2000 0.1269	2.5620*	−2.9784*	3.7906* 0.0000*	4.7129* 5,12E−09*
Net income/sales	37	0.0172 0.0192	0.1303 0.1459	3.2708*	−3.2811*	0.6074 0.1620	3.8679* 5,42E−07*
Net income/PPE	37	0.0386 0.0214	0.1636 0.0968	3.3633*	−3.5189*	2.8923* 0.0494*	4.7555* 6,17E−08*
Unregulated							
Operating income/sales	18	0.1113 0.0763	0.1797 0.1294	1.2527	−0.9808	1.8682 0.0038*	3.8725* 0.0006*
Operating income/PPE	18	0.1206 0.0711	0.2139 0.0788	0.9345	−0.7277	2.4296* 0.0038*	2.5125* 0.0006*
Net income/sales	18	−0.0331 0.0299	0.0461 0.0456	0.9706	−1.0124	−0.7044 0.2403	0.7687 0.0154*
Net income/PPE	18	0.0510 0.0402	0.1273 0.0476	0.9072	−0.5379	2.1953* 0.0481*	2.0011 0.0037*

(Table continues on the following page.)

Table 5A.1 (continued)

Variable	N	Mean before Median before	Mean after Median after	t-statistic for change in mean	Z-statistic for change in median	Test for mean before = 0 median before = 0	Test for mean after = 0 median after = 0
Regulated							
Operating income/sales	19	0.1247 0.0872	0.2291 0.1726	4.7276*	−2.8465*	4.0062* 0.0004*	7.9657* 1,91E−06*
Operating income/PPE	19	0.0744 0.0549	0.1868 0.1649	5.8026*	−3.6347*	4.4425* 0.0004*	8.2944* 1,91E−06*
Net income/sales	19	0.0649 0.0143	0.2101 0.2030	5.1091*	−3.3720*	2.1687* 0.3238	9.6619* 1,91E−06
Net income/PPE	19	0.0268 0.0019	0.1981 0.1607	4.5417*	−4.2478*	1.9231 0.3238	6.7673* 1,91E−06*

* Significant at the 10 percent level.
** Significant at the 5 percent level.
*** Significant at the 1 percent level.
Note: N = number and PPE = property, plant, and equipment.
Source: Authors' calculations.

Figure 5A.1 Cost per Unit before and after Privatization, Adjusted and Unadjusted

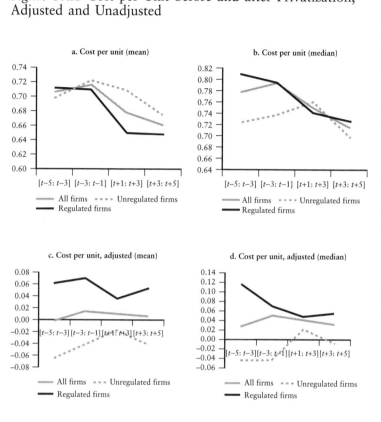

Note: t = year of privatization; the number represents the number of years before or after privatization.
Source: Authors' calculations.

Table 5A.2 Changes in Operating Efficiency of Privatized Firms

Variable	N	Mean before Median before	Mean after Median after	t-statistic for change in mean	Z-statistic for change in median	Test for mean before = 0 median before = 0	Test for mean after = 0 median after = 0
All firms							
Cost per unit	37	0.7049	0.6606	−1.8235	1.2595	22.8569*	21.9694*
		0.7769	0.7149			0.0000*	0.0000*
Sales/PPE	37	1.1686	1.1570	−0.2074	−1.1838	4.3087*	7.2498*
		0.5787	0.7487			0.0000*	0.0000*
Sales/employee	30	69284.4870	102795.0097	3.9218*	−2.1290*	5.4755*	6.5359*
		42013.6095	82924.2615			0.0000*	0.0000*
Operating income/ employee	30	14705.0275	25088.0736	2.8042*	−2.7795*	2.9264*	4.2550*
		4087.5993	13788.9867			0.0000*	0.0000*
Unregulated							
Cost per unit	18	0.6979	0.6747	−0.4239	0.3797	17.4061*	14.3750*
		0.7234	0.6978			0.0000*	0.0000*
Sales/PPE	18	1.7011	1.0906	−1.0359	−5.7266*	3.2401*	4.2907*
		0.6083	0.6532			0.0000*	0.0000*

	N						
Sales/employee	12	1.07647.9371	134806.9036	1.3016	−0.4041	4.0110*	3.7855*
		85164.2136	107110.7778			0.0002*	0.0032*
Operating income/ employee	12	29483.4651	39012.3794	0.8572	−0.1732	2.5880*	2.8487*
		6807.3028	22053.4960			0.0002*	0.0193*
Regulated							
Cost per unit	19	0.7116	0.6473	−2.7041*	1.4159	14.9651*	16.5470*
		0.8083	0.7257			0.0000*	0.0000*
Sales/PPE	19	0.6641	1.1394	1.6805	−1.8539	6.3889*	6.1465*
		0.5589	0.8323			0.0000*	0.0000*
Sales/employee	18	43708.8536	81453.7471	4.0624*	−2.9108*	6.2884*	8.6217*
		34940.3242	82345.8544			0.0000*	0.0000*
Operating income/ employee	18	4852.7357	15805.2031	5.8470*	−3.8915*	3.9250*	6.8893*
		3448.3215	13788.9867			0.0007*	0.0000*

* Significant at the 10 percent level.
** Significant at the 5 percent level.
*** Significant at the 1 percent level.
Note: N = number and PPE = property, plant, and equipment.
Source: Authors' calculations.

Figure 5A.2 Investment as a Fraction of Physical Assets (PPE) before and after Privatization, Adjusted and Unadjusted

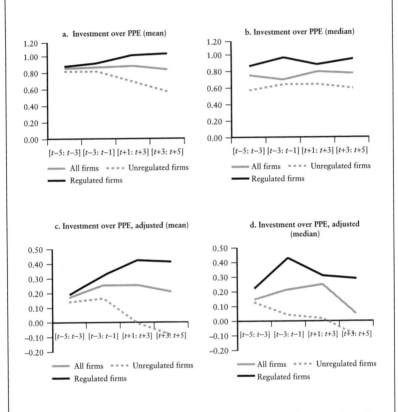

Note: PPE = property, plant, and equipment; t = year of privatization; the number represents the number of years before or after privatization.

Source: Authors' calculations.

Table 5A.3 Changes in Investment and Assets in Privatized Firms

Variable	N	Mean before Median before	Mean after Median after	t-statistic for change in mean	Z-statistic for change in median	Test for mean before = 0 median before = 0	Test for mean after = 0 median after = 0
All firms							
Log(PPE)	36	16.4534	16.7571	1.1599	−0.7658	41.4029*	38.2008*
		16.3349	16.6948			0.0000*	0.0000*
Investment/sales	28	0.1612	0.1074	−0.6339	0.5899	2.6560*	2.1901*
		0.0977	0.0265			0.1725	0.0436*
Investment/ employees	24	4885.4701	18064.6755	1.2613	−0.3093	0.9709	2.0507
		3106.3502	2235.6167			0.1537	0.0758
Investment/PPE	28	0.0537	0.0322	−0.4064	−0.0655	1.3310	1.6093
		0.0443	0.0448			0.1725	0.0436*
PPE/employees	30	233653.7571	330056.5131	2.3351*	−0.7097	2.2491*	2.5458*
		60346.6975	70591.5865			0.0000*	0.0000*
Unregulated							
Log(PPE)	17	16.0596	16.2138	0.2260	−0.3272	21.9867*	19.9756*
		16.0273	16.5830			0.0000*	0.0000*
Investment/sales	12	0.1771	0.0930	−0.3470	0.4041	1.3215	0.9619
		−0.0302	−0.0159			0.3872	0.6128
Investment/ employees	6	6420.8692	54646.7804	1.0025	−0.9608	0.4668	2.3891*
		−10070.6767	65872.1966			0.3438	0.3438
Investment/PPE	12	0.0493	−0.0049	−0.3395	0.1155	0.5256	−0.1229
		−0.0250	0.0268			0.3872	0.6128

(Table continues on the following page.)

Table 5A.3 (continued)

Variable	N	Mean before / Median before	Mean after / Median after	t-statistic for change in mean	Z-statistic for change in median	Test for mean before = 0 / median before = 0	Test for mean after = 0 / median after = 0
PPE/employees	12	470839.7510 / 173215.2970	670100.9661 / 283717.7356	1.6964	−0.7506	1.8877 / 0.0002*	2.2080* / 0.0002*
Regulated							
Log(PPE)	19	16.8058 / 16.5665	17.2432 / 17.1940	3.5192*	−0.8321	44.4567* / 0.0000*	43.4982* / 0.0000*
Investment/sales	16	0.1492 / 0.1132	0.1182 / 0.0265	−0.4954	0.9422	3.6193* / 0.0384*	2.4036* / 0.0106*
Investment/ employees	15	4100.1476 / 3242.7176	8183.0048 / 2307.4099	0.3273	0.0622	3.0199* / 0.0592	2.1897* / 0.0176*
Investment/PPE	16	0.0570 / 0.0494	0.0600 / 0.0448	0.1086	−0.1131	3.4090* / 0.0384*	3.7712* / 0.0106*
PPE/employees	18	75529.7611 / 57560.8634	103360.2111 / 70591.5865	0.6359	−0.8542	5.7723* / 0.0000*	4.6236* / 0.0000*

* Significant at the 10 percent level.
** Significant at the 5 percent level.
*** Significant at the 1 percent level.
Note: N = number and PPE = property, plant, and equipment.
Source: Authors' calculations.

Figure 5A.3 Investment as a Fraction of Sales before and after Privatization, Adjusted and Unadjusted

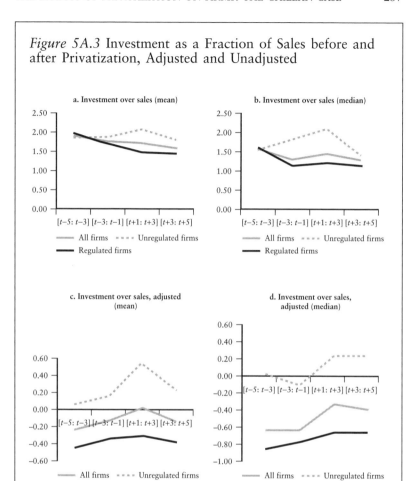

Note: t = year of privatization; the number represents the number of years before or after privatization.

Source: Authors' calculations.

Table 5A.4 Changes in Profitability of Privatized Firms, Adjusted

Variable	N	Mean before Median before	Mean after Median after	t-statistic for change in mean	Z-statistic for change in median	Test for mean before = 0 median before = 0	Test for mean after = 0 median after = 0
All firms							
Operating income/sales	36	-0.0570 -0.0576	-0.0128 -0.0313	2.0203	-1.1374	-2.0925* 0.0005*	-0.5885 0.1214
Operating income/PPE	36	0.0223 -0.0030	0.1093 0.0296	2.1198*	-1.9934*	1.1384 0.2025	2.6297* 0.0662
Net income/sales	36	-0.0621 -0.0405	-0.0355 -0.0328	0.8480	-0.3941	-2.6489* 0.0326*	-1.3586 0.0326*
Net income/PPE	36	0.0149 -0.0110	0.0964 0.0141	2.2858*	-1.6555	1.0682 0.3088	3.0114* 0.1214
Unregulated							
Operating income/sales	18	-0.0170 -0.0072	0.0301 0.0005	1.0079	-0.4113	-0.3470 0.1189	0.8091 0.5927
Operating income/PPE	18	0.0408 -0.0030	0.1410 0.0094	1.0144	-1.0124	1.1243 0.4072	1.7721 0.2403

	N						
Net income/sales	18	−0.0879	−0.0487	0.5670	−0.1898	−2.0494	−1.0150
		−0.0150	−0.0242			0.2403	0.1189
Net income/PPE	18	0.0211	0.0804	0.7612	−0.2214	0.8746	1.4181
		0.0150	−2.3359E−05			0.4072	0.5927
Regulated							
Operating income/sales	18	−0.0970	−0.0559	1.8235	−1.4553	4.4782*	2.8959*
		−0.1085	−0.0714			0.0006*	0.0481*
Operating income/PPE	18	0.0037	0.0776	3.4631*	−1.9299	0.2543	3.0121*
		−0.0031	0.0756			0.2403	0.1189
Net income/sales	18	−0.0363	−0.0222	0.4705	−0.2847	1.9511	1.0098
		−0.0442	−0.0368			0.0481*	0.1189
Net income/PPE	18	0.0087	0.1124	2.9345*	−1.9932*	0.5940	3.6010*
		−0.0140	0.0783			0.1189	0.0481*

* Significant at the 10 percent level.
** Significant at the 5 percent level.
*** Significant at the 1 percent level.
Note: N = number and PPE = property, plant, and equipment.
Source: Authors' calculations.

Figure 5A.4 Net Income as a Fraction of Physical Assets before and after Privatization, Adjusted and Unadjusted

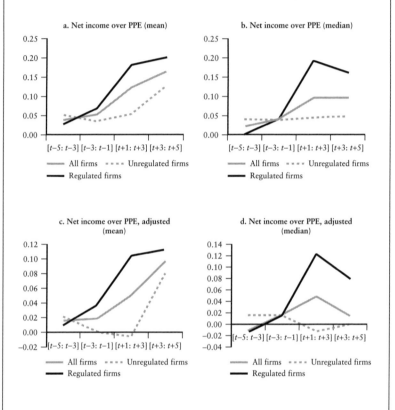

Note: PPE = property, plant, and equipment; t = year of privatization; the number represents the number of years before or after privatization.

Source: Authors' calculations.

Table 5A.5 Changes in Operating Efficiency of Privatized Firms, Adjusted

Variable	N	Mean before / Median before	Mean after / Median after	t-statistic for change in mean	Z-statistic for change in median	Test for mean before = 0 / median before = 0	Test for mean after = 0 / median after = 0
All firms							
Cost per unit	36	−0.0017	0.0055	0.2858	−0.1126	−0.0679	0.2343
		0.0275	0.0322			0.4340	0.1215
Sales/PPE	36	0.6096	0.6121	0.0093	−1.0812	2.3561*	4.0088*
		0.1922	0.2864			0.3089	0.0662
Unregulated							
Cost per unit	18	−0.0652	−0.0419	0.4396	−0.6328	−1.7328	−1.0239
		−0.0441	−0.0093			0.1189	0.2403
Sales/PPE	18	0.8943	0.4995	−0.6096	−0.3797	1.7690	2.0071
		−0.0600	0.1074			0.4073	0.4073
Regulated							
Cost per unit	18	0.0617	0.0529	−0.3107	0.8226	2.2441*	2.8640*
		0.1164	0.0548			0.0481*	0.0038*
Sales/PPE	18	0.3248	0.7248	1.7461	−1.4237	3.1721*	4.0149*
		0.2820	0.4787			0.1189	0.0481*

* Significant at the 10 percent level.
** Significant at the 5 percent level.
*** Significant at the 1 percent level.
Note: N = number and PPE = property, plant, and equipment.
Source: Authors' calculations.

Figure 5A.5 Operating Income as a Fraction of Physical Assets before and after Privatization, Adjusted and Unadjusted

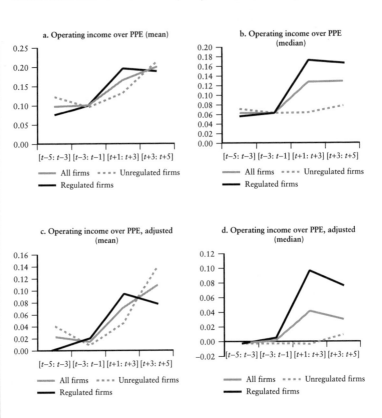

Note: PPE = property, plant, and equipment; t = year of privatization; the number represents the number of years before or after privatization.

Source: Authors' calculations.

Table 5A.6 Changes in Investment and Assets in Privatized Firms, Adjusted

Variable	N	Mean before / Median before	Mean after / Median after	t-statistic for change in mean	Z-statistic for change in median	Test for mean before = 0 / median before = 0	Test for mean after = 0 / median after = 0
All firms							
Log(PPE)	35	0.7909	0.7846	−0.4744	0.3230	39.4821*	39.0845*
		0.7845	0.7779			0.0000*	0.0000*
Investment/sales	28	−1.8959	−1.5611	2.0772*	−2.4089*	−11.7751*	−14.2995*
		−2.0177	−1.6611			0.0000*	0.0000*
Investment/PPE	28	−0.6250	−0.6034	0.2502	−0.8193	−11.1709*	−13.1927*
		−0.5748	−0.5465			0.0000*	0.0000*
Unregulated							
Log(PPE)	17	0.7785	0.7628	−0.4644	0.4650	23.5227*	22.6188*
		0.7845	0.7779			0.0000*	0.0000*
Investment/sales	12	−1.4619	−1.3864	0.1834	−0.6351	−6.1159*	−7.0902*
		−1.6319	−1.3423			0.0032*	0.0002*
Investment/PPE	12	−0.6013	−0.6354	−0.1415	−0.3464	−5.4303*	−6.0524*
		−0.5748	−0.5435			0.0032*	0.0002*
Regulated							
Log(PPE)	18	0.8026	0.8052	0.3869	−0.1898	33.6094*	35.8317*
		0.7866	0.7699			0.0000*	0.0000*
Investment/sales	16	−2.2214	−1.6922	2.8174*	−2.9397*	12.0912*	14.3819*
		−2.2513	−1.6893			0.0000*	0.0000*
Investment/PPE	16	−0.6428	−0.5793	0.8667	−0.6030	11.6052	27.7174*
		−0.5759	−0.5501			0.0000*	0.0000*

* Significant at the 10 percent level.
** Significant at the 5 percent level.
*** Significant at the 1 percent level.
Note: N = number and PPE = property, plant, and equipment.
Source: Authors' calculations.

Figure 5A.6 Operating Income as a Fraction of Sales before and after Privatization, Adjusted and Unadjusted

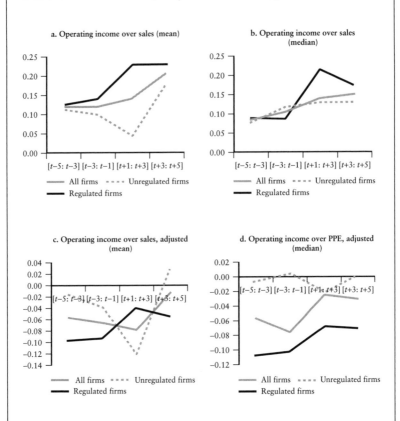

Note: t = year of privatization; the number represents the number of years before or after privatization.

Source: Authors' calculations.

Table 5A.7 Employment in Privatized Firms

Type of firm	N	Mean before Median before	Mean after Median after	t-statistic for change in mean	Z-statistic for change in median	Test for mean before = 0 median before = 0	Test for mean after = 0 median after = 0
All firms	32	1193	1381	1.3374	−0.1880	3.8391*	3.4071*
		380	360			0.0000*	0.0000*
Unregulated	15	1557	1764	0.6502	−0.1867	3.1965*	2.7635*
		754	874			0.0000*	0.0000*
Regulated	17	871	1044	1.2049	−0.3272	2.2127*	2.0096
		179	236			0.0001*	0.0001*

* Significant at the 10 percent level.
** Significant at the 5 percent level.
*** Significant at the 1 percent level.
Note: N = number.
Source: Authors' calculations.

Table 5A.8 Physical Productivity before and after Privatization

Firm	Before	After	Percent variation	Unit of measurement
Unregulated				
CAP	0.0718	0.0629	−0.1233	Tons of steel forged (MT/worker)
Colbún	17.0733			
Electroandina		12.4271		
ENDESA	2.6206	3.6677	0.3995	Energy generated (GWh/workers)
Fepasa	0.4554	0.4123	−0.0947	(Millions of tons km/workers)
Ferronor	0.2891	0.5084	0.7584	(Millions of tons km/workers)
Gener	5.7859	4.7388	−0.1810	Energy generated (GWh/workers)
Laboratorios Chile		1394.5421		
LAN Chile	1.7089	1.0008	−0.4144	(Passengers per kilometer/workers)
Pilmaiquén	7.1905	8.6277	0.1999	Energy generated (GWh/workers)
Telex	39.0387			
Regulated				
Mean			0.0778	
Median			−0.0947	
Standard deviation			0.4002	
Number			7	
Chilectra	1.3412	1.7036	0.2702	Energy purchased (GWh/workers)
Chilquinta	0.8038	1.6152	1.0093	Energy purchased (GWh/workers)
CTC	69.3534	151.1731	1.1797	Number of lines in operation (units/ workers)

Edelaysén	0.3208			
Edelmag	0.6296	0.8611	0.3676	Energy purchased (GWh/workers)
Elecda	0.9252	1.4479	0.5649	Energy purchased (GWh/workers)
Eliqsa	1.6372	2.0288	0.2391	Energy purchased (GWh/workers)
Emec	1.7957	1.4135	−0.2128	Energy purchased (GWh/workers)
Emel	1.2992	0.8345	−0.3577	Energy purchased (GWh/workers)
Emelari	1.0657	1.6876	0.5836	Energy purchased (GWh/workers)
Emelat	1.5176	1.5749	0.0377	Energy purchased (GWh/workers)
Emos	0.1911			
IANSA	278.0696	266.4219	−0.0419	Sugar produced per worker (metric tons/workers)
Saesa	0.6055	0.9196	0.5188	Energy generated (GWh/workers)
Telefónica del Sur	39.0387			
Mean			0.3466	
Median			0.3189	
Standard deviation			0.4612	
Number			12	
All firms				
Mean			0.2475	
Median			0.2391	
Standard deviation			0.4485	
Number			19	

Note: MT = metric tons, GWh = gigawatt hours, and km = kilometers.
Source: Authors' calculations.

Table 5A.9 Concession Projects under Construction

Project name	Percent built (as of December 2001)	Project origin	Bidder's budgeted expense (US$ million)	Franchise length (years)
Cerro Moreno Airport, Antofagasta	100	Private	8	10
International Airport, Santiago	100	Public	170	15
Punta Arenas Airport	98.95	Public	10	9
Santiago-Valparaíso—Viña del Mar highway	77.96	Public	383	25
Litoral Central Road	0	Public	67	30
Route 5, Collipulli—Temuco	91.79	Public	256	25
Route 5, Río Bueno—Puerto Montt	99.3	Public	236	25
Route 5, Santiago—Talca and southern access to Santiago	33.78	Public	698	25
North—South urban highway, Santiago	1.08	Public	517	30
Costanera Norte urban highway	33.4	Public	405	30
El Bato reservoir, Illapel	Auctioned 2001	NA	37	25
Alternate Melipilla road	Auctioned	NA	19	25
Américo Vespucio South urban highway	Auctioned 2001	NA	28	30
Américo Vespucio North urban highway, Santiago	Auctioned 2001	NA	250	30
International road 60	Auctioned January 2002	NA	165	30
Route Talcahuano—Penco	Auctioned 2001	NA	19	25
Group 1 jails (Iquique-La Serena-Rancagua)	Auctioned 2001		75	15 to 20

Source: Ministerio de Obras Publicas.

Table 5A.10 Projects in Concession Process

Project name	Status December 2001	Project cost (US$ million)	Franchise length (years)	Auction date	Bidding date
New regional airport, Atacama	Call for bids	25	20	October 2001	April 2002
Jails, Group 2 (Concepción, Valdivia)	Call for bids	50	22	October 2001	May 2002
Commuter Rail Melipilla—Santiago—Batuco	Call for bids	300	18		July 2002
Chiloé bridge	Call for bids	350	30[a]		August 2002
Airport, Arica	NYA	10	10	June 2002	September 2002
Jails, Group 3 (Santiago1, 2, region V, interior)	NYA	80	20	June 2002	October 2002
International airport, IV region	NYA	45	20	June 2002	November 2002
Intermediate Tech., Recoleta—Independencia	NYA	171	20		December 2002
Ecological complex, Santiago	NYA	50	30	1st half, 2002	2nd half, 2002
North-West access Santiago	NYA	160	30	1st half, 2002	2nd half, 2002
Exchange stations, Quinta Normal, Gran Avenida	NYA	60	30	2nd half, 2002	1st half, 2003
Land Port, Los Andes	NYA	16	25	2nd half, 2002	1st half, 2003
Intermediate highway ring, El Salto—Kennedy	NYA	32	30	2nd half, 2002	1st half, 2003
Convento Viejo Reservoir	NYA	210	20 to 25	2nd half, 2002	1st half, 2003
Improvement, Route 5: La Serena—Caldera	NYA	105	17[a]	2nd half, 2002	1st half, 2003

(Table continues on the following page.)

Table 5A.10 (continued)

Project name	Status December 2001	Project cost (US$ million)	Franchise length (years)	Auction date	Bidding date
Exchange Stations Pajaritos, Santos Dumont	NYA	60	—	1st half, 2003	2nd half, 2003
Jails, Group 4 (Santiago 2, region V)	NYA	50	15 to 20	1st half, 2003	2nd half, 2003
New airport, Region IX	NYA	48	20 to 25	1st half, 2003	2nd half, 2003
Maintenance, Route 66	NYA	64	18	1st half, 2003	2nd half, 2003

— Not available.
NYA Not yet auctioned.
a. Approximate.
Source: Ministerio de Obras Publicas.

Notes

The authors wish to thank Florencio López-de-Silanes for many helpful comments. They also thank Pablo González, Manuel Cruzat, and Ángel Gajardo for their valuable assistance.

1. During the 1980s taxes were reduced and the government was able to finance the transition to a private pension system without going into deficit. Privatization revenues were not used to delay fiscal adjustment, as happened in Argentina.

2. In a personal communication, Rolf Lüders observed that he had not been able to detect improved performance in privatized firms discussed in Hachette and Lüders (1994). His explanation was that managers of state-owned firms were ideologically committed to efficiency during the 1980s. For further evidence of this, see appendix table 5A.1.

3. We do not include the water sanitation companies, which were sold during the late 1990s.

4. A terminal is an autonomous operational unit within a port that consists of adjoining berthing spaces and their associated support and service areas, thereby making it possible to auction them as separate units.

5. Of the 12 companies in the unregulated sector, 4 face no domestic competition (CAP, ENAEX, LAN Chile, and Soquimich), while Colbun, ENDESA, and Gener represent almost all of the generating capacity in the interconnected central electric system.

6. For example, in 1965, value added in state-related firms was just 14.5 percent of GDP.

7. However, CORFO may have only displaced private investment in those sectors.

8. Related firms are those that belong to the same conglomerate.

9. In other words, the Central Bank exchanged fresh money for a claim on profits.

10. The government also privatized a radio company. The only valuable assets in this company were the rights to the FM spectrum, which were sold separately under allegedly questionable circumstances. The remaining AM frequencies were not valuable, and the company went bankrupt very shortly thereafter.

11. Some of these 16 firms had never been publicly traded, while others were taken off the stock market (that is, became private or "closed") after privatization.

12. This is a very slow process, since the firms are not required to provide the information. Obtaining data for Empremar, Fepasa, and Ferronor took almost three months because it required obtaining information not only from the firms but also from the original state-owned firms, which no longer exist.

13. Another source of information at the plant level is the Instituto Nacional de Investigación Agropecuaria survey, which registers quarterly data on many of the variables of interest for this study. Unfortunately, privacy considerations surrounding information provided by the National Institute of Statistics, which owns the survey, make it impossible to use the data for our purposes.

14. The digital form does not include the number of workers, which must be reconstructed from the FECUs in paper form.

15. Circular 239, Superintendencia de Valores y Seguros, Santiago, 1982.

16. We have included the electric-generating companies among unregulated firms because they sell a large fraction of their energy through unregulated long-term contracts.

17. Telex, a long-distance operator, was not regulated during the period under consideration.

18. PPEs appear in the FECUs. The PPE increase is significant for the change in medians.

19. The law excludes mobile telephony (except for access charges) from the requirement that the Antitrust Commission should decide whether the market is competitive, so user prices are free.

20. Initially, the creation in the early 1990s of an independent interconnected system in the northern part of the country helped to increase the use of existing capacity in that area. However, business mistakes in the late 1990s led to overcapacity and large losses.

21. When computing future marginal costs, and very dry conditions are simulated, the regulated or node price is the outage cost (that is, the cost to users of long-run supply failures).

22. Chile has no stranded-cost principle, so the introduction of new technology may reduce the value of existing power plants to zero.

23. The majority of the mobile phones are sold as calling card phones and do not have fixed monthly contracts.

24. The price drop has not been as sharp on other routes. Carriers pay so-called accountancy rates to their foreign counterparts for traffic imbalances on international routes. On those routes where outgoing traffic exceeds incoming calls, the marginal cost of providing service should include the accountancy rate.

25. For more details on these arguments, see Engel, Fischer, and Galetovic (forthcoming). For a different perspective, see Gómez-Lobo and Hinojosa (2000).

26. Some doubts exist about the rationale for this last type of concession contract, since it appears to be a means of evading the standard budgetary process.

27. The franchise was awarded to the firm that had the highest score on an index that weighed (mainly) the toll and the payment to the government. Because of poor auction design, payments to the government had a higher relative weight, so the bidders set tolls at the ceiling and bid positive payments.

28. If the government promised to compensate the franchise-holders for each change in the network that was claimed to affect their traffic flows, there would be endless and expensive negotiation of the impact of the changes. An example of the effects of such restrictions is Orange County's Riverside Freeway, which is terminally congested because its contract with the private 91 Express Lanes does not allow expansion without permission from the owner of the private franchise. See Engel, Fischer, and Galetovic (forthcoming).

29. A similar approach had already been used in the United Kingdom when awarding the franchises of the Second Severn Bridge and the Queen Elizabeth II Bridge over the Thames. The main difference with the U.K. approach is that there were no auctions for the bridges.

30. This requires that the contract specify a minimum toll in order to avoid the threat of expropriation of the franchise-holder.

31. San Antonio is an exception and has been able to expand these support areas.

32. Ex ante rents are dissipated through this cash payment. See Engel, Fischer, and Galetovic (2001) for a detailed analysis.

33. Report of the President of Empresa Portuaria de Iquique, 2000.

34. Empresa Portuaria San Antonio.

References

Beard, T. Randolph, David L. Kaserman, and John W. Mayo. 2001. "Regulation, Vertical Integration and Antitrust." *Journal of Industrial Economics* 49 (3): 319–33.

Bitran, Eduardo, and Raul Sáez. 1994. "Privatization and Regulation in Chile." In Barry Bosworth and others, eds., *The Chilean Economy: Policy Lessons and Challenges*, pp. 329–77. Washington, D.C.: Brookings Press.

Corporación de Fomento de la Producción. n.d. "Privatización de empresas y activos, 1973–1978." Gerencia de Normalización de Empresas, Santiago.

Demsetz, Harold. 1968. "Why Regulate Utilities?" *Journal of Law and Economics* 11: 55–66.

Engel, Eduardo, Ronald Fischer, and Alexander Galetovic. 2001. "How to Auction an Essential Facility When Underhand Integration Is Possible." NBER Working Paper 8146. National Bureau of Economic Research, Washington, D.C.

————. 2002. "Highway Franchising with Subsidies." Cowles Foundation Discussion Paper 1354; Economic Growth Center Discussion Paper 840. Yale University, New Haven, Conn.

————. Forthcoming. "Privatizing Roads: An 'Old' New Approach to Infrastructure Provision." *Regulation*.

Fischer, Ronald, and Pablo Serra. 2000. "Regulation of the Electric Market in Latin America." *Economía* 1 (1): 155–98.

Foxley, Juan, and Jose Luis Mardones. 2000. "Port Concessions in Chile: Contract Design to Promote Competition and Investment." *Public Policy Journal*. Issue 223. World Bank, Washington, D.C.

Galetovic, Alexander. 1998. "Desatando a prometeo: Reformas microeconómicas en Chile 1973–1989." *Perspectivas en política, economía y gestión* 2 (1): 131–56.

Gómez-Lobo, Andrés, and Sergio Hinojosa. 2000. "Broad Roads in a Thin Country: Infrastructure Concessions in Chile." Technical Report 2279. World Bank, Washington, D.C.

Hachette, Dominique. 2000. "Privatizaciones: Reforma estructural pero inconclusa." In F. Larraín and R. Vergara, eds., *La transformación económica en Chile*. Santiago: Centro de Estudios Públicos.

Hachette, Dominique, and Rolf J. Lüders. 1994. *La privatización en Chile*. Santiago, Chile: Centro Internacional para el Desarrollo Económico.

La Porta, Rafael, and Florencio López-de-Silanes. 1999. "The Benefits from Privatization: Evidence from Mexico." *The Quarterly Journal of Economics* 114: 1193–242.

Larraín, Felipe, and Rodrigo Vergara. 1995. *Macroeconomic Effects of Privatization: Lessons from Chile and Argentina*. Washington, D.C.: World Bank.

Larroulet, Cristián. 1984. "Reflexiones en torno al estado empresario en Chile." *Estudios Públicos* (14): 129–51.

Mamalakis, Markos J. 1976. *The Growth and Structure of the Chilean Economy: From Independence to Allende*. New Haven, Conn.: Yale University Press.

Meller, Patricio. 1996. *Un siglo de economía política chilena (1890–1990)*. Santiago: Editorial Andrés Bello.

Rosende, Francisco, and Andrés Reinstein. 1986. "Estado de avance del programa de reprivatización en Chile." *Estudios Públicos* (23): 251–74.

Sáez, Raul E. 1996. "Las privatizaciones de empresas en Chile." In Oscar Muñoz G., ed., *Después de las privatizaciones: Hacia el estado regulador*. Santiago: Dolmen-CIEPLAN.

Sanfuentes, Andrés. 1984. "Los grupos económicos: Control y políticas." *Colección Estudios Cieplan* (15): 131–70.

Valenzuela, Mario. 1989. "Reprivatización y capitalismo popular en Chile." *Estudios Públicos* (33): 175–217.

Vergara, Rodrigo. 1996. "Privatización de la banca: La experiencia chilena." *Estudios Públicos* (63): 335–45.

Williamson, Oliver. 1976. "Franchise Bidding for Natural Monopoly–In General and with Respect to CATV." *Bell Journal of Economics* 7 (spring): 73–104.

6

Privatization in Colombia: A Plant Performance Analysis

Carlos Pombo and Manuel Ramírez

IN THE EARLY 1990S, THE COLOMBIAN government launched an economic liberalization program through the promotion of market competition and institutional deregulation. The economic openness package included major structural reforms encompassing foreign trade policy, the exchange rate regime, capital flow controls, central bank independence, privatization, labor legislation, foreign investment legislation, and social security and pension regimes.[1]

Historically, the size of the public sector in Colombia has been below the average of other Latin American countries such as Argentina, Brazil, Peru, and Venezuela. Yet revenues from privatization have had an important impact on the government's short-run fiscal policy, financing the majority of investment in social programs from 1994 to 1998. During the 1993–98 period, the privatization program in the productive sector was dominated by the sale of assets in the power, natural gas transportation, manufacturing, and, to a lesser degree, the water and sewerage sectors. Reforms in the telecommunications sector have induced new private investment in the public enterprises rather than outright changes in ownership.

Colombia's most important institutional and regulatory reform during the 1990s took place in public utilities, where free entry was granted to private sector providers. This implied the establishment of modern and independent regulatory commissions for electricity and natural gas, water and sanitation, and telecommunications. Hence, economic deregulation in Colombia was part of a comprehensive long-term strategy to promote new roles for the public and private sectors. However, a decade later, economic liberalization has not been well documented or analyzed on a sectoral basis.[2]

Some examination has been undertaken of the privatization process, however, including the work of Zuleta and others (1993) and Montenegro (1994, 1995). These papers document in a preliminary manner the motivations that induced the government to rely on privatization as an economic instrument for promoting market competition, but they do not provide any empirical analysis of efficiency performance after privatization. Papers by Gutierrez and Berg (1999) on telecommunications and Pombo (2001a) on electric utilities document the regulatory reforms in these two sectors and present the evolution of some indicators that provide a partial evaluation of such reforms. Thus, the documentation of Colombia's privatization programs and regulatory reforms during the 1990s is still incomplete; empirical evidence is required to gauge the success of the design and implementation of those economic policies.

This chapter seeks to fill that gap by providing an ex post performance analysis of the privatization programs based on a representative sample with emphasis on manufacturing and power plants, following the benchmark approach of Megginson, Nash, and van Randenborgh (1994) and La Porta and López-de-Silanes (1999). The objectives of the study are twofold. First, it seeks to measure the changes in performance indicators for a sample of manufacturing and power firms that underwent privatization, were restructured because of new regulations, or started operations under the new regulatory environment. Second, the chapter aims to model technical efficiency and profitability variables controlling for industry and plant characteristics, ownership type, and regulatory variables in order to evaluate the effect of privatization on plant performance.

The chapter is organized as follows. The next section analyzes privatization efforts within the context of overall deregulation, private investment in public infrastructure, and the promotion of free market policies. The chapter then examines the privatization programs by economic sector. It begins by analyzing the divestiture program of former Institute for Industrial Promotion (Instituto de Fomento Industrial, or IFI) enterprises from 1986 to 1997 and then continues with a brief summary of the divestiture program for the state oil company, which affected the natural gas and regional gasoline distributing companies. The section ends with an analysis of the regulatory reform of Colombia's power sector, which was greatly affected by privatization. Next we present the core results of the chapter, evaluating the null hypothesis of structural changes in indicator mean and median regarding firm profitability, efficiency, investment, payroll size, and sales. The analysis takes into account industry-adjusted indicators by specific control group for the newly privatized firms in manufacturing and power utilities. It also looks at thermal power generation as a measure of technical efficiency—based on Data Envelopment Analysis (DEA) techniques—before and after the 1994 regulatory reform in the power sector. The chapter then presents the empirical evidence of firms' efficiency and profitability indicators, controlling for plant characteristics, industry-specific variables, ownership structure, and variables related to regulatory policy. The last section offers some concluding remarks.

The Deregulation and Privatization Program in Colombia

Privatization in Colombia was originally approached as a tool for economic deregulation and promotion of market competition. The objective of the privatization program designed during the 1990s was to create incentives for and redirect private investment in public infrastructure and network industries. This was to be achieved through concession contracts, sales contracts, and sectoral regulatory reforms.

Concession contracts are instruments for promoting the involvement of private investment in public works and residential services. Concessions had been virtually abolished in Colombia since 1930, when nationalization and direct government involvement in the market economy became more prevalent. Before that, concessions had been widely used during the 19th century in railroads, mining, and crude oil exploitation. The economic deregulation policy of the 1990s restored concessions as a favored instrument for enhancing investment in strategic infrastructure sectors such as railroads, ports, airports, and highways. In 1991 the constitution was amended to introduce new rules for property rights regarding residential public services and the development of public infrastructure, creating a legal basis for implementing concessions. In 1993 new legislation (Law 80) set up a flexible legal framework regarding public contracting and concession regimes. The main objectives of the law were to introduce equal treatment into the awarding of state contracts to private and public firms and to extend the length of contracts. Specifically, the law allows the signing of contracts of more than 20 years in duration. At roughly the same time, the 1990 Government Development Plan was addressing the new economic agenda: economic deregulation, trade liberalization, and sectoral regulatory reforms. Afterward, a series of documents from the National Council for Economic and Social Policy (Concejo Nacional de Política Económica y Social, or CONPES), as well as the laws governing residential public services, electric power, telecommunications, and privatization, set forth specific rules and guidelines regarding private investment, the upcoming privatizations, and regulatory reform of network industries.[3]

Concession-type contracts were used in public works infrastructure projects such as maritime ports, road construction and maintenance, airports, aqueducts and sewers, railroads, and mobile phone networks. The recent studies of Alonso and others (2001) and Bonilla and others (2000) document the most important concession contracts by economic sector in Colombia. The former focuses on the contracts' characteristics and incentive mechanisms, providing a preliminary assessment. The latter analyzes the provision of utilities and transportation infrastructure in the largest cities of Colombia's Atlantic coast region. This study is important because concessions have been more active in those cities, where a history of poor local governance had translated into low-quality residential public services for decades before private providers were allowed to enter the market.

According to the results of those studies and several follow-up CONPES documents, one can conclude that concessions have not been widely implemented. By 1998, 35 concession contracts were signed (see appendix table 6A.1 for a list of concessions). Out of 1,400 municipal and rural aqueducts within the country, only 4 contracts were written for water companies; out of a possible 20 airports, only 3 contracts were written. The only concessions in telecommunications have been in mobile telephony. Local phone companies have implemented joint-venture contracts with private investors for network expansion, as has the public long-distance carrier, TELECOM. Railroad concessions have been limited to cargo transportation, mainly to one operating concessionaire in coal transportation. In fact, in 1998 the rail network in operation was only half the size of the national network in 1970.[4] Despite their limited coverage, concessions have been important in promoting private investment in road maintenance, maritime ports, and the construction of new gas pipelines.

Concessions were not the only facet of the privatization program. In addition, the program involved the outright sale by local, regional, or national public institutions of equity shares in several enterprises in the manufacturing, network utilities, natural gas distribution, and banking industries.[5] The privatization program was centered on the IFI equity transfers, the Colombian state oil company (ECOPETROL) divestiture program, and the direct sales of municipal or regional public utilities (MPUs and RPUs), most of which were in the power sector. Table 6.1 displays a complete list of the number of privatization contracts that took place in the productive sector between 1986 and 1998.

Three comments are worth making. First, the number of sale contracts as well as their amount is too low in comparison with other international experiences. Aside from public utilities, privatization sales added up to $547 million.[6] This amount is equivalent for instance, to the privatization sale of a government shareholding in a single company such as Volkswagen, Singapore International Airline, or Elf Aquitane.[7] Privatization contracts were generally limited to the sale of equity shares of mixed-capital enterprises in manufacturing, natural gas and gasoline distribution, and, to a lesser degree, in services and mining, according to data up to 1998.

Second, privatization in Colombia was not a centerpiece of policy, but rather a policy instrument designed to complement economic deregulation. In that sense, privatization was intended to ease industrial restructuring processes. Third, privatization of network industries arose as one

Table 6.1 Privatization Program in the Real Sector in Colombia, 1986–98

Industry	Number of contracts	Divesting public institution	Total sale (US$ million)
Manufacturing	27	IFI	288.1
Consumer goods	8	IFI	7.3
Intermediate goods	12	IFI	220.8
Capital goods	7	IFI	60.0
Mining	4	IFI	3.5
Natural gas	2	ECOPETROL	205.5
Gasoline distribution	5	ECOPETROL	41.2
Fishing	1	IFI	1.5
Services	6	IFI	6.9
Power sector	12	MPU	5,060.0
Water and sanitation	1	MPU	2.9
Total	58		5,610

Note: IFI = Instituto de Fomento Industrial, ECOPETROL = Compañía Colombiana de Petróleos, MPU = municipal public utility, and RPU = regional public utility. The privatized firms of IFI and ECOPETROL shareholdings were in all cases mixed-capital enterprises rather than state-owned enterprises.

Source: ECOPETROL, requested files; IFI, requested files; DNP 1993, 1997b, 1997c; Dager 1999; Bonilla and others 2000; Alonso and others 2001; Pombo 2001b.

instrument for promoting market competition. It came as part of ongoing sectoral regulatory reforms aimed at enhancing industry efficiency, channeling private investment, and deregulating market entry, especially in the provision of residential public services. The power sector has been the leader by far in accumulated privatization sales (90 percent of all privatization sales) followed by sales in manufacturing (5.1 percent) and natural gas transportation and gas distribution (3.6 percent).

Hence, one can conclude that privatization in Colombia, in contrast to the experiences of other Latin American countries such as Argentina, Chile, Mexico, and Peru, was not a comprehensive process.

Privatization in Manufacturing

The privatization program in manufacturing was centered around the sale by the Instituto de Fomento Industrial of shares from its investment portfolio in a group of manufacturing and nonmanufacturing enterprises. The IFI was founded by Decree-Law 1157 of 1940 and became a strategic tool for state promotion of industrialization. The IFI's main objectives are to provide long-term credit to private enterprises and to advance risk capital to industrial investment projects. Typically, the IFI's resources come from domestic saving through the issue of certificates of deposit and long-term bonds. In the international market, the IFI leverages loans from multilateral agencies and commercial banks.

The role of the IFI in creating new manufacturing was central during the 1950s and 1960s. Today Colombia's largest private capital enterprises in the steel, chemical, paper, fertilizer, metalworking, and automobile sectors are former IFI-associated companies. The IFI's larger projects were oriented to capital-intensive industries and producers of intermediate materials and were an integral part of Colombia's import substitution industrialization policy, which sought to generate a new supply of manufactured goods for the domestic market. The IFI firms to a large extent drove Colombia's industrialization process during the postwar years. Thus, the formation of mixed-capital enterprises channeled private-sector investments into new activities. IFI also guaranteed a degree of stability in foreign investment participation. The IFI's founding statutes are specific in ordering the sale of equity shares once the government considers the new enterprises to be established in their respective markets. Hence, privatization traditionally has been a financial instrument used by the Colombian government. The role of the IFI, however, made for a different type of privatization than that carried out in other Latin American countries, as most firms in the Colombian case were mixed-capital enterprises rather than state-owned enterprises.

CONPES document 2378 (DNP 1988) set forth an accelerated timetable for the privatization of IFI enterprises. In so doing, the policy placed more emphasis on the transfer of assets than on the IFI's new investments. In December of 1987, the IFI had capital shares in 45 manufacturing and nonmanufacturing enterprises. Thirty of them were in operation and the others had already begun a liquidation process. In addition, there were investments in 6 ongoing projects.[8] Table 6.2 summarizes the IFI's sale program.

The equity transfer program involved three steps in each privatization contract: the selection criteria, the stock assessment, and the method of sale. The selection criteria singled out for sale of equity shares all those operating enterprises that were not subject to special legal procedures, as well as ongoing projects that had not started business operations within three years of initial disbursements.[9] The stock assessment process sought to determine the value of the firms' net assets and the stock price. The assessment studies took into account several parameters such as the present value of company cash flows, asset benchmarking, asset book values, stock exchange prices, and reposition and liquidation costs. In addition, all stocks were listed on the domestic stock exchange markets as well as at the National Stock Registry Office to lend transparency to the process.

Regarding the sale method, the IFI used several bidding procedures: private offers to current shareholders or to the company's employee unions

Table 6.2 IFI Privatization Program, 1986–97

Sector	Company name	Privatization date	IFI share (percent)	Stock assessment (current pesos)	Stock sale (current pesos)	Total sale (million pesos)	Total sale (million US$)	Selling method
Fishing	COPESCOL	July 1991	49.0	1,000	6,505	956	1.5	Public bid
Manufacturing	EMPACA S.A.	May 1986	29.2	10	150	54	0.3	Public bid
Manufacturing	SUCROMILES S.A.	May 1986	15.6	100	2,400	247	1.3	Public bid
Manufacturing	VIKINGOS S.A.	July 1986	35.5	10	16	113	0.6	Stock market
Manufacturing	UNIKA S.A.	March 1988	3.4	10	95	105	0.4	Stock market
Manufacturing	FORJASCOL S.A.	Dec. 1988	n.a	ASSETS		1,700	5.7	Public offer
Manufacturing	SOFASA	Feb. 1989	49.8	1,000	18,362	19,935	52.1	Public offer
Manufacturing	CICOLSA	March 1990	17.4	100	100	14	0.0	Private offer
Manufacturing	AICSA S.A.	April 1990	49.0	10	144	190	0.4	Public offer
Manufacturing	ING RISARALDA S.A.	July 1990	11.7	100	421	972	1.9	Public offer
Manufacturing	PAPELCOL S.A.	Aug. 1990	22.7	ASSETS		16,218	32.3	Public offer
Manufacturing	COLCLINKER S.A.	Oct. 1990	15.7	1,000	16,160	1,909	3.8	Private offer
Manufacturing	RIOCLARO S.A.	Dec. 1990	10.3	100	430	2,185	4.4	Stock market
Manufacturing	CCA[a]	Dec. 1990	0.0	0	0	0	0.0	Private offer
Manufacturing	COSEDA	June 1991	20.0	1,000	1,277	255	0.4	Private offer
Manufacturing	ASTIVAR	Aug. 1991	31.0	100	2,800	130	0.2	Private offer
Manufacturing	TEXPINAL	Sep. 1991	32.4	5	160	3,534	5.6	Private offer
Manufacturing	PROVICA	Sep. 1991	13.2	1,000	1,414	67	0.1	Private offer
Manufacturing	CONASTIL	Jan. 1992	59.9	1,000	1,000	1,014	1.5	Private offer
Manufacturing	FERTICOL	April 1992	0.7	10	10	1	0.0	Preferential offer
Manufacturing	PENNWALT	Nov. 1992	40.7	10	158	1,223	1.8	Private offer

(Table continues on the following page.)

Table 6.2 (continued)

Sector	Company name	Privatization date	IFI share (percent)	Stock assessment (current pesos)	Stock sale (current pesos)	Total sale (million pesos)	Total sale (US$ million)	Selling method
Manufacturing	FATEXTOL	Feb. 1993	16.0	1,000	2,250	540	0.8	Stock market
Manufacturing	FRIGOPESCA	Dec. 1994	47.4	100	440	2,512	3.2	Public bid
Manufacturing	INTELSA	April 1995	15.7	1,500	16,500	130	0.2	Public offer
Manufacturing	COSECHAR	Oct. 1995	1.4	500	695	8	0.0	Public offer
Manufacturing	QUIBI S.A.	April 1996	20.7	10	45	578	0.6	Public offer
Manufacturing	CERRO MATOSO	Feb. 1997	47.7	100	28,264	155,814	150.3	Preferential offer/ public bid
Manufacturing	NITROVEN	Dec. 1997	10.3	1,000	702,933	21,088	20.3	Preferential offer/ public bid
Mining	FOSFONORTE S.A.	Jan. 1989	1.1	1,000	1,250	1	0.0	Private offer
Mining	FOSFOBOYACA S.A.	Feb. 1990	6.4	1,000	1,000	9	0.0	Private offer
Mining	PROCARBON	Sep. 1991	0.1	100	270	9	0.0	Stock market

Mining	PRODESAL	Oct. 1991	11.6	100	921	2,164	3.5	Stock market
Services	PROHOTELES S.A.	May 1986	10.8	10	39	43	0.2	Stock market
Services	CIAC S.A.	March 1989	0.5	10	38	4	0.0	Private offer
Services	COLAR LTDA.	Aug. 1989	n.a	ASSETS		100	0.3	Public offer
Services	CORFERIAS S.A.	Oct. 1989	5.6	10	65	276	0.7	Private offer
Services	CORFIDESARROLLO	Sep. 1993	16.1	100	217	3,295	4.8	Stock market
Services	COKOSILK S.A.	Jan. 1997	16.2	690	690	876	0.8	Preferential offer/ public bid
Manufacturing			23.7			230,536	288.1	
Mining			4.8			2,184	3.5	
Services			9.8			4,593	6.9	
Fishing			49.0			956	1.5	
Total						238,269	300.1	

Note: IFI = Instituto de Fomento Industrial. The stock assessment value is the equity book value after the assessment study, which represents the preprivatization price. After 1995 all privatization contracts were subject to Law 226.

a. CCA: Equity shares seized by Banco Colombia's trust fund in 1986.

Source: IFI, requested files; Dager 1999.

and retirement associations, public bids, and the domestic stock exchange. The first method consisted of one preferential offer to individuals or commercial partners who had a direct involvement in either the company's ownership or control. These transfers followed the logic that block-holders represent the company's best interests. The second method followed a public bid scheme. Specifically, either the IFI or the investment bank in charge of underwriting the sale called for offers from strategic investors. Similarly, the listing on the stock exchange was intended to give small shareholders the opportunity to benefit from privatization. In addition, before 1995 at least 15 percent of the public equity shares in a company had to be offered to cooperatives, investment funds, union associations, and the company's employees.

From May 1986 to December 1997, there were 38 privatizations affecting IFI enterprises. Three aspects merit further comment. First, in all but one case, the shares held by the IFI accounted for less than half of the firm's net worth. In one firm (CONASTIL), the IFI reported a 59 percent shareholding. In three cases the sale was based on book values of assets of firms undergoing liquidation. One of them was a liquidating paper-mill project (PAPELCOL) that never started operations. These data confirm that the role of the IFI was oriented toward promoting technology transfers and fostering entrepreneurship rather than exerting direct control on managing policies. Second, the data suggest that the sales process was successful in the sense that stock prices were in all cases greater than or equal to the preprivatization nominal stock price. However, there is no evidence to ascertain if fixed assets were correctly valued before privatization. Third, the total sales figure for manufacturing was $288 million, which reflects the modest government involvement in manufacturing by the end of the 1980s.

Privatization of Natural Gas and Gasoline Distribution

The state oil company's sale of equity shares from its investments in the natural gas and distribution industry as well as the gasoline retail distribution networks represented the privatization program in the natural gas and gasoline industry. Privatization was restricted to the sale of those assets that were not directly related to crude oil exploration, transportation, and refineries, and other investments in nonoil businesses.[10] Table 6.3 summarizes the divestiture program of ECOPETROL up until mid-1999.

During this period two gas companies were sold. Law 226 of 1995 regulated these transactions and required that privatization sales must give a preferential offer to the *solidarity sector*, which includes the former company's labor union, worker associations, and cooperative firms. For that reason, these sales had two rounds. First was the preferential offer to cooperative associations. The offer price was equal to the assessment price. Cooperatives purchased around 10 percent of shares of Gas Natural and

Table 6.3 ECOPETROL Privatization Program, 1993–99

Company name	Activity	Privatization year	ECOPETROL shareholding (percent)	Stock assessment price (current pesos)	Stock sale price (current pesos)	Value sale (million pesos)	Value sale (US$ million)	Sale method
Natural gas companies								
Gas natural	Transportation distribution	1997	60.6	6,667	19,902	168,494	147.8	Preferential-offer stock market
COLGAS	Distribution	Ongoing	16.2	143				Preferential-offer stock market
Promigas	Transportation	1997	28.8	2,800	3,362	56,830	49.8	Preferential-offer stock market
INVERCOLSA	Distribution	Ongoing	24.8	64				Preferential-offer stock market
Surtigas	Distribution	No sale	15.4	256				
Gases Guajira	Transportation distribution	No sale	6.2	n.a				
Gasoline companies								
Terpel Sabana	Distribution	1993	40.0	n.a	6,562	4,200	5.3	Direct offer
Terpel Bucaramanga S.A.	Distribution	1993	36.1	n.a	7,691	14,477	18.4	Stock market
Terpel del Centro S.A.	Distribution	1993	49.7	n.a	221	10,386	13.2	Stock market
Terpel Sur S.A.	Distribution	1993	45.6	n.a	6,502	1,705	2.2	Stock market
Terpel Norte S.A.	Distribution	1993	18.0	n.a	705	1,615	2.1	Stock market
Total natural gas							197.6	
Total gasoline							41.2	

n.a. Not applicable.
Note: After 1995 all privatizations were subject to Law 226; ECOPETROL stopped the sale of IVERCOLSA in 2000. COLGAS had not been sold as of 2001.
Source: ECOPETROL Planning Office, requested files; Decree 829 of 1999; DNP 1993b, 1997b, 1997c.

2 percent of Promigas at those prices. The second round consisted of a simultaneous first price auction on the country's three stock markets among previously registered bidders. These auctions were successful, particularly for Gas Natural, where the sale price was three times greater than the base price.[11]

Privatization of the gasoline distribution companies took place in 1993, so no preferential offer was made. The sale was through the stock exchange, except in one case where the sale was through a direct offer. Domestic investors bought 100 percent in three TERPEL companies and 50 percent in the other two cases.[12] ECOPETROL also offers financing for these purchases. On average, 36 percent of the shares was financed through direct credits, and the remaining 64 percent was paid in cash.

Two observations are worth mentioning. First, except for Gas Natural, ECOPETROL's shareholdings in the privatized companies were less than 50 percent on the privatization date. Therefore, like the IFI enterprises, firms were not directly subordinated to or controlled by ECOPETROL management policies. Moreover, those companies were independent in their investment expansion plans, and company wage policy was set independently of ECOPETROL. Second, the sale of the TERPEL gasoline stations was the first privatization transfer after the privatization was authorized in 1993. TERPEL was traditionally the competitor of private retailers. Thus, this transfer implied that gasoline retail distribution became wholly privately owned and run, in contrast to other oil producers in Latin American countries such as Ecuador, Mexico, and Venezuela, where gasoline distribution remains vertically integrated with the state oil company.

Industry Restructuring and Privatization in the Power Sector

Regulatory reform in Colombia's electricity supply industry is supported by the Electric Law (Law 143) and by the Residential Public Services Law (Law 142) of July 1994. This reform has been the most important and comprehensive since 1967, when the national grid company, Interconexión Eléctrica S.A. (ISA), was established. The reform changed the structure of the vertically integrated industry. The new regulatory institutions started to operate one year later. The reform's core elements followed the schemes adopted in Great Britain: separating generation, transmission, and distribution markets; setting up an electricity spot market or pool; and developing a long-term contract market for electricity.[13] Law 143 created the Regulatory Commission for Energy and Gas (Comisión de Regulación de Energía y Gas, or CREG) and rules regarding the sector's planning and expansion plans, the regulatory scheme, power generation, transmission and grid operation, grid access fees, the rate-setting regime for electricity sales, concession contracts, and environmental issues.

The power sector reform sought to introduce new competition and set up an independent regulatory system. In that sense, the main purpose was to set the basis for the expansion and diversification of power generation sources, improving both the sector's efficiency and its reliability. Political willingness to support this plan was high after 1992, when the country was caught in the middle of a generalized power shortage and electricity rationing schedules were imposed. The generating system had to be made less vulnerable to abnormal hydrological conditions (namely, El Niño) and more reliant on thermal generation from either coal or natural gas.

There are several points to make about the separation of electricity generation, transmission, and distribution. First, the split among power activities implied the divestiture of the main power holdings that were vertically integrated monopolies. The same happened with the national grid company, which had to sell all of its power-generating units in 1995. The new regulatory framework seeks to promote market entry and competition among generators. They compete openly by sending their bids one day ahead to the pool. The sale price is based on an hour of use, and it differentiates between peak and off-peak hours. The National Dispatch Center, which is located at ISA headquarters, combines information regarding the system's constraints, such as hydrological factors, reservoir levels, and transmission bottlenecks, with final commercial demand in order to determine the dispatch orders. Thus, the market price that the pool sets is the highest marginal bid that clears the market each hour. Based on the above, the pool administrator runs the next-day merit order dispatches.[14] Electric power is bought either through direct purchases from the pool or through contracts signed directly between generators and final users. However, the pool administrator runs the invoicing generated by all financial agreements. That is, that office pays and collects bills derived from contracts.

The regulatory scheme treats power transmission as a natural monopoly, and thus CREG guarantees equal access to the grid to all providers. ISA is not allowed to have an equity share in either power-generating or -distributing companies. Power distributors face two types of regulation. The first one is price regulation. CREG currently sets the markup formula for distributors, as well as determining the nature of the costs that can be passed through to final users. These include the direct purchase costs such as the pool sale price and transportation charges, capacity charges, and costs of the reserve provisions that stabilize the system and prevent bottlenecks in the transmission system. Price regulation at this stage differs from most systems that have moved toward electricity markets that have adopted price-cap rules. The second type of regulation concerns quality control, whereby companies are subject to sanctions if their service fails to meet minimum quality standards. The reform was designed to protect two types of final users. Residential users are mainly consumers whose electricity prices are set by a markup formula, which includes past inflation. The reform also covered large clients, mainly commercial and industrial users that use at least half a megawatt of electricity a month. Large clients may enter into purchase agreements with power distributors, wholesale retailers, or generators, enabling them to hedge against pool price volatility, a sensitive variable especially in hydro-based systems.

The reforms and regulations led to a general divestiture across electricity holdings to fully separate power generation, transmission, distribution, and the setting up of new commercialization activities. Thus, privatization arose as one instrument for promoting market competition and industry restructuring, and it became a complementary policy within a broad deregulatory context. Table 6.4 describes the privatization process in the power sector.

Privatization in the power sector had two phases. The first one was the 1996–97 privatization round, which focused on the sale of thermal plants and hydroelectric stations. Sales reached $3.9 billion and covered half of overall generating capacity. The most important transaction was the sale of 48 percent of the Bogotá Power Company's net worth, which also included the transfer of the local distribution network and the regional grid. The buyers were two holding companies owned by ENDESA and CHILECTRA, Chile's largest power generators.

The second phase of the privatization program took place in 1998 and focused on the capitalization and sale of the CORELCA holding, which covered Colombia's northern Atlantic region. The restructuring involved splitting the holding into several independent companies according to power activity: generation, transmission, and distribution. The national grid company ISA bought 65 percent of the new transmission company's equity share. A holding company formed by American and Venezuelan utilities purchased a 65 percent equity share of the two distribution utilities founded after CORELCA's restructuring. The two transactions added up to $1.16 billion.

Performance Analysis

This section studies firm performance within a sample of former IFI manufacturing enterprises and the privatized power holdings. It also provides an efficiency analysis of the thermal generation sector in which new regulations led to privatization, restructuring, and the entry of new entities. The approach follows the general framework of Megginson, Nash, and van Randenborgh (1994) and La Porta and López-de-Silanes (1999) for performance analysis within the privatized power holdings; in the case of manufacturing, it follows as closely as possible the definition and construction of the performance variables of the benchmark cases. Nonetheless, we include other performance variables regarding efficiency, market power, technology, and profitability indicators that follow standard methodologies in industrial economics and are based on a combination of

Table 6.4 Privatization in the Power Sector, 1995–98

Utility	Capacity (megawatts)	Type	Sale (US$ million)	Seller	Buyer	Buyer share (percent)	Investor country origin
Batania	500	Hydro	497	ICEL	ENDESA	100	Chile
Chivor	1,000	Hydro	645	ISA	CHILGENER	100	Chile
Tasajero	150	Thermal, coal	30	ICEL	Cooperative	58	Colombia
TermoCartagena	180	Thermal, coal	15	CORELCA	Electricidad-Caracas	15	Venezuela
					Cooperative	85	Colombia
EPSA-generation	772	Hydro	535	CVC	Houston Industries	56	United States
	210	Thermal, gas					
EPSA-distribution					Electricidad-Caracas		Venezuela
EEB-generation	2,312	Hydro	810	EEB	Capital-Energia Holding[a] (EMGESA)	48.5	Chile, Spain
	104	Thermal, coal					
EEB-distribution			1,085	EEB	Luz-Bogota Holding[b] (CODENSA)	48.5	Chile, Spain
EEB-transmission			141	EEB	Capital-Energia Holding[a]	5.5	Chile, Spain
			141	EEB	Luz-Bogota Holding[b] (EEB-Head Quarters)	5.5	Chile, Spain
CORELCA							
ElectroCosta-distribution				CORELCA	Houston Inc. - Electricidad Caracas	65	United States, Venezuela

(Table continues on the following page.)

Table 6.4 (continued)

Utility	Capacity (megawatts)	Type	Sale (US$ million)	Seller	Buyer	Buyer share (percent)	Investor country origin
ElectroCaribe-distribution			980	CORELCA	Houston Inc. - Electricidad Caracas	65	United States, Venezuela
Transelca-transmission			180.5	CORELCA	ISA	65	Colombia
Total generation	5,228		2,532				
Total distribution			2,065				
Total transmission			462.5				
Total privatization			5,060				

Note: EEB = Empresa de Energía de Bogota, EPSA = Empresa del Pacifico S.A., CVC = Corporación Autónoma del Cauca, ICEL = Instituto Colombiano de Energía Eléctrica, CORELCA = Corporación Eléctrica de la Costa atlántica, and ISA = Interconexión Eléctrica S.A. (formerly CVC), CVC = Corporación Autónoma del Cauca,

a. Capital Energía = ENDESA (Chile) + ENDESA-Desarrollo (Sapin).

b. Luz Bogota = CHILECTRA (Chile) + ENERSIS (Chile) + ENDESA-Desarrollo (Spain).

Source: MME 1996, 1998; reports to the Congress; ISA 1998, 1999.

physical and financial series at the plant level, which have a similar or equivalent interpretation to those constructed from financial statements.

Data Sets

There were two reasons for taking such measures. One was the lack of availability of data at the plant or firm level. In particular, there were no consistent records of the financial statements at IFI headquarters that would allow us to assemble a data set similar to that of La Porta and López-de-Silanes (1999). The second reason was the quality of data. The most comprehensive longitudinal data set is the Annual Manufacturing Survey (Encuesta Anual Manufacturera, or EAM) of Colombia's National Statistics Department (Departamento Administrativo Nacional de Estadística, or DANE). This survey is a census of medium and large manufacturing enterprises that has been undertaken annually since 1958. The variables and industrial classifications in this data set have been relatively unchanged in format since the 1970 industrial census. In general, the EAM includes around 140 variables, covers 94 specific groups (at the four-digit international standard industrial classification level), and surveys an average of 6,000 plants.[15] The survey reports variables such as gross output, number of employees, wages and benefits, raw materials, electricity consumption, sales, gross investment, and some financial variables such as asset book value and accounting depreciation.

The manufacturing data set consists of 30 former IFI enterprises that were at some point either publicly owned or mixed-capital companies for which IFI was a founding partner or strategic investor. Nineteen of the 30 started business operations between the 1950s and mid-1970s. Among them were the country's largest steel mills, tire and tube plants, pulp and paper mills, and basic industrial chemical plants. Twenty-one firms were part of the 1986–97 IFI transfer program, accounting for 75 percent of total accumulated privatization sales. Four firms in the data set were exiting firms that were liquidated after 1992. The remaining firms are cases in which either the companies were transferred to the private sector before 1987 or the sale was postponed for strategic reasons. The data set is an unbalanced panel that records individual information from 1974 to 1998. Hence, the panel permits analysis of market dynamics at the firm level by tracking entry and exit flows. That feature makes the study sample appealing because of the robustness and length of this data set in contrast to the data sets used in other privatization studies, which at most have available time series with three or four observations before and after privatization (Megginson and Netter 2001).[16]

Table 6.5 shows a summary of the basic variables for the IFI sample and total manufacturing before and after privatization. The sample consists of larger capital-intensive plants in Colombia. For instance, the sample accounts for 5 percent of manufacturing's value added, 3 percent of manufacturing employment, and most important, 20 percent of the total capital stock as well as power consumption of manufacturing.

Table 6.5 Average Changes in Manufacturing Basic Variables
after Privatization for IFI Sample and Total Manufacturing
(US$ million at 1995 prices, unless otherwise specified)

Variable	Manufacturing before privatization, 1974–89			Manufacturing after privatization, 1990–98		
	IFI	Total	Ratio	IFI	Total	Ratio
	1	2	1/2	3	4	3/4
Gross output	1,203	20,145	6.0	1,751	31,052	5.6
Value added	497	9,030	5.5	697	13,495	5.2
Total employment	20,631	495,404	4.2	15,806	622,594	2.5
Gross investment	127	956	13.2	92	1,372	6.7
Capital stock	2,016	9,679	20.8	2,934	14,450	20.3
Number of plants	25	6,356	0.39	27	7,475	0.36
Electricity consumption (gigawatts per year)	1,060	4,953	21.4	1,594	8,299	19.2

Note: IFI = Instituto de Fomento Industrial. Definitions of each variable and its
methodology can be found in appendix table 6.C1.
Source: Authors' estimations based on DANE, various years.

For the privatized power holdings, we were able to collect the financial
reports as far back as 1983 from several sources; this data set allowed us
to replicate similar measures of profitability, efficiency, assets and investment, sales, and employment as in the benchmark study done by La Porta
and López-de-Silanes (1999). See appendix table 6D.1 for a complete
description of the power sector data sets.

Changes in Performance in Manufacturing

The study of IFI enterprises seeks to analyze changes in economic performance before and after privatization. The postprivatization period for
the manufacturing sector has coincided with the economic openness policy that began in the 1990s. In fact, 30 out of 37 IFI privatization contracts
have taken place since March 1990. Thus, the analysis relies on the measurement of five types of indicators of performance and strategic competition: efficiency and productivity, profitability and market concentration,
labor, assets and investment, and sales or total output.

The proxies are measured at the firm level. For incumbent firms the
preprivatization period is 1974–89. Thus, changes in performance capture two effects: privatization and economic deregulation. For entrants,
the time series starts with the first recorded observation, which in most
cases coincides with the start-up year of commercial operations. The

sample has four exiting firms, which shut down operations within the privatization period (1990–98). The time period covered by the data set allows us to assume that in most cases firms have had enough time to complete restructuring processes after privatization. Changes in performance are tested by using the Mann-Whitney (1947) rank sum test of means.

The reading of the results is not straightforward because one has to analyze two forces behind the tests. On one hand, testing differences in sample means and assuming equal variances shows the direction of privatization effects. On the other hand, by testing for differences in medians, one is evaluating a change in the distribution shape, which may or may not coincide with the direction of the change in means. For example, increases in the sample mean with a negative change in the median show that a few individuals in the sample might explain overall variation. Thus, privatization effects are not equally distributed or might have opposite results across firms.

The basic results regarding performance changes in manufacturing are summarized in table 6.6, which depicts the raw indicators, and table 6.7, which presents the industry-adjusted indicators. The latter are ratios relative to specific industry classification groups. These results call for several comments. The effects of structural changes on profitability are mixed. The traditional ratios of operating income to sales, operating income to capital stock, and net income to sales show that changes in means are not statistically significant and that the companies therefore were not necessarily unprofitable before privatization. The industry-adjusted ratios show that changes in medians rather than means are significant, in all cases at the 5 percent level. The median of the three indicators for the privatizing firms fell 25 points, on average, relative to their private competitors. At first glance, this outcome suggests that at least half of the IFI companies became less profitable after privatization.

We analyzed those results further by constructing a set of complementary profitability indicators that either are similar or have the same interpretation. These nontraditional indicators are the Lerner index as a proxy for the markup rates, the gross margin, and market share.[17] According to the Lerner index, IFI enterprises were highly profitable before privatization. For example, the mean of the Lerner index as a proxy of the markup rate is 14.8 percent. That rate fell to 12.7 percent during the 1990s. Moreover, the adjusted indicator shows that, on average, IFI firms were more than twice as profitable as their private competitors before privatization. After privatization this ratio fell slightly. The median of the markup rate, although statistically insignificant, increased from 6.6 percent to 10 percent, meaning that there was a positive convergence within the sample, partly due to the exit of less profitable plants after 1990. Changes are statistically significant at the 5 and 10 percent levels. This result is contrary to most privatization studies, which have found that unprofitable public enterprises constituted a central argument in favor of equity transfers.

Table 6.6 Changes in Performance for the Sample of Privatized IFI Firms

Variable	N before	N after	Mean before Median before	Mean after Median after	t-statistic Z-statistic
Profitability					
Traditional indicator					
Operating income/sales	394	227	0.2289	0.2206	−0.37
			0.2476	0.2403	0.43
Operating income/	393	227	0.8684	0.8286	−0.28
capital stock			0.4580	0.3045	1.96**
Net income/sales	394	227	0.1328	0.1793	1.33
			0.1953	0.2033	−1.19
Nontraditional indicator					
Lerner index	394	227	0.148	0.127	−1.59**
			0.066	0.101	1.07
Gross margin	394	227	0.557	0.534	−0.34
			0.608	0.689	3.16***
Market share	394	227	0.135	0.108	−2.50***
			0.073	0.079	1.32
Efficiency					
Traditional indicator					
Cost per unit	394	227	0.5757	0.5159	−1.35*
			0.5452	0.5312	1.45*
Log(sales/employees)	394	227	10.562	11.037	6.59***
			10.527	11.177	−6.28***
Log(sales/capital stock)	393	227	0.442	0.313	−1.03*
			0.777	0.435	2.41***
Nontraditional indicator					
Capital: partial	394	227	6.02	4.68	−1.10
productivity			1.29	0.75	2.65***
Labor: partial	394	227	30,487	43,837	4.97***
productivity			21,161	29,207	−4.33***
Translog index TFP	394	227	118.85	140.39	2.36***
			93.76	81.89	2.38***
Labor					
Log(workers)	394	226	5.59	5.47	−1.07
			5.84	5.62	1.58
Log(technicians)	354	221	3.04	2.89	−1.34*
			3.00	2.75	1.12
Log(administrative	394	222	4.53	4.56	0.34
employees)			4.71	4.54	0.33
Assets and investment					
Log(capital stock)	393	246	8.98	9.44	2.42***
			9.20	10.00	−2.34 ***

Table 6.6 (continued)

Variable	N before	N after	Mean before Median before	Mean after Median after	t-statistic Z-statistic
Capital/labor	394	227	173,184	228,968	1.28*
			16,446	32,928	−4.08***
Investment/value added	394	225	0.861	0.187	−1.02
			0.069	0.055	2.41***
Investment/before	393	225	0.091	0.059	−3.53***
capital stock			0.059	0.025	5.27***
Machinery/investment	389	221	0.860	0.757	−0.41
			0.724	0.703	−0.78
Investment/total	393	225	8,360	6,418	−0.76
employees			1,533	1,529	1.13
Output					
Log(gross output)	394	227	16.69	17.07	2.61***
			16.89	17.48	−2.74***

* Significant at the 10 percent level.
** Significant at the 5 percent level.
*** Significant at the 1 percent level.
Note: IFI = Instituto de Fomento Industrial, N = sample size, and TFP = total factor productivity. This table presents raw results for 28 manufacturing enterprises that were included in the 1988 IFI divestiture program. The data set includes 4 plants that shut down operations after 1990. The panel is unbalanced by construction, and the sample size refers to firm-year observations for two time periods: 1974–89, the years before privatization, and 1990–98, the years after privatization. The maximum number of firm-year observations before privatization is 394; after privatization, 227. The table presents for each empirical proxy the number of usable observations, the mean, and the median values before and after 1990. The table reports *t*-statistics and *Z*-statistics (Mann-Whitney nonparametric rank sum) as the test for significance for the change in mean and median values, respectively. Capital and labor productivities and capital/labor and investment/employee ratios are in 1995 US$. Definitions of each variable and its methodology can be found in appendix table 6C.1.
Source: Authors' calculations.

Part of the explanation can be found in the economic openness program and the corporate structure of these firms. IFI firms were a central piece within the mixed strategy of import substitution and export diversification implemented since the mid-1960s.[18] These firms enjoyed high effective protection until 1990. The drop observed in the mean of firm market share from 13.5 percent to 10.8 percent reflects the increase of imports within industry-specific domestic supply. Figure 6.1 depicts the markup rate evolution for the IFI sample and total manufacturing. Clearly, profitability shows a decreasing trend, although IFI firms still show above-average profitability in manufacturing.

Table 6.7 Industry-Adjusted Changes in Performance for the
Sample of Privatized IFI Firms

| | | | Industry-adjusted | | |
| | N | N | Mean | Mean | t-statistic |
Variable	before	after	Median	Median	Z-statistic
Profitability					
Traditional indicator					
Operating income/sales	394	227	0.9165	0.8788	−0.26
			0.9401	0.8018	2.46***
Operating income/	393	227	2.1877	1.8446	−0.95
capital stock			1.1061	0.6317	2.53***
Net income/sales	394	227	0.6348	0.6212	−0.03
			0.9157	0.7554	2.51***
Nontraditional indicator					
Lerner index	394	227	2.181	1.936	−1.35*
			1.416	1.398	0.20
Gross margin	394	227	0.190	1.281	1.23
			1.022	1.000	3.62***
Market share	394	227	0.197	0.150	−2.35***
			0.052	0.063	1.32
Efficiency					
Traditional indicator					
Cost per unit	394	227	1.012	0.964	−0.89
			0.948	0.984	−0.49
Log(sales/employees)	393	227	0.998	1.008	1.99**
			1.005	1.016	−2.11**
Log(sales/capital stock)	393	227	0.535	1.705	1.87**
			1.018	1.127	−2.05**
Nontraditional indicators					
Capital: partial	393	227	8.681	7.197	−0.85
productivity			1.733	0.986	2.72***
Labor: partial	394	227	1.321	1.385	0.76
productivity			1.069	1.022	0.98
Translog index TFP	391	158	1.408	1.609	1.66*
			1.043	1.026	−0.22
Labor					
Size	394	227	5.584	6.265	0.93
			3.643	2.961	0.59
Size-workers	394	227	5.628	6.370	1.02
			3.739	3.128	0.48
Assets and investment					
Capital stock	393	227	10.576	11.433	0.45
			2.504	3.327	−0.70

Table 6.7 (continued)

| | | | Industry-adjusted | | |
| | N | N | Mean | Mean | t-statistic |
Variable	before	after	Median	Median	Z-statistic
Capital/labor	393	227	4.915	4.153	−0.77
			0.674	0.966	−2.12**
Investment/value added	394	225	2.580	1.399	−0.99
			0.736	0.560	1.83*
Investment/capital stock	393	225	1.186	1.068	−0.49
			0.577	0.382	3.57***
Investment machinery/	393	225	1.612	1.190	−0.90
investment			1.018	0.974	1.61*
Investment/employees	393	225	1.744	1.646	−0.22
			0.746	0.616	1.13
Output					
Scale	394	227	6.313	7.846	1.81**
			3.377	2.674	−0.46

* Significant at the 10 percent level.
** Significant at the 5 percent level.
*** Significant at the 1 percent level.
Note: IFI = Instituto de Fomento Industrial, N = sample size, and TFP = total factor productivity. The industry control group is the four-digit international standard industrial classification group to which a specific firm belongs. For each year and firm we compute industry-adjusted indicators by taking the ratio of the value of the indicator for the IFI firm to its industry control group. See table 6.6 for an explanation of the data set and significance tests on which this table is based. Definitions of each variable and its methodology can be found in appendix table 6C.1.
Source: Authors' calculations.

The gross margin rate is an indicator of working capital that shows how firms are restricted by payroll structures.[19] The change in medians of this indicator is positive and significant at the 5 percent level, increasing from 60.8 percent before privatization to 68.9 percent afterward. This result indicates that half of the distribution was able to adjust its payroll structure to efficiency parameters. Most former IFI firms have had strict union convention clauses. The 1990 labor market reform (Law 50) eliminated wage rigidities such as the retroactive severance pay system and the mandatory reinstatement regime for workers with more than 10 years on the payroll.[20] Thus, IFI firms could ease their payroll constraint and speed up the benefits derived from the 1990 labor reform after privatization. However, the industry-adjusted margin rate shows an opposite change in medians, which moved from 1.02 to 0.92 times, meaning that despite the IFI firms' new contracting flexibility, private competitors increased their gross margin faster than IFI firms during the 1990s.

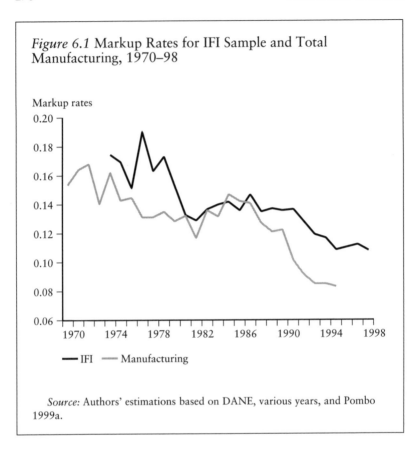

Figure 6.1 Markup Rates for IFI Sample and Total
Manufacturing, 1970–98

Source: Authors' estimations based on DANE, various years, and Pombo
1999a.

Corporate structure is another explanatory factor of IFI firms' profitability levels. As was pointed out earlier, the IFI companies were mixed-
capital enterprises. At the time of privatization, the share of IFI in manufacturing company equity was on average 24 percent and the accumulated
sales were under US$300 million (see table 6.2). These numbers under-
score the state's limited participation in manufacturing, where the IFI's
policy of capital rotation implied a sale of equity once companies became
incumbents and mature within the market. This limited state role in the
economy was a sharp contrast to other Latin American countries. State-
owned enterprises (SOEs) in Mexico, for example, represented 38 percent of the economy's capital stock by 1982, and there were SOEs in
almost all manufacturing groups. In Chile SOE sales represented 14 percent of gross domestic product in 1965, and the government controlled
the key foreign export sector of copper mining, as well as most large
manufacturing enterprises located in industries such as paper and pulp
manufacturing.[21]

Efficiency gains underpin part of the pro-competitive pricing strategy that followed trade liberalization. In contrast to the profitability results, the efficiency outcomes are in the expected direction: there is evidence that IFI firms improved technical efficiency during the 1990s. The average (median) cost per unit decreased 6 percent (1.4 percent), while the mean and the median ratio of sales to employees rose 48 percent. At the same time, the median ratio of sales to capital stock fell 34 percent. These changes are all significant at either the 5 or the 10 percent level. The industry-adjusted ratios of these indicators behave in different directions. On one side, the average and median ratios of sales to employees rise only slightly, but on the other side the average of sales to capital stock triples from 0.54 to 1.71 times. The median increases more moderately, moving from 1.02 to 1.13 times relative to their control group. These changes are significant at the 5 percent level. Last, neither the mean nor the median change in the industry-adjusted cost per unit is significant.

These results indicate at least two things. First, an efficiency gain resulted from the large increase in labor productivity that improved firms' total factor productivity (TFP). Second, evidence of gains is not conclusive concerning capital productivity in the raw indicator of sales-to-capital ratio. Nonetheless, the change in the industry-adjusted indicator implies that even if IFI firms did not improve their capital productivity, they did much better than their private peers, which experienced a large drop in capital input productivity after 1990. To pin down the source of efficiency gains, we constructed nontraditional indicators of partial and total factor productivity. Ratios of value added to capital or labor are direct measures of partial input productivity. These measures are more accurate than sales-to-input ratios because changes in quality in raw materials are in fact a source of a firm's efficiency gains that might influence the direction of these performance indicators.

The measuring of partial and total productivity shows that average (median) firm labor productivity increased 43 percent (13 percent) at constant prices,[22] and the average TFP index rose by 22 basis points, which is equivalent to a 2.4 percent annual productivity growth rate. The TFP median fell 11 basis points, meaning that efficiency gains were asymmetric across plants. The median for capital partial productivity contracted 58 percent, moving from $1.29 per unit of installed fixed capital to $0.75 at constant prices. These changes are significant at the 5 percent level.

These results illustrate the direction of plant restructuring in these companies. IFI firms represent 20 percent of Colombia's manufacturing capital stock (see table 6.5). The study sample consists of large capital-intensive plants. In fact, the measurements of capital-to-labor ratios show that before privatization, IFI firms were 4.9 times more capital intensive than their counterparts in the private sector. That number dropped to 4.1 after 1990. The behavior of the TFP index for the IFI sample closely follows the cycle for total manufacturing (figure 6.2). Productivity for IFI companies

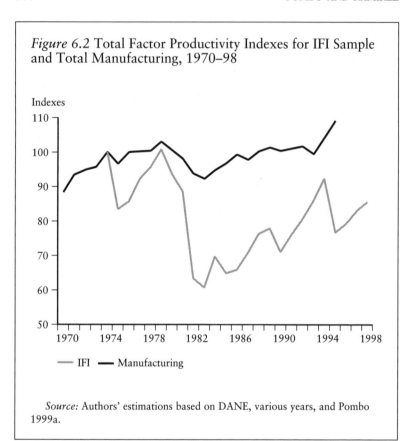

Figure 6.2 Total Factor Productivity Indexes for IFI Sample and Total Manufacturing, 1970–98

Source: Authors' estimations based on DANE, various years, and Pombo 1999a.

plummets by 40 basis points between 1979 and 1983, according to the TFP index. This means a –10 percent TFP growth per year, whereas the average efficiency loss in manufacturing was −2.6 percent per year. This productivity shock implied that even 15 years later the surviving firms had not been able to reach the TFP levels of the mid-1970s.

One factor that explains this cycle in productivity is the crisis in capital productivity of the 1980s and its slow pace of recovery. The adjusted indicator shows that for IFI firms the median of capital productivity was 1.8 times that of their private competitors. During the 1990s the number converged to 0.99 times, meaning that productivity was about the same in both groups and reaching industry benchmarks. Moreover, investment plummeted because of an overinvestment problem. In fact, the mean (median) rate of capital accumulation dropped from rates of 9.1 percent (5.9 percent) per year before privatization to rates of 5.9 percent (2.5 percent) per year while the median investment rate fell from 6.9 percent to 5.5 percent per

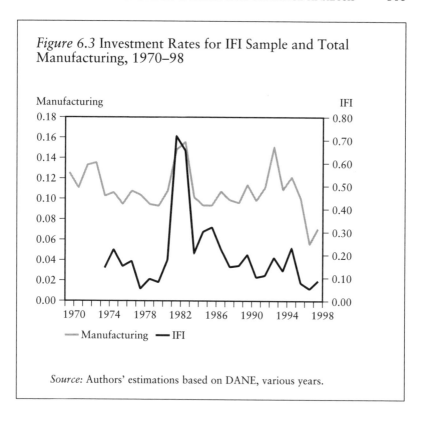

Figure 6.3 Investment Rates for IFI Sample and Total Manufacturing, 1970–98

Source: Authors' estimations based on DANE, various years.

year after 1990. These changes are significant at the 5 percent level. At the same time, the mean of investment per employee decreased from $8,360 to $6,418 per year at constant prices, while the median remained unchanged. The change in the last indicator is not statistically significant. The changes in the adjusted indicators of investment rates are in the same direction.

Figure 6.3 illustrates the overinvestment problem for IFI companies, where investment rates were 2.5 times the level for total manufacturing until 1989. Thereafter the gap decreased to 1.4 times. Thus, IFI firms strongly rationalized capital spending in order to pin down excess capacity. Various factors help explain the sample's overinvestment. One is associated with the macroeconomic disequilibriums of the late 1970s generated by coffee boom prices that led to the appreciation of the Colombian peso. Temporary trade liberalization, which enhanced capital goods imports, was another factor. Microeconomic factors also came into play. During the 1977–83 period, the IFI and private investors undertook the two largest industrial investment projects since the 1960s. One was a cement mill (Compañía Colombiana de Clinker, or Colclinker) that began operations in 1977 and still is the country's largest. The second, the establishment of one of the largest nickel processing plants in Latin America (Cerromatoso), began operations in 1983. As a founding partner, IFI had a 45 percent equity share in this nickel plant.

Similar results have been found in other country-specific studies of privatization. Equity transfers to private holders do not necessarily boost investment, as many government officials argue when calling for privatization. By the late 1980s, most IFI-associated firms clearly had an excess capacity problem, which became a bottleneck once the domestic market started to peter out as a source of demand growth.[23] Nonetheless, even with decreasing trends in overall investment rates, one might expect investment to become more selective through spending on new machinery to replace worn-out capital equipment. This was not the case for the IFI companies. The mean (median) embodied investment rate—the ratio of investment spending on machinery to total investment—declined from 86 percent before 1990 (72 percent) to 76 percent (70 percent) after privatization. However, these changes are not statistically significant. The adjusted embodied investment rate shows that the median changed from 1.02 to 0.97 times after privatization and is significant at the 10 percent level. These results on investment behavior suggest that one aspect of firm restructuring after privatization was the reduction of excess capacity.

Labor productivity is the other component explaining the direction of the firms' restructuring after privatization. As was pointed out, IFI firms were able to increase their TFP growth by 2.4 percent per year after 1990. However, those rates have not allowed a full recovery from the dramatic loss in capital productivity that those companies experienced during the 1980s. The mean (median) of labor productivity rose from $30,487 ($21,161) to $43,837 ($29,207) at constant prices during the 1990s. This change means a 43 percent real increase in value added per worker. As reported in table 6.2, around 4,800 workers were laid off, representing a 23 percent total payroll reduction within IFI companies after privatization. The layoff composition was 3,700 workers, 750 administrative employees, and 340 technicians. However, the changes in means and medians of the labor series by type of occupational category are not statistically significant.

The adjusted labor indicators given by plant size show an increase in the mean from 5.58 to 6.26, while the medians decrease from 3.64 to 2.96. These measurements also show the asymmetric effects of labor layoffs across plants, but the direction of change in medians implies a lower plant operating scale. Again these changes are not statistically conclusive; therefore, one might have some caveats about the labor adjustment direction. In any case, labor cuts were small in comparison with other national experiences. The Mexican manufacturing payroll was halved during privatization (La Porta and López-de-Silanes 1999), for example, while the privatization of British Telecom involved the layoff of more than 5,000 workers (Armstrong, Cowan, and Vickers 1994).

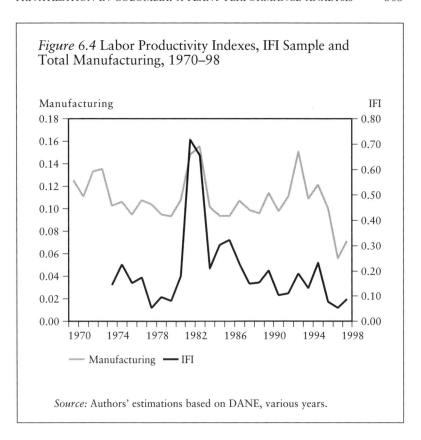

Figure 6.4 Labor Productivity Indexes, IFI Sample and Total Manufacturing, 1970–98

Source: Authors' estimations based on DANE, various years.

Figure 6.4 depicts the labor productivity indexes for the IFI sample and for total manufacturing. One sees a positive gap between IFI firms and the average for total manufacturing, starting in 1984 and coinciding with the turning point for the IFI firms' productivity trends. The average value of the labor productivity gap was 20 points during the 1980s and nearly triple that in the 1990s. Thus, IFI firms made greater efforts in increasing labor productivity relative to their private competitors. This is partly explained by the moderate levels of layoffs but also by adjustment in plant efficiency scales, which by definition eliminates any diseconomies in production.

The positive but lower rates of capital accumulation plus the payroll contraction after 1990 explain changes in the ratio of plant capital to labor. The mean (median) capital units per employee rose 32 percent (100 percent) at constant prices after privatization. The adjusted indicator also shows that IFI firm plants became more capital-intensive relative to their control group. The median changed from 0.67 to 0.97 times—that is, these firms effectively substituted capital for labor input, adjusting their relation to industry benchmarks. The changes are significant at the 5 percent level.

Another important result is that IFI firms were able to increase their sales despite the payroll contraction and the lower rates of capital accumulation. Mean (median) gross output increased 38 percent (59 percent). This increase implies a 4.2 percent (6.5 percent) output growth rate per year during the 1990s. The adjusted indicator shows that, on average, output rises from 6.3 to 7.8 compared with the control group. These results complement those found regarding plant size. On one hand, plant size adjustment implies a correction in plant scale but on the other hand, IFI firms were able to exploit new economies of scale. Thus, part of the observed TFP growth is explained by economies of scale and the rest might be attributable to changes in technology.[24]

Another issue that is important to analyze is the role of labor costs in explaining cost reductions that allow firms to set lower prices and behave more competitively. According to the redistribution hypothesis, one can expect a drastic fall in wages after privatization because of lower labor productivity and a renegotiation of unions' convention clauses. In the case of the IFI firms, we do find that the mean (median) of the industry-adjusted value added per worker before privatization was 1.3 (1.07) (see table 6.7). Hence, the argument does not apply.

Table 6.8 presents the wage data by type of worker. The striking result here is the large increase in real wages of workers in the privatized IFI firms. The increase in means (median) in the per capita wage for blue-collar workers was 30 percent (17 percent) after privatization in real terms. For white-collar workers, the mean (median) increase was 36 percent (27 percent) at 1995 prices. More interesting are the changes in the industry-adjusted per capita wages. Wages for both blue- and white-collar workers increased relative to private competitors. La Porta and López-de-Silanes (1999) document similar results for Mexico. All tests are significant at the 5 percent level.

To summarize, the analysis of changes in performance indicates that IFI firms followed pro-cyclical trends relative to their control group. That is, there was no asymmetric performance of these companies in contrast to their private peers. Part of the explanation for this is that IFI firms were mixed-capital enterprises and followed profit-maximizing pricing rules rather than pursuing second-best prices or net transfers through subsidized sale prices. As a result, management strategies followed private-sector benchmarks, although rate-setting policy favored, at some points and for some cases, the dominant position of IFI firms within domestic markets. Because IFI's role was the strategic but supportive one of promoting firm capitalization, it never sought to control company management policies. The results regarding plant efficiency are consistent with the expected effects, but in this case, privatization helped to speed up firm labor restructuring, which implied a strong change in magnitude in the labor productivity indexes. Finally, the wage data

Table 6.8 IFI Firms: Role of Transfers from Workers

Variable	N before	N after	Mean before Median before	Mean after Median after	t-statistic Z-statistic
Total wages/sales	394	227	0.1154	0.0988	−2.33***
			0.0914	0.0691	4.06***
Log(total employees)	394	227	5.98	5.90	−0.74
			6.12	5.96	1.28
Real wages per	394	226	338.4	437.1	5.96***
blue-collar worker			312.5	363.1	−3.98***
Industry-adjusted real	394	226	1.06	1.18	3.28***
wages per blue-collar			1.04	1.09	−2.30***
worker					
Real wages per	394	222	543.43	738.71	6.34***
white-collar worker			492.02	625.07	−5.01***
Industry-adjusted real	394	222	1.09	1.26	3.80***
wages per white-collar			1.04	1.14	−3.14***
worker					
Real wages per worker	394	227	386.7	500.1	6.83***
			355.8	448.4	−5.23***
Industry-adjusted real	394	227	1.16	1.34	3.32***
wages per worker			1.05	1.12	−1.79*

* Significant at the 10 percent level.
** Significant at the 5 percent level.
*** Significant at the 1 percent level.
Note: IFI = Instituto de Fomento Industrial and N = sample size. The series of per capita wages are expressed in US$ at 1995 prices. See tables 6.6 and 6.7 for an explanation of the data set and significance tests on which this table is based. Definitions of each variable and its methodology can be found in appendix table 6C.1.
Source: Authors' calculations.

indicate that we can reject the hypothesis of transfers from workers to shareholders after privatization.

Changes in Performance in the Power Sector

Our analysis of the performance in the power sector takes into account the effects of the 1994 reform on firm entry, market competition, and efficiency gains. In that sense, the analysis focuses on firm changes in means and medians of direct measures of profitability, efficiency, assets and investments, and sales of the privatized power holdings. The study sample covers the equity transfers in three of five regional power systems where privatization took place in both power generation and power distribution, as described earlier. They are the former Bogotá Power Company, Cauca Valley Corporation (CVC), and the Corporación Regional de la

Costa Atlántica (CORELCA) holding. The control group is Public Enterprises of Medellín (EPM), which is a municipally owned company and has been traditionally the most efficient public utility. Series were chained after 1995 keeping the prereform holding structure in order to have comparable statistics.

Tables 6.9 and 6.10 present the main results regarding the performance effects of privatization on the power holdings. Several facts are worth noting. First, the reform has had a direct and positive effect on operating efficiency. The average cost per unit dropped 45 percent at constant prices after reform, compared with the preprivatization rate. The mean (median) ratio of sales to assets (property, plant, and equipment, or PPE) rose 17 percent (18 percent), while the mean (median) ratio of sales to employees rose 20.3 percent (15.7 percent). The same happened with the ratio of operating income to employee, where the mean (median) increase was 63 percent (48 percent) at constant prices after the reform. Changes are significant at the 5 percent level.

There are at least three important sources of these efficiency gains. First, utilities made an effort to reduce both power losses and the tariff-collecting problem in power distribution. This was the case for the Bogotá Power Company in particular, which drastically reduced its power loss indexes from 53 percent in 1985 to 22 percent in 1996.[25] Second, the reform and privatization induced new investment in incumbent firms, in contrast to what was observed for manufacturing. All investment rates at least doubled, on average. Notice that capital stock remained unchanged, but this finding is not statistically significant. Total assets usually have several biases depending on the depreciation schedules. For that reason a more accurate indicator is the current investment rate. Notice that in most cases the industry-adjusted changes in performance of operating efficiency and investment-adjusted indicators are not statistically significant, meaning that despite their efforts, the newly privatized power holdings could not match EPM's efficiency changes. Third, employment cuts were not as significant as in the case of manufacturing. The four electric holdings altogether had, on average, 13,300 employees before the reform. This number only decreased to 11,600 employees during the 1995–99 period. Thus, the observed 23 percent real increase in labor productivity resulted from an increase in sales rather than drastic employment cuts. In fact, mean (median) sales increased by 16.4 percent (21.1 percent).

The new regulation has used two instruments to encourage market entry. One is a guaranteed minimum return on installed capacity. The second instrument is the power purchase agreement (PPA). These agreements are long-term contracts that allow generators to hedge against unexpected changes in demand and distributors to hedge against system constraints. One type of PPA initially implemented in Colombia is to pay what is generated, which involves an advance purchase of plant capacity by a power distribution company Most thermal generators are marginal producers

Table 6.9 Changes in Performance in the Sample of Privatized Power Utilities and Public Enterprises of Medellín

Variable	N before	N after	Mean before Median before	Mean after Median after	t-statistic Z-statistic
Profitability					
Operating income/ sales	48	20	0.3208 0.3587	0.1891 0.2262	-3.093*** 2.410**
Net income/sales	48	20	0.1382 0.1992	0.0882 0.0998	-0.693 0.794
Operating income/ PPE	48	20	0.0562 0.0556	0.0288 0.0397	-3.060*** 2.544**
Operating income/ net worth	48	20	0.0997 0.0958	0.0463 0.0452	-3.155*** 3.876***
Operating efficiency					
Cost per unit	48	20	0.0292 0.0226	0.0207 0.0194	-1.790** 1.561
Log(sales/PPE)	48	20	1.2574 1.2278	1.4289 1.4101	3.260*** -2.907***
Log(sales/employees)	48	20	2.0020 2.0021	2.2035 2.1578	4.469*** -3.957***
Operating income/ employees	48	20	112.82 105.54	183.91 156.68	4.367*** -4.321***
Labor					
Log(employees)	48	20	3.4354 3.5205	3.3987 3.4255	-0.4701 0.8080

(Table continues on the following page.)

Table 6.9 (continued)

Variable	N before	N after	Mean before Median before	Mean after Median after	t-statistic Z-statistic
Assets and investment					
Log(PPE)	48	20	4.1807	4.1733	−0.1135
			4.1513	4.1509	0.1750
Investment/sales[a]	48	8	0.0039	0.0066	1.9950**
			0.0033	0.0063	−1.1710
Investment/	48	8	0.4869	0.8374	1.6493*
employees[a]			0.2721	0.6909	−1.5220
Investment/PPE[a]	48	8	0.0742	0.1579	3.1909***
			0.0647	0.1521	−1.9900**
Log(PPE/total	48	20	0.7453	0.7746	0.4286
employees)			0.7817	0.7960	−0.2690
Output					
Log(sales)	48	20	5.4382	5.6023	2.5933***
			5.4771	5.6886	−2.6250***

* Significant at the 10 percent level.
** Significant at the 5 percent level.
*** Significant at the 1 percent level.

Note: N = sample size and PPE = property, plant, and equipment. This table presents raw results for three privatized power holdings and for public enterprises of Medellín. The data set is a balanced panel by construction, and the sample size refers to firm-year observations for two time periods: 1983–94, the years before the regulatory reform, and 1995–99, the postreform years. The maximum number of firm-year observations before the reform is 40; after the reform, 20. The table reports for each empirical proxy the number of usable observations, the mean, and the median values before and after the sector regulatory reform (1995), and the *t*-statistic and Z-statistic (Mann-Whitney nonparametric rank sum) as the test for significance of the change in mean and median values. Value variables before transformations in logs are in millions of pesos at 1995 prices. Definitions of each variable as well as details on Colombia's power sector data sets and definitions can be found in appendix table 6.C1.

a. Postreform years are 1995–96 due to unavailability of appropriate data for later years.

Source: Authors' calculations.

Table 6.10 Industry-Adjusted Changes in the Performance of Privatized Power Utilities

Variable	N before	N after	Mean before / Median before	Mean after / Median after	t-statistic / Z-statistic
Profitability					
Operating income/ sales	36	15	0.7122 / 0.8264	0.4088 / 0.6109	2.308** / 1.757*
Net income/sales	36	15	0.1677 / 0.1949	0.0504 / −0.0076	0.341 / 0.537
Operating income/PPE	36	15	0.7458 / 0.6933	0.3206 / 0.4037	2.018** / 2.233**
Operating income/ net worth	36	15	0.7647 / 0.7559	0.3152 / 0.3729	1.996** / 1.736*
Mean tariff	26	6	1.7088 / 1.4213	1.0469 / 1.0296	2.032** / 1.977**
Operating efficiency					
Cost per unit	36	15	0.5101 / 0.4162	0.6649 / 0.5036	−1.242 / −1.137
Log(sales/PPE)	36	15	1.0055 / 0.9663	1.0488 / 0.9989	−0.828 / −1.116
Log(sales/employees)	36	15	1.0296 / 1.0324	0.9910 / 0.9955	1.394 / 1.220
Operating income/ employees	36	15	1.2877 / 1.2240	1.1073 / 1.0026	1.142 / 1.199
Labor					
Log(employees)	36	15	1.0013 / 1.0477	0.9974 / 0.9974	0.128 / 0.475

(Table continues on the following page.)

Table 6.10 (continued)

Variable	N before	N after	Mean before / Median before	Mean after / Median after	t-statistic / Z-statistic
Assets and investment					
Log(PPE)	36	15	1.0133 / 1.0031	0.9763 / 0.9593	1.826** / 2.150**
Investment/sales[a]	36	6	1.1585 / 0.9723	1.0014 / 0.9074	0.371 / 0.539
Investment/employees[a]	36	6	1.6667 / 0.8622	0.6618 / 0.3741	1.350 / 1.546
Investment/PPE[a]	36	6	1.2120 / 1.0115	1.0372 / 1.4047	0.411 / 0.108
Log(PPE/employees)	36	15	1.0733 / 1.2772	0.9021 / 0.9461	1.386 / 1.530
Output					
Log(sales)	36	15	1.0115 / 1.0361	0.9937 / 1.0081	1.225 / 1.199

*Significant at the 10 percent level.
**Significant at the 5 percent level.
***Significant at the 1 percent level.

Note: N = sample size and PPE = property, plant, and equipment. This table presents the industry-adjusted results for three privatized power holdings. Performance proxies are adjusted relative to Public Enterprises of Medellin. The data set is a balanced panel by construction, and the sample size refers to firm-year observations for two time periods: 1983–94, the years before the regulatory reform, and 1995–98, the postreform years. The maximum number of firm-year observations before the reform is 36; afterwards it is 15. See table 6.9 for an explanation of the significance tests; see appendix table 6C.1 for definitions of the variables.

a. Postreform data are for 1995–96 due to unavailability of appropriate data for later years.

Source: Authors' calculations.

whose objective is to generate a hedge for the system. In fact, thermal units are spread across electricity holdings, and some of them became independent companies after privatization as mentioned earlier (see table 6.4). Overall, 63 thermal plants with an effective capacity of 3,800 megawatts were operating in 1998; that represented a 32 percent share of all generated electricity. Among those thermal units, 21 started commercial operations after 1993, and 16 are privately owned. This is not a coincidence since the government had already undertaken an emergency plan to expand thermal generators to overcome the 1992 power generation crisis.[26]

Figure 6.5 illustrates the evolution of the country's effective and available capacity from 1991 to 1999. The available capacity rose from 1,000 gigawatt hours (GWh) in 1990 to around 2,500 GWh in 1998.[27] In sum, fixed investment in thermal generation has played a central role in improving system reliability as well as promoting market entry in power generation.

The behavior of profitability indicators, however, did not mirror the efficiency gains. Notice the striking result that all profitability indicators, adjusted and unadjusted, dropped after the regulatory reform. The mean (median) ratio of operating income to sales was 32.1 percent (35.8 percent) before the reform for the study sample (see table 6.9). The indicator fell to 18.9 percent (22.6 percent) during the postreform years. The ratios of operating income to PPE and to net worth, indicators of firms' profit rates on gross and net fixed assets, respectively, were reduced by close to one-half. These changes are significant at the 5 percent level. The adjusted indicators show the same behavior, that is, the privatized holdings lost relative profitability compared with their control group.

As in the case of manufacturing, these results are the opposite of the expected effects of privatization on firm profitability. The conventional wisdom would say that any gains in input productivity must have a direct impact on firm profitability rates if and only if there are no drastic changes in market competition. The 1994 regulatory reform implied more market competition for both power generation and distribution. First, ownership composition changed drastically within the first five years after the regulatory reform, which led to a balanced distribution of power-generating capacity between public and private utilities. By 1998 public utilities accounted for 42 percent of the power-generating capacity, while private and mixed-capital utilities held a 58 percent share. The largest generator had a 21 percent market share.[28] This outcome contrasts with the initial divestiture in the United Kingdom where nonnuclear generation was split into a duopoly, and in Chile, where the three largest power generators control 85 percent of the market.

On the power distribution side, privatized utilities dropped their rates for final users after 1995. Moreover, they have converged to EPM's final-user rate. The industry-adjusted rate for residential users dropped from 1.70 to 1.04 after the reform. If one takes into account the unregulated

Figure 6.5 Thermal Capacity versus Thermal Generation, 1991–99

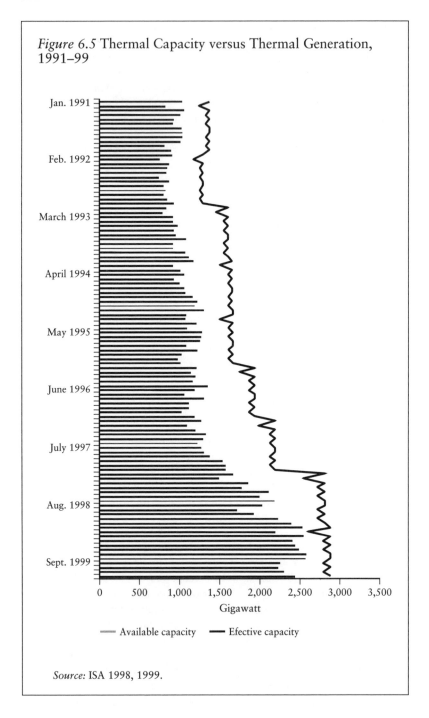

Source: ISA 1998, 1999.

electricity market (industrial users), the drop must be even greater. Table 6.11 summarizes the main variables of the wholesale electricity market. Two facts are noteworthy. First, the evolution of electricity spot prices suggests that buyers—power distributors—have effectively hedged against pool price volatility. Real contract prices dropped 42 percent from 1996 to 2000. That outcome is important since contracts have a 75 percent market share in bulk electricity. Another important outcome is that market deregulation has sharply increased the number of unregulated users, most of which are large industrial and commercial clients.

A sharp increase in financial costs during the first half of the 1990s also contributed to narrowing gross and net utility profits. The four regional markets under study had, on average, a 90 percent real increase in their financial costs relative to the average of the 1980s. The Bogotá Power Company faced most of the indebtedness burden because of the overcosts generated by the five-year delay in the start-up of the Guavio hydroelectric plant.

An Analysis of the Productive Efficiency of Thermal Plants

The previous section shows that the 1994 regulatory reform and resulting market competition encouraged power firms to achieve improvements in efficiency, to try to stop theft and other nontechnical losses of power, and to undertake new investments in power-generating capacity. This section presents the measurement of productive efficiency at the plant level for a sample of thermal plants that belong to public, private, and mixed-capital utilities. Of the 63 plants that belong to the interconnected system, only 32 units have been active, having a permanent or temporary production within a specific year. Because of changes in the statistical sources, the data set was divided into two samples. The first sample has records for 33 thermal plants, on average, for the 1988–94 period, that is, the years before reform. The second one has records for 32 thermal units for the postreform years (1995–2000).

The measurement of plant technical efficiency is based on Data Envelopment Analysis techniques and requires information about inputs and output for each thermal unit. Plant inputs are capital, or capacity in megawatts (MW); labor (number of employees); and fuel consumption (coal, gas, fuel oil, and diesel oil). All fuels must have a common measure unit, such as British thermal units (Btus) or thermal calories.[29] Output is given in gigawatt hours (millions of kilowatt hours). Information for power generation, consumption by type of fuel, and capacity at the plant level is available by crossing the different data sets before and after 1994.

Labor input is not directly observable for most units. There are two reasons for that problem. One is that before privatization thermal units were vertically integrated with power utilities; thus, payroll series were recorded following accounting criteria. Power companies kept labor

Table 6.11 Annual Averages for Wholesale Electricty Market Efficiency Variables, 1996–2000

Year	Mean spot price (US$/kWh)	Mean PPA price (US$/kWh)	Spot price index (Dic98=100)	PPA price index (Dic98=100)	Commercial demand (GWh)	Unregulated demand (GWh)	Regulated demand (GWh)	Unregulated demand share (percent)	Unregulated users (number)
1996	0.0084	0.0348	52.8	125.0	3,329.6	454.5	2,875.0	0.1365	11.2
1997	0.0548	0.0321	342.7	115.2	3,410.1	453.9	2,956.2	0.1336	95.3
1998	0.0374	0.0288	233.7	103.4	3,452.5	659.5	2,793.0	0.1910	678.8
1999	0.0159	0.0220	99.3	79.1	3,316.5	676.1	2,640.4	0.2038	891.6
2000	0.0204	0.0203	127.7	72.9	3,387.3	843.7	2,543.6	0.2489	2,377.0

Note: GWh = gigawatt hour, kWh = kilowatt hour, and PPA = power purchase agreement. This table shows the main variables of the wholesale electricity market. The spot price indicates the pool daily prices, and the PPAs are forward contracts of electricity prices and dispatched quantities. Both are market prices. Final residential and small commercial users, whose price formula is set by the regulatory commission, form the regulated demand. Unregulated users are large clients that underwrite purchase contracts with power generators and distributors. Commercial demand is equal to the sum of the regulated and unregulated demand. The last column reports the average number of large clients that are registered in the electricity market for a given year. Prices per kilowatt hour are in US$ at 1998 prices. Value series were deflated by the U.S. consumer price index.

Source: ISA 1998, 1999; Mercado de Energía Mayorista (MEM) requested files.

314

records to fulfill the requirements of financial reporting. Second, there was no regulator requesting information by power activity. Labor statistics after 1996 have improved sharply since the regulator (Superintendent of Domiciliary Public Services) has been in charge of the SIVICO database. Labor series by power company are broken down by occupational categories, sectoral activities (that is, generation, transmission, and distribution), and by type of power generation. In addition, after privatization the plants that were sold became new utilities. This allowed for making direct inferences about labor input (number of employees) by thermal substations. Fixed coefficients of labor to capacity were assumed based on the information sent by power generators to complete labor series before 1995. The results of the efficiency frontier measurement exercise based on 42 thermal plants that were active as marginal producers before and after the 1995 regulatory reform are displayed in appendix table 6E.1. The results show that the most efficient plants before the reform were not the most efficient afterward. Entrants indeed pushed efficiency up and became benchmark technologies. Thus, the 1994 reform that sought to promote plant entry also spurred gains in technical efficiency through the new plants and the overhaul of others. Such was the case of Termo-Barranquilla, which is the country's largest thermal plant.

Econometric Analysis of IFI Manufacturing Plants

This section analyzes the role that plant characteristics, foreign trade variables, and privatization played in determining privatization outcomes for the sample of IFI firms. The econometric analysis focuses on two key performance variables: plant profitability rates (Lerner indexes) and the translog indexes of total factor productivity as a proxy for technological change. This econometric exercise hopes to shed light on plant efficiency and markup determinants as well as to evaluate the significance of privatization within the model. The data set is an unbalanced panel of 28 IFI firms that records information for the 1974–98 period. The estimating equation follows the baseline pooled regression model:

$$performance_{it} = (\beta_0 + \alpha_i) + X_{it}B + Z_{it}\Lambda + \varepsilon_{it} \qquad (6.1)$$

where i equals 1, ..., n is the number of individual firms; t = 1, 2,..., T is the number of observations in each panel; X is equal to firm characteristics variables; and Z is equal to specific industrial classification variables. Equation 6.1 allows the running of several types of regression models according to specific assumptions on the residual variance covariance matrices and individual effects α_i. In particular, the estimations relax the assumptions of constant variance across panels, the nonexistence of individual effects, and instruments for endogeneity on right-hand-side variables.

Plant characteristic variables are related to technology structures, labor composition, and the firm's market positioning actions. One expected result is that technology-related variables have a positive impact on profitability gains. In that sense, plant size, operative scale, quality of raw materials, capital intensity, and relative labor productivity result in lower average costs that represent productivity gains due to new economies of scale. Plant payroll composition reflects quality in labor input. Thus, technicians should lead overall plant labor productivity because skilled workers are more dynamic and generate productivity spillovers. Administrative employees, in turn, may generate inflexibilities that end up hurting profitability. Market positioning variables are those actions that strengthen a firm's market share. The firm's signals are investment rates, the use of technological licenses, and product differentiation tactics such as advertising. These actions may persuade rivals to soften competition and adopt collusive prices, but because a competitor's best response might include hardening competition and setting dumping prices, there is no expected sign.

Industry-specific variables are mostly related to foreign trade. Three main variables are used in the estimating equations: nominal tariffs, effective protection rates, and Grubel and Lloyd (1975) indexes. The last is a proxy for trade in differentiated goods.[30] Protectionism increases domestic profitability by deterring entry. Intraindustry trade, in contrast, implies trade in similar goods that makes entry credible because of the monopolistic competition market structure, which drives sale prices to second-best prices.[31] Hence, profitability decreases.

Table 6.12 displays the main results for the markup determinants; these results call for several comments. First, in all cases, the firm's market share is the robust determinant. This is consistent with the observation that economic openness reduces the firm's market power and therefore decreases markup rates. Estimations show that a 10 percent decrease in market share reduces profitability by 9 percent.

Second, the foreign trade variables are robust regressors and show the expected sign. On average, an increase of 10 percent in the effective protection rate increases markups by 4 percent. In contrast, if intraindustry trade indexes rise 10 percent, markups will decrease on average by 3 percent. This finding is important from the perspective of strategic trade policy. Competition through similar goods forces firms to undertake further specialization strategies to promote efficiency gains in order to compensate for the reduction in markup rates. Third, plant size and productive efficiency are important sources of profitability gains. IFI firms are on average seven times larger than their competitors. As a result the observed gains in TFP partially offset the falling trend in firm markup. On average, if TFP indexes rise 10 points, they will increase markup rates by between

Table 6.12 Markup Determinants for IFI Firms

Independent variable	Equation 1 Pooled OLS[a]	Equation 2 Panel FGLS	Equation 3 Panel FGLS	Equation 4 Within FE	Equation 5 Pooled 2SLS[a]	Equation 6 FE + IV
Market share	0.8751***	0.9318***	0.9264***	0.8931***	0.9641***	0.9459***
	(0.0470)	(0.0263)	(0.0255)	(0.0305)	(0.0311)	(0.0341)
Labor productivity industry-adjusted	0.0195***	0.0085***	0.0089***	0.0108***	—	—
	(0.0039)	(0.0017)	(0.0016)	(0.0024)		
Translog index TFP	0.0001*	0.0001***	0.0001***	0.0001*	0.0003***	0.0002**
	(0.00003)	(0.00001)	(0.00001)	(0.00004)	(0.00011)	(−0.00006)
Size	0.0012**	0.0008***	0.0009***	—	—	—
	(0.0006)	(0.0002)	(0.0002)			
Human capital	−0.0226***	—	—	—	—	—
	(0.0054)					
Grubel and Lloyd index	−0.0521***	−0.0280***	−0.0385***	−0.0170*	−0.0400**	−0.0182*
	(0.0160)	(0.0079)	(0.0084)	(0.0094)	(0.0156)	(0.0095)
Effective protection	—	0.0381***	0.0433***	0.0337***	0.0878***	0.0328***
		(0.0055)	(0.0059)	(0.0079)	(0.0136)	(0.0080)
Dummy privatization	—	—	0.0125***	—	—	—
			(0.0029)			
Dummy foreign investment	—	—	−0.0144***	—	—	—
			(0.0031)			
Constant	0.0084	−0.0228***	−0.0214***	−0.0039	−0.0470**	−0.0016
	(0.0076)	(0.0035)	(0.0041)	(0.0069)	(0.0206)	(0.0089)

(Table continues on the following page.)

Table 6.12 (continued)

Independent variable	Equation 1 Pooled OLS[a]	Equation 2 Panel FGLS	Equation 3 Panel FGLS	Equation 4 Within FE	Equation 5 Pooled 2SLS[a]	Equation 6 FE + IV
Regression statistics						
R^2	0.6315			0.6699	0.6249	0.6245
Number of groups		28	28	28		28
Number of observations	613	621	621	621	620	564
Observations per group:						
Minimum		13	13	13		13
Maximum		25	25	25		25
F-test	116.03			238.69	145.15	235.16
	[0.0000]			[0.0000]	[0.0000]	[0.0000]
Wald-Chi$^2(k-1)$		2741	2932			
			[0.0000]			
F-test for all $\alpha_i = 0$				[0.0000]		
				93.6		
				[0.0000]		
Heteroscedasticity tests						
Cook-Weisberg	267.79					
	[0.0000]					
White	293.58					
	[0.0000]					

Variance matrix residuals						
Homoscedastic panels	Yes	No	No	Yes	Yes	Yes
Instrumental variable	No	No	No	No	Yes	Yes
RHS endogenous variables					TFP	TFP
Other equations in system	TFP = F(partial labor productivity, industry-adjusted; scale; capital/labor ratio, industry-adjusted).					

* Significant at the 10 percent level.
** Significant at the 5 percent level.
*** Significant at the 1 percent level.

Note: FE = fixed effects, FGLS = feasible generalized least squares, IFI = Instituto de Fomento Industrial, OLS = ordinary least squares, IV = instrumental variables, 2SLS = two-stage least squares, and TFP = total factor productivity. The table reports results from ordinary least squares, feasible generalized least squares, fixed effects, two-stage ordinary least squares, and fixed effects with instrumental variables for an unbalanced panel of 28 IFI firms for the 1974–98 period that were included in the 1988 privatization program. The maximum number of observations is 621. The dependent variable in all equations is the Lerner index, or markup rate. Standard errors appear in parentheses and p-values in brackets. Definitions of each variable and its methodology can be found in appendix table 6C.1.

a. White-Hubert robust heteroskedastic standard errors.

Source: Authors' calculations.

0.005 and 0.02 points in markup rates. Fourth, privatization shows a consistent sign. Privatization induced a 1.2 percent increase in profit rates (column 3 in table 6.12). Finally, the foreign investment dummy has the opposite sign. In the context of the IFI sample, this result is not surprising since some firms are located in industries that were once highly protected and that kept lower efficiency levels with respect to parent firms and international standards.

The econometric results on productive efficiency are displayed in table 6.13. Five comments are worth making. First, plant characteristics are relevant for TFP indexes. All the regression equations show that plant labor productivity, licensing, and number of technicians have positive effects. On average, an increase of 10 percent in partial labor productivity relative to the specific control group raises TFP by 3.2 percent. The effect of licensing is the largest. If plants expand their spending on technological licensing relative to their value added by 1 percent, they boost productivity by between 5.5 and 8.2 times. This finding is consistent with previous results for total manufacturing and calls attention to the short-run effectiveness of using patented licenses for improving productivity rather than engaging in direct research and development spending.[32] The number of technicians is a proxy for labor input quality. A 10 percent increase in this variable improves productivity by 1.12 percent.

Second, the equation includes two variables to capture demand effects on TFP measured by either the growth in value added or the log value of a firm's specific control group. The sign matches with the expected one, which is consistent with the traditional hypothesis derived from the Verdoom law by which growth and productivity are constrained by effective demand. The impact of aggregate demand is twofold: domestic demand and export demand induce growth and improve productivity by learning. This in turn leads to improvements in price competitiveness, which induces higher levels of effective demand (Dixon and Thirlwall 1975).[33] Third, privatization has a positive effect on productivity, causing an increase ranging from 0.27 to 0.53 points on TFP indexes. Fourth, the scale and the adjusted capital partial productivity coefficients have a negative impact on productivity. The interpretation of this result is not straightforward. The losses in capital productivity due to overinvestment suggest that IFI firms adjusted capital spending to close gaps with industry benchmarks.

Fifth, markups are inversely related with TFP, which is not consistent with the self-investment-financing hypothesis of endogenous growth models (Romer 1990; Barro and Sala-i-Martin 1995). In particular, one should expect a positive impact since larger profitability rates ease the self-financing of capital equipment and spending on research and development. After controlling for fixed effects, however, the expected sign is recovered. The within-regression coefficients show that a 10 percent increase in markups improves TFP by 13 percent.

Table 6.13 Total Factor Productivity Determinants for IFI Firms

Independent variable	Equation 1 Pooled OLS[a]	Equation 2 Panel FGLS	Equation 3 Panel FGLS	Equation 4 Within FE	Equation 5 Pooled 2SLS[a]	Equation 6 FE + IV
Labor productivity, industry-adjusted	0.3803***	0.3633***	0.3295***	0.2219***	0.4811***	0.2384***
	(0.0598)	(0.0321)	(0.0318)	(0.0248)	(0.0769)	(0.0223)
Capital productivity, industry-adjusted	−0.0094***	−0.0049***	−0.0050***	—	−0.0103***	—
	(0.0017)	(0.001)	(0.0009)		(0.0019)	
Demand growth[b]	0.2011***	0.0812**	0.0977**	—	0.1915**	—
	(0.0782)	(0.0457)	(0.0444)		(0.0783)	
Scale	−0.0316***	−0.0190***	−0.0175***	−0.0136***	−0.0262***	−0.0185***
	(0.0043)	(0.0023)	(0.0023)	(0.0038)	(0.0045)	(0.0035)
Licensing	7.9312***	7.9246***	8.1922***	—	5.3740**	—
	(1.9463)	(1.3614)	(1.4664)		(2.1096)	
Compensation per worker, industry-adjusted	−0.3283***	−0.1031***	−0.1135***	—	−0.2392**	—
	(0.0943)	(0.0424)	(0.0432)		(0.1125)	
Advertising coefficient	−2.2255***	−1.6442***	−1.4812***	—	−2.2842***	—
	(0.5537)	(0.4407)	(0.4422)		(0.5543)	
Log technicians	0.1152***	0.1019***	0.0778***	0.1418***	0.1875***	0.1071***
	(0.0324)	(0.0176)	(0.0163)	(0.0262)	(0.0353)	(0.0215)
Privatization dummy	0.3626***	0.0525	—	—	0.2700	—
	(0.1073)	(0.0438)			(0.1118)	
Lerner index	—	−0.4968***	−0.4130***	1.3185***	−2.1912***	1.3116***
	—	(0.1570)	(0.1502)	(0.2899)	(0.4225)	(0.3626)

(*Table continues on the following page.*)

321

Table 6.13 (continued)

Independent variable	Equation 1 Pooled OLS[a]	Equation 2 Panel FGLS	Equation 3 Panel FGLS	Equation 4 Within FE	Equation 5 Pooled 2SLS[a]	Equation 6 FE + IV
Log value added[b]	—	—	—	0.3308***	—	0.2702***
				(0.0462)		(0.0412)
Relative capital/labor ratio	—	—	—	—	—	-0.0339***
						(0.0040)
Constant	0.9934***	0.6140***	0.7227***	-5.7045***	0.8739***	-4.3417***
	(0.1497)	(0.0762)	(0.0691)	(0.8684)	(0.1591)	(0.7796)
Regression statistics						
R^2	0.1954			0.2708	0.1663	0.4047
Number of groups		28	28	28		28
Number of observations	554	554	554	575	554	476
Observations per group:						
Minimum		4	4	5		5
Maximum		24	24	25		25
F-test	22.9			40.25	20.73	54.93
	[0.0000]			[0.0000]	[0.0000]	[0.0000]
Wald-chi$^2(k-1)$		289.6	296.4			
		[0.0000]	[0.0000]			
F-test for all $\alpha_i = 0$			142.5			
			[0.0000]			

Heteroscedasticity tests

Cook-Weisberg	73.51 [0.0000]				
Breuch-pagan LM stat	158.9 [0.0000]				

Variance matrix residuals

Homoscedastic panels	Yes	No	No	Yes	Yes
Instrumental variables	No	No	No	No	Yes
RHS endogenous variables				LERNER	LERNER
Other equations in system				LERNER	LERNER

Lerner = F(market share, Grubel & Lloyd index, effective protection)

* Significant at the 10 percent level.
** Significant at the 5 percent level.
*** Significant at the 1 percent level.

Note: FE = fixed effects, FGLS = feasible generalized least squares, IFI = Instituto de Fomento Industrial, OLS = ordinary least squares, IV = instrumental variables, and 2SLS = two-stage least squares. The table reports results from ordinary least squares, feasible generalized least squares, fixed effects, two-stage ordinary least squares, and fixed effects with instrumental variables for an unbalanced panel of 28 IFI firms for the 1974–98 period that were included in the 1988 privatization program. The maximum number of observations is 621. The dependent variable in all equations is the translog index of total factor productivity (1974 = 100). For each year and firm, we compute industry-adjusted indicators by taking the ratio of the value of the indicator for the IFI firm to its industry control group. Industry control group is the four-digit standard industrial classification group to which a specific firm belongs. Standard errors appear in parentheses and *p* values in brackets. Definitions of each variable and its methodology can be found in appendix table 6C.1.

a. White-Hubert robust heteroskedastic standard errors.
b. By specific industrial classification.

Source: Authors' calculations.

Power Plants: Statistical Analysis of Efficiency Scores

This section reports the results of an econometric analysis of thermal power plant DEA efficiency scores. The exercise follows a limited dependent variable model because the dependent variable under analysis is censored by construction. It takes positive values and is bounded at 1.00; thus, the efficient plants record an efficiency score, y_{it}, of 1. Otherwise, $0 \leq y_{it} < 1$. The sample might also be truncated because there is knowledge of independent variables only if y_{it} is observed. This is particularly important for marginal power producers when the thermal plants are shut down by maintenance, transmission, and generation constraints because there is no power dispatch. The baseline-censored model follows a linear specification:

$$y_{it} = \begin{cases} x'_{it}B + e_{it} & 0 < y_{it} \leq 1 \\ 0 & otherwise \end{cases} \tag{6.2}$$

and the residuals follow a normal distribution with zero mean and constant variance.

Equation 6.2 models efficiency scores as a function of plant characteristics, ownership structure, and regulatory policy dummies. Plant characteristics include plant age, capital-to-labor ratio, technology type, and load factor. Controlling for the load factor indicates how marginal a given producer is. A dummy that takes the value of 1 for all private plants captures ownership. The regulatory dummy tries to capture the effect of large customer definition. Thus, for each plant that dummy takes a value of 1 after 1998 (when the minimum usage limit was lowered, thus increasing the number of unregulated users from 100 to 900). The data set includes all observed records from all active thermal plants during the 1995–2000 period. Therefore, the data set is an unbalanced panel with 166 observations.

Table 6.14 displays the Tobit regressions. The dependent variable in the first two equations is Score1, which represents plant efficiency scores measured under the assumption of constant returns to scale, and capital input is adjusted by its effective utilization. This adjustment normalizes plant capacity by load factor, which means that all producers are treated as if they were off-peak generators. The dependent variable in the third equation is Score2, in which the measure of plant efficiency relaxes the assumption of constant returns to scale. The reading of those results is as follows. First, the equations exhibit high quality of fit, reported by the R^2 of the OLS regressions.[34] In particular, the overall effect of the plant characteristics, ownership structure, and regulatory policy dummy explains 90 percent of the efficiency scores once capital input is adjusted by capacity utilization; that number falls to 78 percent when the assumption of constant returns to scale is relaxed. Second, dummy variables for technology

Table 6.14 Determinants of Thermal Plants' Efficiency Scores

Independent variable	Equation 1 Pooled Tobit Score1	Equation 2 Pooled Tobit Score1	Equation 3 Pooled Tobit Score2
Adjusted capacity	−0.0004*		
	(0.0002)		
Age	−0.0155***	−0.0175***	−0.0183***
	(0.0018)	(0.0018)	(0.0029)
Age^2	0.0004***	0.0005***	0.0005***
	(6E-04)	(6E-05)	(9.5E-05)
Load factor	0.4169***	0.3700***	0.1128***
	(0.0445)	(0.031)	(0.0428)
Load factor^2	−5.1005***	−4.5298***	
	(1.207)	(1.125)	
Capital/labor ratio	0.0010		
	(0.0006)		
Gas dummy	0.3653***	0.3704***	0.3960***
	(0.0118)	(0.0122)	(0.0196)
Combined cycle dummy	0.1431		
	(0.0923)		
Private ownership dummy	0.0323***		
	(0.0116)		
Public ownership dummy		−0.0423***	
		(0.0117)	
Regulatory policy dummy	0.0201*	0.0229**	0.0432**
	(0.0108)	(0.0112)	(0.1762)
Constant	0.4098***	0.4593***	0.5020***
	(0.0206)	(0.0208)	(0.0315)
Sigma	0.0660	0.0691	0.1122
Regression statistics			
R^2-OLS	0.9104	0.9074	0.775
Uncensored observations	155 156	152	
Censored observations	7 10	14	
LR~Chi($k-1$)	377.3	379.5	228.9
	[0.0000]	[0.0000]	[0.0000]
Test residuals			
Cook-Weisberg (OLS)	0.00	0.04	2.46
	[0.9924]	[0.8445]	[0.1168]
Breuch-Pagan (OLS)	6.87		
	[0.4416]		

(Table continues on the following page.)

Table 6.14 (continued)

	Equation 1 Pooled Tobit	Equation 2 Pooled Tobit	Equation 3 Pooled Tobit
Independent variable	Score1	Score1	Score2
Ramsey-RESET (OLS)	1.83	0.59	0.28
	[0.1439]	[0.6225]	[0.8391]
Swilk (OLS)	4.99	4.67	3.35
	[0.0000]	[0.0000]	[0.0004]

* Significant at the 10 percent level.
** Significant at the 5 percent level.
*** Significant at the 1 percent level.
Note: OLS = ordinary least squares. This table reports results from Tobit regressions for an unbalanced panel of 33 thermal plants for the 1995–2000 period. The total number of observations is 166. The dependent variables are Score1 and Score2. Score1 is equal to plant efficiency scores measured under the assumptions of constant return to scale and convex technology. Capital input is multiplied by its effective utilization rate. Score2 is equal to plant efficiency scores measured under the assumptions of variable returns to scale and convex technology. Capital input is multiplied by its effective capacity utilization rate. Gas technology is a dummy that takes the value of 1 if plant technology is gas based, and 0 otherwise; combined cycle is a dummy that takes the value of 1 if plant technology, whether a thermal plant, has a combined cycle technology, and 0 otherwise; private ownership is a dummy that takes the value of 1 if the plant is privately owned, and 0 otherwise; public ownership is a dummy that takes the value of 1 if the plant is publicly owned, and 0 otherwise; and regulatory policy is a dummy that takes the value of 1 for the years that the definition of a large client was set to a minimum consumption of 0.5 megawatt per month. Standard errors appear in parentheses and p-values in brackets.
Source: Authors' calculations.

are robust and statistically significant in all equations. This implies that new gas-based technologies improve system efficiency, because they save on fuel consumption. Entrants played a central role in this particular issue. Third, the load factor is positively related, meaning that power losses associated with the frequent and costly plant start-ups are effectively reduced. The square of the variable is negatively related, however, showing that there are decreasing returns to scale at full plant capacity.

Fourth, plant age is negatively related, meaning that older plants lose relative efficiency. Nonetheless, the behavior of the square of the age variable shows the presence of positive learning effects that partially offset plant aging. For example, the accumulated efficiency loss after 10 years is 17 percent, but the learning effect represents a 4.5 percent efficiency gain. Fifth, regulatory policy has had positive effects. The regression coefficients indicate that, on average, the three equations show an overall efficiency gain of 2.8 percent. Sixth, the exercise is inconclusive about whether ownership leads to structural differences in productive efficiency. The private ownership dummy was not significant once capital input was corrected for capacity utilization and the assumption of constant returns to scale was relaxed (see table 6.14, column 3). This result is in line with other studies. Pollit (1995) reports statistically insignificant regression coefficients for his ownership dummy based on a cross-sectional data set of 768 thermal power plants for 14 countries.

Concluding Remarks

This chapter has given an overview of the privatization program in Colombia, gathering detailed information in a comprehensive way that sets this process in context within the global economic deregulation and market promotion competition strategy. In that sense, the chapter offers for the first time a complete description of Colombia's privatization experience in the 1990s and is also the first to provide empirical evidence based on an ex post performance evaluation for the privatized plants. The chapter has explored in-depth the cases of IFI manufacturing enterprises and power holdings. These sectors account for 95 percent of the privatization sales up to 1998, which undoubtedly make the results comprehensive in terms of the overall effects of privatization on firm performance.

The study yielded several interesting results. For the case of manufacturing, we found that IFI firms followed the cycles and trends of their private competitors across the manufacturing industry. This was proved through the study's measurement of 25 indicators of economic performance. The evolution of firm market power and profitability rates indicates that privatized firms are pricing more competitively and still adjusting to global economic deregulation and foreign competition. In particular, the decreasing trends in firms' markup after 1990 is a counterintuitive result. Most studies on privatization show an opposite result because when they were state-owned, the privatized firms were unprofitable or experiencing permanent operative deficits. The IFI firms were different because the government did not exercise control of the companies' management policies. As a result, the IFI companies behaved more like their private competitors than like typical state-owned enterprises. Thus, the lower markup rates after privatization show that the markets are more competitive because of deregulation on entry and the exposure to international competition brought about by lower tariffs.

The study also shows that privatization had a positive effect on firm efficiency. The analysis of the changes in performance of the efficiency indicators shows a sharp increase in labor productivity as well as a reduction in the cost per unit. In contrast, IFI firms experienced a drastic reduction in the median of the ratios of sales and value added to capital stock. This was a direct consequence of the overinvestment problem of the late 1970s and 1980s that hit the IFI companies harder because of their capital-intensive technologies. Privatization in this case did not boost investment. Instead, IFI companies rationalized capital spending to overcome their fall in sales per unit of capital. Nonetheless, the measurements of total factor productivity had a net positive change for these firms—the industry-adjusted indicators even showed that their overall efficiency gain was greater than their private competitors. Thus, privatization was important as a complementary mechanism that facilitated and sped up industrial restructuring in these plants. This observation is supported in econometric results in which the privatization dummy turned out to be a robust determinant of the indexes of total factor productivity.

The analysis of the power sector also yielded important results. The general trends of electricity contract prices, the evolution of plant entry in thermal generation, and the increasing share of unregulated users in commercial demand suggest that the regulatory reform has been effective in promoting market competition and system efficiency. As was true for the IFI manufacturing firms, the performance analysis shows that the 1994 regulatory reform and the privatization program had a positive impact on the efficiency of electric utilities but a negative impact on their profitability.

The sources of efficiency gains are explained by market competition in power generation; the reduction of nontechnical power losses, such as theft, in distribution; and the new investment in gas-based thermal technologies. The measurement of efficiency scores by thermal units reinforces the evidence in favor of the existence of an overall gain in system efficiency and reliability. Regulatory policy has had positive effects on plant efficiency based on the econometric results. The increasing number of unregulated users has led generators to offer more competitive prices to secure generating contracts and thus a steady flow of business. Consistent with other studies, we found no evidence that private ownership of electricity utilities had a positive impact on efficiency. Instead, regulation and market reform pin down the positive change in technical efficiency across thermal units.

The results of the reform on utilities' profitability do not go in the expected direction; instead of rising, they have fallen. This outcome is partially explained by the introduction of market competition in electricity generation. Competition implies that utilities have less market power, which limits their capacity to obtain extra profits through power generation. In fact, the wholesale electricity market in Colombia is one of the most competitive given the number of power generators relative to the size of the market. Two additional facts are worth noting. First, power holdings faced financial burdens caused by an increase in their external debt service and delays in start-up in some hydro units at the beginning of the 1990s. Second, power distributors have decreased real prices to final users. This is a consequence of a deregulated market that has introduced competition in the market of forward contracts.

Finally, although privatization in Colombia has been small in size and scope, this study provides elements to conclude that the experiment was successful because it helped to consolidate entry and market competition in previously protected industries and to break up vertically integrated monopolies.

Appendix 6A

Table 6A.1 Infrastructure Concession Projects with Ongoing Private Investment by 1998

Project name		Project name	
Roads		*Airports*	
Armenia–Pereira–		Bogota-Second Track	
Manizale		Barranquilla, Aereopuerto	
Barranquilla–Cienaga		del Caribe S.A.	
Bogota–Facatativa		Cartagena, Airport	
Bogota–Villavicencio		*Water and sanitation*	
Buga–Tulua–Paila		ACUACAR-Cartagena	
Carreteras Meta		Triple A-Bquilla	
Cartagena–Barranquilla		Sta Marta	
Cortijo–Vino		Metro-Agua	
Espinal Neiva		TIBITOC Plant for	
Medellin–RioNegro		water treatment	
Patios–Guasca		Bogota Water Company	
Sta–Marta–			
Paraguanchon		*Railroads*	
Total road kilometers	1,388	Atlantic Line–cargo	
under concession		*Maritime ports*	
Gas pipelines		Total ports under concession	15
Sebastopol–Medellin		*Telecomunications*[a]	
Barranca–B/manga		COMCEL (mixed capital)	
Sur–Huila		CELCARIBE (mixed capital)	
Mariquita–Cali		OCCEL (mixed capital)	
Huila–Tolima		CELUMOVIL (private)	
Total length in kilometers	861	CELUMOVIL COSTA (private)	
under concession		COCELCO (private)	

Note: This table excludes the power sector. Concession contracts are either build-operate-maintain-transfer or rehabilitate-operate-maintain-transfer.

a. Refers to mobile phone company names and their capital structure by 1998.

Source: Law 37 of 1993; DNP 1993, 1995, 1997c; Bonilla and others (2000); Alonso and others (2001).

Appendix 6B

Table 6B.1 List of IFI Enterprises in the Sample

Number	Name	Startup	ISIC4	ISIC–name
1	Acerías Paz del Río	1947	3710	Iron and steel basic industries
2	Aicsa	1977	3845	Manufacture of aircraft
3	Alcalis-Betania	1951	3511	Basic industrial chemicals except fertilizers
4	Alcalis-Mamonal	1967	3511	Basic industrial chemicals except fertilizers
5	Astivar	1974	3841	Shipbuilding and repairing
6	Catsa Compañía Colombiana	1978	3116	Grain mill products
7	Automotriz	1974	3843	Manufacture of motor vehicles
8	Cementos Boyacá	1955	3523	Cement, lime, and plaster
9	Cementos Rioclaro	1986	3692	Cement, lime, and plaster
10	Cerromatoso	1979	3722	Recovery and founding of tin and nickel
11	Colclinker	1974	3692	Cement, lime, and plaster
12	Conastil	1969	3841	Shipbuilding and repairing
13	Empaques del Cauca	1965	3211	Spinning, weaving, and finishing textiles
14	Fatextol	1988	3220	Wearing apparel
15	Federaltex	1987	3211	Spinning, weaving, and finishing textiles

16	Ferticol	1966	3511	Fertilizers and pesticides
17	Frigopesca	1978	3114	Canning, processing of fish, shellfish
18	Icollantas	1942	3551	Tire and tube industries
19	Ingenio de Risaralda	1978	3118	Sugar refineries
20	Intelsa	1979	3832	Manufacture of radio, tv, and telecommunications equipment
21	Monomeros	1967	3512	Fertilizers and pesticides
22	Penwalt	1967	3512	Fertilizers and pesticides
23	Propal	1961	3411	Pulp, paper, and paperboard
24	Quibi	1968	3522	Manufacture of drugs and medicines
25	Simesa	1938	3710	Iron and steel basic industries
26	Sofasa	1969	3843	Manufacture of motor vehicles
27	Sucromiles	1973	3511	Basic industrial chemicals except fertilizers
28	Tejidos Unica	1953	3216	Weaving and cotton manufactures
29	Texpinal	1973	3211	Spinning, weaving, and finishing textiles
30	Vikingos de Colombia	1968	3114	Canning, processing of fish, shellfish

Note: IFI = Instituto de Fomento Industrial.
Source: DANE, *Industrial Directory*; IFI, Investment Department.

Appendix 6C

Performance Indicators for IFI Firms: Definitions and Methodology

The Annual Manufacturing Survey of Colombia (Encuesta Anual Manu-facturera, or EAM) is in practice a census of medium and large enterprises in manufacturing. The EAM has undergone three methodological changes affecting the following time periods: 1970–91, 1992–93, and 1994 to date. The changes have affected the inclusion or exclusion of variables within chapters; the addition or suppression of new information across chapters; the modification of the format or variable classification criteria; and the rescaling of the sample cohorts.

Some specific examples are the changes of the payroll classification, the inclusion of temporary workers after 1987, the exclusion of direct exports as a component of a firm's sales, the elimination of the direct tax variables after 1991, the redefinition of large enterprise according to number of employees, and the addition of new components for fixed investment after 1992, among many others.

Despite the format modifications, the survey has kept the basic variables and structure across time. The database cleanup process was a two-step procedure. First, we worked with the basic variables of the 1970–91 survey. Second, all basic series were overlapped and grouped, keeping the original definitions of the older survey.[35] The manufacturing survey offers the following five types of variables:

• *Identification variables*—location, specific standard industrial classi-fication, firm's legal capital structure, and size classification.
• *Labor variables*—wages, benefits, permanent and temporary employees, administrative employees, workers, technicians, and gender statistics.
• *Output-related variables*—gross output, value added, intermediate consumption components, industrial expenditures, and inventories of final products and raw materials.
• *Finance-related variables*—fixed asset investment, accounting depreciation, sales, marketing spending, paid royalties, and other general expenditure variables.
• Consumption, generation, and sales of electricity.

The survey recorded data for 133 variables from 1970 to 1991. The survey recorded 380 variables during 1992 and 1993. Since 1994 the survey has worked with 200 variables. The 1992–93 period is problematic because the survey included information that was not comparable with previous data. However, the core variables were recorded.

Table 6C.1 The Indicators for IFI Firms in the Sample

Variable	Description
Fixed capital stock series by type of depreciable assets	$k_t = k_{t-1}(1 - \delta) + I_t$, perpetual inventory method, and K_0 is the initial capital $k_0 = \dfrac{IB_0}{g + \delta}$, where g is the historic growth rate of the fixed assets gross investment series; δ is the economic depreciation rate; IB_0 is gross investment at the initial date. Depreciation rates are taken from Pombo (1999b).
Cost per unit	The ratio of cost of sales to net sales. Cost of sales is equal to the direct expenses involved in the production of a good, including raw materials expenditures plus compensation paid to blue-collar workers. Sales are equal to the total value of products and services sold nationally and internationally.
Log(sales/employees)	The log of the ratio of sales to the total number of employees. Sales are equal to the total value of products and services sold nationally and internationally. Employees correspond to the total number of paid workers who depend directly on the company.
Log(sales/capital stock)	The log of the ratio of sales to capital stock. Sales are equal to the total value of products and services sold nationally and internationally. Capital stock series follow the perpetual inventory method, defined above.
Value added/capital	Partial capital productivity is the ratio of value added to capital stock. Capital stock series follow the perpetual inventory method, defined above.
Value added/labor	Partial labor productivity is the ratio of value added to labor. Capital stock series follow the perpetual inventory method, defined above. Labor is the total number of permanent employees.
Value added/workers	Partial labor productivity. Workers stand for the number of blue-collar workers by firm.
Total factor productivity (TFP)	TFP decomposition following the methodology in Jorgenson and Grilliches (1967), using a translog technology.
Operating income/sales	Operating income is equal to sales minus operating expenses, the cost of sales, and depreciation. Sales are equal to the total value of products and services sold nationally and internationally.

(Table continues on the following page.)

Table 6C.1 (continued)

Variable	Description
Net income/sales	Net income is equal to operating income minus interest expenses and net taxes paid. Sales are equal to the total value of products and services sold nationally and internationally.
Operating income/ capital stock	The ratio of operating income to capital stock. Operating income is equal to sales minus operating expenses, the cost of sales, and depreciation. Capital stock series follow perpetual inventory method.
Gross margin rate	$\dfrac{VA_i - W_i}{VA_i}$ The ratio of value added minus wages over value added.
Lerner index	$\dfrac{\alpha_i}{\varepsilon}$ The ratio of firm's market share over demand elasticity.
Capital intensity ratio 1	Ratio of capital over permanent employment.
Capital intensity ratio 2	Ratio of capital over blue-collar workers.
Plant size	Ratio of total workers of firm i in sector j over plant average workers in industry j.
Permanent workers/average permanent workers	Ratio of permanent blue-collar workers of firm i in sector j over average permanent blue-collar workers in industry j.
Output scale indicator	$\dfrac{Y_{ij}}{\overline{Y}_j}$ Ratio of output of firm i in sector j over average plant output in sector j.
Gross investment rate	$\dfrac{I_i}{Y_i}$ Ratio of investment of firm i over output in firm i.
Machinery and equipment investment rate/output	The ratio of new investment of firm i in machinery and equipment to the total output of firm i.
Machinery and equipment investment rate/total investment	The ratio of new investment of firm i in machinery and equipment to the total output of investment of firm i.
Real wages per worker	Real average wages paid per worker by firm. The consumer price index was used as deflator to calculate real wages at constant pesos. The monthly average

Table 6C.1 (continued)

Variable	Description
	official exchange rate of 1995 is used to convert series to constant prices in US\$. A similar procedure is used for the calculation of real wages per blue-collar and per white-collar workers.
Industry-adjusted real wages per worker	Industry control group is the four-digit standard industrial classification to which a specific firm belongs. For each year and firm we compute the industry-adjusted indicator by taking the ratio of the value of the indicator for the IFI firm to its industry control group. A similar procedure is used for blue-collar and white-collar workers.
Total wages/sales	The ratio of total wages paid by the firm to the sales of the firm. Total wages is equal to the total wage bill paid to all workers in payroll. Sales are equal to the total value of products and services sold nationally and internationally.
Wage rate	The ratio of total wages paid by the firm to the firm's value added. Total wages is equal to the total wage bill paid to all workers in payroll. Value added is equal to the firm's gross output minus intermediate consumption.
Compensation rate	The ratio of total compensation paid by the firm to the firm's value added. Total compensation is equal to wages plus social benefits paid to workers in payroll. Value added is equal to the firm's gross output minus intermediate consumption.
CR4 entropy index	The output of the four largest plants of industry j over industry j output.
Herfindal index	$\sum_{i=1}^{n} s_{ij}^2$ Summation of market shares (s) of firm i in industry j.
Imported raw material/domestic raw materials	A measure of quality in intermediate consumption, where imported raw materials stand for the raw materials used in a production process whose country of origin is not Colombia. Domestic raw materials are raw materials produced in Colombia.

(Table continues on the following page.)

Table 6C.1 (continued)

Variable	Description
Human capital	Ratio of technicians over workers.
Advertising rate	Ratio of advertising expenditures over value added.
Licensing indicator	Ratio of paid royalties on value added.
Intraindustry trade coefficient	Grubel and Lloyd index of intraindustry trade by industry.
Gross output	For the manufacturing industry, gross output is equal to the total of product sales plus sales of all self-produced electricity plus income for industrial services plus sales of all nontransformed goods.
Intermediate consumption	For manufacturing, intermediate consumption is the combination of raw materials plus industrial expenses plus purchases of electricity.
Value added	Gross output minus intermediate consumption.

Note: IFI = Instituto de Fomento Industrial.

Appendix 6D

The Power Sector Indicators and Data Sets

The performance indicators for the power sector are based on the financial statements. These indicators follow the definition and methodology of the privatization studies of Megginson, Nash, and van Randenborgh (1994) and La Porta and López-de-Silanes (1999). Most of the variables are defined in appendix table 6C.1.

The cost per unit indicator is expressed in pesos per kilowatt at 1995 prices. Output is in gigawatts.

The Data Sets

Currently, the power sector statistics in Colombia are split among the the National Grid Company (Interconexión Eléctrica S.A, or ISA); the Mining and Energy Planning Unit; the Electricity and Gas Regulatory Commission; the National Planning Department; and the Superintendent of Domiciliary Public Services (SSPD). As a result, each source has a different format and contents.

The information is sorted by plant, utilities, regional electricity markets, and geographical regions, or at a countrywide aggregate level. Table 6D.1 describes the contents of the collected data sets.

Table 6D.1 Colombia: Power Sector Statistics and Description of the Data Sets

Data sources	Contents
ISA Reports (1995–99)	Operative reports of the National Interconnected System Hydrology Grid constraints Generation Demand Available effective capacity The Electricity Spot Market Report Pool's prices and contacts Total traded amount (gigawatts) Pool's marginal supply prices by type of generation
SIVICO 1997–99 *Source:* SSPD	The following data are available by utility level: Financial statements Income statement Balance sheet Labor statistics Number of employees by sector's activity Number of employees by occupational category Number of employees by type of generation Market composition by type of user Consumption Invoicing Number of subscribers Average tariffs by users Results and performance control process indicators Quality service indicators Spending and indebtedness indicators
SIEE 1970–98 *Source:* Organización Latinoamericana de Energía	The Energy and Economic Information System (SIEE) is a data set covering the Latin American economies' energy-related statistics. The SIEE sections are Prices Demand and supply Energy-related equipment Environmental impact

(Table continues on the following page.)

Table 6D.1 (continued)

Data sources	Contents
	Economic + energy indicators
	Worldwide energy statistics
FEN	The power sector historical financial data
1983–94	compiled by the Financiera Electrica
Source: FEN	Nacional (FEN). The database offers a
	summary by power company of
	Income statements
	Balance sheets
	Other variables: purchase + sales of
	bulk electricity; available capacity;
	power losses
SINSE	The power sector national system is a
1970–94	comprehensive database. The data are
Source: MME	available by utility and regional market.
	The SINSE chapters are
	Energy balances
	Generation and electricity demand
	Number and type of subscribers
	Average tariffs by users

In addition to the data sets, we made direct requests to ISA for the monthly indicators of the Mercado de Energia Mayorista, starting in July 1995, and the Thermal Park Data Set. The crossing of information among ISA's thermal park data set, SIVICO, and SINSE allowed us to collect the input-output variables by thermal unit that are depicted in appendix table 6D.2 To make direct inferences of labor input by plant *after* 1996, a survey was carried out among the members of the Colombian Generators Association. The collected information allowed for distinguishing benchmarks of capacity-to-labor ratios; under normal assumptions of Leontief technology of noninput substitution, that coefficient turns out a constant parameter. The data provided by the power utilities along with SIVICO allowed us to identify the number of employees by thermal plants for the period 1996–99, given the reported capacity per unit. The estimated benchmark labor-to-capacity ratios by occupational category for a base-technology thermal plant were 0.036597 (directors), 0.151852 (administrative), and 0.527731 (operative).

For the 1988–94 period, the FEN books recorded some physical variables per power utility, among them the permanent employment series.

Table 6D.2 Thermal Plants: Input and Output Variables

Sample	Variables
1988–1994	Generation (gigawatt hours)
	Gross capacity (megawatts)
	Net capacity (megawatts)
	Coal (tons)
	Fuel oil (gallons)
	Diesel oil (gallons)
	Gas (cubic feet)
1995–1999	Generation (gigawatt hours)
	Effective capacity (megawatts)
	Labor (number of employees)[a]
	Heat rate

Note: Labor information is recorded by power utility and industry activity: generation, transmission, and distribution (SIVICO).

a. Since 1996.

Source: SINSE, ISA, SIVICO.

Thus, the inference of labor series by the thermal units followed a constant distributing capacity assumption, that is:

Thermal Unit Labor (L_1) = (Max Theoretical Thermal Plant Unit Capacity in GWh/Utility Available Capacity in GWh) * Total Permanent Utility Employees

Other formulas were used to generate alternative labor series by thermal plants. One was based on power generation:

Thermal Unit Labor (L_2) = (Thermal Plant Generation in GWh/Utility Available Capacity in GWh) * Total Permanent Utility Employees

Then an adjusted L_2 series was generated under the assumption:

$$\left(\frac{L}{MW}\right)_{thermal} = \left(\frac{L}{MW}\right)_{hydro} / (1+x); \text{ where: } x = \text{avg} \frac{MgP_{hydro}}{MgP_{thermal}};$$

Rationing Price: $MgP_{hydro} > MgP_{thermal} = 1.8$;
Without Rationing: $MgP_{hydro} < MgP_{thermal} = 0.6$,

where MgP = marginal price, MW = megawatts of installed capacity.

The above coefficients are observed parameters. L_1 and L_2 were used as the labor input series in the estimation of plant efficiency scores.

Appendix 6E

Table 6E.1 DEA Efficiency Scores in Thermal Generation before and after the Regulatory Reform

Decision-making unit	Plant name	Startup year	Capacity megawatts	Owner-ship	Score before	Score after	Score1 before	Score1 after	Relative effic.	Relative effic.1
1	Barranca1	1982	13	Public	0.7859	0.5932	0.7859	0.7939	−	+
2	Barranca2	1982	13	Public	0.7203	0.5932	0.7448	0.7702	−	+
3	Barranca3	1972	66	Public	0.8798	0.6404	0.8798	0.8211	−	−
4	Barranca4	1983	32	Public	0.6625	0.6118	0.6625	0.8110	−	+
5	Barranca5	1983	21	Public	0.7023	0.6176	0.7023	0.8217	−	+
6	Bquilla1	1980	58	Public	0.9211	.	0.9139	.		
7	Bquilla3	1980	66	Private	1.0000	0.6624	1.0000	0.7156	−	−
8	Bquilla4	1980	69	Private	0.9699	0.7439	0.9803	1.0000	−	+
9	Cartagena1	1980	66	Private	0.8677	0.6428	1.0000	0.7447	−	−
10	Cartagena2	1980	54	Private	0.7932	0.6515	0.7437	0.8274	−	+
11	Cartagena3	1980	67	Private	0.8712	0.6815	0.8603	0.8245	−	−
12	Chinu4	1982	14	Public	0.4242	.	0.7097	.		
13	Cospique1	1960	4	Public	0.9086	.	1.0000	.		
14	Cospique2	1960	4	Public	0.7277	.	1.0000	.		
15	Cospique3	1967	8	Public	1.0000	.	0.9722	.		
16	Cospique4	1966	9	Public	1.0000	.	0.7791	.		
17	Cospique5	1965	12	Public	0.4487	.	0.8584	.		
18	Flores1	1993	152	Private	0.9881	1.0000	0.9881	1.0000	+	+

19	Guajira1	1987	160	Public	1.0000	0.8563	1.0000	0.7743	—	—
20	Guajira2	1987	160	Public	1.0000	0.8374	1.0000	0.8915	—	—
21	Paipa 1	1963	31	Public	0.4048	0.4977	0.3208	0.8859	+	+
22	Paipa 2	1975	74	Public	0.7307	0.3794	0.4755	0.7891	—	+
23	Paipa3	1978	74	Public	0.6331	0.4154	0.3874	0.7735	—	+
24	Palenque 3-4	1972	15	Public	0.8780	0.4586	1.0000	0.8011	—	—
25	Palenque5	1985	21	Public	0.6706	.	0.6706	.	·	·
26	Proeléctrica1	1993	46	Private	0.9993	0.9695	0.9993	0.8857	—	—
27	Proeléctrica2	1993	46	Private	1.0000	0.9695	1.0000	0.9654	—	—
28	Tasajero	1985	163	Private	1.0000	0.6755	1.0000	0.8241	—	—
29	Tibú1	1965	6	Public	0.1669	.	0.3157	.		
30	Tibú2	1965	6	Public	0.1632	.	0.8026	.		
31	Zipa2-3	1976	104	Mixed	0.4904	0.8888	0.4213	0.6721	+	+
32	ZIPA3	1976	66	Mixed	.	0.2235	.	0.8021	·	·
33	Zipa4	1981	66	Mixed	0.4626	0.1879	0.4601	0.6797	—	+
34	Zipa5	1985	66	Mixed	0.2692	0.3213	0.3042	0.8655	+	+
35	Flores2	1996	100	Private	.	0.9199	.	0.9205		
36	Flores3	1998	152	Private	.	1.0000	.	1.0000		
37	Merilectrica	1998	157	Private	.	0.7887	.	0.9273		
38	TebsaB1	1998	768	Private	.	1.0000	.	0.9141		
39	Termocentro1	1997	99	Public	.	0.9160	.	1.0000		
40	Dorada1	1997	52	Public	.	0.2554	.	0.8010		
41	Sierra1	1998	150	Public	.	0.1442	.	0.8564		

(Table continues on the following page.)

Table 6E.1 (continued)

Decision-making unit	Plant name	Startup year	Capacity megawatts	Owner-ship	Score before	Score after	Score1 before	Score1 after	Relative effic.	Relative effic.1
42	Termovalle1	1998	214	Private	.	0.8237	.	0.8858	19	12
					Total decrease (plants)				19	12
					Share capacity (percent)				35.3	24.6

. No data are available.

Note: This table shows the results of the efficiency frontier measurement on 42 thermal plants that were active as marginal producers before and after the 1995 regulatory reform. The first three columns depict the plant name, startup year, and plant capacity in megawatts. All thermal units before the reform belonged to one of the five electric holdings in the country as described in text. The fourth column indicates the ownership status by the year 2000, that is, whether the thermal unit belonged to a public, private, or a mixed-capital electric utility. The next four columns describe the efficiency scores before and after the 1994 reform. The table presents two types of scores. The first one is the variable Score, which uses megawatts of capacity as total capital input. The second one is the variable Score1, in which capacity is adjusted by its effective utilization, and this is the definition of capital input used in these estimations. The reason to make such an adjustment is that most thermal units are marginal producers. In Colombia the base system is hydro. The efficiency measures assume constant return to scale assumption, that is, the value of total output is equal to total input spending and therefore the sum of inputs weights is equal to 1.

Source: Authors' estimations based on EMS 1.3 software written by Scheel (2000).

Notes

The authors wish to give special thanks to the following people and institutions: Eduardo Granados (DANE), Francisco Ochoa (ACOLGEN), Adriana Calderon (IFI), Gerson Castaneda (SSPD), Alberto Jose Uribe (Banco de la República), Ferney Niño (Banco de la República), and Diana Espinoza (ECOPETROL). The authors are grateful for the comments of Florencio López-de-Silanes, Alberto Chong, and other IDB seminar participants; Claude Crampes and the electricity workshop participants at the Institut d'Economie Industrialle, Toulouse; and Luis Eduardo Fajardo at the Universidad del Rosario. Rodrigo Taborda provided superb research assistance. Financial support from the IDB's Latin American Research Network is gratefully acknowledged.

1. The general objectives and the scope of the economic openness program are in the 1990–94 Development Plan (DNP 1991a). The main institutional reforms are embodied in the following laws and CONPES (National Council for Economic and Social Policy) documents: foreign control regime (Law 9/1991), foreign trade reform (Law 7/1991), financial reform (Law 45/1990), new statute of foreign investment (CONPES document, January 22/1991), labor reform (Law 50/1990), and privatization of maritime ports (Law 1/1991). See DNP (1991b).

2. One example is the study by Spiller and Guasch (1998) on the regulatory process in Latin America, in which they skip over the Colombian experience despite the country's advances in public utilities regulation. Furthermore, in the collective studies of privatization in Latin America, such as those by Glade (1996), Baer and Conroy (1994), and Baer and Birch (1994), references to Colombia are usually limited, in contrast to other Latin American countries.

3. The CONPES documents are 2648 (DNP 1993); 2775 (DNP 1995); and 2929 (DNP 1997c). Law 37 of 1993 deals with concessions contracts for telecommunications; Law 142 of 1994, the residential public services reform; Law 143 of 1994, the power sector reform; and Law 226 of 1995, the privatization transfers.

4. For details, see Alonso and others (2001) and DNP 1993, 1995, 1997b, and 1997c.

5. The schedule for public divestiture of public and mixed-capital enterprises and public financial institutions was laid out in CONPES documents 2378 (DNP 1988) and 2648 (DNP 1993).

6. All dollar values are in U.S. dollars unless otherwise indicated.

7. For details, see Megginson, Nash, and van Randenborgh (1994).

8. It is important to highlight that the IFI made major transfers of assets to the private sector before the privatization program of the 1990s. One example was Icollantas, in which the IFI sold its equity shares in 1980 and 1985. In 1994 the IFI participated in a 20 percent share of the company's capitalization of $60 million.

9. "Special legal procedures" were applied to companies with property shares from two or more public institutions, companies with direct investments from foreign government agencies, and companies with ongoing settlement processes with their lenders. For details, see DNP (1988).

10. For instance, by March 1993 ECOPETROL had equity shares in three domestic investment banks (Corficaldas, Corfinorte, Corfinanza), one power utility (ESSA), one fertilizer plant (FERTICOL), and one craft enterprise (Artesanias de Colombia). For details, see DNP (1993).

11. For details, see ECOPETROL's press release of June 6, 1997. According to that bulletin there was tight competition among the winner (Gas Natural of Spain) and British Petroleum, Amoco, Empresas Públicas de Medellín, and France Gas.

12. These cases were TERPEL CENTRO and TERPEL SUR, which sold 60 percent and 38 percent of their shares, respectively.

13. The national grid company Interconexión Eléctrica S.A. (ISA) was founded in 1967. By that time, the sectoral development view was to consolidate ISA as the largest nationwide power generator and transporter of bulk electricity following the vertically integrated natural monopoly model. For more details, see World Bank (1991). A complete description of the regulatory reform in Colombia's power sector is in Pombo (2001b) and ISA reports. Historically, Colombia's power sector has been divided into five regional markets: Bogotá Power Company (EEB), the Atlantic Coast Regional Electric Corporation (CORELCA), Public Enterprises of Medellín (EPM), Public Enterprises of Cali and the Cauca Valley Corporation (EMCALI and CVC), and the Colombian Power Institute (ICEL). Only three of the five regional power distribution networks have been privatized, leaving 70 percent of the distribution network in the National Interconnected System in public ownership. Hence, privatization and entry competition remain a pending and unfinished task for local distribution.

14. The power market in Colombia parallels the British pool of the early 1990s. For more details on electricity markets and the British experience, see Armstrong, Cowan, and Vickers (1994) and Newbery (2000). For Latin America, good reviews are found in Spiller and Guasch (1998) and the Inter-American Development Bank's 2001 annual report.

15. Although the survey is conducted annually, dissemination of the information at the plant level is restricted to protect the sources' identities. We were able to access the plant level data thanks to a technical cooperation agreement between the Universidad del Rosario in Bogotá and DANE. All the information was processed at DANE's headquarters.

16. See appendix table 6B.2 for a list of the companies in the date set and appendix 6C for a description of Colombia's Annual Manufacturing Survey.

17. Again we want to point out that although the use of nontraditional indicators is not that common within the privatization or financial economics literature, these indicators are widely used in industrial economics.

18. Ocampo (1994) presents a comprehensive analysis of the trade policy and industrialization in Colombia for the 1967–91 period.

19. Firm i's gross margin is equal to $GM_i = (VA_i - W_i)/W_i$, where VA is the firm's value added and W denotes wages.

20. For details of the reforms of the 1990s, see Montenegro (1995).

21. See La Porta and López-de-Silanes (1999) for more details about the Mexican privatization program. For more details on Chile's privatization process, see, for example, Maloney (1994); Hachette, Lüders, and Tagle (1993); and the study on Chile in this volume.

22. Partial productivities are expressed in U.S. dollars at 1995 prices. Thus, average labor productivity per worker before privatization was $30,487, and average productivity per unit of capital stock was $6.02.

23. Garay's (1998) study presents a demand-side growth decomposition exercise for Colombian manufacturing. The main result is that the contribution of import-substituting industrialization to manufacturing growth has not been positive since the mid-1970s. For the case of Mexico, La Porta and López-de-Silanes (1999) found that the mean (median) ratio of investment to sales of privatized firms is 3.58 (5.80) percentage points lower than the control group levels after privatization. In the study of Mexico, the adjusted indicators are differences rather than ratios, which is the methodology used in this study.

24. Unfortunately, we do not have detailed discrete information across IFI firms regarding plant restructuring such as firms' labor training programs, adjustments in plant automation, administrative adjustments, and reengineering in processes and products. What we do have, from some internal IFI documents and special publications sponsored by IFI (1987) and MDE (1995), is partial information regarding the technological history for some companies.

25. See Pombo (2001b) for more details. The point here is that there are two sources of power losses. One is the technical loss due to the power losses in transmission necessary to maintain the system's stability. The nontechnical loss is the difference between real consumption and invoicing. Cities such as Bogotá used to have power stealing, illegal connections, and adulterated meters, among other irregularities.

26. See Pombo (2001b) for an analysis of the 1992 blackout. The official version of the blackout causes and policy measures is in the 1993 Ministry of Mining report to the Congress.

27. Effective capacity refers to all plants generating at full capacity. Available capacity does not take into account units that are shut down for maintenance and the fraction of power that is used to stabilize the electric system, such as the load factor and voltage.

28. See Pombo (2001b) for more details.

29. One kilowatt hour (kWh) = 3,412.1 Btus; 1 gigawatt hour = 0.86 thermal calories; 1 megawatt of capacity = 1,000 kWh. The literature of DEA as well as its applications is extensive. Good introductions can be found in Coelli, Prasada Rao, and Battesse (1998) and Thanassoulis (2002).

30. See Pombo (2001a) for a specific study on intraindustry trade and technology applied to the case of Colombia.

31. This idea is similar to the competition behind contestability in which firms apply the hit-and-run strategy in order to capture profits. However, in this case there are significant sunk costs. For theoretical details, see Baumol (1982) and Baumol, Panzar, and Willig (1988).

32. For details, see Pombo (1999b).

33. Notice that the possible simultaneity bias that arises from running TFP against value added growth is partially avoided here because value added growth refers to the overall industry-specific group.

34. In general, the variables included in the Tobit regressions are robust. Residuals are homoskedastic according to the reported OLS tests. The residuals are not normal, which is associated with the distribution Kurtosis. The distribution of the residuals is symmetric.

35. The main problem with the methodological changes was the modification in the basic plant identification (ID) variable from 1991 to 1992 and 1993. This is troublesome if one wants to track the information at plant level. We ran a cross-matching program throughout plant commercial names, recorded at the industrial directories, and generated an identification key for the ID variables in the 1991–92 and 1992–93 surveys.

References

Alonso, Juan, Juan Benavides, Israel Fainboim, and Carlos Rodríguez. 2001. "Participación privada en proyectos de infraestructura y determinantes de los esquemas contractuales: El caso colombiano." Latin American Research Network Working Paper R-412. Inter-American Development Bank, Research Department, Washington, D.C.

Armstrong Mark, Steven Cowan, and John Vickers. 1994. *Regulatory Reform: Economic Analysis and British Experience*. Cambridge, Mass.: MIT Press.

Baer, Werner, and Michelle Birch, eds. 1994. *Privatization in Latin America*. Westport, Conn.: Praeger.

Baer, Werner, and Michael Conroy. 1994. "Latin America: Privatization, Property Rights, and Deregulation." *Quarterly Review of Economics and Finance* Special Issue 34. December.

Barro, Robert, and Xavier Sala-i-Martin. 1995. *Economic Growth.* New York: McGraw Hill.

Baumol, William. 1982. "Contestable Markets: An Uprising in the Theory of Industry Structure." *American Economic Review* 72(1): 1–15.

Baumol, William, John Panzar, and Robert D. Willig. 1988. *Contestable Markets and the Theory of Industrial Structure.* Rev. ed. San Diego: Harcourt Brace Jovanovich.

Bonilla, J., V. Cantillo, A. Escudero, C. González, and A. Herrera. 2000. "Los servicios públicos en las ciudades puerto del Caribe colombiano." Universidad del Norte, Barranquilla, Colombia.

Coelli, Tim, D. S. Prasada Rao, and George Battesse. 1998. *An Introduction to Efficiency and Productivity Analysis.* London: Kluwer Academic Publishers.

Dager, Vanessa. 1999. "Proceso de venta de empresa del IFI." Departamento Ingeniería Industrial, Universidad de los Andes, Bogotá.

DANE (Departamento Administrativo Nacional de Estadística). Various years. "Annual Manufacturing Survey." Bogotá.

DNP (Departamento Nacional de Planeación). 1988. *Venta de las empresas del IFI.* Documento CONPES 2378, Bogotá, Colombia: Departamento Nacional de Planeación.

———. 1991a. *La revolución pacífica: Plan Nacional de Desarrollo 1990–1994.* Bogotá.

———. 1991b. *Modernización y apertura de la economía,* vol. 1. Bogotá.

———. 1993. *Nuevos espacios para la inversión privada en Colombia.* Documento CONPES 2648. Bogotá.

———. 1995. *Participación del sector privado en infraestructura física.* Documento CONPES 2775. Bogotá.

———1997a. *Asignación de utilidades de la nación y saneamiento de las empresas industriales y comerciales del sector eléctrico.* Documento CONPES 2923. Bogotá.

———. 1997b. *Balance de los procesos de vinculación de capital privado: Las privatizaciones.* Documento CONPES 2929. Bogotá.

———. 1997c. *La participación privada en infraestructura: Seguimiento.* Documento CONPES 2928. Bogotá.

Dixon, R., and P. Thirlwall. 1975. "A Model of Regional Growth Rate: Differences on Kaldorian Lines." *Oxford Economic Papers* 27 (2): 201–14.

Garay, Luis Jorge. 1998. "Colombia: estructura industrial e industrialización: 1967–1996." Departamento Nacional de Planeación, Colciencias, Bogotá.

Glade, William., with Rosanna Corona, eds. 1996. *Bigger Economies, Smaller Governments: Privatization in Latin America.* Boulder, Colo.: Westview Press in cooperation with Institute of the Americas.

Grubel, Herbert, and Peter Lloyd. 1975. *Intraindustry Trade: The Theory and Measurement of International Trade in Differentiated Goods.* London: Macmillan.

Gutierrez, Luis, and Sanford Berg. 1999. "Telecommunications Liberalization and Regulatory Governance: Lessons from Latin America." *Telecommunications Policy* 24: 865–84.

Hachette, Dominique, Rolf Lüders, and Guillermo Tagle. 1993. "Five Cases of Privatization in Chile." In Rosanna Corona and Manuel Sánchez, eds., *Privatization in Latin America.* Washington, D.C.: Johns Hopkins University Press for the Inter-American Development Bank.

IFI (Instituto de Fomento Industrial). 1987. *Aporte al progreso de una nación.* Bogotá.

ISA (Interconexión Eléctrica S.A.). 1998, 1999. *Informes de gestión.* On CD. Medellín.

Jorgenson, Dale W., and Zvi Grilliches. 1967. "The Explanation of Productivity Change." *Review of Economic Studies* 34(3): 249–80.

La Porta, Rafael, and Florencio López-de-Silanes. 1999. "The Benefits of Privatization: Evidence from Mexico." *Quarterly Journal of Economics* 114: 1193–242.

Maloney, William. 1994. "Privatization with Share Diffusion: Popular Capitalism in Chile." In Werner Baer and Michelle Birch, eds., *Privatization in Latin America: New Roles for the Public and Private Sectors.* Westport, Conn.: Praeger.

Mann, H. B., and D. R. Whitney. 1947. "On a Test of Whether One of Two Random Variables Is Stochastically Larger than the Other." *Annals of Mathematical Statistics* 18: 50–60.

MDE (Ministerio de Desarrollo Económico). 1995. *Instituto de Fomento Industrial: 1940–1995.* Bogotá.

Megginson, William, and Jeffry Netter. 2001. "From State to Market: A Survey of Empirical Studies on Privatization." *Journal of Economic Literature* 39(2): 321–89.

Megginson, William, Robert Nash, and Matthias van Randenborgh. 1994. "The Financial and Operating Performance of Newly Privatized Firms: An International Analysis." *The Journal of Finance* 49(2): 403–52.

MME (Ministerio de Minas y Energía). 1996, 1998. *Memorias al Congreso Nacional.* Bogotá.

Montenegro, Armando. 1994. "El sector privado y la reforma del estado." *Revista Planeación y Desarrollo* 24(2): 153–66.

———. 1995. "Economic Reforms in Colombia: Regulation and Deregulation 1990–1994." EDI Working Paper 95-04. World Bank, Economic Development Institute, Washington, D.C.

Newbery, David. 2000. *Privatization, Restructuring, and Regulation of Network Utilities.* Cambridge, Mass.: MIT Press.

Ocampo, Jose Antonio. 1994. "Trade Policy and Industrialization in Colombia, 1967–1991." In G. Helleiner, ed., *Trade Policy and Industrialization in Turbulent Times.* London: Routledge.

Pollit, Michael. 1995. *Ownership and Performance in Electric Utilities.* Oxford, U.K.: Oxford University Press.

Pombo, Carlos. 1999a. "Economías de escala, markups, y determinantes del cambio técnico en la industria en Colombia." *Coyuntura Económica* 29(4): 107–32.

———. 1999b "Productividad industrial en Colombia: una aplicación de números índices." *Revista de Economía del Rosario* 2(1): 107–39.

———. 2001a. "Intraindustry Trade and Innovation: An Empirical Study of the Colombian Manufacturing Industry." *International Review of Applied Economics* 15(1): 77–106.

———. 2001b. "Regulatory Reform in Colombia's Electric Utilities." *Quarterly Review of Economics and Finance* 41(5): 683–711.

Romer, Paul. 1990. "Endogenous Technical Change." *Journal of Political Economy* 98: 71–102.

Scheel, Holger. 2000. "EMS: Efficiency Measurement System User's Manual." Available at http://www.wiso.uni-dortmund.de/lsfg/or/scheel/ems/.

Spiller, Pablo, and José Guasch. 1998. "Managing the Regulatory Process: Design, Concepts, Issues and the Latin American and the Caribbean Story." World Bank, Washington, D.C.

Sprent, Peter, and Nigel Smeeton. 2001. *Applied Non-Parametric Statistical Methods*, 3d ed. New York: Chapman and Hall.

Thanassoulis, Emmanuel. 2002. *Introduction to the Theory on Application of Data Envelope Analysis*. London: Kluwer Academic Publishers.

World Bank. 1991. "Colombia: The Power Sector and the World Bank 1970–1987." In Comision Nacional de Energía, *Evaluación del Sector Eléctrico Colombiano*. Bogotá: Ministerio de Minas.

Zuleta, L. H., L. Jaramillo, E. Ballen, and A. M. Gomez. 1993. "Privatization in Colombia: Experiences and Prospects." In Manuel Sanchez and Rosanna Corona, eds., *Privatization in Latin America*. Washington, D.C.: Johns Hopkins University Press for the Inter-American Development Bank.

7

Privatization in Mexico

Alberto Chong and Florencio López-de-Silanes

WHAT SHOULD PRIVATIZATION ATTEMPT TO achieve? Why does it work? How does it affect firm performance? What are the determinants of privatization prices? What are the effects in terms of fiscal policy? How should a privatization program be structured? What role should deregulation or reregulation have in a privatization policy, and why? In this chapter, we provide empirical answers to these questions through a micro- and macroeconomic analysis of the Mexican privatization program. The Mexican program, carried out since the mid-1980s, has been one of the largest in the world in its scale and scope. It implied the reversal of 40 years of state interventionism and profoundly transformed the economic landscape of Mexico.

Recently, politicians and the media have harshly questioned the effect of privatization, claiming that benefits are greatly exaggerated and that privatization invariably leads to welfare losses for society. This chapter's key finding is that privatization leads to dramatic improvements in firm performance and that those improvements result from efficiency gains, not from transfers from workers or exploitation of consumers. We find that the operating-income-to-sales ratio for the median firm increased 24 percentage points, and by assuming that quality is unchanged and that fired workers have zero productivity, we estimate that price increases and transfers from workers can account for at most 5 percent and 31 percent of the increase in profitability, respectively. Similar improvements are observed for operating efficiency and output. Furthermore, we calculate industry-adjusted indicators to ensure that the results obtained are directly attributable to the transfer of control to the private sector and not a reflection of general macroeconomic trends or a sector-specific phenomenon.

Even when this initial objection is overcome, many argue that privatization should be opposed because benefits accrue to the new owners only, while consumers and the poor are left behind. It is claimed that the sale of state-owned enterprises (SOEs) amounts to a privatization of benefits while the government is left to foot the bill if things go wrong. Contrary to this belief, we find that there are significant social benefits to privatization, particularly in greater access to goods and services. It is precisely the poor who are usually left out of the telephone, electricity, and water networks when they are public and therefore it is the poor who have the most to gain from increased coverage. Moreover, although it is true that the government has sometimes footed the bill for botched privatizations, an often-overlooked aspect is its beneficial fiscal effect. Lower subsidies, increased taxes, and of course, the direct revenues from the sale provided Mexico with the revenues needed to dramatically reduce its stock of external debt and increase spending on education and poverty alleviation programs.

Among those who accept that privatization is a positive force, there is a widespread belief that SOEs need extensive restructuring and nurturing before they are fit for sale. With this in mind, governments often pour vast sums of money and spend valuable time implementing investment and efficiency plans which are not valued by bidders. In the case of Mexico, the presence of an efficiency restructuring program or an investment plan reduced the net privatization price received by the government by 56 percent and 95 percent, respectively. Furthermore, each additional month taken to complete the privatization decreased prices by 2.2 percent. This evidence clearly suggests that governments should think twice before engaging in these types of restructuring programs and that often the best solution is simply to concentrate on the sale of SOEs and leave the restructuring to the market. If politicians wish to help displaced workers, there is sure to be a more cost-effective way to do it than by trying to fix public firms before they are sold. An additional lesson that can be drawn from the Mexican experience is that simplicity and transparency are paramount to a successful program. Special requirements such as cash-only sales reduced net prices by 30 percent, while allowing foreign participation boosted prices by 32 percent, and the presence of an additional bidder in the final round increased them by 17 percent.

Finally, this chapter attempts to make sense of the cases of failed privatization by analyzing the importance of a set of complementary policies such as the design of the privatization contracts, deregulation and reregulation of privatized firms, and the corporate governance framework. We find that the main instances of botched privatization can be traced back to mistakes in one or more of these complementary policies. Although more attention is clearly needed in these areas, the good news is that the failures seen so far seem to have a readily available solution.

The Mexican SOEs and Privatization

To understand the opportunities presented by the Mexican privatization program, it is helpful to analyze first the role of the government in the economy and the motives behind this role. The 1917 Mexican constitution established the general jurisdictional framework under which the role of the state in the economy was defined. From this foundation, the Mexican government launched a gradual takeover of the economy, and by 1982, the year in which banks were nationalized, the government controlled more than 1,100 firms in all sectors of the economy, including having monopolistic control of strategic areas such as energy and infrastructure. Since then, government ownership of enterprises has declined precipitously and is now significant only in some entrenched sectors, most notably oil and electricity, that have successfully used their political clout to resist divestiture. This section analyzes the rise of the SOE sector and the subsequent privatization program in more detail.

The Growth of the SOE Sector

Table 7.1 shows the main focus of state expansion for different periods during 1917–2003, as well as the number of SOEs at the end of each

Table 7.1 State-Owned Enterprises in Mexico, 1917–2003

Main focus of state activity	Period	Number of state-owned enterprises (end of period)
Public administration, creation of infrastructure, administration of natural resources, and provision of basic services	1917–40	36
Import-substitution-oriented investments (capital-intensive and long-maturity areas; industry input suppliers); transportation and communications; and social security institutions	1941–54	144
Stable development, unplanned expansion: regional development, production expansion, and creation of employment	1955–70	272
Planned expansion: oil bonanza, government as an industrial investment engine	1971–75	504
Planned expansion: bank nationalization, government investment in strategic areas, and takeover of firms in distress	1976–82	1,155
Main program of liberalization of the economy and divestiture of the state-owned sector	1983–93	258
Consolidation of the privatization program: public utilities and pension system	1994–2003	210

Source: Aspe 1993; Presidencia de la República, 1982–2003.

period. During the 1920s government operations mostly reflected attempts to regulate the economy; the central bank (Banco de Mexico) was established to control monetary policy, and investments in infrastructure were used to stimulate the economy.[1] The Great Depression in the United States and the worldwide economic crises that accompanied it led the Mexican government to take direct responsibility for the provision of many basic services. In 1934 the "Cardenista" era began with the implementation of a six-year plan that emphasized the role of agricultural development and the provision of basic services. Predictably, this approach quickly spawned an array of funding institutions that would outlive their initial mandate and become engines for state expansion.[2] Pemex, the national oil company and probably the most prominent SOE in Mexican history, was created during this period and remains in state hands today.

By 1940 the government owned 36 enterprises, and the stage was set for a massive expansion of the state-owned sector. The period from 1940 to the mid-1950s witnessed the state's implementation of an import-substitution model and the undertaking of capital-intensive and long-maturity investments such as steel mills, coal mines, paper mills, and oil refineries. The government also took over the social security system during this period and created two institutions to run it: the National Institute for Social Security (to manage private sector pensions) and the Social Security of Government Employees. Until 1947 each company was almost completely responsible for its own operations, and the whole SOE sector was managed in a decentralized fashion. In that year, however, as the size of government operations increased, centralized control was established under two ministries.[3]

The late 1950s and 1960s were known as a period of stable development, during which the economy grew swiftly and the government expanded its influence in a seemingly random way. The number of SOEs more than doubled, and public ownership of firms expanded to new sectors including sugar cane mills and the manufacture of textiles, tobacco, and food processing. The state's major investments were directed toward regional development with the aim of increasing employment and production across the nation. Supervision became more complex as the number of SOEs increased, and in 1970 control of these firms was centralized under the control of three ministries: the Ministry of Finance (SHCP), the Secretariat of the Presidency (SP), and the Secretariat of National Patrimony (SENEPAL).

Starting in the first half of the 1970s, a fall in private investment and stricter restrictions imposed by the government consolidated the role of the public sector as the main engine of investment. The government borrowed heavily and used income from high oil prices to expand the number of SOEs under its control. During the 1970s and early 1980s, the government followed a haphazard strategy of taking over companies that fell into financial distress or were of particular interest to the politicians in charge. By 1982 the number of SOEs reached 1,155, and their weight in the economy was unprecedented: they accounted for 4.4 percent of the country's labor force and 30 percent of fixed capital formation, and they received subsidies equivalent to almost 13 percent of gross domestic product (GDP).[4]

The Privatization Program

The Mexican privatization program was one of the world's largest, in terms of both the number of companies privatized and their relative size. Between 1982 and 2003 the number of SOEs dropped from 1,155 to 210. Table 7.2 shows the evolution of the SOE sector from 1982 to 2003, while table 7.3 shows the number of privatized firms and the number of privatization contracts per year for the same period.[5] The scope of the program entailed the privatization of close to 440 companies in 49 four-digit Standard Industrial Classification (SIC) codes.

Table 7.2 State-Owned Enterprises, 1982–2003

State-owned enterprises	1982–88	1989–93	1994–2003
Total at the beginning of period	1,155	666	258
Creation	59	39	108
Liquidations/shutdowns	294	193	58
Mergers	72	17	16
Transfers	25	11	26
Privatizations	157	226	56
In process[a]			37
Total at the end of the period	666	258	210

Note: To obtain the total number of state-owned enterprises (SOEs) at the end of each period, we add the number of created SOEs to the number at the beginning of the period and subtract the liquidations, shutdowns, mergers, transfers, and privatizations. *Total at the beginning of period* is the number of legal entities forming part of the parastatal sector at the start of each period; *creation* is the number of created companies by the state in the specified period; *liquidations/shutdowns* is the number of companies shut down by the state in the specified period; *mergers* is the number of SOEs that merged with other SOEs in the specified period; *transfers* is the number of SOEs that were transferred to other levels of government, including firms that ceased to be treated as state-owned by legal mandate (Ley Federal de Entidades Paraestatales); *privatizations* is the number of SOEs sold in the specified period; *in process* is the number of SOEs pending privatization in the specified period; this number reflects the number of ongoing privatizations, liquidations, shutdowns, mergers, or transfers in 2003.

a. The most important ongoing processes are Banrural System (13 institutions), FIDELIQ, and Nacional Hotelera de Baja California S.A. de C.V.

Source: Presidencia de la República 1982–2003.

Table 7.3 The Privatization Program in Perspective

Year	Companies privatized	Number of transactions (privatization contracts)
1983	4	2
1984	3	1
1985	32	10
1986	30	16
1987	22	17
1988	66	51
1989	37	29
1990	91	63
1991	65	37
1992	21	10
1993	12	8
1994	1	1
1995	1	7
1996	1	16
1997	2	12
1998	3	13
1999	32	5
2000	16	2
2001	0	0
2002	0	0
2003	0	0
Total	439	300

Note: The difference between the number of companies privatized and the number of privatization contracts stems from the fact that some companies were sold in a bundle with other privatized firms, while others were split up before the sale.
Source: Presidencia de la República 1983–2003.

The first period, which lasted from 1982 through 1988, began as the result of a restructuring program intended to increase the overall efficiency of the public sector. The program involved restructuring measures as well as a general "cleaning up" of the sector through liquidations, mergers, transfers, and privatizations. This period was also marked by constitutional reforms aimed at reducing the economic role of the government; a new federal law for SOEs clarified the relationship and obligations between each SOE and the state and led to a large reduction of unviable operations. Nearly 300 SOEs were liquidated or shut down, and 157 were privatized.

The privatization program reached its peak in both size and scope during the Salinas administration, from late 1988 to 1993. Firms sold during this period represented over 96 percent of all assets privatized and employed 311,000 workers, or 35 percent of the total work force of SOEs (López-de-Silanes 1994). To manage this huge task in such a short time, the president created a special unit within the Ministry of Finance, the Office of Privatization of State-Owned Enterprises (OP), to coordinate a decentralized process that encouraged the involvement of commercial banks, foreign businesses, and financial valuators.

The third period, from 1994 to 2003, was characterized by the consolidation of the previous efforts of divestiture of the parastatal sector. The administration in charge undertook the privatization of strategic areas of the economy and public utilities such as telecommunications (satellites), ports, airports, toll roads, railroads, and the distribution of natural gas. A major reform to the private sector pension system took place in 1995. By 2003 the privatization program had lost its appeal, and in fact the government marginally reversed the process by expropriating some previously privatized companies.[6] All in all, net privatizations of SOEs were negative in 2003.

A central objective of divestiture in Mexico was to transfer control of SOEs to privately owned groups that could provide the necessary alignment in incentives for better financial and investment decisions of the firms. As a general rule, the government sold 100 percent of its ownership in each SOE privatized, retaining a minority share in only eight cases.[7] Six of these companies were instances where the companies were already trading in the stock market, and the intention was to sell secondary packages through the stock exchange.[8]

The Benefits of Privatization

Critics often argue that the benefits of privatization come at significant cost to society through higher prices, lower wages, and reduced income for the government (Campbell-White and Bhatia 1998; Bayliss 2002). In this section we analyze the validity of these claims for the case of Mexico and find evidence that points to the contrary. We study unadjusted and industry-adjusted performance ratios to quantify the effects of privatization on firms and to ensure that these are not explained by macroeconomic factors. We then examine the importance of price increases, market power, and worker exploitation as potential determinants of the observed increase in profitability. Finally, we analyze the effect of privatization on the quality and accessibility of services.

Raw Data

We rely on seven broad indicators to measure performance: profitability, operating efficiency, employment and wages, capital investment, output, taxes, and prices. For each firm, we measure the change in any given indicator by comparing its value in 1993 to the average value during the four years preceding privatization.[9]

The results, shown in table 7.4, reveal several interesting phenomena. Profitability increased significantly after privatization according to all indicators: the mean (median) change in profitability ranges from a low of 24.1 (12.1) percentage points for operating income to sales to a high

Table 7.4 Changes in Performance for the Sample of Privatized Firms

Variable	Number	Mean change	Median change
Profitability			
Operating income/sales	170	0.2411***	0.1208***
Operating income/PPE	170	0.3450***	0.1347***
Net income/sales	170	0.3996***	0.1447***
Net income/PPE	170	0.2713***	0.1567***
Operating efficiency			
Cost per unit	170	−0.2149***	−0.1676***
Log (sales/PPE)	170	0.6464***	0.2385***
Log (sales/employees)	169	1.0530***	0.9909***
Labor			
Log (employees)	169	−64.89***	−56.75***
Log (blue-collar workers)	168	−53.44***	−60.87***
Log (white-collar workers)	169	−53.52***	−46.34***
Assets and investment			
Investment/sales	170	0.0150*	0.0103***
Investment/PPE	170	0.0474***	0.0216***
Output			
Log (sales)	170	0.5428***	0.6816***
Net taxes			
Net taxes/sales	170	0.1301***	0.0763***
Prices			
Index of real prices (Paasche)	83	1.31	1.27

* Significant at the 10 percent level.
** Significant at the 5 percent level.
*** Significant at the 1 percent level.

Note: PPE = property, plant, and equipment. This table presents raw results for a subsample of 170 privatized firms between 1983 and 1992. The table presents, for each empirical proxy, the number of usable observations, the mean change, and the median change before and after privatization. *Before privatization* refers to the average value for the four years before privatization, while *after privatization* refers to the value as of 1993. We report t-statistics and Z-statistics (Wilcoxon rank sum) as our test for significance for the change in mean and median values, respectively. All variables definitions can be found in the appendix.

Source: La Porta and López-de-Silanes (1999).

of 40.0 (14.5) percentage points for net income to sales. All t-statistics and Z-statistics are significant at the 1 percent level.

This increase in profitability seems to stem from significant gains in efficiency. The mean (median) cost per unit decreased 21.5 (16.8) percentage points, while the mean (median) ratio of sales to physical assets (property, plant, and equipment, or PPE) increased 64.6 (23.9) percent. Regarding the efficiency of employees, both mean and median sales per employee double. Once again, all changes are significant at the 1 percent level.

The higher profitability and especially the higher levels of sales per employees can be partially explained by reduced employment levels, as the mean (median) numbers of employees plummet by 64.9 (56.8) percent. This reduction is shared more or less equally between blue- and white-collar workers: the mean (median) number of white-collar workers falls by 53.5 (46.3) percent, while the mean (median) number of blue-collar workers falls by 53.4 (60.9) percent.[10]

The data indicate that investment increases only slightly and therefore cannot be responsible for the vast increase in profitability and operating efficiency documented above. The mean (median) investment-to-sales ratio increased 1.5 (1.0) percentage points and the investment-to-PPE ratio increased by a mean (median) of 4.7 (2.2) percentage points.

One of the most surprising findings is that privatized firms increased their sales substantially despite a reduced labor force and only marginal increments in their capital stock. The mean (median) real growth in sales is 54.3 (68.2) percent and is statistically significant at the 1 percent level.[11] Once we consider that there is no statistically significant increase in product prices of privatized firms, the increase in production suggests that consumer surplus should also have increased significantly.

To assess the social impact of privatization, we must also account for the taxes paid by newly privatized firms and the prices paid by consumers. The ratio of net taxes to sales increased by a mean (median) of 13.0 (7.6) percent, a significant increase when we consider that sales increased substantially. The magnitude of this change is more evident when we consider that the average firm received a small subsidy before privatization but paid approximately $8.55 million in taxes in 1993.

Contrary to predictions, we find that the prices of the products of the mean (median) firm increased only 1.3 (1.3) percent in real terms. One way to gauge the contribution of price hikes to the observed change in profitability is to compare the observed percentage-point increase in the ratio of operating income to sales to that which would take place if privatized firms had increased output but left prices unchanged in real terms.[12]

Our results suggest that price increases account for 1.24 (0.9) percentage points of the ratio of operating income to sales. Accordingly, price increases explain about 5.1 percent of the observed change in mean operating income to sales and 7.4 percent of the change in the observed median operating income to sales. The evidence above does not support the hypothesis that price increases play a substantial role in the increased profitability of privatized firms.

Industry-Adjusted Data

During the early 1990s the Mexican economy experienced a significant structural transformation, and growth accelerated. To ensure that the increases in performance documented in the previous section were not driven by macroeconomic factors, we measure the performance of privatized firms relative to those of the industry to which they belong.

Figure 7.1 illustrates the closing gap between privatized and private firms. After dramatically underperforming their private peers in net-income-to-sales, operating-income-to-sales, and costs-per-unit ratios, privatized firms caught up with and even surpassed them. The most remarkable results are found for the ratio of net income to sales, where private firms were 17.2 percentage points less profitable than private firms before

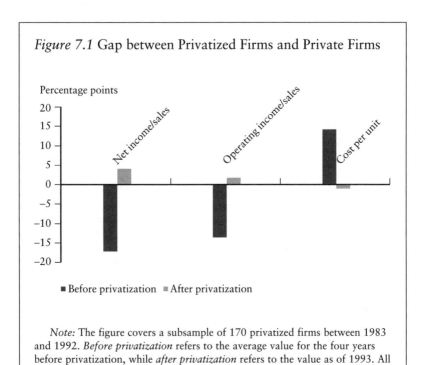

Figure 7.1 Gap between Privatized Firms and Private Firms

Percentage points

■ Before privatization   ■ After privatization

Note: The figure covers a subsample of 170 privatized firms between 1983 and 1992. *Before privatization* refers to the average value for the four years before privatization, while *after privatization* refers to the value as of 1993. All variables definitions can be found in the appendix.
Source: La Porta and López-de-Silanes 1999.

privatization and 4 points more profitable afterward. Costs per unit show a similar converging trend, albeit from a different starting point. Before privatization SOEs had median costs per unit 14.2 percentage points higher than their private competitors. After privatization they closed this gap completely and even experienced costs per unit 1 percentage point below their control group.

Table 7.5 shows that controlling for industry factors explains a nontrivial fraction of the employment cuts. Relative to industry benchmarks, mean (median) employment in privatized firms fell by roughly 35.4 (34.4) percent. Growth in sales remains strong relative to industry as the mean (median) industry-adjusted growth in sales is 43.2 (48.9) percent. Macroeconomic factors can therefore account for only about 21.4 (28.2) percent of the mean (median) growth in sales while firm restructuring accounts for the rest.[13]

Although some of the improvements in performance are attributable to macroeconomic factors, the bulk of the observed increase in performance results from privatization. The next step is to address a number of issues relating to the robustness of our results. In particular, we explore the hypothesis that the increased profitability of privatized firms comes from exploitation of consumers through the use of market power and of workers through wage cuts.

Market Power

One of the main criticisms of privatization is that the increase in profitability is attributable to transfers from consumers extracted through market power. To test this hypothesis, we compare the profitability of privatized firms in competitive and noncompetitive industries. If newly privatized firms use market power to extract rents, the social view of privatization predicts that noncompetitive firms would experience larger increases in profitability than would competitive firms, as well as lower growth in output, employment, and investment. In table 7.6 we classify firms as operating in competitive or noncompetitive industries based on two objective criteria.[14] The table shows, for each ratio, the median change for competitive and noncompetitive firms following privatization as well as the difference between these changes.

Changes in the ratios of operating income to sales and operating income to PPE are higher in competitive industries than in noncompetitive ones. In contrast, both net-income-to-sales and net-income-to-PPE ratios increase more in the noncompetitive sector than in the competitive one. With one exception (net income to sales in the classification based on the number of firms), all differences between the competitive and noncompetitive sectors are statistically insignificant.

By construction, three factors can account for the conflicting behavior of operating income and net income: taxes, extraordinary items, and

Table 7.5 Industry-Adjusted Changes in Performance for the
Sample of Privatized Firms

Variable	Number	Mean change	Median change
Profitability			
Operating income/sales	168	0.3264***	0.1531***
Operating income/PPE	168	2.4274***	0.1492***
Net income/sales	168	0.4144***	0.2121***
Net income/PPE	168	0.2524***	0.1736***
Operating efficiency			
Cost per unit	168	−0.1848***	−0.1528***
Log (sales/PPE)	168	0.4684***	0.2014**
Log (sales/employees)	168	0.9157***	0.8834***
Labor			
Log (employees)	169	−35.35***	−34.37***
Log (blue-collar workers)	168	−36.78***	−32.61***
Log (white-collar workers)	168	−32.21***	−31.59***
Assets and investment			
Investment/sales	168	−0.0474***	−0.0495***
Investment/PPE	168	−0.0328***	−0.0503***
Output			
Log (sales)	170	0.4324***	0.4891***
Net taxes			
Net taxes/sales	168	0.1609***	0.0757***

* Significant at the 10 percent level.
** Significant at the 5 percent level.
*** Significant at the 1 percent level.

Note: PPE = property, plant, and equipment. This table presents industry-adjusted results for a subsample of 170 privatized firms between 1983 and 1992. The table presents, for each empirical proxy, the number of usable observations, the mean change, and the median change before and after privatization. *Before privatization* refers to the average value for the four years before privatization, while *after privatization* refers to the value as of 1993. We constructed the industry control groups using all private firms trading in the Mexican Stock Market (three-digit SIC code level). For each privatized firm and for each year, we compute industry-adjusted indicators by taking the difference between the value of the indicator for the firm and its industry control group. We use economywide aggregates, if available, for those firms for which we cannot find a matched industry sample. We report *t*-statistics and *Z*-statistics (Wilcoxon rank sum) as our test for significance for the change in mean and median values, respectively. All variables definitions can be found in the appendix.
Source: La Porta and López-de-Silanes 1999.

interest expense. The increase in taxes paid is larger for noncompetitive firms than for competitive firms and therefore its explanatory power is diminished. Changes in leverage provide a more promising explanation. We conjecture that firms in oligopolistic and monopolistic sectors,

Table 7.6 Median Performance Changes in Privatized Firms in Competitive versus Noncompetitive Industries

| | Sorted by number of firms | | | | | Sorted by market share | | | | |
Variable	N	Competitive	N	Non-competitive	Difference in medians	N	Competitive	N	Non-competitive	Difference in medians
Profitability										
Operating income/sales	124	0.1365	42	0.1334	0.0031	104	0.1799	62	0.0712	0.1087
Operating income/PPE	124	0.1714	42	0.1698	0.0016	103	0.1832	62	0.1222	0.0610
Net income/sales	122	0.1838	41	0.4260	−0.2422**	101	0.2263	62	0.2524	−0.0261
Net income/PPE	122	0.2102	41	0.2781	−0.0679	101	0.2015	62	0.2716	−0.0701
Operating efficiency										
Cost per unit	124	−0.1255	42	−0.2362	0.1107***	104	0.1415	62	0.1907	−0.0492
Log (sales/employees)	126	1.0353	43	0.7875	0.2478	107	1.0877	62	0.7474	0.3403**
Log (sales/PPE)	124	0.5882	42	0.3313	0.2569	104	0.6429	62	0.2859	0.3570
Operating income/employees	125	19.7240	43	20.9320	−1.2080	106	21.6320	62	14.9110	6.7210
Labor										
Log (total employment)	126	−0.4339	43	−0.3592	−0.0747	107	−0.4338	62	−0.3645	−0.0693
Log (blue-collar workers)	126	−0.4365	43	−0.2473	−0.1892	107	−0.4495	62	−0.2518	−0.1977

(Table continues on the following page.)

Table 7.6 (continued)

Variable	Sorted by number of firms					Sorted by market share				
	N	Competitive	N	Non-competitive	Difference in medians	N	Competitive	N	Non-competitive	Difference in medians
Log (white-collar workers)	126	−0.4264	43	−0.3342	−0.0922	107	−0.3327	62	−0.4443	0.1116
Assets and investment										
Investment/sales	123	0.0059	42	0.0098	−0.0039	104	0.0048	62	0.0096	−0.0048
Investment/PPE	123	0.0144	42	0.0180	−0.0036	104	0.0144	62	0.0191	−0.0047
Output										
Log (sales)	124	0.6479	42	0.3752	0.2727	105	0.6479	61	0.4419	0.2060
Prices										
Index of real prices (Paasche)	66	4.60	17	−3.64	8.24	53	9.29	30	−2.82	12.1148*
Net taxes										
Net taxes/sales	124	0.0717	41	0.0897	−0.0180	104	0.0675	61	0.0815	−0.0140

* Significant at the 10 percent level.
** Significant at the 5 percent level.
*** Significant at the 1 percent level.

Note: N = number of observations and PPE = property, plant, and equipment. This table presents median performance results for a subsample of 170 privatized firms between 1983 and 1992. In the first measure, firms are considered competitive if they are in an industry with more than 10 firms and as noncompetitive otherwise; in the second measure, firms are considered competitive if they have less than 10 percent of market share and as noncompetitive otherwise. For each group of firms, the table presents median change in each indicator following privatization and their difference. We report Z-statistics (Wilcoxon rank sum) as our test for significance for the change in median values between competitive and noncompetitive firms. All definitions of the variables can be found in the appendix.

Source: La Porta and López-de-Silanes 1999.

perhaps because of their greater access to government-backed capital before privatization, exhibit greater reductions in leverage after privatization than do firms in competitive sectors. Finally, it is also possible that the net income of SOEs was unduly depressed by restructuring changes before privatization. The bottom line is that operating income, in contrast to net income, is unaffected by changes in leverage and is thus a better gauge for the impact of market power on profits. In any event, differences in profitability changes are not statistically significant.

We also analyze the behavior of investment, employment, and output and find no statistically significant evidence to suggest that market power plays a significant role in explaining the increased profitability of privatized firms. In any case, the differences that exist point toward a more dynamic restructuring in the noncompetitive sector relative to the competitive one. For example, according to the classification of competitiveness based on number of firms, costs per unit decreased 11 percentage points more in noncompetitive firms, while according to the classification of competitiveness based on market share, sales per employees increased 34 percent more in noncompetitive firms than in competitive ones.

Perhaps the most interesting result is the behavior of real prices. Not only does the increase in the noncompetitive sector lag behind that of the competitive sector, but prices in the former actually fell. According to the market-share classification, the growth of prices in the competitive sector was 9.29 percent while that of the noncompetitive sector was −2.82 percent. This difference is statistically significant at the 10 percent level. All in all, we find no evidence that market power or the exploitation of consumers explains the increased profitability of privatized firms.

Transfers from Workers

In this section we consider the role of labor retrenchment in explaining the large gains in profitability experienced by privatized firms. The redistribution hypothesis links postprivatization gains in profitability to transfers from workers to shareholders, as wages fall from above-market levels induced by income-redistribution goals. Political models of state ownership also imply that SOE workers are overpaid, but unlike redistribution models, these models lack strong predictions regarding the behavior of wages in the postprivatization period. This uncertainty comes from the fact that public sector jobs are attractive for several reasons besides pay; for example, they may be desirable because they do not require much effort or because they provide the opportunity to collect bribes in exchange for public services. We try to quantify the contribution of layoffs and wage cuts to the observed changes in profitability. Examining changes in real wages is a natural way to test competing hypotheses regarding the channels through which privatization works.

Contrary to the predictions of the redistribution hypothesis, available evidence shows that real wages increased substantially for the mean and median firm (table 7.7). Real wages per worker increased by a mean (median) of almost 80 (125) percent. This is even more striking since overall real wages in Mexico stagnated during the sample period. Furthermore, gains by blue-collar workers are larger than gains by white-collar workers. Even though white-collar wages increased substantially, the mean and median index of industry-adjusted blue-collar wages rose much more— well over 100 percent. Although both skilled and unskilled workers experience impressive increases in wages, it is the lowest-paid workers who gain the most.

To provide an estimate of the cost savings attributable to layoffs, we make the extreme assumption that the marginal product of all fired workers is zero and calculate what the increase in profitability would have been if no workers were fired. Even in this extreme case, savings that come from layoffs are not as large as the reductions in employment suggest. This is so for two reasons: first, total wages represent only 23.38 percent of sales in the preprivatization period, and second, labor costs in the postprivatization period are spread over a much wider base since sales increase significantly. Our estimate yields a saving from layoffs equivalent to 6.80 (4.45) percent of sales in 1993. During the same period, the mean (median) ratio of operating income to sales increased 22.12 (9.59) percentage points. Therefore, savings from layoffs account for only 31 to 46 percent of the observed gains in profitability. If, instead of assuming that fired workers' value added is equal to zero, we assume they are half as productive as retained workers, savings from layoffs drop to between 15 and 23 percent of the increase in profitability.

In conclusion, real wages experience large increases in the postprivatization period probably because those workers who are retained are required to work and are paid accordingly.[15] Overall, the high level of labor redundancy in the preprivatization period, the observed increases in real wages, and the productivity gains in the postprivatization period are consistent with the political view.

Services and Access

The Mexican privatization program spread benefits to society beyond its direct effects on prices and firm profitability. These benefits take the form of greater access to, extended coverage of, and enhanced quality of the services provided by the privatized firms. Table 7.8 summarizes some of these benefits. Among the most important improvements are a dramatic increase in freight road transport and in the provision of natural gas, a substantial increase in the capacity and efficiency of the port system, and substantial investments and increased coverage in the provision of running water and sanitation.

Table 7.7 The Role of Transfers from Workers

Variable	N	Mean		Median	
		Before privatization	After privatization	Before privatization	After privatization
Index of real wages per worker	101	100.00	179.64***	100.00	224.92***
Index of industry-adjusted real wages per worker	101	100.00	209.30 ***	100.00	198.96***
Index of real wages per blue-collar worker	101	100.00	235.43***	100.00	248.14***
Index of industry-adjusted real blue-collar wages	101	100.00	265.61***	100.00	222.43***
Index of real wages per white-collar worker	101	100.00	158.26***	100.00	200.95***
Index of industry-adjusted white-collar wages	101	100.00	177.97***	100.00	147.92***
Index of total employment	101	100.00	57.92***	100.00	58.05***
Total wages/sales	101	0.2338	0.1441***	0.1506	0.1143***
Operating income/sales	101	−0.1530	0.0682***	−0.0251	0.0708***

*** Significant at the 1 percent level.

Note: N = number of observations. The table presents data of total number of workers, blue-collar workers, and white-collar workers for a subsample of 101 privatized firms between 1983 and 1992 for which we have full employment data. For each empirical proxy we show mean and median real wages per worker and the index of industry-adjusted real wages per worker for all three groups. Before privatization refers to the average value for the four years before privatization, while after privatization refers to the value as of 1993. We report t-statistics and Z-statistics (Wilcoxon rank sum) as our test for significance for the change in mean and median values, respectively. All variables definitions can be found in the appendix.

Source: La Porta and López-de-Silanes 1999.

Table 7.8 Other Benefits of Privatization Programs

Program	Impacts
Freight road transport	Between 1988 and 1993, the number of firms providing freight road transport service nearly tripled—from 4,456 to 12,972. The number of trucks increased from 58,133 to 142,973.
Natural gas	Between 1996 and 2000, the Comisión Reguladora de Energía (CRE) awarded 21 gas distribution permits under which concessionaires were obligated to serve 2.3 million customers by 2004. This represents a 15-fold increase in the customer base relative to 1995.
Passenger road transport	The impact of the reform has been seen in increased entry of new firms or regularization and registration of existing firms; increased demand (between 1990 and 1996 the number of total passengers transported increased from 1.97 million to 2.75 million and the number of vehicles rose from 36,593 to 53,133); and in significantly improved quality and reliability of services.
Ports	There have been huge increases in installed capacity (from 59 million tons in 1993 to 94 million tons in 1998) and capacity utilization (from 41 percent in 1993 to 59 percent in 1998). In 1993 the port of Veracruz was handling 43 containers/hour per ship. In 2003 this figure was 84. Manzanillo moves 65 containers/hour per ship, and Altamira has achieved the international standard of 50 moves per hour. In Veracruz the total capacity for loading and unloading agricultural bulk cargo improved from 2,500 to 9,000 tons per day between 1995 and 1998, with the port of Progreso showing similar improvement.
Railroads	New operators invested more than P$3 billion on maintenance of infrastructure and the renewal of rolling stock during 1997–98 and another P$3.3 billion during 1999. Between 1997 and 1998 the total volume of freight handled by the rail system in Mexico increased by 21.5 percent.
Telecommunications	During the 1990s the number of wire-line telephones in service doubled; wireless telephony grew from negligible levels to nearly 40 percent of all telephones; and waiting lists for service virtually disappeared during the first decade after privatization.

(Table continues on the following page.)

Table 7.8 (continued)

Program	Impacts
Toll roads	The highway concession program doubled the length of existing toll highways (from 4,500 kilometers in 1989 to 9,900 kilometers in 1994).
Urban water supply and sanitation	A 1994 amendment to the federal water law initiated a program of concessions in water supply and sanitation. By the year 2000, approximately 14 million Mexicans were served by water systems with varying degrees of private participation (including the Federal District service contracts). Private investments totaling $400 million have been committed, and private operators are handling approximately 16 percent of the 43 meters per second of wastewater effluent that is treated.

Source: Rogozinsky and Tovar 1998; World Bank 2003.

Fiscal Impact

This section explores the fiscal impact of the privatization program as well as its effects on other macroeconomic variables. There are four primary components to the fiscal impact of privatization: the direct revenue generated from the sale; the costs incurred by restructuring before the sale; the elimination of the net flow of subsidies and transfers from the government to the SOEs; and the new stream of tax payments generated under private ownership.

Direct revenues from the sale of SOEs were a major source of government revenue. The aggregate value of the program from 1983 to 2003 amounts to slightly over 5.3 percent of 2003 GDP (table 7.9), with the 1989–93 period accounting for the vast majority of these sales (79 percent). About one-third of privatization contracts required "cash-only" payment, and the vast majority of the remaining contracts allowed only very short-term debt lasting no more than a few years. Because most firms were sold for cash and no long-term debt was exchanged, the cash-versus-debt component of privatization plays only a marginal role in the case of Mexico.

The costs of restructuring were by no means negligible; the government spent substantial resources restructuring firms before privatization, particularly through labor retrenchment programs. Although the first period (1982–88) had fewer prior restructuring measures, their costs amounted to one-half of total direct revenues. During the second period (1989–93),

Table 7.9 The Fiscal Impact of Privatization: 1983–2003
(percentage of 2003 GDP)

Period	Nominal price of privatization contract	Privatization restructuring costs	Net subsidies during the four years before privatization
1983–88	0.40	0.20	0.18
1989–93	4.20	1.30	0.35
1994–2003	0.73	n.a.	n.a.
Total	5.32	1.51	0.53
Number of privatization contracts	255	220	95

n.a. = Not available.
Source: Data collected by the authors from the original privatization sales and prospectuses from the Secretaría de Hacienda y Crédito Público and Secretaría de Comunicaciones y Transportes (2000).

firms were restructured more often, but total costs were equivalent to only one-third of total revenues. In any case, it is clear that restructuring costs were significant.

Subsidies and transfers accounted for a significant percentage of the overall government budget—totaling almost 13 percent of GDP in 1982.[16] Table 7.9 provides a measure of subsidies net of dividends, revenues, and restructuring costs associated with privatization during the four-year period before privatization; it reveals that these operations imposed a large net burden on the public finances. During the first privatization period, net subsidies during the four years before privatization equaled 0.18 percent of 2003 GDP, almost half of the sale price of the firms privatized during the period. During the second period, net subsidies were more than twice their previous value but represented only about 8 percent of the nominal price of privatization contracts.

Overall, the evidence suggests that privatization had a positive and significant impact on the fiscal position of the government. The operating balance and total public-sector borrowing requirements show a significant turnaround. In fact, during the second period the government's budget deficit (without considering direct privatization revenues) climbed from 16 percent of GDP to a small budget surplus (figure 7.2). Furthermore, the greater fiscal discipline afforded by privatization contributed to a sharp reduction in inflation and therefore to improved macroeconomic stability (López-de-Silanes 1994).

The funds obtained from the sale of SOEs were allocated to three principal uses: an emergency contingency fund to protect against nonrecurrent external shocks; a fund destined to reduce the stock of external debt; and

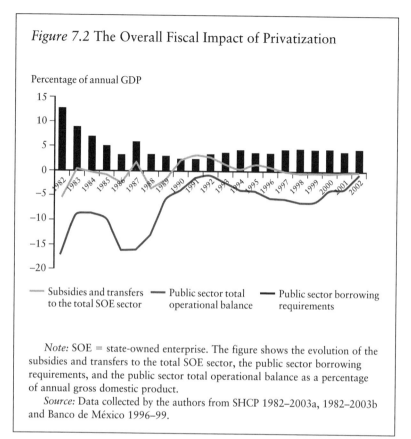

Figure 7.2 The Overall Fiscal Impact of Privatization

Percentage of annual GDP

— Subsidies and transfers   — Public sector total   — Public sector borrowing
   to the total SOE sector   operational balance   requirements

Note: SOE = state-owned enterprise. The figure shows the evolution of the subsidies and transfers to the total SOE sector, the public sector borrowing requirements, and the public sector total operational balance as a percentage of annual gross domestic product.
Source: Data collected by the authors from SHCP 1982–2003a, 1982–2003b and Banco de México 1996–99.

a permanent increase in the budget for education and social assistance. The relative composition of public and private investment also changed because of privatization: total government investment in the economy shrank from more than 10 percent of GDP in 1982 to less than 3 percent in 2001 (SHCP 1982–2003b). During this period, investments by SOEs fell from more than one-half of private investment to less than one-tenth, reflecting the joint effect of lower government involvement in the economy and a recovery of private investment.

The privatization program also encouraged foreign direct investment. Although foreign investors won only 9 percent of all privatization contracts auctioned, they engaged in joint ventures with domestic investors for an additional 11 percent of privatization contracts, including several of the largest firms (table 7.10).

The net effect of these factors contributed to the radical reduction of government debt experienced by Mexico since the mid-1980s. As shown in figure 7.3, total debt, both internal and external, dropped from a high

Table 7.10 Foreign Direct Investment in Privatization

Winner's nationality	Number of privatization contracts in the sample			Present value of sale price as a percentage of average FDI flows
	1938–88	*1989–93*	*1994–2003*	
Foreign	6	8	9	15.58
Foreign–domestic joint venture	4	16	8	67.35
Domestic	77	110	18	171.96
Total	87	134	35	255.17

Note: FDI = foreign direct investment.
Source: Data collected by the authors from the original privatization sales and prospectuses from the Secretaría de Hacienda y Crédito Público, Secretaría de Comunicaciones y Transportes, and Banco de México.

of 80.7 percent of GDP in 1986 to only 38.7 percent in 1991 and to 27 percent in 2001. Although the stock of external debt increased sharply before the 1995 financial crisis, and the stock of internal debt has increased continuously since 1996, it is clear that Mexico's debt situation is very different from what it once was. The privatization program, through its fiscal windfall and especially the lower financial requirements of a reduced SOE sector, is one of the main factors explaining this transformation.

Allocative Efficiency

Allocative efficiency refers to the idea that firms should be placed in the hands of those who value them the most. The guiding principle behind the idea of maximizing allocative efficiency is that any other mechanism would provide an inferior potential welfare outcome because any distribution goal can be achieved by giving the asset to whoever values it the most and then taxing them to compensate others. Some privatization programs, particularly in former communist countries, used voucher mechanisms to achieve a direct transfer of resources. These programs gave each individual a share of the former national industry with the objective of achieving a more equitable distribution of wealth and to prevent a few rich investors from pocketing most of the potential gains from privatization.

Recent literature on the subject (Galal and others 1994; Maskin 1992) has emphasized that voucher programs are less efficient than fiscal policy in achieving wealth distribution and are subject to more problems. Diffused

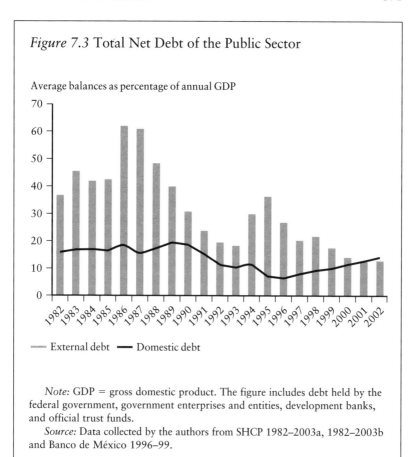

Figure 7.3 Total Net Debt of the Public Sector

Average balances as percentage of annual GDP

— External debt   —— Domestic debt

Note: GDP = gross domestic product. The figure includes debt held by the federal government, government enterprises and entities, development banks, and official trust funds.
Source: Data collected by the authors from SHCP 1982–2003a, 1982–2003b and Banco de México 1996–99.

shareholders are often bought out at deep discounts by agents with asymmetric information, and entrenched management can more easily resist reform because there is no organized pressure from the new owners. Because of this, it seems a wiser idea for governments to follow a process similar to Mexico's, which focused its attention on maximizing allocative efficiency and then used the proceeds from privatization to benefit the rest of the population. As of June 1992 the Mexican privatization program involved a total of more than 2,200 interested individuals and companies who formally requested information and 839 actual bidders. This wide participation is one of the main reasons for the high prices paid for privatized firms in Mexico (López-de-Silanes 1997).

As a result of the income derived from privatization programs, spending on education and social assistance increased dramatically. The resources generated and liberated by privatization account for a significant share of these programs, and have helped the levels of education, health, and regional development regain their pre-1982-crisis levels (around 9 percent of GDP). For example, in 1992 the education budget increased 9.5 percent in real terms, while the health and social services sector received an increase of 7.7 percent, and transfers to rural development programs increased almost 40 percent (López-de-Silanes 1994).

Dos and Don'ts in Privatization

The Mexican privatization program provides an excellent opportunity to study the effects of different privatization policies and restructuring programs. Privatization requires heavy government involvement and is usually fraught with conflicts of interest as politicians set up the method and run the process through which they end up either "selling their own firms" or "firing themselves or their friends" (Perotti 1995; Biais and Perotti 2002; Bortolotti, Fantini, and Scarpa 2001; Earle and Gehlbach 2003). Table 7.11 shows the most common restructuring measures adopted before privatization and their frequency in the different periods of the Mexican privatization program.

The most popular restructuring measures in both periods (1983–88 and 1989–92) are labor retrenchment and debt absorption, which were carried out with the hope that bidders would be willing to pay more for firms that had been restructured in this way. During the second period, other restructuring mechanisms such as changing the management team, firing the chief executive officer (CEO), and implementing investment and efficiency programs became much more common.

To assess the impact of different restructuring measures on the price paid for privatized firms, we need to construct a variable that controls for the value of the firm sold and captures the resources that accrue to the government from the sale of the SOE. We propose an approximation of Tobin's Q—the ratio of the firm's market value to the replacement cost of its physical assets—which we call privatization Q (PQ) and estimate as:

$$PQ = \frac{\dfrac{GNPP}{sh} + TD}{TA}$$

where GNPP is the price received by the government once all restructuring costs have been deducted; sh is the number of shares sold; TD are total liabilities at the time of privatization; and TA are total assets at the time of privatization.[17] The PQ standardization considers $GNPP_i$ as the proxy for market value of stock while controlling for debt and assets and allows for the calculation of a good proxy for Tobin's Q.[18]

Table 7.11 Restructuring Actions before Privatization

Actions	Number of privatization contracts	
	1983–88	*1989–92*
Management		
Chief executive officer replaced	11	25
Change of management team	15	54
Change or creation of board of directors	1	30
Labor		
Labor cuts	24	65
Collective contract canceled	4	13
Collective contract renegotiated	3	10
Debt absorption		
Outsiders debt	23	53
Cross liabilities	10	45
Fiscal debt	11	37
Efficiency programs		
Performance measures	6	29
Increased management responsibilities	0	27
Investment programs		
Investment-performance agreements	10	29
Other investment programs	5	1
Deinvestment measures	9	32
Legal measures		
Legal debt absorption or solution of disputes	2	15
Negotiations with minority shareholders	11	9
Reorganization or changes in legal status	7	11
Assets restructuring		
Clarify or document assets ownership	7	22
Patent registrations	1	5
Breaking up companies for sale	3	37
Bundling companies for sale	14	4
Assets spin-offs	10	14
Number of privatization contracts in the sample	87	134

Note: The table shows the main groups of restructuring actions before privatization and their frequency by period for a subsample of 221 privatization contracts in Mexico between 1983 and 1992. Some privatization contracts did not undergo any of the actions listed above, while others underwent several restructuring actions simultaneously. The exact definition of each restructuring group can be found in the appendix.

Source: Data collected by the authors from the original privatization sales and prospectuses from the Secretaría de Hacienda y Crédito Público.

The estimations shown in this section regarding the effects of the sale process on privatization prices consider PQ as the dependent variable and firm-specific characteristics, industry characteristics, auction requirements, and restructuring measures undertaken before privatization as the independent variables. Ordinary least square (OLS) results as well as instrumental variable (IV) results that take into account the possible endogeneity of our proposed measures are shown in table 7.12.

Firm and Industry Characteristics

All firm and industry characteristics show their expected effect on PQ and are statistically significant. An increase of 10 percentage points on the ratio of net income to sales increases PQ by 16 (15) percent using estimates from an ordinary least squares (instrumental variables) regression. A more aggressive labor force, measured by the cost of firing workers or by the number of strikes suffered in the years leading up to privatization, significantly reduces the price received for privatized firms. For example, an additional strike in the five years leading up to privatization lowers PQ by 17 (23) percent. Government involvement in the industry significantly increases the price paid for a privatized firm, but privatizations that do not transfer control of the firms to private hands are sold at a significant discount. A 10 percentage point increase in the market share of public enterprises increases PQ by about 7 percent, probably as a result of protection against competition granted to sectors under heavy state control.[19] In contrast, the sale of government holdings in private firms is heavily penalized. The average noncontrol privatization fetched PQs 91 (78) percent lower than those privatizations where the government owned the controlling interest, probably as a result of poor corporate governance and deficient enforcement of shareholder's rights, which fueled investors' fears that they would be exploited by the current majority shareholder.

Auction Process and Requirements

Auction requirements make a substantial difference in the net price received by the government. Bans on foreign participation reduced PQs by 32 (30) percent. Cash-only sales, another common restriction, were popular because they lowered the government's risk to future breaches of contract and provided an instant infusion into the treasury. Nevertheless, these advantages must be carefully weighed against the 30 (27) percent discount in PQ they entailed. It is important to point out that these penalties are independent of the fact that they lower auction competition, a substantial factor when we consider that an additional bidder in the final round increased PQ by 17 (12) percent for the average firm.

Table 7.12 Prior Restructuring: Dos and Don'ts

Independent variables	Percentage change in privatization Q (OLS)	Percentage change in privatization Q (IV)
Firm and industry characteristics		
Net income/sales	15.83***	15.33***
Contingent labor liabilities per worker	−1.97**	−1.38*
Number of strikes	−16.98**	−23.12**
Government in industry	7.06*	7.12*
Noncontrol package dummy	−90.89***	−78.28**
Auction process and requirements		
Total length of sale	−2.23***	−3.35***
Additional bidder in final round	16.96***	11.64**
FDI allowed dummy	31.56*	29.63*
Cash-sale only dummy	−30.41	−26.52
Prior restructuring policy		
CEO change dummy	34.13	54.88**
Percentage of labor cuts	−2.82	12.28*
Debt absorbed/total liabilities	−40.89	11.44
Efficiency measures dummy	−14.71	−56.09
Investment measures dummy	2.40	−95.31
Deinvestment measures dummy	−16.57	3.96

* Significant at the 10 percent level.
** Significant at the 5 percent level.
*** Significant at the 1 percent level.

Note: OLS = ordinary least squares, IV = instrumental variables, FDI = foreign direct investment, and CEO = chief executive officer. The table shows the effect of firm and industry characteristics, auction characteristics and requirements, and prior restructuring policies on the mean privatization Q for a subsample of 140 firms privatized in Mexico between 1983 and 1992 for which full information is available. We calculate the effect of a 10 percentage point increase in the net-income-to-sales ratio; an additional strike; a 10 percentage point increase in the government's preprivatization market share of the industry of the privatized firms; an additional month in the length of sale; and a 10 percent reduction in the labor force. For all other variables, we show the discrete change of the dummy from 0 to 1. The first column considers prior restructuring measures and the rest of the variables as "exogenous" and uses estimates from an OLS regression. The second column shows the second step of the two-step instrumental variables procedure in which prior restructuring measures, total length of sale from rumors to completion, and the number of bidders in the final round are treated as potentially endogenous variables. All variables definitions can be found in the appendix.

Source: López-de-Silanes 1997.

The speed at which privatization takes place also has important effects on the net price raised. While there are potential costs of rushing a sale, the benefits of a quick process include disposing of money-losing firms and avoiding costly restructuring. Additionally, a lengthy process usually leads to a deterioration of the operating performance of the firm as managers' incentives collapse and workers are disgruntled about the possibility of losing their jobs. Evidence from Mexico suggests this is the case, as each additional month taken to complete the privatization process costs an average of 2.2 (3.4) percent of PQ.[20]

Prior Restructuring Policies

Government restructuring of SOEs before their sale is fraught with political difficulties. Direct costs of restructuring are quite substantial— equivalent, on average, to about 30 percent of the sale price. As with other policies, restructuring programs can be defended rationally on the grounds that they increase revenues from the sale, or that they minimize layoffs and contribute to the future success of the privatized firm. As a result, there is great ambivalence about the optimal policy approach toward restructuring before privatization. Analyzing this question is not a straightforward proposition because restructuring measures are not undertaken randomly but are selectively targeted to firms that need them most.[21] To solve this problem, we use an instrumental variable approach to capture the true effect of restructuring measures on privatization prices.[22]

In this section, we look at six types of prior restructuring: change in management, labor retrenchment, debt absorption, efficiency programs, investment measures, and deinvestment measures. Restructuring measures are almost certainly endogenous, and therefore we focus on the results provided by the instrumental variable regression.

On one hand, management shake-ups before privatization can lead to lower privatization prices if the loss of experienced managers leads to deteriorating performance (Bolton and Roland 1992). On the other hand, removing an entrenched team can improve the operating performance of a firm as well as make it easier to tackle mismanagement and corruption. This is especially likely if management was appointed for political rather than technical reasons (Barberis and others 1996). The empirical evidence supports the second hypothesis, as firing the CEO leads to a statistically significant increase of 55 percent in the PQ.[23]

The argument against restructuring labor contracts or firing workers before privatization rests on the assumption that the new owner will be better suited to choose which workers to retain and which to dismiss and can therefore restructure the labor force to suit the firm's needs at a lower cost than the government could. This may be particularly true if unions have significant power to influence the political process through elections or collective action (Freeman 1986). Conversely, the public sector may have a comparative advantage in bargaining with unions if it can convince workers that social mechanisms will be put in place to assist them. For our sample of Mexican privatized firms, labor retrenchment had a slight negative effect on PQ under the OLS regression but a significant positive impact once we account for its endogenous nature. Under this specification, a 10 percent reduction in the labor force is associated with a statistically significant 12 percent increase in PQ. This evidence should be taken with care, as recent investigations dealing specifically with the effects of labor retrenchment on privatization suggest that these programs are seldom the optimal policy (Chong and López-de-Silanes 2003).

Classical finance theory holds that government's absorption of SOEs' debt should have a neutral effect on price because potential acquirers would simply increase their bids by the same amount as the decrease in debt (Donaldson and Wagle 1995). However, one can imagine scenarios under which debt absorption could have a positive or negative effect on net prices if the borrowing terms for the private buyers are different from those for the government or if debt absorption reduces the expected cost of financial distress for excessively leveraged companies (Bolton and Roland 1992). Once we control for endogeneity, the effect of debt absorption on PQ becomes quantitatively and statistically insignificant.

Some of the most frequent restructuring policies undertaken include investment programs and efficiency measures. We would expect a premium in PQ for restructured firms if the government is able to improve the operating performance of firms at a lower cost than the private sector could. However, if restructuring decisions are driven by political motivations or if the government is unable to match the know-how of private firms, the restructuring effort will be a waste of resources and therefore lower PQ. The latter seems to be the case in Mexico as, controlling for endogeneity, firms subject to efficiency measures and investment plans were sold for PQs 56 and 95 percent lower, respectively.

If bidders value investments by the government at less than their cost, it is worth investigating whether PQ could be increased by cutting the flow of resources and canceling previously approved investment programs. This may not be straightforward, however, as deinvestment may hurt the long-term profitability of firms and lead to lower prices. Our results find that, on average, undertaking deinvestment measures has no significant effect.

Available empirical evidence strongly suggests that restructuring policies do not lead to better net prices per dollar of assets sold. We find that the optimal policy seems to be to refrain as much as possible from engaging in SOE restructuring. Some of the most popular measures such as debt absorption do not increase net prices, while others such as investment and efficiency programs actually reduce net prices. These results are actually quite intuitive once we realize that all they imply is that new owners are able to satisfy their own goals better than politicians could.

Complementary Policies of Privatization

Privatization should not be looked at in isolation. Its success or failure is likely to depend on a set of complementary policies that are sometimes neglected. First, the outcome of a privatization process depends crucially on the quality and appropriateness of the contracts written, particularly when dealing with the provision of public services or public-private ventures. Policymakers should not rely on the good will of the private sector to act in the best interest of society. If the privatization contracts do not establish the right incentives, it should come as no surprise that newly privatized firms will try to use market power to increase their benefits or that concession holders may manipulate their accounts to extract rents from the government. Second, it is crucial to consider carefully the necessary deregulation or reregulation for sectors with market power or in which government ownership represented a substantial percentage of total assets before privatization. Without adequate deregulation, firms may not restructure as planned, and potential efficiency gains may be lost, as it is easier to extract rents from the government. Conversely, without a program to reregulate privatized firms, those with market power may use their ability to influence prices to exploit consumers, and those in sectors with protective regulations may benefit from barriers to entry and other measures originally intended to protect SOEs from competition. Finally, it is important to establish a set of institutions that promote good corporate governance and strengthen shareholder and creditor rights in order to facilitate firms' access to capital and allow recently privatized firms to finance their growth without dependence on the state.

The Type of Contract Written

The type of privatization contract written is of the utmost importance to ensure that no room is left for opportunistic behavior at the hands of politicians or private buyers. The simplest contracts are straightforward sales of assets in which the government disconnects itself completely from the operational future of the privatized firm. Other types of contracts may lead to a perverse relationship between the privatized firm and the state as managers and bureaucrats collude to serve their own interests at the expense of consumers and taxpayers.

Most vulnerable to this sort of manipulation are the provision of services, the construction of infrastructure projects, and the establishment of joint ventures between private companies and the government.

The common element in these cases is that the umbilical cord between the government and the firm has not been severed, leaving room for rent-seeking behavior. When privatized firms depend on the state for funding or need permission to undertake certain decisions, it is likely that the incentives to restructure will not be as strong and that management will instead focus its efforts on extracting rents from the government. These perverse incentives are fed by politicians who often aspire to transform firms into national champions by subsidizing them and shielding them from competition. This collusion with business is often rewarded directly by economic support from firms and by the political benefits derived from being perceived as standing up for labor and against foreign competitors. To minimize the potential losses from these arrangements and to ensure that privatized firms live up to their commitments, clear disclosure and monitoring mechanisms are needed.

The importance of writing adequate contracts can be illustrated by one of the major instances of failure in Mexico's privatization program, the concessions to construct and manage highways. As Rogozinsky and Tovar (1998) explain, to encourage private sector participation in highways, the government included clauses in its contracts guaranteeing minimum traffic growth rates. If revenues fell below the guaranteed level, the private party would be entitled to claim a revision of the length of the concession. Moreover, under this scheme, the only variable of adjustment was the length of the concession. These incentives created perverse rent-seeking incentives for concession holders to inflate construction costs and to charge excessively high toll charges. With the peso devaluation of 1994, a bad situation was made much worse as lower than expected revenues and higher interest rates pushed many concession holders to the brink of bankruptcy. Banks that had supplied much of the debt were themselves hard hit and thus unable or unwilling to provide relief through debt restructuring (World Bank 2003).

The World Bank's 2003 report on private solutions for infrastructure in Mexico points out four basic causes for the failure of road privatization. First, the program as a whole was not financially sound; concessions with the highest profit potential were awarded first, but the overall program was too extensive for each concession to be financially self-sufficient. Second, the decision to award concessions based on the shortest period of private ownership led to excessively high toll levels. The average duration of concessions was 12 years, and in two cases an award was given for only 5 years. This led to inefficiencies as several newly built toll roads were virtually empty while parallel public roads remained heavily congested; truck traffic, in particular, fell below forecast levels. Third, poor feasibility studies led to overgenerous contracts. The Secretaría de Comunicaciones y Transportes did not have the necessary experience or resources to carry out appropriate cost and demand forecasts for such an extensive program and, in particular, it seems to have substantially underestimated the demand elasticity of toll roads. Finally, underbidding and overvaluation of contractor contributions were widespread. Contractors overvalued their contributions, especially once financial problems emerged, because they could then press for extensions on the concession.

The policy lesson is clear: contracts must be designed to take into account moral hazard incentives and the asymmetries of information between the government and the private sector. The design of the contracts should be based on considerations of economic efficiency rather than on political or macroeconomic ones and, in particular, contracts should help limit rent-seeking behavior.

Deregulation

An appropriate regulatory framework after privatization is a key component of the success or failure of the program. A common element across many failed examples of privatization is inadequate deregulation, which may lead to suboptimal levels of competition and allows producers to keep the gains from privatization without sharing them with consumers.[24] Deregulation is particularly important in sectors where the state owned most of the assets before privatization, as they tend to be protected by a web of regulations originally instituted to cut the losses of state-owned firms and reduce fiscal deficits. Without a thorough review of these regulations, privatized firms will be artificially shielded from competition and able to make extraordinary gains at the cost of consumers.

Deregulation complements privatization in two ways. First, product market competition provides a tool for weeding out the least efficient firms. This process may take too long—or not work at all—if regulation inhibits new entry or makes exit costly. Second, deregulation may also complement privatization by raising the cost of political intervention. Whereas an inefficient monopoly can squander its rents without endangering its existence, an inefficient firm in a competitive industry would have to receive a subsidy to stay afloat.

Figure 7.4 shows the frequency and composition of deregulation measures taken in Mexico from 1983 to 1992 before privatization. These include price and quantity deregulation, simplified entry and exit barriers, lower restrictions on foreign direct investment and ownership, increased international competition, and the elimination or reduction of subsidies. During the De la Madrid administration, 87 privatization contracts were carried out, with trade liberalization and changes in specific regulatory schemes as the most popular measures. During the Salinas administration, 134 privatization contracts were signed, and deregulation was undertaken much more aggressively. In particular, price and quantity quotas were disbanded and entry barriers were lowered, both directly and by granting a more prominent role to foreign direct investment. Although it is clear that

Figure 7.4 Deregulation Actions Taken before Privatization

Number of privatization contracts

[Bar chart showing deregulation actions across eight categories. Each category has two bars: 1983–88 (gray) and 1989–92 (black).]

- Price deregulation: 9 (1983–88), 57 (1989–92)
- Quantity/quotas/routes deregulation: 9 (1983–88), 38 (1989–92)
- Foreign direct investment: 2 (1983–88), 29 (1989–92)
- Trade liberalization: 17 (1983–88), 35 (1989–92)
- Changes to specific regulation schemes: 14 (1983–88), 43 (1989–92)
- Lower entry barriers: 1 (1983–88), 19 (1989–92)
- Elimination/reduction of subsidies: 10 (1983–88), 24 (1989–92)

■ 1983–88 ■ 1989–92

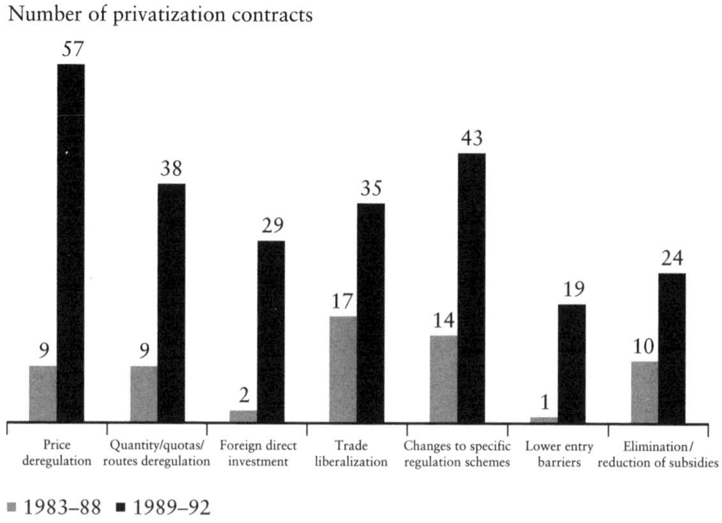

Note: The figure shows the main groups of deregulation actions taken before privatization for a subsample of 221 privatization contracts between 1983 and 1992. Not every privatization contract underwent some form of deregulation, while others underwent several. Eighty-seven privatization contracts were carried out during the first period (1983–88) and 134 during the second period (1989–92). The exact definition of each restructuring group can be found in the appendix.

Source: Data collected by the authors from the original privatization sales and prospectuses from the Secretaría de Hacienda y Crédito Público.

the Salinas administration engaged in deregulation with greater alacrity than the previous administration, privatization coupled with deregulation played a key role throughout the period.

Reregulation

Regulation should be carefully revised in conjunction with privatization for firms in industries characterized as natural monopolies or in oligopolistic markets. The reasoning behind the first case is that firms with market power may have ample opportunities to exploit consumers and that the institutions necessary to supervise them either are nonexistent or do not have the necessary experience to do the job appropriately. When firms with market power are in public hands, it is likely that the profit-maximizing incentive is held in check as the government places priorities on other goals such as providing subsidized services to certain sectors or maximizing employment. Once firms are handed over to the private sector, however, it is likely that the new owners will use whatever means they have at their disposal to increase profits. It is therefore necessary to complement privatization with adequate reregulation and with the creation of institutions that ensure fair competition and a level playing field to all participants.

A clear example of the perils of not reregulating privatized SOEs appropriately is that of the Mexican banking industry. During the years under state management, banks functioned as an annex to the national treasury and served mainly as a tool for financing state deficits and handing out favors to politically influential sectors. As a result, banks did not develop the necessary experience in valuing the risks associated with particular loans or the skills needed to value collateral. Moreover, when banks were privatized, no supervisory mechanism was in place to ensure that bank loans to related parties were in the best interests of the bank or that reserves were proportional to the riskiness of the loans undertaken. The combination of these two shortcomings proved fatal for the banks' future and to the thousands of shareholders who purchased minority stakes in them.

The changes made in the regulatory framework of the banking industry were structured around three main objectives: First, they aimed to decrease the role of the government in determining the allocation of bank loans; second, they tried to create a new market structure for financial services as a whole; and third, they attempted to curtail barriers to entry. Unfortunately, the reforms carried out to achieve these objectives were executed in a piecemeal fashion and not within the context of a comprehensive plan to provide the banking industry with adequate regulation. In the end, the greater flexibility granted to private banks allowed them to engage in risky behavior and to extract benefits from consumers and the government without providing incentives for banks to reform and become more efficient.

Following privatization, lending increased rapidly and was accompanied by improvements in bank profitability. The average bank increased its operating margin by almost 2 percentage points to 10.85 percent, and profit margins increased from 5.37 percent to 6.36 percent (figure 7.5). Interest margins, however, remained steady at about 7 percent despite the fact that nominal interest rates fell from 80 percent to only 35 percent.[25]

Two hypotheses can be used to explain the higher profitability of privatized banks without resorting to charges of collusion and market power: the employee-wealth-transfer hypothesis, and the reduced-agency-cost

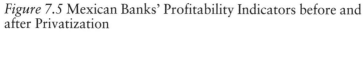

Figure 7.5 Mexican Banks' Profitability Indicators before and
after Privatization

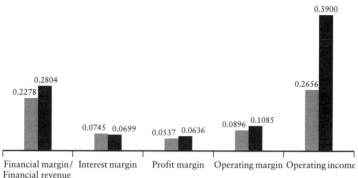

Financial margin / Interest margin   Profit margin   Operating margin Operating income
Financial revenue

■ Before privatization   ■ After privatization

Note: This figure shows mean performance indicators before and after
privatization for the cross section of banks privatized in Mexico. *Financial
margin/financial revenue* is the ratio of the financial margin to financial
revenue; *interest margin* is the financial margin divided by the sum of loans
portfolio plus securities portfolio; *profit margin* is the ratio of period net
income to the period total revenue; *operating margin* is the ratio of period
operating income to the period total revenue; *operating income* is the real
annual growth rate in the operating income. *Before privatization* refers to the
period between January 1989 and the month of privatization of each bank,
while *after privatization* is the period ranging from the month of privatization
to the end of 1992, or for the largest period for which information is available.
The banks included in the sample are Atlantico, Banpais, Banamex, Banco del
Centro, Bancomer, Bancrecer, Banco Oriente, Banoro, Banorte, B.C.H., Cremi,
Confia, Comermex, Internacional, Mercantil, Serfin, Somex, and Promex.
Source: López-de-Silanes and Zamarripa 1995.

hypothesis. The former argues that wealth is transferred to investors by
laying off workers and reducing the wages of remaining employees
(Shleifer and Summers 1988), while the latter argues that proper incentives
reduce agency costs and lead to higher profitability.

Figure 7.6 shows that the average annual change in employment
after privatization is −1.64 percent, which would seem to lend credence
to the employee-wealth-transfer hypothesis. However, the real annual
growth rate of personnel expenses per employee more than doubled in

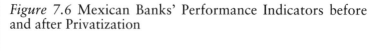

Figure 7.6 Mexican Banks' Performance Indicators before
and after Privatization

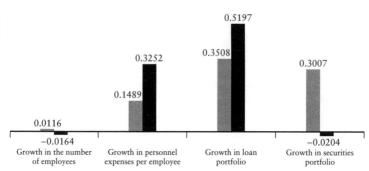

■ Before privatization ■ After privatization

Note: This figure shows mean performance indicators before and after
privatization for the cross-section of Mexican privatized banks. *Growth in the
number of employees* is the annual percentage increase in the number of
employees; *growth in personnel expenses per employee* is the real annual growth
in the monthly personnel expense per employee; *growth in loan portfolio* is the
real growth rate in the loan portfolio; *growth in securities portfolio* is the real
growth rate in the securities portfolio. *Before privatization* refers to the period
between January 1989 and the month of privatization of each bank, while *after
privatization* is the period ranging from the month of privatization to the end of
1992, or for the longest period for which information is available. The banks
included in the sample are Atlantico, Banpais, Banamex, Banco del Centro,
Bancomer, Bancrecer, Banco Oriente, Banoro, Banorte, B.C.H., Cremi, Confia,
Comermex, Internacional, Mercantil, Serfin, Somex, and Promex.
Source: López-de-Silanes and Zamarripa (1995).

the period following privatization, jumping from 14.9 percent to 32.5
percent.[26] When put together, these two pieces of evidence show that
labor costs did not decrease, but that they in fact increased significantly
following privatization. The employee-wealth-transfer hypothesis,
therefore, cannot explain the increased operating performance of
banks.

In terms of the reduced-agency-costs hypothesis, two elements point
toward possible savings. The first concerns banking operations as such.
Under government ownership, banks had deviated from their main
lending activity and entered the securities market, possibly in reaction to

increased competition from brokerage houses. This deviation reflected management or political objectives, such as size or growth, which are common for SOEs all over the world. After privatization, the growth rate of the loan portfolio increased from 35.08 percent to 51.97 percent, while the securities portfolio decreased at an annual rate of 2.04 percent (see figure 7.6). Given that the financial margin on loans ranged from 3 to 15 percent, while that of securities was only about 1 to 3 percent (López-de-Silanes and Zamarripa 1995), it is tempting to argue that privatization reduced the agency problem because resources were channeled toward lending and not toward other objectives. A second source of reduced agency costs can be found in the ownership structure that emerged after privatization. Most bank managers were also shareholders, which helps increase the incentives to maximize shareholder value. In addition, although management had seats on the board of directors, the board was controlled by outsiders, a management structure that is more likely to allow the board of directors to act as an effective mechanism of corporate governance (Fama and Jensen 1983).

These two pieces of supporting evidence notwithstanding, the banking crisis of the mid-1990s and the role that related lending played in bringing about the collapse of the banking system seriously undermine the idea that reduced agency costs can explain the increase in profitability experienced by privatized banks. The conclusion we are left with, therefore, is that inadequate competition allowed banks to collude and increase their profitability without really restructuring.

In terms of failed supervision, the government turned a blind eye to overdue loans. The supervisory system was not modernized, and the government did not require banks to increase their reserves or to tie them to the underlying riskiness of the loans. Meanwhile, banks continued to pay high dividends and reserves were progressively decapitalized, leaving the whole system vulnerable to collapse. Signs of stress in the financial sector first appeared in 1993 as the economy slipped into a recession, and by July 1994 most financial institutions were experiencing serious difficulties.

As the financial crisis evolved, the government took over financially distressed banks with the goal of restructuring them and finding a buyer for them in better times. Once the dust settled, however, only 3 out of 18 commercial banks remained independent, and none escaped unscathed. As of the year 2000, 7 banks were under government management, 5 had been acquired by foreign financial institutions, and 3 had been acquired by domestic financial institutions.

Interestingly, many, if not most, of the defaulted loans that led to the collapse of the banking industry were related loans, or loans granted to directors of the bank or companies in the same industrial conglomerate as others owned by bank directors. Many economists have argued that related lending is beneficial to banks as it allows them to better assess the risks related to particular projects and to monitor the compliance of debtors. If this is true, banks may be able to get higher ex post returns from preferential loans granted to related parties than from arm's-length transactions at full rates. In the Mexican case, however, there is evidence that related lending was used by controlling shareholders to loot banks.

There are four basic results that, when put together, overwhelmingly support the looting view of related lending. First, the borrowing terms offered to related parties were substantially better than those available to unrelated ones (figure 7.7). Controlling for observable financial characteristics, the interest rate for fixed-rate related loans in pesos was a mean of 6.88 percentage points lower than that of unrelated loans. The smallest difference is 2.25 percent for floating-rate dollar-denominated loans, still a significant margin and, like all the others, statistically significant at the 1 percent level. Moreover, loans to related parties posted collateral or personal guarantees less often than unrelated loans, and when they did it was for a lower amount. Finally, the maturity of related loans was an average of three months longer and the grace period seven months longer than those of unrelated loans. These facts clearly establish that related loans were given preferential treatment over unrelated ones.

The second point is that the default rate on related loans was 70 percent compared with only 39 percent for unrelated parties and recovery rates were 19 to 40 cents per dollar lower for related borrowers than for unrelated ones (figure 7.8). This clearly undermines the idea that preferential loans can be justified by higher ex post returns.

Third, related lending represented about 20 percent of all loans outstanding, the limit established by law. Moreover, as the economy slipped into recession, the fraction of related lending doubled for banks that subsequently went bankrupt, while it increased only slightly for the banks that survived. This suggests that when bankers thought they might lose their investment, they stepped up the rate of looting to extract as much value as possible while they still controlled the bank, and it is consistent with what a theoretical model of looting would predict.

Finally, and most interestingly, the worst-performing loans were those made to persons or companies closest to the controllers of the banks. In most cases, a dollar lent to a firm owned by the bank's owners turned out to be a dollar lost.

The evidence provided here clearly shows that related lending had a negative effect on the banking sector in Mexico. Loans to related parties were granted not because compliance was easier to supervise or because related parties were more suitable candidates. Instead, there is clear evidence that related loans were used to divert funds away from banks and to exploit minority shareholders. Even so, bank owners emerged from the crisis relatively unscathed; after "tunneling" money out of their bank, they lost control of the bank but not of their industrial assets.

Figure 7.7 Terms of Related and Unrelated Loans

a. Real interest rates

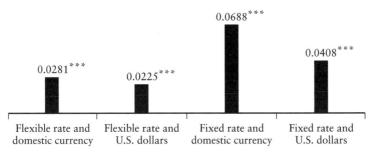

| Flexible rate and domestic currency | Flexible rate and U.S. dollars | Fixed rate and domestic currency | Fixed rate and U.S. dollars |

0.0281***   0.0225***   0.0688***   0.0408***

b. Collateral and guarantees

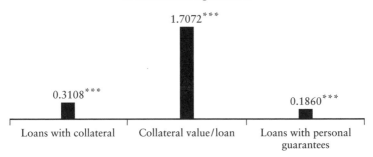

1.7072***   0.3108***   0.1860***

Loans with collateral   Collateral value/loan   Loans with personal guarantees

c. Maturity and grace period

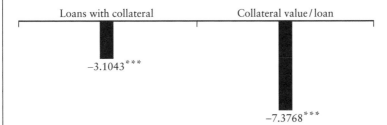

Loans with collateral   Collateral value/loan

−3.1043***   −7.3768***

*** Significant at the 1 percent level.
Note: This table shows the main characteristics of related and unrelated loans in Mexico for a random sample of loans between 1995 and 1999. Panel a shows the mean change in real interest rates for the sample of related versus unrelated loans. Panel b shows the mean difference of the percentage of loans with collateral; percentage points difference in the collateral to value of the loan ratio; and the difference in the percentage of loans backed up with personal guarantees. Panel c shows the mean difference in months to maturity of the loan and the difference in months of grace granted to the loans. For a description of the sample and definitions of all variables, refer to the appendix.
Source: La Porta, López-de-Silanes, and Zamarripa 2003.

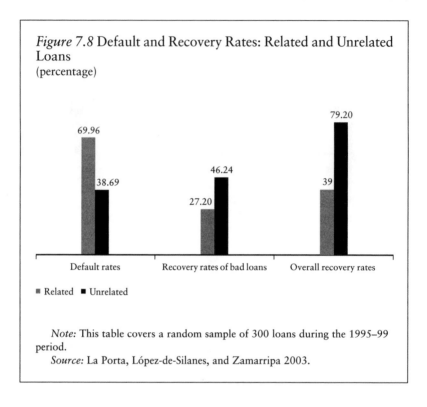

Figure 7.8 Default and Recovery Rates: Related and Unrelated Loans
(percentage)

Default rates   Recovery rates of bad loans   Overall recovery rates

■ Related ■ Unrelated

Note: This table covers a random sample of 300 loans during the 1995–99 period.
Source: La Porta, López-de-Silanes, and Zamarripa 2003.

Although related lending explains a significant part of the problem in financial institutions, it cannot be blamed completely for the current malaise of the banking sector. The other aspect of lending is collecting, and banks need to have effective collecting mechanisms in place. Effective corporate governance through creditor protection has recently proven to be a key component of the development of financial systems around the world. As the next section shows, the problems brought on by related lending were exacerbated and in part instigated by deficient shareholder and creditor rights.

Privatization and Corporate Governance

The development and appropriate functioning of stock and credit markets need a solid regulatory framework that promotes investor protection and disclosure. Recent research shows a strong link between firms' access to capital and efficiently enforced laws (La Porta and Florencio López-de-Silanes 1999; La Porta and others 1997, 1998, 2000a, 2000b; La Porta, López-de-Silanes, and Shleifer 2002). In countries where large numbers of firms have been privatized and deregulation has increased competition and lowered trade barriers, institutions are urgently needed that can efficiently channel resources to the private sector. The old laws and institutions that might have been efficient in covering the needs of state-owned enterprises will probably not suffice for the requirements of private enterprises and privatized firms. This section focuses on the role of shareholder rights and creditor rights as important determinants of the success of stock markets and credit institutions.

Modigliani and Miller (1958) argue that the size of capital markets is determined only by the cash flows that accrue to investors; roughly speaking, this implies that the size of capital markets should be proportional to gross national product. To explain the large discrepancies in the size of financial markets across countries with similar gross national products, however, we need to recognize that securities are more than the cash flows they represent. They entitle investors to exercise certain rights and to exercise control over management through the voting process. Similarly, debt not only entitles creditors to receive interest payments, but also to regain their collateral in the event of bankruptcy.

Countries differ enormously in the extent to which they afford legal protection to investors. Not only does a shareholder in Mexico have a very different set of rights from a shareholder in the United Kingdom or the United States, but his/her recourse to redress is also likely to be significantly different—that is, weaker. The legal theory (La Porta and others 1997, 1998) predicts larger capital markets in countries where agency costs are reined in by the law and the institutions built to support their enforcement. The evidence presented in these studies shows that, all in all, Mexico offers investors a rather unattractive legal environment.

Figure 7.9 shows market capitalization as a percentage of GDP and the number of listed firms in the Mexican stock exchange. Not surprisingly, the Mexican market has a low capitalization by international standards. The stock market enjoyed a significant boom during the Salinas administration, as many privatized firms were subsequently listed and those that already were privatized increased their capitalization considerably. Market capitalization increased from slightly over 5 percent in 1988 to almost 45 percent in only six years. Following the 1994–95 crisis, capitalization plunged to 25 percent and has dropped further since. Moreover, the number of listed firms itself is declining, which suggests that firms are either going bankrupt or being taken private. In either case, it is a clear sign that corporate governance structures are not functioning efficiently.

Some recent attempts have been made to strengthen shareholder rights in Mexico. Most notably, the 1997 and 2001 securities acts moved from a merit to a disclosure system of regulation. They also established requirements for a minimum number of independent directors on boards of listed companies and mandated the creation of an independent audit committee. A forthcoming securities act attempts to expand protection further

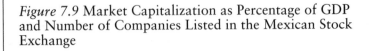

Figure 7.9 Market Capitalization as Percentage of GDP and Number of Companies Listed in the Mexican Stock Exchange

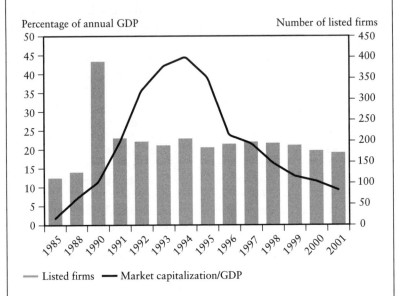

— Listed firms   — Market capitalization/GDP

Note: This table shows the number of firms listed on the Mexican stock exchange and their market capitalization as a percentage of GDP (gross domestic product).

Source: For market capitalization/GDP, Standard and Poor's Emerging Market Database (and Emerging Stock Markets Factbook); for the number of listed companies in 1985 and 1988, Banco de México and BMV 1985–92); for the number of listed companies 1990 to 2001, the World Federation of Exchanges.

by making the economic group the subject of regulation, establishing the duty of loyalty and care for directors, improving disclosure requirements, improving the enforcement powers of the Securities and Exchange Commission, and establishing a special committee to monitor conflicts of interest and related-party transactions. Furthermore, the new securities act seeks to limit the issuing of nonvoting shares and expand the rights of minority shareholders to obtain information about the firm, convene shareholder meetings, designate comptrollers, and even challenge unfair actions through the judicial system. Although these reforms are expected to have a significant effect, their scope is inherently limited as they apply only to listed companies. The next step will be to expand some of these best practices to a broader set of firms.

Another source of finance for privatized firms and other businesses is bank lending. However, if financing for privatized SOEs is expected to come from privatized banks—or from any other private credit institution— then creditor rights, embedded in bankruptcy laws and the efficiency of courts, must be strengthened and streamlined.

Without proper bankruptcy procedures that allow for the expedient recovery of assets, financial institutions will be reluctant to lend and may end up failing to satisfy the financial needs of the private sector. La Porta and others (1997) empirically confirmed the existence of a strong link between efficient creditor rights and an efficient judiciary with deeper debt markets. In a more recent paper, Djankov and others (2003) studied the costs, in both time and money, involved in collecting a bounced check or evicting a tenant in 109 countries. Their results show that Mexico ranks among the worst countries, which suggests that if there are considerable difficulties in using the court system for simple procedures, foreclosing on defaulted loans would be even more maladroit. The lesson is clear: if banks are to function appropriately, they must have mechanisms in place to recover the costs of loans in the case of default. Otherwise, the possibility of having a large number of irrecoverable loans default will drive up the interest rates for all projects, stifling growth and aggravating adverse selection problems.

Two types of reforms may be key to building stronger and sounder financial institutions. First, potential conflicts of interest in boards of directors of banks must be reduced. These boards have allowed large-scale, unprofitable related lending to occur, which has increased the fragility of the banks and of the overall financial system. Corporate governance reform must be designed to prevent interested directors from voting on approving related transactions that do not benefit the institution as a whole. Tougher limits on related loans, disclosure of related credits, and laws that effectively punish directors who vote in favor of unprofitable transactions should be among the first group of reforms. Second, in the event that a borrower defaults on its loans, financial institutions need to be able to exercise their rights to collect their debts. An essential condition for improved creditor protection is to strengthen bankruptcy laws and to increase efficiency in the implementation of these rights.

Conclusion

Empirical evidence shows that the Mexican government was effective in improving its fiscal discipline, increasing the efficient allocation of resources and restructuring inefficient SOEs. Success, however, has not been absolute. Although the privatization process was drastic and far-reaching, public utilities and firms in the energy sector remain in state possession. Moreover, there have been important failures in the Mexican privatization process, such as banks and highways.

The Mexican experience provides valuable insights into what to do and what not to do regarding large-scale privatization programs. Mexico's program should be considered a success, as the performance of firms increased dramatically according to all performance measures and both the government and consumers are better off as a result. Nevertheless, particular care should be taken to provide appropriate regulation to oligopolistic sectors or those that have spent considerable time under the control of the state.

This study provides three useful lessons that any privatization program should heed to maximize the probability of success. First, the privatization process must be carefully designed. Special requirements such as a ban on foreign direct investment or cash-only payments lead to substantial price discounts for firms sold. Simplicity and transparency, in contrast, increase prices because they expedite the whole process and increase the number of bidders. Speed is important because the operational efficiency of SOEs tends to atrophy once rumors of divestiture arise. The ability to draw on a wide pool of bidders is crucial to maximize the price received for privatized firms and therefore to obtain the most social benefit from the program. Privatization of services and infrastructure provides a valuable opportunity to enhance social welfare, but contracts must be carefully designed. Special attention is needed to ensure that the incentives of future owners are aligned with those of the government.

Second, restructuring firms before privatization is usually counterproductive in raising net sale prices. Restructuring programs are usually politically motivated and cost more than the value they add to companies; this is in addition to the fact that they lengthen the privatization process and therefore increase the costs related to the sale. Although the evidence from Mexico shows that labor retrenchment paid off, this is probably due to the abnormally bloated work force of most Mexican SOEs. Labor retrenchment is fraught with difficulties because the most politically palatable option, voluntary retirement programs, is plagued by adverse selection problems. Under these schemes, the most experienced and productive workers tend to leave and the least productive stay. The government is thus left with a steep bill from severance payments and bidders are left with a lower-quality work force that may not possess the skills necessary to run the firm successfully.

Third, reregulation of sectors with market power, deregulation of industries previously protected by the government, and efficient corporate governance institutions are important complementary measures to privatization. Mounting evidence is underscoring the importance of good corporate governance institutions in ensuring positive results from privatization and avoiding debacles similar to the related-lending problems suffered by the Mexican banking industry. The need for better regulation and corporate governance is not an argument for slower privatization, but it does point to the need for studying similar privatization programs to anticipate the regulatory framework and best practices codes needed for firms to have a smooth transition into the private sector.

Privatization and deregulation have allowed the Mexican government to withdraw from virtually all commercial and industrial activities and to concentrate on providing a stable economic environment. The proceeds from privatization helped deal with a crushing debt burden and allowed the government to invest in education and poverty alleviation. The evidence provided in this chapter leaves but one conclusion: The overall effect of privatization has been positive for Mexico.

Appendix 7A Description of Variables

This appendix describes all variables used to compute the results presented in the chapter. It contains three sections, each based on a different section of the chapter. The first section describes the restructuring actions undertaken for a cross section of 221 privatized SOEs in the 1983–92 period. We gathered these data from the original privatization sales and prospectuses from the Mexican Ministry of Finance and Public Credit (SHCP). The second section corresponds to the quantitative variables collected for a cross section of 170 nonfinancial firms privatized in Mexico during the 1983–92 period and used to measure the performance of privatized firms. We gather the preprivatization data from the original privatization sales and prospectuses from SHCP. For each firm, we compute the preprivatization value of each variable or ratio by averaging its value in the four years before the privatization of the firm. The postprivatization data come from the 1994 economic census from the Mexican National Statistics Institute (INEGI) and refer to 1993 data for each firm. When necessary, industry adjustments are made to various variables and ratios with the use of financial data of publicly traded firms in the Mexican stock market, INEGI's "Monthly Survey of Industry," and the producer price index at the sector level. The third section of the table defines the loan characteristic variables used in our related-lending section. Regulation in 1995 required banks to submit a list of the 300 largest loans, as well as their size and detailed information about the borrowers. Our sources are the SAM-300 database (largest 300 loans for each bank), the SENICREB database (complete list of loans made by each of the privatized banks), and banks' individual databases as reported to the Mexican Banking Commission.

Table 7A.1 Definition of Variables

Variable	Definition
Restructuring action	
Management	These actions include changes of the CEO (chief executive officer) and in the next level of the management team, as well as the creation of or changes in the board of directors in the two years before privatization.
Labor	These actions include preprivatization labor reductions of union or nonunion workers with their related severance payment costs, as well as varying forms of labor contract restructuring, plans for worker ownership of shares, cancellation of collective contracts in some subsidiaries or for the whole company, and union unification under the same contract.
Debt absorption	The actions include the government's engagement in partial or total debt absorptions of outsiders' debt (that was owed to private companies or private banks), cross liabilities, and the absorption of the company's past-due fiscal liabilities or taxes.
Efficiency programs	This category includes all of those detected actions that increased the management responsibility, increased the flexibility of investment policies, or referred to the installation of programs with defined performance targets and internal restructuring of operations.
Investment programs	These actions involve only detectable programs of rehabilitation and maintenance plans, agreements of financial restructuring tied to inflow of resources for operation improvements, and temporary reopenings of the plant.
Deinvestment measures	These actions include partial or total shutdown of operation, stopping of major investment programs, declarations of emergency-only expenditure taking place, and stopping of all government funding.
Legal measures	This group involves the solution or clarification of legal disputes, the reorganization and consolidation of all legal information and demands against the company, renewal or creation of necessary operation concessions and permits, and changes in the legal incorporation or in the company's by-laws. Under this category are also considered negotiations with other shareholders regarding either their "preference status" in the case of sale or their agreement to sell their shares to the new buyer or to put them in the government's hands for privatization of a larger package.

Table 7A.1 (continued)

Variable	Definition
Assets restructure	The actions include the government's engagement, before the sale, in clarification, or sometimes documentation, of fixed-assets ownership, especially in the cases of broken-up corporations; patent registrations and changes in assets classification mechanisms; break-ups or splits of the SOE for its sale; and spin-offs of specific assets.
Deregulation	These measures reflect deregulatory actions undertaken by the government tied to privatization. The range of actions includes price and quantity deregulations, foreign direct investment and ownership restrictions, international trade quotas or tariffs, entry or exit barriers for domestic or international competitors, changes in the regulation scheme of the company or the industry, and elimination or reduction of subsidies.

Firm characteristics

Privatization Q	The value of the government's net privatization price (*GNPP*) adjusted by the fraction of shares sold plus total liabilities at the time of privatization, divided by total assets of the company at the time of privatization. *GNPP* is calculated as follows:

$$GNPP = B' - P * R - GC - Adj$$

where (B') is the present value of the nominal price of sale as registered in the sale contract that is adjusted in the following ways: subtraction of the cost of the restructuring measures $(P*R)$ undertaken by the government before the sale; subtraction of the costs of the "government commitments" and the "special clauses" promised by the government at the time of the sale (GC), matching them with the actual bills paid later on; and addition and subtraction of the adjustments made to the sale contract (Adj), which includes reimbursements on both sides when the financial statements differ from the ones given to the bidders before the sale.

Operating income/sales	The ratio of operating income to sales. Operating income is equal to sales minus operating expenses, minus cost of sales and depreciation. Sales are equal to the total value of products and services sold, nationally and internationally, minus sales returns and discounts.

(Table continues on the following page.)

Table 7A.1 (continued)

Variable	Definitions
Operating income/PPE	The ratio of operating income to property, plant, and equipment. Operating income is equal to sales minus operating expenses, minus cost of sales and depreciation. PPE is equal to the value of a company's fixed assets adjusted for inflation.
Net income/ sales	The ratio of net income to sales. Net income is equal to operating income minus interest expenses and net taxes paid, as well as the cost of any extraordinary items. Sales are equal to the total value of products and services sold, nationally and internationally, minus sales returns and discounts.
Net income/PPE	The ratio of net income to property, plant, and equipment. Net income is equal to operating income minus interest expenses and net taxes paid, as well as the cost of any extraordinary items. PPE is equal to the value of a company's fixed assets adjusted for inflation.
Cost per unit	The ratio of cost of sales to net sales. Cost of sales is equal to the direct expense involved in the production of a good (or provision of a service), including raw material expenditure plus total compensation paid to blue-collar workers. Sales are equal to the total value of products and services sold, nationally and internationally, minus sales returns and discounts.
Log (sales/PPE)	The log of the ratio of sales to property, plant, and equipment. Sales are equal to the total value of products and services sold, nationally and internationally, minus sales returns and discounts. PPE is equal to the value of a company's fixed assets adjusted for inflation.
Log (sales/ employees)	The log of the ratio of sales to total number of employees. Sales are equal to the total value of products and services sold, nationally and internationally, minus sales returns and discounts. Employees correspond to the total number of workers (paid and unpaid) who depend directly on the company.
Log (total employment)	The log of the total number of employees. Employees correspond to the total number of workers (paid and unpaid) who depend directly on the company. They receive, in general, either salary or wage payments on a regular schedule and work at least 15 hours

Table 7A.1 (continued)

Variable	Definitions
	a week. A minimal number of these workers do not receive a regular salary. This number includes all workers on strike, as well as workers who still report to officials of the company despite different work locations, and workers on sick-leave or vacation. It does not include individuals who are retired or working on commission.
Log (white-collar workers)	The log of the total number of white-collar workers. White-collar workers perform skilled labor and administrative tasks for modest to high salaries. They are individuals involved in sales, administration, and management.
Log (blue-collar workers)	The log of the total number of blue-collar workers. Blue-collar workers perform unskilled or semiskilled labor for modest to low wages. They perform tasks directly related to the (mass) production process or menial services. Typically, they are factory line or maintenance workers.
Investment/sales	The ratio of investment to sales. Investment is equal to the value of expenditure to acquire property, equipment, and other capital assets that produce revenue. Sales are equal to the total value of products and services sold, nationally and internationally, minus sales returns and discounts.
Investment/PPE	The ratio of investment to property, plant, and equipment. Investment is equal to the value of expenditure to acquire property, equipment, and other capital assets that produce revenue. PPE is equal to the value of a company's fixed assets adjusted for inflation.
Log (sales)	The log of sales. Sales are equal to the total value of products and services sold, nationally and internationally, minus sales returns and discounts.
Index of real prices (Paasche)	The Paasche price index is the ratio (expressed as a percentage) of the total value in the given year of the quantity of each commodity produced in the given year to what would have been the total value of these quantities in a base year. To isolate changes in relative prices, for each firm and for each of the firm's line of business, we found an appropriate control group among the 61 sectors that have official producer price index statistics and report the

(Table continues on the following page.)

Table 7A.1 (continued)

Variable	Definitions
	postprivatization behavior of the firm-level price index relative to its control group.
Net taxes/sales	The ratio of net taxes to sales. Net taxes are equal to corporate income taxes paid net of direct subsidies received during the fiscal year. Sales are equal to the total value of products and services sold, nationally and internationally, minus sales returns and discounts.
Index of total employment	For each firm, the index takes a value of 100 for the preprivatization period. The 1993 value is computed by augmenting the preprivatization value by the difference between the cumulative growth rate of employment of the firm and the cumulative growth rate of employment of the control group in the postprivatization period relative to the average employment in the four years that preceded privatization. Industry control groups are given by three digit SIC code sectors for all manufacturing firms, and an index of economywide total employment for firms in the mining and the service sectors. A similar procedure is used for the calculation of the index of blue-collar workers and the index of white-collar workers.
Index of real wages per worker	For each firm, the index takes the value of 100 for the preprivatization period. This refers to the real average wages paid per worker in each firm. The consumer price index was used as a deflator to calculate real wages. A similar procedure is used for the calaculation of the index of real wages per blue-collar and per white-collar worker.
Index of industry-adjusted real wages per worker	For each firm, the index takes the value of 100 for the preprivatization period. The 1993 value is computed by augmenting the preprivatization value by the difference between the cumulative growth rate of real wages per worker of the firm and the cumulative growth rate of real wages per worker of the control group in the postprivatization period relative to the average real wage per worker in the four years before privatization. Industry control groups are given by three-digit SIC code sectors for all manufacturing firms, and an index of economywide real wages per worker for firms in the mining and the service sectors. A similar procedure is used for

Table 7A.1 (continued)

Variable	Definitions
Total wages/sales	the calculation of the index of industry-adjusted real wages per blue-collar worker and the index of industry-adjusted real wages per white-collar worker. The ratio of the total wages paid by the firm to the sales of the firm. Total wages are equal to the total wage bill paid by the firm to blue- and white-collar employees. Sales are equal to the total value of products and services sold, nationally and internationally, minus sales returns and discounts.

Loan characteristics

Real interest rate	The average real interest rate paid during the duration of the loan. The average real interest rate is computed as:

$$\frac{1}{T} \sum_{t=1}^{T} \frac{(1 + i_t + s)}{(1 + \pi_t)},$$

where i is the reference interest rate assigned to the loan, s is the spread above the interest rate, and π the inflation rate. For loans in Mexican pesos, the inflation rate was calculated using the producer price index (INPP) excluding oil products. For loans in U.S. dollars and other foreign currencies, the inflation rate was calculated using the U.S. producer price index of finished products.

Collateral	Variable that takes a value equal to 1 if the loan is backed by collateral, and 0 otherwise. Definitions from collateral include physical tangible assets, financial documents (such as title documents or securities), intangibles, and business proceeds pledged by the borrower to ensure repayment on the loan. Collateral does not include personal guarantees such as obligations backed only by the signature of the borrower or the submission of wealth statements from guarantors to the bank—a usual practice in Mexico.
Collateral value/ loan value	The ratio of collateral value to loan value when the loan was first granted.
Personal guarantees	Variable that takes a value equal to 1 if the loan is secured by a personal guarantee, and 0 otherwise. A personal guarantee is defined as the obligation of repayment by a letter of compromise. Usually the

(Table continues on the following page.)

Table 7A.1 (continued)

Variable	Definitions
	debtor must submit wealth statements from a guarantor who is willing to back his/her loan.
Maturity	The number of months to maturity of the loan, starting the moment the loan was granted.
Grace period	The number of months beyond maturity given to a debtor to repay the balance due. A grace period is granted to a debtor on an individual basis. A loan may have no grace period at all, but, if granted, the grace period may vary according to the loan type and terms established in the loan contract.
Loan in domestic currency	Variable that takes a value equal to 1 if the loan is denominated in Mexican pesos or in Mexican inflation-adjusted currency units (UDIs or *Unidad de Inversión*), and 0 otherwise.
Loan with fixed interest rate	Variable that takes a value equal to 1 if the loan pays a fixed interest rate, and 0 otherwise. A fixed interest rate loan pays an annual percentage rate on a fixed rate for the duration of the loan.

Source: Authors' calculations.

Notes

The authors thank Patricio Amador and José Caballero for excellent research assistance. The authors would also like to thank Guillermo Babatz, José Antonio González, and Abraham Zamora from Secretaría de Hacienda y Crédito Público (SHCP) and Rodolfo Salgado, Alonso Martínez, and Linda del Barrio from Secretaría de Comunicaciones y Transportes (SCT) for facilitating access to part of the data.

1. For example, the National Commission of Irrigation and the National Commission of Highways and Roads were in charge of providing investments to rural areas and of encouraging trade by improving the infrastructure of Mexico.

2. Among the most important firms and funding institutions created during this period are the National Commission of Electricity, the National Railway Company, the Exporting and Importing Mexican Company (CEIMSA), the National Bank of Agricultural Credit, and the National Bank of Ejido Credit.

3. The Ministry of Finance and the Ministry of National Goods and Administrative Inspection were the two entities with overseeing powers established by the 1947 Law for the Federal Government's Control of Decentralized Institutions and Enterprises of State Participation.

4. According to Aspe (1993), even this number does not capture the true magnitude of the drain on the government from the SOE sector. If we include the banking sector operations that led to the nationalization of commercial banking in September 1982, the corrected figure would increase to a staggering 18.5 percent of GDP.

5. We group our observations in three periods, and for each, the privatization strategy often involved splitting companies into smaller units or making multifirm conglomerates For instance, Ferrocarriles Nacionales was split into 8 railroads, whereas 35 local airports were sold in packages of about 10 each.

6. For example, in 2001 the government expropriated several sugar mills for questionable public interest reasons. In addition, between 2001 and 2003 the government created the following enterprises: Consejo Nacional para Prevenir la Discriminacion (National Council to Prevent Discrimination); Servicio de Administracion y Enajenacion de Bienes (Service of Administration and Alienation of Goods); Consejo Nacional de la Cultura Física y el Deporte (National Council of Physical Culture and Sport); and Instituto Nacional de Lenguas Indígenas (National Institute of Indigenous Languages).

7. For a detailed description of the auction process followed for SOE divestitures, see López-de-Silanes (1994, 1997).

8. The clearest case is Telmex (the telephone communications monopoly), where the government originally kept 31 percent of shares and now owns only 4.75 percent. The other five cases include three banks (Bancomer, Banca Serfín, and Banco International) and two companies in transportation (Cia. Mexicana de Aviación and Transportación Marítima Mexicana).

9. We use industry-matched producer price indexes (PPI) to adjust all product prices and the aggregate consumer price index (CPI) to adjust the values of all other nominal values. The choice of deflator is not irrelevant since the CPI series shows higher inflation than the PPI series over the sample period. Therefore, the use of the CPI index imparts a conservative bias against finding significant increases in sales, earnings, fixed assets, wages, and taxes in the postprivatization period.

10. Even though these figures seem large, they probably underestimate the true level of labor retrenchment experienced by privatized firms. In fact, looking at the subsample of firms for which we have complete employment data for all four preprivatization years (117), we find that the mean (median) number of workers falls 16.5 (4.2) percent between t-4 and t-1 and a further 62.4 (64.7) percent between t-1 and 1993, where t is the year of privatization.

11. It is possible that this increase in output overestimates the true impact of privatization as some of the observed gains may simply reflect redistribution away from customers. Some SOEs priced their output below market levels or failed to charge for goods and services produced because of corruption, political meddling, or sheer incompetence. Although there is no way to directly quantify the importance of these factors in our sample, available evidence regarding the evolution of prices for the products of privatized firms suggests this is not the driving force behind increased sales.

12. Specifically, we define $Sales_{1993}$ and $Cost_{1993}$, respectively, as sales and operating costs in the postprivatization period and π as the increase in real prices, and compute the following measure for the contribution of price increases to higher profitability:

$$Price\ Contribution = [(Sales_{1993} - Cost_{1993})/Sales_{1993}]$$
$$- \{[(Sales_{1993}/1 + \pi) - Cost_{1993}]/[Sales_{1993}/1 + \pi]\}$$

13. We can calculate the macroeconomic contribution to the growth in sales by measuring the difference in raw and industry-adjusted indicators (0.1164 and 0.1925, respectively) as a proportion of the raw increase (0.5428 and 0.6816, respectively).

14. Under the first classification, firms are considered competitive if they are in an industry with more than 10 firms and as noncompetitive otherwise. Under the second classification, firms are considered competitive if they have less than 10 percent of market share and as noncompetitive otherwise.

15. To confirm the robustness of our interpretations, we carried out a poll to determine the principal perceived reasons for increased wages. The essential element of the respondents' explanation was that SOE jobs were desirable not because they paid well, but because they required little effort. After privatization, employers quickly moved to dismiss workers who did not increase their productivity and hired new workers from a different pool than those who were hired under state management. Firms retained the most productive workers and offered them conditions similar to both those prevailing in the private sector and those offered to new hires. We therefore believe that higher wages are explained by improvements in worker productivity.

16. Based on data from SHCP 1982–2003a, 1982–2003b.

17. For the calculation of *GNNP*, see the definition of privatization Q in the appendix.

18. As a robustness check, an additional standardization was calculated in the same fashion but using total shareholders' equity (defined as the sum of total assets and total liabilities at the time of privatization) to normalize the privatization Q. The results obtained from this estimate are very similar and are thus omitted.

19. An alternative hypothesis is that sectors under control of the state tend to be those with the greatest untapped capacity for efficiency gains. In this case the premium is explained because of a higher perceived future growth rate and not because of the belief that protective regulations will be maintained.

20. This hypothesis is supported by López-de-Silanes (1997), who finds that the discount in privatization Q is explained by "internal speed," the length of time between the moment when the first rumors of privatization arise to the time of the public announcement, and not by "public length," the time elapsed from the formal announcement to the conclusion of the sale.

21. We would expect the government to absorb debt of highly indebted SOEs, to fire workers when firms face serious overemployment, or to invest in new machinery when production processes are outdated. If the endogenous nature of these measures is not considered, we run the risk of reaching the wrong conclusions as regression coefficients would capture not only the effect of the restructuring measure, but also the negative effects of being in distress or having a bloated work force.

22. We apply a two-step instrumental variables approach by estimating a nonlinear reduced-form equation that describes the probability that a particular labor-restructuring policy will be implemented. The instruments used are classified in two groups: firm-level and macroeconomic-level determinants. The firm-level variables include the presence of a leading agent bank, involvement of a government ministry before privatization, the political affiliation of unions, and sectoral dummies. The macroeconomic variables include the average GDP growth rate, the degree of openness in the three years before privatization, and the legal origin of the country. None of these variables is statistically significant when included in the price equation. The *F* statistic for the excluded instruments is statistically significant at 1 percent in all cases.

23. We also investigated the effects of changing the management team independently of the CEO and found no significant effect. We can therefore tentatively conclude that the main benefit stems from changing the head and not the body of the management team.

24. Megginson and Netter 2001; Boubakri and Cosset 1998.

25. For this section, we consider the period *before privatization* as the time elapsed from the beginning of 1989 to the time of privatization of each bank; *after privatization* corresponds to the period from the time banks were privatized until the end of 1992, or for the longest period for which we have data. This division biases our findings against finding dramatic improvements in bank performance, which had been increasing since 1986, first because of a partial flotation of bank

shares through the Mexican stock market and, second, because of the deregulation measures adopted between 1987 and 1988. For example, although the ratio of financial margin to financial revenue increased almost 6 percentage points between 1988 and 1994, it increased a further 12 percentage points between 1987 and 1989. For a detailed analysis of bank performance during this period, see López-de-Silanes and Zamarripa (1995).

26. The most likely explanation for this increase in personnel expenses despite the reduction in employment is that wages increased as private financial institutions competed for talented employees. This conjecture is reinforced by the fact that the cuts in employment show a higher concentration in unskilled labor.

References

Aspe, Pedro. 1993. *Economic Transformation The Mexican Way.* Cambridge, Mass: MIT Press.

Banco de México. 1996–99. "The Mexican Economy." Annual publication of the Dirección de Organismos y Acuerdos Internacionales of the Bank of Mexico, Mexico D.F.

Barberis, Nicholas, Maxim Boycko, Andrei Shleifer, and Natalia Tukanova. 1996. "How Does Privatization Work? Evidence from the Russian Shops." *Journal of Political Economy* 104: 764–90.

Bayliss, Kate. 2002 "Privatization and Poverty: The Distributional Impact of Utility Privatization." *Annals of Public and Cooperative Economics* 73: 603–25.

Biais, Bruno, and Enrico Perotti. 2002. "Machiavellian Privatization." *American Economic Review* 92: 240–58.

BMV (Bolsa Mexicana de Valores). Various issues for 1985 through 1992. *Indicadores Bursatiles.* Mexico City.

Bolton, Patrick, and Gerald Roland. 1992. "Privatization Policies in Central and Eastern Europe." *Economic Policy* 15: 275–303.

Bortolotti, Bernardo, Marcela Fantini, and Carlo Scarpa. 2001. "Privatisation: Politics, Institutions and Financial Markets." *Emerging Markets Review* 2: 109–36.

Boubakri, Narjess, and Jean Claude Cosset. 1998. "The Financial and Operating Performance of Newly Privatized Firms: Evidence from Developing Countries." *Journal of Finance* 53(3): 1081–110.

Campbell-White, Oliver, and Anita Bhatia. 1998. "Privatization in Africa." Directions in Development series. World Bank, Washington, D.C.

Chong, Alberto, and Florencio López-de-Silanes. 2003. "Privatization and Labor Restructuring Around the World." Yale University, New Haven, Conn.

Djankov, Simeon, Rafael La Porta, Florencio López-de-Silanes, and Andrei Shleifer. 2003. "Courts." *Quarterly Journal of Economics* 118: 453–517.

Donaldson, David J., and Dileep M. Wagle. 1995. "Privatization: Principles and Practice." *Lessons of Experience Series*, 1. World Bank, International Finance Corporation, Washington, D.C.

Earle, John, and Scott Gehlbach. 2003. "A Spoonful of Sugar: Privatization and Popular Support for Reform in the Czech Republic." *Economics and Politics* 15 (1): 1–32.

Fama, Eugene, and Michael Jensen. 1983. "Separation of Ownership and Control." *Journal of Law and Economics* 26 (2) (June): 301–25.

Freeman, Richard. 1986. "Unionism Comes to the Public Sector." *Journal of Economic Literature* 24 (March): 41.

Galal, Ahmed, Leroy Jones, Pankay Tandon, and Ongo Vogelsang. 1994. *Welfare Consequences of Selling Public Enterprises.* Oxford, U.K.: Oxford University Press.

La Porta, Rafael, and Florencio López-de-Silanes. 1999. "The Benefits of Privatization: Evidence from Mexico." *Quarterly Journal of Economics* 4: 1193–242.

La Porta, Rafael, Florencio López-de-Silanes, and Andrei Shleifer. 2002. "Government Ownership of Banks." *Journal of Finance* 57: 265–302.

La Porta, Rafael, Florencio López-de-Silanes, and Guillermo Zamarripa. 2003. "Related Lending." *Quarterly Journal of Economics* 118 (1): 231–68.

La Porta, Rafael, Florencio López-de-Silanes, Andrei Shleifer, and Robert Vishny. 1997. "Legal Determinants of External Finance." *Journal of Finance* 52 (3): 1131–50.

———. 1998. "Law and Finance." *Journal of Political Economy* 106:1113–55.

———. 2000a. "Agency Problems and Dividend Policies Around the World." *Journal of Finance* 55: 1–33.

———. 2000b. "Investor Protection and Corporate Governance." *Journal of Financial Economics* 58: 1–25.

López-de-Silanes, Florencio. 1994. "A Macro Perspective on Privatization; The Mexican Program." In S. Levy and L. Svensson, eds., *Macroeconomic Aspects of Privatization.* Washington, D.C.: World Bank.

———. 1997. "Determinants of Privatization Prices." *Quarterly Journal of Economics* 112 (4): 965–1025.

López-de-Silanes, Florencio, and Guillermo Zamarripa. 1995. "De-regulation and Privatization of Commercial Banking." *Revista de Análisis Económico* ILADES/Georgetown University 10: 113–64.

Maskin, Eric. 1992. "Auctions and Privatization." In Horst Siebert, ed., *Privatization*, pp.115–36. Tübingen, Germany: J. C. B. Mohr Publisher.

Megginson, William, and Jeffry Netter. 2001. "From State to Market: A Survey of Empirical Studies on Privatization." *Journal of Economic Literature* 39 (2): 321–89.

Modigliani, Franco, and Merton Miller. 1958. "The Cost of Capital, Corporation Finance, and the Theory of Investment." *American Economic Review* 48 (June): 261–97.

Perotti, Enrico. 1995. "Credible Privatization." *American Economic Review* 85: 847–59.

Presidencia de la República. 1982–2003. "Informe de Gobierno." Mexico City: Presidencia de la Republica Mexicana, Direccion General de Comunicacion Social.

Rogozinsky, Jacques, and Ramiro Tovar. 1998. "Private Infrastructure Concessions: The 1989–1994 National Highway Program in Mexico." In *High Price for Change: Privatization in Mexico.* Washington, D.C.: Inter-American Development Bank.

Secretaría de Comunicaciones y Transportes. 2000. *El Sector Comunicaciones y Transportes 1994–2000.* Mexico City.

SHCP (Secretaria de Hacienda y Crédito Público). 1982–2003a. *Cuenta Pública.* Mexico City.

———. 1982–2003b. *Situación Económica de México.* Mexico City.

Shleifer, Andrei, and Lawrence Summers. 1988. "Breach of Trust in Hostile Takeovers." In Alan J. Auerbach, ed., *Corporate Takeovers: Causes and Consequences.* Chicago: University of Chicago Press. Reprinted in R. Romano, ed., *Foundations of Corporate Law,* Oxford University Press, 1993.

World Bank. 2003. *Private Solutions for Infrastructure in Mexico.* Washington, D.C.: World Bank.

8

Peruvian Privatization: Impacts on Firm Performance

Máximo Torero

SINCE THE EARLY 1980S, COUNTRIES AROUND the world have embarked on major privatization programs. Yet many remain reluctant to privatize, while still more have had to halt ongoing processes of privatization. This is particularly true in developing countries, where state-owned enterprises (SOEs) still account for more than 10 percent of gross domestic product, 20 percent of investment, and about 5 percent of formal employment (Kikeri, Nellis, and Shirley 1994). The aversion to privatization appears to be associated with public distrust of the privatization process. Unions and other traditional opponents of privatization have argued that it results in layoffs and poorer services. Political leaders, meanwhile, fear that the higher profitability of private companies comes at the expense of the rest of society, especially during the difficult transition period from state ownership to private ownership.

The transfer from the public to the private sector (Vickers and Yarrow 1988) necessarily implies a change in the relationships between those responsible for the firm's decisions and the beneficiaries of the profit flows (the social view and the agency view). In theory, the transfer of property rights leads to a different structure of management incentives, causing changes in managerial behavior, company performance, and quality of service in terms of access and use. To prove these theories, however, empirical work is crucial.

Yet little empirical knowledge is available about how well privatization has worked. There are difficult methodological problems as well as special problems with data availability and consistency. Furthermore, the possibility of bias in the sample selection can arise from several sources, including a government's desire to sugarcoat the process by privatizing the healthiest firms first. Megginson and Netter (2001) carried out a detailed review of 22 studies on privatization in nontransitional economies and concluded that Galal and others (1994), La Porta and López-de-Silanes (1999), and the studies summarized in D'Souza and Megginson (1999) are the most solid and persuasive supporting the proposition that privatization improves the operating and financial performance of firms. The author of this chapter considers La Porta and López-de-Silanes (1999) the finest study of an individual country, since it examines nearly the entire universe of Mexican privatizations.

These studies, especially La Porta and López-de-Silanes (1999), investigate whether companies increase profits after privatization and whether privatization inflicts significant social losses, and, if so, through which channels. They conclude that the improved performance of privatized firms is the result of significant restructuring efforts, not of market power exploitation nor massive layoffs and lower wages. In other words, firms undergo a harsh restructuring process following privatization and do not simply mark up prices and lower wages, as many economists have predicted. Deregulation, particularly the removal of price or quantity controls and trade protections, is associated with faster convergence to industry benchmarks. The authors suggest that the sale profits and increased tax revenues the government receives from privatizations are probably enough to offset the cost of job losses to society.

According to these studies, newly privatized firms cut employment, usually reducing the roll of white- and blue-collar workers by nearly half. These numbers may actually underestimate the effects of privatization, since in the preceding years most companies have already trimmed payrolls to prepare for divestiture. These findings suggest that transfers from workers to shareholders play a role in the success of privatization. Even so, productivity gains resulted in large real wage increases of 114 percent in the postprivatization period.

La Porta and López-de-Silanes showed, for example, that privatized firms increased sales 54.3 percent, despite work force reductions and only modest increases in capital. Surprisingly, prices rose only 2.9 percent relative to the producer price index. La Porta and López-de-Silanes also decomposed reported increases in profitability. Approximately 10 percent of the gain in profits was attributable to higher prices and 33 percent to worker layoffs, while productivity gains accounted for the remaining 57 percent. Some of the social effects of higher prices and layoffs were offset by corporate taxes, which absorbed slightly more than half of the gains in operating income.

In this study, the author follows an approach similar to that of La Porta and López-de-Silanes (1999) by collecting information on nearly the entire population of privatized firms in Peru to evaluate the impact of privatization there. The author then compares the performance of those firms with the remaining SOEs and, when possible, with industry-matched private firms. Through this method, the impact of privatization on profitability ratios, operating efficiency ratios, labor indicators, and capital-deepening indicators is analyzed. Even though the ultimate effect of changes in management incentives depends on the competitive and regulatory environment in which a given firm operates, it is argued that the degree of market competition and the effectiveness of regulatory policy have more important effects on performance than does change of ownership (Vickers and Yarrow 1988). This is extremely important in the case of the Peruvian privatization process because it was accompanied by large-scale sectoral reforms in which competitive structures and independent regulatory agencies were established to monitor and promote competition in each sector. Therefore, variables needed to identify the roles played by the regulatory agencies and the competitive forces that determine firm performance (existence of a regulatory framework, autonomy of the regulatory agency, and so forth) are taken into account in the analysis.

Peru's privatization experience was rated one of the early success stories in Latin America. The privatization process, begun by then-president Alberto Fujimori, was launched as part of a rigorous process of stabilization and structural reform initiated in response to a crisis in the Peruvian economy. At the time, inflation had reached an annualized rate of 36,000 percent, and per capita income had dropped to its lowest level in 30 years. Although privatization was not part of the initial set of reforms, it soon became a central plank of the overall reform program.

By 2001 the privatization process had involved 252 transactions, including 42 SOEs; had brought $9.2 billion in revenue (including capitalization) to the national treasury; and had mobilized an additional $11.4 billion in new investments.[1] Nevertheless, Peru's considerable success in attracting private participation and capital was focused on a few sectors such as telecommunications, electricity, banking, hydrocarbons, and mining. Unlike some countries, such as Argentina and Bolivia, there has been virtually no private participation in the transportation, water, or sanitation sectors. Furthermore, as is the case in other countries, public support for privatization has been declining steadily—from 65 percent in May 1992 to less than 25 percent by 2000. This decline has brought the privatization process nearly to a halt. This report, written during a period of antiprivatization sentiment, is of special importance because it aims to analyze empirically the impact on performance of privatized SOEs.

This study reviews the privatization process and its principal results. It then summarizes the empirical methodology followed by the author, details the database developed, and presents the results of the calculations of the differences in pre- and postprivatization performance, difference-in-difference comparisons for which control groups were developed, and a panel data regression analysis of the static and dynamic performance of privatized firms relative to SOEs.

The Privatization Process

At the beginning of 1990, Peru faced its worst macroeconomic situation ever.[2] The country had never experienced such large and prolonged periods of inflation and recession. The economic model implemented in response to the crisis assigned the state a central role in economic policymaking. The policies adopted by the government were not up to the challenge at hand: public expenditure and public internal credit rose impressively, price controls and subsidies were established, tariffs on public services were fixed, and exchange rate controls were set. These policies translated into a persistent fiscal imbalance, a considerable drop in tax revenues and a striking decline in financial intermediation.[3]

The macroeconomic crisis was hardest on Peru's poorest citizens, around 43 percent of the 1990 population. The situation worsened as public services, such as education and health, deteriorated. In addition, by the end of the 1980s, informal economic activity, delinquency, drug trafficking, and terrorism had all increased. In 1990 Peru reached record underemployment (86.4 percent), while unemployment was around 8.3 percent, and formal employment barely reached 5.3 percent.[4]

In this context, public enterprises were characterized by inefficient provision of goods and services, ambiguous objectives, extensive intervention by politicians, decapitalization of investment resources, and a lack of fresh investment. Not surprisingly, public firms registered accumulated losses of more than $4 billion in 1989–90.[5] In an effort to reverse this situation, the Peruvian government decided to design an attractive normative and institutional framework to promote private investment as the main vehicle of economic growth. One of the key aspects of this new framework was a program to privatize public-sector companies in 1991.

In February 1991 the privatization process was launched with the enactment of Supreme Decree 041, which regulated and restructured the managerial activity of the state, even though the state was limited to managing no more than 23 companies. In November 1991 the government extended more active and decisive support for the privatization process by enacting Legislative Decree (LD) 674, also known as the Promotion of Private Investment in State Companies. LD 674 introduced the Commission for the Promotion of Private Investment (COPRI) and the Special Privatization Committees (CEPRIs), as well as private investment promotion schemes, which included sales of stocks and assets, service provision, concessions, and other items. One of the most important laws enacted was LD 662, or the "Law of Foreign Investment Promotion," which mandated equal treatment of national and foreign capital. This law permitted foreign investment in all economic sectors and its execution through any legal administrative means.

To give more dynamic and political support to the process, President Fujimori appointed five state ministers to lead COPRI. These ministers were in charge of the general management of the privatization process; they had to establish the policies and objectives of the process, appoint the CEPRIs that were responsible for the planning and execution of individual privatizations, and approve the most important decisions.

Diverse reforms were instituted in 1992 to facilitate the privatization process. The government was authorized to grant the safeguards and guarantees necessary to protect foreign acquisitions and investments. Foreign investors were also granted facilities for the payment of taxes and debts owed by SOEs in the privatization process. In some cases, these commitments were suspended until the end of the process.

In 1993 all of these reforms were codified into law with the approval of the new Political Constitution. The new constitution included the promotion of free private initiative, the establishment of equality between national and foreign investors, the encouragement of competition and equal treatment for all economic activities, and a guarantee of the possibility of the signing of stability agreements between private investors and the state. In addition, the state subscribed to many international agreements for the protection of foreign investment and conflict resolution through international arbiters.

Together with the launching of the privatization program, the government undertook another set of structural reforms. Through these reforms, the government promoted market-based competition and free international trade, installed policies to create a more flexible labor market, liberalized the financial system, eliminated price controls, and implemented sector reforms for the deregulation of markets. All the reforms carried out were complementary and necessary to the privatization program. In so doing, the government recognized that adequate regulatory and institutional frameworks and a competitive market, not just ownership, were determining factors in the success of the privatization process.

Peru's privatization scheme began in earnest between November 1991 and February 1992. Its main objective was simple: privatize as many public companies as quickly as possible. The initial tasks were defining privatization methods, prioritizing the public enterprises to be privatized (which depended on their importance and the ease with which they could be privatized), and creating the CEPRIs.[6] Because of its transparent and competitive scheme, the public auction was the most common practice adopted for privatization.

In the following years, the design of an appropriate juridical-legal framework for the development of private investment continued. One particularly important law provided for the regulation of immigration applications and facilitated the nationalization of foreign citizens who wanted to provide capital and invest in Peru.

The results of the privatization process were outstanding. Beyond the simple transfer of assets, companies were purchased and significant amounts of investment were committed (see table 8.1 for details). In 1991 two public companies were privatized (Sogewiese Leasing and Buenaventura Mine). In 1992, under an operational COPRI and various CEPRIs, 10 SOEs were privatized, drawing in revenues of $208 million and another $706 million in projected investment. In 1993 the process gathered momentum, with 13 companies privatized for a total of $317 million and projected investment of $589 million. The next year the government sold its natural monopolies in the telecommunications and electricity sectors,

Table 8.1 Privatization Revenues and Investment, 1991–2001
(US$ million)

| Year | Sale of shares and assets | Transactions | | | Total | Projected investment |
		Concessions	Option rights, small assets, and others	Capitalizations		
1991	2.6				2.6	0.0
1992	207.5		1.4		208.9	706.0
1993	316.7	20.7	6.5		343.9	589.3
1994	2,579.2		4.7	610.8	3,194.7	2,050.0
1995	1,089.0	6.6	9.1	120.1	1,224.8	70.1
1996	2,281.8	344.2	2.7	40.0	2,668.7	2,695.0
1997	447.1	99.0	8.8	126.4	681.3	706.2
1998	251.6	35.1	5.2		291.9	220.6
1999	285.8	10.9	3.1		299.8	323.3
2000	95.1[a]	209.9[a]			317.0[b]	4,480.0
2001	19.5[a]	65.4[a]			261.0[b]	98.0
Total	7,575.9	791.8	41.5	897.3	9,494.6	11,938.5

Note: Sale of shares and assets includes resources obtained through private purchases of public firms; concessions are resources acquired through concession contracts with private agents; option rights, small assets, and others are resources obtained through sales of minor assets like machines or equipment from companies; and capitalizations are resources assigned to raise a firm's equity.

a. The information for these items is incomplete because of unavailability of data, particularly for the year 2001.

b. These numbers are gross amounts for annual totals, so they do not equal the sum of the first four columns.

Source: PROINVERSION.

which resulted in $2,579 million in revenues collected and a total amount of $2,050 million of projected investments.

During 1995 and 1996 the privatization process accelerated and deepened. Sixty-four companies were privatized, producing revenue of $3.4 billion and investment commitments of $2.8 billion. This continued in 1997 when 25 more companies were transferred for $447 million and projected investments of $706 million. In 1998 the privatization process made way for the concessionary process of transportation infrastructure.[7] CEPRIs were created to handle the concessions of airports, ports, road networks, and mobile telephone bands, among other facilities.

Between 1991 and 2001, Peru's privatization and concessionary processes generated revenues totaling $9.5 billion (including capitalizations) and investment commitments of approximately $11.45 billion. Figure 8.1 shows the evolution of the privatization process and the timeline for the transfer of nearly all of the public enterprises since 1991. Figure 8.2 shows the revenues and projected investment resulting from privatization outlined by sector.[8] Altogether 203 privatization operations were carried out, representing $7.85 billion in revenues and $6.4 billion of investment commitments. Concessions raised $726 million in revenue and $4.60 billion in investment commitments.

Most of the privatization process occurred in the telecommunications, electricity, finance, mining, and hydrocarbons sectors. Figure 8.3 shows the percentage privatized in various sectors. Telecommunications and finance are already entirely privatized. Those two sectors, along with electricity and mining, represent more than 80 percent of privatization revenues collected by the Peruvian government. Yet, to date, there has been virtually no private participation in the transportation, water, or sanitation sectors, and there are still sectors, such as agriculture, where much remains under public ownership.

Despite the increase in government revenues and investment commitments, public approval of the privatization process has decreased steadily, as shown in figure 8.4. Therefore, to develop a complete picture of the impact of privatization on other fundamental areas of the Peruvian economy, the results of previous privatization studies must be complemented by a detailed analysis of the impact on firm performance.

This chapter evaluates the privatization process by analyzing the performance of all privatized firms in Peru. The report studies a sample of firms representing 63 percent of the privatized SOEs and 91 percent of the transactions involved in the privatization process. In addition, this study analyzes in detail the three sectors where most of the privatization took place: telecommunications, electricity, and financial services.

In the telecommunications sector, the Peruvian government sold both Compañía Peruana de Teléfonos (CPT) and Empresa Nacional de Telecomunicaciones (ENTEL). CPT provided basic telecommunications services in the Lima area, and ENTEL provided national and international long-distance services, as well as local service for the rest of Peru.

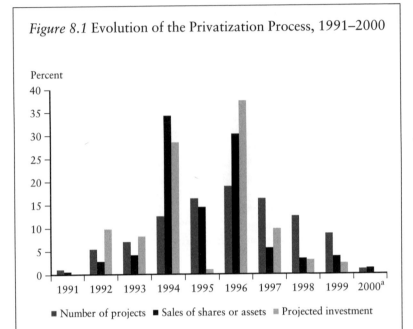

Figure 8.1 Evolution of the Privatization Process, 1991–2000

Percent

■ Number of projects   ■ Sales of shares or assets   ■ Projected investment

Note: The bars represent the number of projects completed in one year as a percentage of projects privatized between 1991 and 2000, the amount of sales in one year as a percentage of total sales of shares or assets made between 1991 and 2000, and the amount of projected investments in one year as a percentage of total investments made between 1991 and 2000.
ᵃ Through June 30.
Source: PROINVERSION.

Divestiture took place in 1994 after an auction to the highest bidder. Using a first-price sealed bid mechanism, approximately 35 percent of CPT and ENTEL common shares (the minimum required to give the buyer control of the merger) were sold to Spain's Telefónica de España.[9] The results of the auction were impressive: Telefónica paid a little more than $2 billion, far larger than the second highest bid of $800 million—a bid that was closer to the base price set by the government. Soon after buying both companies, Telefónica de España merged them and created Telefónica del Perú S.A. (TdP). Initially, TdP was granted a five-year national monopoly for the provision of lines, local calls, national long-distance, and international long-distance throughout the country.[10] Simultaneously, the government created the Supervisory Agency for Private Investment in Telecommunications (OSIPTEL).

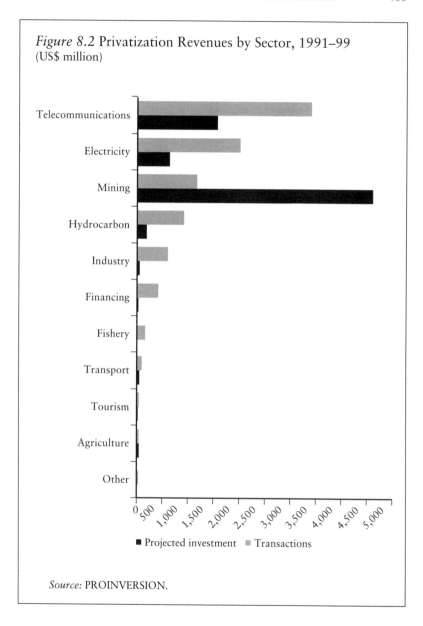

Figure 8.2 Privatization Revenues by Sector, 1991–99
(US$ million)

Source: PROINVERSION.

The privatization of TdP continued over the following years. In 1996, 65 percent of the company's shares were divided between minor shareholders (36.3 percent) and the Peruvian government (28.7 percent). The latter decided to sell 26.6 percent of its shares to small individual investors

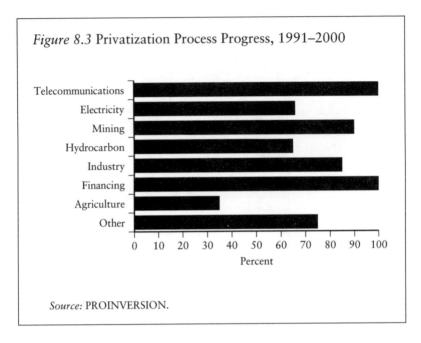

Figure 8.3 Privatization Process Progress, 1991–2000

Source: PROINVERSION.

through a process known as Sistema de Participación Ciudadana (Citizen Participation System). In total, privatization in the telecommunications sector raised $3.6 billion in revenues and $1.56 billion in investment commitments for the government.

For the electricity sector, the government approved in 1992 the Law of Electric Concessions (LD 25844), which split power generation from electricity distribution and transmission. Power generation is a market open to competition, whereas transmission and distribution are usually considered natural monopolies. Between 1994 and 1997, the government privatized 10 electricity SOEs (5 in distribution and 5 in generation) for a total of $1.43 billion. There was also a significant investment commitment to increase the total capacity of the privatized generation companies by 560 megawatts (MW). At present, the privatized companies represent 64 percent of the total power generation capacity of the national electric system and 79 percent of the distribution service.

The government also created two regulatory bodies for the electricity sector: the Supervisory Agency for Private Investment in Energy (OSINERG) and the Commission of Energy Tariffs, which was absorbed later by OSINERG. The privatization process in this sector is not yet concluded because one of the major generating enterprises in the south of Peru, Central Hidroelectrica del Mantaro, and all of the region's distribution enterprises are not yet privatized. Even though the privatization is incomplete,

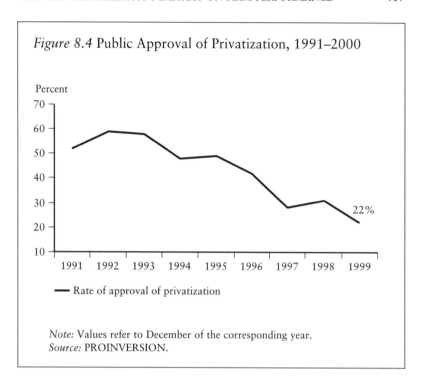

Figure 8.4 Public Approval of Privatization, 1991–2000

— Rate of approval of privatization

Note: Values refer to December of the corresponding year.
Source: PROINVERSION.

the electric sector has already become the second largest generator of privatization revenues and investment commitments for the state: $2.3 billion in revenue and $716 million in investment commitments.

Water and sanitation is the only public utility where no privatization has occurred, although a concession was given to the Italian company Impregilo to operate wells and a water treatment plant in the Chillón river basin to sell water to the Lima water company. Instead of privatizing, the government sought to improve the organization and management of the water and sanitation system by decentralizing it. This new reform gave municipalities control over water services. The only exception was the most important municipal water service, Empresa de Servicio de Agua Potable y Alcantarillado de Lima (SEDAPAL), which remains a state company. SEDAPAL was the only water-service provider included in the privatization program, but it has yet to be privatized. Despite this, the government has tried to improve SEDAPAL's services and coverage. Additionally, in 1992 the government created the Superintendencia Nacional de Servicios de Saneamiento (SUNASS), the National Office for Services of Sanitation, as the regulatory body for this sector. SUNASS is responsible for controlling the quality of the service provided, the pricing system, and regulation, as well as intersector coordination, establishment of norms for the execution of investment plans, and supervision of those plans.

With respect to the financial sector, on July 20, 1994, 99.86 percent of the government's shares in Interbanc were auctioned. The winner was a consortium formed by International Financial Holding (Grand Cayman) and IFH Peru S.A., with the advice of Banco Osorno and La Union (Chile), for $51 million (workers paid $4.83 million of this for a total of 9.46 percent of the bank's shares). Interbanc branches Financiera Peruana (Interfip), Internacional de Inmuebles, and Empresas de Servicios Internacionales (Interserv) were also included in the auction.

And on April 18, 1995, 60 percent of the shares of Banco Continental were awarded to the consortium formed by Banco Bilbao Vizcaya (Spain) and the companies Inversiones Breca, Inversiones San Borja, Urbanizadora Jardin, and Minsur (all belonging to the Brescia Group of Peru). In August 1995, in agreement with the share purchase sale contract of Banco Continental, 15,325,388 shares belonging to the state were transferred to Holding Continental S.A for $32 million.[11] By July 21, 1998, the Peruvian government had managed to sell 19 percent of Banco Continental's remaining shares on the international and local markets.

Methodology

Following Boubakri and Cosset (1998), the analysis conducted in this chapter tries to determine whether firms improve their performance after privatization. Firm performance is measured by profitability, operating efficiency, capital expenditures, output, employment, and leverage. Table 8.2, taken from Megginson, Nash, and van Randenborgh (1994), shows details on the proxies for these performance measures as well as the predicted relationships.

Based on these performance measures, the empirical approach consists of two stages. In the first stage, a simple statistical analysis is conducted to study the postprivatization changes in firms' performance. In the second stage, a regression analysis is performed, controlling most of the differences between firms and variables, other than privatization, that could explain the performance of the firm.

The statistical analysis consists of computing the performance variables for each company in the sample for a 15-year period (1986–2000). Then the means for each performance variable (Y) for the preprivatization and postprivatization periods are computed. To avoid any bias resulting from a preprivatization restructuring of the firm, all years in which restructuring took place before the divestiture are excluded.[12] After the

Table 8.2 Firm Performance Measures

Performance measure	Proxies	Predicted relationship
Profitability	Return on sales (ROS) = net income/sales	ROSA > ROSB
	Return on assets (ROA) = net income/total assets	ROAA > ROAB
	Return on equity (ROE) = net income/equity	ROEA > ROEB
Operating Efficiency	Sales efficiency (SALEFF) = sales/number of employees	SALEFFA > SALEFFB
	Net income efficiency (NIEFF) = net income/number of employees	NIEFFA > NIEFFB
Capital Investment	Capital expenditure to sales (CESA) = capital expenditures/sales	CESAA > CESAB
	Capital expenditure to assets (CETA) = capital expenditures/total assets	CETAA > CETAB
Output	Real sales (SAL) = nominal sales/consumer price index	SALA > SALB
Employment	Total employment (EMPL) = total number of employees	EMPLA < EMPLB
Leverage	Debt to assets (LEV) = total debt/total assets	LEVA < LEVB
	Long-term debt to equity (LEV2) = long-term debt/equity	LEV2A < LEV2B
Payout	Dividends to sales (DIVSAL) = cash dividends/sales	DIVSALA > DIVSALB
	Dividends payout (PAYOUT) = cash dividends/net income	PAYOUTA > PAYOUTB

Note: This table presents some of the most common firm performance measures found in the literature (see appendix table 8B.1 for variable definitions). Each type of measure is associated with one or more proxy variables (column 2). For each proxy there is a predicted relationship between two firms (column 3). Firm A (the postprivatization firm) would have a better performance than firm B (the preprivatization firm) if the predicted relationship stated is satisfied.

Source: Megginson, Nash, and van Randenborgh 1994.

means are calculated, using differences from the sample counterpart of the privatization effect and the performance variables, the following is obtained:

$$\Delta\overline{Y} = [\overline{Y}^{postprivatization} - \overline{Y}^{preprivatization}]$$

The two-tailed Wilcoxon signed-rank test and the Hotelling test are then used to test for significant changes in performance variables after privatization. Both tests are based on the assumption that the distributions are normal. If the sample size is small and the true distribution of differences is far from normal, the stated probability levels may be significantly in error. Specifically, when looking at each individual firm, the central limit theorem cannot be applied since the sample of years for each is small. For that reason, it is necessary to verify the normality of the series. Therefore, the Shapiro-Francia test for normality is used. When the Shapiro-Francia test rejects the null hypothesis of normality, a nonparametric test, the Kolmogorov-Smirnov (K-S) statistic, is used to formally test the equality of the empirical hazards functions of the different pre- and postprivatization performance indicators.[13]

The above methodology is equivalent to considering the simplest possible model for capturing the effect on performance with no regressors; it can easily be derived so that performance depends only on the date of the privatization dummy,

$$Y_{i,t} = \alpha + \gamma \ Privatization_{i,t} + u_{i,t} \quad E(u_{i,t}/Privat_{i,t}) = 0 \quad (8.1)$$

Nevertheless, the above result is likely to be biased for two reasons. First, the two groups of years may have different characteristics and thus different performance behavior. Second, the two groups of years may be subject to different shocks. Part of the differences in pre- and postprivatization performance patterns may simply be a result of these differences.

An alternative way to solve this problem is to develop a benchmark to control for these different characteristics and shocks. In this sense, a difference-in-difference measure is calculated for each economic sector in which privatization is important:

$$\Delta^2\overline{Y} = [\overline{Y}^{post-priv^{year}} - \overline{Y}^{pre-priv^{year}}]priv. \ firms \ -$$

$$[\overline{Y}^{post-priv^{year}} - \overline{Y}^{pre-priv^{year}}]notpriv. \ firms \quad (8.2)$$

The main caveat of the difference-in-difference measure is the lack of an appropriate control group with which to compare the difference in performance of the privatized firms. It is not possible to use an optimal matching methodology such as propensity scores, as detailed in Rubin (1974, 1977, 1979), Heckman and Smith (1995), Heckman and others

(1996), Heckman, Ichimura, and Todd (1997), and Heckman, Lalonde, and Smith (1999), because in all sectors under analysis, except banking, there are not enough cases to find the appropriate control group. For this reason, the author tries to reduce this problem by complementing the above equations with a regression analysis.

The regression analysis added to equations 8.1 and 8.2 incorporates into the model regressors that control for observable characteristics at the firm level. It also includes sectoral and macroeconomic variables. The latter variables try to capture different shocks, thereby isolating the impact of privatization.

The regression analysis consists primarily of an attempt to model each of the performance measures (P) as a function of the following variables:

$$Y_{i,t} = f(X_{i,t}, T_i, P_{i,t}, P_{i,r}, S_j, R_j, Z_t)$$

where $Y_{i,t}$ are the different performance measures previously detailed for firm i in period of time t; $X_{i,t}$ are firm characteristics; T_i are the characteristics of the privatization process of the specific firm; $P_{i,t}$ is the date in which the firm was privatized or given in concession; $P_{i,r}$ is a dummy indicating whether the firm is privatized or not; S_j are variables at the sector level of the firm; R_j are characteristics of the regulatory agency (for details, see Guasch and Spiller 1999), and Z_t are other controls such as macroeconomic variables.

Additionally, the author explored interaction effects of the privatization dummy, and carried out panel estimations using differences to drop out all firm-observed and -unobserved time-invariant fixed effects. Therefore, the three econometric specifications regressed are:

$$P_{i,t} = \alpha_0 + \beta_0 P_{i,t} + \beta_1 t + \beta_2 X_{i,t} + \beta_3 S_j + \beta_4 T_i \\ + \beta_5 R_j + \beta_6 Z_1 + \mu_{i,t} \tag{8.3}$$

$$P_{i,t} = \alpha_0 + \beta_0 P_{i,t} + \gamma_0 P_{i,r} + \beta_1 t + \beta_2 X_{i,t} + \beta_3 S_j + \beta_4 T_i \\ + \beta_5 R_j + \beta_6 Z_1 + \mu_{i,t} \tag{8.4}$$

$$P_{i,t} = \alpha_0 + \beta_0 P_{i,t} + \gamma_0 P_{i,r} + \beta_1 t + \gamma_1 t P_{i,r} + \gamma_2 P_{i,r} t + \beta_2 X_{i,t} \\ + \beta_3 S_j + \beta_4 T_i + \beta_5 R_j + \beta_6 Z_1 + \mu_{i,t} \tag{8.5}$$

Equation 8.3 is the same as equation 8.1 but includes firm, sector, and macroeconomic variables and, when available, some variables for the characteristics of the regulatory agency. Equation 8.4 includes a privatization dummy and a control group in the sample to be able to carry out a difference-in-difference estimation as in equation 8.2, but again with the controls previously specified. Finally, equation 8.5 includes additional interactions of the year-privatized dummy $(P_{i,t})$ and the dummy of whether the firm is privatized or not $(P_{i,r})$, and a time trend to capture trend and convergence over time of newly privatized firms with firms in the control group (public firms or already private firms).

Equations 8.3, 8.4, and 8.5 are estimated using simple ordinary least squares (OLS) panel data of firms, as detailed below. In addition, it is necessary to account for unmeasured industry and industry/year effects. Making establishment fixed effects allows all firm-observed and -unobserved time-invariant fixed effects to drop out. However, since these performance models could suffer from endogeneity problems, simultaneous determination and reverse causality of the explanatory variables are used, following what is now standard procedure in the literature of instrumental variables.[14] Because the privatization process directly affects most of the explanatory variables for many of the performance indicators, reverse causality or simultaneous determination is a latent problem. Additionally, the GMM-IV (generalized method of moments instrumental variables) estimation allows for heteroskedasticity of unknown form.[15] In order to have appropriate instruments, the lags of the instrumentalized variables as well as the privatization variables are used. Also, a test of overidentifying restrictions—Hansen's J statistic (1982)—is provided to check whether the equation is overidentified by an abundance of instruments. If this statistic rejects the null hypothesis, the validity of the model is called into question.[16]

Although this estimator is restricted to models linear in the parameters, it is relatively more efficient than an OLS with instrumental variables, even with correction for heteroskedasticity with the White procedure. The efficiency gain is derived from the GMM-IV estimator's use of an optimal weighting matrix (rather than the identity weighting matrix implicit in any least squares estimator) to define the appropriate combination of moment conditions.[17] In this context, the moment conditions are the orthogonality conditions of each instrument with the error process. A discussion of the development of the estimator is given in Greene (2000).

The Data

The construction of the database required several sources of statistical information. For the preprivatization period, the primary sources of information were the White Books (a collection of all information available for firms to be privatized) and the published histories of the respective firms. This information was complemented by sources such as the fiscal statistical summary of the Central Reserve Bank of Peru, the National Institute of Statistics and Computing, annual economic surveys, and others (for further details on data sources, see appendix 8A).

For the postprivatization period, the author collected information from various sources. Again, company histories were an excellent source of information. Data on the characteristics of the firms were complemented by statistics from the Supervising Committee of Companies and Securities, annual economic surveys, and monthly financial reports of the Bank and Insurance Superintendent. The author also collected data for sectoral indicators from statistics published by the regulatory agencies. To provide enough preprivatization sectoral data, the data collected include information for the period 1986–2000. The preprivatization data allowed the author to control for the period of restructuring that many enterprises experienced before they could be privatized.

One major problem was the merger, absorption, or division of many companies or business units during the privatization process. This sort of restructuring made it difficult to follow companies as a single unit through the privatization process. Two alternative methods were adopted to resolve the issue. In the first method, the author aggregated preprivatization accounting information provided in the White Books; the second alternative relied on the fact that in most of the privatization agreements, such as the merger of CPT and ENTEL into TdP, the privatized entities were required to keep separate accounting books. Thus, the author could either aggregate a company's important data or follow the merged unit over time.

A second problem of data collection was that some privatization strategies required that SOEs be divided and each individual unit offered separately. The registers kept before the privatization processes were based on aggregated data, since all the different business units operated as a single enterprise. However, from the day of the decision to privatize, the registers were kept separately for each unit and then consolidated into one record for the company.

Although the companies were considered single units after the privatization process, in some cases there existed a combination of private businesses and SOEs that were only partially privatized. Mixed ownership in a firm's record complicated the measurement of the impact of privatization. To control partially for this problem, the author generated a variable based on the percentage of the firm still owned by the government to measure the intensity of the privatization process and added a discrete dummy of the period in which the privatization started.

The final problem was that parts of the SOE portfolios had been liquidated. Those companies usually represented inefficient units of SOEs that had not been absorbed by the private system. In these cases, when possible, the unit of the company liquidated was excluded, or it was assumed that the new private owner decided to shut down that unit for efficiency reasons.

Between the years 1992 and 2000, 185 transactions took place. This process included 42 privatized SOEs. However, for several important reasons, the sample of companies in this chapter does not include all of the privatized SOEs:

• Some state companies were divided horizontally or vertically into small units and privatized separately. In most cases, it was possible to join all the parts in which the company was divided and to assume that it remained a single operating unit. In the case of Telefónica del Perú, information from CPT and ENTEL Perú has been added. This was not possible in other cases due to lack of information about some of the units into which the company was divided.

• Most of the concessions and projects were not included due to the lack of financial information from the preprivatization period.

• Several firms were liquidated or had their operations stopped.

• Some firms were absorbed, or another firm acquired some of their business units.[18]

• In some cases, information was unavailable.

Despite these limitations, the sample includes 86 percent of the total value of transactions undertaken and 47 percent of the privatized SOEs involved in the process. These percentages increase to 91 percent and 63 percent, respectively, when liquidated or extinct companies are not considered. Table 8.3 presents the set of nonfinancial SOEs included in the study; nonfinancial companies not included in the study are listed in table 8.4.

A separate database was constructed for the financial sector. It consists of annual data and considers private banks during the period as the control group and the Banco de la Nación as a state-owned enterprise. The privatized banks are detailed in table 8.5. The evolution of privatization in the financial sector is given in appendix table 8C.2.

Appendix table 8B.1 gives a detailed explanation of the variables constructed and the manner in which they were calculated. Figure 8.5 plots all of the performance indicators for the entire database of privatized firms using a nonparametrical approximation (kernel densities) for the distribution of the values of the pre- and postprivatization performance indicators.[19] A clear increase (larger for the privatized firms than for the SOEs) of the performance indicators can be seen since 1994, when the process of privatization accelerated. For some indicators, such as return on assets, the difference between SOEs and privatized firms is not clear. This could occur because privatized firms significantly increased their possession of assets, which, in turn, reduces the impact of an increase in sales. When looking at employment, income, sales, and asset efficiency, the positive impact of privatization on the efficiency of firms is even more apparent, even though the reduction in total number of workers is similar for both SOEs and privatized firms.

Furthermore, after analyzing the performance indicators for each individual firm, it becomes apparent that the distributions of privatized firms shifted to the right for practically all of the performance indica-

Table 8.3 Nonfinancial Companies Included in the Study

| | | Firm data availability (years) | |
		Under public ownership	*Under private ownership*
Name of state-owned enterprise	*Name of private firm*	1986–93	1994–99
Electrolima	Edelnor	1986–93	1994–99
	Luz del Sur		
	Edegel		
	Ede – Cañete		
	Ede – Chancay		
Electroperú	Electroperú	1986–94	1995–99
	Egenor		
	Egesur		
	Cahua		
Empresa Eléctrica de Piura	Empresa Eléctrica de Piura	—	1997–99
—	Electro Andes	—	1997–99
Electro Centro	Electro Centro	1986–98	1999
Electro Noroeste	Electro Noroeste	1986–98	1999
Electro Norte	Electro Norte	1986–98	1999
Electro Norte Medio	Electro Norte Medio	1986–98	1999
Electro Oriente	—	1986–99	—
Electro Sur	—	1986–99	—
Electro Sur Este	—	1986–99	—
Electro Sur Medio	Electro Sur Medio	1986–96	1997–99
Etevensa	Etevensa	1994–95	1996–99
Seal	—	1986–99	—
Cemento Sur	Cemento Sur	1986–89, 1994	1996–98

(Table continues on the following page.)

425

Table 8.3 (continued)

Name of state-owned enterprise	Name of private firm	Firm data availability (years)	
		Under public ownership	Under private ownership
Cementos Lima	Cementos Lima	1987–93	1994–2000
Cementos Norte Pacasmayo	Cementos Norte Pacasmayo	1992–93	1994–2000
Cemento Yura	Yura	1986–90	1994–95
Centromín	—	1986–90	—
Sociedad Minera Cerro Verde	Sociedad Minera Cerro Verde	1993	1994–96, 1999–2000
Compañía Minera Condestable	Compañía Minera Condestable	1987–90	1992–2000
Hierro Perú	Shougan Hierro Perú	1986–90	1998–99
Minero Perú	—	1986–90	—
Empresa Minera Especial Tintaya	—	1986–89	—
Empresa de la Sal	Empresa de la Sal	1991–94	1995–2000
Petroperú	Petroperú	1986–91	1992–98
Petroperú - Refinería la Pampilla	Refinería la Pampilla	—	1996–98
Química del Pacifico	Química del Pacifico	1988–92	1993–2000
Certificaciones del Perú	Certificaciones del Perú	1991–93	—
Reactivos Nacionales	Reactivos Nacionales	1987–89, 1991–92	1993–2000
Industrias Navales	Industrias Navales	1991–92	1993–96
Sudamericana de Fibras	Sudamericana de Fibras	1991–92	1993–96
Siderperú	Siderperú	1986–90, 1993–95	1996–97
Solgas	—	1986–90	—
Compañía Peruana de Teléfonos			
Entel Perú	Telefónica	1986–93	1994–2000
SEDAPAL	—	1986–99	—

— Not applicable.
Source: Author's data.

Table 8.4 Nonfinancial Companies Not Included in the Study

Ceased or liquidated	Divided	Land privatizations	Absorbed by another firm	Information not found
Minpeco USA	Sociedad Paramonga	Proyecto Especial Chavimochic	Lar Carbón	Petrolera Transoceánica
Aeroperú	Epsep	Tierras del Proyecto Especial Pastogrande	Sia	Refinería Cajamarquilla
Petromar		Tierras del Proyecto Especial Chinecas	Nisa	Pesca Perú
Ecasa		Tierras del Proyecto Especial Majes-Siguas	Planta de Cemento Rioja	Enafer
Flopesca		Tierras del Proyecto Especial Jequetepeque-Zaña	Petrolube	Empresa Minera Yauliyacu
Pesquera Grau		Tierras Eriazas	Enata	Empresa Radio Panamericana
Fertisa		Tierras del Proyecto Especial Chira-Piura	Empresa Minera Mahr Túnel	Empresa Difusora Radio Tele
Epersur			Empresa Minera Paragsha	Pletasa
Plesulsa				Planta Lechera de Iquitos
Metaloroya				
Amfa				
Talleres de Moyopampa				
Empresa Minera Cobriza				
Cedega T				
Enatru Perú				
Ertur Arequipa				
Eretru				
Ertsa Puno				
Entur Perú				
Emturín				
Kuélap				
Complejo Pesquero de Samanco				
Ergusa				
Incasa				
Ertur				

Note: See text for an explanation of why firms were excluded from the study.
Source: Author's data.

427

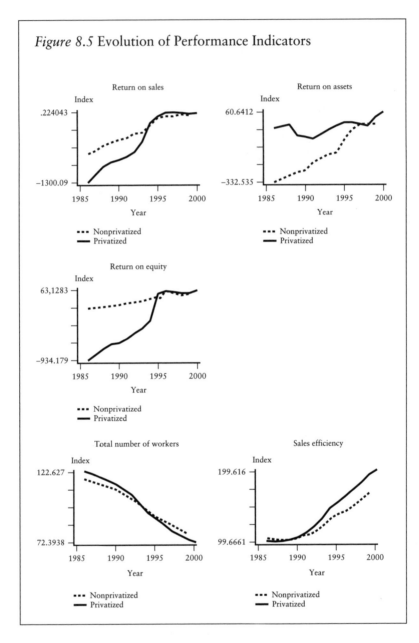

Figure 8.5 Evolution of Performance Indicators

tors. This signifies that the mean value of the specific performance indicator is bigger than it was when the firms were SOEs. The profitability ratios and the operating efficiency ratios increased after the privatization process. It must be mentioned, however, that the positive tendency

Figure 8.5 (continued)

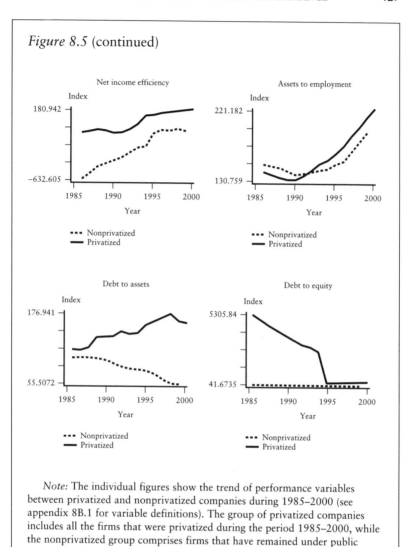

Note: The individual figures show the trend of performance variables between privatized and nonprivatized companies during 1985–2000 (see appendix 8B.1 for variable definitions). The group of privatized companies includes all the firms that were privatized during the period 1985–2000, while the nonprivatized group comprises firms that have remained under public ownership. Values have been estimated using lowess smoothing—KSM (kernel densities). Banks have been excluded from the estimations.

in profitability ratios emerged a few years before the actual process began, since many of the privatized enterprises had to undertake a restructuring process instituted through the implementation of reforms in all these sectors.

Additionally, it should be noted that the profitability indicators for the banks under examination showed an important decline a few years after

Table 8.5 Privatized Banks Included in the Study

| | | Number of yearly observations | |
Bank	Privatization date	Preprivatization	Postprivatization
Continental	April 1995	9	6
Interbank	July 1994	8	7
Comercio	June 1992	6	9
Popular	November 1993	6	—

— Not applicable.
Source: Author's data.

the privatization process. This result can be explained by the severe global financial crisis at the end of the 1990s.

Improvement in the operating efficiency ratios demonstrated not only a recovery in sales and income of companies across sectors, but also the strong decline in postprivatization total employment across sectors. These indicators had a positive, but weak, evolution in the years before the privatization process, but only after privatization occurred did their pace accelerate.

The capital-deepening indicator (the ratio of assets to employment) showed a very important increase after the privatization process. In all sectors, this indicator was more or less stagnant before the process occurred, but afterward, it started rising very rapidly. Furthermore, leverage indicators, which had a very negative and unstable tendency before privatization, began to improve, although not immediately. In all sectors the negative tendency was reversed after the privatization process began, but many sectors faced a relapse during the global financial crisis. The means and variances for these ratios during the period of analysis, as well as for the values of the most important indicators for all sectors, can be found in appendix 8D.

Even though businesses in the sanitation sector (specifically SEDA-PAL) have not been privatized, they are included in this project as a control group for the privatized firms in the utilities sector. SEDAPAL is used as a control group because it is a utility, like telephones or electricity, and because it had a similar evolution in performance indicators for the preprivatization period. That occurred because the government initially prepared SEDAPAL for privatization. This similarity presents an opportunity to compare an "untreated group" (a firm that was prepared for privatization but then not privatized) with a "treated group" (TdP). In the case of electricity, as detailed in appendix table 8C.1, state-owned firms still exist. Thus, there are enough controls to evaluate the impact of privatization in the utilities sector under the difference-in-difference methodology.

Empirical Results

In this section, the methodologies outlined earlier are used to analyze the impact of the privatization process on firm performance. First, a detailed analysis of performance indicators is carried out for all the privatized firms in the sample; then the three major privatized sectors are analyzed: telecommunications, electricity, and the financial sector.

Each of the tables consists of two tests comparing pre- and postprivatization. The first test is a first-difference analysis using firm and year fixed effects to analyze the difference between pre- and postprivatization information for all firms under study. The second test is a difference-in-difference test, as detailed in the methodological section. The difference-in-difference statistic both tests for the change in firm performance compared with the privatization period and takes into account relative firm performance when compared with a control group of SOEs that did not undergo the privatization process. In the all-firm panel, the control groups are all the SOEs present for every year for which information was collected. The gross national product per capita for each sector is also included to control for the size of the sector to which the specific firms belong.

When analyzing the two principal sectors where privatization took place, the control firms were those identified as most similar to the ones under analysis. In the case of telecommunications, the control group is SEDAPAL, the main firm in the water and sanitation sector. This firm was not privatized but underwent a preprivatization reform process similar to that of the telecommunications firm.[20] For the electricity sector, the control group is a group of nonprivatized electric companies (Electro Oriente, Electro Sur, Electro Sur Este, and Electro Sur Medio). Finally, for the case of the two privatized banks, Banco Continental and Interbanc, two different control groups were used. The first group consisted of all private banks in operation between 1986 and 2000; the comparison was between privatized banks and private banks. The second control was the state-owned bank, Banco de la Nación.

Since there were enough private banks to develop the control group, a propensity score, in which the probability of belonging to the treated group, given observable characteristics (interbank funds, assets, total liabilities, and equity),[21] was used as a summary of those characteristics in order to measure the average treatment effect on the treated variables in comparison with the performance variables.

Finally, a regression analysis and the estimation of equation 8.5 were carried out to find a possible convergence of performance indicators. The regression analysis also allowed controlling for different variables mentioned in the literature that could explain the impact of the privatization of the SOEs. In addition to characteristics of the firm such as size, sector, gross domestic product, and assets over employment, controls that helped measure the size of market failure were included.

As noted above, and as mentioned by Megginson and Netter (2001), welfare theory argues that privatization tends to have the greatest positive impact in cases where the role of the government in minimizing market failure is the weakest, that is, for SOEs in competitive markets or markets that can readily become competitive. In contrast, Shleifer (1998) and others have argued that both in natural monopolies and in the markets for public goods, where competitive considerations are weaker, government-owned firms are rarely the appropriate solution.

Consistent with this literature, the regression analysis includes a set of variables that control for the degree of competition approximated by concentration indexes, as well as variables that measure the type of regulatory processes that accompanied the privatization process. In addition, and of utmost importance, the inclusion of such variables allows for the separation of the effects of market power from those of privatization. It is possible that some companies may have had market power before their sale but did not exploit it because they were under state control. If this is the case, then part of the improvement in firm performance could be a result of exploitation of consumers through market power and not a consequence of efficiency and incentive improvements resulting from privatization.

Results for All Privatized Firms

Table 8.6 presents the results for all of the privatized firms in the sample. In the table, first and second differences in performance changes are presented using both the mean and the median. The second differences are presented using as a control group all the firms not privatized in the respective periods of analysis. In all performance indicators and as mentioned in the methodological section, a simple regression was carried out (equation 8.1) in which fixed effects were included at the level of the firm (figure 8.5 plots each of the indicators). Additionally, a test for normality was carried out as well as the Kolmogorov-Smirnov nonparametric test to determine if the difference in the distribution of the performance indicators was significant. In all the performance indicators, with the exception of leverage and assets to employee, the test showed significant differences.

Even accounting for the wide range of firms included in the study, the performance indicators show a significant improvement after privatization. Specifically, when analyzing three basic indicators, sales, cost per unit, and labor, the results obtained are as expected: privatized firms significantly increase their sales compared with nonprivatized SOEs. At the same time, there is a statistically significant reduction in cost per unit, and direct employment falls significantly, in line with the restructuring process that the privatized firms went through.

Table 8.6 Changes in Performance for the Privatized Firms

Variable	First difference		t-statistic[a] t-statistic[b]	Difference in difference t-statistic[a] t-statistic[b]
	Mean before Median before	Mean after Median after		
Profitability				
Operating income/	0.053	0.187	2.70	2.700
sales	0.083	0.207	5.57	4.850
Net income/sales	−0.293	0.028	2.41	2.410
	−0.128	0.074	0.30	0.300
Net income/PPE	−0.062	0.010	1.41	1.410
	−0.027	0.042	1.56	1.090
Operating efficiency				
Cost per unit	0.947	0.813	−2.70	−2.700
	0.917	0.793	−2.81	−2.980
Sales/employee[c]	110.317	242.909	11.91	11.910
	105.089	249.802	2.12	1.970
Log(sales/	5.336	5.770	10.85	10.850
employees)	5.377	5.789	3.35	2.550
Sales/PPE	1.215	1.007	−1.43	−1.430
	1.167	0.936	0.25	−0.260
Log(sales/PPE)	−0.443	−0.321	1.98	1.980
	−0.377	−0.323	0.14	0.240
Output				
Log(sales)	6.590	11.636	8.47	8.470
	7.596	11.674	1.25	0.350
Labor				
Employee[c]	114.621	68.621	−13.93	−13.930
	116.612	67.377	−4.88	−2.740
Log(employee)	6.145	5.635	−14.65	−14.650
	6.183	5.622	−0.28	−5.740
Assets				
Log(PPE)	11.641	11.722	0.73	0.730
	11.594	11.768	1.22	0.490

Note: PPE = property, plant, and equipment. See text for an explanation of the empirical results; see appendix table 8B.1 for variable definitions. Pre- and postprivatization categories are defined according to the privatization date for each company. Second differences (last column) calculated from a panel regression are presented using as a control group all the firms not privatized in the period of analysis.

a. Corresponds to the test of significance of an ordinary least squares regression with fixed effects.

b. Corresponds to the test of significance of an LMS (Lagrange multiplier statistic) regression with fixed effects.

c. Index (year 1993 = 100).

Source: Author's calculations.

Moreover, the profitability indicators and all the operating efficiency indicators show significant improvement for both the privatized firms and in comparison with the nonprivatized firms. The ratio of net income to assets (property, plant, and equipment, or PPE) shows no significant difference between the pre- and postprivatization periods. This result was expected because both the denominator and the numerator increase with the privatization given the high levels of investments made by new companies to increase efficiency.

Results for Public Utilities Sector. A detailed analysis of the two major privatized sectors (public utilities and finance) is carried out for the firms included in the panel and the different time periods over which they were privatized. As previously mentioned, these two sectors represent about 80 percent of the total revenue collected by the privatization process.

The results of estimating equation 8.5 for public utilities (electricity, telephones, and water as a control) are shown in table 8.7. As expected, the results are consistent with the literature: privatized firms are more profitable and productive than are public firms (Boardman and Vining 1989; Vining and Boardman 1992; La Porta and López-de-Silanes 1999). The results of the privatization date dummy are significant only for the debt indicators. At the same time, the time trend is positive and significant, which means that over time all the performance measures improved. This finding, together with the insignificant dummy that captures the date of privatization, suggests that the performance indicators started to improve before the privatization process and that only the debt indicators improved significantly faster after the privatization process.

When examining the dummy that captures a firm's privatization status, through a treatment on the treated type of analysis (similar to the second difference) in the return on sales, debt indicators, sales efficiency, and the ratio of assets to employment, the privatized utilities show a significant improvement compared with SEDAPAL, which is used as a control group. However, the variable of time trend times the privatized firm dummy is significant and negative, meaning that over time, the privatized firms are converging to the lower performance of SEDAPAL. This finding is very important because it sheds light on the decline in recent years in the financial performance of both the telephone company and the electric utilities, which could be a consequence of increased market competition.

At the same time, the coefficient on the percent of government participation has a negative and significant sign for two of the three profitability indicators (return on assets and return on sales), although it shows a positive and significant sign in sales efficiency and ratio of assets to employment. These results sharply contradict expectations. In

Table 8.7 Performance Indicators of Privatized Utilities, Difference in Difference
(Generalized method of moments instrumental variables estimator)

Variable	ROS	ROA	ROE	Debt to assets	Debt to equity	Sales efficiency	Net income efficiency	Assets/ employment
Dummy for date of privatization (*fpriv*)	−0.5355	0.0788	−0.0263	−0.5594	−1.9622	−3.9619	20.346	4,453.08
	(0.8867)	(0.1070)	(0.1706)	(0.2133)***	(0.6373)**	(324.041)	(186.8696)	(4209.4528)
Dummy if firm is privatized (*epriv*)	1.3155	0.0114	−0.008	0.4892	1.4444	233.929	40.0353	5,574.28
	(0.4665)***	(0.0242)	(0.0425)	(0.0549)***	(0.2800)***	(47.0005)***	(32.4350)	(1,771.816)***
Time trend (*t*)	0.1517	0.0113	0.0176	0.0097	0.0162	34.3105	11.3793	35.6078
	(0.0292)***	(0.0038)***	(0.0063)***	(0.0046)**	(0.0130)	(4.6841)***	(2.7264)***	(84.3298)
*t * fpriv*	0.1455	−0.0026	0.0077	0.0502	0.1705	53.5472	13.581	192.7965
	(0.0885)	(0.0074)	(0.0123)	(0.0174)***	(0.0525)***	(28.5794)	(15.1040)	(372.0849)
*t * epriv*	−0.1305	−0.0067	−0.0093	−0.0345	−0.1115	−26.3847	−6.3136	−443.6183
	(0.0425)***	(0.0032)**	(0.0061)	(0.0071)***	(0.0306)***	(5.0188)***	(3.3763)	(148.8121)***
Concentration index	−0.004	0.0002	0.0003	0.0000	−0.0017	1.1352	0.1334	−15.8996
	(0.0025)	(0.0003)	(0.0006)	(0.0006)	(0.0025)	(1.0208)	(0.4399)	(14.9523)
Percent change of GDP per capita	0.0484	0.0012	0.0015	0.0013	0.0033	20.0098	4.6774	−72.6033
	(0.0141)***	(0.0018)	(0.0030)	(0.0022)	(0.0101)	(2.0111)	(1.9953)**	(66.4124)
Percent government participation	1.1136	20.0448	−0.0635	0.1108	0.1387	513.6258	104.3681	6,369.42
	(0.7313)	(0.0184)**	(0.0310)**	(0.0603)	(0.1850)	(122.735)***	(78.5154)	(1,345.163)***

(Table continues on the following page.)

Table 8.7 (continued)

Variable	ROS	ROA	ROE	Debt to assets	Debt to equity	Sales efficiency	Net income efficiency	Assets/ employment
Dummy regulation by price cap	-0.4064	0.0602	0.1393	0.1374	0.3629	-66.4621	-58.5637	-626.2109
	(0.2648)	(0.0352)	(0.0569)**	(0.0622)**	(0.1887)	(77.8893)	(36.9691)	(1017.4182)
Dummy regulation based on costs	0.0522	-0.0177	-0.0137	-0.0415	0.0214	222.233	22.2343	21,485.57
	(0.3372)	(0.0303)	(0.0530)	(0.0469)	(0.2030)	(56.4033)***	(39.7200)	(1524.1113)
Log(employment)	0.2742	0.0247	0.0463	0.0138	0.0598	104.4154	40.8697	-572.6417
	(0.1328)**	(0.0094)***	(0.0176)***	(0.0182)	(0.0818)	(19.5389)***	(13.6881)***	(714.1734)
Assets/employment	-0.0002	0.0000	0.0000					
	(0.0001)	(0.0000)***	(0.0000)***					
Constant	-4.4631	-0.2313	-0.4215	-0.0884	-0.4686	-1,450.22	-505.2756	-1,151.88
	(1.5426)***	(0.0860)***	(0.1583)***	(0.1853)	(0.6785)	(256.104)***	(175.467)***	(6526.9513)
Observations	93	93	93	96	96	98	98	93
Pseudo-R²	0.349	0.335	0.335	0.569	0.502	0.741	0.371	0.426

* Significant at the 10 percent level.
** Significant at the 5 percent level.
*** Significant at the 1 percent level.

Note: ROA = return on assets, ROE = return on equity, and ROS = return on sales. This table reports difference-in-difference panel data GMM-IV (generalized method of moments instrumental variables estimator) results of performance indicators for utilities. SEPADAL, the most important water and sanitation enterprise, is used as a control group. There are eight different regressions with distinct dependent performance variables; see appendix table 8B.1 for variable definitions. Standard errors are in parentheses. Log(employment) has been instrumented using one period lag, fpriv and epriv by GMM-IV. Pseudo-R² is the R² using IV regression with robust standard errors. Hansen J-statistic (1982) has been used to test for overidentifying restrictions. In every case the null hypothesis that the additional moment conditions are approximately satisfied was rejected, validating the use of the instruments.

Source: Author's calculations.

addition, the dummy variable for price cap regulation is significant and positive for the return on equity and on the debt-to-assets ratio, implying that the type of regulation carried out by the regulatory agency also has an important impact on firm performance. Finally, the concentration index is not significant, possibly because there is competition in the electricity sector, especially in distribution, and a monopoly in the telephone sector: the effects of the two different market structures go in opposite directions.

When examining each of the privatized firms, the results of the first- and second-difference statistics for the privatized SOEs are completely consistent with the findings shown in table 8.7. In the cases of Telefónica del Perú S.A. and Electrolima, both the first and second differences are significant and in the expected direction. In the case of the telephone company, only the difference in means in the leverage indicators in both the first and second differences were not significant (see appendix table 8E.1).

Similarly for Electrolima, all the performance indicators, including leverage, improved significantly (appendix table 8E.2). This also holds when a control group is included and the second difference is calculated. The profitability ratios moved from being negative on average to positive in magnitudes from 8 percent to 20 percent. Another significant change occurred in debt ratios, which fell more than 50 percent. Furthermore, sales efficiency increased by 400 percent, and net income efficiency reached high levels compared with previously negative results. One of the expected explanations for such a significant increase in operating efficiency would be the reduction of employment by more than half (55.6 percent) after privatization. This reduction, however, only doubles the ratio and is thus not sufficient to explain the improvement. It is safe to conclude that efficiency gains through restructuring and improved incentives play a key role in contributing to the rise in operating efficiency. In summary, the results for Electrolima showed that although the reduction in employment affected labor productivity, labor productivity and total factor productivity increased after the privatization process.

The results for Electroperú, which was privatized between 1995 and 1996, two years after Electrolima, are shown in appendix table 8E.3. The results in this case are not as significant as the results for Electrolima. Only two indicators improved: operating efficiency, as observed in the first difference, and the ratio of debt to assets, as observed in the difference in difference when the performance of this firm is compared to other firms not yet privatized. The state's assumption of Electrolima's long-term debts just before privatization explains the improvement in the ratio of debts to assets. These unsatisfactory results could be a consequence of the incomplete privatization process in this sector. One of the major electricity-generating enterprises, Central Hidroeléctrica del

Mantaro, and all of the distribution enterprises in the south of Peru are not yet privatized.

Results for the Financial Sector. The results for simple differences in mean for the financial sector were similar to those of the public utilities sector. There was no significant impact on profitability measures and leverage indicators, but there was a significant increase in the operating efficiency and coverage of the privatized banks (Interbanc and Banco Continental). The increase in operating efficiency is mainly explained by the 50 percent reduction in employment, which practically duplicates the indicator of operating efficiency. At the same time, the difference-in-difference indicators are similar to the first-difference indicators when public banks are used as a comparison. When a comparison is made with private banks of similar size, the private banks still demonstrate better performance measures than privatized banks. Finally, when the control group was defined with propensity scores, and the difference-in-difference estimation for privatized banks against matched private banks was carried out, private banks still performed better.

Furthermore, when analyzing indicators specific to banks, such as personnel expenses per employee, bad loan portfolios, administrative expenses, and financial margin per branch, an increase in the performance was discovered. These results even hold for personal expenses per employee in the difference-in-difference indicators despite the fact that the comparison group is preexisting private banks (see table 8.8).

The results of estimating equation 8.5 can be observed in table 8.9. The table shows that, unlike the results for the utilities sector, the date of privatization (*fpriv*) is significant for all the performance indicators. This finding reveals that there was an important change after the privatization process. At the same time, there is no direct difference between the privatized banks (*epriv* = 1) and the already private banks (the control group). These results are consistent with the fact that privatized banks are being compared to banks that were always private, and their performance is therefore expected to be better or similar to the private banks.

When analyzing the interaction between the time trend and the dummy for privatized banks (*epriv*), there is a significant and positive effect for the return on sales, indicating that over time newly privatized banks improve in comparison with banks that were always private. This result reflects a possible convergence of performance. As expected, there is also a negative time trend, which could be explained by the international financial crisis that affected all the banks in the region. Additionally, the interaction between the time trend and dummy for year of privatization is significant and negative, implying that the growth rate of performance since privatization is declining. The decline can also be explained by the international effects of the Japanese and Russian financial crises. However, the

Table 8.8 Changes in Performance in the Financial Sector after Privatization
(Differences between means and difference-in-difference tests)

| Sector | Means | | First Differences | | Difference in difference | S-Francia[c] Prob > Z | Kolmogorov-Smirnov |
	Preprivatization	Postprivatization	t-test[a]	Hotelling[b]	Hotelling[b]		
Performance measure (P_i)							
Profitability							
Return on sales (ROS)	0.0545	0.0784	-1.320*	1.743	2.971	0.116	0.476
	(0.010)	(0.016)					
Return on assets (ROA)	0.0112	0.0099	0.383	0.147	0.167	0.314	0.994
	(0.002)	(0.002)					
Return on equity (ROE)	0.1467	0.1193	0.629	0.395	0.429	0.291	0.994
	(0.029)	(0.027)					
Operating efficiency							
Sales efficiency (SALEFF)[d]	188.85	404.10	-7.122***	50.725***	35.071***	0.125	0.007***
	(17.921)	(24.582)					
Net income efficiency (NIEFF)[d]	10.70	22.60	-2.641**	6.973**	12.031**	0.178	0.082**
	(2.403)	(4.249)					
Employment							
Total employment (EMPL)	3132.5	1831.2	7.101***	50.419***	44.613***	0.146	0.001***
	(95.085)	(177.859)					
Leverage							
Debt to assets (LEV)	0.9125	0.9175	-0.555	0.308	0.758	0.077	0.329
	(0.007)	(0.002)					
Debt to equity (LEV2)	12.134	11.189	0.485	0.235	0.733	0.029	0.476
	(1.432)	(0.304)					

(Table continues on the following page.)

Table 8.8 (continued)

Sector	Means		First Differences		Difference in difference	S-Francia[c]	Kolmogorov-
	Preprivatization	Postprivatization	t-test[a]	Hotelling[b]	Hotelling[b]	Prob > Z	Smirnov
Coverage							
Loans per worker (LOAW)	354.17	1440.36	−13.329***	177.654***	120.006***	0.015	0.001***
	(40.902)	(81.520)					
Deposit per worker (DEPW)	513.23	1742.60	−9.216***	84.940***	93.298***	0.051	0.001***
	(52.243)	(154.157)					
Indicators specific to banks							
Personal expenses per employee	−31.45	−53.48	6.74***	45.41***	22.79***	0.665	0.007***
	(1.98)	(2.54)					
Bad loan portfolio	0.08	0.08	−0.26	0.07	0.60	0.671	0.721
	(0.07)	(0.01)					
Administrative expenses	0.49	0.42	1.19	1.43	3.91*	0.010	0.216
	(0.04)	(0.01)					
Financial margin per branch	1913.80	2374.20	−1.27	1.62	1.30	0.724	0.476
	(253.46)	(145.10)					

* Significant at the 10 percent level.
** Significant at the 5 percent level.
*** Significant at the 1 percent level.

Note: This table reports results for two privatized banks, Banco Continental and Interbank First, and second differences for changes in performance are shown, for each empirical proxy, using the mean values (see appendix table 8B.1 for variable definitions). Columns 1 and 2 present the mean values before and after privatization (the year of privatization is 1995). Columns 3 and 4 show results for two tests for significance in changes in performance after privatization (first differences): t-test (two-tailed Wilcoxon signed-rank test) and the Hotelling test. Column 5 displays significance of difference-in-difference results using a Hotelling test (control group is based on propensity score matching). Column 6 presents Shapiro-Francia test for normality. Finally, column 7 shows the results for the Kolmogorov-Smirnov (K-S) statistic, a nonparametric test used to formally test the equality of the empirical hazards functions of the different pre- and postprivatization performance indicators.

a. t-test for Ho (null hypothesis) for difference between means. Numbers are unequal.

$$t = \frac{(\bar{X}_1 - \bar{X}_2)}{S\bar{x}_1 - \bar{x}_2} = \frac{(\bar{X}_1 - \bar{X}_2)}{\sqrt{\frac{(n_1 - 1)\, s_1^2 + (n_2 - 1)\, s_2^2}{(n_1 + n_2 - 2)}} * \sqrt{\frac{1}{n_1} + \frac{1}{n_2}}}$$

where x is an $l \times k$ matrix of the means and S is the estimated covariance matrix.

b. Test of equality:

$$T^2 = (\bar{x}_1 - \bar{x}_2)\, S^{-1} (\bar{x}_1 - \bar{x}_2)'$$

c. Shapiro-Francia test for normality. Ho (null hypothesis) variable is normally distributed.

d. Thousands of nuevos soles.

Table 8.9 Performance Indicators of Privatized Banks, Difference in Difference
(Generalized method of moments instrumental variables estimator)

Variable	ROS	ROA	ROE	Debt to assets	Debt to equity	Sales efficiency	Net income efficiency	Assets/employment
Dummy for date of privatization (fpriv)	0.3092 (0.1237)**	0.0538 (0.0182)***	0.4506 (0.2096)**	-0.0922 (0.0323)***	-11.4328 (4.1852)***	-1.4313 (112.163)	111.1536 (36.1325)***	-900.2763 (627.2483)
Dummy if firm is privatized (epriv)	-0.1219 (0.0508)**	-0.0114 (0.0080)	0.0778 (0.0696)	0.0334 (0.0227)	7.1600 (4.0179)	-96.5512 (82.2342)	-40.8681 (20.4276)**	-27.2020 (461.7338)
Time trend (t)	-0.0208 (0.0085)**	-0.0023 (0.0009)***	-0.0132 (0.0070)	-0.0002 (0.0010)	-0.0470 (0.0648)	6.4866 (2.8684)**	-2.9459 (1.1379)**	121.4275 (19.2942)***
t * fpriv	-0.0247 (0.0102)**	-0.0041 (0.0017)***	-0.0260 (0.0185)	0.0108 (0.0036)***	1.4272 (0.5373)***	12.5945 (13.5645)	-8.1146 (3.7083)**	175.8407 (77.6577)**
t * epriv	0.0116 (0.0059)**	0.0014 (0.0011)	-0.0096 (0.0080)	-0.0054 (0.0029)	-1.0251 (0.5275)	4.9709 (11.7789)	4.2447 (2.9500)	-51.8588 (68.2979)
Participation in total credit allocations (share)	-0.1551 (0.6042)	0.0567 (0.0601)	1.1762 (0.7128)	0.0521 (0.0696)	12.3772 (6.2735)**	1748.686 (202.047)***	274.5105 (61.9442)***	14982.4047 (1,549.272)***
Percent change of GDP per capita	0.0006 (0.0017)	-0.0005 (0.0003)	-0.0035 (0.0021)	0.0019 (0.0006)***	0.0754 (0.0423)	-12.4515 (1.8376)***	-1.8681 (0.8185)**	-56.0758 (9.3183)***

Dummy for closed state-owned banks	-0.0548 (0.0301)	-0.0067 (0.0048)	-0.0125 (0.0818)	0.0127 (0.0106)	1.4007 (1.0590)	-76.3966 (27.8619)***	-24.4158 (10.8307)**	-67.1054 (157.1675)
Log(employment)	0.0283 (0.0451)	-0.0026 (0.0045)	-0.0549 (0.0479)	0.0126 (0.0055)**	0.3098 (0.3564)	-115.6341 (14.6869)***	-19.1690 (6.4199)***	-942.4289 (97.4552)***
Loans per worker	0.0001 (0.0001)**	0.0000 (0.0000)	0.0001 (0.0000)					
Constant	-0.0258 (0.2340)	0.0347 (0.0252)	0.4267 (0.2199)	0.8055 (0.0325)***	7.0200 (1.8918)***	878.7896 (95.6279)***	154.4391 (46.8079)***	5849.7005 (594.3191)***
Observations	285	285	285	285	285	285	285	285
Pseudo-R^2	0.111	0.115	0.06	0.162	0.144	0.411	0.146	0.4755

* Significant at the 10 percent level.
** Significant at the 5 percent level.
*** Significant at the 1 percent level.

Note: ROA = return on assets, ROE = return on equity, and ROS = return on sales. This table reports difference-in-difference panel data GMM-IV (generalized method of moments instrumental variables estimator) results of performance variables. Private banks are used as a control group. There are eight different regressions with distinct dependent performance variables (see appendix table 8B.1 for variable definitions). Standard errors are in parentheses. *Log(employment)* and *loans per worker* have been instrumented using one period lag, *fpriv* and *epriv* by GMM-IV. Pseudo-R^2 is the R^2 using IV regression with robust standard errors. Hansen J-statistic (1982) has been used to test for overidentifying restrictions. In every case the null hypothesis that the additional moment conditions are approximately satisfied was rejected, validating the use of the instruments.

Source: Author's calculations.

size of the coefficient is less than a tenth of the coefficient of the date of the privatization dummy, implying that the overall effect of privatization on performance is positive.

Employment

The impact of privatization on the welfare of displaced public workers has received little attention in the literature. One of the main problems faced by researchers is the lack of available data, since information for displaced workers is provided for only one period of time (the moment of displacement from the SOE). In fact, it would require large amounts of time, effort, and resources to trace displaced public workers for the purpose of analyzing the long-term impact of privatization on their welfare and earnings. This is possibly the reason why most of the studies analyze the effects of privatization on employment, welfare, and wage levels using gross national figures or industry and firm information.

The employment indicators make clear that direct employment was reduced significantly after privatization (table 8.10). On average, employment in the former SOEs fell almost 35 percent after privatization, although when the figures are compared with industry averages, the average decrease in employment is 0.7 percent higher than the average for the industry.[22] When decomposing the employment data by white- and blue-collar employees, the privatized firms show a smaller overall reduction than the industry average of 4.1 percent, but the reduction in employment of blue-collar workers is 17.6 percent higher for the privatized firms than

Table 8.10 Changes in Employment after Privatization

Variable	Before privatization 1993	After privatization 1997	Change (percent)
Total			
Mean	2461.17	1605.75	−34.76
Median	2237.50	1393.50	−37.72
	(1508.536)	(1300.427)	
White-collar			
Mean	2049.17	1387.00	−32.31
Median	1746.50	1102.00	−36.90
	(1457.232)	(1153.019)	
Blue-collar			
Mean	412.00	218.75	−46.91
Median	210.00	149.50	−28.81
	(495.463)	(247.820)	

Note: See text for explanation. Standard deviations are in parentheses.
Source: Author's calculations.

for the industry average, which means that the main reduction of direct employment took place among blue-collar workers.

One of the chief criticisms of the privatization process is that the major reason for improvement in performance is a significant reduction in the number of employees, rather than a real increase in total factor productivity. To address this issue, the author follows La Porta and López-de-Silanes (1999) to calculate the impact on privatized companies if all the layoffs were instead kept on at their original salaries.[23] For this purpose, the cost of layoffs was calculated as: $(L_{pre} - L_{1994}) * W_{pre}$, where W_{pre} is the average wage in the year preceding privatization, L_{pre} is the average number of employees in the years preceding privatization, and L_{1994} is the level of employment in 1994 after privatization.

The results are shown in table 8.11. There is no significant difference between the postprivatization performance indicators and the postprivatization performance indicators under the assumption that there were no layoffs. For utilities, the percentage change in the profit indicators goes from −2 percent to −5 percent, while in the case of the banks the impact is bigger, averaging −12 percent and −26 percent for Banco Continental and Interbanc, respectively. After including all laid-off workers at their original salaries, net income efficiency (a variable that is directly affected by the number of employees) fell substantially; the percentage change for TdP was −12 percent, for Interbanc −34 percent, and for Continental −14 percent.

In the case of TdP, contracting service companies created a significant amount of indirect employment. These service companies frequently consisted of personnel laid off as a result of the privatization. This required an additional exercise that involved subtracting the costs from all service payments carried out by the company to find the net employment layoff. This resulted in a positive percentage change for some of the profitability indicators since the wage costs before privatization were smaller than the fees the company pays the service companies. Furthermore, the number of employees in the telecommunications sector rose from 13,000 employees in 1993 to 34,000 employees in 1998, according to OSIPTEL.

In general, for all the companies studied, the results of the modified version of La Porta and López-de-Silanes' (1999) exercise can be explained through the following reasons: total wages of laid-off employees represented only 1.4 percent of total sales, since the average wages paid before privatization were extremely low; postprivatization sales increased significantly, which spread labor costs over a wider base; and there was also a significant increase in the productivity of other factors, especially capital, because of the increase in coverage and the new investments undertaken by privatized firms.[24]

In the case of utility companies, there was a clear and significant increase in sales. In telecommunications, the number of fixed-line phones per 100

Table 8.11 Impact of Layoffs on Performance Indicators for Major Privatized Firms

Firm	Postprivatization				Postprivatization without layoffs			
	ROS	ROA	ROE	Net income efficiency	ROS	ROA	ROE	Net income efficiency
Telefonica	0.385	0.162	0.287	81.385	0.366	0.155	0.272	71.883
	(0.09)	(0.05)	(0.08)	(42.84)	(0.09)	(0.05)	(0.07)	(40.57)
Electrolima	0.170	0.056	0.072	136.742	0.165	0.054	0.069	132.152
	(0.08)	(0.03)	(0.03)	(72.01)	(0.08)	(0.03)	(0.03)	(69.05)
Electroperú	0.257	0.030	0.050	258.850	0.252	0.029	0.049	252.863
	(0.22)	(0.02)	(0.04)	(206.78)	(0.22)	(0.02)	(0.04)	(206.65)
SEDAPAL	0.160	0.027	0.034	33.496	0.154	0.026	0.032	25.160
	(0.04)	(0.01)	(0.01)	(7.70)	(0.04)	(0.01)	(0.01)	(11.61)
Continental	0.091	0.011	0.130	23.434	0.080	0.010	0.115	20.051
	(0.05)	(0.01)	(0.09)	(13.67)	(0.06)	(0.01)	(0.09)	(13.70)
Interbank	0.066	0.010	0.116	17.323	0.048	0.007	0.087	11.457
	(0.06)	(0.01)	(0.10)	(14.27)	(0.06)	(0.01)	(0.11)	(16.37)

Note: ROA = return on assets, ROE = return on equity, and ROS = return on sales. See text for explanation. See appendix table 8B.1 for variable definitions.

Source: Author's calculations.

inhabitants grew from 2.9 in 1993 to 7.8 in 1998. Cellular phones grew from 50,000 to 735,000 in the same two years. In the electricity sector, the coefficient of electrification grew an average of 27 percent, and the generation of electricity grew an average of 25 percent as a result of the heavy volume of investments (approximately $682 million). Even more important, prices for telephone and electricity services were brought into line with the costs of producing those services; before privatization, prices typically covered 75 percent or less of the costs (see Torero and Pascó-Font 2001).

In summary, the results show a clear improvement in firm performance following privatization; a relative improvement compared with industry control groups; and an improvement in both labor productivity and total factor productivity.

Conclusions

Privatization began in Peru in 1991 to generate vital fiscal revenues for the government and improve the quality and coverage of infrastructure and other services. Privatization took place in the telecommunications, electricity, mining, financial services, and hydrocarbons sectors. The process was accompanied by sector reforms aimed at establishing competitive markets and autonomous regulatory agencies. The result was one of Latin America's greatest privatization success stories. A strong record of economic policy and performance underpinned the success of the privatization process, however. Macroeconomic stability, an open policymaking environment, and competitive sector markets gave the firms a stable and certain environment through 1998. Without such conditions, success would not have been achieved.

Unfortunately, the depth of the reforms, especially the extent of privatization, was uneven across sectors. Despite this reform mixture, the results in terms of improvement on the supply side are positive and very significant. The analysis clearly shows a significant improvement in firm performance since privatization.

It is clear from the analysis that privatization had an impact on privatized public utility firms in comparison to firms that went through a similar preprivatization restructuring but then were not privatized. Although over time there was a decrease in the performance of the privatized utilities, implying lower profits, this could have resulted from increased competition in the sector and a slowdown in certain services such as electricity due to the incomplete privatization process.

Results for the financial sector are similar. The main difference is that privatized banks performed better than they had before they were privatized, but not as well as the private banks in the control group. The results also show that privatized banks have a convergence tendency toward the best performers in the private sector.

It is clear that in the short run, the impact of privatization on employment is negative since SOEs usually hired people based on political rather than technical criteria. The privatized firms had to adjust to the new market conditions and reduce the level of employment by 35 percent, on average. Two effects have been demonstrated: a significant increase in indirect employment through services, and an average growth of 28 percent in total employment—both direct and indirect—since privatization. Nevertheless, to measure the real impact on employment in the medium run, it is inadequate to study only employment in a specific sector. One also has to study the effects on other sectors stemming from the higher demand for services by the privatized firms.

Despite the success in terms of firm performance, service quality and consumer benefits must be taken into account to make a balanced judgment of the privatization process. As mentioned in Torero and Pascó-Font (2001), there exist important problems in the privatization process that could explain why positive welfare impacts on consumers were not very significant, or were even negative in electricity. Although, the electricity sector has shown important improvements, the positive effects of privatization had not yet reached important regions of urban Peru. This could explain why, on average, consumers are not experiencing an increase in welfare. In contrast, telephony is the sector that has experienced the most significant improvements since privatization. In terms of both supply and demand, the results show a positive balance, including an increase in absolute levels of consumer surplus and in progressiveness, for the telecommunications sector. However, since 1997 the positive trend of gains in consumer surplus was reduced.

In summary, improved firm performance clearly suggests the necessity of continuing the privatization process, especially in electricity, water, and other SOEs where major reforms need to be concluded—or in some cases begun. This is only a supply-side analysis, but when combined with results from the demand-side analysis (see Torero, Schroth, and Pascó-Font 2004), it is apparent that firms and regulatory agencies must develop adequate policies to facilitate the transfer of performance benefits from privatized firms to consumers. In so doing, even further increases in the gains in welfare derived from the process will be possible. Policymakers must fortify the regulatory agencies and increase their independence. They also must work with privatized firms to identify vulnerable groups and to develop tailored measures, such as appropriate consumption plans, that will help increase consumer welfare.

Appendix 8A

Data Sources

Banco Central de Reserva del Perú (BCRP). 1986–2000. *Annual Report.* Lima.

———. Web page: http://bcrp.gob.pe.

Cementos Lima S.A. 1988–98. *Annual Report.* Lima.

Comisión de Promoción de la Inversión Privada (COPRI). 1996. *White Book.* Cementos Lima S.A. Lima.

———. *White Book.* CEPREL – Electrolima S.A. Lima.

———. *White Book.* Electroperú, S.A. Lima.

———. *White Book.* Electro Sur Medio, S.A. Lima.

———. *White Book.* Empresas Regionales de Electricidad: Electro Norte, S.A., Electro Norte Medio, S.A., Electro Noroeste, S.A., and Electro Centro, S.A. Lima.

———. Web page: http://www.copri.org.

Comisión de Tarifas Eléctricas (CTE). 1984, 1985, 1986–89, 1990–91, 1996, 1999. *Annual Report.* Lima.

———. 1992–93, 1994, 1995, 1996, 1997, 1998, 1999. *Statistical Yearbook.* Lima.

Comisión Nacional Supervisora de Empresas y Valores (CONASEV). Web page: http://www.conasevnet.gob.pe.

Compañía Peruana de Teléfonos S.A. 1985–87, 1990–93. *Annual Report.* Lima.

Electrolima, S.A. 1985–88, 1990–94, 1997. *Annual Report.* Lima.

Electroperú, S.A. 1985–99. *Annual Report.* Lima.

Entel Perú, S.A. 1990, 1991, 1993. *Annual Report.* Lima.

———. 1985–92. *Statistical Yearbook.* Lima.

SEDAPAL, S.A. 1984–99. *Annual Report.* Lima.

———. 1997. "Historia del abastecimiento del agua potable de Lima 1535–1996." Lima.

Superintendencia de Banca y Seguros (SBS). 1986–2000. *Weekly Notes.* Lima.

Superintendencia Nacional de Servicios de Saneamiento (SUNASS). 1996–99. *Annual Report.* Lima.

———. 1998. "Indicadores de Gestión 1996–1998." Lima.

————. Centro de Documentación, Web page: http://www.sunass.gob.pe/
cendoc.html.

Telefónica del Perú, S.A. 1994–2000. *Annual Report*. Lima.

Other Data Sources

From the Commission of Energy Tariffs:

Commercial Information (First quarter, 2000).
Publication containing results from the processing and analysis of commercial information provided by the electric sector companies.

CTE Informs (June 1999–November 2000).
Monthly publication with news about regulation, markets, agents, and
other current topics of interest in the electricity and hydrocarbon sectors in Peru and all around the world.

Electric Sector Operations (January 2000–November 2000).
Monthly publication containing information on production and demand
of electricity, prices, and other information related to the operation of
the sector.

El Informativo (June 1996–November 2000).
Periodical publication containing technical articles, market information,
evolution of rates, company news, statistics, and sector news.

The Statistical Yearbook (1994–98).
A yearly publication that details regulation of electricity rates and economic results for the Peruvian electricity market.

Yearly Report (1994–1999).

From OSIPTEL (Supervisory Agency for Private Investment in Telecommunications):

The Transformation of Telecommunications in Peru. 1995 Report.

Regulation and the Telecommunications Market. 1996 Report.

The Opening of the Telecommunications Market. 1997 Report.

Consumers and Telecommunications. 1998 Report.

Five Years in the Telecommunications Market. 1999 Report.

Institutional Report. 2000.

Technical studies (various titles).

Studies in telecommunications (various titles).

Bulletins (various titles).

Appendix 8B

Table 8B.1 Description of Variables

Variable	Description
Performance variable	
ROS	Return on sales is the ratio of net income to sales. Net income is equal to total income minus operating and administrative expenses, plus financial income minus financial expenses, and net taxes paid. Sales are equal to the total value of products and services sold, nationally and internationally, minus sales returns and discounts.
ROA	Return on assets is the ratio of net income to assets. Net income is equal to total income minus operating and administrative expenses, plus financial income minus financial expenses, and net taxes paid. Assets are the total value of the entire property of the firm on December 31.
ROE	Return on equity is the ratio of net income to equity. Net income is equal to total income minus operating and administrative expenses, plus financial income minus financial expenses, and net taxes paid. Equity is the value of the participation that the partners or owners have in the company.
Debt/assets	Debt/assets is the ratio of liability to assets. Liability is the value of the debt owed by the company. Assets are the total value of the entire property of the firm on December 31.
Debt/equity	Debt/equity is the ratio of liability to equity. Liability is the value of the debt owed by the company. Equity is the value of the participation that the partners or owners have in the company.
Sales efficiency	Sales efficiency is the ratio of sales to employment. Sales are equal to the total value of products and services sold, nationally and internationally, minus sales returns and discounts. Employment is measured as the total number of employees in the firm, including white- and blue-collar workers.

(Table continues on the following page.)

Table 8B.1 (continued)

Variable	Description
Net income efficiency	Net income efficiency is the ratio of net income to employment. Net income is equal to total income minus operating and administrative expenses, plus financial income minus financial expenses, and net taxes paid. Employment is measured as the total number of employees in the firm, including white- and blue-collar workers.
Total employment	Total employment is the total number of employees. The employees include white-collar workers and blue-collar workers at full time.
Assets/employment	The ratio of assets to employment indicates the proportion of assets that on average, would correspond to each employee. Assets are the total value of the entire property of the firm on December 31. Employment is measured as the total number of employees in the firm, incuding white- and blue-collar workers.
Sector variable	
Share rate	The share rate is the ratio of participation of the firm in its economic sector. In the case of utilities, participation is constructed by the contribution of the firm to total invoicing of the sector. In other words, it is the ratio of the firm's invoicing to the total invoicing of the sector. In the case of banks, the rate is constructed by the participation of the bank in total credit allocations.
Concentration index by sector	The concentration index of the sector is the CI4. This index is the sum of the share rate of the four firms with the highest participation in the sector. The share rate is the ratio of participation of the firm in its economic sector. In the case of utilities, participation is constructed by the contribution of the firm to total invoicing of the sector. In the case of banks, the rate is constructed by the participation of the bank in total credit allocations. The highest value the CI4 can take is 1, which indicates the existence of a monopoly.
Utilities	A dummy that takes the value 1 if the firm belongs to the utilities sector, and 0 otherwise.

Table 8B.1 (continued)

Variable	Description
Privatization variable	
Privatization	A dummy that takes the value 1 for all years the firm has been in private hands, and 0 otherwise.
Concession	A dummy that takes the value 1 for all years the firm has been in private hands, and 0 otherwise.
Value of transactions	The value of transactions is the amount, in current US$ millions, paid by the investor for the available share package or management rights.
Projected investment	The projected investment is the amount, in current US$ millions, that the investor commits to invest.
Operator's characteristic	
Foreign participation	A dummy that takes the value 1 if foreign investors hold a greater percentage of stocks than any other investor, and 0 otherwise.
Buyer's experience	A dummy that takes the value 1 if the buyer owns and manages one or more companies that belong to the same sector of the privatized firm, and 0 otherwise. Industries or sectors considered are telecommunications, electricity, water and sanitation, and banking.
Regulatory agency variable	
Regulated industry	A dummy that takes the value 1 if the firm belongs to a regulated industry, and 0 otherwise. A regulated industry is characterized by the presence of a regulatory agency. Industries or sectors considered are telecommunications, electricity, water and sanitation, and banking.
Regulatory agency	A dummy that takes the value 1 if a regulatory agency operated in the firm's sector in that year, and 0 otherwise. Industries or sectors considered are telecommunications, electricity, water and sanitation, and banking.
Price cap regulation	A dummy that takes the value 1 if there was a price cap regulation in a specific year, and 0 otherwise. Industries or sectors considered are telecommunications, electricity, water and sanitation, and banking.

(Table continues on the following page.)

Table 8B.1 (continued)

Variable	Description
Rate of return regulation	A dummy that takes the value 1 if the rate of return is regulated, and 0 otherwise. Industries or sectors considered are telecommunications, electricity, water and sanitation, and banking.
Discretionary prices	A dummy that takes the value 1 if the regulatory agency adopts a discretionary price regulation in that year, and 0 otherwise. Industries or sectors considered are telecommunications, electricity, water and sanitation, and banking.
Macro variable	
Peruvian per capita real GNP	Per capita real GNP is the gross national product by inhabitant at 1994 prices.
Average precipitation	Average precipitation is the average annual rain precipitation, measured in cubic millimeters.
Average exchange rate	The annual average exchange rate, measured as the value of a U.S. dollar in Nuevos Soles.
IPG	The IPG (generalized price index) is a modification of the consumer price index (CPI). It has the advantage of solving problems that are found in traditional estimations of changes in prices, and that become particularly severe in hyperinflation periods. It is a measure of how much the average price has changed since the base year (1994).
GNP	The gross national product is the value of goods and services produced by a country's residents over a year at 1994 prices. GNP is the sum of the value of consumption, investment, government expenses, and exports, minus imports.
Population	The total number of inhabitants in Peru.
Agriculture GNP	The value of the goods and services produced in the agricultural sector in a specific year at 1994 prices.
Fishing GNP	The value of the goods and services produced in the fishing sector in a specific year at 1994 prices.
Mining and hydrocarbons GNP	The value of the goods and services produced in the mining and hydrocarbons sector in a specific year at 1994 prices.

Table 8B.1 (continued)

Variable	Description
Manufacturing GNP	The value of the goods and services produced in the manufacturing sector in a specific year at 1994 prices.
Construction GNP	The value of the goods and services produced in the construction sector in a specific year at 1994 prices.
Total domestic savings (percent of GNP)	The change in the value of the economy's assets as a whole, calculated as a percentage of GNP.
Public savings (percent of GNP)	The change in the value of the Peruvian public sector's assets calculated as a percentage of the GNP.
Private savings (percent of GNP)	The change in the value of the Peruvian private sector's assets, calculated as a percentage of the GNP.
Total investment (percent of GNP)	The value of total purchases of capital goods as a percentage of GNP.
Public investment (percent of GNP)	The value of public purchases of capital goods as a percentage of GNP.
Private investment (percent of GNP)	The value of private purchases of capital goods as a percentage of GNP.
Current account balance (percent of GNP)	The value of goods produced by domestic residents (including the net factor income from abroad) plus net transfers from abroad, minus the expenditure by domestic residents on goods as a percentage of the GNP. When the current account balance is positive (negative), there is a surplus (deficit) in the current account.
Trade balance (percent of GNP)	The value of exports of goods minus the value of imports of goods, expressed as a percentage of GNP.
Services balance (percent of GNP)	The value of exports of services minus the value of imports of services, expressed as a percentage of GNP.
Net factor income (percent of GNP)	The net income from labor or capital factors, which includes claims on assets abroad and debt interest payments. It is calculated as a percentage of GNP.
Current transfers (percent of GNP)	The value of received foreign assets minus assets transferred outside the country. Any extraordinary contributions, such as donations, are included. It is calculated as a percentage of GNP.

(Table continues on the following page.)

Table 8B.1 (continued)

Variable	Description
Total exports	Total exports, measured in $US millions at 1994 prices.
Total imports	Total imports measured in $US millions at 1994 prices.
Private and public total external debt	The value of debt contracted with foreign agents by public and private organizations, measured in US$ millions at 1994 prices.
Public total external debt	The value of debt contracted with foreign agents by the government, measured in US$ millions at 1994 prices.
RIN (net international reserves)	The value, in US$ millions at 1994 prices, of liquid assets, including international currency, which the Central Bank uses for international transactions.
Inflation (percent)	The percentage change in the general level of prices, as measured by the IPG (defined above).
Export (percent of GNP)	The value of exports as a percentage of GNP. Exports are goods that are produced by the residents of a country and sold to foreigners.
Import (percent of GNP)	The value of imports as a percentage of GNP. Imports are goods that are produced by foreigners and sold to the residents of a country.
Export + import (percent of GNP)	The value of exports plus imports as a percentage of GNP. Exports are goods that are produced by the residents of a country and sold to foreigners. Imports are goods that are produced by foreigners and sold to the residents of a country.
Terms-of-trade index	The price of Peru's tradable goods expressed relative to the price of a market basket of the world's tradable goods. It is approximated by the ratio of Peru's export prices to import prices.
Potable water	The national production of potable water in a year, measured in cubical meters.
Electricity	The national production of electricity in a year, measured in kilowatts per hour.
Telephony	The number of telephone calls in a year.
Vital minimum wage	Legal minimum wage that a firm can pay.
Index of total employment (Jan. 1995 = 100)	The number of persons working at jobs in the market sector divided by the number of workers in January 1995 and multiplied by 100.

Table 8B.1 (continued)

Variable	Description
Strikes	Number of strikes in a year for all industries of the economy. The Ministry of Labor registers the strikes, the number of affected workers, and the total loss of work hours as a result of strikes.
Affected workers	Total number of workers affected by strikes in a year for all industries of the economy.
Man-hours lost	The sum of all lost work hours per worker due to strikes.
Subversive activity	The number of subversive attacks in a year within the Peruvian territory.
Financial variables	
Personal expenses per employee	The ratio of total personal expenses to the total number of employees. Personal expenses are equal to all resources dedicated to labor issues and services in a firm. Total number of employees is the total employment. The employees include white-collar workers and blue-collar workers at full time.
Bad loan portfolio	The ratio of bad loans to the net loan portfolio. Bad loans are defined as expired loans plus legal costs. Net loan portfolio is equal to current accounts less discounts, plus long- and short-term loans, refinanced loans, mortgages, and other loans.
Administrative expenses	The ratio of total administrative expenses to financial income. Administrative expenses are equal to personal expenses, general expenses, depreciation, and amortization. Financial income is equal to income obtained by commissions and interests on loans.
Financial margin per branch	The ratio of the financial margin to the number of branches. Financial margin is equal to financial income (income obtained by commissions and interests on loans) less financial expenses. Branch is defined as the total number of offices.

Source: Author's calculations.

Appendix 8C

Table 8C.1 Evolution of Privatization in the Electricity Sector

1986–93	1994	1995	1996	1997	1998	1999
Electroperú	Electroperú[b]	Electroperú	Electroperú	Electroperú	Electroperú	Electroperú
		Egenor	Egenor	Egenor	Egenor	Egenor
		Egesur	Egesur	Egesur	Egesur	Egesur
		Cahua	Cahua	Cahua	Cahua	Cahua
Electrolima[a]	Luz del Sur	Luz del Sur	Luz del Sur	Luz del Sur	Luz del Sur	Luz del Sur
	Edegel	Edegel	Edegel	Edegel	Edegel	Edegel
	Edelnor	Edelnor[d]	Edelnor	Edelnor	Edelnor	Edelnor
	Electrolima[c]	EDE-Chancay[d]	EDE-Cañete	EDE-Cañete	EDE-Cañete	EDE-Cañete
		EDE-Cañete				
Elec. Centro		Elec. Centro	Elec. Centro	Elec. Centro	Elec. Centro	Elec. Centro
Elec. Nor Oeste		Elec. Nor Oeste	Elec. Nor Oeste	Elec. Nor Oeste	Elec. Nor Oeste	Elec. Nor Oeste
Elect. Norte		Elect. Norte	Elect. Norte	Elect. Norte	Elect. Norte	Elect. Norte
Elec. Nor. Medio		Elec. Nor. Medio	Elec. Nor. Medio	Elec. Nor. Medio	Elec. Nor. Medio	Elec. Nor. Medio
Elec. Oriente		Elec. Oriente	Elec. Oriente	Elec. Oriente	Elec. Oriente	Elec. Oriente
Elec. Sur		Elec. Sur	Elec. Sur	Elec. Sur	Elec. Sur	Elec. Sur
Elec. Sur Este		Elec. Sur Este	Elec. Sur Este	Elec. Sur Este	Elec. Sur Este	Elec. Sur Este
Elec. Sur Medio		Elec. Sur Medio	Elec. Sur Medio	Elec. Sur Medio	Elec. Sur Medio	Elec. Sur Medio
Seal	Seal	Seal	Seal	Seal	Seal	Seal
		Emsemsa	Emsemsa	Emsemsa	Emsemsa	Emsemsa
		Etevensa	Etevensa	Etevensa	Etevensa	Etevensa

Egasa	Egasa	Electro Andes	Egasa	Electro Andes	Egasa	Electro Andes
Gera	Gera	Eepsa	Gera	Eepsa	Gera	Eepsa
Egemsa	Egemsa	Chavimochic	Egemsa	Chavimochic	Egemsa	Chavimochic
Etecen	Etecen		Etecen	Shougesa	Etecen	Shougesa
Etesur	Etesur		Etesur	Pariac	Etesur	Pariac
Electro Ucayali	Electro Ucayali		Electro Ucayali	Electro Pangoa	Electro Ucayali	Electro Pangoa
	Coelvisa		Coelvisa		Coelvisa	Emseusa
	Sers		Sers		Sers	Electro Tocache
	C.H. Virú					Electro Puno
						San Gabán

a. Electrolima was divided into four different companies: Edelnor (distribution), Luz del Sur (distribution), Edegel (generation), and Electrolima (residual company).

b. Electroperú split into four different companies: Electroperú, Egenor, Egesur, and Cahua.

c. Electrolima (residual company) was again divided into two companies: EDE-Chancay and EDE-Cañete.

d. The merger between Edelnor and EDE-Chancay resulted in Edelnor.

Source: Author's tabulations.

Table 8C.2 Evolution of Privatization in the Financial Sector

Name	Birth year	State participation	Financial reform: 1992–98	1986	1987	1988	1989	1990	1991	1992
Amazónico	1962	Yes	Liquidación	Amazónico	Amazónico	Amazónico	Amazónico	Amazónico	Amazónico	Amazónico
America	1966			America	America	America				
Bandesco	1980			Bandesco	Bandesco	Bandesco	Bandesco	Bandesco	Bandesco	Bandesco
Central de Madrid	1984			Central de Madrid	Central de Madrid					
CCC	1988						CCC	CCC	CCC	
Citibank	1920			Citibank	Citibank	Citibank	Citibank	Citibank	Citibank	Citibank
Comercio	1967			Comercio	Comercio	Comercio	Comercio	Comercio	Comercio	Comercio
Continental	1951	Yes	Privatización	Continental	Continental	Continental	Continental	Continental	Continental	Continental
Continorte	1961	Yes	Liquidación	Continorte	Continorte	Continorte	Continorte	Continorte	Continorte	
Crédito	1889			Crédito	Crédito	Crédito	Crédito	Crédito	Crédito	Crédito
De los Andes	1962	Yes	Liquidación	De los Andes	De los andes	De los andes	De los Andes	De los andes	De los Andes	
Del Norte	1960			Del Norte	Del Norte	Del Norte	Del Norte	Del Norte	Del Norte	Del Norte
Extebandes	1982			Extebandes	Extebandes	Extebandes	Extebandes	Extebandes	Extebandes	Extebandes
Financiero	1986				Financiero	Financiero	Financiero	Financiero	Financiero	Financiero
Interamericano	1991								Interamericano	Interamericano
Interandino	1990						Interandino	Interandino	Interandino	Interandino
Interbank	1897	Yes	Privatización	Interbank	Interbank	Interbank	Interbank	Interbank	Interbank	Interbank
Latino	1982			Latino	Latino	Latino	Latino	Latino	Latino	Latino
Lima	1952			Lima	Lima	Lima	Lima	Lima	Lima	Lima
Londres	1936			Londres	Londres					
Manhattan	1984			Manhattan						
Mercantil	1984			Mercantil	Mercantil	Mercantil	Mercantil	Mercantil	Mercantil	Mercantil
Popular	1889	Yes	Liquidación	Popular	Popular	Popular	Popular	Popular	Popular	
Probank	1990							Probank	Probank	Probank
Sur Perú	1962	Yes	Liquidación	Sur Perú	Sur Perú	Sur Perú	Sur Perú	Sur Perú	Sur Perú	Sur Perú
Surmebanc	1962	Yes	Liquidación	Surmebanc	Surmebanc	Surmebanc	Surmebanc	Surmebanc	Surmebanc	
Tokyo	1965			Tokyo	Tokyo					

Name		1993	1994	1995	1996	1997	1998	1999	2000
Wiese	1943			Wiese	Wiese	Wiese	Wiese	Wiese	Wiese
Sudamericano	1993								
Banex	1993								
Nuevo Mundo	1993								
Del Libertador	1994								
Del Trabajo	1994								
Solventa	1994								
Serbanco	1996								
Boston	1996								
Republica	1980								
Orion	1995								
Del pais	1997								
Mibanco	1998								
BNP-andes	1999								
Amazónico									
America									
Bandesco		Bandesco	Bandesco						
Central de Madrid									
CCC									
Citibank		Citibank	Citibank	Citibank	Citibank	Citibank	Citibank	Citibank	Citibank
Comercio		Comercio	Comercio	Comercio	Comercio	Comercio	Comercio	Comercio	Comercio
Continental		Continental	Continental	Continental	Continental	Continental	Continental	Continental	Continental
Continorte									
Crédito		Crédito	Crédito	Crédito	Crédito	Crédito	Crédito	Crédito	Crédito
De los Andes									
Del Norte		Del Norte	Del Norte	Del Norte	Del Norte	Del Norte	Del Norte	Del Norte	NBK-Boston
Extebandes		Extebandes	Extebandes	Extebandes	Extebandes	Extebandes	Standard	Standard	Standard
Financiero		Financiero	Financiero	Financiero	Financiero	Financiero	Financiero	Financiero	Financiero

(Table continues on the following page.)

Table 8C.2 (continued)

Name	1993	1994	1995	1996	1997	1998	1999	2000
Interamericano	Interamericano	Interamericano	Interamericano	Interamericano	Interamericano	Interamericano	Interamericano	Interamericano
Interandino	Interandino	Interandino	Santander	Santander	Santander	Santander	Santander	Santander
Interbank	Interbank	Interbank	Interbank	Interbank	Interbank	Interbank	Interbank	Interbank
Latino	Latino	Latino	Latino	Latino	Latino	Latino	Latino	Latino
Lima	Lima	Lima	Lima	Lima	Lima	Lima	→ Fusión con Wiese	
Londres								
Manhattan								
Mercantil	Mercantil	Mercantil	Mercantil	→ Fusión con Santander				
Popular								
Probank	Probank	Probank	Probank	Probank	Probank	Probank	→ Fusión con Del Norte	
Sur Perú	Sur Perú	Sur Perú	Sur Perú	Sur Perú	Sur Perú	Sur Perú	Sur Perú	→ Fusión con Del Norte
Surmebanc								
Tokyo								
Wiese	Wiese	Wiese	Wiese	Wiese	Wiese	Wiese	Wiese	Wiese
Sudamericano	Sudamericano	Sudamericano	Sudamericano	Sudamericano	Sudamericano	Sudamericano	Sudamericano	Sudamericano
Banex	Banex	Banex	Banex	Banex	Banex	Banex		
Nuevo Mundo	Nuevo Mundo	Nuevo Mundo	Nuevo Mundo	Nuevo Mundo	Nuevo Mundo	Nuevo Mundo	Nuevo Mundo	Nuevo Mundo
Del Libertador		Del Libertador	Del Libertador	← Fusión con Sur Peru				
Del Trabajo		Del Trabajo	Del Trabajo	Del Trabajo	Del Trabajo	Del Trabajo	Del Trabajo	→ Fusión con Del Norte
Solventa			Solventa	Solventa	Solventa	Solventa	→ Fusión con Del Norte	
Serbanco				Serbanco	Serbanco	Serbanco	Serbanco	
Boston				Boston	Boston	Boston	Boston	Boston
Republica				Republica	Republica	Republica		
Orion					Orion	Orion	Orion	
Del pais					Del pais	Del pais	→ Fusión con Nuevo Mundo	
Mibanco						Mibanco	Mibanco	Mibanco
BNP-Andes							BNP-Andes	BNP-Andes

Source: Superintendencia de Banca y Seguros, Memorias 1986–1991.
Superintendencia de Banca y Seguros, Información Financiera Mensual 1992–2000.

Table 8D.1 Basic Statistics of Privatized Firms

Firm	Number	ROS	ROA	ROE	Debt to assets	Debt to equity	Sales efficiency	Net income efficiency	Number of workers	Assets to employment	Net income	Assets
Nonfinancial firms	336	−0.249	−0.039	0.595	0.469	33.372	369.818	−43.185	1,337	1,443.96	−70,480	1,540,130
		(0.72)	(0.23)	(12.18)	(0.55)	(519.60)	(554.37)	(262.36)	(2,533.35)	(3,508.70)	(802,842)	(3,612,434)
		332	298	297	301	300	317	317	336	296	331	311
Telecommunications												
Telefonica	15	0.174	0.077	0.136	0.462	1.047	270.121	37.457	10,523	663.55	343,455	5,398,240
		(0.22)	(0.09)	(0.17)	(0.15)	(0.77)	(177.89)	(51.47)	(4,284.89)	(490.97)	(427,695)	(2,266,784)
			10	10	10	10	13	13	14	11	14	11
Energy												
Electro Centro	14	−0.443	−0.034	−0.053	0.263	0.407	146.745	−43.999	618	722.48	−31,089	388,853
		(0.76)	(0.05)	(0.08)	(0.14)	(0.29)	(72.39)	(60.80)	(150.04)	(338.59)	(42,847)	(99,896)
		14	10	10	10	10	14	14	14	11	14	11
Electro Nor Oeste	13	−0.600	−0.141	−0.259	0.459	1.140	203.269	−94.758	372	695.36	−35,737	240,917
		(0.95)	(0.25)	(0.43)	(0.18)	(1.07)	(89.24)	(114.65)	(87.02)	(283.27)	(47,839)	(103,963)
		13	10	10	10	10	13	13	13	11	13	11
Electro Norte	14	−0.473	−0.105	−0.534	0.455	2.030	156.803	−54.046	327	405.53	−18,137	125,990
		(0.60)	(0.08)	(1.20)	(0.22)	(4.00)	(85.14)	(44.42)	(46.00)	(135.30)	(15,795)	(33,007)
		13	10	10	10	10	13	13	14	11	13	11
Electro Norte Medio	14	−0.367	−0.025	−0.066	0.387	1.010	260.329	−69.090	550	1,024.26	−41,454	468,014
		(0.66)	(0.04)	(0.10)	(0.24)	(1.14)	(183.68)	(116.46)	(140.05)	(777.21)	(71,836)	(298,246)
		14	10	10	10	10	14	14	14	11	14	11

(Table continues on the following page.)

Table 8D.1 (continued)

Firm	Number	ROS	ROA	ROE	Debt to assets	Debt to equity	Sales efficiency	Net income efficiency	Number of workers	Assets to employment	Net income	Assets
Electro Oriente	14	-0.437	-0.046	-0.074	0.329	0.555	237.351	-84.553	199	1,285.01	-17,795	240,264
		(0.61)	(0.04)	(0.07)	(0.14)	(0.39)	(86.83)	(95.37)	(32.33)	(475.32)	(20,692)	(82,307)
		14	10	10	10	10	14	14	14	11	14	11
Electro Sur	14	-0.408	-0.124	-0.010	0.419	0.333	187.524	-50.600	152	519.93	-8,429	74,913
		(0.61)	(0.23)	(0.73)	(0.41)	(1.71)	(67.67)	(71.51)	(23.42)	(327.13)	(11,603)	(50,539)
		14	10	10	10	10	14	14	14	11	14	11
Electro Sur Este	14	-0.283	-0.027	-0.054	0.313	0.578	203.681	-51.568	313	778.74	-16,760	233,936
		(0.46)	(0.03)	(0.08)	(0.21)	(0.62)	(60.11)	(70.13)	(35.53)	(333.17)	(23,075)	(87,921)
		14	10	10	10	10	14	14	14	11	14	11
Electro Sur Medio	14	-0.248	-0.044	-0.100	0.295	0.516	140.550	-15.698	368	337.86	-7,816	110,249
		(0.45)	(0.08)	(0.18)	(0.18)	(0.47)	(74.78)	(26.94)	(124.89)	(135.52)	(13,078)	(36,632)
		14	10	10	10	10	14	14	14	13	14	11
Electrolima	14	-0.031	0.012	0.012	0.345	0.577	415.272	47.692	3,252	1,370.89	51,941	3,533,158
		(0.30)	(0.05)	(0.08)	(0.12)	(0.29)	(323.15)	(94.74)	(1,275.97)	(967.23)	(221,382)	(1,480,396)
							14	14	14	13	14	13
Electroperú	14	-0.475	0.010	0.017	0.453	0.905	540.289	69.958	1,503	8,463.11	-26,213	12,500,000
		(1.52)	(0.03)	(0.05)	(0.10)	(0.47)	(497.82)	(240.49)	(806.17)	(3,448.23)	(320,191)	(9,487,072)
							14	14	14	13	14	13
Sanitation												
SEDAPAL	14	-0.279	-0.002	-0.001	0.192	0.241	133.730	-0.536	2,514	1,059.30	-47,248	2,500,485
		(0.70)	(0.03)	(0.04)	(0.05)	(0.08)	(78.19)	(40.12)	(954.74)	(408.21)	(183,016)	(1,143,402)
Mining												
Centromin	5	-0.133	-0.069	-0.541	0.877	8.169	1,909.095	-206.377	714	3,935.96	-147,339	2,810,561
		(0.17)	(0.10)	(0.70)	(0.04)	(3.71)	(578.95)	(257.10)	(0.00)	(2,321.44)	(183,552)	(1,657,888)

Cerro Verde	6	−0.191 (0.73) 5	−0.095 (0.36) 5	−0.157 (0.68) 5	0.445 (0.22) 6	1.025 (0.75) 6	257.143 (127.13) 5	−25.517 (148.92) 5	556 (114.88) 6	545.46 (347.76) 6	−15,259 (80,744) 5
											293,492 (165,074) 6
Condestable	14	−0.097 (0.45) 14	−0.020 (0.21) 14	20.031 (52.62) 14	0.797 (0.23) 14	676.505 (2,395.99) 14	775.598 (326.46) 7	97.327 (160.30) 7	28 (0.00) 7	902.60 (694.27) 7	150 (5,534) 13
											24,341 (13,553) 14
Hierro Peru	8	−0.293 (0.60) 8	−0.082 (0.14) 8	−0.457 (0.85) 8	0.628 (0.20) 8	2.743 (2.72) 8	98.712 (8.29) 3	−0.329 (6.73) 3	2003 (145.42) 3	177.58 (28.59) 3	−26,824 (67,554) 8
											493,081 (287,769) 8
Minero Peru	5	−1.213 (1.81) 5	−0.215 (0.26) 5	−0.976 (1.10) 5	0.810 (0.04) 5	4.474 (1.24) 5	716.930 (479.05) 3	−634.945 (717.66) 3	984 (0.00) 3	3,152.68 (2,747.58) 3	−624,833 (706,262) 8
											3,102,620 (2,704,137) 8
Tintaya	4	−0.190 (0.37) 4	−0.050 (0.08) 4	−0.805 (1.61) 4	−0.232 (1.89) 4	13.902 (26.50) 4	3,292.367 (786.45) 3	−541.116 (1,263.80) 3	88 (0.00) 3	21,114.60 (17,047.68) 3	−47,634 (111,257) 8
											1,858,315 (1,500,480) 8
Industry											
Cemento Sur	13	0.135 (0.20) 8	0.059 (0.16) 8	0.076 (0.26) 7	0.365 (0.28) 8	0.407 (0.21) 7	198.682 (86.87) 8	24.380 (36.09) 8	141 (15.04) 13	270.92 (138.58) 8	2,873 (4,010) 8
											35,505 (14,562) 8
Cemento Yura	10	−1.152 (1.65) 7	−0.087 (0.23) 7	−2.199 (5.64) 7	0.608 (0.22) 7	6.184 (12.30) 7	299.780 (166.06) 7	−274.507 (595.65) 7	199 (10.12) 10	1,436.22 (1,081.74) 7	−56,090 (119,813) 7
											284,337 (220,114) 7
Cementos Lima	14	0.144 (0.14) 14	0.080 (0.07) 14	0.115 (0.10) 14	0.241 (0.13) 14	0.353 (0.24) 14	785.835 (268.28) 14	138.690 (111.02) 14	340 (56.83) 14	1,886.88 (1,052.64) 14	43,628 (35,490) 14
											657,215 (451,104) 14
CNP S.A.	15	−0.234 (0.51) 9	−0.100 (0.21) 9	−0.823 (2.47) 9	0.747 (0.26) 9	0.421 (6.92) 9	49.333 (17.35) 9	−6.827 (12.94) 9	399 (48.77) 15	57.97 (20.28) 9	−2,157 (4,419) 9
											21,189 (5,758) 9

(Table continues on the following page.)

Table 8D.1 (continued)

Firm	Number	ROS	ROA	ROE	Debt to assets	Debt to equity	Sales efficiency	Net income efficiency	Number of workers	Assets to employment	Net income	Assets
Cerper	3	0.065	0.105	0.176	0.412	0.707	0.000	0.000	0	0.00	1,213	11,460
		(0.10)	(0.13)	(0.22)	(0.04)	(0.12)	(0.00)	(0.00)	(0.00)	(0.00)	(1,469)	(217)
		10	10	10	10	10	10	10	12	10	10	10
Sider Peru S.A.	12	−0.149	−0.051	−0.105	0.505	1.414	138.729	−14.741	3,271	262.68	−73,433	848,168
		(0.55)	(0.21)	(0.76)	(0.19)	(1.17)	(64.26)	(47.50)	(1,052.99)	(166.00)	(153,536)	(724,436)
		10	10	10	10	10	10	10	12	10	10	10
Empresa de la Sal	10	−0.051	−0.023	−0.041	0.358	0.575	113.040	−1.783	187	162.10	−458	19,505
		(0.16)	(0.09)	(0.15)	(0.07)	(0.18)	(60.39)	(11.86)	(147.11)	(90.17)	(1,858)	(1,952)
		10	10	10	10	10	10	10	10	10	10	10
Industrias Navales	6	0.018	0.069	0.062	0.333	0.675	90.090	6.622	34	140.94	279	4,483
		(0.37)	(0.12)	(0.28)	(0.20)	(0.73)	(40.56)	(22.17)	(13.29)	(48.94)	(657)	(1,076)
La Pampilla	1	0.024	0.025	0.039	0.362	0.566	1,486.441	35.453	341	1,442.04	12,089	491,734
Petroperu S.A.	13	−0.540	−0.403	−1.394	1.422	2.455	1,055.132	−274.642	4,772	793.46	−1,592,135	3,835,390
		(1.10)	(0.81)	(2.28)	(2.04)	(11.70)	(1,216.42)	(657.35)	(1,733.10)	(759.62)	(3,759,827)	(4,588,286)
		13	13	13	13	13	13	13	13	13	13	13

	(1)											
Quimica del Pacifico	6	0.129	0.081	0.118	0.314	0.497	154.684	18.946	323	210.63	6,379	66,508
		(0.11)	(0.05)	(0.06)	(0.11)	(0.30)	(77.20)	(19.41)	(95.18)	(117.05)	(8,553)	(49,123)
Renasa	13	0.050	0.024	0.042	0.357	0.576	170.530	7.394	82	221.96	1,235	17,262
		(0.21)	(0.14)	(0.21)	(0.08)	(0.19)	(64.52)	(33.13)	(31.24)	(93.80)	(4,067)	(10,391)
SEAL	14	−0.224	−0.005	−0.017	0.377	0.781	263.449	−27.685	433	636.37	−16,490	245,730
		(0.38)	(0.06)	(0.11)	(0.17)	(0.77)	(167.86)	(54.21)	(146.53)	(351.27)	(27,328)	(185,602)
		14	10	10	11	11	14	14	14	11	14	11
Solgas	5	−0.003	0.042	0.060	0.323	1.743	309.336	−0.852	230	184.35	−196	42,403
		(0.07)	(0.13)	(0.14)	(0.35)	(3.32)	(154.65)	(29.10)	(0.00)	(124.02)	(6,694)	(28,530)
Sufisa	6	−0.047	−0.075	−8.294	0.757	24.466	339.473	−6.461	401	451.71	−7,384	159,632
		(0.18)	(0.20)	(20.30)	(0.32)	(46.83)	(81.74)	(51.93)	(124.37)	(236.92)	(26,100)	(47,332)
Financial firms	340	0.725	0.080	1.600	0.883	9.462	277.628	269.940	1179	1636.41	1,904,351	1,738,226
		(12.85)	(1.32)	(28.00)	(0.07)	(4.43)	(182.05)	(4,621.28)	(1,573.68)	(1,182.42)	(34,800,000)	(2,983,462)
Continental	15	0.080	0.012	0.167	0.920	13.073	273.887	18.716	2913	1,656.87	52,323	4,491,742
		(0.05)	(0.01)	(0.11)	(0.02)	(6.10)	(109.48)	(12.73)	(491.96)	(923.11)	(34,154)	(1,929,788)
Interbank	15	0.056	0.011	0.121	0.908	10.313	254.653	12.846	2361	1,310.12	28,045	2,408,220
		(0.05)	(0.01)	(0.10)	(0.02)	(2.22)	(141.65)	(12.25)	(911.15)	(974.21)	(27,476)	(886,993)

Note: This table reports raw results for performance indicators (see appendix 8B for variable definitions). The results are simple means for each one of the variables. Standard deviations are shown in parentheses. Column (1) presents the number of available observations per firm or group of firms used to obtain the estimations. However, when there are fewer observations for a specific variable, this number is shown under the standard deviation for such a variable.

Source: Author's calculations.

Table 8E.1 Changes in Performance after Privatization for Telefónica del Perú

Sector	Means		First differences		Diff. in diff.	S-Francia[c] prob > z	Kolmogorov-Smirnov
	Pre-privatization	Post-privatization	t-test[a]	Hotelling[b]	Hotelling[b]		
Performance measure (P_i)							
Profitability							
Return on sales (ROS)	-0.0099 (0.029)	0.4083 (0.028)	-10.2639***	105.3480***	49.6114***	0.1974	0.001***
Return on assets (ROA)	0.0024 (0.014)	0.1714 (0.021)	-6.9935***	48.9086***	24.4539***	0.3279	0.001***
Return on equity (ROE)	0.0036 (0.032)	0.3128 (0.014)	-7.8995***	62.4022***	33.4508***	0.2083	0.007***
Operating efficiency							
Sales efficiency (SALEFF)[d]	143.9187 (23.373)	455.3162 (47.931)	-6.3317***	40.0909***	42.5110***	0.0382	0.007***
Net income efficiency (NIEFF)[d]	-0.9794 (3.662)	93.7577 (12.355)	-8.3231***	69.2732***	47.2743***	0.0299	0.008***
Employment							
Total employment (EMPL)	14125.6 (575.074)	5992.17 (543.713)	9.9687***	99.3749***	38.4810***	0.1090	0.001***
Leverage							
Debt to assets (LEV)	0.4999 (0.055)	0.4584 (0.049)	0.5444	0.2964	1.9149	0.8725	0.921
Debt to equity (LEV2)	1.2433 (0.339)	0.9228 (0.170)	0.7603	0.5781	1.6069	0.0026	0.921

Coverage

Lines per worker (LINES)	39.6038	261.0051	−8.0536***	64.8610***	0.0047	0.001***
	(9.763)	(78.008)				

* Significant at the 10 percent level.
** Significant at the 5 percent level.
*** Significant at the 1 percent level.

Note: First and second differences for changes in performance are shown, for each empirical proxy, using the mean values (see appendix table 8B.1 for variable definitions). Columns 1 and 2 present the mean values before and after privatization (the year of privatization is 1994). Columns 3 and 4 show results for two tests for significance in changes in performance after privatization (first differences): *t*-test (two-tailed Wilcoxon signed-rank test) and the Hotelling test. Column 5 displays significance of difference-in-difference results using a Hotelling test (control group is the water and sanitation enterprise SEDAPAL). Column 6 presents Shapiro-Francia test for normality. Finally, column 7 shows the results for the Kolmogorov-Smirnov (K–S) statistic, a nonparametric test used to formally test the equality of the empirical hazards functions of the different pre- and postprivatization performance indicators.

a. *t*-test for Ho (null hypothesis) for difference between means. Numbers are unequal.

$$t = \frac{(\bar{X}_1 - \bar{X}_2)}{S\,\bar{x}_1 - \bar{x}_2} = \frac{(\bar{X}_1 - \bar{X}_2)}{\sqrt{\dfrac{(n_1 - 1)\,s_1^2 + (n_2 - 1)\,s_2^2}{(n_1 + n_2 - 2)}} * \sqrt{\dfrac{1}{n_1} + \dfrac{1}{n_2}}}$$

where x is an $l \times k$ matrix of the means and S is the estimated covariance matrix.

b. Test of equality:

$$T^2 = (\bar{x}_1 - \bar{x}_2)\,S^{-1}(\bar{x}_1 - \bar{x}_2)'$$

c. Shapiro-Francia test for normality. Ho (null hypothesis) variable is normally distributed.
d. Thousands of nuevos soles.
Source: Author's calculations.

Table 8E.2 Changes in Performance after Privatization for Electrolima

| | Means | | First differences | | Diff. in diff. | S-Francia[c] | Kolmogorov- |
	Pre-privatization	Post-privatization	t-test[a]	Hotelling[b]	Hotelling[b]	prob > z	Smirnov
Sector							
Performance measure (P_i)							
Profitability							
Return on sales (ROS)	−0.1811	0.2018	−2.6239**	6.8848**	3.6440*	0.0032	0.017***
	(0.320)	(0.024)					
Return on assets (ROA)	−0.0205	0.0661	−4.2075***	17.7033***	7.5367**	0.2327	0.017***
	(0.016)	(0.004)					
Return on equity (ROE)	−0.0335	0.0850	−3.2998***	10.8884***	2.4812	0.0583	0.017***
	(0.028)	(0.005)					
Operating efficiency							
Sales efficiency (SALEFF)[d]	162.9284	803.5256	−12.5352***	157.1316***	119.0269***	0.0155	0.002***
	(16.391)	(60.559)					
Net income efficiency (NIEFF)[d]	−19.0959	163.0455	−9.4166***	88.6730***	33.3117***	0.0424	0.017***
	(11.569)	(16.074)					
Employment							
Total employment (EMPL)	4210.3	1855.60	7.2221***	52.1582***	50.8770***	0.1292	0.002***
	(239.607)	(138.342)					
Leverage							
Debt to assets (LEV)	0.4302	0.2208	5.1558***	26.5819***	15.2595***	0.6949	0.001***
	(0.023)	(0.037)					
Debt to equity (LEV2)	0.7739	0.2952	4.7567***	22.6259***	48.3539***	0.8744	0.002***
	(0.069)	(0.062)					

Coverage						
Lines per worker (LINES)	229.3598	794.4770	−8.8517***	78.3535***	0.0183	0.002***
	(57.742)	(169.273)				

* Significant at the 10 percent level.
** Significant at the 5 percent level.
*** Significant at the 1 percent level.

Note: First and second differences for changes in performance are shown, for each empirical proxy, using the mean values (see appendix table 8B.1 for variable definitions). Columns 1 and 2 present the mean values before and after privatization (the year of privatization is 1994). Columns 3 and 4 show results for two tests for significance in changes in performance after privatization (first differences): *t*-test (two-tailed Wilcoxon signed-rank test) and the Hotelling test. Column 5 displays significance of difference-in-difference results using a Hotelling test (control group is basd on Electro Oriente, Electro Sur, Electro Sur Este, and Electro Sur Medio for SALEFF, NIEFF, and EMPL). Column 6 presents Shapiro-Francia test for normality. Finally, column 7 shows the results for the Kolmogorov-Smirnov (K-S) statistic, a nonparametric test used to formally test the equality of the empirical hazards functions of the different pre- and postprivatization performance indicators.

a. *t*-test for Ho (null hypothesis) for difference between means. Numbers are unequal.

$$t = \frac{(\bar{X}_1 - \bar{X}_2)}{S \, \bar{x}_1 - \bar{x}_2} = \frac{(\bar{X}_1 - \bar{X}_2)}{\sqrt{\dfrac{(n_1 - 1) \, s_1^2 + (n_2 - 1) \, s_2^2}{(n_1 + n_2 - 2)}} \, \sqrt{\dfrac{1}{n_1} + \dfrac{1}{n_2}}}$$

where x is an $l \times k$ matrix of the means and S is the estimated covariance matrix.

b. Test of equality:

$$T^2 = (\bar{x}_1 - \bar{x}_2) \, S^{-1} (\bar{x}_1 - \bar{x}_2)'$$

c. Shapiro-Francia test for normality. Ho (null hypothesis) variable is normally distributed.
d. Thousands of nuevos soles.
Source: Author's calculations.

Table 8E.3 Changes in Performance after Privatization for Electroperú
(Differences between means and difference-in-difference tests)

Sector	Means		First differences		Diff. in diff.	S-Francia[c] prob > z	Kolmogorov-Smirnov
	Pre-privatization	Post-privatization	t-test[a]	Hotelling[b]	Hotelling[b]		
Performance measure (Pi)							
Profitability							
Return on sales (ROS)	-0.8485 (0.605)	0.2229 (0.096)	-1.1486	1.3194	1.6025	0.0001	0.274
Return on assets (ROA)	0.0008 (0.008)	0.0300 (0.012)	-1.9676*	3.8716*	1.6639	0.4842	0.234
Return on equity (ROE)	0.0021 (0.015)	0.0483 (0.021)	-1.7341	3.0070	0.2457	0.5607	0.234
Operating efficiency							
Sales efficiency (SALEFF)[d]	205.7400 (57.770)	1222.7810 (51.656)	-10.7568***	115.7089***	45.2077***	0.0177	0.003***
Net income efficiency (NIEFF)[d]	-26.6490 (65.580)	285.7193 (119.717)	-2.4842**	6.1711**	3.3408*	0.6345	0.197

Employment

Total employment (EMPL)	1976.7 (194.342)	593.00 (30.257)	4.6217***	21.3599***	9.9168***	0.3306	0.003***

Leverage

Debt to assets (LEV)	0.4757 (0.035)	0.4010 (0.049)	1.1977	1.4345	3.5220*	0.0858	0.749
Debt to equity (LEV2)	1.0039 (0.185)	0.7000 (0.125)	1.0279	1.0565	2.4812	0.0005	0.749

Coverage

Lines per worker (LINES)	0.0034 (0.002)	0.0216 (0.008)	−6.8787***	47.3159***		0.0031	0.003***

* Significant at the 10 percent level.
** Significant at the 5 percent level.
*** Significant at the 1 percent level.
Note: For explanation, see appendix table 8E.2.
Source: Author's calculations.

Notes

This chapter has been prepared for the project "Costs and Benefits of Privatization in Latin America" of the Inter-American Development Bank's Latin American Research Network. Dean Hyslop gave valuable advice on the econometric analysis of these results; and Florencio López-de-Silanes, Alberto Chong, Alberto Pascó-Font, and all the participants in the IDB Research Network on Costs and Benefits of Privatization offered numerous and helpful comments. The author is also indebted to the enormous effort and support of Virgilio Galdo throughout this project, as well as to his remarkably talented team of research assistants: Daniel Oda, Jorge de la Roca, Gissele Gajate, and Linette Lecussan. Finally, the author thanks the Comisión de Promoción de la Inversión Privada (COPRI) for granting access to the White Books of all the privatized firms.

1. All dollar amounts are U.S. dollars unless otherwise indicated.
2. For the period 1987–92 the annual change in gross domestic product at constant prices was −4.9 percent, annual inflation was 733.1 percent (reaching a high of 7,649.6 percent in 1990), and the real effective exchange rate depreciation for the period was −2.04 percent.
3. According to Apoyo (2002), during the second half of 1985, the amount of banking deposits reached 23 percent of gross national product (GNP); five years later, in May 1990, bank deposits fell to 5 percent of GNP. A similar drop also occurred in the net internal credit of the banking system to the private sector (interest rates rose between 200 and 400 percent annually in real terms).
4. These figures are for the Lima metropolitan area; see *Perú en Números* 1991, Cuánto S.A.
5. Apoyo (2002).
6. The first 26 CEPRIs initiated their operations in February 1992.
7. This entailed the creation of the Commission for the Promotion of Private Concessions in 1997, which was later absorbed by COPRI.
8. The slowdown in privatizations between 1997 and 2000 is attributable to domestic and foreign factors, among them, the Russian financial crisis, "El Niño," and the Peruvian political crisis.
9. Telefonica was no stranger to the acquisition of Latin American telecommunications providers, having already bought the former Teléfonos de Chile, currently known as CTC, and Argentina's ENTEL.
10. Although the monopoly was initially scheduled to expire in June 1999, the TdP moved the expiration forward to August 1, 1998.
11. This transaction corresponds to the shares not purchased by the workers of Banco Continental and subsidiaries as part of their preferential right conferred by LD 674. In agreement with the contract, these shares had to be purchased by Holding Continental S.A. at the auction price.
12. The privatization year is the year in which the government sold, for the first time, a certain amount of shares.
13. The test evaluates the closeness of the distributions $\lambda^{pre-priv}$ and $\lambda^{post-priv}$ by computing the least upper bound of all pointwise differences $|\lambda^{post-priv}(x) - \lambda^{pre-priv}(x)|$. The K-S statistic can be written as:

$$D = \sup_x[|\lambda^{post-priv}(x) - \lambda^{pre-priv}(x)|]$$

The null hypothesis ($H_0 : \lambda^{post-priv} = \lambda^{pre-priv}$) is accepted if $\lambda^{post-priv}$ is sufficiently close to $\lambda^{pre-priv}$, in other words, if the value of D is sufficiently small or smaller than the critical value at a certain significance level.

14. Heterogeneity may also be present but can be controlled by pooling the data.

15. For further details, see Arellano and Bond (1991, 1998).

16. This statistic is distributed Chi-squared in the number of overidentifying restrictions. The null hypothesis is that the additional moment conditions are approximately satisfied.

17. Hansen (1982) showed that the optimal weighting matrix for this class of estimators is $W = \text{AsyVar}[1/N \, Z'e]$, where Z is the $N \times L$ matrix of instruments and e is the $N \times 1$ matrix of the GMM residuals. For the procedure followed for N observations, the optimal W is given by:

$$W = (1/N^2) \sum_{i=1}^{N} z_i z_i^T e_i^2$$

where z_i is the ith row of Z and e_i is the ith element of e, and GMMIV saves W in $e(W)$.

18. Among the companies acquired, the most important are Lar Carbon, Sia, and Nisa, acquired by Cementos Lima; Petrolube, acquired by Mobil Oil; Enata, acquired by Tabacalera del Sur S.A.; Compania Minera Mahr Tunel and Compania Minera Paragsha, acquired by Volcan; and Planta de Cemento Rioja, acquired by Cementos Norte Pacasmayo.

19. An unweighted and locally weighted smoothing is carried out.

20. Barber and Lyon (1996) suggest that sample firms must be matched to control firms with similar pre-event performance, which is especially difficult in studies of privatized firms, but SEDAPAL went through the same reform as the privatized firms.

21. For this purpose a probit model was used to estimate the propensity score. For further reference, see Heckman and Hotz (1989); Heckman and others (1996); Heckman, Ichimura, and Todd (1997).

22. It is important to mention that Peru had possibly the most restrictive and protective labor legislation of any Latin American country. After the successive waves of reform in 1991 and 1995, no other country had so liberalized its labor market (Lora and Márquez 1998; Márquez and Pagés 1998; Saavedra and Torero 1999). Such drastic reform must be considered when looking at the impact of privatization on employment.

23. Wages of the privatized firms increased significantly after privatization, in both absolute and relative terms with respect to the industry. On average, salaries increased 180 percent in the privatized companies and were 91 percent higher than the average of the specific industry of the privatized firm.

24. Note that, as in La Porta and López-de-Silanes (1999), the methodology overstates the contribution of layoffs, given the assumption that laid-off workers had zero productivity.

References

Arellano, M., and S. Bond. 1991. "Some Tests of Specification for Panel Data: Monte Carlo Evidence and an Application to Employment Equations." *Review of Economic Studies* 58: 277–97.

———. 1998. *Dynamic Panel Data Estimation Using DPD98 for Gauss: a Guide for Users.* Oxford, U.K.: Oxford University.

Apoyo. 2002. *Análisis de coyuntura, perspectivas económicas, tendencias.* Apoyo, Lima.

Barber, B., and J. Lyon. 1996. "Detecting Abnormal Operating Performance: The Empirical Power and Specification of Test Statistics." *Journal of Financial Economics* 41: 539–99.

Boardman, Anthony, and Aidan R. Vining. 1989. "Ownership and Performance in Competitive Environments: A Comparison of the Performance of Private, Mixed, and State-Owned Enterprises." *Journal of Law and Economics* 32: 1–33.

Boubakri, Narjess, and Jean Claude Cosset. 1998. "The Financial and Operating Performance of Newly Privatized Firms: Evidence from Developing Countries." *Journal of Finance* 53 (3): 1081–110.

D'Souza, Juliet, and William L. Megginson. 1999. "The Financial and Operating Performance of Privatized Firms during the 1990s." *Journal of Finance* 54 (4): 1397–438.

Galal, A., L. Jones, P. Tandon, and I. Vogelsang, 1994. *Welfare Consequences of Selling Public Enterprises.* Washington, D.C.: Oxford University Press for the World Bank.

Greene, W. 2000. *Econometric Analysis,* 4th ed. New York: Prentice-Hall.

Guasch, José Luis, and P. Spiller. 1999. *Managing the Regulatory Process: Design, Concepts, Issues, and the Latin America and Caribbean Story.* Washington, D.C.: World Bank.

Hansen, L. 1982. "Large Sample Properties of Generalized Methods of Moments Estimators." *Econometrica* 50: 1029–54.

Heckman, J., and J. Hotz. 1989. "Choosing among Alternative Nonexperimental Methods for Estimating the Impact of Social Programs: The Case of Manpower Training." *Journal of the American Statistical Association* 84: 862–80.

Heckman, J., and J. Smith. 1995. "Assessing the Case of Social Experiments." *Journal of Economic Perspectives* 9: 85–110.

Heckman, J., H. Ichimura, and P. Todd. 1997. "Matching as an Econometric Evaluation Estimator: Evidence from Evaluating a Job Training Program." *Review of Economic Studies* 64: 605–54.

Heckman, J., R. LaLonde, and J. Smith. 1999. "The Economics and Econometrics of Active Labor Market Programs." In O. Ashenfelter and D. Card, eds., *Handbook of Labor Economics,* vol. III. Elsevier, Amsterdam: North-Holland Press.

Heckman, J., H. Ichimura, J. Smith, and P. Todd. 1996. "Characterizing Selection Bias Using Experimental Data." *Econometrica* 66: 1017–98.

Kikeri, Sunita, John Nellis, and Mary Shirley. 1994. "Privatization: The Lessons from Market Economies." *World Bank Research Observer* 9: 241–72.

La Porta, Rafael, and Florencio López-de-Silanes. 1999. "Benefits of Privatization: Evidence from Mexico." *Quarterly Journal of Economics* 114(4): 1193–242.

Lora, Eduardo, and G. Márquez. 1998. "El problema del empleo en América Latina: Percepciones y hechos estilizados." Paper prepared for the meeting of the Governors of the Inter-American Development Bank, Cartagena, Colombia.

Mackenzie, G. 1998. "The Macroeconomic Impact of Privatization." *IMF Staff Papers* 45 (2): 363–73.

Márquez, G., and C. Pagés. 1998. *Ties That Bind: Employment Protection and Labor Market Outcomes in Latin America.* Paper prepared for the meeting of Governors of the Inter-American Development Bank, Cartagena, Colombia.

Megginson, William, and Jeffry Netter. 2001. "From State to Market: A Survey of Empirical Studies on Privatization." *Journal of Economic Literature* 39: 321–89.

Megginson, William, Robert Nash, and Matthias van Randenborgh. 1994. "The Financial and Operating Performance of Newly Privatized Firms: An International Empirical Analysis." *Journal of Finance* 49(2): 403–52.

Rubin, D. 1974. "Estimating Causal Effects to Treatments in Randomized and Nonrandomized Studies." *Journal of Educational Psychology* 66: 688–701.

———. 1977. "Assignment to Treatment Group on the Basis of a Covariate." *Journal of Educational Studies* 2:1–26.

———. 1979. "Using Multivariate Matched Sampling and Regression Adjustment to Control Bias in Observational Studies." *Journal of the American Statistical Association* 74: 318–28.

Saavedra, J., and Máximo Torero. 1999. "Labor Market Reforms and Their Impact on Formal Labor Demand and Job Market Turnover: The Case of Peru." Working Paper R-394. Inter-American Development Bank, Research Department, Washington, D.C.

Shleifer, Andrei. 1998. "State versus Private Ownership." *Journal of Economic Perspectives* 12(4):133–50.

Torero, Máximo, and Alberto Pascó-Font. 2001. "The Social Impact of Privatization and Regulation of Utilities in Peru." WIDER Discussion Paper 2001-XX.

Torero, Máximo, Enrique Schroth, and Alberto Pascó-Font. 2004. "The Impact of Telecommunications Privatization in Peru on the Welfare of Urban Consumers." *Economía* 4(1).

Vickers, John, and George Yarrow. 1988. *Privatization: An Economic Analysis.* Cambridge, Mass.: MIT Press.

Vining, Aidan R., and Anthony Boardman. 1992. "Ownership versus Competition: Efficiency in Public Enterprises." *Public Choice* 73: 205–39.

Acronyms and Abbreviations

Afps	Administradoras de Fondos de Pensiones (Private pension funds) (Chile)
BCRA	Banco Central de la Republica Argentina
BNDES	National Social and Economic Development Bank (Brazil)
Btu	British thermal unit
CAP	Compañía de Acero del Pacífico (Chile)
CEO	Chief executive officer
CEPRI	Comité Especial de Privatizaciones (Special Privatization Committee) (Peru)
CIIU	Clasificación Industrial Internacional Uniforme (Manufacturing Industry Survey) (Bolivia)
CONPES	Concejo Nacional de Política Económica y Social (National Council for Economic and Social Policy) (Colombia)
COPRI	Comision de Promoción de la Inversión Privada (Commission for the Promotion of Private Investment) (Peru)
CORFO	Corporación de Fomento (Chile)
CPI	Consumer price index
CPT	Compañía Peruana de Teléfonos (Peru)
CREG	Comisión de Regulación de Energía y Gas (Regulatory Commission for Energy and Gas) (Colombia)
CST	Companhia Siderúrgica de Tubarão (Brazil)

DANE	Departamento Administrativo Nacional de Estadística (National Statistics Department) (Colombia)
DEA	Data Envelopment Analysis
EAM	Encuesta Anual Manufacturera (Annual Manufacturing Survey) (Colombia)
EDS	Encuesta de Desarrollo Social (Argentina)
ENAP	Empresa Nacional del Petróleo (Chile)
ENDE	Empresa Nacional de Electricidad (Bolivia)
ENDESA	Empresa Nacional de Electricidad S.A. (Chile)
ENFE	Empresa Nacional de Ferrocarriles (Bolivia)
ENTEL	Empresa Nacional de Telecomunicaciones (Bolivia, Chile, Peru)
EPM	Public Enterprises of Medellín (Colombia)
FECUs	Ficha Estadística Codificada Uniforme (Chile)
FFDP	Fondo Fiduciario para el Desarrollo Provincial (Argentina, a World Bank–IDB-created fund)
FGLS	Feasible generalized least squares
FGTS	Fundo de Garantia de Tempo de Serviço (Workers' Tenure Guarantee Fund) (Brazil)
GDP	Gross domestic product
GLS	Generalized least squares
GMM-IV	Generalized method of moments instrumental variables
GNP	Gross national product
GWh	Gigawatt hour
IFI	Instituto de Fomento Industrial (Institute for Industrial Promotion) (Colombia)
ISA	Interconexión Eléctrica S.A. (Colombia)
IV	Instrumental variable
kWh	Kilowatt hour
LAB	Lloyd Aéreo Boliviano (Bolivia)
LAD	Least absolute deviation

LD	Legislative decree
MPU	Municipal public utility
MW	Megawatt
NPD	National Program of "Destatization" (Brazil)
OLS	Ordinary least squares
OSINERG	Organismo Supervisor de la Inversión en Energía (Supervisory Agency for Private Investment in Energy) (Peru)
OSIPTEL	Organismo Supervisor de Inversión Privada en Telecomunicaciones (Supervisory Agency for Private Investment in Telecommunications) (Peru)
OSN	Obras Sanitarias de la Nación (Argentina)
PCS	Personal communications services
PPA	Power purchase agreement
PPE	Property, plant, and equipment
PPI	Producer price index
PQ	Privatization Q
PVR	Present value of revenue
ROA	Return on assets
ROE	Return on equity
RPU	Regional public utility
SEDAPAL	Empresa de Servicio de Agua Potable y Alcantarillado de Lima (Peru)
Sendos	Servicio Nacional de Obras Sanitarias (Chile)
SIC	Standard Industrial Classification
SIRESE	Sistema de Regulación Sectorial (Bolivia)
SOE	State-owned enterprise
Subtel	Subsecretaría de Telecomunicaciones (Chile)
SUNASS	Superintendencia Nacional de Servicios de Saneamiento (National Office for Services of Sanitation) (Peru)
TdP	Telefónica del Perú S.A. (Peru)

TFP   Total factor productivity

WSP   Water and sewerage provider

YPF   Yacimientos Petrolíferos Fiscales (Argentina)

YPFB   Yacimientos Petrolíferos Fiscales Bolivianos

Index